ORGANIZATIONAL BEHAVIOR

Understanding Life at Work

ORGANIZATIONAL BEHAVIOR

SECOND EDITION

Understanding Life at Work

GARY JOHNS

Concordia University
Montreal

HarperCollins*Publishers*

For my parents, BILL and JEAN

Cover: Jasper Johns, *Between the Clock and the Bed,* 1981, encaustic on canvas, 6'1/8″ × 10'6-3/8″. Collection, The Museum of Modern Art, New York. Given anonymously.

Library of Congress Cataloging-in-Publication Data

Johns, Gary, 1946-
    Organizational behavior : understanding life at work / Gary Johns.
  -- 2nd ed.
        p.   cm.
    Includes bibliographies and index.
    ISBN 0-673-18418-8
    1. Organizational behavior. 2. Organization. 3. Management.
  I. Title.
  HD58.7.J6 1987
  658.3--dc19   87-23296
                                                              CIP

Preface

The preface of the first edition of *Organizational Behavior* began with the following words:

> In writing this book I have been guided by two goals. First, I wished to convey the genuine excitement inherent in the subject of organizational behavior. Second, I wanted the presentation of the material to have both academic and practical integrity, acknowledging the debt of the field to both behavioral science research and organizational practice. To put this another way, I wanted to develop a book that would be useful as well as enjoyable to read without oversimplifying key subjects on the premise that this somehow makes them easier to understand.

These two goals have continued to guide me in the preparation of this, the second edition of *Organizational Behavior*. However, they have been supplemented by two additional goals. One is a revision of content to reflect current concerns and to effect an enhanced balance between micro and macro organizational behavior topics. The product of this goal is most apparent in the presence of two new chapters, one on careers and another that expands upon the macro coverage of the first edition. Another goal in preparing the second edition involves the subtitle of the book, *Understanding Life at Work*. To further enhance student understanding of life at work, real-world problems and practices dealing with organizational behavior have been highlighted in the cases and exercises and in the In–Focus sections new to the current edition. The details of these are noted below.

FEATURES

A number of features of the second edition of *Organizational Behavior* are worthy of attention. Although it is necessary to list these features in a sequential manner, it is important to note that they were designed to work *together* to produce an effective text:

■ The writing style is personal and conversational. Excessive use of jargon is avoided, and important ideas are well defined and illustrated. Special attention has been paid to the *consistency* of terminology throughout the book. Key concepts, listed at the end of each chapter, are in boldface type when they are discussed in the body of the text to provide ready references for students.

■ Believing that a well-tailored example can illuminate the most complex concept, I have used examples liberally throughout the text to clarify the points under consideration. The reader is not left wondering how a key idea applies to the world of organizations. The book is illustrated with exhibits, cartoons, and excerpts from the press as well to enhance the flow of the material and reinforce the relevance of the examples for the student.

■ I have treated the subject matter generically, recognizing that organizational behavior occurs in *all* organizations. The reader will find examples, cases, and In–Focus selections drawn from a variety of settings, including large and small businesses, high technology firms, social service agencies, hospitals, schools, and the military. In addition, care has been taken to demonstrate that the material covered is relevant to various levels and jobs within these organizations.

■ Rather than comprising a laundry list of marginally related concepts, each chapter is organized in an interlocked topical manner. Topics are actively interrelated and treated in enough detail to ensure understanding. Special attention has been devoted to the flow and sequencing of these topics.

■ All chapters begin with a short case (or, for Chapter 2, a short quiz) designed to stimulate interest in the subject matter to be covered. This case is carefully analyzed at several points in the chapter to illustrate the ideas under consideration.

■ New to the second edition, all chapters contain In–Focus selections to supplement, complement, or illustrate the textual material. These selections are derived from the practicing-management literature, the research literature, and the popular press. They are chosen to exemplify real-world problems and practices as they relate to organizational behavior.

■ Each chapter now concludes with one or more case studies or exercises. There are twenty-four of these, nineteen of which are new to the second edition. The cases are of medium length, thus allowing great flexibility in tailoring the use of them to one's personal instructional style.

■ The material covered is authoritative and up-to-date, reflecting current research and practical concerns. In addition to traditional subjects, the second edition presents new or expanded coverage of topics such as careers, resource dependency, organizational strategy, advanced technology, culture, attribution theory, and social learning.

■ A comprehensive *Instructor's Resource Book* has been prepared by the author to accompany *Organizational Behavior*.

ORGANIZATION

The book is organized in a simple but effective building block manner. Part One (An Introduction) defines organizational behavior, discusses the nature of organizations, and explains how we acquire knowledge about organizational behavior. Part Two (Individual Behavior) covers the topics of learning, perception, attribution, attitudes, job satisfaction, and motivation. Part Three (Social Behavior and Organizational Processes) discusses groups, socialization, culture, leadership, communication, decision making, power, politics, conflict, and stress. Part Four (The Total Organization) considers organizational structure, environment, strategy, technology, change, and careers. Some instructors may prefer to revise the order in which particular chapters are read, and this can be accomplished easily. However, Chapter 6 (Theories of Work Motivation) should be read before Chapter 7 (Motivation in Practice). Also, Chapter 15 (Organizational Structure) should be read before Chapter 16 (Environment, Strategy, and Technology). The book has been designed to be used in either a quarter or semester course.

ACKNOWLEDGMENTS

Books are not written in a vacuum. In writing and revising *Organizational Behavior,* I have profited from the advice and support of a number of individuals. This is my chance to say thank you.

In preparing this revision, I have received ongoing encouragement from the Concordia University administration. Thanks to Dean Steve Appelbaum, Management Department Chairman Vishwanath Baba, and Past Chairman Jack Goodwin. I'm also grateful to my other management department colleagues for their support and ideas. Special thanks to J. Bruce Prince, who authored Chapter 18.

The individuals who reviewed the initial drafts of *Organizational Behavior* went well beyond the call of duty. Invariably, their reviews were detailed, informative, and supportive. Large portions of the manuscript were reviewed by Professors David Cherrington (Brigham Young University), W. Clay Hamner, Linda Jewell, and Richard Mowday (University of Oregon). In addition, the entire manuscript was reviewed by Professors Richard Blackburn (University of North Carolina), James McFillen (Bowling Green State University), and Lyman Porter (University of California, Irvine). Special thanks to Lyman Porter for his continuing advice and support. Also, thanks to all my colleagues who have taken time to suggest ideas for the revision when we have met at professional conferences.

Three friends who are skilled authors have been an ongoing source of amusement and academic acumen. Thanks to Evan Douglas (Bentley College), Nigel Nicholson (University of Sheffield), and Steve Robbins (San Diego State University).

Once again, the people at Scott, Foresman have applied their considerable skills in turning a concept into reality. Thanks to Jim Sitlington, John Nolan, and

Kathy Richmond. Also, special thanks to Mary Espenschied for managing the detailed mechanics of turning *that* manuscript into *this* book.

Finally, thanks to Laurie St. John and the Concordia academic support staff for their patience, good humor, and efficiency.

Gary Johns

Contents

4 Perception, Attribution, and the Judgment of Others   79

7   Motivation in Practice   184

10 Leadership   307

11 Communication   346

12 Decision Making   384

13   Power, Politics, and Conflict   425

17 Organizational Change and Development   575

ORGANIZATIONAL BEHAVIOR

Understanding Life at Work

Part One

An Introduction

Chapter 1

Organizational Behavior and Organizations

RUSS MICHAELS

One day last winter, Russ Michaels quit his job. Russ had been the news anchorperson for a small New England television station affiliated with one of the major networks. His newscasts had become the most popular in the viewing area during his three years there, and this enabled the station to command premium prices for the commercials aired during these periods. When Russ announced his resignation, the station manager instructed the producer of the news show to ''scour the country'' for a replacement for Russ. Dozens of long-distance telephone calls were made, and a number of candidates were flown in for auditions. The process cost several thousand dollars. When the replacement broadcaster went on the air, a substantial number of irate viewers called to enquire as to Russ's status and to report that they didn't like the new announcer. In addition, several major advertisers indicated that their commercials should be reduced in frequency or suspended until the acceptability of the new anchor was determined. Two weeks later, the station's newswriter, who had worked very well with Russ, reported that she didn't feel comfortable with the new broadcaster's style and let it be known that she was looking for work in a warmer climate.

This scenario raises some obvious questions. Could Russ's resignation have been anticipated? Why did he resign? Could the resignation have been prevented? In the pages that follow, you will learn that the field of organizational behavior attempts to provide answers to questions such as these. In the chapters that follow, you will learn that it sometimes succeeds.

In this chapter, we will define organizational behavior and discuss why its study is important. We will also discuss the goals of the field of organizational behavior. Then we will define the term *organization* and discuss some general characteristics of organizations that have implications for the study of organizational behavior. Finally, a framework for the remainder of the book will be presented.

WHAT IS ORGANIZATIONAL BEHAVIOR?

Organizational behavior is a rather general term that refers to the attitudes and behaviors of individuals and groups in organizations. The discipline or **field of organizational behavior** involves the systematic study of these attitudes and behaviors. Thus, the field is concerned with both personal and interpersonal issues in an organizational context. Attitudes of interest might include how organizational members feel about their jobs, co-workers, or pay, or how committed they feel to the goals of the organization. Behaviors of interest might include conflict, cooperation, productivity, absence, or resignation.

Why Study Organizational Behavior?

Why should you attempt to read and understand the material in this book? For one thing, like human behavior in general, organizational behavior is *interesting*. You have probably had experiences observing people who were extremely productive or especially unproductive and wondered why such differences exist. Similarly, you may have observed groups whose members worked well together as well as those riddled with conflict and dissension and wondered what prompted these differences. Although you may have some tentative explanations for these differences, studying organizational behavior should improve your understanding of them.

In addition to the intrinsic interest of its subject matter, the field of organizational behavior is *practical*. To say the least, ours is a highly "organized" society, and we are all involved with a number of organizations. Most of us are members of organizations, and all of us are consumers of their products and services. In addition, some of us are managers of organizations. Thus, the behavior that occurs in organizations should be of great practical concern. The study of the field should enable you as an organizational member to better understand your own organizational behavior, as well as that of your peers, superiors, and subordinates. This study will suggest what you can do as a manager to increase the effectiveness of your organization and meet the diverse needs of its members. The study of organizational behavior should help you as a consumer to comprehend why some organizations are able to offer their products and services effectively and efficiently while others are not. Such knowledge should make you a wiser consumer of these products and services.

The behavior that occurs in organizations is *important* to their functioning. For example, the story presented earlier demonstrates the profound impact that an apparently routine incident can have. Russ's resignation influenced the work activities of the station manager and the news producer, not to mention the career plans of the newswriter. In addition, it influenced the consumers of the station's services, including the viewing public and the advertisers in the viewing area. These consequences had obvious short-term costs, and they had the potential to adversely influence the long-term effectiveness of the station. Of course, not all examples of organizational behavior inspire such dramatic consequences. Nevertheless, all of the activities that occur in organizations have the potential to affect how well organizations operate to achieve their own goals and those of society.

Errors in organizations often reveal the importance of organizational behavior. In–Focus 1-1 illustrates how even apparently simple incidents of such behavior can have an important impact on organizations.

Goals of the Field

Like any discipline, the field of organizational behavior has a number of commonly agreed upon goals. Chief among these are the *prediction, explanation,* and *control* of the behavior that occurs in organizations. For example, in a later chapter we will discuss the factors that predict which organizational reward systems are most effective in stimulating employee performance. We will then explain the reasons for this differential effectiveness and describe how effective systems can be implemented to enhance performance. As another example, we will discuss the kinds of job characteristics that are predictive of worker satisfaction. We will then explain why these characteristics are satisfying and describe how jobs can be designed to capitalize on these characteristics. Let us now examine the concepts of prediction, explanation, and control in more detail.

PREDICTION.   The **prediction** of the behavior of others is an essential requirement of our everyday lives, both inside and outside of organizations. Our lives are made considerably easier by the ability to anticipate when our friends will get angry, when our professors will respond favorably to a finished assignment, and when salespeople and politicians are telling us the truth about a new product or the state of the nation. With regard to organizational behavior, there is considerable interest in predicting the conditions under which people will be productive, or make good decisions, or be absent from work, or be happy with their jobs.

The very regularity of behavior in organizations permits us to make some predictions about the future occurrence of this behavior. If we see enough friendly supervisors with satisfied subordinates, we become pretty skillful at anticipating the reactions of the subordinates of the next friendly supervisor we encounter. However, as we will see in the following chapter, there are several factors that often reduce the accuracy of our casual predictions of organizational behavior. Through systematic study, analysts of organizational behavior seek to improve the accuracy of such predictions in order to reduce the uncertainty with which organizations must cope. Throughout this book, we will discuss matters that should enable you to become more effective in predicting organizational events.

In the story that began the chapter, it would have been advantageous if the station manager had been able to predict Russ's resignation and the events that followed. Minimally, some of the problems that followed the resignation might have been precluded. Under the best of circumstances, it might have been possible to prevent the resignation. Of course, being able to predict some behavior does not mean that we will be able to explain the reason for the behavior and develop an effective strategy to control it. This brings us to the second goal of the field of organizational behavior.

EXPLANATION.   Another goal of organizational behavior is **explanation** of the events that occur in organizations. Notice that prediction and explanation are not synonymous processes. Primitive societies were certainly capable of predicting the regular setting of the sun, but were unable to explain where it went or why it went there. Similarly, average students may be able to predict with terrible regularity the appearance of *C* grades on assignments but be unable to explain why their hard work does not result in *As*. In general, the ability to accurately predict an event precedes the explanation of that event. Thus, the very regularity of the disappearance of the sun at the end of the day gave some clues about why it was disappearing.

In organizational behavior, we are especially interested in determining why people are more or less productive, satisfied, or prone to resign. As the previous paragraph implies, the explanation of these events is much more complicated than their prediction. For one thing, a given behavior may have multiple causes. For example, some individuals may quit an organization because they are dissatisfied with their pay, while others may quit because they dislike the nature of the work they are required to perform. Clearly, an understanding of which of these factors (if either) was motivating Russ's intended resignation would have been extremely helpful for the station manager. Also, the explanation of some event may change over time or circumstances. For example, the reasons people quit organizations may vary greatly from times of full employment to times of high unemployment. Thus, consideration of the current job market for news broadcasters might have given the station manager some clues about the motives for Russ's behavior.

In the next chapter, we will discuss some factors that interfere with the accurate explanation of organizational behavior. In addition, throughout the book you will encounter material that should enhance your understanding of organizational events. The ability to explain these events is a necessary prerequisite for taking action to control them.

CONTROL.   The third goal of the field of organizational behavior is the **control** of the behavior that occurs in organizations. It is safe to say that explicit interest in this goal is fairly recent. As it developed, the field was primarily descriptive rather than prescriptive. That is, attempts were made to specify what happens in organizations (prediction) and why it happens (explanation) in order to develop the observational and analytical skills of workers and managers. What *should* be done in response to this information was usually contained in courses in supervision, general management, and personnel management, which were generally more prescriptive. Thus, a knowledge of organizational behavior was seen primarily as a ''tool'' in the management ''tool kit'' provided by other courses.

However, as more and more organizational events were described, and the accuracy with which behavior in organizations could be predicted and explained increased, it became obvious that such behavior was susceptible to special forms of control. Thus, organizational behavior has developed a number of its own technologies or interventions to supplement those offered by traditional management courses. Clearly, these technologies represent the bottom line for practicing managers and ultimately validate the practicality of our attempts to accurately predict and explain organizational behavior. In the following chapters, you will encounter examples of interventions designed to control the performance, attendance, and job satisfaction of organizational members. These interventions involve changes in

---

EXHIBIT 1-1   **Relationships between goals of the field of organizational behavior and important managerial tasks.**

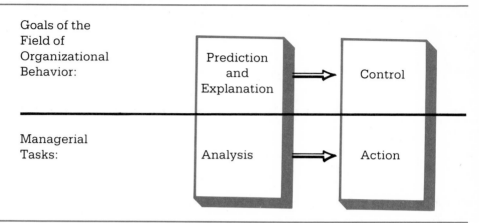

Goals of the Field of Organizational Behavior:

Prediction and Explanation ⟹ Control

Managerial Tasks:

Analysis ⟹ Action

---

reward systems, supervision, and the design of jobs, to name just a few. The important thing to remember is that such interventions should be based on the careful, systematic study of organizational behavior and grounded in previous prediction and explanation. (See the top half of Exhibit 1-1.)

Some individuals react negatively to the notion that knowledge of organizational behavior can be used to control the behavior of people at work. Somehow, this use of knowledge smacks of manipulation. However, several factors suggest that such concerns are exaggerated. For one thing, the word *control* is simply a managerial term for affect or influence. Also, every discipline that deals with the management of organizations has implications for the control of behavior. For example, standard accounting practices and procedures, such as budgeting and record keeping, are designed in part to provide performance standards that control the spending behavior of organizational members and units. Finally, it is important to understand that *all* organizations have some kind of reward system, provide some kind of supervision, and provide jobs of a particular design. These factors control the behavior of organizational members, like it or not, and it only seems reasonable to design them to support the effective functioning of the individual and the organization. If this book has a bias, it is that the knowledge derived from studying organizational behavior can be used to control behavior in a way that balances the needs of individual employees with the requirements of the larger organization. Achieving this balance is an important determinant of organizational effectiveness (Exhibit 1-2). Clearly, this is an important, practical concern for both the manager who implements control and the recipients of the control. Also, it does not rule out the possibility that employees can effectively control their own behavior via self-management to achieve both personal and organizational goals.

EXHIBIT 1-2   **Controlling organizational behavior to balance the needs of individuals with the requirements of the organization.**

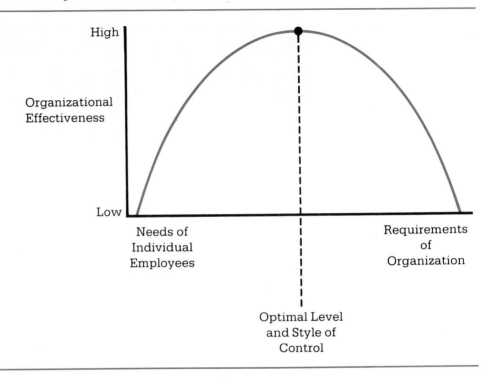

To illustrate this point, let's return to the story of Russ. If the station manager can predict Russ's impending resignation and can truly explain the reason for this behavior, he may be able to act to prevent the resignation, satisfying both the station and the news anchor. Suppose that the manager determines that Russ is not happy with simply broadcasting the news twice a night and wishes to participate in getting the facts behind important local stories. This factor could certainly explain his intention to resign. To control (in this case, prevent) the resignation, the manager might be able to redesign Russ's job to include occasional opportunities to research key stories and go into the field to report on them. As you will discover in a later chapter, this particular intervention is known as job enrichment. Of course, the success of this attempt at control would be dependent on the adequacy of the manager's explanation for the intended resignation.

MANAGEMENT ANALYSIS AND ACTION.   In this section we have said that the goals of the field of organizational behavior involve the prediction, explanation, and control of behavior in organizations. These three goals are closely related to each other. In order to generate a possible explanation for Russ's impending resignation, the station manager would have to be aware of the cues that might predict resignation. In order to control this or future resignations, the manager would have to generate an accurate explanation for the behavior.

A clear understanding of how to predict, explain, and control behavior is necessary to effectively accomplish two important managerial tasks: analysis and action. As shown in Exhibit 1-1, prediction and explanation are necessary components for the adequate analysis of organizational problems. With adequate analysis, the manager has a better chance of engaging in actions that will effectively control the behavior in question and deal with the problems. There is a strong tendency for managers to attempt to solve behavioral problems without adequate analysis. I hope this book will improve your analytical abilities and thus improve your attempts to control organizational behavior.

Contingencies in Organizational Behavior

Predicting, explaining, and controlling organizational behavior is not an easy task, partly because human nature is so complex. The admission of this complexity, however, does little to illuminate behavior in general or behavior in organizations. In this book you will find ample evidence that human nature expressed in organizations is indeed complex. Consequently, this is not a "cookbook" of organizational behavior, because such a book cannot be written. You will not find formulas to improve performance or job satisfaction with one cup of leadership style and two cups of group dynamics. We have not discovered a simple set of laws or principles of organizational behavior that can be memorized by students and retrieved from the memory bank when necessary to solve any organizational problem.

This does not mean that we are ignorant of the factors that influence what happens in organizations. However, the general answer to many of the questions that will be posed in the following chapters is, "It depends." Which leadership style is most effective? It depends. Will an increase in pay lead to an increase in performance? Again, it depends. These dependencies are often called **contingencies.** Thus, the effectiveness of a particular leadership style is contingent upon the nature of the task being performed, and the consequence of a pay increase is contingent upon how it is administered. Earlier, it was indicated that the reasons for resignation from organizations might be contingent upon the general employment situation. These contingencies reveal the complexity of organizational behavior and provide evidence of the need for its systematic study. Throughout the book we will discuss organizational behavior in a contingency framework.

WHAT ARE ORGANIZATIONS?

Since this book concerns events in organizations, it might be a good idea to consider briefly the nature of the beast. **Organizations** are social inventions for accomplishing goals through group effort. This fairly simple definition can be dissected to make some important points about organizational behavior and further justify its systematic study.

Social Inventions

The plain and simple fact is that organizations are, by definition, social inventions or contrivances. That is, they basically require the coordinated presence of *people,* not things. This is admittedly a difficult concept, and it is hard to separate the "coordinated presence of people" who work at General Motors from the physical existence of buildings, trucks, and assembly lines. However, if your favorite restaurant or tavern closes its doors due to lack of patronage, it ceases to be an organization, despite the fact that its physical trappings remain behind those doors. Similarly, given our definition, if *everyone* had resigned from the television station and had not been replaced, it would have ceased to be an organization. Of course, none of this should be taken to imply that the material technology of organizations is unimportant. General Motors simply wouldn't *be* General Motors without buildings and assembly lines. Thus, you will learn in Chapter 16 that particular technologies have an important impact on the behavior that occurs in organizations.

This perspective suggests that organizational behavior is pervasive, and that its study is basic to the understanding of any organization. There are organizations (such as neighborhood associations) that exist without balance sheets, capital assets, financial plans, or formal marketing strategies, but not without people. It is worth noting, however, that established organizations are not usually dependent upon the presence of *specific* individuals for their existence and continuity. In fact, one of the very reasons that our society supports the formation of organizations is to ensure that "the work gets done," independent of the whim and fancy of specific individuals. That is, organizations are designed to continue achieving their goals even if certain members are replaced. Thus, the television station remained in existence even though Russ, a key member, resigned.

Goal Achievement

Organizations are not random collections of people. Individuals are assembled into organizations for some reason. Thus, the organizations mentioned above have (or had) as one goal the production and sale of cars, the preparation and sale of food, or the transmission of television signals. Nonprofit organizations have goals such as saving souls, curing the sick, or educating people. Two points about these examples of goals are rather obvious. First, they hardly represent the only goals that their respective organizations have. In addition to producing and selling cars, General Motors has the goal of reducing the pollution created by its products and facilities. Similarly, in addition to saving souls, a church seeks to help the needy in its community. Thus, organizations have multiple goals. Secondly, the goals just cited are general and abstract. Such goals have been referred to as **official goals,** and one finds evidence of their existence in charters, annual reports, and official public pronouncements by organizational representatives.[1] But official goals provide little day-to-day guidance for operating a firm or institution. How are such vague official goals translated to guidelines for organizational activities? It has been proposed that **operative goals** are developed to bridge this gap.[2] These goals, which may reflect the modification or even subversion of official goals by internal interest groups, guide organizational activities by virtue of their specificity. Examples of such goals for an automobile producer might be the development and testing of a diesel-powered passenger car within two years or a decrease of 10 percent in the average fuel consumption of its passenger fleet over three years. A university might resolve to secure funding for a new building to house its school of business administration or to develop a new course registration system. The television station might plan to develop a hard-hitting public affairs show to lure viewers away from competitors.

One important, although often implicit, official goal of virtually all organizations is survival. In fact, it can be argued that most other official organizational goals are ultimately directed toward survival. Thus, when the crippling disease polio was effectively eradicated in the United States during the 1960s, the March of Dimes developed another official goal—the eradication of birth defects. This change in official goals ensured its survival as an organization. There are several *behaviors* that appear to be necessary for an organization's survival to be assured:

- Individuals must be induced to join and remain in the organization.
- Members must carry out their assignments reliably.
- Members must occasionally engage in innovative activities that go beyond their usual assignments.[3]

These organizational behaviors are important because they represent a subset of people-related operative goals which help guide organizations in achieving other operative goals (such as developing that diesel car or public affairs show). Some of the operative goals that are of particular concern to the field of organizational behavior include things such as:

- The maintenance of a work environment that is satisfying to present members and attractive to potential members.
- A reasonable level of turnover from the organization.
- A minimal level of absence from work.
- A reasonable level of high-quality performance from both individuals and groups.
- Creative, realistic decision making and problem solving.
- The avoidance or resolution of dysfunctional conflict and other problematic interpersonal behaviors.

Clearly, these (often implicit) people-related operative goals are not separate and independent from official goals. If the television station seeks to survive (official goal), it must produce a profit (official goal). To do this, it may have to develop a hard-hitting public affairs show (operative goal), and the achievement of this outcome depends upon the general attainment of the people-related operative goals listed above. In fact, when we speak of the overall performance or effectiveness of an organization, we are usually referring to how well it achieves such goals.

Group Effort

Organizations achieve their goals with people who operate in some *coordinated* manner. Sometimes this coordination is a matter of efficiency rather than absolute necessity. For example, an artists' cooperative might purchase art supplies and help market its members' work. The members could do these things themselves, but find that such things are accomplished more efficiently through group means. On the other hand, Boeing Corporation *must* use group means to design and build products such as the 747 jumbo jet. Though he certainly could have understood all of the physical and aerodynamic properties of such an aircraft, even Albert Einstein could not have mastered all of the applied skills needed to design one, and he obviously couldn't have built one by himself! Individuals have intellectual and physical limitations which can only be overcome by organized group effort.

The grouping that characterizes organizations is of interest to the field of organizational behavior for several reasons. First, much of the work (both intellectual and physical) done in organizations is quite literally performed by groups, whether they are short-term task forces or formal work groups shown on an organizational chart. We are therefore interested in predicting and explaining the functioning of these groups and controlling them so that they function effectively. You will recall that the two-person newswriting/news reading team was severely disrupted by Russ's resignation. Secondly, everyone is aware that informal grouping occurs in all organizations. That is, friendships develop and informal alliances are formed to accomplish required work. Such grouping is not prescribed by the organization and not shown on the chart, but it can have an important impact upon goal achievement. Consequently, we are interested in how such groups form and what their exact impact is. Finally, the field of organizational behavior is concerned with the influence that both formal and informal grouping has on the individuals who enter organizations with their own particular needs and values.

A LOOK AHEAD

Now that we have discussed organizational behavior and the nature of organizations, let's have a look at the "organization" of the book. In Chapter 2 we will examine some sources of information about organizational behavior and suggest that common sense provides a rather limited basis for understanding this behavior.

We will then discuss some research methods that behavioral scientists have employed to find out about organizational behavior. This should enable you to see the source of the material discussed in this book.

Part Two (Chapters 3 to 7) is concerned with personal or individual behavior in organizations. These chapters consider how individual characteristics influence organizational behavior and how organizations influence individual members. Most behavior of interest in organizations is learned, and in Chapter 3 we will discuss how this learning occurs and how undesirable behavior can be "un-learned." Since everyone has a somewhat different learning history, it is not surprising that organizational members might have different perceptions of organizational reality. Thus, in Chapter 4 we will study the perceptual process as it relates to organizations. In addition, we will examine the process by which people form judgments of the motives, qualifications, and performance of others. Chapter 5 will consider the development of attitudes in the work setting, with special emphasis on the causes and consequences of job satisfaction. Chapter 6 presents several theories of motivation in the work setting. Given these theories, Chapter 7 discusses a number of practical strategies to enhance motivation. These strategies are especially clear examples of the *control* goal of the field of organizational behavior.

Part Three (Chapters 8 to 14) is concerned with social or interpersonal behavior and important processes in organizations. As we have already discussed, organizations are social inventions that accomplish goals through group effort, and these chapters will concentrate on groups and the processes that are necessary for goal accomplishment. In Chapter 8 we will examine how and why groups are formed in organizations. The following chapter will discuss how groups influence their members and how people are socialized into groups and organizations. It will also cover the related topic of organizational culture. One important factor in groups is leadership, and all but the most primitive groups have leaders. In Chapter 10 we will see how leadership affects the activities of groups and their members. By definition, communication is an important social process, and we will investigate communication problems and their solutions in Chapter 11. Decision making is one of the key work activities in any organization, and Chapter 12 will consider how organizational decisions are made and how they can be improved. Power, politics, and conflict are natural occurrences in organized life, and these topics will be investigated in Chapter 13. Finally, many of these processes have the potential to generate stress among organizational members, and this is the topic of Chapter 14.

Part Four (Chapters 15 to 18) will view organizational behavior from the perspective of the entire organization. Chapter 15 will consider the topic of organizational structure and the various forms of structure that organizations might exhibit. Chapter 16 will cover environment, strategy, and technology, with special emphasis on the implications of these factors for structure. Chapter 17 is concerned with organizational change and in developing organizations so that they can better achieve their goals. Finally, Chapter 18 examines careers in organizations from both the organization's perspective and your own perspective as an employee. Exhibit 1-3 shows the relationships among Chapters 3 to 18. As you can see, a

EXHIBIT 1-3 **Relationships among individual behavior, social behavior, organizational processes, and the total organization.**

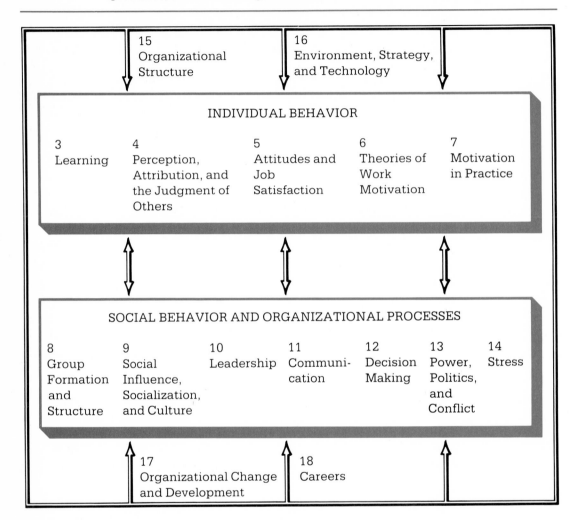

reciprocal relationship exists between individual or personal behavior and social behavior and organizational processes. In addition, the structure, strategy, and technology of organizations and organizational change and career paths influence individual behavior, social behavior, and critical processes. For pedagogical purposes, we will move from individual to group to entire organization. However, you should be on the lookout for examples of interrelationships among these levels of analysis.

SUMMARY

■ The term *organizational behavior* refers to the attitudes and behaviors of individuals and groups in organizations. The field of organizational behavior involves the systematic study of these attitudes and behaviors.

■ The study of organizational behavior is interesting, but it is also practical, because the behavior that occurs in organized settings is an important determinant of how well organizations function. The field of organizational behavior seeks to predict, explain, and control organizational behavior, and often deals with contingencies. Contingencies refer to the fact that many of the relationships that exist in organizations are dependent upon some other factor which must be taken into account.

■ Organizations are social inventions for accomplishing goals through group effort. These characteristics have important consequences for the behavior that occurs in organizations. In this book we will move from the study of individuals in organizations to the study of groups to the study of organizations as a whole.

KEY CONCEPTS

Organizational behavior   Contingencies
The field of organizational behavior   Organizations
Prediction   Official goals
Explanation   Operative goals
Control

DISCUSSION QUESTIONS

1.   What are your goals in studying organizational behavior? What practical advantages might this study have for you?

2.   Consider absence from work as an example of organizational behavior. What are some of the factors that might *predict* who will tend to be absent from work? How might you *explain* absence from work? What are some techniques organizations use to *control* absence?

3.   Consider an organization with which you are familiar. What are some of its official goals? What are some of its operative goals? How do these goals affect the behavior that occurs in the organization?

4.   In order to demonstrate that you grasp the idea of contingencies in organizational behavior, consider how closely managers should supervise the work of their subordinates. What are some factors upon which closeness of supervision might be contingent?

FOR FURTHER READING

Cummings, L. L. (1978). Toward organizational behavior. *Academy of Management Review, 3,* 90–98.

> Discusses the discipline of organizational behavior and distinguishes it from other related disciplines. Argues that organizational behavior is a way of thinking, a body of models and facts, and a set of technologies for changing organizations.

Lorsch, J. W. (1979, March–April). Making behavioral science more useful. *Harvard Business Review,* 171–180.

> Discusses why many managers fail to make use of behavioral science concepts. Argues that the contingency approach of matching the concept to the situation can reduce confusion about the applicability of many techniques.

Miner, J. B. (1980). *Theories of organizational behavior.* Hinsdale, IL: Dryden.

> Systematically presents various theories of organizational behavior and examines their research support. A good overview of the coverage of the discipline.

Miner, J. B. (1984). The validity and usefulness of theories in an emerging organizational science. *Academy of Management Review, 9,* 296–306.

> The author had experts nominate important theories about organizations and rate their scientific validity and practical usefulness. Found little relationship among the importance, validity, and usefulness of theories, suggesting that what is applied is not always the "best."

Case Study

Monitex Medical Systems

Sharon could not believe the words she was hearing:

Look, I am sorry I have to do this, but things can't continue the way they have the last few months. We are going to have to let you go. You can stay for a couple of months to give you time to find something else, but you are finished here!

The fact that Robert Delorme, General Manager of Monitex Medical Systems, was giving her time to make personal adjustments did little to ease the shock of her being fired or the unreality of the situation. Sharon had thought that she was indispensable, and while she knew her commitment to Monitex had lessened in recent months, she had no idea that her position had deteriorated so severely.

Sharon had risen quickly in the firm in the last three years. She had been hired by Monitex to be a customer service representative because of her technical background as a certified X-ray technician. The firm, which offered hospitals and clinics a monitoring process that substantially improved both the quality and cost performance of various radiographic tests, had increased sales revenues by a factor of 10 in a three-year period. Total employment had grown from 8 to 24 employees during this time, and as the sales force grew, Sharon's position had naturally expanded to the point where she effectively was the head of all sales personnel. Her enthusiasm, her aggressiveness, and her buoyant nature had been key elements in her ability to personally capitalize on the firm's rapid growth.

In the early periods of Sharon's employment at Monitex she had been extremely satisfied with her job. The growth of the firm, the success of its innovative process, and the autonomy the Monitex unit was granted by its conglomerate parent company had created a dynamic work environment with tremendous opportunities for everyone in the firm. The team spirit that developed among all of the employees had made Monitex an exciting and fun place to work. It was very satisfying at the end of the month when the sales results were calculated, and the firm would take everyone to a restaurant to celebrate what had been accomplished. Many close relationships had developed among the young staff members.

The relationship between Sharon and her boss, Delorme, had slowly deteriorated over the last year or so. While no one incident had initiated this change, Delorme had criticized Sharon for being too emotional and for not using a more businesslike approach in carrying out her duties. On one occasion, Sharon had predicted that certain competitors would go after some major segments of the market. Delorme would not approve the expenditures to counter these potential entries in the market without facts. ''Back up what you are arguing,'' he had told Sharon. Sharon had been unable to do this, but she knew she was right and subsequent events had proved the accuracy of her intuition.

Things had really deteriorated four months ago when Delorme had announced the decision to appoint a sales manager. Sharon had not been consulted on this move, nor was she consulted on the selection of the individual who was eventually hired.

Source: Prepared by William D. Taylor and Shara Rosen. Reprinted by permission.

She had felt very awkward when the new sales manager, Richard Martin, had not invited her to his first sales meeting when he arrived at Monitex. She had been the one who had built the sales group, and many of the group were her close personal friends.

As she walked back to her office after her meeting with Delorme, Sharon realized that she had been difficult to work with in the last few months. She had been short-tempered, she had snapped responses to those who had requested information, and she had made no real effort to help Martin, whom she regarded as incompetent. With respect to Martin she felt little guilt: her friends in the sales group had kept her informed of his many "goofs" and she, herself, had seen the way he had fumbled the development of a marketing plan for Monitex which was eventually written by Delorme.

When she reached her desk, her mood had changed. Sharon began to feel more and more anger towards Delorme and his "buddy" Martin. She resented Delorme's insinuation that she had not learned to work within an organization. In her mind, she knew that she had made a major contribution to Monitex's success, and everyone knew it!

■ ■ ■

1. In retrospect, which factors in the case might have *predicted* Sharon's firing from Monitex?
2. What are some possible explanations for the events described in the case? In other words, what are some possible reasons for Sharon's problem at Monitex?
3. In retrospect, could Robert Delorme have behaved more effectively? Could Sharon have behaved more effectively? Could a better understanding of the field of organizational behavior have helped both of them?

REFERENCES

1.   Perrow, C. (1961). The analysis of goals in complex organizations. *American Sociological Review, 26,* 854–866.
2.   Perrow, 1961.
3.   Katz, D. (1964). The motivational basis of organizational behavior. *Behavioral Science, 9,* 131–146.

Chapter 2

Finding Out About Organizational Behavior

A QUIZ

Although this is probably your first formal course in organizational behavior, you already have a number of opinions about the subject. To illustrate this, let's begin this chapter with a short quiz. Are the following statements true or false? Please jot down a one-sentence rationale for your answer. There are no tricks involved!

1. Workers who are more satisfied with their jobs tend to be much more productive than those who are less satisfied.
2. Individuals who become organizational leaders tend to possess similar personality traits.
3. Nearly all workers prefer stimulating, challenging jobs.
4. Experienced employment interviewers do a fairly good job of selecting successful performers.
5. Managers have a very accurate idea about how much their peers and superiors are paid.

Now that you have answered the questions, do one more thing. Assume that the correct answer is opposite to the one you have given. That is, if you answered true to a statement, assume it is actually false, and vice versa. Now, give a one-sentence rationale why this opposite answer could also be correct.

Each of these statements concerns the behavior of people in organizations. Furthermore, each statement has important implications for the functioning of organizations. If satisfied workers are indeed more productive, organizations might sensibly invest considerable time, energy, and money in fostering satisfaction. Similarly, since the employment interview is a component of over 90 percent of selection decisions, its accuracy should be a matter of some concern. In this book we will investigate the extent to which statements such as these are true or false and why they are true or false. The answers to our brief quiz will be presented shortly.

In this chapter we will examine some of the factors that contribute to our commonsense understanding of organizational behavior and challenge the notion that common sense is the best source of knowledge about organizational behavior. Then, we will examine some research techniques that contribute more accurate knowledge about what happens in organizations.

HOW MUCH DO YOU KNOW ABOUT ORGANIZATIONAL BEHAVIOR?

Let's now return to our quiz. If this were an introductory course in accounting, statistics, computer science, or art appreciation, the reader would likely cry "Foul!" upon encountering such a test. How could one be expected to know that the standard deviation equals the square root of the variance or that Picasso painted his final cubist work in 1921? While we will readily concede ignorance when approaching subjects such as these, our direct and indirect experiences have enabled us to "know" a fair amount about organizational behavior in advance of its formal study. Thus, it is likely that you easily and willingly completed the quiz.

Now to the answers. Substantial research (systematic study) indicates that each of the statements in the quiz is essentially false. There are exceptions, but in general satisfied workers are not more productive, leaders do not have special personality traits, many people prefer routine jobs, employment interviewers are not especially good at predicting candidates' success, and managers are not well informed about the pay of their peers and superiors. However, you should not jump to unwarranted conclusions based on the inaccuracy of these statements until we determine *why* they tend to be incorrect. There are good reasons for an organization to attempt to satisfy its work force and to retain employment interviewers. Also we *can* predict who might assume a leadership role and who might prefer challenging jobs. These issues will be discussed in more detail in later chapters.

Experience indicates that people are amazingly good at giving sensible reasons as to why the same statement is either true or false. Thus, satisfied workers are especially productive because they identify with their work, or they are paying the organization back for providing them with satisfactory employment. Conversely, workers are satisfied because they have developed rewarding social contacts in the workplace, but these relationships interfere with productivity. The ease with which people can generate such contradictory responses suggests that our "common sense" has been developed by the unsystematic and incomplete experiences we have had with organizational behavior.

COMMON SENSE AND ORGANIZATIONAL BEHAVIOR

In case you are wondering, there is a tendency for beginning students of organizational behavior to assume that the statements included in the quiz are true.

"After all, it's only common sense. . . ." Where does this **common sense** come from? By the time we reach adulthood we have acquired considerable *direct experience* with behavior, with organizations, and with behavior in organizations. Since birth, we have been "behaving" in the informal organization of the family and in formal organizations such as schools, colleges, and places of employment. Most of us have had reasonable success in negotiating the challenges these organizations have presented for us. Furthermore, as consumers of the outputs of organizations, we have had the opportunity to observe those behaviors that seem to lead to efficient performance (e.g., the typical McDonalds restaurant) or inefficient performance (e.g., the typical college course change system). Finally, *indirect experience* is a powerful shaper of our views concerning the nature of work and organizations. When a friend says, "You wouldn't believe what happened to me at work today," or informs us that her bank credit card limit was raised on the same day her loan application was refused, we form implicit assumptions about the nature of behavior in organizations. Similarly, when we follow the progress of a political campaign, a coal strike, or military action on television, or read about the "blue collar blues" in *David Copperfield* or *Newsweek,* we add to our arsenal of knowledge about organizational behavior. Just how systematic this study has been is debatable.

Although we rely on common sense every day, this reliance often results in curious contradictions. For example, in completing a questionnaire concerning the traits of a particular ethnic group, otherwise sensible individuals will report that the group's members are continually attempting to force themselves upon the rest of society. Several questions later, they will agree equally vigorously that the ethnic group sets itself apart and behaves in an excessively clannish manner. In a similar vein, consider the following "wisdom of the ages":

■ Look before you leap BUT He who hesitates is lost.

■ Better safe than sorry BUT Nothing ventured, nothing gained.

■ Absence makes the heart grow fonder BUT Out of sight, out of mind.

■ Many hands make light work BUT Too many cooks spoil the broth.

■ Two heads are better than one BUT If you want something done, do it yourself.

The common sense provided by these old sayings is certainly common, but is it sensible? These sayings tend to be so abstract that it is impossible to deduce when they are applicable The last two pairs of sayings have some clear relevance to the design of work groups and to decision making in organizations, but one is hard pressed to know when to implement which advice. The failure of general common sense to provide us with truly useful information suggests that we should carefully differentiate opinions about organizational behavior from actual behavior that occurs in organizations.

WHAT CREATES INACCURATE OPINIONS?

There are a number of reasons for our developing inaccurate opinions about organizational behavior. These reasons stem from the nature and quality of our direct and indirect experiences with organizations.

Overgeneralization

Individuals have a tendency to assume that their experience with a particular organization is typical and general. Thus, the student politician who has acquired considerable expertise in furthering the goals of his constituency in a university setting may find it difficult to translate this expertise to a management trainee job with a bank after graduation. Although both the university and the bank are organizations, and "people are people," the knowledge acquired in one setting may not apply directly to the other. Additionally, people may assume that their own experiences in organizations are shared by other people. Thus, workers who are both satisfied with their jobs and productive assume that other satisfied workers will also be productive. Overgeneralization is often a function of *selective perception,* or seeing what we want to see or expect to see. If we know a couple of executives who are extremely dominant and aggressive, we may tend to perceive these traits in other executives while ignoring contrary instances.

Practice and Media Attention

Some ideas about behavior in organizations have acquired general acceptance simply by virtue of their visibility. This visibility may stem from actual organizational practices or from the exploration of an issue by the media.

Many people think that the employment interview must be an effective selection tool based upon the frequency with which it is used: "If organizations use it, then it must work." Likewise, it is often assumed that pay and fringe benefit increases must be an attempt to bolster productivity through increased satisfaction. Such assumptions do not take into account the nonrational actions of organizations, which are more frequent than might be expected. In fact, organizations have exhibited excessive faddishness and a tendency to follow the leader in areas such as the design of pay systems and management training and development.

Media attention can also provide us with oversimplified or sometimes inaccurate ideas about the relationships between people and organizations. Magazine and television portrayals of high-profile organizational people and events (Silicon Valley computer whiz kids, thirty-year-old Wall Street millionaires, Japanese management, and lusty corporate takeovers) surely shape our views about work. However, the critical observer must wonder whether the issue deserves attention or attention creates the issue. Also, in recent years there has been a phenomenal upsurge of popular books about business and management (see In–Focus 2-1).

IN–FOCUS 2-1 BUSINESS BOOKS BIG SELLERS

Dieting, sex, whimsey, food, money, and gossip are no longer first in the hearts of bibliophiles. Bookstores are not yet putting their torrid autobiographies and Chinese cookbooks on the half-price tables, but they know that the new darlings of the sales charts are business books. And the newly-blessed business scribes watch thousands of new readers a day loosening their purse strings to buy their dollops of management wisdom. Some specifics are: *In Search of Excellence* (Peters & Waterman, 1982); *Megatrends* (Naisbitt, 1982); and *The One Minute Manager* (Blanchard & Johnson, 1982). These took the first, second, and fourth spots on the 1983 nonfiction bestseller list (derived from *Publishers Weekly* annual bestseller reports.)

For three or four years now people have had an outlandishly zesty appetite for these books. They have sold by the millions. True, an occasional business book of yore made a cameo appearance on a weekly bestseller list, but runaway sales of *Search's* caliber were never seen. The rare business books that made it to the annual top ten list typically had sales in the neighborhood of 200 thousand copies. In contrast, *Search* sold 122 thousand copies within a scant two months after its November 1982 release. The next year it shattered records, selling over one million copies, persistently refusing to fall from first place on the weekly nonfiction bestseller list.

The 1980s bestsellers have been far more successful than any previous management books. Why these books? Why now? Some evidence emerges from the themes of past bestsellers and the cultural context in which they were penned. If you look over the oldies, most are critical of management and business—some lambastingly so, some with the bite of satire, still others with a mantle of pessimism in tune with the times. *The Organization Man* accused business of promoting deadening conformity; *Parkinson's Law* scoffed dryly at organizational inefficiency. Perhaps the *Peter Principle* sold well because its critique of the executive ranks fit the antibusiness temper of the late 1960s.

This publishing phenomenon may not be so much a unique event as it is just another sign that we are now in the *business decade.* Corporate America is back in good standing, along with a reemergence of pride and hope in the business citizenry. These new bestsellers, these epistles to managers, fairly shimmer with *optimism.* They are *enthusiastic* about the business world, about the possibility of organizational transformation, about a new culture of management. Boosterism like this means that the authors often eschew the syntax of reservation and qualification common to academic prose. This, of course, makes them prime targets for potshots from the academic community.

Going hand-in-hand with the times, though, is not enough to make a book a bestseller. What other features do these books share? One is *practicality.* They all have an explicit or implicit message of "how you can do it, too."

The real impact of these new bestsellers on managers and company culture is unknown. Some critics have charged that the advice they give is simplistic and that its wholesale acceptance would cause more harm than good. It appears, though, that this phenomenon is more fad than trend, and as such will have no major impact on organizational life 10 years hence. The residue of the spent fad probably will be healthy—perhaps as basic as an increased awareness that most people like to work toward productive ends in an environment of trust and encouragement.

Source: Excerpted from Freeman, F. H. (1985). Books that mean business: The management best sellers. *Academy of Management Review, 10,* 345–350.
Reprinted by permission.

Titles such as *In Search of Excellence, A Passion for Excellence, Iacocca,* and *The One Minute Manager* have dominated the best seller lists, reaching a much larger audience than the typical college textbook. Although such books vary tremendously in quality, some do contain valuable insights about organizational behavior. However, it would be a mistake to assume that all such books contain wisdom *because* they are popular. Frequently, popularity stems from catering to what the reader wishes were true rather than what is true. Avid readers of such books might be excused for thinking that some phenomenal advance in organizational behavior research and management occurred sometime around 1982! In fact, research evidence and practical management experience accumulate gradually, by trial and error.

Value Judgments

Our values—our feelings about what is good or bad and right or wrong—often influence our views about what happens or should happen in organizations. These values often differ according to our background and particular position in the social structure. Thus, it is unlikely that managers and unionists would have similar views about the nature of blue-collar work. The values of society and its subgroups also change over time, and this change is reflected in thinking about organizational behavior. It is safe to say that North Americans during the present century have come to value a mildly participative leadership style within organizations—somewhere between rigid authoritarianism and "giving away the shop." Such a change in values was probably prompted by the rise of unionism and observations of the adverse effects of the authoritarianism that led to World War II.

The point, however, is that such value orientations often influence our views about behavior in organizations in spite of the actual consequences of these values. We favor what *we* perceive as "good" even if this goodness is unsupported by evidence or is contrary to the values of others. If we see stimulating, challenging work in a positive light, we expect to encounter such work in organizations. Also, people seem to have an unwarranted tendency to assume that linkages exist between valued phenomena. If we assume that it is good for workers to be satisfied with their jobs and that it is good for workers to be productive, we may tend to assume that these favorable events occur together in some natural relationship— that satisfied workers are productive workers. As was pointed out earlier, this assumption is essentially inaccurate.

The purpose of the preceding discussion has been to differentiate the reality of organizational behavior from opinions about organizational behavior. Our common sense is frequently a product of overgeneralization, media attention, and unwarranted value judgments. However, this does not mean that such opinion is unimportant. On the contrary, it frequently influences our expectations and our behavior. The manager who assumes that people prefer stimulating, challenging work may arrange subordinates' tasks very differently from one who assumes the contrary. The organization whose president thinks that money is an important motivator of productivity may distribute wages and salaries very differently from one whose president does not. So, you can see that opinions about organizational behavior affect the practice of management. However, such practice should be based upon informed opinion and systematic study.

RESEARCH IN ORGANIZATIONAL BEHAVIOR

In a general sense, research is a way of finding out about the world by some objective, systematic means of gathering information. The key words here are *objective* and *systematic,* and it is these characteristics that separate the outcomes of the careful study of organizational behavior from opinion and common sense.

We will spend the remainder of this chapter discussing research methods for several reasons. For one thing, you should be aware of the manner in which the information presented in this book was collected. This should increase your confidence in the advantages of systematic study over common sense. Furthermore, you will likely encounter reports in management periodicals and the popular press of interventions designed to improve organizational behavior, such as job redesign or employee development programs. A critical perspective is necessary to differentiate carefully designed and evaluated interventions from useless or even damaging ones. Those backed by good research deserve the greatest confidence. Occasionally, a manager may be called upon to evaluate a research proposal or consultant's intervention to be carried out in his or her own organization. A brief introduction to research methodology should at least enable this person to ask some intelligent questions about such ventures. Research in organizational behavior is carried out by trained behavioral scientists who have backgrounds in management, applied psychology, or applied sociology. While this introduction will not make you a trained behavioral scientist, it should provide some appreciation of the work that goes into generating accurate knowledge about organizational behavior.

Observational Techniques

Observational research techniques are the most straightforward ways of finding out about behavior in organizations and thus come closest to the ways we develop commonsense views about such behavior. In this case, *observation* means just what it implies—the researcher proceeds to examine the natural activities of real people in an organizational setting by listening to what they say and watching what they do. The difference between our everyday observations and the formal observations of the trained behavioral scientist is expressed by those key words *systematic* and *objective*. First, the behavioral scientist attempts to keep a careful ongoing record of the events that are observed, either as they occur or as soon as possible afterward. Thus, excessive reliance upon memory is unnecessary. Secondly, the researcher approaches the setting of interest with extensive training concerning the nature of human behavior and a particular set of questions that the observation is designed to answer. These factors provide a systematic framework for the business of observing. Finally, the behavioral scientist is well informed of the dangers of influencing the behavior of those who are being observed, and trained to draw reasonable, warranted conclusions from his or her observations. These factors help ensure objectivity. The products of observational research are summarized in a narrative form (sometimes called a *case study*) which specifies the nature of the organization and people studied, the particular role and techniques of the observer, the research questions, and the events observed.

PARTICIPANT OBSERVATION.   One obvious way for a researcher to find out about organizational behavior is to actively participate in this behavior. In **participant observation,** the researcher becomes a functioning member of the organizational unit being studied. At this point, you might well respond, "Wait a minute. What about objectivity? What about influencing the behavior of those being studied?" These are clearly legitimate questions, and they might be answered in the following way: In adopting participant observation, the researcher is making a conscious bet that the advantages of participation outweigh these problems. It is doubtless true in some cases that "There is no substitute for experience." This is nicely illustrated in George Plimpton's book *Paper Lion*.[1] Plimpton, a journalist and good amateur athlete rather than a behavioral scientist, was permitted to practice with the Detroit Lions football team and act as quarterback in some plays during pre-season games. Obviously, being faced with third down and fifteen yards to go in the rain is a very different event when viewed from the stands, and such an experience can only be captured by participation. Another advantage to participant observation is its potential for secrecy—the subjects need not know they are being observed. There are some clear ethical issues to be confronted in this case, however. One sociologist served as an industrial worker in two plants in England to study the factors that influenced productivity.[2] Although he could have acted in secrecy, he was required to inform management and union officials of his presence to secure records and documents, and he thus felt it unfair not to inform his work mates of his purpose. It should be stressed that his goals were academic, and he was *not* working for the managements of the companies involved. Sometimes, secrecy seems necessary to accomplish a research goal, as the following study of "illegal" industrial behavior shows.

Bensman and Gerver investigated an important organizational problem: What happens when the activities that appear to be required to get a job done conflict with official organizational policy?[3] Examples of such conflicts include the punch press operator who must remove the safety guard from his machine to meet productivity standards, the executive who must deliver corporate money to a political slush fund, or the police officer who can't find time to complete an eight-page report to justify having drawn her revolver on a night patrol.*

The behavior of interest to Bensman and Gerver was the unauthorized use of taps by aircraft plant workers. A tap is a hard steel hand tool which is used to cut threads into metal. The possession of this device by aircraft assemblers was

---

*These examples represent conflicting operative goals or conflicts between operative goals and official goals.

Investigating "illegal" behavior in an aircraft plant like this one required participant observation by the investigators.

strictly forbidden because it could be used to correct sloppy or difficult work, such as the misalignment of bolt holes in two pieces of aircraft skin or stripped lock nuts, leading to potential structural weaknesses or maintenance problems. Possession of a tap was a strict violation of company policy, and a worker could be fired on the spot for it. On the other hand, supervisors were under extreme pressure to maintain a high quota of completed work, and the occasional use of a tap to correct a problem could save hours of disassembly and realignment time. How was this conflict resolved? The answer was provided by one of the authors, who served as a participant observer while functioning as an assembler. Put simply, the supervisors and inspectors worked together to encourage the cautious and appropriate use of taps. New workers were gradually introduced to the mysteries of tapping by experienced workers, and the supervisors provided refinement of skills and signals as to when a tap might be used. Taps were not to be used in front of inspectors or to correct chronic sloppy work. If "caught," promiscuous tappers were expected to act truly penitent in response to a chewing out by the supervisors, even if the supervisors themselves had suggested the use of the tap. In short, a *social ritual* was developed to teach and control the use of the tap to facilitate getting the work out without endangering the continued presence of the crucial tool. Clearly, this is the kind of information about organizational behavior that would be extremely difficult to obtain except by participant observation.

DIRECT OBSERVATION.   This research technique involves observation without participation in the activity being observed. There are a number of reasons why one might choose **direct observation** over participant observation. First, there are many situations where the injection of a new person into an existing work setting would severely disrupt and change the nature of the activities in that setting. These are cases where the "influence" criticism of participant observation is especially true. Secondly, there are many tasks that a trained behavioral scientist could not be expected to learn for research purposes. For example, it seems unreasonable to expect a person to spend years acquiring the skills of a pilot or banker in order to be able to investigate what happens in the cockpit of an airliner or in a boardroom. Finally, participant observation places rather severe limitations upon the observers' opportunity to record information. Existence of these conditions suggests the use of direct observation. In theory, such observation could be carried out covertly, but there are few studies of organizational behavior in which the presence of the direct observer was not known and explained to those being observed.

An excellent example of the use of direct observation is provided by Mintzberg's study of the work performed by chief executives of two manufacturing companies, a hospital, a school system, and a consulting firm.[4] At first glance, this might appear to be an inane thing to investigate. After all, everybody knows that managers plan, organize, lead, and control, or some similar combination of words. In fact, as Mintzberg forcefully argues, we actually know very little about the routine, everyday behavior managers enact to achieve these vague goals. Furthermore, if we ask managers what they do (in an interview or questionnaire) they usually respond with a variation of the plan-organize-lead-control theme.

Mintzberg spent a week with each of his five executives, watching them at their desks, attending meetings with them, listening to their phone calls, and inspecting their mail. He kept detailed records of these events and gradually developed a classification scheme to make sense of them. What Mintzberg found belies the commonsense view that some hold of managers: They sit behind a large desk, reflecting on the state of affairs of their organizations or affixing their signatures to impressive documents all day. In fact, Mintzberg found that his managers performed a terrific amount of work and had little time for reflection. On an average day they examined thirty-six pieces of mail, engaged in five telephone discussions, attended eight meetings, and made one tour of their facilities. Work-related reading encroached upon home lives. The activities managers engaged in were varied, unpatterned, and of short duration. Half of the activities lasted less than nine minutes, and 90 percent less than one hour. Furthermore, these activities tended to be directed toward current, specific issues rather than historical, general issues. Finally, the managers revealed an extensive preference for verbal communications, either by telephone or unscheduled face-to-face meetings, and two thirds of their contacts were of this nature. In contrast, they generated an average of only one piece of mail a day.

In summary, both observational techniques capture the depth, breadth, richness, spontaneity, and realism of organizational behavior. However, they also involve some weaknesses. One of these weaknesses is a lack of control over the environment in which the study is being conducted. Thus, Mintzberg could not ensure that unusual or atypical events would not occur to affect the behavior of the executives he observed. Also, the small number of observers and situations in the typical observational study is problematic. With only one observer (measuring instrument) there is a strong potential for selective perceptions and interpretations of observed events. Since only a few situations are analyzed, the extent to which the observed behaviors can be generalized to other settings is limited. (Do most executives behave like the five Mintzberg studied?) It is probably safe to say that observational techniques are best used to make an initial examination of some organizational event on which we have little information and to generate ideas for further investigation with the more refined techniques we will now discuss.

Correlational Techniques

Correlational research sacrifices some of the breadth and richness of the observational techniques for more precision of measurement and greater control. It necessarily involves some abstraction of the real event that is the focus of observation in order to accomplish this precision and control. More specifically, correlational approaches differ from observational approaches in terms of the nature of the data collected and the issues investigated.

The data of observational studies is most frequently notes made by the observer. We hope that it exhibits **reliability;** that is, we hope that other observers would see the same thing, and that any one observer would report seeing the same thing if it occurred again tomorrow. We also hope that this data exhibits **validity;** that is, we hope that it is a true reflection of what was actually observed or that it measures what it is supposed to measure. Unfortunately, because observations are generally the products of a single individual viewing a unique event, we have very little basis on which to judge their reliability and validity.

The data of correlational studies involves interviews and questionnaires as well as existing data. Existing data comes from organizational records and includes productivity, absence, and biographical information (age, sex, etc.). Variables often measured by questionnaires and interviews involve things like:

- subordinates' perceptions of how their supervisors behave on the job
- the extent to which employees are satisfied with their jobs
- reports by employees about how much freedom of action they have on their jobs.

It is possible to determine in advance of our research the extent to which such measures are reliable and valid. Thus, when constructing a questionnaire to measure job satisfaction, we can check its reliability by repeatedly administering it to a group of workers over a period of time. If individual responses remain fairly stable, we have evidence of reliability. Evidence of the validity of our questionnaire might come from its ability to predict who would quit the organization for work elsewhere. It seems reasonable that dissatisfied employees would be more likely to quit, and such an effect is partial evidence of the validity of our satisfaction measure. The point here is that in doing correlational research we can choose to use measurement instruments with known reliability and validity.

In addition to the nature of the data collected, it was pointed out that correlational studies differ from observational studies in terms of the kinds of events they investigate. Although the questions investigated by observational research appear fairly specific (What maintains an "illegal" behavior such as tapping? What do executives do?) virtually any event deemed relevant to the question is fair game for observation. Thus, such studies are extremely broad based. Correlational research sacrifices this broadness to investigate the relationship (correlation) between specific, well-defined variables. The relationship between the variables of interest is usually stated as a **hypothesis,** which is a prediction about the way variables are expected to be connected. Using the variables mentioned above, we can construct three sample hypotheses and describe how they would be tested:

- Employees who are satisfied with their jobs will tend to be more productive than those who are less satisfied. (To test this we might administer a reliable, valid questionnaire concerning satisfaction and obtain production data from company records.)

- Employees who perceive their supervisor as friendly and considerate will be more satisfied with their jobs then those who do not. (To test this we might use reliable, valid questionnaires or interview measures of both variables.)

- Older employees will be absent less than younger employees. (To test this we might obtain data concerning the age of employees and their absenteeism from organizational personnel records.)

In each case, our interest lies in a very specific set of variables, and we take pains to measure them precisely.

A good example of a simple correlational study is reported by Waters, Roach, and Waters.[5] They were interested in the relative ability of biographical variables, job satisfaction, and intent to remain with the organization to predict turnover among female clerks in an insurance company. Based on some previous research, they hypothesized that intent to remain would be the best predictor. This intention was measured in a questionnaire, as were several dimensions of job satisfaction (pay, promotions, co-workers, supervision, and work). In this case, biographical information (age, marital status, job grade, and tenure) was also obtained in the questionnaire. Two years later, company records were examined to determine who had quit. Useful predictors of turnover included intent, dissatisfaction with the work itself, and three of the biographical variables. Specifically, older employees, those with more tenure, and those with higher job grades were less likely to have quit. Intent to remain was the best predictor, with 78 percent of those who claimed they would stay remaining and 76 percent of those who reported they would leave quitting. The researchers suggested the inclusion of such an intentions measure in attitude surveys to aid in personnel planning.

A final important point should be made about correlational studies. Suppose we hypothesize that friendly, considerate supervisors will have more productive subordinates than unfriendly, inconsiderate supervisors. In this case, we might have some subordinates describe the friendliness of their supervisors on a reliable, valid questionnaire designed to measure this variable and obtain subordinates' productivity levels from company records. The results of our hypothetical study are plotted in Exhibit 2-1, where each dot represents a subordinate's response to the questionnaire in conjunction with his or her productivity. In general, it would appear that our hypothesis is confirmed—that is, subordinates who describe their supervisor as friendly tend to be more productive than those who describe him or her as unfriendly. Because of this study, should an organization attempt to select friendly supervisors or perhaps train existing supervisors to be more friendly in order to facilitate productivity? The answer is *no*. The training and selection proposal assumes that friendly supervisors *cause* their subordinates to be productive, and this may not be the case. Put simply, supervisors may be friendly *if* their subordinates are productive. This is hardly an impossible interpretation of our data, and such an interpretation does not suggest selection or training to make supervisors friendly. This line of argument should not be unfamiliar to you: Heavy smokers and cigarette company lobbyists like to claim that smoking is related to the incidence of lung cancer because cancer proneness prompts smoking, rather than vice versa. The point here is that *correlation does not imply causation*. How

EXHIBIT 2-1 **Hypothetical data from a correlational study of the relationship between supervisory friendliness and subordinate productivity.**

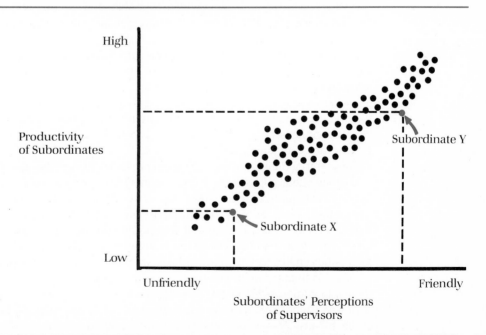

can we find out which factors cause certain organizational behaviors? The answer is to perform an experiment.

Experimental Techniques

If observational research involves observing nature, and correlational research involves measuring nature, **experimental research** *manipulates* nature. In an experiment, some variable is manipulated or changed under controlled conditions, and the consequence of this manipulation for some other variable is measured. If we have truly controlled all other conditions, and a change in the second variable follows the change we have introduced in the first variable, we can infer than the first change caused the second change. In experimental language, the variable that the researcher manipulates or changes is called the **independent variable.** The variable that the independent variable is expected to affect is called the **dependent variable.** Consider the following hypothesis: The introduction of recorded music into the work setting will lead to increased productivity. In this hypothesis, the independent variable is music, which is expected to affect productivity, the dependent variable. Consider another hypothesis: Stimulating, challenging jobs will increase the satisfaction of the work force. Here, the design of the job is the independent variable and satisfaction is the dependent variable.

Let's return to our hypothesis that friendly, considerate supervisors will tend to have more productive subordinates. If we wish to determine if friendly supervision causes (leads to, contributes to) subordinate productivity, the nature of supervision becomes our independent variable and productivity becomes our dependent variable. This means we must manipulate or change the friendliness of some supervisors and observe what happens to the productivity of their subordinates. In practice, this would probably be accomplished by exposing the bosses to some form of human relations training designed to teach them to be more considerate and personable toward their workers.

Exhibit 2-2 shows the results of such a hypothetical experiment. The line on the graph represents the average productivity of a number of subordinates whose supervisors have received our training. It can be seen that this productivity increased and remained higher following the introduction of the training. Does this mean that friendliness indeed increases productivity, and that we should proceed to train all of our supervisors in this manner? The answer is again no. We cannot be sure that *something else* didn't occur at the time of the training to influence productivity (such as a change in equipment or job insecurity prompted by rumored layoffs). In order to control this possibility, we need a **control group** of supervisors who are not exposed to the training and we need productivity data for their subordinates (see the cartoon). Ideally, these supervisors would be as similar as possible in experience and background to those who receive the training, and their subordinates would be performing at the same level. The results of our improved experiment are shown in Exhibit 2-3. Here, we see that the productivity of the subordinates whose supervisors were trained increases following training,

EXHIBIT 2-2 **Hypothetical data from an experiment concerning human relations training.**

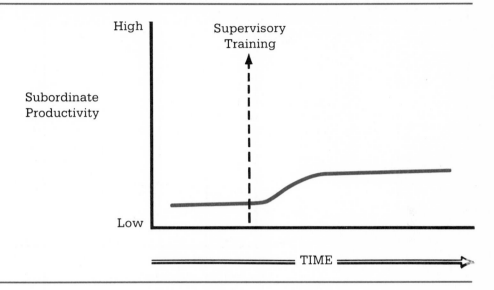

You won't be needing those, sir, you're in the control group.

Source: *Psychology Today,* December 1986, p. 14.

EXHIBIT 2-3   **Hypothetical data from an improved experiment concerning human relations training.**

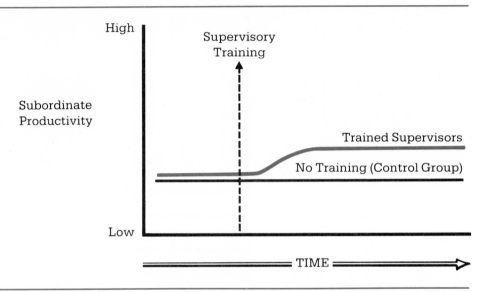

while that of the control supervisors remains constant. We can thus infer that the friendliness acquired by training affected subordinate productivity.

Ivancevich and Lyon conducted an interesting experiment concerning the effects of a shortened workweek on the operative employees of a company which manufactures food packaging equipment.[6] The independent variable was the length of the workweek (4 days, 40 hours versus 5 days, 40 hours). Two of the company's divisions were converted to a 4-40 week from a 5-40 week. A third division, remaining on the 5-40 schedule, served as a control group. Workers in the control division were similar to those in the other divisions in terms of age, seniority, education, and salary. The dependent variables (measured one month before the conversion and several times after) included questionnaire responses concerning job satisfaction and stress, absence data from company records, and performance as rated by supervisors. After twelve months, several aspects of satisfaction and performance showed a marked improvement for the 4-40 workers when compared with the 5-40 workers. However, at twenty-five months, this edge existed for only one aspect of satisfaction. The authors concluded that benefits that have been proposed for the 4-40 workweek may be of short-term duration.

A Continuum of Research Techniques

You might reasonably wonder which of the research techniques just discussed is best. As shown in Exhibit 2-4, the methods we have been discussing can be placed

EXHIBIT 2-4   **Continuum of research techniques.**

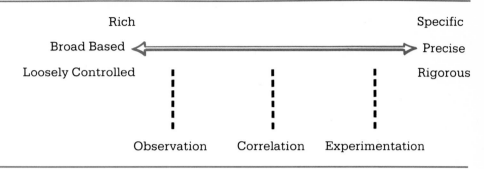

on a continuum ranging from rich, broad based, and loosely controlled (observation) to specific, precise, and rigorous (experimentation). The position on this continuum at which we choose to investigate organizational behavior should be dictated by the nature of the problem that interests us. In the writing of this section of the chapter special pains were taken to choose examples of problems that were well suited to the research techniques employed to investigate them. Bensman and Gerver, as well as Mintzberg, were interested in variables that were not well defined. The variables were thus not easy to isolate and measure precisely, and observation was the appropriate technique. Furthermore, ''tapping'' was a delicate issue, and considerable trust would had to have been developed to investigate it with questionnaires or formal interviews. Similarly, Mintzberg insists that such instruments have failed to tell us what executives do. The researchers who were concerned with predicting turnover were interested in a specific set of variables that were relatively easily measured. On the other hand, experimentally manipulating ''intent to stay'' would seem unethical, even if we knew how to do it. Ivancevich and Lyon were also interested in a specific set of variables, and they conducted their research on the shortened workweek in a situation where it was both possible and ethical to manipulate the workweek. In all of these cases, the research technique chosen was substantially better than dependence on common sense or opinion.

Issues in Organizational Research

In every field of study there are particular issues that confront the researcher, and the field of organizational behavior is no exception. To conclude this chapter, we will consider three issues that have concerned researchers in organizational behavior—sampling, Hawthorne effects, and ethical issues.

SAMPLING.   If we wish to generalize the results of our research beyond the particular setting being studied, we can have the greatest confidence in results that are based on large, random samples. Large samples ensure that the results obtained are truly representative of the individuals, groups, or organizations being studied, and not merely the product of an extreme case or two. Similarly, random samples that ensure that all relevant individuals, groups, or organizations have an equal probability of being studied also give confidence in the generality of findings. As was noted earlier, observational studies usually involve small samples, and they are seldom randomized. Thus, generalizing from such studies is a problem. However, a well designed observational study that answers important questions is surely superior to a large-sample, randomized correlational study that enables us to generalize about a trivial hypothesis.

In experimental research, randomization means randomly assigning subjects to experimental and control conditions. To illustrate the importance of this, we can return to our hypothetical study of the effects of human relations training. Suppose, instead of assigning supervisors to the experimental and control groups randomly, we have managers nominate supervisors for training. Suppose further that to "reward" them for their long service, more experienced supervisors are nominated for the training. This results in an experimental group of more experienced supervisors and a control group of less experienced supervisors. If supervisory experience promotes subordinate productivity, we may erroneously conclude that it was the *human relations training* that led to any improved results and that our hypothesis is confirmed. Poor sampling has biased the results in favor of our hypothesis. To be sure that randomization has been achieved, it would be a good idea to ascertain that the subordinates of the experimental and control supervisors were equally productive *before* the training began.

HAWTHORNE EFFECTS.   The term Hawthorne effect stems from a series of studies conducted at the Hawthorne plant of the Western Electric Company near Chicago many years ago. These studies were designed to examine the effects of independent variables such as rest pauses, lighting intensity, and pay incentives on the productivity of assemblers of electrical components.[7] In a couple of these loosely controlled experiments, unusual results occurred (In–Focus 2-2). In the illumination study, both experimental and control workers improved their productivity. In another study, productivity increased and remained high despite the introduction and withdrawal of factors such as rest pauses, shortened work days, and so on. These results gave rise to the **Hawthorne effect,** which might be defined as a favorable response on the part of subjects in an organizational experiment that is due to some factor other than the independent variable being manipulated. This "other factor" is generally thought to be psychological in nature, although it is not well understood.[8] Likely candidates include reactions to being given special attention, including feelings of prestige, heightened morale, and so on. The point is that the researcher may misinterpret the true reason for any observed change in behavior.

To return to the human relations training experiment, a Hawthorne effect might occur if the experimental subjects are grateful to management for selecting them for this special training and resolve to work harder back on the job. These

IN–FOCUS 2-2   THE HAWTHORNE EFFECT

Begun in November of 1924, it was not until the third illumination study, later in the project, that the first glimpse of the important role of human factors was provided. Placed in separate enclosures, control subjects received a constant illumination of 10 foot-candles while the illumination for experimental subjects, begun at this level, was decreased in 1-foot-candle steps in successive work periods. Throughout the experiment, both sets of subjects increased their performance, slowly but steadily. It was not until illumination in the experimental room reached 3 foot-candles that subjects started to complain that they could hardly see what they were doing, and productivity finally started to decline. Something other than level of illumination was affecting productivity.

Subsequent informal experimentation clearly indicated the contribution of psychological factors. In one instance the illumination was reduced to .06 of a foot-candle, the level of ordinary moonlight, and yet efficiency was maintained!

The Hawthorne effect probably owes its existence to a second experiment, called the Relay Assembly Test Room Study. Five female employees who spent each work day assembling relays, were separated from their large department and placed into a special test room where all relevant variables could be better controlled or evaluated. The study was designed to explore the optimal cycle of rest and work periods. However, to make the subjects independent of influences from their former department and sensitive to experimental manipulations, the investigators began by changing the method of determining wages. During the experiment the investigators also manipulated, on different occasions and sometimes concurrently, the length and timing of rest periods, the length of the work week, the length of the work day, and whether or not the company provided lunch and/or beverage. Productivity seemed to increase regardless of the manipulation introduced. Finally, well into the second year the investigators decided to discontinue all treatments and to return the workers to full work days and weeks without breaks or lunches. Unexpectedly, rather than dropping to preexperiment levels, productivity was maintained. Obviously the worker's behavior was influenced by the effects of some other variable that the investigators had unintentionally manipulated.

Before the experiment had begun, the investigators had feared that workers taken from their regular work to be placed in a test room would be negative and resistant to the experiment. To overcome this anticipated negative set supervision was removed, special privileges were allowed, and considerable interest and attention was expressed toward the worker, all changes intended to provide for a controlled experiment. However, it was these unintentional manipulations, researchers were forced to conclude, that had caused the subjects to improve their overall productivity and that had given birth to the Hawthorne effect.

Source: Excerpted from Adair, J. G. (1984). The Hawthorne effect: A reconsideration of the methodological artifact. *Journal of Applied Psychology, 69,* 334–345, pp. 336–337. Reprinted by permission.

supervisors might put in longer hours thinking up ways to improve productivity that have nothing to do with the training they received. However, the researcher could easily conclude that the human relations training itself had improved productivity.

It is very difficult to prevent Hawthorne effects. However, it is possible, if expensive, to see if they have occurred. This is usually done by establishing a second experimental group that receives special treatment and attention but is not exposed to the key independent variable. In the human relations experiment, this might involve training that is not expected to increase productivity. If the productivity of the subordinates of the subjects in both experimental groups increases equally, the Hawthorne effect is probably operating. If productivity increases only in the human relations training condition, it is unlikely due to the Hawthorne effect.

ETHICS.   Researchers in organizational behavior, no matter who employs them, have an ethical obligation to do rigorous research and to report that research accurately. In all cases, the psychological (and physical) well-being of the research subjects is of prime importance. In general, ethical researchers avoid unnecessary deception, inform participants about the general purpose of their research, and protect the anonymity of research subjects. For example, in a correlational study involving the use of questionnaires, the general reason for the research should be explained, and potential subjects should be afforded the opportunity not to participate. If names or company identification numbers are required to match responses with data in personnel files (e.g., absenteeism or subsequent turnover), guarantees must be given and honored that responses of individuals will not be made public. In some observation studies and experiments, subjects may be unaware that their behavior is under formal study. Here, researchers have special obligations to prevent negative consequences for subjects. Ethical research has a practical side as well as a moral side. Good cooperation from research subjects is necessary to do good research. Such cooperation is easier to obtain when people are confident that ethical procedures are the rule, not the exception.

SUMMARY

- Common sense provides a somewhat limited basis for understanding organizational behavior. This is because knowledge derived from common sense is often a function of overgeneralization and value judgments. In addition, we frequently assume that actual organizational practices or media presentations of them yield correct pictures of organizational behavior.

- The systematic study of organizational behavior, using carefully designed research, represents a useful alternative to reliance only on common sense. Observational research techniques are closest to commonsense methods for finding out about organizational behavior, in that they involve one or a few observers assessing one or a few instances of the activity in question. In participant observation, the observer actually takes part in the activity being observed. In direct observation, the assessment occurs without the active participation of the researcher.

■   Compared with observation, correlational research techniques attempt to measure the variables in question more precisely by using questionnaires, interviews, and existing data. One problem with correlational research is its inability to reveal which variables cause other variables. Experiments are used to overcome this problem.

■   In experimental research, the investigator actually manipulates some factor in the organizational setting and measures the effect that this manipulation has. Each of the three basic research techniques is useful for answering certain kinds of questions about behavior in organizations.

■   Proper sampling, attention to Hawthorne effects, and ethical considerations are all components of good organizational research.

KEY CONCEPTS

Common sense	Hypothesis
Observational research	Experimental research
Participant observation	Independent variable
Direct observation	Dependent variable
Correlational research	Control group
Reliability	Hawthorne effect
Validity	

DISCUSSION QUESTIONS

1.   Describe the assumptions about organizational behavior that are reflected in television shows such as situation comedies and police dramas. How accurate are these portrayals? Do they influence our thinking about what occurs in organizations?

2.   Discuss an example in which an inaccurate assumption about organizational behavior caused you a problem.

3.   State three very specific hypotheses about behavior in organizations and describe how you would test them.

4.   Review the comparative strengths and weaknesses of experimental research, correlational research, and observational research.

5.   A researcher finds that superior ratings of subordinate performance are reliable but not valid. What does this mean?

6.   A company introduces a complicated new bonus plan for its factory workers. To explain how it works, it holds a number of meetings, puts up posters, and

prepares a video information campaign. After the bonus plan is introduced, productivity increases for awhile and then reverts to pre-plan levels. Interpret what happened in terms of the Hawthorne effect.

FOR FURTHER READING

Daft, R. L. (1983). Learning the craft of organizational research. *Academy of Management Review, 8,* 539–546.

> A nice essay that portrays the research process as a craft, not just the slavish application of science. Advocates building room for error and surprise into research, getting involved in the organization being studied, and relating research ideas to common sense. Talks about research as storytelling and poetry.

Stone, E. F. (1978). *Research methods in organizational behavior.* Glenview, IL: Scott, Foresman.

> An excellent short introduction to correlational and experimental research methods. Discusses the research process, measurement methods, research design, sampling, and ethical issues.

Thomas, K. W., & Tymon, W. G. (1982). Necessary properties of relevant research: Lessons from recent criticisms of the organizational sciences. *Academy of Management Review, 7,* 345–352.

> Discuss the conditions under which organizational research is most relevant to managers. Contend that relevant research is timely, descriptively accurate of managerial experience, and possible to put into practice. Suggest that nonobvious research findings have special value for managers.

Van Maanen, J. (Ed.) (1979). Qualitative methodology. *Administrative Science Quarterly, 24,* 519–679.

> Special issue of this journal devoted to "qualitative" methodologies such as observational techniques. Some articles compare qualitative methods with quantitative methods such as correlation and experimentation.

Case Study

Electric City

Twenty–five years ago, Ollie Grayson had a good idea. Over the years, the fruits of that idea provided him with a lot of personal satisfaction and made him a lot of money. At the time, Ollie owned a modest appliance store on the main street of a medium-sized southern city. Ollie's store prospered by selling stoves, refrigerators, washers, dryers, and televisions to the good citizens of that city. Ollie's main competitors were two large chain department stores located on the same street. However, a combination of lower overhead and more personalized selling techniques enabled Ollie's store to more than hold its own against the department stores.

During this period, Ollie accurately foresaw several trends that were to radically reshape American retailing. One of these was the rise in popularity of large suburban shopping malls located on relatively low–priced land outside of city centers. Another was a boom in the home appliance and consumer electronics market. Electric dishwashers and trash compactors were coming onto the market already, and Ollie knew that microwave ovens for home use were not far behind. And the home entertainment market had nowhere to go but up, as his increased sales of color televisions were already showing. Ollie was a great fan of classical music, and he had recently purchased a sophisticated, expensive component stereo system from a very small specialist music shop. His own store did not carry such equipment, only low-priced one-unit record player systems and overpriced (he thought) console versions of the same thing. But Ollie read all the electronics trade magazines, and he foresaw the day when most American homes would have component sound systems. And Ollie felt that when the market for such sound systems was saturated, new devices such as video recorders or even home computers might come along to take up the slack.

What Ollie saw was space in the marketplace for a new kind of store that wasn't a department store, a specialist shop, or even a traditional appliance store like his own. Rather, it was predicated on selling large volumes of appliances and electronic gear at very competitive prices—a "warehouse-type operation" Ollie called it at the time. Ollie predicted that when the big department stores moved to the malls they would think twice about devoting much floor space to bulky, low-turnover items like appliances. And he felt that they would not attract the sales talent to do a good job of selling the more sophisticated electronic equipment. On the other hand, he felt that as the mystique disappeared from sound systems, price, not esoteric music knowledge, would be key to sales. This would make the small specialist shops less competitive.

When he heard rumors of a large mall development just outside of town, Ollie jumped into action. He took an option on a piece of property on the main road between the city and the proposed mall, and he began to turn his dream into a reality. Ollie named his new store Electric City, and it was immediately successful. As he says today, "I let the glitzy shopping mall attract the customers, and I peddled them low-cost appliances and electronics gear from my rather spartan premises."

Over the years, using basically the same tactics,

Ollie repeated his success, gradually opening eighteen Electric City stores throughout the south. All the stores are profitable, although this varies according to store location. The average store employs twenty–five people, most of whom are sales personnel, and none of whom are unionized. Nowadays, Ollie spends most of his time touring his stores and "managing by walking around." He visits each store at least three times a year and is well-liked and respected by almost all personnel. For relaxation, Ollie listens to classical music on a top-of-the-line compact disc system readily available in any Electric City outlet.

In the mid 1980s Ollie became aware that the profitability of the Electric City chain was gradually leveling off. In response, he called in a consulting firm that he had employed successfully in the past and asked them to do a thorough analysis of the situation. They examined financial data, visited Electric City stores, talked to store managers and personnel, and visited competing electronics and appliance outlets. The partner who headed the consulting project summarized the results for Ollie:

"Mr. Grayson, you have prime store locations, a good selection of merchandise, a good pricing policy, and an efficient distribution system. What we think you need to do is pursue a more aggressive selling policy in the stores. Competition has increased tremendously in your market sector, and clinching sales on the premises seems to be the key to continued success. We recommend a two–part strategy. First, we think you need to institute a formal sales training program for your personnel. This may cover some product knowledge, but they seem pretty good there. What they need more is some advanced sales skills training. To reinforce your concern with sales, we also recommend that you replace your current hourly pay plan for sales personnel with a system based partly on hourly pay and partly on commission. Here, let me show you some projected figures. . . ."

Ollie Grayson pondered the consultant's recommendations. It was true that Electric City had never used formal sales training. Sales personnel had been viewed more as order takers in the warehouse-type operation. Sales training was expensive. Would it be effective? Ollie also debated the question of commissions. How would the sales staff react? How would the non-sales staff react? Electric City stores had always had good labor relations, and Ollie didn't want this to change. And how would customers react to all this? Would the sales staff become overly aggressive? Could training be used without the commission scheme, or vice-versa? Ollie just wasn't sure.

■ ■ ■

1. Construct a research design to help Ollie Grayson solve his dilemmas. Justify the logic behind your choice of research techniques, and state the hypotheses being tested.
2. Discuss the issue of measurement in your proposed research design. What should be measured, how should it be measured, and when should it be measured?
3. Discuss any problems that might occur in performing the research you propose.
4. Could the Hawthorne effect come into play in your research study?

REFERENCES

1. Plimpton, G. (1966). *Paper lion.* New York: Harper & Row.
2. Lupton, T. (1963). *On the shop floor.* Oxford: Pergamon.
3. Bensman, J., & Gerver, I. (1963). Crime and punishment in the factory: The function of deviancy in maintaining the social system. *American Sociological Review, 28,* 588–598.
4. Mintzberg, H. (1973). *The nature of managerial work.* New York: Harper & Row.
5. Waters, L. K., Roach, D., & Waters, C. W. (1976). Estimates of future tenure, satisfaction, and biographical variables as predictors of termination. *Personnel Psychology, 29,* 57–60.

6. Ivancevich, J. M., & Lyon, H. L. (1977). The shortened workweek: A field experiment. *Journal of Applied Psychology, 62,* 34–37.

7. Roethlisberger, F. J., & Dickson, W. J. (1939). *Management and the worker.* Cambridge, MA: Harvard University Press; Greenwood, R. G., & Wrege, C. D. (1986). The Hawthorne studies. In D. A. Wren & J. A. Pearce II. *Papers dedicated to the development of modern management.* The Academy of Management.

8. Adair, J. G. (1984). The Hawthorne effect: A reconsideration of the methodological artifact. *Journal of Applied Psychology, 69,* 334–345.

44

Part Two

Individual
Behavior

Chapter 3

Learning

ELLEN WILDER

Ellen Wilder had just been promoted to supervisor of the Accounts Payable department of a large urban department store. Anxious to perform her new job well, she paid particular attention to the supervisory techniques of her counterpart in Accounts Receivable, Gail Marcus. Gail was a very experienced supervisor, and was generally conceded to be one of the best in the company. Over a period of a couple of weeks, Ellen noticed that Gail frequently resorted to praising her subordinates to acknowledge good performance. This appeared logical enough to Ellen, but there seemed to be some inconsistency in the way Gail used praise. Some subordinates were the object of frequent and immediate praise, while others were praised much less frequently, even though they were performing just as well. Once, Gail had actually interrupted a conversation with Ellen to go over and praise a new teller who had just done a good job of handling a very irate customer. On the other hand, Ellen had seen Gail delay praising some subordinates for work well done until the end of the week. Gail also had some curious habits regarding the way she criticized ineffective behavior. Some undesirable activities, such as disruptive shouting and quarreling among the staff, were actually ignored. Ellen wondered why Gail resisted the temptation to jump in and straighten these incidents out. This is not to say that Gail never criticized her subordinates. In fact, she had the reputation for giving a very harsh dressing down in the privacy of her office or after working hours. Ellen wondered why Gail didn't offer criticism in front of the rest of the staff to make an example of the offender.

After several months Ellen had her first performance review since becoming Accounts Payable supervisor. In the review, Ellen's boss was especially complimentary of how she dealt with her subordinates. Ellen smiled and thought to herself, "I just did everything Gail did."

You may have some of the same questions about Gail's supervisory style that Ellen had. Why did Gail praise some subordinates frequently and immediately while delaying the praise given to others? Why did Gail ignore some instances of ineffective performance and refuse to "make an example" of poor performers? In this chapter you will discover that Gail Marcus is a good learning theorist and practitioner. She knows what to say to whom (and when) in order to aid her subordinates in learning effective organizational behavior, and Ellen was able to acquire her skill by observing her closely.

To some important degree, people *learn* to show up for work, to be motivated on the job, to be good leaders, and to create conflict in organizations. In the following pages we will define learning and discuss the learning process. We will examine how the work environment can be managed to encourage the learning of effective organizational behavior and the errors that organizations sometimes make in trying to do this. In addition, we will investigate how the environment can be managed to terminate unwanted organizational behavior.

WHAT IS LEARNING?

Learning occurs when practice or experience leads to a relatively permanent change in behavior potential. The words *practice or experience* rule out viewing changes in behavior caused by factors like drug intake or biological maturation as learning. One does not learn to be relaxed after taking a tranquilizer, and a boy does not suddenly learn to be a bass singer at the age of fourteen. The practice or experience that prompts learning stems from an environment that gives feedback concerning the consequences of behavior. Gail's praise and criticism provided such experience for her subordinates.

When we say that the change induced by learning is *relatively permanent,* we mean that it is not a function of incidental temporary factors, such as warmup effects or fatigue. If I arrive at the golf driving range shortly after you begin to practice and observe you hitting a series of hooks and slices, you will correctly protest that this doesn't indicate your true level of learning in golf, since you have not yet warmed up. Similarly, if I encounter this same performance after you have practiced for two hours in the hot sun, you could rightly make the claim that fatigue has affected your shots.

When we say that learning indicates a change in *behavior potential* we mean that what is learned may not always be reflected in performance. The word *learning* is psychological shorthand for a process that cannot be observed directly. We assume that learning has occurred when we see a change in an individual's behavior or performance. While learning and performance are usually correlated, there are cases when this may not be true. Consider the bright new business administration graduate who accepts a management trainee position. His corporation requires trainees to rotate through several departments to acquire a feel for the organization. Such an individual may not perform up to his potential while in these departments because of the boredom of a series of short-term, disconnected assignments. In this case, learning is not reflected in performance. Similarly, consider the worker who limits her productivity as a machine operator because her work mates label high producers as "workhorses" and isolate them socially. Again, it can be said that her learning is not reflected in her performance.

OPERANT LEARNING AND SOCIAL LEARNING

In the 1930s the American psychologist B. F. Skinner investigated the behavior of rats that were confined in a box containing a lever that delivered food pellets when pulled. Initially, the rats ignored the lever, but at some point they would accidently operate it and a pellet would appear. Over time, the rats gradually acquired the lever-pulling response as a means of obtaining food. In other words, they *learned* to pull the lever. The term **operant learning** has been used to describe the kind of learning studied by Skinner, because the organism learns to operate on the environment to achieve certain consequences. The rats learned to operate the lever to achieve food. Notice that operantly learned behavior is controlled by the consequences that follow it. These consequences are usually contingent upon (depend upon) the behavior, and this connection is what is learned. For example, salespersons have learned effective sales techniques to achieve commissions and to avoid criticism from the sales manager. The consequences of commissions and criticism depend upon which sales behaviors are exhibited.

Besides experiencing consequences directly, humans can learn by observing the behavior of others. This form of learning is called **social learning.** Generally, social learning involves examining the behavior of others, seeing what consequences they experience, and thinking about what might happen if we act the same way. If we expect favorable consequences, we may imitate the behavior. For example, the rookie salesperson may be required to make calls with a seasoned sales veteran. By simply observing the veteran in action, the rookie may begin to acquire considerable skill without yet having personally made a sale. Obviously, operant learning theory and social learning theory complement each other in explaining organizational behavior.[1]

INCREASING THE PROBABILITY OF BEHAVIOR

One of the most important consequences that promotes behavior is called reinforcement. **Reinforcement** is the process by which stimuli strengthen behaviors. Thus, a *reinforcer* is a stimulus that follows some behavior and increases or maintains the probability of that behavior. The sales commissions and criticism mentioned above are reinforcers. In each case reinforcement serves to strengthen behaviors of interest to the organization (proper sales techniques). In general, organizations are interested in maintaining or increasing the probability of behaviors such as correct performance, prompt attendance, and accurate decision making. As we shall see, some reinforcers work by their application *to* a situation, while others work by their removal *from* a situation.

Positive Reinforcement

Positive reinforcement increases or maintains the probability of some behavior by the *application* or *addition* of a stimulus to the situation in question. Such a stimulus is called a positive reinforcer. In the basic Skinnerian learning situation described earlier, we can assume that reinforcement occurred because the probability of lever operation increased over time. We can further assume that the food pellets were positive reinforcers because they were applied to or injected into the situation after the lever was pulled.

Imagine a new telephone operator who has been instructed in the proper language and demeanor to use when answering the telephone, and whose performance is being monitored by a supervisor. Suppose the supervisor praises each correct handling of a call and remains silent when errors are made. Over time, if the operator's performance improves, we can assume that the praise offered by the supervisor served as a positive reinforcer for this performance. In fact, returning to the story that began the chapter, it would appear that Gail Marcus used praise to positively reinforce the good performance of her subordinates. Similarly, consider the experienced securities analyst who tends to read a particular set of financial newspapers regularly. If we had been able to observe the development of this reading habit, we might have found that it occurred as the result of a series of successful business decisions. That is, the analyst has learned to scan those papers whose reading has been positively reinforced by subsequent successful decisions. In these examples, something has been added to the situation (praise, favorable decisions) which has increased the probability of certain behaviors (correct telephone performance, selective reading). Also, in both cases, the appearance of the reinforcer is dependent or contingent upon the occurrence of those behaviors.

In general, positive reinforcers tend to be pleasant stimuli such as food, praise, or business success. However, the intrinsic character of stimuli do not determine whether they are positive reinforcers, and pleasant stimuli are not positive reinforcers when considered in the abstract. Whether or not something is a positive reinforcer depends only upon whether it increases or maintains the occurrence of some behavior by its application. Thus, it is improbable that the Christmas turkey given to all the employees of a manufacturing plant positively reinforces anything. The only behavior upon which receipt of the turkey is contingent is being employed by the company during the third week of December. It is unlikely that the turkey increases the probability that employees will remain for another year or work harder. On the other hand, stimuli that most of us find unpleasant may serve as positive reinforcers for the behavior of masochists, who seek pain. Reinforcers are designated by what they do and how they do it, not by their surface appearance.

Negative Reinforcement

Negative reinforcement increases or maintains the probability of some behavior by the *removal* of a stimulus from the situation in question. Also, negative reinforcement occurs when a response *prevents* some event or stimulus from occurring.

In each case, the removed or prevented stimulus is called a negative reinforcer. Negative reinforcers are usually aversive or unpleasant stimuli, and it stands to reason that we will learn to repeat behaviors that remove or prevent these stimuli.

Let's repeat this point, because it frequently confuses students of learning: Negative reinforcers *increase* the probability of behavior. Suppose we rig a cage with an electrified floor so that it provides a mild shock to its inhabitant. In addition, we install a lever that will turn off the electricity. On the first few trials a rat put in the cage will become very upset when shocked. Sooner or later, however, it will accidently operate the lever and turn off the current. Gradually, the rat will learn to operate the lever as soon as the shock is felt. The shock serves as a negative reinforcer for the lever pulling, increasing the probability of the behavior by its removal.

Managers who continuously nag their subordinates unless they work hard are attempting to use negative reinforcement. The only way subordinates can stop the aversive nagging is to work hard and "toe the line." The nagging maintains the probability of productive responses by its removal. In this situation, subordinates often get pretty good at anticipating the onset of nagging by the look on the boss's face. This look serves as a signal that nagging can be avoided altogether if they work harder.

Mechanics are often guided in correct work performance by negative reinforcement. Suppose that a loud squeaking or grinding noise indicates the improper functioning of a machine. The maintenance person who is assigned to correct this problem knows that repairs have been properly performed when the noise goes away. Thus, the noise increases the probability of proper repairs in the future when it is removed. It has functioned as a negative reinforcer.

Negative reinforcers generally tend to be unpleasant stimuli such as shock, threat, nagging, or nasty noises. Again, however, negative reinforcers are defined only by what they do and how they work, not by their unpleasantness. Above, we indicated that nagging could serve as a negative reinforcer to increase the probability of productive responses. However, nagging could also serve as a positive reinforcer to increase the probability of unproductive responses if a subordinate has a need for attention and nagging is the only attention provided by the manager. In the first case, nagging was a negative reinforcer—it was terminated following productive responses. In the second case, nagging was a positive reinforcer, because it was applied following unproductive responses. In both cases, the responses increased in probability.

ORGANIZATIONAL ERRORS INVOLVING REINFORCEMENT

Now that we have established the basic dynamics of reinforcement, we can consider some of the more interesting implications of the concept for behavior in organizations. It is, of course, not surprising that people tend to repeat those behaviors that lead to valued outcomes or terminate unfavorable states of affairs. However, a learning analysis can sometimes reveal effects that are not revealed by casual observation. Such analyses show that organizations frequently commit the following errors when attempting to implement reinforcement: They confuse *rewards* with reinforcers, neglect *individual preferences* for reinforcers, and neglect *important sources* of reinforcement.

Confusing Rewards With Reinforcers

Organizations and individual managers frequently "reward" workers with things such as pay, promotions, fringe benefits, paid vacations, overtime work, and the opportunity to perform special tasks. Such rewards may fail to serve as reinforcers, however, because they are not made contingent upon specific behaviors that are of interest to the organization, such as attendance, punctuality, or productivity. Thus, these rewards are poorly tied to the organization's people-related operative goals and fail to aid in the achievement of these goals. For example, many organizations assign overtime work on the basis of seniority, rather than on performance or good attendance, even when not required to do so by union contract. Although the opportunity to earn extra money may have strong potential as a reinforcer, it is seldom made contingent upon some desired behavior.

For another instance of a "lost" reinforcer, take an advertising manager whose graphic artist has trouble meeting deadlines for the completion of projects. When the artist completed his work on an especially crucial sales presentation well before the deadline, the manager waited until a slack period two weeks later to reward him with an afternoon off work. Not only did the manager fail to specify why she was granting the time off, but during the two-week interval the artist failed to complete two other projects on time! The long period of time between the good performance and the reward destroyed any contingent reinforcing effects, and one might suspect that, if anything, the tardy completions were more likely reinforced.

Neglecting Individual Preferences for Reinforcers

Organizations often fail to appreciate individual differences in preferences for reinforcers. In this case, even if rewards are administered after a desired behavior, they may fail to have a reinforcing effect. Intuitively, it seems questionable to reinforce a workaholic's extra effort with time off from work, yet such a strategy is fairly common. A more appropriate reinforcer might be the assignment of some special preferred task, such as work on a very demanding key project. Some labor contracts include clauses that dictate that overtime be assigned to those workers with the greatest seniority. Not surprisingly, high seniority workers may also be the best paid and the least in need of the extra pay available through overtime. Even if it is administered so that the best performing high seniority workers get the overtime, such a strategy may not prove reinforcing—the usual time off may be preferred over extra money.

Managers should carefully explore the possible range of stimuli under their control (such as task assignment and time off from work) for their applicability as reinforcers for particular subordinates. Furthermore, organizations should attempt to administer their formal rewards (such as pay and promotions) to capitalize upon their reinforcing effects for various individuals. We will have more to say about these matters in Chapter 7.

Neglecting Important Sources of Reinforcement

There are many reinforcers of organizational behavior that are not especially obvious. While concentrating upon potential reinforcers of a formal nature, such as pay or promotions, organizations and their managers often neglect those which are administered by co-workers or intrinsic to the jobs being performed. Many managers cannot understand why a worker would persist in potentially dangerous horseplay despite threats of a pay penalty or dismissal. Frequently, such activity is positively reinforced by the attention provided by the joker's co-workers. In fact, on a particularly boring job, even such threats may act as positive reinforcers for horseplay by relieving the boredom, especially if the threats are never carried out.

One very important source of reinforcement that is often ignored is that which accompanies the successful performance of tasks. This reinforcement is available on jobs that provide *feedback* concerning the adequacy of performance. If someone blindfolds you, gives you a pencil, and tells you to draw a three-inch line, you might practice for hours without improving your line-drawing performance. On the other hand, if someone sits beside you and tells you whether you are too long or too short on each trial, you will gradually learn to perform the task quite well—you are receiving feedback on your activity.

On some jobs, feedback contingent upon performance is readily available. Doctors can observe the success of their treatment by observing the progress of their patients' health, and mechanics can take the cars they repair for a test drive. In other cases, some special feedback mechanism must be designed into the job. Consultant Edward J. Feeny, former vice-president of Emery Air Freight, has described that company's experience in providing such a system. Emery's profits were highly dependent upon the use of large containers to forward smaller pieces of freight to a common destination. Costs soared when these containers were not fully utilized. For this reason, warehouse workers and their supervisors were carefully trained to use the containers when possible, and both parties felt that they were achieving around 90 percent utilization. In fact, a performance audit indicated a rate of 45 percent. The change in the job implemented by Feeny was very simple. Workers had to keep a checklist to provide themselves with feedback concerning container utilization. This feedback so reinforced correct performance that utilization jumped to 95 percent within a very short time. Emery estimated that this simple change saved $650,000 in one year.[2]

A similar feedback system is in place at Fleming Foods, a large wholesaler headquartered in Oklahoma City:

Fleming is getting workers to make themselves more productive. Each warehouse worker about to start a task inserts a card into a computer terminal that tells him how long management thinks a job should take. When the job is done, the worker reinserts the card. If he beats the clock, the screen flashes ''good job.'' If he doesn't, the screen tells him how far below capacity he's working.[3]

In Chapter 7 we will consider further how jobs can be designed to provide feedback that reinforces effective performance.

REINFORCEMENT STRATEGIES AND THEIR EFFECTS

What is the best way to administer reinforcers? Should we apply a reinforcer immediately after the behavior of interest occurs, or should we wait for some period of time? Should we reinforce every correct behavior, or should we reinforce only a portion of correct responses? You will recall that Ellen Wilder was confused by Gail Marcus's differential use of these strategies in praising her subordinates. Obviously, pragmatic factors sometimes dictate the answer to these questions. The busy manager who wishes to use praise or nagging to reinforce performance or attendance may find it physically impossible to immediately and continuously reinforce each and every desired response of subordinates. On the other hand, it should be equally apparent that some responses are well enough learned that they do not have to be reinforced quickly or even every time they occur. To make the most of reinforcers, we need to know when to use which strategies.

In order to obtain the *fast acquisition* of some response, **continuous** and **immediate reinforcement** should be used—that is, the reinforcer should be applied every time the behavior of interest occurs, and it should be applied without delay after each occurrence. Many conditions exist in which the fast acquisition of responses is desirable. These include correcting the behavior of ''problem'' employees, training employees for emergency operations, and dealing with unsafe work behaviors. Consider the otherwise excellent performer who tends to be late for work. Under pressure to demote or fire this good worker, the boss might sensibly attempt to positively reinforce instances of prompt attendance with compliments and encouragement. In order to modify the subordinate's behavior as quickly as possible, the supervisor might station herself near the office door each morning to supply these reinforcers regularly and immediately.

You might wonder when one would *not* want to use a continuous, immediate reinforcement strategy to mold organizational behavior. Put simply, behavior learned under such conditions tends not to persist when reinforcement is made less frequent or stopped. Intuitively, this should not be surprising. For example, under normal conditions, operating the power switch on your stereo system is continuously and immediately reinforced by music. If the system develops a short circuit and fails to produce music, your switch-operating behavior will extinguish very quickly. In the example in the preceding paragraph, the use of continuous, immediate reinforcement was justified by the need for fast learning. Under more typical circumstances, we would hope that prompt attendance could occur without such close attention.

Behavior tends to be *persistent* when it is learned under conditions of **partial** and **delayed reinforcement.** That is, it will tend to persist under reduced or terminated reinforcement when not every instance of the behavior is reinforced during learning, or when some time period elapses between its enactment and reinforcement. In most cases, the supervisor who wishes to reinforce prompt attendance knows he will not be able to stand by the shop door every morning to compliment his crew's timely entry. Given this constraint, the supervisor should compliment prompt attendance occasionally, perhaps later in the day. This should increase the persistence of promptness and reduce the subordinates' reliance on the boss's monitoring.

To repeat, fast learning is facilitated by continuous, immediate reinforcement, and persistent learning is facilitated by delayed, partial reinforcement (Exhibit 3-1). There are two important implications here. First, it is impossible to maximize both speed and persistence with a single reinforcement strategy. The strategy must be matched to the requirements of the situation. Secondly, many responses in our everyday lives cannot be continuously and immediately reinforced, so in many cases it pays to sacrifice some speed in learning to prepare the learner for this fact of life. The "spoiled brat" has been continuously and immediately reinforced for correct behavior. When such a child finds that the world outside his or her home does not provide such reinforcement, this correct behavior may extinguish rapidly.

All of this suggests that reinforcement strategies have to be tailored to the needs of the situation. Often, this means that they must be altered over time to achieve effective learning and maintenance of behavior. For example, the manager breaking in a new subordinate should probably use a reinforcement strategy that is fairly continuous and immediate (whatever the reinforcer). "Looking over the subordinate's shoulder" to obtain the fast acquisition of behavior is appropriate.

EXHIBIT 3-1   **Summary of reinforcement strategies and their effects.**

Strategy   Effect

Frequency of reinforcement

    • Continuous ════════════════════▶ Fast
    • Partial   acquisition

Delay of reinforcement

    • Short
    • Long ══════════════════════▶ Persistence

Gradually, however, the supervisor should probably reduce the frequency of reinforcement and perhaps build some delay into its presentation to reduce the subordinate's dependency upon his or her attention. Since the manager has other subordinates to attend to, and since it is desirable to build long-term persistence into the subordinate's behavior, such a strategy seems reasonable. In addition, as the subordinate learns the job, other sources of reinforcement (feedback from co-workers, customers, and the job itself) will come into play.

This should clarify the rationale for Gail Marcus's seemingly inconsistent use of praise as a reinforcer. Gail was quick to provide immediate, on-the-spot reinforcement for her new teller, on the presumption that her good performance was not well learned and was thus in special need of attention. Furthermore, we can assume that Gail provided less frequent and delayed praise for experienced workers whose correct work behaviors were better established.

SCHEDULES OF PARTIAL REINFORCEMENT

Earlier it was indicated that many responses in everyday circumstances are only partially reinforced—not every response that occurs is followed by reinforcement. In this section we will consider the different ways this partial reinforcement might be scheduled and the particular effects that these schedules have upon behavior. This topic is important for two reasons. First, a consideration of reinforcement schedules enables us to explain many natural variations in behavior that appear somewhat puzzling at first glance. Secondly, reinforcers are often expensive and time-consuming to administer, and we need to know which schedules will enable us to achieve most efficiently the behaviors we desire.

One kind of reinforcement schedule we will consider is called an *interval* schedule. Under interval schedules, some *time period* must elapse after a reinforced response before another reinforcement is available. In this case, the number of responses following a reinforcement is irrelevant to how quickly the next reinforcement becomes available, since interval schedules are time-dependent. (Of course, responses must be made for reinforcement to occur.) The other kind of schedule to be examined is called a *ratio* schedule. Under ratio schedules, some *number of responses* must occur after a reinforced response before another reinforcement is available. Here, the responses following a reinforcement determine how quickly the next reinforcement becomes available. In other words, "fast work equals more reinforcement" under ratio schedules, which are response-dependent. Each of these types of schedules has two subtypes, which we will discuss below.

Fixed Interval

Under a **fixed interval schedule,** some *fixed* time period occurs between a reinforced response and the availability of the next reinforcement. Under ideal conditions, mail is delivered according to this schedule—every twenty-four hours your mailbox-checking activity is reinforced by the mail carrier's visit. Similarly, if you have three equally spaced announced tests during the semester in your organizational behavior class, you can see a fixed interval schedule at work. Your studying behavior is reinforced by the opportunity to demonstrate your knowledge and receive a grade. Notice the kind of behavior this schedule induces (Exhibit 3-2). The individual in question learns to anticipate when reinforcement is available and tends to respond more rapidly as this time approaches. After reinforcement, the behavior subsides because the individual has learned that no further reinforcement will occur for awhile. If you are expecting an important letter and the mail is habitually delivered at 10:00 A.M., you might check the mailbox at 9:15, 9:30, and 9:45 in anticipation. If the mail finally comes at 10:00 and does not include your letter, it is unlikely that you will look again at 10:15. Similarly, the fixed interval exam schedule often leads to "cramming" behavior on the part of students in advance of "E day," followed by a moratorium on studying until the next exam approaches.

EXHIBIT 3-2   **Idealized response curves for reinforcement schedules. The steeper the curve, the higher the rate of response. Reinforcements are indicated by short diagonal lines.**

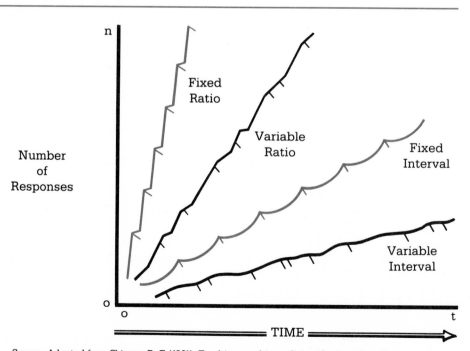

Source: Adapted from Skinner, B. F. (1961). Teaching machines. *Scientific American, Inc.*

Organizations abound with examples of fixed interval schedules. Yearly performance reviews are arranged in this manner. On a certain date, or on an employee's anniversary date with the firm, his or her supervisor sits down and discusses the employee's previous year's performance. In advance of this reinforcement, many managers have observed a tendency for performance to improve as the date for the review draws near. Again, the individual learns to anticipate the reinforcing event. Similarly, considering pay as a reinforcer for performance and attendance, organizational records often reveal that the best attendance occurs on paydays and falls off afterwards.

Variable Interval

Under this schedule, some *variable* time period occurs between a reinforced response and the chance for the next reinforcement. As shown in Exhibit 3-2, **variable interval schedules** lead to a slow, steady rate of response, because the individual cannot anticipate when a reinforcement will occur and cannot influence its occurrence by responding faster. A random "pop quiz" system, in which the students do not know when they will be examined during the semester, is an example of a variable interval schedule. Not surprisingly, such a system makes "cramming" impossible and tends to distribute study time more evenly over the semester. For obvious reasons, bank examiners tend to schedule their visits to banks according to a variable interval schedule, arranged around some average number of inspections per year. By the same token, some managers have learned to overcome the deficiencies of the formal yearly performance appraisal system by providing unannounced informal reviews during the year.

Fixed Ratio

Under **fixed ratio schedules,** after a reinforced response, some *fixed* number of responses must be made before another reinforcement becomes available. Hand-operated water pumps work according to a fixed ratio schedule. A given number of pumping movements is necessary before the water flows. As shown in Exhibit 3-2, this schedule leads to a high rate of response followed by a short pause after reinforcement. The loading dock supervisor who permits his workers to take a rest break after they stack a hundred crates is implementing a fixed ratio schedule. He is assuming that the break will serve as a reinforcer for high performance when coupled with a specific, known performance goal of a hundred crates. The firm that gives its office workers an extra vacation day for every forty working days they complete without being absent is applying a fixed ratio schedule to reinforce attendance.

Variable Ratio

With this schedule, some *variable* number of responses is necessary after a reinforcement before another reinforcement is offered. As shown in Exhibit 3-2, **variable ratio schedules** typically lead to a very high response rate with little or no pause after reinforcement. Slot machines are programmed according to a variable ratio schedule, paying off after some variable number of attempts by the players. The ratio of payoffs to plays is designed around some average that nets the casino a handsome profit. (You should consider why the other three schedules are inappropriate for slot machines.) Door-to-door salespeople are reinforced by sales according to a variable ratio schedule. The more houses they call on the more likely they are to make a sale, but the number of houses called on between sales varies. Lower level managers have their suggestions accepted by top management according to this schedule. The more suggestions offered, the greater the chance of having one approved, although the number of ideas generated between approvals varies.

Pay as a Scheduled Reinforcer

The pay offered to employees is a reward for work behaviors of interest to the organization. The potential reinforcing effects of this reward depend upon exactly how it is administered. An hourly pay scheme is an example of a fixed interval reinforcement schedule. In theory, employees are paid at the end of each hour they work (although they are typically paid at the end of the work week). Just what is being reinforced under an hourly pay schedule? Hourly pay is contingent upon putting in time on the job and performing at the minimal acceptable level. Thus, these are the behaviors that the hourly schedule reinforces. Hourly pay can be contrasted with a piecerate scheme. Under piecerate, workers are paid a certain amount of money for producing a particular number of objects, or pieces. For example, sewing machine operators might be paid one dollar for every two jackets they stitch, or electronics factory workers might earn five dollars for every seven radios they assemble. It can be seen that piecerate pay represents a fixed ratio schedule of reinforcement—a certain number of responses are necessary for payment to occur. Under this pay scheme, *productivity* is reinforced, because pay is contingent upon performance of the job; that is, more work equals more pay. The information presented earlier indicated that fixed ratio schedules lead to higher response rates than fixed interval schedules, and such is the case here. In general, studies reveal that piecerate pay leads to greater productivity than hourly pay.*[4] This demonstrates the importance of reinforcement schedules in affecting organizational behavior.

---

*There are a number of exceptions to this rule, and there are certain problems involved in the introduction of piecerate pay systems. We will discuss these matters in Chapter 7.

ORGANIZATIONAL BEHAVIOR MODIFICATION

From what has been said thus far, it should be clear to you that much of the behavior that occurs in organizations is the product of reinforcement. Most of this reinforcement occurs naturally, rather than as the result of a conscious attempt to control behavior. However, the description of the feedback procedure instituted at Emery Air Freight is an example of **organizational behavior modification,** the systematic use of learning principles to influence organizational behavior. The results achieved at Emery have been essentially anecdotal. In this section we will report several attempts to scientifically monitor practical applications of organizational behavior modification. In each case, you will observe that an attempt was made to positively reinforce employee behaviors that were of interest to the organization. In general, research supports the effectiveness of such programs.[5]

Reinforcing Punctuality

The first situation involves a manufacturing firm that was having trouble with workers reporting for work after scheduled starting time. Such behavior is disruptive to production scheduling, and it occurred in spite of the fact that the company had devised a yearly bonus for the workers with the best attendance and punctuality records. Clearly, the reinforcing properties of such a bonus are questionable, because its very long delay characteristic obscured the contingency between any instance of punctuality and the subsequent achievement of money. In fact, the bonus probably rewarded workers who would have been prompt even without such a scheme while having no effect on problem employees. Researchers suggested a behavior modification plan in which chronically tardy workers received a small bonus for every day they arrived at work on time. You will recall that such a continuous, low-delay reinforcement strategy is especially effective for teaching proper organizational behavior because it clarifies the contingency between the reinforcer and the behavior. The plan was implemented by having the gate guard give each chronically tardy person in the experimental group a credit slip when he or she arrived on time. Compared with a control group of chronic tardies who did not receive this treatment, the experimental subjects showed a clear increase in on-time arrival. Thus, the company used money (in the guise of credit slips) as a continuous, immediate reinforcer of punctual arrival at the workplace.[6]

Reinforcing Attendance

In the previous study, the major concern was punctuality, although workers obviously had to show up for work to be on time. In another study, the organization in question was primarily interested in attendance, although punctuality was also reinforced. Workers in four sections served as control subjects, while those in another section were confronted with the following behavior modification plan:

> Each day an employee comes to work on time, he is allowed to choose a card from a deck of playing cards. At the end of the five-day week, he will have five cards or a normal poker hand. The highest hand wins $20. There will be eight winners, one for approximately each department.[7]

Supervisors were in charge of monitoring attendance, passing out the cards, and posting on a large chart the poker hands held by subordinates as the week progressed. Over four months, the attendance rate increased by 18 percent for workers exposed to the behavior modification plan, while the attendance rate for control workers actually decreased somewhat. Notice that at least two reinforcers were probably responsible for this success. First, the $20 that could be won evidently worked according to a variable ratio schedule. That is, more instances of prompt attendance increased the probability of winning $20, but a certain level of attendance did not guarantee reinforcement in any given week. Secondly, the cards themselves and the attendant discussion concerning the progress of the week's hands as revealed on the chart probably acquired continuous and immediate reinforcing properties. These reinforcers were available even for those who did not win the $20.

Reinforcing Safe Work Practices

A final example of the use of organizational behavior modification involves the reinforcement of safe working behavior in a food manufacturing plant. At first glance, accidents appear to be chance events or wholly under the control of factors such as equipment failures. However, the researchers felt that accidents could be reduced if specific safe working practices could be identified and reinforced. These practices were identified with the help of past accident reports and advice from supervisors. Systematic observation of working behavior indicated that safe practices were being followed only about 74 percent of the time. A brief slide show was prepared to illustrate safe versus unsafe job behaviors. Then, two reinforcers of safe practices were introduced into the workplace. The first consisted of a feedback chart that was conspicuously posted in the workplace to indicate the percentage of safe behaviors noted by observers. This chart included the percentages achieved in observational sessions before the slide show, as well as those achieved every three days after the slide show. This approximated a fixed interval schedule of reinforcement. In addition, supervisors were encouraged to praise instances of safe performance that they observed, approximating a variable interval schedule. These interventions were successful in raising the percentage of safe working practices to around 97 percent almost immediately. When the reinforcers were terminated, the percentage of safe practices quickly returned to the level exhibited before the reinforcement was introduced (See Exhibit 3-3).[8]

EXHIBIT 3-3   **Percentage of safe working practices achieved with and without reinforcement.**

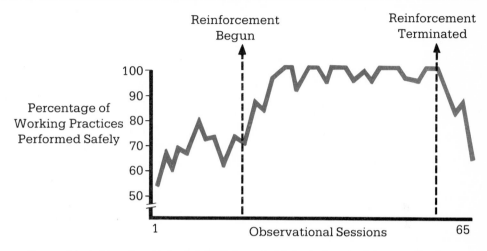

Source: Adapted from Komaki, J., et al. (1978, August). A behavioral approach to occupational safety: Pinpointing and reinforcing safe performance in a food manufacturing plant. *Journal of Applied Psychology,* 63(4), 439. Copyright © 1978 by American Psychological Association. Adapted by permission of the author.

MODELING

Organizational behavior modification programs involve the conscious use of reinforcement to manage organizational behavior. However, it has perhaps occurred to you that much learning can occur in organizations without the conscious control of positive and negative reinforcers by managers. Often, effective (or ineffective) behavior seems to occur "automatically," without the benefit of gradual shaping through trial and error and selective reinforcement. For instance, after experiencing just a couple of executive committee meetings, a newly promoted vice-president may look like an "old pro," bringing appropriate materials to the meeting, asking questions in an approved style, and so on.

How are we to account for such learning? One important factor is **modeling,** the process of imitating the behavior of others. With modeling, learning occurs by observing or imagining the behavior of others, rather than through direct personal experience.[9] Thus, the new vice-president doubtless modeled his behavior on that of his more experienced peers on the executive committee. Also, in the story that began the chapter, Ellen Wilder evidently modeled her supervisory style on that of Gail Marcus. But has reinforcement occurred here? It is probably *self*-reinforcement that occurs in the modeling process. For one thing, it is reinforcing to acquire an understanding of others who are viewed positively. In addition, we are able to imagine the reinforcers that the model experiences coming our way when we imitate his or her behavior. Surely this is why children imitate the behavior of sports heroes. In any event, modeling is an aspect of what we earlier called social learning.

What kinds of models are likely to provoke the greatest degree of imitation? In general, attractive, credible, competent, high-status persons stand a good chance of being imitated. Gail Marcus fulfilled this role in the department store. In addition, it is important that the model's behavior provoke consequences that are seen as positive and successful to the observer. Finally, it helps if the model's behavior is vivid and memorable—bores do not make good models.[10] In business schools, it is not unusual to find students who have developed philosophies or approaches that are modeled on credible, successful, high-profile business leaders. Current examples include Chrysler's Lee Iacocca and Apple Computer co-founder Steven Jobs, both of whom have been the object of extensive splashy coverage in the business and popular press.

The extent of modeling as a means of learning in organizations suggests that managers should pay more attention to the process. For one thing, managers who operate on a principle of ''do as I say, not as I do'' will find that what is done is more likely to be imitated, including undesirable behaviors such as expense account abuse. Also, in the absence of credible management models, workers may imitate dysfunctional peer behavior if peers meet the criteria for strong models. On a more positive note, well designed performance evaluation and reward systems permit organizations to publicize effectively the kind of organizational behavior that should be imitated.

REDUCING THE PROBABILITY OF BEHAVIOR

Thus far in our discussion of learning, we have been interested in *increasing* the probability of various work behaviors, such as attendance or good performance. Both positive and negative reinforcement can be used to accomplish this goal. However, in many cases we encounter learned behaviors that we wish to *stop* from occurring. Such behaviors are detrimental to the operation of the organization and may be detrimental to the health or safety of the individual worker. There are two strategies that can be used to reduce the probability of learned responses. One is called extinction and the other is called punishment.

Extinction

The process of **extinction** simply involves doing away with the reinforcer that is maintaining some unwanted behavior. If the behavior is not reinforced, it will gradually dissipate or be extinguished. In a large university, the heads of the accounts and records departments were upset by the tendency for their employees to leave their job stations on paydays in order to pick up their paychecks halfway across campus. This resulted in a twenty-minute absence during the working day which was often disruptive. In response to this problem, the department heads arranged with the treasurer's office to have the checks delivered to the departments for direct distribution. After this, the reinforcer for leaving the job station was removed and the dysfunctional behavior stopped.

People running programs that provide job training for the chronically unemployed have found that such persons must sometimes be absent from work because they are unable to find babysitters for their children. In order to deal with this problem, these programs have attempted to arrange reliable babysitting before the person acquires a job. Again, a reinforcer of a dysfunctional behavior is removed in hope of extinguishing this behavior. The workers no longer have to remain at home to ensure care for their children.

As a final example of the extinction process, consider the case of a bright young marketing expert who was headed for the "fast track" in his organization. Although he was being considered for a promotion by his boss, the vice-president of marketing, he had developed a very disruptive habit—the tendency to play comedian during department meetings. The vice-president observed that this wisecracking was reinforced by the appreciative laughs of two other department members. He proceeded to enlist their aid to extinguish the joking. After having the problem explained to them, they agreed to ignore the disruptive one-liners and puns. At the same time, the vice-president took special pains to positively reinforce constructive comments by the young marketer. Very quickly, joking was extinguished and the young man's future with the company was improved.[11]

The preceding example illustrates that extinction works best when coupled with the reinforcement of some desired substitute behavior. It should be noted that behaviors that have been learned under delayed or partial reinforcement schedules are more difficult to extinguish than those learned under continuous, immediate reinforcement. Ironically, it would be harder to extinguish the joke-telling of a partially successful committee member than one who was always successful at getting a laugh.

Punishment

The process of **punishment** involves following an unwanted behavior with some unpleasant, aversive stimulus. In theory, this should reduce the probability of the response when the actor learns that the behavior leads to unwanted consequences. Notice the difference between punishment and negative reinforcement. In negative reinforcement, a nasty stimulus is *removed* following some behavior, increasing the probability of that behavior. With punishment, a nasty stimulus is *applied* after some behavior, *decreasing* the probability of the behavior. If a boss yells at her secretary after seeing the office phone used for personal calls, we expect to see less of this activity in the future.

The word *punishment* has a rather negative connotation. It is important for you to understand, however, that many of our everyday activities are controlled by punishing consequences. Little League baseball players learn the proper way to slide into a base by experiencing the painful consequences of improper techniques. Losing a golf game because you hooked a shot or failing an exam because you studied the wrong material represent negative consequences that influence your future golfing and studying behaviors. While we readily accept the operation of punishment in these natural circumstances, we tend to feel uncomfortable when discussing the use of punishment in an organizational context. One reason for this discomfort is the fact that punishment is difficult to administer effectively and fairly. We will discuss some of the reasons for this difficulty shortly.

There is consensus that organizations and individual managers rely rather heavily upon punishment to control behavior.[12] Why is this so? After all, we have discussed techniques for influencing behavior (positive reinforcement and extinction) that do not have the negative connotations of punishment. First, there are some cases in which dangerous behaviors must be terminated immediately. For example, one cannot hope that smoking in an area where combustible chemicals are kept will somehow extinguish through boredom. For safety's sake, immediate attention is necessary to stop this activity. Secondly, many lower level managers do not have a wide range of formal organizational rewards (such as money and promotional opportunities) under their control for use as positive reinforcers. Thus, they feel that punishment is the only tool available to control behavior.[13] Finally, busy managers have some tendency to notice problematic behaviors while ignoring instances of correct performance. For example, instead of positively reinforcing prompt attendance, they develop a strategy of punishing lateness and absence. While such an approach may save time in the short run, its long-term consequences may be less than successful.

Using Punishment Effectively

If punishment is used so frequently as a tool of control by management, we would hope that it is fairly effective. In theory, punishment should be good at eliminating unwanted behavior. After all, it seems unreasonable to repeat actions that cause us trouble. Unfortunately, punishment has some special characteristics that often limit its effectiveness in stopping unwanted activity. First of all, while punishment provides a clear signal as to which activities are inappropriate, it does not by itself demonstrate which activities should *replace* the punished response. Reconsider the executive who chastises her secretary for making personal calls at the office. If the secretary only makes personal calls when she has caught up on her work, she might legitimately wonder what she is supposed to be doing during her occasional free time. If the boss fails to provide substitute activities, the message contained in the punishment may be lost.

Both positive and negative reinforcers specify which behaviors are appropriate. Punishment only indicates what is not appropriate. This characteristic has some important consequences. Since no reinforced substitute behavior is provided, punishment only temporarily suppresses the unwanted response. When surveillance is removed, the response will tend to recur. Constant monitoring is very time-consuming, and individuals become amazingly adept at learning when they can get away with the forbidden activity. The secretary will soon learn when personal calls can be made without detection. The moral here is clear—*provide an acceptable alternative for the punished response.*

A second difficulty with punishment is that it has a tendency to provoke a strong emotional reaction on the part of the punished individual.[14] This is especially likely when the punishment is delivered in anger or perceived to be unfair. (See In–Focus 3-1 and 3-2.) Managers who try overly hard to be patient with subordinates and then finally blow up risk overemotional reactions. So do those who tolerate unwanted behavior on the part of their subordinates and then impulsively decide to make an example of one individual by punishing him or her. At best, emotional reactions to punishment may interfere with the learning of acceptable alternative behavior. The worker who is "chewed out" for the unsafe operation of his machine may be so angered and humiliated that he fails to hear the valuable safety instructions the boss proceeds to provide. At worst, emotional reactions may lead to acts of revenge or sabotage. To avoid such reactions, managers should be sure that their own emotions are under control before punishing, and punishment in front of observers should be avoided. Because of the emotional problems involved in the use of punishment, some organizations have downplayed its use in discipline systems (In–Focus 3-2).

In addition to providing correct alternative responses and limiting the emotions involved in punishment, there are several other principles that can increase the effectiveness of punishment:

■   *Make sure the chosen punishment is truly aversive.* Organizations frequently "punish" chronically absent employees by making them take several days off work. Managers sometimes "punish" ineffective performers by requiring them to work overtime, which allows them to earn extra pay. In both cases, the presumed punishment may actually act as a positive reinforcer for the unwanted behavior.

■   *Punish immediately and intensely.* Managers frequently overlook early instances of rules violations or ineffective performance, hoping that things will "work out."[15] This only allows these behaviors to gain strength through repetition. In addition, many organizational disciplinary programs start off with mild punishment for some offense (a note in the person's file) and proceed to stronger punishment (perhaps firing) if the offense continues.[16] Ironically, there is evidence that responses acquired in the presence of mild punishment may become especially persistent. Thus, the mild early warnings may have an effect opposite to that which is intended. Sometimes immediate punishment is difficult to apply because of the presence of observers. In this case, the manager should delay action until a more appropriate time and then reinstate the circumstances surrounding the problem behavior. For example, the bank manager who observes inappropriate behaviors by one of her tellers might ask this person to remain after work. She should then carry out punishment at the teller's window rather than in her office, perhaps demonstrating correct procedures and roleplaying a customer to allow the subordinate to practice them. Of course, such delay tactics must be balanced with the seriousness of the infraction. (See the accompanying cartoon for an example of a punishment dilemma!)

■   *Do not reward unwanted behaviors before or after punishment.* Many supervisors join in horseplay with their subordinates until they feel it's time to get some work done. Then, unexpectedly, they do an about-face and punish those who are "goofing around." Sometimes, managers feel guilty about punishing their subordinates for some rule infraction and then quickly attempt to make up with displays of good-natured sympathy or affection. For example, the boss who criticizes her secretary for personal calls might show up an hour later with a gift of flowers. Such actions present subordinates with extremely confusing signals about how they should behave, since the manager may be inadvertently reinforcing the very response he or she wants to terminate.

■ *Do not inadvertently punish desirable behavior.* During a California drought, a public campaign was conducted to convince residents to reduce their household water consumption. The campaign was so successful that water companies proceeded to raise their rates in order to make up for lost revenues due to decreased consumption, in effect punishing conservation efforts! Examples of such inconsistencies abound in organizations. Managers who

"I realize these days it is only money, Miss Debbett, but in the interest of tidiness, could we try not to spill?"

© Norris—Vancouver Sun/Rothco

do not use all of their capital budget for a given fiscal year may have their budget for the next year reduced, punishing their prudence. Government employees who "blow the whistle" on wasteful or inefficient practices may find themselves demoted.[17] University professors who are considered excellent teachers may be assigned to onerous, time-consuming duty on a curriculum committee, cutting into their class preparation time.

In summary, punishment can be an effective means of stopping undesirable behavior. However, it must be applied very carefully and deliberately in order for this effectiveness to be achieved. In general, reinforcing correct behaviors and extinguishing unwanted responses may be safer strategies for the practicing manager than the frequent use of punishment. In all cases, the manager must become adept at discovering what controls behavior.

A FOOTNOTE CONCERNING SELF-MANAGEMENT

Much of this chapter has been concerned with how organizations and individual managers can use learning principles to manage the behavior of organizational members. If the principles of learning are used wisely, they can contribute to safe, productive, satisfying behavior in the workplace. However, it must be emphasized that employees can use learning principles to manage their *own* behavior, making the use of external control less necessary. This process is called **self-management.**[18] In many respects, it is economical for the organization while building trust and self-confidence among employees.

How can self-management occur? You will recall that our discussion of social learning and modeling involved factors such as observation, imagination, imitation, and self-reinforcement. Advocates of self-management argue that these and similar techniques can be used in an intentional way to control one's own behavior. The basic process involves observing one's own behavior, comparing the behavior with a standard, and rewarding oneself if the behavior meets the standard.[19]

To illustrate some specific self-management techniques, consider the executive who finds that he is taking too much work home to do in the evenings and over weekends. While his peers seem to have most evenings and weekends free, his own family is ready to disown him due to lack of attention! What can he do?[20]

- *Collect self-observation data.* This involves collecting objective data about one's own behavior. For example, the executive might keep a log of phone calls and other interruptions for a few days if he suspects these contribute to his inefficiency.

- *Observe models.* The executive might examine the time-management skills of his peers to find someone successful to imitate.

- *Goal setting.* The executive might set specific short-term goals to reduce telephone interruptions and unscheduled personal visits, enlisting the aid of his secretary and using self-observation data to monitor his progress. Longer-term goals might involve four free nights a week and no more than four hours of work on weekends. (We will examine goal setting in some detail in Chapter 7.)

- *Rehearsal.* The executive may anticipate that his co-workers will have to be educated about his reduced availability. So as not to offend them, he may practice explaining the reason for his revised accessibility.

- *Self-reinforcement.* The executive may promise himself a weekend at the beach with his family the first time he gets his take-home workload down to his target level.

As you can see, self-management involves a package of interrelated processes. Managers can encourage their subordinates to practice self-management by doing it themselves and by reinforcing attempts at self-management. Also, unnecessary rules, regulations, and procedures do not provide a conducive climate for self-management.

SUMMARY

- Learning occurs when practice or experience leads to a relatively permanent change in behavior potential. Operant learning occurs as a function of the consequences of behavior. Social learning occurs by observing the behavior of others.

■   If you see some behavior that is occurring regularly or increasing in probability you can assume that it is being reinforced (Exhibit 3-4). The consequence that is maintaining the behavior is the reinforcer. If the reinforcer is

---

EXHIBIT 3-4   **Summary of learning effects.**

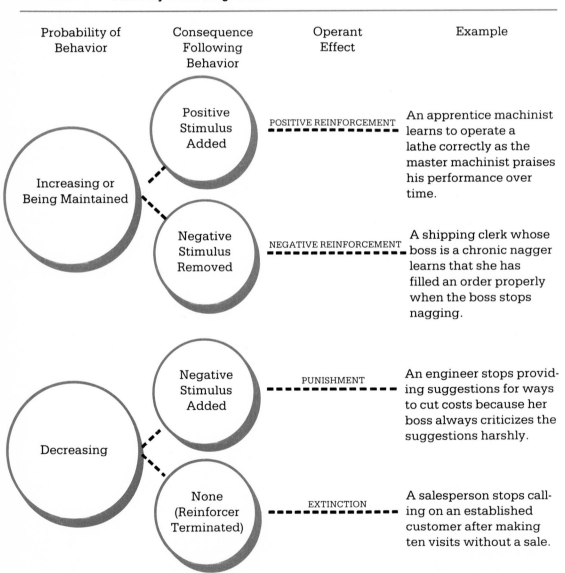

Probability of Behavior	Consequence Following Behavior	Operant Effect	Example
Increasing or Being Maintained	Positive Stimulus Added	POSITIVE REINFORCEMENT	An apprentice machinist learns to operate a lathe correctly as the master machinist praises his performance over time.
	Negative Stimulus Removed	NEGATIVE REINFORCEMENT	A shipping clerk whose boss is a chronic nagger learns that she has filled an order properly when the boss stops nagging.
Decreasing	Negative Stimulus Added	PUNISHMENT	An engineer stops providing suggestions for ways to cut costs because her boss always criticizes the suggestions harshly.
	None (Reinforcer Terminated)	EXTINCTION	A salesperson stops calling on an established customer after making ten visits without a sale.

added to the situation following the behavior it is a positive reinforcer. These are usually pleasant consequences. If the reinforcer is removed from the situation following the behavior it is a negative reinforcer. These are typically unpleasant stimuli.

■ Organizations and managers often confuse rewards with reinforcers, neglect individual preferences for reinforcers, and neglect important sources of reinforcement.

■ Behavior is learned quickly when it is reinforced immediately and continuously. Behavior tends to be persistent under reduced or terminated reinforcement when it is learned under conditions of delayed and/or partial reinforcement. Partial reinforcement can be administered under interval or ratio schedules. The former are time dependent and the latter are response dependent. Ratio schedules usually lead to higher response rates, because the individual can increase the frequency of reinforcement by responding faster.

■ Organizational behavior modification is the systematic use of learning principles to influence organizational behavior. It has been used successfully to improve punctuality and attendance and reinforce safe work practices.

■ Modeling, an example of social learning, is the process of imitating others. Models are most likely to be imitated when they are high in status, attractive, competent, credible, successful, and vivid.

■ If you see some behavior decrease in probability you can assume that it is either being extinguished or punished (Exhibit 3-4). If the behavior is followed by no observable consequence, it is being extinguished. That is, some reinforcer that was maintaining the behavior has been terminated. If the behavior is followed by the application of some unpleasant consequence, it is being punished.

■ Self-management occurs when workers use learning principles to manage their own behavior, thus reducing the need for external control. Aspects of self-management include collecting self-observation data, observing models, goal setting, rehearsal, and self-reinforcement.

KEY CONCEPTS

Learning	Fixed interval schedule
Operant learning	Variable interval schedule
Social learning	Fixed ratio schedule
Reinforcement	Variable ratio schedule
Positive reinforcement	Organizational behavior modification
Negative reinforcement	Modeling
Continuous versus partial reinforcement	Extinction
	Punishment
Immediate versus delayed reinforcement	Self-management

DISCUSSION QUESTIONS

1. Consider some examples of behavior that you repeat fairly regularly (such as studying or going to work every morning). What are the positive and negative reinforcers that maintain this behavior?

2. It was pointed out that managers frequently resort to punishing ineffective behavior. What are some of the practical demands of the typical manager's job that lead to this state of affairs?

3. Discuss a situation you have observed in which the use of punishment was ineffective in terminating some unwanted behavior. Why was punishment ineffective in this case?

4. Describe a situation in which you think organizational behavior modification could be used to improve or correct employee behavior. Can you anticipate any dangers in using this approach?

5. A supervisor in a textile factory observes that one of her subordinates is violating a safety rule which could result in severe injury. What combination of reinforcement, punishment, extinction, or modeling could she use to correct this behavior?

6. Contrast the reinforcement strategies that a supervisor might use to manage the work behavior of an experienced versus an inexperienced subordinate. Be sure to consider the issue of self-management.

FOR FURTHER READING

Arvey, R. D., & Jones, A. P. (1985). The use of discipline in organizational settings: A framework for future research. *Research in Organizational Behavior, 7,* 367–408.

> The role of discipline and punishment in organizations is discussed. Factors that prompt discipline and determine disciplinary methods are considered. The impact of various forms of discipline on worker attitudes and behavior is reviewed.

Locke, E. A. (1977). The myths of behavior mod in organizations. *Academy of Management Review, 2,* 543–553.

> Argues that operant learning principles do not really explain the effects of behavior modification and that they provide a poor model for managers. Discusses how the effects of feedback and pay have been misinterpreted by learning theorists. See a response to this article by Jerry Gray in the January 1979 issue of the same journal (pp. 121–129) and Locke's rejoinder to Gray (pp. 131–136).

O'Brien, R. M., Dickinson, A. M., & Rosnow, M. P. (Eds.). (1982). *Industrial behavior modification: A management handbook.* New York: Pergamon.

> Various chapters describe a wide variety of organizational behavior modification efforts. An especially interesting chapter explains how the sales performance of Scandinavian Airlines reservations personnel was increased.

Case Study

Denver Department Stores

Source: Ritchie, J. B., & Thompson, P. (1984). *Organization and people: Readings, cases, and exercises in organizational behavior* (3rd ed.). St. Paul, MN: West. Reprinted by permission.

(A)

In the early spring of 1974 Jim Barton was evaluating the decline in sales volume experienced by the four departments he supervised in the main store of Denver Department Stores, a Colorado retail chain. Barton was at a loss as to how to improve sales. He attributed the slowdown in sales to the current economic downturn affecting the entire nation. However, Barton's supervisor, Mr. Cornwall, pointed out that some of the other departments in the store had experienced a 15 percent gain over the previous year. Cornwall added that Barton was expected to have his departments up to par with the others in a short period of time.

Background

Jim Barton had been supervisor of the sporting goods, hardware, housewares, and toy departments in the main store of Denver Department Stores for three of the ten years he had worked for the chain. The four departments were situated adjacent to each other on the ground floor of the store. Each department had a head sales clerk who reported to Mr. Barton on merchandise storage and presentation, special orders, and general department upkeep. The head sales clerks were all full-time, long-term employees of Denver Department Stores, having an average of about eight years' experience with the chain. The head clerks were also expected to train the people in the department they supervised. The rest of the staff in each department was made up of part-time employees who lived in or near Denver. Most of the part-time people were students at nearby universities who worked to finance their education. In addition, there were two or three housewives who worked about ten hours a week in the evenings.

All sales personnel at Denver Department Stores were paid strictly on an hourly basis. Beginning pay was just slightly over the minimum wage and raises were given based on length of employment and work performance evaluations. The salespeople in the housewares and sporting goods departments were paid about forty cents an hour more than the clerks in the other departments because it was thought that more sales ability and experience were needed in dealing with the people who shopped for items found in those departments.

As a general rule the head sales clerk in each department did not actively sell, but kept the department well stocked and presentable, and trained and evaluated sales personnel. The part-time employees did most of the clerk and sales work. The role of the sales clerk was seen as one of answering customer questions and ringing up the sale rather than actively selling the merchandise except in the two departments previously mentioned where a little more active selling was done.

The sales clerks in Barton's departments seemed to get along well with each other. The four department heads usually ate lunch together. If business was brisk in one department and slow in another, the sales people in the slower area would assist in the busy department. Male clerks often helped female clerks unload heavy merchandise carts. Store procedure was that whenever a cash register was low on change a clerk would go to a master till in the stationery department to get more. Barton's departments, however, usually supplied each other with change, thus avoiding the longer walk to the master till.

Barton's immediate supervisor, Mr. Cornwall, had the reputation of being a skilled merchandiser and in the past had initiated many ideas to increase the sales volume of the store. Some of the longer-term employees said that Mr. Cornwall was very impatient and that he sometimes was rude to his subordinates while discussing merchandising problems with them.

The store manager, Mr. Blanding, had been with Denver Department Stores for twenty years and would be retiring in a few years. Earlier in his career Mr. Blanding had taken an active part in the merchandising aspect of the store, but recently he had delegated most of the merchandising and sales responsibilities to Mr. Cornwall.

(The exhibit on p. 75 is an organization chart of the store.)

Situation

Because of Mr. Cornwall's concern, Barton consulted with his department supervisors about the reason for the declining sales volume. The consensus reached was that the level of customer traffic had not been adequate to allow the departments to achieve a high sales volume. When Barton presented his problem to Mr. Cornwall, Cornwall concluded that since customer traffic could not be controlled and since the departments had been adequately stocked throughout the year, the improvement in sales would have to be a result of increased effort on the part of the clerks in each department. Cornwall added that if sales didn't improve soon the hours of both the full- and part-time sales clerks would have to be cut back. Later Barton found out that Cornwall had sent a letter around to each department informing employees of the possibility of fewer hours if sales didn't improve.

A few days after Barton received the assignment to increase sales in his department, Mr. Cornwall called him into his office again and suggested that each sales person carry a personal tally card to record daily sales. Each clerk would record his or her sales and at the end of the day the personal sales tally card would be totaled. Cornwall said that by reviewing the cards over a period of time he would be able to determine who were the "deadwood" and who were the real producers. The clerks were to be told about the purpose of the tally card and that those clerks who had low sales tallies would have their hours cut back.

Barton told Cornwall he wanted to consider this program and also discuss it with the head salespeople before implementing it. He told Mr. Cornwall that the next day was his day off but that when he returned to work the day after he would discuss this proposal with the head sales clerks.

(B)

Upon returning to the store after his day off, Mr. Barton was surprised to see each of his salespeople carrying a daily tally sheet. When he asked Mr. Cornwall why the program had been adopted so quickly, Cornwall replied that when it came to improvement of sales, no delay could be tolerated. Barton wondered what effect the new program would have on the personnel in each of his departments.

Before reading Part (C) of the case, answer these questions:

1. At the beginning of the case exactly what is the problem facing this branch of Denver Department Stores? What are the various possible reasons for this problem?
2. What are the strengths and weaknesses of the various personnel mentioned in the case (Mr. Cornwall, Mr. Barton, the clerks)?
3. In learning theory terms, describe precisely the system that Mr. Cornwall implemented. What are its possible strengths and weaknesses?
4. Predict in detail what you think will happen. To do so, you may wish to consider the various employee behaviors that are necessary for the store to function effectively.

(C)

When Mr. Cornwall issued the tally cards to Barton's salespeople, the head sales clerks failed to fill them out. Two of the head clerks had lost their tally cards when Cornwall came by later in the day to see how the program was progressing. Cornwall issued the two head clerks new cards and told them that if they

EXHIBIT 1   **Denver Department Stores organization chart.**

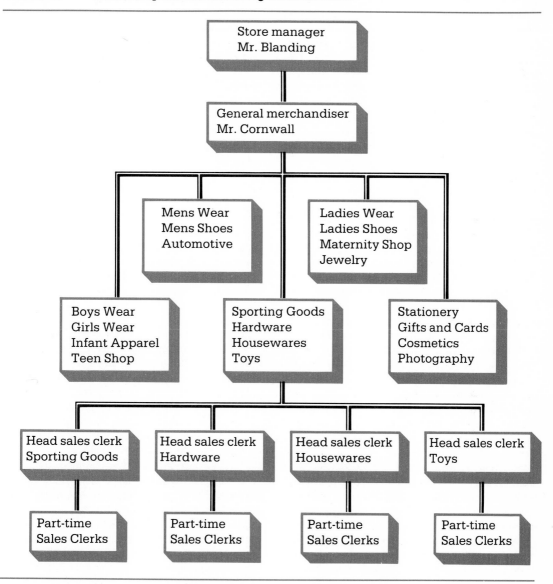

didn't "shape up" he would see some "new faces" in the departments.

The part-time salespeople filled out the cards completely, writing down every sale. The rumor that those clerks who had low sales tallies would have their hours cut spread rapidly. Soon the clerks became much more active and aggressive in their sales efforts. Customers were often approached more than once by different clerks in each department. One elderly lady complained that while making her way to the restroom in the back of the hardware department she was asked by four clerks if she needed assistance in making a selection.

When Barton returned the day after the institution of the program, the head sales clerks asked him about the new program. Barton replied that they had no alternative but to follow Cornwall's orders or quit. Later that afternoon the head clerks were seen discussing the situation on their regular break. After the break the head clerks began waiting on customers and filling out their sales tally cards.

Not long after the adoption of the program, the stock rooms began to look cluttered. Unloaded carts lined the aisles of the stock room. The shelves on the sales floor were slowly emptied and remained poorly stocked. Sales of items that had a large retail value were especially sought after and the head sales clerks were often seen dusting and rearranging these more expensive items. The head clerks' tally sheets always had the greatest amount of sales when the clerks compared sheets at the end of each day. (Barton collected them daily and delivered them to Cornwall.) The friendly conversations among salespeople and between clerks and customers were shortened and sales were rung up on the cash register and completed in a much shorter time. Breaks were no longer taken as groups and when they were taken they seemed to be much shorter than before.

When sales activity was slow in one department, clerks would migrate to other departments where there were more customers. Sometimes conflicts between clerks arose because of competition for sales. In one instance the head clerk of the hardware department interrupted a part-time clerk from the toy department who was demonstrating a large and expensive table saw to a customer. The head clerk of the hardware department introduced himself as the hardware specialist and sent the toy clerk back to his own department.

Often customers asked for items which were not on the shelves of the sales floor. When the clerk looked for the item it was found on the carts which jammed the stock room aisles. Some customers were told the item they desired wasn't in stock and later the clerk would find it on a cart in the stock room.

When Barton reported his observations of the foregoing situations to Mr. Cornwall, he was told that it was a result of the clerks' adjusting to the new program and to not worry about it. Cornwall pointed out, however, that sales volume had still not improved. He further noted that the sum of all sales reported on the tally sheets was often $500 to $600 more than total department sales according to the cash register.

A few weeks after the instigation of the tally card system Cornwall walked through the hardware department and stopped beside three carts of merchandise left in the aisle of the stock room from the morning of the day before. He talked to the head clerk in an impatient tone and asked him why the carts weren't unloaded. The clerk replied that if Mr. Cornwall had any questions about the department he should ask Mr. Barton. Cornwall picked up the telephone and angrily dialed Barton's office. Barton told him that the handling of merchandise had been preempted by the emphasis on the tally card system of recording sales. Cornwall slammed down the receiver and stormed out of the department.

That afternoon, at Barton's request, Blanding, Cornwall, and Barton visited the four departments. After talking with some of the salespeople, Mr. Blanding sent a memo announcing that the tally card program would be discontinued immediately.

After the program had been terminated, sales clerks still took their breaks separately and conversations seemed to be limited to only the essential topics needed to run the department. Barton and the head sales clerks didn't talk as freely as they had before and some of the head clerks said that Mr. Barton had failed to represent their best interests to Cornwall. Some of the clerks said they thought the tally card system was Barton's idea. The part-time people resumed the major portion of the sales and clerking jobs and the head clerks returned to merchandising. Sales volume in the departments didn't improve.

■ ■ ■

5. What behaviors were reinforced, extinguished, and punished by the system that Mr. Cornwall implemented?
6. Are there any conditions under which the tally system might have been effective?

7. What are some alternative methods by which sales might have been increased?
8. Summarize the mistakes Mr. Cornwall made in attempting to improve sales.

REFERENCES

1. For a presentation of operant learning theory, see Honig, W. K., & Staddon, J. E. R. (Eds.), (1977). *Handbook of operant behavior.* Englewood Cliffs, NJ: Prentice-Hall; for a presentation of social learning theory see Bandura, A. (1977). *Social learning theory.* Englewood Cliffs, NJ: Prentice-Hall.
2. (1972). Performance audit, feedback, and positive reinforcement. *Training and Development Journal, 26,* 8-13; (1973, Winter). At Emery Air Freight: Positive reinforcement boosts performance. *Organizational Dynamics,* 41–50.
3. Dumaine, B. (1985, January 21). Fleming's fast rise in wholesale foods. *Fortune,* 54.
4. Lawler, E. E., III (1971). *Pay and organizational effectiveness: A psychological view.* New York: McGraw-Hill; Locke, E. A., Feren, D. B., McCaleb, V. M., Shaw, K. N., & Denny, A. T. (1980). The relative effectiveness of four methods of motivating performance. In K. D. Duncan, M. M. Gruneberg, & D. Wallis (Eds.). *Changes in working life.* London: Wiley & Sons.
5. O'Hara, K., Johnson, C. M., & Beehr, T. A. (1985). Organizational behavior management in the private sector: A review of empirical research and recommendations for further investigation. *Academy of Management Review, 10,* 848–864.
6. Hermann, J. A., De Montes, A. I., Dominguez, B., Montes, F., & Hopkins, B. L. (1973). Effects of bonuses for punctuality on the tardiness of industrial workers. *Journal of Applied Behavior Analysis, 6,* 563–570.
7. Pedalino, E., & Gamboa, V. U. (1974). Behavior modification and absenteeism: Intervention in one industrial setting. *Journal of Applied Psychology, 59,* 694–698.
8. Komaki, J., Barwick, K. D., & Scott, L. R. (1978). A behavioral approach to occupational safety: Pinpointing and reinforcing safe performance in a food manufacturing plant. *Journal of Applied Psychology, 63,* 434–445. For a similar study see Haynes, R. S., Pine, R. C., & Fitch, H. G. (1982). Reducing accident rates with organizational behavior modification. *Academy of Management Journal, 25,* 407–416.
9. Luthans, F., & Kreitner, R. (1985). *Organizational behavior modification and beyond: An operant and social learning approach.* Glenview, IL: Scott, Foresman; Manz, C. C., & Sims, H. P., Jr. (1981). Vicarious learning: The influence of modeling on organizational behavior. *Academy of Management Review, 6,* 105–113.
10. Bandura, 1977; Goldstein, A. P., & Sorcher, M. (1974). *Changing supervisor behavior.* New York: Pergamon.
11. Luthans, F., & Kreitner, R. (1975). *Organizational behavior modification.* Glenview, IL: Scott, Foresman.
12. Luthans, F., & Kreitner, R. (1972). The role of punishment in organizational behavior modification (o.b.mod.). *Public Personnel Management, 2,* 156–161.
13. Ashour, A. S., & Johns, G. (1983). Leader influence through operant principles: A theoretical and methodological framework. *Human Relations, 36,* 603–626.

14. However, more research is necessary to establish the extent of this in organizations. See Arvey, R. D., & Ivancevich, J. M. (1980). Punishment in organizations: A review, propositions, and research suggestions. *Academy of Management Review, 5,* 123–132.

15. Organ, D. W., & Hamner, W. C. (1982). *Organizational behavior: An applied psychological approach* (Revised ed.). Plano, TX: Business Publications.

16. Organ & Hamner, 1982.

17. See Parmerlee, M. A., Near, J. P., & Jensen, T. C. (1982). Correlates of whistle-blowers' perceptions of organizational retaliation. *Administrative Science Quarterly, 27,* 17–34.

18. Manz, C. C., & Sims, H. P., Jr. (1980). Self-management as a substitute for leadership: A social learning theory perspective. *Academy of Management Review, 5,* 361–367.

19. Kanfer, F. H. (1980). Self-management methods. In F. H. Kanfer & A. P. Goldstein (Eds.). *Helping people change: A textbook of methods* (2nd ed.). New York: Pergamon.

20. Luthans & Kreitner, 1985; Manz & Sims, 1980.

Chapter 4

Perception, Attribution, and the Judgment of Others

ZACK THOMAS

It was 9:10 when Zack Thomas rolled his Corvette into the staff parking lot at First Seaway National Bank. Zack, branch accountant at First Seaway, had a 9 o'clock appointment with his boss, branch manager Henry Pellan. The purpose of the appointment was to discuss Pellan's review of Zack's past year's performance at the bank. Zack had begun his job there exactly one year ago, and according to bank policy, this was his first yearly performance review.

Fighting his way over the congested Narrows Bridge, Zack had had mixed feelings about the upcoming performance review session. On the one hand, Zack knew he had experienced a good year. Several changes in procedure he had suggested had saved dozens of hours a week in clerical time. In addition, some dedicated detective work on his part had uncovered a case of embezzlement at the head office and led to the apprehension of a particularly troublesome bad check writer. Although such activities required a lot of uncompensated overtime, Zack felt good about his performance. On the other hand, he was not exactly looking forward to sitting down with Henry Pellan. Zack wasn't sure why, but he and the branch manager had never hit it off very well, right from the start. However, Zack felt he got along great with the assistant manager and the tellers.

After exchanging formalities and describing the bank's performance appraisal philosophy, Henry Pellan handed Zack the rating form he had completed. Zack did a double take, as if he didn't believe his eyes.

"Mr. Pellan, I don't understand this. You've rated me below average on quality of work, quantity of work, promptness, and initiative. This doesn't make sense!"

"Zack, I just don't think you've exhibited a strong sense of commitment to the bank and dedication to your job. I'm not sure you fit in well here."

"Look, sir, what possible evidence do you have for that statement?" Zack said desperately.

"Zack, you were fifteen minutes late for work a year ago today—your first day on the job! And you've been late often ever since. That's no example to set for the others."

Zack remembered that first day with a mixture of exasperation and embarrassment. There had been an accident on the Narrows Bridge, and the traffic had been unbelievable.

"Look, Mr. Pellan, other people around here are late too, and I live in Roxboro. You know the traffic across the bridge is absolutely unpredictable."

"Our other employees are very seldom late, Zack. In fact, if I remember correctly, you were late for the bank's awards dinner and for our golf tournament too. And you know how furious I was when Gravitz was down here from the head office and you didn't get in until 10:30!"

Zack knew, all right. The Corvette had broken down on the way to work. Zack had shown Pellan the towing bill, but Pellan was so angry it hadn't seemed to register.

"My car broke down," Zack said quietly.

"Speaking of that car, Zack, are you sure a Corvette is appropriate transportation for a branch accountant? I'm certain the female tellers like it, but what image does it convey?"

Zack was flabbergasted. "Mr. Pellan, that Corvette is an eight-year-old, secondhand car. I'm happily married, and I have a kid. What about the clerical procedures I instituted? What about the bad check artist I helped nail?"

Zack left Pellan's office depressed and irritated. How could two people see things so differently? Zack resolved to cool off and enlist the help of the assistant manager in dealing with his problem.

How *could* two people see things so differently? Why did Pellan place so much emphasis on Zack's tardiness to the exclusion of his achievements? How did he form his overall impression of Zack? Was Zack just inventing excuses for his behavior? These are the kinds of questions we will attempt to answer in this chapter. First, we will define perception and examine how various aspects of the perceiver, the object or person being perceived, and the situation influence perception. Following this, a model of the perceptual process will be presented, and we will consider some of the perceptual tendencies we employ in forming impressions of people and attributing causes to their behavior. Finally, we will examine the perceptual problems of employment interview and performance evaluation situations. In general, you will learn that the perceptual system influences who gets into organizations, how they are treated as members, and how they interpret this treatment.

WHAT IS PERCEPTION?

Perception is the process of interpreting the messages of our senses to provide order and meaning to the environment. The world is a complex place, and perceptions helps us sort out and organize the input received by our senses of sight, smell, touch, taste, and hearing. The key word in this definition is *interpreting*. Mr. Pellan interpreted Zack's lateness as a lack of dedication. People frequently base their actions on the interpretation of reality provided by their perceptual system, rather than the reality itself. If you perceive your pay to be very low, you may seek employment in another firm. The reality—that you are the best paid person in your department—will not matter if you are unaware of the fact. However, to go a step further, you may be aware that you are the best paid person and *still* perceive your pay as low compared to that of the company president or your ostentatious next-door neighbor. Again, this perception may prompt you to look for work elsewhere.

Some of the most important perceptions that influence organizational behavior are the perceptions that organizational members have of each other. Such perceptions have strong potential to influence the interactions between members, as the case that began the chapter indicates. Because person perception is such an important aspect of organizational behavior, we will concentrate on person perception in this chapter.

COMPONENTS OF PERCEPTUAL EVENTS

Any perceptual event has three components—a perceiver, a target that is being perceived, and some situational context in which the perception is occurring. Each of these components influences the perceiver's impression or interpretation of the target.

The Perceiver

The perceiver's experience, motives, and emotions can affect his or her perceptions. Let's explore each of these more closely.

EXPERIENCE.   One of the most important characteristics of the perceiver that influences his or her impressions of a target is experience. Past experiences lead us to develop expectations, and these expectations affect current perceptions. In Mr. Pellan's experience, responsible bankers did not drive Corvettes, and those who did were perceived with vague distrust.

An interesting example of the influence of experience upon perceptions is revealed by the responses of executives in a development seminar who were required to read a case study regarding the operation of a steel company.[1] They were asked to specify the company's most pressing problem. Not only did their perceptions of the key problem differ, but they tended to differ according to the executives' specialties. That is, sales executives tended to see marketing problems, the industrial relations specialist identified human relations problems, and so on. As you might imagine, such differences in perceptions due to experience can sometimes lead to communication problems and conflict within organizations.

MOTIVATIONAL STATE.   In addition to experience, a major characteristic of the perceiver that influences his or her perceptions is motivational state. Motivational state refers to the particular needs that an individual has at any given point in time. These might be needs for things such as water, food, affection, or money. Frequently, our motivational state has an unconscious influence on our perceptions by causing us to perceive what we wish to perceive. Research has demonstrated that perceivers who have been deprived of food will tend to "see" more edible things in ambiguous pictures than will well-fed observers. Similarly, lonely university students may misperceive the most innocent actions of members of the opposite sex as indicating interest in them.

Consider the case of a sales representative who was puzzled by the actions of his colleagues. These sales reps worked on an incentive system, in which the individual who achieved the best sales every month was awarded a prize. What surprised the representative was the attention that the current prize was receiving—a trip to Mexico with the company president. The trip was the talk of the office. In contrast, the previous month's prize, a very expensive diamond ring, had provoked little interest. The sales rep knew that, in fact, the ring was worth about three times as much as the trip. However, it was as if the sales representatives *perceived* the trip as more valuable. It is probable that this phenomenon was caused by the motivational state of the workers. In short, they were very well paid, and it would appear that the dollar value of the trip was less important to them than its symbolic value. The chance to "hobnob" with the company president in Mexico matched their evident need for prestige and recognition, which appeared stronger than their current need for a diamond ring.

EMOTIONAL STATE.   Emotional state refers to the particular emotions that an individual is experiencing at any given point in time. Emotions such as anger, happiness, or fear can influence our perceptions. We have all had the experience of misperceiving the innocent comment of a friend or acquaintance when angry. For example, a worker who is upset about not getting a promotion might perceive the consolation provided by a co-worker as gloating condescension. On the other hand, consider the worker who does get a promotion. He is so happy that he fails to notice how upset his co-worker is because she wasn't the one promoted. Mr. Pellan was so upset with one of Zack's lateness episodes that he failed to register Zack's excuse.

In some cases, our perceptual system serves to defend us against unpleasant emotions. This phenomenon is known as **perceptual defense.** We have all experienced cases in which we ''see what we want to see'' or ''hear what we want to hear.'' In many of these instances, our perceptual system is working to ensure that we don't see or hear things that are threatening. For example, some executives fail to perceive signals that their organization is in financial trouble because they cannot handle the emotions aroused by this knowledge. Such defensivesnses can have serious consequences. One writer has made a detailed study of the planning of the disastrous Cuban Bay of Pigs invasion by President John Kennedy and his advisors. Evidence suggests that there were plenty of signals to indicate that such an invasion would fail. However, the seriousness of these signals was evidently misperceived, partly to defend the planners from the unpleasant message they contained.[2]

The Target

In addition to the experience, motivational state, and emotional state of the perceiver, perceptions are affected by characteristics of the target. Two of the most important characteristics are the degree of ambiguity of the target and the target's social status.

AMBIGUITY.   Theoretically, an ambiguous target should not present problems for a perceiver. Its characteristics or motives should simply be perceived as unclear, and that should be that. However, if you have been reading carefully, you realize how naive this viewpoint is. Perception involves interpretation and the addition of meaning to the target, and ambiguous targets are especially susceptible to interpretation and addition. Perceivers seem to have some need to resolve such ambiguities. Psychotherapists sometimes ask their clients to report what they see in ink blots. The assumption behind this is that the client's interpretation of the ambiguous blots will reveal something about the inner workings of the personality.

A word of warning should be offered about ambiguous targets. You may be tempted to believe that providing more information about the target will necessarily improve perceptual accuracy. Unfortunately, this is not always the case. Writing clearer memos may not always get the message across. Similarly, assigning minority workers to a prejudiced manager will not always improve his or her perceptions of their true abilities. As we shall see shortly, the perceiver does not or cannot always use all of the information provided by the target. In these cases, a reduction in ambiguity may not be accompanied by greater accuracy. Just ask the executive who has a hundred pages of computer printout on plant operations to guide his or her next decision!

SOCIAL STATUS.   In the case of person perception, another factor that influences our perceptions of the target is the target's social status. Social status refers to the person's position in society, and is generally determined by factors such as income, occupation, location of residence, and so on. At a simple level, status can influence our perceptions of physical characteristics. An individual was introduced to several groups of Australian students as a visitor to their university. Although he was always portrayed as coming from Cambridge University, his social status was varied by changing his academic standing (professor, senior lecturer, laboratory assistant, student). The students were then asked to estimate the height of their visitor. Perceptions of height were neatly correlated with academic standing, and the "professor" was seen as being two-and-a-half inches taller than the "student"![3]

The status of the target also affects our perceptions of what the target says. If a co-worker warned you about your attendance or work habits, you would probably perceve it differently than a warning from your boss. Organizations frequently use their high status members to make important pronouncements to enhance perceptions of the validity of these statements. Several years ago, when poisoned bottles of the headache remedy Tylenol turned up on drugstore shelves, Johnson & Johnson's chief executive officer personally represented the company's position on *Donahue* and *60 Minutes*. Although a subordinate could have made a technically accurate presentation, it was assumed that the presentation would be more believable when it came from a high-status organizational member.

The Situation

Thus far we have discussed certain characteristics of the perceiver and certain characteristics of the target that affect the former's perception of the latter. In addition, every instance of perception occurs in some situational context, and this context can affect what is perceived. The most important effect that the situation can have is to add information about the target. Imagine a casual critical comment about your performance from your boss the week before she is to decide whether or not you will be promoted. You will likely perceive this comment very differently than you would if you were not up for promotion. Also, a worker might perceive a racial joke overheard on the job very differently before and after racial strife has occurred in the plant. In both of these examples, the perceiver and the target are the same, but the perception of the target changes with the situation. Again,

EXHIBIT 4-1 **Factors that influence perception.**

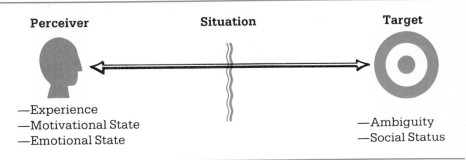

Perceiver

Situation

Target

—Experience
—Motivational State
—Emotional State

—Ambiguity
—Social Status

perception involves interpreting or adding meaning to a target, and the situation can serve to influence this interpretation and addition.

Exhibit 4-1 summarizes the factors that influence perception.

A MODEL OF THE PERCEPTUAL PROCESS

In the previous section we discussed the way the perceiver, the target, and the situation influence perception. In this section we will consider exactly how the perceiver goes about putting together the information contained in the target and the situation to form a picture of the target. In other words, how does the perceiver form his or her perceptions?

Psychologist Jerome Bruner has developed a model of the perceptual process that can provide a useful framework for our discussion.[4] A key concept in this model is cue. **Cues** are nothing more than the bits and pieces of information contained in the target and the situation that we use (or ignore) in forming our perceptions of the target. In the story at the beginning of the chapter, Zack's tardiness, his car, and his style with tellers were cues Mr. Pellan used in developing perceptions of him. The bigoted manager who underrates the performance of her minority subordinates may ignore the cues contained in their work behavior and concentrate on the cues provided by their skin color.

According to Bruner, when we encounter an unfamiliar target we are very open to the cues contained in the target and the situation surrounding it. In this unfamiliar state, we are "hard up" for information upon which to base our perceptions of the target, and we will actively seek out cues to resolve this ambiguity. Gradually, we will encounter some familiar cues (note the role of the perceiver's experience here) that enable us to crudely categorize the target in some manner. At this point, our cue search becomes less open and more selective. We begin to search out cues that confirm our categorization of the target. As this categorization becomes stronger, we tend to actively ignore or even distort cues that violate our initial perceptions. (See left side of Exhibit 4-2.) This does not mean that our early

EXHIBIT 4-2   **Bruner's model of the perceptual process and an example.**

Model	Example
Unfamiliar target encountered	New co-worker
⇓	⇓
Openness to target cues	Observation; search for information
⇓	⇓
Familiar cues encountered	Co-worker is Stanford graduate with good grades
⇓	⇓
Target categorized	Co-worker is "good man" with "great potential"
⇓	⇓
Cue selectivity	Co-worker's poor performance ignored or distorted
⇓	⇓
Categorization strengthened	Co-worker is still "good man" with "great potential"

Reprinted by permission.

categorization can't be changed. It does mean, however, that it will take a good many contradictory cues before we recategorize the target, and that these cues will have to overcome the expectations we have developed.

Let's clarify your understanding of Bruner's perceptual model with an example, shown on the right side of Exhibit 4-2. Imagine that a woman who works as an engineer for a large aircraft company is trying to size up a newly hired co-worker. Since he is an unfamiliar target, she will probably be especially open to any cues that may provide information about him. In the course of her cue search, she discovers that he has a Master's degree in aeronautical engineering from Stanford University and that he graduated with top grades. These are familiar cues, because she knows that Stanford is a top school in the field, and she has worked with many excellent Stanford graduates. She then proceeds to categorize her new co-worker as a "good man" with "great potential." With these perceptions, she takes a special interest in observing his performance, which is good for several months. This increases the strength of her initial categorization. Gradually, however, the performance of the engineer deteriorates for some reason, and his work becomes less and less satisfactory. This is clear to everyone except the other engineer, who continues to see him as adequate and excuses his most obvious errors as stemming from external factors beyond his control.

Several aspects of this example and Bruner's general model deserve elaboration. You will notice that selectivity is often exhibited in perception. Not all of the available cues are used, and those that are used are thus given special emphasis. The established engineer was especially interested in the new recruit's academic credentials and his job performance. A different observer might be interested in different cues, but would doubtless be just as selectve in forming an impression of the target. An employment interviewer will not and cannot be interested in everything a job candidate says, does, and wears. This selectivity means that our perception is efficient, and this efficiency can both aid and hinder our perceptual accuracy. The interviewer screening applicants for a sales job will sensibly pay more attention to a candidate's social skills than whether the person is wearing designer clothes. Of course, the efficiency provided by selectivity can also hurt perceptual accuracy. The engineer in the above example, in concentrating upon her new co-worker's academic background, probably ignored other cues that might have predicted the subsequent performance problem. Similarly, an interviewer who concentrates upon an applicant's sex or race at the expense of the person's past achievements will likely provide inaccurate recommendations.

Bruner's model and the accompanying example also illustrate that our perceptual system works to paint a constant and consistent picture of the target. Perceptual constancy refers to the tendency for the target to be perceived in the same way over time or across situations. We have all had the experience of "getting off on the wrong foot" with a teacher or a boss and finding it difficult to change their constant perception of us. The engineer's image of the new co-worker's performance remained constant despite objective reality. Perceptual consistency refers to the tendency to select, ignore, and distort cues in such a manner that they fit together to form a homogeneous image of the target. We strive for consistency in our perception of people. We do not tend to see the same person as both good and bad or dependable and untrustworthy. For the engineer, consistency demanded that a Stanford graduate be a good performer. Often, cues that are discrepant with our general image of a person are distorted to make them consistent with this image. An individual who has a generally good impression of an executive may perceive some of her actions as indicative of confidence. Another observer with an unfavorable image may see the same actions as evidence of conceit.

In summary, Bruner's model suggests that our perceptual system works selectively and efficiently, if not always accurately, to present us with a constant and consistent image of the target. In the next section we will consider some specific perceptual biases that contribute to selectivity, constancy, and consistency in our perception of people.

BASIC BIASES IN PERSON PERCEPTION

For accuracy's sake, it would be convenient if we could encounter others under laboratory conditions, in a vacuum or a test tube, as it were. Because the real world lacks such ideal conditions, the impressions we form of others are susceptible to a number of perceptual biases.

Primacy and Recency Effects

Given the examples of person perception that have been discussed thus far, you might gather that we form our impressions of others fairly quickly. One reason for this fast impression formation is our tendency to rely on the cues that we encounter early in a relationship. This reliance on early cues is known as the **primacy effect.** First impressions due to primacy often have a lasting impact. Thus, the worker who can favorably impress his or her boss in the first days on the job is in an advantageous position due to primacy. Similarly, the labor negotiator who comes across as ''tough'' on the first day of contract talks may find this image difficult to shake as the talks wear on. Primacy is a form of selectivity, and its lasting effects illustrate the operation of constancy. Sometimes, a **recency effect** may occur in which cues encountered most recently are given undue weight. Landing a big contract today may be perceived as excusing a whole year's bad sales performance. In the story that began the chapter, Zack Thomas may have been the victim of both primacy and recency. He was late the first day of work and the very day of his performance review.

Reliance on Central Traits

Even though perceivers tend to rely upon early information when developing their perceptions, these early cues do not receive equal weight. There is evidence that people tend to organize their perceptions around the presence of certain traits or characteristics that are of interest to them. In developing her perceptions of her new co-worker, the experienced engineer seemed to organize her impressions around his intellectual capacity. For her, this was a **central trait** that influenced her overall image of him. The centrality of traits depends upon the perceiver's interests and the situation. Thus, not all engineers would organize their perceptions of the new worker around his intellectual abilities, and the established engineer might not use this trait as a central factor in forming impressions of the people she meets at a party. Central traits often have a very powerful influence on our perceptions of others. Researchers presented groups of English university students with contrived newspaper stories about a soccer club manager and a local constable. There were two forms of each story. In one form of the soccer story, the manager was described by the team captain as ''warm-hearted.'' In the other, he was called ''a cold fish at times.'' The constable was alternately described as ''humane'' and ''ruthless.'' These traits were mixed with a number of others which remained constant across stories. Evidently, the varied traits were central to the impressions the students formed of the manager and the constable, because they strongly influenced their descriptions of the targets on other dimensions. For example, the ruthless constable was seen as more self-centered, blunt, irritable, and evasive than the humane constable.[5] Thus, it would appear that central traits are a basis for the development of consistent perceptions. Clearly, tardiness was a central trait around which Mr. Pellan organized his perceptions.

Implicit Personality Theory

In the previous example, how was it that the ruthless constable was also seen as blunt, irritable, and evasive when no information about these characteristics was presented in the newspaper stories? It has been suggested that each of us has an implicit, personal "theory" about which personality characteristics go together. Thus, the students saw ruthlessness as indicative of other traits, even though they had no objective cues to this effect. Perhaps you expect hardworking people to also be honest. Perhaps you feel that people of average intelligence tend to be most friendly. These assumed connections are examples of **implicit personality theories.** To the extent that such theories are inaccurate, they provide a basis for misunderstanding. The worker who assumes that her dominant boss is also insensitive may be reluctant to discuss a work-related problem with him that could be solved fairly easily. Mr. Pellan, the bank manager, seemed to hold an implicit personality theory that tied together lateness, lack of commitment, and flirtatious behavior.

Projection

In the absence of information to the contrary, and sometimes in spite of it, people often assume that others are like themselves. This tendency to attribute one's own characteristics and feelings to others is called **projection.** In some cases, projection is an efficient and sensible perceptual strategy. After all, people with similar backgrounds or interests often *do* think and feel similarly. Thus, it is not unreasonable for a capitalistic business person to assume that other business people favor the free enterprise system and disapprove of government intervention in this system. However, projection can also lead to perceptual difficulties. The chairperson who feels that an issue has been resolved and perceives committee members to feel the same way may be very surprised when a vote is taken. The honest warehouse manager who perceives others as honest may find stock disappearing. In the case of threatening or undesirable characteristics, projection can serve as a form of perceptual defense. The dishonest worker may say "Sure I steal from the company, but so does everyone else." Such perceptions can be used to justify the perceiver's thievery. In the story that began the chapter, Zack projected his own tardiness onto his co-workers to justify his behavior.

Stereotyping

One way to form a consistent impression of other people is simply to assume that they have certain characteristics by virtue of some category they fall into. This perceptual tendency is known as **stereotyping,** and the categories upon which a stereotype might be based include race, age, sex, ethnic background, social class, occupation, and so on. There are actually three specific aspects to stereotyping.[6]

- We distinguish some category of people (College professors).

- We assume that the individuals in this category have certain traits (Absentminded, disorganized, ivory tower mentality).

■   We perceive that everyone in this category possesses these traits ("All of my professors this year will be absent-minded, disorganized, and have an ivory tower mentality.").

People can evoke stereotypes with incredibly little information. In one study, students were asked to describe the traits of a number of ethnic groups, including several fictional ones. Although the students had never met a Danerian, a Pirenian, or a Wallonian, this did not inhibit them from assigning traits, and those assigned were usually unfavorable.[7] Of course, not all stereotypes are unfavorable. You probably hold favorable stereotypes of the social categories of which you are a member, such as student. However, it is worth noting that these stereotypes may be less well developed and less rigid than others you hold. Stereotypes help us develop impressions of ambiguous targets, and we are usually pretty familiar with the people in our own groups. In addition, this contact helps us appreciate individual differences among group members, and such differences work against the development of stereotypes. It is worth noting that the language can be easily twisted to turn neutral or even favorable information into a basis for unfavorable stereotypes. For example, if British people do tend to be reserved it is fairly easy to interpret this reserve as snobbishness. Similarly, if women who achieve executive positions have had to be aggressive, it is easy to interpret this aggressiveness as pushiness.

On the average, not all stereotypes are inaccurate. You probably hold fairly correct stereotypes about the educational level of the typical college professor and the on-the-job demeanor of the typical telephone operator. These accurate stereotypes ease the task of developing perceptions of others. However, it is probably safe to say that most stereotypes are inaccurate, especially when we use them to develop perceptions of specific individuals. This follows from the fact that stereotypes are most likely to develop when we don't have good information about a particular group.

This raises an interesting question: If many stereotypes are inaccurate, why do they persist? After all, reliance upon inaccurate information to develop our perceptions would seem to be punishing in the long run. In fact, it would appear that a couple of factors work to *reinforce* inaccurate stereotypes. For one thing, even incorrect stereotypes help us process information about others quickly and efficiently. Sometimes, it is easier for the perceiver to rely on an inaccurate stereotype than it is to discover the true nature of the target. The male manager who is required to recommend one of his twenty subordinates for a promotion may find it easier to automatically rule out promoting a woman than to carefully evaluate all of his subordinates, regardless of sex. Also, inaccurate stereotypes are often reinforced by selective perception and the selective application of language that was discussed above. The black worker who stereotypes all white managers as "honkies" or "the man" may be on the lookout for behaviors to confirm these stereotypes and fail to notice examples of fair and friendly treatment. If such treatment *is* noticed, it may be perceived as patronizing rather than helpful.

OCCUPATIONAL STEREOTYPES.   Knowing a person's occupation, we often make assumptions about his or her behavior and personality. Accountants may be stereotyped as compulsive, precise, and one-dimensional, while engineers may be perceived as cold and calculating. Labor and management representatives often hold stereotypic views of each other. One study asked union and management people to "analyze the personalities" of men shown in photographs. Each picture included a fictional description of the history of the man, who was incidentally said to be a plant manager or union official. These descriptions were manipulated so that the same picture with the same history was sometimes portrayed as a manager and sometimes as a unionist. When actual managers or unionists saw their "opposites" in the pictures, they responded with negative stereotypes—the person portrayed was seen as undependable and intellectually, emotionally, and interpersonally deficient. This occurred despite the fact that both had viewed the same photograph with the same history, except for the manipulated group membership of the portrayed person.[8] Mr. Pellan had a stereotype of bank accountants that Zack Thomas did not match.

SEX STEREOTYPES.   One of the most problematic stereotypes for organizations is the sex stereotype. Considering their numbers in the work force, women are severely underrepresented in managerial and administrative jobs. There is evidence that sex stereotypes are partially responsible for this state of affairs, discouraging women from business careers and blocking their ascent to managerial positions. It would appear that this happens because stereotypes of women do not correspond especially well with stereotypes of businesspeople or managers.

What is the nature of sex stereotypes? One researcher had managers describe men in general, women in general, and typical "successful middle managers." She determined that successful middle managers were perceived as having traits and attitudes that were more similar to those generally ascribed to men. That is, successful managers were seen as more similar to men in factors such as leadership ability, competitiveness, self-confidence, ambitiousness, and objectivity.[9] Thus, the respondents' stereotypes of successful middle managers did not correspond to their stereotypes of women. These results are especially interesting because *both* male and female managers held similar stereotypes. While it might be expected that younger women would be less likely to voice these stereotypes, such was not the case. However, there was evidence that stereotypes were weaker among women who had been managers for a longer period of time.

Granting that sex stereotypes exist, do they matter? That is, do they lead to biased personnel decisions? The answer would appear to be yes. In a typical study, male bank supervisors were asked to make hypothetical personnel decisions about workers who were described equivalently except for sex.[10] Women were discriminated against for promotion to a branch manager position. They were also discriminated against when they requested to attend a professional development conference. In addition, female supervisors were less likely than males to receive support for their request that a problem employee be fired. In one case, bias worked to *favor* women. The bank supervisors were more likely to approve a request for a

IN–FOCUS 4-1 SEXISM AND "BEAUTYISM" IN HIRING DECISIONS

By the late 1970s, there was already a sizable body of literature documenting the problems women face because of sex-role stereotypes. We speculated that attractive women might be at a real disadvantage when they aspire to occupations in which stereotypically masculine traits—such as being strong, independent and decisive—are thought to be required for success.

To test that possibility we did a study with [Barry] Gillen and Steve Burns . . . in which professional personnel consultants were hired to rate a "job applicant's" suitability for six positions. We matched the positions for the skill required, the prestige offered, and the degree of supervisory independence allowed. Two jobs were stereotypically masculine (automobile salesperson and wholesale hardware shipping and receiving clerk), two feminine (telephone operator and office receptionist) and two were sex-neutral (motel desk clerk and photographic darkroom assistant).

Each of the 72 personnel consultants who participated received a résumé package for an individual that contained the typical kinds of information that a job applicant might submit: academic standing, a list of hobbies and interests, specific skills and recommendations from teachers and counselors. All of the résumés were identical with the exception of the name ("John" vs. "Janet" Williams) and the inclusion of a photograph of the applicant. Photographs showed either an extremely attractive applicant or an unattractive one, previously judged on an attractiveness scale.

The results documented the existence of both sexism and "beautyism." On the sexism front, men were given stronger endorsements by the personnel consultants for the traditionally masculine jobs, while women were rated higher for the traditionally feminine jobs. Men were also judged to have just as much chance of success on the neutral jobs as on the masculine ones, while women were perceived to be less likely to succeed on the neutral jobs than on the feminine ones.

"Beautyism" had several facets: Attractive men were favored over their less attractive male competitors for all three types of jobs. Similarly, attractiveness gave women a competitive edge against other women, but only for traditionally female or neutral jobs. When it came to jobs inappropriate to society's traditional sex roles, the attractive women were rated lower than their less attractive female competitors.

These findings gain support from a subsequent study by Madeline Heilman and Lois Saruwatari, psychologists at Yale University. They examined the effects of appearance and gender on selection for both managerial and nonmanagerial jobs. Male and female students in a business administration class received résumé packages for equally qualified candidates. Each résumé included a photograph of either an attractive or unattractive man or woman. Being attractive was always an advantage for men. Attractive men received stronger recommendations for hiring, were judged to have better qualifications and were given higher suggested starting salaries than unattractive men for both the managerial and the nonmanagerial positions.

Among women, however, those who were less attractive actually had a significant edge over their more attractive peers when seeking a place in management, a traditionally masculine occupation. Good looks were an advantage only when women were applying for the nonmanagerial positions. Attractiveness resulted in lower salary recommendations when the women were viewed as stepping into an out-of-sex-role position.

Source: Abridged from Cash, T. F., & Janda, L. H. (1984, December). The eye of the beholder. *Psychology Today*, 46–52. Reprinted by permission.

leave of absence to care for one's children when it came from a female. This finding is similar to others which show that sex stereotypes tend to favor women when they are being considered for "women's" jobs (such as editorial assistant) or for "women's" tasks (such as supervising other women).[11] (See In–Focus 4-1.)

In general, research suggests that the above findings are fairly typical. Women suffer from a sex stereotype that is detrimental to their hiring, starting salaries, development, and promotion. Furthermore, it appears that this stereotype is held by men and women as well as managers and college students. However, the picture is not entirely bleak. There is growing evidence that the detrimental effects of sex stereotypes are reduced or removed when decision makers have good information about the qualifications and performance of particular women and an accurate picture of the job which they are applying for or seeking promotion into.[12] In particular, several field studies reveal convincingly that women do not suffer from sex stereotypes in *performance evaluations* provided by their supervisors.[13] This is not altogether surprising. Stereotypes help us process information in ambiguous situations. To the extent to which we have good information upon which to base our perceptions of people, reliance on stereotypes is less necessary. Day-to-day performance is often fairly easy to observe, and sex stereotypes do not intrude on evaluations. On the other hand, hiring and promotion decisions may confront managers with ambiguous targets or situations and prompt them to resort to sex stereotypes in forming impressions.

AGE STEREOTYPES. Another kind of stereotype that presents problems for organizations is the age stereotype. Knowing that a person falls into a certain age range, we have a tendency to make certain assumptions about the person's physical, psychological, and intellectual capabilities. Again, it would appear that such stereotypes may be partially responsible for unfair treatment of older workers. In a recent four-year period, state and federal age discrimination complaints rocketed from around 5,000 to over 19,000.[14]

What is the nature of age stereotypes that are relevant to organizational behavior? Older workers are seen as having less *capacity for performance*. They tend to be viewed as less productive, creative, logical, and capable of performing under pressure than younger workers. In addition, older workers are seen as having less *potential for development*. Compared with younger workers, they are considered more rigid and dogmatic and less adaptable. Not all stereotypes of older workers are negative, however. They tend to be perceived as more honest, dependable, and trustworthy (in short, more *stable*). In general, these stereotypes are held by both younger and older individuals. In addition, it is worth noting that there is evidence that these stereotypes are essentially inaccurate.[15]

Again, the relevant question arises—do age stereotypes affect personnel decisions? It would appear that such stereotypes may affect decisions regarding hiring, promotion, and skills development. In one study, university students were required to make hypothetical recommendations regarding younger and older male workers. An older man was less likely to be hired for a finance job that required rapid, high-risk decisions. An older man was considered less promotable for a

Do age and sex stereotypes help keep some workers in lower-level jobs?

marketing position which required creative solutions to difficult problems. Finally, an older worker was less likely to be permitted to attend a conference on advanced production systems.[16] These decisions reflect the stereotypes of the older worker depicted above. Again, however, it should be recognized that age stereotypes may have less impact upon personnel decisions when managers have good information about the capacities of the particular worker in question.

In summary, the accurate perception of others is difficult and subject to bias. Primacy, recency, central traits, implicit personality theories, projection, and stereotypes may all reduce the accuracy of impression formation.

ATTRIBUTION: PERCEIVING CAUSES AND MOTIVES

Thus far we have considered a general model of perception and discussed some specific perceptual tendencies that operate as we form impressions of others. We will now consider a further aspect of impression formation—how we perceive people's motives. This process is called attribution. **Attribution** is the process by which we assign causes or motives to people's behavior. The attribution process is important because many rewards and punishments in our society are based upon judgments about what really caused a target person to behave in a certain way.

In making attributions about behavior, an important goal is to determine whether the behavior is caused by dispositional or situational factors. **Dispositional attributions** suggest that some personality characteristic ''inside the person'' is responsible for the behavior, and that the behavior thus reflects the ''true person.'' If we explain a behavior as a function of intelligence, greed, friendliness, or laziness we are making dispositional attributions. **Situational attributions** suggest that the external situation or environment in which the target person exists was responsible for the behavior, and that the person may have had little control over the behavior. If we explain behavior as a function of bad weather, good luck, proper tools, or poor advice, we are making situational attributions. In the story that began the chapter, Zack Thomas explained his lateness in situational terms (the Narrows Bridge bottleneck), while Mr. Pellan attributed it to dispositional factors (Zack lacked commitment and dedication).

Obviously, it would be nice to be able to read minds in order to understand people's motives. Since we can't do this, we are forced to rely on external cues and make inferences from these cues. Research indicates that as we gain experience with the behavior of a target person, three implicit questions guide our decisions as to whether the behavior should be attributed to dispositional or situational causes:[17]

■   Does the person engage in the behavior regularly and consistently? **(Consistency cues)**.

■   Do most people engage in the behavior, or is it unique to this person? **(Consensus cues)**.

■   Does the person engage in the behavior in many situations, or is it distinctive to one situation? **(Distinctiveness cues)**.

Let's examine consistency, consensus, and distinctiveness cues in more detail.

Consistency Cues

Unless we see clear evidence of the operation of external constraints, we tend to perceive behavior that is performed regularly as indicative of a person's true motives. In other words, high consistency leads to dispositional attributions. Thus, one might assume that the professor who has generous office hours and is always there for consultation really cares about students. Similarly, we are likely to make dispositional attributions about workers who are consistently good or poor performers, perhaps perceiving the former as ''dedicated'' and the latter as ''lazy.'' When behavior occurs inconsistently, we begin to consider situational attributions. For example, if a person's performance cycles between mediocre and excellent, we might look to variations in workload to explain the cycles.

Consensus Cues

In general, acts that deviate from social expectations provide us with more information about the actor's motives than conforming behaviors do. Thus, unusual, low-consensus behavior leads to more dispositional attributions than typical, high-consensus behavior. The person who acts differently from the majority is seen as revealing more of his or her true motives. In a department where the norm is not to keep regular office hours, the professor who is available is seen as especially concerned with students. The informational effects of low-consensus behavior are magnified when the actor is expected to suffer negative consequences due to the deviance. Consider the job applicant who makes favorable statements about the role of big business in society while interviewing for a job at General Motors. Such statements are so predictable in this situation that the interviewer can place little confidence in what they really indicate about the candidate's true feelings and motives. On the other hand, imagine an applicant who makes critical comments about big business in the same situation. Such comments are hardly expected, and could clearly lead to rejection. In this case, the interviewer would be more confident about the applicant's true disposition regarding big business. A corollary to this would suggest that we place more emphasis upon people's private actions than their public actions when assessing their motives.[18] When our actions are not open to public scrutiny, we are more likely to act out our genuine motives and feelings. Thus, we place more emphasis upon a co-worker's private statements about his boss than we do on his public relations with the boss.

Distinctiveness Cues

When a behavior occurs across a variety of situations, it lacks distinctiveness, and the observer is prone to provide a dispositional attribution about its cause. We reason that the behavior reflects a person's true motives if it "stands up" in a variety of environments. Thus, the professor who has generous office hours, stays after class to talk to students, and attends student functions is seen as truly student-oriented. The worker whose performance was good in his first job as well as several subsequent jobs is perceived as having real ability. When a behavior is highly distinctive, in that it occurs in only one situation, we are likely to assume that some aspect of the situation caused the behavior. If the only student-oriented behavior we observe is generous office hours, we assume they are dictated by department policy. If a worker performed well on only one job, back in 1975, we suspect that his uncle owned the company!

Attribution in Action

Frequently, observers of real life behavior have information at hand about consistency, consensus, and distinctiveness. Let's take an example that shows how the observer puts such information together in forming attributions. At the same time, the example will serve to review the previous discussion. Imagine that Smith, Jones, and Kelley are employees who work in separate firms. Each is absent from work today, and an organizational observer must develop an attribution about the cause in order to decide which personnel action is warranted.

- *Smith*—Smith is absent a lot, his peers are seldom absent, and he was absent a lot in his previous job.

- *Jones*—Jones is absent a lot, her peers are also absent a lot, but she was almost never absent in her previous job.

- *Kelley*—Kelley is seldom absent, his co-workers are seldom absent, and he was seldom absent in his previous job.

Just what kind of attributions are likely to be made regarding the absences exhibited by Smith, Jones, and Kelley? Smith's absence is highly consistent, it is a low-consensus behavior, and it is not distinctive, since he was absent in his previous job. As shown in Exhibit 4–3, this combination of cues is very likely to prompt a dispositional explanation, perhaps that Smith is lazy or irresponsible. Jones is also absent consistently, but the behavior is high-consensus in that her peers also exhibit absence. In addition, the behavior is highly distinctive—she is only absent on this job. As indicated, this combination of cues will usually result in a situational attribution, perhaps that working conditions are terrible or that the boss is nasty. Finally, Kelley's absence is inconsistent. In addition, it is similar to that of co-workers and not distinctive, in that he was inconsistently absent on his previous job as well. As shown, this combination of cues suggests that some temporary, short-term situational factor causes his absence. It is possible that a sick child occasionally requires him to stay home.

In the story that began the chapter, Mr. Pellan perceived Zack's lateness as highly consistent and a low-consensus behavior, in that he felt that Zack's co-workers were seldom late. In addition, the lateness was not seen as distinctive to the work setting, because Zack was also late for activities away from work. Thus, Mr. Pellan developed the dispositional attribution that Zack's lateness stemmed from lack of dedication and commitment.

EXHIBIT 4-3   **Cue combinations and resulting attributions.**

	Consistency	Consensus	Distinctiveness	Likely attribution
Smith	High	Low	Low	Disposition
Jones	High	High	High	Situation
Kelley	Low	High	Low	Temporary situation

Biases in Attribution

As the preceding section indicates, observers often operate in a rational, logical manner in forming attributions about behavior. The various cue combinations and the resulting attributions have a sensible appearance. This does not mean that such attributions are always correct, but that they do represent good bets about why some behavior occurred. This having been said, it would be naive to assume that attributions are always free from bias or error. Earlier, a number of very basic perceptual biases were noted, and it only stands to reason that the complex task of attribution would be open to further problems. Let's consider three attribution biases.[19]

FUNDAMENTAL ATTRIBUTION ERROR.   Suppose you make a mistake in attributing a cause to someone else's behavior. Would you be likely to err on the side of a dispositional cause or a situational cause? Substantial evidence indicates that when we are making judgments about the behavior of people other than ourselves we tend to overemphasize dispositional explanations at the expense of situational explanations. This is called the **fundamental attribution error.**[20] For example, Marine Corps recruits see their gruff and demanding drill sergeant as a cold, uncaring person and discount the fact that the philosophy of the Marine training program (a situational factor) causes his behavior.

Why does the fundamental attribution error occur? For one thing, we often discount the strong effects that social roles can have on behavior. We may see bankers as truly conservative people because we ignore the fact that their occupational role and their employer dictate that they act conservatively. Second, many people we observe are seen in rather constrained, constant situations (at work, at school, etc.) which reduce our appreciation of how their behavior can vary in other situations. Thus, we fail to realize that the observed behavior is distinctive to a particular situation. That conservative banker may actually be a weekend skydiver!

The fundamental attribution error can lead to problems for the managers of poorly performing subordinates. It suggests that dispositional explanations for the poor performance will sometimes be invoked even when situational factors are the true cause. Laziness or low aptitude may be cited, while poor training or a bad sales territory are ignored. However, this is less likely when the manager has had actual experience performing the subordinate's job and is thus aware of situational roadblocks to good performance.[21]

ACTOR-OBSERVER EFFECT.   It is not surprising that actors and observers often view the causes for the actor's behavior very differently. Recall that Zack Thomas and Mr. Pellan viewed Zack's lateness from very different perspectives. This difference in attributional perspectives is called the **actor-observer effect.**[22] Specifically, while the observer may be busy committing the fundamental attribution error, the actor may be emphasizing the role of the situation in explaining his or her own behavior. Thus, as actors, we are often particularly sensitive to those environmental events that led us to be late or absent. As observers of the same

IN–FOCUS 4-2 ATTRIBUTION AND ILLEGAL BUSINESS PRACTICES

James A. Waters studied a number of cases of unethical or illegal organizational practices, such as price fixing and the bribery of government officials. Waters argues that the public, as well as organizational observers, frequently assume that the involved executives are intrinsically immoral and dishonest. Such a position is reflected in media coverage implying that formerly respected pillars of the business community were really crooks deep down. This corresponds to the proposition that observers tend to explain the behavior of others dispositionally, via personality characteristics. However, Waters contends that the unethical and illegal activities are a function of potent situational factors. In addition, he presents testimony from congressional hearings that suggests that those convicted of such activities saw themselves at the mercy of situational forces. This corresponds to the proposition that people are more likely to explain their own behavior in situational, rather than dispositional, terms. Some of the situational factors that Waters identifies as contributing to illegal and unethical business activities include the following:

■ Respected higher-status organizational members or more experienced peers serve as models, implying that such activities are acceptable practice in spite of official policy.
■ Strict chains of command inhibit conscience-stricken managers from "going over the heads" of unresponsive direct superiors.
■ When such activities are planned and carried out by special groups, there may be severe pressure to go along with the group.

■ ■ ■

Jeffrey Sonnenfeld conducted lengthy interviews with executives in the folding carton industry shortly after twenty-two companies were convicted of a massive price-fixing conspiracy. None of the executives interviewed had themselves been indicted or convicted. Sonnenfeld found that top corporate executives explained the price fixing differently from divisional executives. He determined that corporate executives, removed from the day-to-day demands of the marketplace, adopted the perspective of an external observer and attributed price fixing to dispositional factors such as low intelligence or weak morals. One said:

The individual salesman seems to think that the company message is for everyone else but them. There seem to be pretty low standards in the folding carton industry and a lot of stupid people there. Now we hear them cry, but we thought it didn't mean us. You begin to wonder about the intelligence of these people. Either they don't listen or they're just plain stupid.

Sonnenfeld found that divisional executives, closer to "the line of fire" of falling demand and tough competition, were more likely to identify with the situational constraints faced by the price fixers. One reported:

Conditions here are volatile because the very big buyers can create cyclicality. The financial pressures are very strong. We are hurting for investment due to our bad earnings record. With declining demand and no new capital, price level is crucial. The drive to stay alive has led to price collusion. Here you aren't working with a stable product or a price list. We have the same paper and equipment as our competitors. We can all make the same boxes and pictures.

Source: Waters, J. A. (1978, Spring). Catch 20.5. Corporate morality as an organizational phenomenon. *Organizational Dynamics*, 2–19 and Sonnenfeld, J. (1981). Executive apologies for price fixing: Role biased perceptions of causality. *Academy of Management Journal, 24*, 192–198.

behavior in others, we are more likely to invoke dispositional causes. (See In–Focus 4-2.)

Why are actors prone to attribute much of their own behavior to situational causes? First, they may be more aware than observers of the constraints and advantages the environment offered. At the same time, they are aware of their private thoughts, feelings, and intentions regarding the behavior, all of which may be unknown to the observer. Thus, I may know that I sincerely wanted to get to the meeting on time, that I left home extra early, and that the accident that delayed me was truly unusual. My boss may be unaware of all of this information.

SELF-SERVING BIAS. It has probably already occurred to you that certain forms of attributions have the capacity to make us feel good or bad about ourselves. In fact, people have a tendency to take credit and responsibility for successful outcomes of their behavior and to deny credit and responsibility for failures.[23] This tendency is called **self-serving bias,** and it is interesting because it suggests that the very same behavior will be explained differently due to events that happened *after* the behavior occurred. If the vice-president of marketing champions a product that turns out to be a sales success, she may attribute this to her retailing savvy. If the very same marketing process leads to failure, she may attribute this to poor performance by the marketing research firm she used. Notice that the self-serving bias can overcome the tendency for actors to attribute their behavior to situational factors. In this example, the vice-president invokes a dispositional explanation ("I'm an intelligent, competent person") when the behavior is successful.

Much self-serving bias may represent intentional self-promotion or excuse-making. However, again, it is possible that it reflects unique information on the part of the actor. Especially when behavior has negative consequences, the actor may scan the environment and find situational causes for the failure (see In–Focus 4-3).

To review the basics of the attribution process, people often use consistency, consensus, and distinctiveness cues in a sensible and rational manner when trying to explain some observed behavior. However, the fundamental attribution error suggests that observers are often overly ready to invoke dispositional explanations for the behavior of actors. The actor-observer effect suggests that the actor is more ready to attribute his or her own behavior to situational factors. According to the self-serving bias, this is especially likely if the behavior is unsuccessful.

THE ACCURACY OF PERSON PERCEPTION IN ORGANIZATIONS

How accurate are our perceptions of others? Given the attribution process just discussed, you might predict that they are not especially accurate. In fact, this would appear to be correct, especially when the perceptual task increases in complexity. At one extreme, people are good at detecting basic, simple emotions in facial exprssions, even across cultures. Americans, Japanese, and members of primitive New Guinea tribes can accurately detect anger, surprise, fear, and sadness in the same set of photographs of faces.[24] However, when the perceptual task becomes more complex, accuracy deteriorates rapidly. To illustrate this, let's consider two complex perceptual tasks common to all organizations—the employment interview and performance evaluation.

Interviewers' Perceptions of Job Applicants

In the discussion of the quiz that began Chapter 2, it was pointed out that employment interviewers are not especially good at selecting successful job applicants. Now we will explore why this is so. A typical research study of the accuracy of interviewers was often conducted like this: Several interviewers would individually interview an applicant for some job and then rate the potential successfulness of the candidate. The results? Typically, the interviewers would strongly disagree in their ratings. Obviously, this means that some of them must have been wrong in their perceptions. In summary, a large body of research shows that interviewers do not agree in their ratings of applicants and do a pretty bad job of predicting actual success.[25]

Why do experienced interviewers have so much trouble selecting successful performers? It is apparent that perceptual errors are partially responsible. To consider the most obvious problem first, applicants are usually motivated to present an especially favorable impression of themselves. As our discussion of the perception of people implies, it is difficult enough to gain a clear picture of another individual without having to cope with active deception! A couple of the perceptual tendencies we have already discussed have also been shown to operate in the interview context. For one thing, there is evidence that interviewers compare applicants with a stereotype of the ideal applicant.[26] In and of itself this is not a bad thing. However, this ideal stereotype must be accurate, and this requires a clear understanding of the nature of the job in question and the kind of person who can do well in this job. This is a tall order, especially for the interviewer who is hiring applicants for a wide variety of jobs. Secondly, interviewers have a tendency to exhibit primacy reactions. One study revealed that decisions were reached after less than five minutes time in fifteen-minute interviews.[27] Evidently the rest of the time is spent in small talk or selectively justifying the early decision.

A couple of perceptual tendencies not discussed earlier have also been observed in interviews. First, interviewers have a tendency to *underweight positive information* about the applicant.[28] This means that negative information has undue impact on the decision. This may occur because interviewers get more feedback about unsuccessful hiring than successful hiring (''Why did you send me that idiot?'') It may also happen because positive information isn't perceived as telling the interviewer much, since the candidate is motivated to put up a good front. In addition, **contrast effects** sometimes occur in the interview.[29] This means that the applicants who have been interviewed previously affect the interviewer's perception of a current applicant. For example, if the interviewer has seen two excellent candidates, and then encounters an average candidate, she may rate this person lower than if he had been preceded by two average applicants. You will note that this is an example of the impact of the situation upon perception.

This section should not be taken as an attack on employment interviewers. It is clear that the interview encounter represents a very difficult situation in which to form accurate impressions about others. It is of short duration, a lot of information is generated, and the applicant is motivated to present a favorable image. Thus, it is no wonder that interviewers often adopt ''perceptual crutches'' that hinder accurate perception. By the way, interviewers can serve a very useful function by presenting a clear and realistic picture of the job in question and the organization to applicants.[30] This may provide candidates with accurate expectations and allow them to decide if they are really cut out for the job.

Observers' Perceptions of Job Performance

Once a person is hired, however imperfectly, further perceptual tasks confront organization members. Specifically, the organization will want some index of the person's job performance for decisions regarding pay raises, promotions, transfers, and training needs. Measures of job performance are also useful for evaluating the impact of changing factors like job design or pay plans.

OBJECTIVE AND SUBJECTIVE MEASURES.   It is possible to find objective measures of performance for certain aspects of some jobs. These are measures that do not involve a substantial degree of human judgment. Accurate attendance records are examples of objective performance measures. So are the dollar sales achieved by salespeople or the number of defect-free pieces turned out by machine operators. Unfortunately, objective performance measures have many problems associated with them. In general, as we move up the organizational hierarchy, it becomes more difficult to find objective indicators of performance. Thus, it is often hard to find countable evidence of a manager's success or failure. When objective indicators of performance do exist, they are often contaminated by situational factors. For example, it may be very difficult to compare the dollar sales of a snowmobile salesperson whose territory covers dealers in Maryland and Virginia with one whose territory is Minnesota and Wisconsin. Also, objective performance measures for a given job may be deficient in their coverage of all the relevant areas of performance. While dollar sales may be a good indicator of current sales performance, they may say little about a person's capacity for sales management. Thus, dollar sales may be a weak foundation on which to base a promotion to district sales manager.

Because of the difficulties that objective performance indicators present, organizations must often rely upon subjective measures of effectiveness. Thus, perceptual judgments of performance are made by observers of the job incumbents. These observers are usually the workers' direct superiors, and they typically report their judgments on rating scales designed to tap several dimensions of effectiveness (e.g., quantity of work, quality of work, leadership capacity, etc.). Compared with the employment interviewer, the performance evaluator should be in a better perceptual position. After all, such a person should have ample opportunity to observe examples of real performance over an extended period of time. However, the performance evaluator is also confronted by a number of perceptual roadblocks. The evaluator may not be in a position to observe many instances of effective and ineffective performance. This is especially likely when the subordinate's job activities cannot be monitored directly by the boss. For example, a police sergeant cannot ride around in six squad cars at the same time, and a telephone company supervisor cannot visit customers' homes or climb telephone poles with all of his or her installers. Such situations mean that the target (the subordinate's performance) is frequently ambiguous, and we have seen that the perceptual system resolves ambiguities in an efficient but often inaccurate manner. Even when performance is observable, performers may alter their behavior to look good when the boss is around.

RATER ERRORS.   Subjective performance evaluation is surely susceptible to some of the perceptual biases discussed earlier, including primacy and stereotypes. In addition, a number of other perceptual tendencies occur in performance evaluation. One class of these tendencies includes leniency, harshness, and central tendency (Exhibit 4-4). **Leniency** refers to the tendency to perceive the performance of one's ratees as especially good, while **harshness** is the tendency to see their performance as especially ineffective. Lenient raters tend to give ''good'' ratings, and harsh raters tend to give ''bad'' ratings. Professors with

EXHIBIT 4-4   **Leniency, harshness, and central tendency rater errors.**

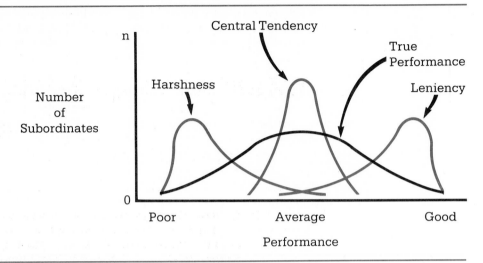

reputations as easy graders or tough graders exemplify these types of raters. **Central tendency** involves assigning most ratees to a middle-range performance category—the extremes of the rating categories are not used. The professor who assigns 80 percent of her students *C*s is committing this error. Each of these three rating tendencies is probably partially a function of the rater's personal experiences. For example, the manager who has had an especially good group of subordinates may respond with special harshness when transferred to supervise a group of slightly less able workers. It is worth noting that not all instances of leniency, harshness, and central tendency represent perceptual errors. In some cases, raters may intentionally commit these errors, even though they have accurate perceptions of workers' performance. For example, a manager might use leniency or central tendency in performance reviews so that his subordinates do not react negatively to his evaluation.

Another perceptual error frequently committed by performance raters is called **halo.**[31] The halo effect occurs when the observer allows the rating of an individual on one trait or characteristic to color ratings on other traits or characteristics. For example, in a teacher evaluation system, a student may perceive his instructor as a nice person, and this may favorably influence his perception of the instructor's knowledge of the material and speed in returning exams and papers. Similarly, a manager may rate a subordinate as frequently late for work, and this may in turn lead her to devalue the subordinate's productivity and quality of work, as Mr. Pellan did in the story that began the chapter. As these examples illustrate, halo can work either for or against the ratee. In both cases, the rater fails to perceive differences *within* ratees. It is probably safe to assume that halo tends to be organized around central traits that the rater considers important. The student feels that being nice is an especially important quality, while the manager places

Do people succeed in their fields because of similar-to-me errors?

special emphasis upon promptness. Ratings on these characteristics then affect the rater's perceptions of other characteristics.

The **similar-to-me effect** is an additional rater error that may in part reflect perceptual bias. The rater tends to give more favorable evaluations to persons who are similar to the rater in terms of background or attitudes. For example, the manager with an M.B.A. degree who comes from an upper middle class family may perceive a similar subordinate as a good performer even though the person is only average. Similarly, a rater may overestimate the performance of an individual who holds similar religious and political viewpoints. Such reactions probably stem from a tendency to view our own performance, attitudes, and background as "good." We then tend to generalize this evaluation to others who are to some degree similar to us.

A final rater error that may often be perceptual in nature is called **knowledge of predictor bias.** This unusual name refers to cases in which the rater gains knowledge of some factor that may predict the success of the ratee, and then rates the subordinate to confirm this prediction. For example, there is a large retail food chain that puts certain store employees through a series of exercises and tests designed to predict promotability to managerial positions. The superiors of the employees are made aware of their subordinates' scores on these tests and exercises. Promotions are based upon these scores and on subsequent ratings of managerial potential made by the superiors. Not surprisingly, the managers always see the high-scoring subordinates as most promotable! This is probably a partial function of selective perception. Knowing which subordinates are *supposed* to be most promotable (from their test and exercise scores), the superiors tend to see their effective behaviors and miss their ineffective behaviors. Thus, the high scorers are invariably perceived as promotable and are given good ratings by the boss. The same effect can occur in other settings. A friend whose judgment you trust may tell you that Professor Bloggs is an excellent teacher. When you take Bloggs's class, you may be predisposed to notice his good aspects and deemphasize his bad characteristics. As we said earlier, expectations held by the perceiver influence his or her perception of the target.

Given all of these problems, it should be clear that it is difficult to get good subjective evaluations of employee performance. Because of this, personnel specialists have explored various techniques for reducing perceptual errors and biases. Obviously, knowledge of predictor bias can be controlled by being sure that predictors of performance are unavailable to the performance rater. Halo can be reduced by requiring the rater to evaluate all ratees on a given performance characteristic before going to the next characteristic, rather than rating one person on all characteristics before turning to the next person. In recent years, there has been a tendency to attempt to reduce rater errors by going to rating scales with more specific behavioral labels. The assumption here is that giving specific examples of effective and ineffective performance will facilitate the rater's perceptual processes and recall. Exhibit 4-5 shows a traditional rating scale that could be used to measure police patrol officer performance on the dimension of judgment. Clearly, such a scale is open to most of the perceptual errors discussed above. It simply does little to help the rater avoid these errors. Exhibit 4-6 shows a behaviorally anchored rating scale that gives very specific behavioral examples of good, average, and poor judgment. With such an aid, the rater may be less likely to succumb to perceptual errors when completing the rating task, although the evidence for this is mixed.[32]

EXHIBIT 4-5   **Traditional rating scale that might be used to evaluate a police officer's judgment.**

This Officer's Judgment is:

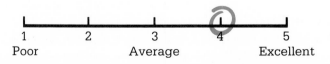

EXHIBIT 4-6   **Behaviorally anchored scale for rating police officer judgment.**

HIGH

Calls for assistance and clears the area of bystanders before confronting a barricaded, heavily-armed suspect.

Notices potentially dangerous situations before anything actually occurs.

Radios in his position and discontinues a high-speed chase before entering areas of high vehicle and pedestrian traffic, such as school areas.

AVERAGE

Issues warnings instead of tickets for traffic violations which occur at particularly confusing intersections for motorists.

Permits traffic violators to explain why they violated the law and then decides whether or not to issue a citation.

Does not leave a mother and daughter in the middle of a fight just because no law is being violated.

LOW

Enters a building with a broken door window instead of guarding the exits and calling for a backup unit.

Does nothing in response to a complaint about a woman cursing loudly in a restaurant.

Continues to write a traffic violation when he hears a report of a nearby robbery in progress.

Judgment—Observation and assessment of the situation and taking appropriate action.

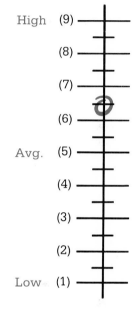

The rater observes the examples to the left in order to understand instances of high, average, and poor judgment. The rater then marks the scale with a circle to indicate the officer's level of performance on judgment.

Source: From Landy, F. J., & Farr, J. L. (1975). *(A) Performance Description Scales* and *(B) Instructions and Examples for Performance Description Scales (Supervisor).* © 1975. Reprinted by permission.

In conclusion, the perceptual task confronting the performance evaluator is difficult but subject to improvement. Such improvements are necessary to provide the organization with accurate information on which to base decisions regarding pay, promotions, and training needs.

SUMMARY

■ Perception involves interpreting the input from our senses to provide meaning to our environment, and any instance of perception involves a perceiver, a target, and a situational context. The experience, motivational state, and emotional state of the perceiver affect perception, as do the ambiguity and social status of the target.

■ Bruner's model of the perceptual process suggests that we are very receptive to cues provided by the target and the situation when we encounter an unfamiliar target. However, as we discover familiar cues we quickly categorize the target and process other cues to maintain a consistent and constant picture of the target. When the target is a person, this drive for constancy and consistency is revealed in a number of specific perceptual biases, including primacy, recency, implicit personality theory, reliance on central traits, projection, and stereotyping. Sex and age stereotypes are especially problematic for organizations.

■ Attribution is the process of assigning causes or motives to people's behavior. The observer is often interested in determining whether the behavior is due to dispositional (internal) or situational (external) causes. Behavior is likely to be attributed to the disposition of the actor when the behavior 1) is performed consistently, 2) differs from that exhibited by other people, and 3) occurs in a variety of situations or environments. An opposite set of cues will prompt a situational attribution. Observers are biased toward making dispositional attributions, while actors are more likely to explain their own behavior in situational terms, especially when its outcomes are unfavorable.

■ Judging the suitability of job applicants in an interview and evaluating job performance are especially difficult perceptual tasks, in part because the target is motivated to convey a good impression. In addition, interviewers and performance raters exhibit a number of perceptual tendencies that are reflected in inaccurate judgments.

KEY CONCEPTS

Perception	Fundamental attribution error
Perceptual defense	Actor-observer effect
Cues	Self-serving bias
Primacy effect	Contrast effects
Recency effect	Leniency
Central trait	Harshness
Implicit personality theory	Central tendency
Projection	Halo
Stereotyping	Similar-to-me effect
Attribution	Knowledge of predictor bias
Dispositional attributions	
Situational attributions	
Consistency cues	
Consensus cues	
Distinctiveness cues	

DISCUSSION QUESTIONS

1. Discuss how differences in the experiences of students and professors might affect their perceptions of students' written work and class comments.

2. Discuss the occupational stereotypes you hold of computer programmers, the clergy, truck drivers, bartenders, and bankers. How do you think these stereotypes have developed? Has an occupational stereotype ever caused you to commit a socially embarrassing error when meeting someone for the first time?

3. Use Bruner's perceptual model (Exhibit 4-2) to explain why performance evaluation and interviewers' judgments are frequently inaccurate.

4. Discuss the assertion that "the perception of reality is more important than reality itself" in the context of organizations.

5. Suppose an employee does a particularly poor job on an assigned project. Discuss the attribution process this person's manager will use to form judgments about this poor performance. Be sure to discuss how consistency, consensus, and distinctiveness cues will be used.

6. A study of small business failures found that owners generally cited factors such as economic depression or strong competition as causes. However, creditors of these failed businesses were much more likely to cite ineffective management. What attribution bias is indicated by these findings? Why do you think the difference in attribution occurs?

7. Discuss the factors that make it difficult for employment interviewers to form accurate perceptions of interviewees.

8. Using the material in the chapter, explain why managers and subordinates often differ in their perceptions of subordinate performance.

FOR FURTHER READING

Carroll, S. J., & Schneier, C. E. (1982). *Performance appraisal and review systems: The identification, measurement, and development of performance in organizations.* Glenview, IL: Scott, Foresman.

An excellent discussion of performance appraisal and its perceptual problems. Discusses how to develop, use, and evaluate appraisal systems to combat perceptual errors and bias.

Rosen, B., & Jerdee, T. H. (1984). *Older employees: New roles for valued resources.* Homewood, IL: Dow Jones-Irwin.

Discusses the fact and fiction of performance capabilities of older employees. Provides useful guidelines for communicating with and managing such workers.

Zalkind, S. S., & Costello, T. W. (1962). Perception: Some recent research and implications for administration. *Administrative Science Quarterly, 7,* 218–235.

A much-reprinted article that discusses the nature of the perceptual process and how perception influences organizational behavior.

Case Study

The Tale of the Gordian Knot

To say that the Marketing Department at Blanchard Manufacturing Company was demoralized would, most certainly, be an understatement. The morale decline had started almost two years ago as the market for barber chairs (the firm's major product line) began to decline. Retail barbers were suffering from changes in men's attitudes about hair styles. Few new shops were opening and many established barbers were cautious about remodeling their shops during an industry recession.

But the devastating blow for Blanchard occurred ten months ago when a Japanese manufacturer, Toyo-Satumi, introduced a high-quality barber chair into the American market at slightly more than two thirds the cost of the equivalent Blanchard chair. The move was unexpected, swift, and comprehensive. Toyo-Satumi had carefully established a large dealer network, promoted heavily within the trade and, within months, made significant inroads into traditional Blanchard markets.

Morton Feinstein, then the Director of Marketing, was summarily terminated for having failed to anticipate or have knowledge of the planned move by Toyo-Satumi. Feinstein was well liked by the marketing staff who viewed his dismissal as a pure case of company "scapegoat."

Feinstein was replaced by his assistant, Larry Golden. Golden, an unimaginative paper shuffler, muddled and further confused the staff for several months before he resigned under top management pressure. For the last two months the position of

Source: Joyce, R. D. (1972). *Encounters in organizational behavior: Problem situations.* Elmsford, NY: Pergamon, pp. 14–16.

Marketing Director has been open. Owen Blanchard, the president, has been personally covering the position while actively shopping for a high powered marketing man to head the department.

Today was the big day. Owen Blanchard smiled broadly as he personally introduced Harvey Grainger to the marketing staff and extolled Grainger's past marketing accomplishments in other industries.

The staff anxiously waited to hear what Grainger would say . . . to find out what kind of person he was and what direction he would move the stalled department. Blanchard then turned the group meeting over to Grainger.

"Ladies and gentlemen," said Grainger, "in a very short period of time I will be better acquainted with each of you and your respective roles in our mutual marketing effort. I am new to Blanchard and an unknown quantity to most of you. Let me take a few moments to give you a better idea by illustration of my way of working, my 'style' so to speak."

Grainger continued, "There is an old legend from Greek mythology about a small village which was constantly under attack by local barbaric tribes. The problem was one of leadership. There were sufficient men in the village to successfully ward off the attacks but the men were disorganized and ineffective. There was no one person or symbol around which they could rally.

"One year a stranger by the name of Gordias came to their village and provided leadership when the village was next attacked. A grateful village honored Gordias by naming him king for life.

"Gordias was a wise man. He knew it was a change in attitude among the men which had saved the village and not his sword alone. He decided to provide the village with a symbol of unity and strength which would bind them together even after his eventual death.

"And so a chariot was moved to the outskirts of the village and Gordias took a very long rope and tied a large knot around the yoke of the chariot. When he finished, he had fashioned the most complex knot known to man. No ends of the rope showed to even indicate how one might begin to unravel it. He named it the Gordian Knot.

"Then he proclaimed, 'My leadership of this village is hereby established and will remain so in perpetuity through my descendants. This village shall never be ruled by anyone else unless he has the great wisdom to untie the Gordian Knot. If he can do this he is truly fit to become your leader.'

"Many years passed and Gordias eventually died. His son ruled after him and his son after that. There was never again so great a leader but the village remained secure for, although many knew of the legend, no one could ever untie the Gordian knot.

"One day the army of Alexander the Great marched to the edge of the remote Asian village. Alexander asked the meaning of the strange knot tied to the chariot yoke and was told of the legend.

"Alexander stared at the knot for some time but did not attempt to untie it. Then he unsheated his sword, raised it above his head, and slashed the knot to its very core! 'Thus do I untie the Gordian Knot' he proclaimed and marched his army into the village."

There was complete silence when Grainger finished. Then he added, "Symbols of strength will not stop us. We will cut through to the very core and march on!"

Later in the hallway, three marketing people discussed their reactions to Grainger's speech:

"What do you think of Grainger?" asked one.

"Don't know for sure, but I get the feeling he's action oriented," said the second.

"But I read in his remarks that it might get a little bloody if you stand in his way," said the third.

"Well," asked one, "what kind of a leader was Grainger trying to tell us he is? I got the impression that he's a hard headed pragmatist."

"Time will tell," said the second, "but a more descriptive word might be *dictator*."

"Or maybe that he's a Greek God," offered the third with tongue in cheek.

■ ■ ■

1. Having heard the story of the Gordian Knot, what are your impressions of Grainger and his motives?
2. Account for the different perceptions of Grainger. After all, all of the staff heard the same speech.
3. Debate: The different perceptions of Grainger are interesting, but irrelevant. How Grainger acts toward his staff in succeeding days will be much more important than anything he says at this meeting.
4. Regardless of Grainger's exact intentions in telling the story of the Gordian Knot, evaluate the general effectiveness of the way he chose to introduce himself.
5. Generalize from the story of Grainger and the Gordian Knot to other first encounters you have had. Consider, for example, your first encounter with your organizational behavior instructor.

REFERENCES

1. Dearborn, D. C., & Simon, H. A. (1958). Selective perception: A note on the departmental identification of executives. *Sociometry, 21,* 140–144.
2. Janis, I. (1982). *Groupthink: Psychological studies of policy decisions and fiascoes.* Boston: Houghton Mifflin.
3. Wilson, P. R. (1968). The perceptual distortion of height as a function of ascribed academic status. *Journal of Social Psychology, 74,* 97–102.
4. Bruner, J. S. (1957). On perceptual readiness. *Psychological Review, 64,* 123–152.
5. Warr, P. B., & Knapper, C. (1968). *The perception of people and events.* London: Wiley.

6. Secord, P. F., Backman, C. W., & Slavitt, D. R. (1976). *Understanding social life: An introduction to social psychology.* New York: McGraw-Hill.

7. Hartley, E. L. (1946). *Problems in prejudice.* New York: King's Crown Press.

8. Haire, M. (1955). Role-perceptions in labor-management relations: An experimental approach. *Industrial and Labor Relations Review, 8,* 204–216.

9. Schein, V. E. (1975). Relationships between sex role stereotypes and requisite management characteristics among female managers. *Journal of Applied Psychology, 60,* 340–344.

10. Rosen, B., & Jerdee, T. H. (1974). Influence of sex role stereotypes on personnel decisions. *Journal of Applied Psychology, 59,* 9–14.

11. Cohen, S. L., & Bunker, K. A. (1975). Subtle effects of sex role stereotypes on recruiters' hiring decisions. *Journal of Applied Psychology, 60,* 566–572. See also Rose, G. L., & Andiappan, P. (1978). Sex effects on managerial hiring decisions. *Academy of Management Journal, 21,* 104–112.

12. Tosi, H. L., & Einbender, S. W. (1985). The effects of the type and amount of information in sex discrimination research: A meta-analysis. *Academy of Management Journal, 28,* 712–723.

13. For a review see Dipboye, R. L. (1985). Some neglected variables in research on discrimination in appraisals. *Academy of Management Review, 10,* 116–127; For a representative study see Peters, L. H. et al. (1984). Sex bias and managerial evaluations: A replication and extension. *Journal of Applied Psychology, 69,* 349–352.

14. Faley, R. H., Kleiman, L. S., & Lengnick-Hall, M. L. (1984). Age discrimination and personnel psychology: A review and synthesis of the legal literature with implications for future research. *Personnel Psychology, 37,* 327–350.

15. Rosen, B., & Jerdee, T. H. (1976). The nature of job-related age stereotypes. *Journal of Applied Psychology, 61,* 180–183; For a more complete review of age-related characteristics see Rhodes, S. R. (1983). Age-related differences in work attitudes and behavior. *Psychological Bulletin, 93,* 328–367; For a review of the age-performance relationship see Waldman, D. A., & Avolio, B. J. (1986). A meta-analysis of age differences in job performance. *Journal of Applied Psychology, 71,* 33–38.

16. Rosen, B., & Jerdee, T. H. (1976). The influence of age-stereotypes on managerial decisions. *Journal of Applied Psychology, 61,* 428–432; Also see Cleveland, J. N., & Landy, F. J. (1983). The effects of person and job stereotypes on two personnel decisions. *Journal of Applied Psychology, 68,* 609–619.

17. Kelley, H. H. (1972). Attribution in social interaction. In E. E. Jones et al. (Eds.), *Attribution: Perceiving the causes of behavior.* Morristown, NJ: General Learning Press.

18. Baron, R. A., Byrne, D., & Griffitt, W. (1974). *Social psychology: Understanding human interaction.* Boston: Allyn and Bacon.

19. This discussion of attribution biases draws upon Fiske, S. T., & Taylor, S. E. (1984). *Social cognition.* Reading, MA: Addison-Wesley.

20. Ross, L. (1977). The intuitive psychologist and his shortcomings: Distortions in the attribution process. In L. Berkowitz (Ed.), *Advances in experimental social psychology* (Vol. 10). New York: Academic Press; Jones, E. E. (1979). The rocky road from acts to dispositions. *American Psychologist, 34,* 107–117.

21. Mitchell, T. R., & Kalb, L. S. (1982). Effects of job experience on supervisor attributions for a subordinate's poor performance. *Journal of Applied Psychology, 67,* 181–188.

22. Watson, D. (1982). The actor and the observer: How are their perceptions of causality divergent? *Psychological Bulletin, 92,* 682–700.

23. Greenwald, A. G. (1980). The totalitarian ego: Fabrication and revision of personal history. *American Psychologist, 35,* 603–618.

24. Ekman, P. (Ed.). (1982). *Emotion in the human face* (2nd ed.). Cambridge: Cambridge University Press.

25. Ulrich, L., & Trumbo, D. (1965). The selection interview since 1949. *Psychological Bulletin, 63,* 100–116.

26. Schmitt, N. (1976). Social and situational determinants of interview decisions: Implications for the employment interview. *Personnel Psychology, 29,* 70–101.

27. Springbett, B. M. (1958). Factors affecting the final decision in the employment interview. *Canadian Journal of Psychology, 12,* 13–22.

28. Hollman, T. D. (1972). Employment interviewers' errors in processing positive and negative information. *Journal of Applied Psychology, 56,* 130–134.

29. Schmitt, 1976.

30. Wanous, J. P. (1980). *Organizational entry: Recruitment, selection and socialization of newcomers.* Reading, MA: Addison-Wesley.

31. Cooper, W. H. (1981). Ubiquitous halo. *Psychological Bulletin, 90,* 218–244.

32. Kingstrom, P. D., & Bass, A. R. (1981). A critical analysis of studies comparing behaviorally anchored rating scales (BARS) and other rating formats. *Personnel Psychology, 34,* 263–289; Landy, F. J., & Farr, J. L. (1983). *The measurement of work performance.* New York: Academic Press.

Chapter 5

Attitudes and Job Satisfaction

"PLUM" JOBS

Candice Rowe and Mike Sherrill landed what were generally considered by their M.B.A. graduating class to be the "plum" jobs of the year. Both were corporate planning jobs in the large conglomerate United Products. United had a reputation for offering good salaries and job security. However, new M.B.A.s usually began their jobs "in the trenches" in one of the firms held by United and gradually worked their way up to a headquarters posting. Candice's and Mike's planning jobs were already at headquarters. By most standards, they paid well and offered some interesting opportunities for expense account travel. Candice and Mike were the envy of their classmates when they received their offers from United. Thus, most were amazed to learn that Mike had quit his job only seven months after being hired. Mike's boss was also surprised, since his performance had been fine during the seven months.

The person who wasn't surprised about Mike's quitting was Candice. Between trips, they frequently compared notes on the jobs they held, jobs that were essentially identical except for the specific project each was working on. Early on, Mike began to indicate that he was less than happy with what he had gotten himself into.

"This travel is really getting to me, Candice. My wife and kids look at me like I'm a deserter when I tell them I've got another business trip coming up."

Candice, who was single, responded, "Yes, I guess it's tough when you have a family. It's funny, though, I really like the travel. It's like a fringe benefit for me, getting to see so many places."

"Also," continued Mike, "the extra hours I'm putting in here when I'm not travelling are causing the same problem. I'm often working until seven every night. When I was an engineer, we'd get paid overtime for doing that!"

Candice looked thoughtful and then said, "I guess I don't mind putting in the extra hours because everyone else here is doing it. If others were taking off early, I'm sure I'd change my tune."

On another occasion, Mike and Candice had discussed the actual kind of work done in corporate planning. Candice said, "I'm glad this is a staff job. I'm good at digging out information, doing financial projections, and writing reports. I don't think I'd be very good at line management—telling people what to do."

Mike laughed. "I got out of engineering and took an M.B.A. so I *could* tell people what to do. Somehow, though, I've landed another staff position here at United, and I don't have any slaves at my beck and call!"

Shortly after this discussion, Mike told Candice that he had landed a management position back at his old engineering firm, and that he would be leaving United in two weeks.

Candice marvelled at how two people could view the same job so differently.

This familiar scenario raises some interesting issues. How do attitudes toward the job develop, and how can two employees exhibit such different attitudes toward the same job? How important are such attitudes to individuals and organizations? And why didn't Mike's performance suffer because of his unhappiness? In this chapter, we will attempt to answer questions of this kind. First we will examine the nature of attitudes and their major components, beliefs and values. Then we will discuss techniques that organizations attempt to use to change employee attitudes and the factors that contribute to the success of these endeavors. Finally, we will consider job satisfaction, an attitude of special interest to organizations. Both its causes and consequences will be examined.

WHAT ARE ATTITUDES?

Although your conception of the meaning of the term *attitude* may be vague, you are probably aware that you hold attitudes toward many people and things in your environment. Thus, you might have attitudes regarding diet soda, French food, the Middle East conflict, and your organizational behavior professor. In this section, we will attempt to clarify the meaning of attitude.

An **attitude** is a fairly stable emotional tendency to respond consistently to some object, situation, person, or category of people. First, notice that attitudes involve *emotions*. If I inquire about your attitude toward diet soda, you will probably tell me something about how well you *like* it. Similarly, if I ask you about the Middle East conflict, you may tell me that you *favor* the Arab or the Israeli position. These responses are indicative of your emotional reactions toward the subject in question. *Emotional* should not be equated with *irrational*. It simply connotes some tendency to approach or avoid a subject.

Secondly, notice that attitudes are *relatively stable*. Under normal circumstances, our attitudes are not subject to especially rapid change. If you truly dislike diet soda or the Arab position today, you will probably dislike them tomorrow. Of course, some attitudes are less strongly held than others and are thus more open to change. Your ethnic background may dictate a very fixed attitude toward the Middle East situation, but your attitude toward diet soda may not be backed by direct experience. By simply buying you a diet soda I may be able to change your attitude toward it.

Third, our definition indicates that attitudes represent *tendencies to respond* to the subject of the attitude. This means that attitudes often influence our behavior toward some object, situation, person, or group:

ATTITUDE ⤳ BEHAVIOR

This is hardly surprising. If you truly dislike diet soda, I would not expect to see you drinking it. By the same token, if you favor the Israeli position in the Middle East, it would not be surprising to see you send a letter to the *New York Times* to discuss the reasons for your support of this position:

DISLIKE DIET SODA $\rightsquigarrow$ DON'T DRINK DIET SODA

SUPPORT ISRAEL $\rightsquigarrow$ SEND LETTER TO *TIMES*

Of course, not everyone who supports Israel sends letters to the *Times*. Often, our attitudes are not reflected in observable behavior. For example, you may strongly dislike one of your professors, but this dislike may not be reflected in your actions or speech. Anyone who "sweet talks" a despised in-law can attest to this phenomenon. These examples indicate that attitudes are not always consistent with behavior, and that attitudes provide useful information over and above the actions we can observe.

The story that began the chapter illustrates the attitudes of Candice and Mike toward their jobs at United Products. Both were emotionally disposed toward the travel required and the nature of the work that the planning job involved. Over the seven months, these attitudes revealed some stability and consistency. In one sense, Mike's behavior corresponded to his unfavorable attitudes, since he quit his job. Notice, however, that his performance had not deteriorated. The attitudes exhibited by Candice and Mike are called *job satisfaction*. We shall examine these attitudes in detail later in the chapter.

THE FORMATION OF ATTITUDES

Where do attitudes come from? Put simply, attitudes are a function of what we think and what we feel. Thus, an attitude is a product of an interrelated thought and feeling. These thoughts are called beliefs and these feelings are called values.

Beliefs

Beliefs are assumed facts or statements about the nature of the world that do not involve evaluation. As such, they merely describe how certain concepts or ideas are perceived to fit together. Some examples of beliefs might include the following:

- Steel is hard.
- Diet soda has fewer calories than regular soda.
- The four-day workweek improves job satisfaction.
- Close, directive supervision leads to high productivity.

You will notice that beliefs do indeed reveal relationships between concepts (e.g., length of workweek and satisfaction). Beliefs are learned by the processes we discussed in Chapter 3. In some cases, the reinforcers for our beliefs have been acquired through direct experience. This is probably how you know that steel is hard. In many cases, however, our beliefs have been reinforced indirectly. Thus, you probably believe that diet soda has reduced calories because it is so advertised, not because you have measured your waistline or done a chemical analysis. Some of the most potent indirect reinforcers of beliefs are social reinforcers. Thus, you probably believe that obtaining a college degree will enhance your earning power because someone whose opinion you respect has told you that this is the case.

What is the relationship between beliefs and attitudes? In a sense, our beliefs set the stage for the development of attitudes. If you have absolutely no beliefs about phargs (whatever they are), it is unlikely that you will develop attitudes concerning phargs. Of course, not all beliefs have attitudes associated with them. You may believe that steel is hard but simply not *care* about this hardness. In this case, it is unlikely that you have attitudes about steel. Beliefs contribute to the development of attitudes when some emotion or feeling is attached to one of the components of the belief. If you think that the four-day workweek improves job satisfaction, your attitude toward the short workweek will depend on how you feel about satisfaction. That is, do you see work force satisfaction as good, bad, or indifferent? Thus, we should explore the emotional or feeling aspect of attitudes—values—in greater detail.

Values

Anything "for which the individual strives, or approaches, extols, embraces, voluntarily consumes, incurs expense to acquire is a positive value. Anything that the individual avoids, escapes from, deplores, rejects, or attacks is a negative value."[1] This quotation indicates that **values** connote goodness or badness. It also indicates that the feelings or emotions inherent in values are *motivational,* since they signal the attractive and unattractive aspects of our environment that should be sought out or avoided. It is useful to separate values into the following categories: intellectual; economic; aesthetic; social; political; and religious.[2]

Everyone does not hold the same values. Managers may value high productivity (an economic value) while union officials may be more concerned with enlightened supervision and full employment (social values). Similarly, professors probably value clear, accurate writing (an intellectual value) more than illiterates do. Of course, individuals may value the same factor for different reasons. Economically-oriented students may value clear, accurate writing because it enables them to do well in school and ultimately obtain a good job, not because such writing furthers knowledge per se. Like beliefs, values are learned by the processes discussed in Chapter 3. Most are socially reinforced by parents, teachers, and representatives of religions. In fact, our entire social system is designed to teach and reinforce those values our society has decided are appropriate. In the story that began the chapter, Mike expressed some values that had to do with family life and with directing the work of others.

Values are not randomly distributed across the population. Of particular interest is the fact that members of different occupational groups espouse different values. A psychologist presents evidence that university professors, city police, oil company salespeople, and operators of small businesses have values that distinguish them as groups from the general population.[3] For example, the professors valued "equal opportunity for all" more highly than the average American. On the other hand, the salespeople and business proprietors ranked social values (peace, equality, freedom) lower than the average American. Value differences such as these may be partially responsible for the occupational stereotypes discussed in Chapter 4. Also, such differences may be responsible for conflict between organizations and within organizations when members of different occupations are required to interact with each other. For instance, the evidence cited above indicates that police officers and professors differ rather radically in the value they place on equal opportunity. This suggests that the average professor who is asked to serve as a consultant in developing a community relations program for a police force might encounter a severe case of value conflict. The same kind of problem can exist within an organization. Doctors frequently report that their social values are at odds with the economic values of hospital administrators. Do differences in occupational values develop after a person enters an occupation, or do such differences cause people to gravitate to certain occupations? Given the fact that values are relatively stable and that many values are acquired early in life, it would appear that people choose occupations that correspond to their values.

Of course, not everyone in a particular occupational group holds the same values, and this raises an interesting question: Within a given occupation, do people with certain values tend to be more successful? It would appear that the answer is yes. Two researchers assessed the values of nearly two thousand managers in Australia, India, Japan, and the United States. The managers' success was measured in terms of annual income, controlling for age. The results indicated that values were related to success. High earners tended to value concepts such as productivity, ability, aggressiveness, creativity, competition, and change. Lower earners valued concepts such as obedience, security, trust, conformity, and social welfare. In summary, the more successful subjects valued taking an active role in a dynamic, risky environment, while those who were less successful preferred passive roles in static, safe environments. Surprisingly, the patterns of values associated with success were fairly similar across countries. The authors present indirect evidence suggesting that value differences cause success, rather than vice versa.[4]

These studies indicate that values are important in their own right in their effect on organizational behavior. We shall now examine how values exert additional impact through their influence on attitudes.

Belief + Value = Attitude

Attitudes are the product of a related belief and value. If you believe that diet soda has reduced calories and you value calorie reduction, we can assume that you might have a favorable attitude toward diet soda. We can represent this relationship in the form of a simple syllogism:[5]

If diet soda has reduced calories (Belief)

And calorie reduction is good (Value)

Then diet soda is good (Attitude)

By the same token:

If the four-day workweek improves satisfaction (Belief)

And high satisfaction is good (Value)

Then the four-day workweek is good (Attitude)

Given this point of view, we can now expand the attitude model presented earlier to include the thinking and feeling aspects of attitudes represented by beliefs and values:

$$\begin{array}{c} \text{BELIEF} \\ + \\ \text{VALUE} \end{array} \Rightarrow \text{ATTITUDE} \rightsquigarrow \text{BEHAVIOR}$$

Thus, we can imagine the following sequence of ideas in the case of the dissatisfied corporate planner Mike Sherrill:

"My job is interfering with my family life." (Belief)
"I dislike anything that hurts my family." (Value)
"I dislike my job." (Attitude)
"I'll search for another job." (Behavior)

In attempting to understand attitudes, it is important to distinguish between their belief components and their value components. For example, consider the manager of a manufacturing plant that is plagued by low productivity. Working backward through our attitude model, the manager might assume that low productivity (a behavior) is caused by "poor attitudes" toward performance on the part of the work force. Are such "poor attitudes" likely to stem from the employees' values or their beliefs about performance? Either might be true. First, the work force might *value* high performance but *believe* that such performance is impossible to achieve. Beliefs of this nature might include: "My performance depends on the performance of my work group." "My equipment is unreliable." On the other hand, the work force might *believe* that it can perform at a high level but not *value* high performance: "I value a lack of fatigue more than I value making a buck for the company." "I value social interaction on the job more than I value working hard."

The preceding discussion illustrates a couple of important points. First, on a general level, behavioral scientists have not developed the concepts of beliefs, values, and attitudes as an exercise in semantics. In order to understand the employees' attitudes toward performance, the manager must understand both their belief and value systems. Knowledge of only one system may lead to inaccurate conclusions about what is limiting performance. Secondly, the kind of administrative action that may be necessary to change the work force's attitudes toward performance depends upon the accurate assessment of these beliefs and values. For example, if the beliefs listed above appear to limit performance, management will have to carefully explore the basis for these beliefs (Is the organization of work into groups limiting productivity? Is equipment really unreliable?). On the other hand, if values appear to be the problem, a different intervention may be called for (such as attempting to hire workers whose value systems correspond more closely to those desired by the organization).

CHANGING ATTITUDES

In our everyday lives we frequently try to change other people's attitudes. By presenting ourselves in a favorable light (putting our best foot forward) we attempt to get others to develop favorable attitudes toward us. By arguing the case for some attitude we hold, we attempt to get others to embrace this attitude. Thus, it should not surprise us that organizations are also involved in the modification and management of attitudes. Some examples of cases where attitude change might be desired include the following:

- Managers' attitudes toward racial minorities, women, or older workers
- Managers' attitudes on how to praise or discipline subordinates
- Attitudes toward anticipated changes, such as the introduction of a four-day workweek or new technology
- Attitudes toward safety practices and the use of safety equipment

Most attempts at attitude change are initiated by a communicator who tries to use persuasion of some form to modify the beliefs or values of an audience that supports a currently held attitude. For example, a seminar might be held to persuade managers to modify discriminatory attitudes, or a training program might be developed to change attitudes toward the praise and discipline of subordinates. An information campaign might be implemented in the company newsletter to change attitudes toward conversion to a shortened workweek. Demonstrations and poster messages might be used to persuade workers of the advantages of safety practices and equipment. Persuasion that is designed to modify or emphasize certain values is usually emotionally oriented. A safety message that concentrates upon a dead worker's weeping, destitute family exemplifies this approach. Persuasion that is slanted toward modifying certain beliefs is usually rationally oriented. A safety message that tries to convince workers that hard hats and safety glasses are not uncomfortable to wear reveals this angle. You have probably seen both of these approaches used in seat belt and antismoking campaigns.

Now for the crucial question—under what circumstances will attempts at attitude change be most effective? That is, which factors influence the extent to which persuasion will actually change attitudes? In order to answer these questions, we must investigate the answers to at least three other questions: First, who should do the persuading? Secondly, which techniques should the persuader use? Finally, who is most likely to be affected by persuasion attempts? Some answers to these questions have been provided by a large number of experiments that were begun at Yale University in the 1950s.[6]

The Communicator

Who would be most able to change the beliefs or values that support a currently held attitude? Research indicates that **communicators** who are perceived as *credible* and *believable* are most effective at inducing attitude change. In general, we tend to perceive others as credible and believable then they are seen as expert, unbiased, and likeable. In order to induce attitude change, experts must be perceived as having special skills and knowledge relevant to the *subject at hand*. Thus, an experienced line manager might be an especially credible trainer in a program designed to change new supervisors' attitudes toward praising and disciplining subordinates. In fact, many organizations have begun to use such individuals to do such training exactly because outside experts lack credibility as trainers. On the other hand, such a manager would probably not be perceived as an expert on the ramifications of introducing a shortened workweek, and would be unlikely to induce much attitude change concerning this subject.

Besides having expertise, the communicator who wishes to change attitudes must also be seen as unbiased. A safety campaign initiated by a union safety officer is probably more convincing than one initiated by the company's accident insurance carriers. The former will probably be seen as caring for the health and welfare of the work force, while the latter may be seen as attempting to reduce claims costs. This may occur in spite of the fact that both parties are perceived as equally expert in matters of safety. By the same token, union support for a shortened workweek will probably induce more favorable attitudes than will exhortations from the company president, who may be perceived as seeing increased productivity as the main goal of the change.

Finally, likeable communicators will usually be able to induce more attitude change than disliked individuals. It is easy to imagine the thoughts of an audience confronted by a disliked persuader: "If a jerk like this supports a four-day workweek, there must be something wrong with the idea." Not surprisingly, cagey managers often attempt to effect attitude changes among subordinates by converting a well-liked subordinate to their cause.

Persuasion Techniques

There are many **persuasion techniques** used to effect attitude change. Face-to-face persuasion is more likely to change attitudes than indirect communication by memo, newsletter, or posters. This probably occurs because such persuasion is flexible, demands attention, and gives the audience the opportunity to be surer about the credibility of the source. Written communications such as posters and newsletters cannot offer active counterarguments or demand attention, and they may be of ambiguous origin (who knows whether the union or the insurance company supplied that safety poster?)

How much attitude change should the communicator try to induce? It is usually best to stick with arguments that are moderately discrepant with the audience's viewpoint. Especially "soft" or "hard" positions are less likely to induce change. For example, consider a seminar leader who is attempting to change the attitudes of male managers regarding the evaluation and promotion of females. Attitudes that females are not cut out for business, and especially for managerial positions, are often strongly ingrained by years of social stereotyping. Thus, the seminar leader would probably hit pretty hard at the inconsistent belief and value system supporting these attitudes. However, it is possible to hit too hard and induce backlash on the part of the audience. Thus, it would probably be wise for the leader to stick to job-related issues of performance and promotion rather than trying to change the managers' attitudes toward women in general.

Finally, should the communicator attempt to present the audience with both sides of the attitude change argument, or just stick to the side in favor of change? Only presenting the case for change is effective if the audience if basically receptive and unlikely to generate counterarguments or hear them from others. However, when the audience is not especially receptive and knows (or will be exposed to) counterarguments against change, the communicator should present both points of view. For example, arguments that safety equipment is cumbersome or uncomfortable should be raised and discussed by the communicator. Similarly, the seminar leader should probably acknowledge that in the past many women have been inadequately prepared for business careers.

The Audience

The nature of the **audience** is important to changing established attitudes. Some organizational attitude change programs, such as those aimed at safety or awareness of minority employee concerns, are voluntary. In this case, who is likely to show up? Evidence indicates that volunteers to such programs tend to be individuals who are already convinced and least in need of attitude change. This is hardly surprising—one finds more black activists than Ku Klux Klan enthusiasts at an NAACP meeting! In general, individuals who are more fixed in the belief and value structures that support a particular attitude are less likely to change that attitude. Sometimes this fixation is a function of self-esteem—individuals who think highly of themselves may be more confident of their existing beliefs and values. In other cases, individuals are reluctant to change their attitudes because the consequences of such a change are anticipated to be punishing. The person who knows that a shortened workweek will lead to transportation problems will not be very susceptible to well-reasoned arguments favoring the change.

Cognitive Dissonance Theory

When communicators are successful in changing attitudes, exactly why are they successful? The **theory of cognitive dissonance** provides an explanation for many instances of attitude changes.[7] Cognitions are simply thoughts or knowledge that people have about their own beliefs, values, attitudes, and behavior. Dissonance refers to a feeling of tension that is experienced when certain cognitions are contradictory or inconsistent with each other (i.e., dissonant). For example, knowing that you have spent a great deal of money on a car that has turned out to be a "lemon" involves inconsistent cognitions that should arouse dissonance. Also, seeing that a workmate's shattered safety glasses protected her eyes in an accident is inconsistent with your having a negative attitude toward wearing your glasses. Again, dissonance should be felt. These examples suggest that dissonance is an unpleasant feeling, and individuals are usually motivated to reduce this feeling.

There are several ways by which dissonance might be reduced. One of them is to downplay the importance of the inconsistency ("I have more important things to worry about than my car.") Another is to marshal additional cognitions which can reduce the dissonance ("At least the car looks classy and prestigious—it impresses my friends.") For our purposes, however, the most interesting way to reduce dissonance is to *change* one of the dissonant cognitions to bring it in line with the other and reduce the tension-producing inconsistency ("My car really isn't so bad.") Notice that this example illustrates a *change in attitude* toward the car that now corresponds to the belief that one paid a lot for it. Similarly, one obvious way to reduce the dissonance between the belief that safety glasses saved a co-worker's eyesight and your own negative attitude toward safety glasses is to change your attitude to a favorable one. Thus, it can be argued that communicators attempt to change attitudes by stressing beliefs and values that are inconsistent with currently held attitudes. It is hoped that this will arouse dissonance, which will be reduced by changing one's attitudes to correspond to the new cognitions.

Changing Behavior to Change Attitudes

You will observe that in our discussion of using persuasion to change attitudes we have been moving from left to right in our attitude model:

CHANGED BELIEFS AND/OR VALUES → CHANGED ATTITUDES → CHANGED BEHAVIOR

Indeed, this is the traditional way most organizational attitude change programs are designed. However, our discussion of dissonance theory suggests an alternative approach. Specifically, would it be sensible to change a person's behavior *first,* with the assumption that the person would realign his or her attitudes to support this behavior? Dissonance theory suggests that engaging in behavior that is not supported by our attitudes may indeed lead us to change our attitudes to reduce the tension produced by inconsistency. Such effects have been observed in studies where people were required to role-play behaviors that were inconsistent with their attitudes. For example, heavy smokers were required to role-play lung cancer victims and prejudiced whites were required to advocate pro-black positions. Evidence indicated that attitude change in the expected direction followed the role-playing—the smokers smoked less and the whites became less negative toward blacks.[8]

In an excellent book, Goldstein and Sorcher argue that the traditional view of attitude change has not proven very effective in business and industry (Exhibit 5-1).[9] They suggest that attempts to use persuasion to change beliefs and values often fail to lead to attitude change because the audience is unable to see how the new beliefs or values will be applicable to their on-the-job behavior. For example, trainees may learn that women can be good performers and that they have been discriminated against, but not understand how to apply this knowledge to dealing with women on the job. In order to deal with this problem, Goldstein and Sorcher suggest that individuals should be taught specific *behaviors* that they can apply

---

EXHIBIT 5-1   **Models of attitude change.**

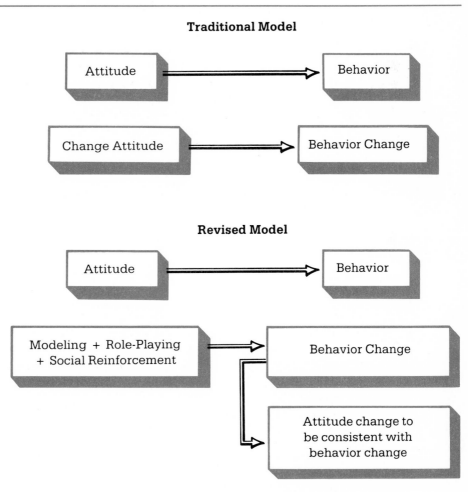

Source: Reprinted with permission from Goldstein, A. P., & Sorcher, M. (1974). *Changing supervisor behavior*. New York: Pergamon Books Ltd.

on the job which correspond to the desired attitude change. When the trainees find out that these behaviors are successful in carrying out their daily activities, dissonance theory suggests that attitudes will change to correspond to the newly learned behaviors. To teach the new behaviors, Goldstein and Sorcher recommend three techniques:

- Modeling of correct behaviors. Videotape is usually employed for this purpose.

- Role-playing of correct behaviors by those being trained. In this phase, trainees get a chance to actually *practice* the desired behaviors.

- Social reinforcement of role-played behaviors. Trainers and fellow trainees provide reinforcement for correct role-playing performance.

The revised model of attitude change suggested by Goldstein and Sorcher is shown in the lower portion of Exhibit 5-1. These techniques have been applied with apparent success by organizations such as Agway, AT&T, IBM, and General Electric. (See In–Focus 5-1.)

A Footnote Concerning Attitude Change

You should be aware that attitude change must be reinforced by the organizational environment. Earlier in the chapter we pointed out that attitudes are not always predictive of behavior. One of the reasons for this is that members are sometimes *punished* for engaging in behavior that corresponds to their newly acquired attitudes. For example, the male manager who changes his attitudes toward the promotion of female subordinates may find that *his* boss does not accept such recommendations. Similarly, the worker who acquires a favorable attitude toward the use of safety glasses may find that her co-workers make fun of her new safety consciousness. Thus, not all examples of attitude change will reveal the favorable behavioral consequences expected. This suggests that attitude change programs must be designed as total packages that anticipate roadblocks to effective implementation.

WHAT IS JOB SATISFACTION?

Recall the story about the corporate planners that began the chapter. The attitudes that they revealed about their jobs are examples of job satisfaction. Job satisfaction is such an important attitude that we will spend the remainder of the chapter discussing it. Exactly what does this term mean? **Job satisfaction** refers to a collection of attitudes which workers have about their jobs. At least two aspects of satisfaction can be differentiated. The first of these is called **facet satisfaction,** the tendency for an employee to be more or less satisfied with various facets of the job. The notion of facet satisfaction is especially obvious when we hear someone say "I love my work but hate my boss" or "This place pays lousy but the people I work with are great." Both of these statements represent different attitudes toward separate facets of the speakers' jobs. In theory, one can conceive of literally hundreds of facets that might provoke more or less favorable attitudes, ranging from the size of the parking spaces in the company lot to the color scheme of the cafeteria. In fact, however, research suggests that the most relevant attitudes toward jobs are contained in a rather small group of facets: the work itself; pay; promotions; recognition; benefits; working conditions; supervision; co-workers; and organizational policy.[10]

In addition to facet satisfaction, we can also conceive of **overall satisfaction,** an overall or summary indicator of a person's attitude toward his or her job that cuts across the various facets. The statement, "On the whole, I really like my job, although a couple of aspects could stand some improvement," is indicative of the nature of overall satisfaction. In a sense, overall satisfaction is an average or total of the attitudes held toward various facets of the job. Thus, two workers might express the same level of overall satisfaction for different reasons. Specifically, they would have offsetting attitudes toward various facets of the job.

In order to provide you with a better understanding of what we actually mean when referring to job satisfaction, it will be useful to discuss briefly how this attitude is typically measured. The most popular measure of job satisfaction is the

Job Descriptive Index (JDI).[11] This questionnaire is designed around five facets of satisfaction. Employees are asked to respond "yes," "no," or "?" (Can't decide) in describing whether or not a particular word or phrase is descriptive of particular facets of their jobs. Some sample JDI items under each facet, shown scored in the "satisfied" direction, are shown in Exhibit 5-2. A scoring system is available to provide an index of satisfaction for each facet. In addition, an overall measure of satisfaction can be calculated by adding the separate facet indexes.

Another carefully constructed measure of satisfaction, developed around a somewhat different set of facets, is the *Minnesota Satisfaction Questionnaire* (MSQ).[12] On this measure, respondents are asked to indicate how happy they are with various aspects of their job on a scale ranging from "very satisfied" to "very dissatisfied." Sample items from the short form of the MSQ include:

- The chance to work alone on the job
- The competence of my supervisor in making decisions
- The way my job provides for steady employment
- The chance to do things for other people
- My pay and the amount of work I do

The responses of these items can be scored to provide an index of overall satisfaction and to measure satisfaction on the facets on which the MSQ is based.

WHAT DETERMINES JOB SATISFACTION?

When the JDI or the MSQ are completed by workers on a variety of jobs, we often find differences in the average scores across the jobs. Of course, this could almost be expected. The various jobs may differ objectively in the facets that contribute to satisfaction. Thus, you would not be astonished to learn that a corporate vice-president was more satisfied with her job than a janitor in the same company. Of even greater interest is the fact that we frequently find decided differences in job satisfaction expressed by individuals performing the same job in a given organization. For example, two nurses who work side by side might indicate radically different satisfaction in response to the MSQ item "The chance to do things for other people." In fact, Candice and Mike, the planners who were described at the beginning of the chapter, had decidedly different attitudes toward the same job. How does such a state of affairs occur?

Discrepancy Theory

You will recall that attitudes such as job satisfaction are the product of associated beliefs and values. It would appear that these two factors operate to cause differences in job satisfaction even when jobs are identical. First, workers may differ in their beliefs about the job in question. That is, they may differ in their *perceptions*

EXHIBIT 5-2   **Sample items from the Job Descriptive Index with "satisfied" responses indicated.**

Work

- N Routine
- Y Creative
- N Tiresome
- Y Gives sense of accomplishment

People

- Y Stimulating
- Y Ambitious
- N Talk too much
- N Hard to meet

Promotions

- Y Good opportunity for advancement
- Y Promotion on ability
- N Dead-end job
- N Unfair promotion policy

Supervision

- Y Asks my advice
- Y Praises good work
- N Doesn't supervise enough
- Y Tells me where I stand

Pay

- Y Income adequate for normal expenses
- N Bad
- N Less than I deserve
- Y Highly paid

Source: The Job Descriptive Index, revised 1985, is copyrighted by Bowling Green State University. The complete forms, scoring key, instructions, and norms can be obtained from the Department of Psychology, Bowling Green State University, Bowling Green, Ohio, 43404. Reprinted with permission.

concerning the actual nature of the job. Given our detailed discussion of perception in Chapter 4, this should not surprise you. For example, one of the nurses may perceive that most of her working time is devoted to direct patient care, while the other may perceive that most of her time is spent on administrative functions. To the extent that they both value patient care, the former nurse should be more satisfied with this aspect of the job than the latter nurse. Secondly, even if individuals perceive their jobs as equivalent, they may differ in what they *want* from the jobs. Such desires are preferences which are dictated in part by the workers' value systems. Thus, if the two nurses perceive their opportunities to engage in direct patient care as high, the one who values this activity more should be more satisfied with the patient care aspect of work. This point of view concerning the causes of job satisfaction is sometimes called a **discrepancy theory** of satisfaction.[13] This theory holds that satisfaction is a function of the discrepancy between the job outcomes a person wants and the outcomes that are perceived to be obtained. The individual who desires a job entailing interaction with the public but who is required to sit alone in an office should be dissatisfied with this aspect of the job.

Similarly, the person who is especially concerned with having a pleasant supervisor may be very dissatisfied with one who is cold and distant. In general, employees who have more of their job-related desires met will report more overall job satisfaction.

Equity Theory

Above we indicated that what people want from their jobs is a partial function of their value systems. In fact, however, there are practical limitations to this notion. You may value money and the luxurious lifestyle that it can buy very highly, but this does not suggest that you expect to receive a salary of $200,000 a year. In the case of many job facets, individuals probably want "what's fair." And how do we develop our conception of what is fair? **Equity theory** suggests that the inputs we perceive ourselves as investing in our job and the outcomes the job provides for us are compared against the inputs and outcomes of some other relevant person or group.[14] Equity will be perceived when the following ratios exist:

$$\frac{\text{My outcomes}}{\text{My inputs}} = \frac{\text{Other's outcomes}}{\text{Other's inputs}}$$

Inputs consist of anything that individuals consider relevant to their exchange with the organization, anything that they give up, offer, or trade to the organization. These might include factors such as education, training, seniority, hard work, high quality work, and so on. **Outcomes** are those factors that the organization is perceived to offer in return for the inputs. The most relevant outcomes are represented by the job facets discussed earlier—things such as pay, promotions, supervision, the nature of the work, and so on. The "other" might be a co-worker performing the same job, a number of co-workers, or even one's conception of all the individuals in one's occupation. For example, the president of the Ford Motor Company probably compares his outcome/input ratio with those that he assumes exist for the presidents of General Motors and Chrysler. You probably compare your outcome/input ratio in your organizational behavior class with that of one or more fellow students.

Equity theory has important implications for job satisfaction. First, inequity itself is a dissatisfying state of affairs, especially when we ourselves are on the "short end of the stick." For example, suppose you see the hours spent studying as your main input to your organizational behavior class and the final grade as an important outcome. Imagine that a friend in the class is your comparison person. Under these conditions, the following situations appear equitable and should not provoke dissatisfaction on your part:

$$\frac{\text{YOU}}{\frac{\text{C grade}}{\text{50 hours}}} = \frac{\text{FRIEND}}{\frac{\text{A grade}}{\text{100 hours}}} \quad \text{or} \quad \frac{\text{YOU}}{\frac{\text{A grade}}{\text{60 hours}}} = \frac{\text{FRIEND}}{\frac{\text{C grade}}{\text{30 hours}}}$$

In each of these cases, a "fair" relationship seems to exist between study time and grades received. Now consider the following relationships:

$$\frac{\text{YOU}}{\text{C grade}} \neq \frac{\text{FRIEND}}{\text{A grade}} \text{ or } \frac{\text{YOU}}{\text{A grade}} \neq \frac{\text{FRIEND}}{\text{C grade}}$$
$$\frac{\text{C grade}}{\text{100 hours}} \neq \frac{\text{A grade}}{\text{50 hours}} \text{ or } \frac{\text{A grade}}{\text{30 hours}} \neq \frac{\text{C grade}}{\text{60 hours}}$$

In each of these situations, an unfair connection appears to exist between study time and grades received, and you should perceive inequity. However, the situation on the left, where you put in more work for a lower grade, should be most likely to prompt dissatisfaction. This is a "short end of the stick" situation. Conditions such as this often lead to dissatisfaction in organizational life. For example, the worker who frequently remains on the job after regular hours (input) and receives no special praise or extra pay (outcome) may perceive inequity and feel dissatisfied. Similarly, the teacher who obtains a master's degree (input) and receives no extra compensation (outcome) might react the same way if others have been rewarded for achieving extra education. Equity considerations also have an indirect effect on job satisfaction by influencing what people want from their jobs. If you study 100 hours while the rest of the students average 50 hours, you will expect a higher grade than the class average. By the same token, in a school system that usually provides higher pay for extra education, the teacher who receives a master's degree will demand a raise.

A Model of Satisfaction

Exhibit 5-3 summarizes what has been said thus far about the determinants of job satisfaction. To recapitulate, satisfaction is a function of the discrepancy between the job outcomes a person wants and the outcomes that are perceived to be received. More specifically, greater satisfaction will be experienced to the extent that these outcomes are met or exceeded, and to the extent that they are perceived as equitable compared to the outcomes others receive. The outcomes people want from a job are a function of their personal value systems, moderated by equity considerations. The outcomes that people perceive themselves as receiving from the job represent their beliefs about the nature of that job. Again, we note that job satisfaction represents a set of attitudes about the job stemming from the beliefs and values of the worker.

In the story that began the chapter, Mike Sherrill encountered a discrepancy between what he wanted from his job and what it offered. He desired a chance to spend some time with his family and the opportunity to supervise others, and the job offered neither. For Candice Rowe, the requirement to travel and the lack of supervisory responsibilities corresponded to what she wanted from a job. In addition, Mike felt inequity because the extra hours he put in on the job were unpaid. In this regard, he chose to compare his situation with that of his ex-colleagues in his old engineering job. Candice did not experience inequity, since she compared her inputs and outcomes with those of her co-workers who were also putting in unpaid overtime. Thus, Candice was more satisfied with the United job than Mike.

EXHIBIT 5-3   **How discrepancy and equity affect job satisfaction.**

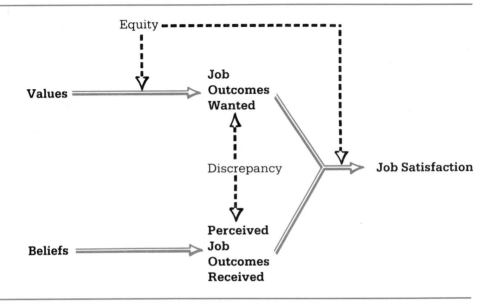

Key Contributors to Job Satisfaction

From what has been said thus far, you might expect that job satisfaction is a highly personal experience. While this is essentially true, we can make some general statements about the facets that seem to contribute the most to feelings of job satisfaction for most workers.[15]

MENTALLY CHALLENGING WORK.   This is work that tests employees' skills and abilities and allows them to set their own working pace. Such work is usually perceived as personally involving and important, and provides the worker with clear feedback regarding performance. Of course, some types of work can be too challenging, and this may result in feelings of failure and reduced satisfaction. In addition, some employees seem to prefer repetitive, unchallenging work that makes few demands on them.

HIGH PAY.   In most societies money is a valued commodity. Thus, it should not surprise you that pay and satisfaction are positively related. However, not everyone is equally desirous of money, and some workers are certainly willing to accept less physically demanding work, less responsibility, or fewer working hours for lower pay. Individual differences in preferences for pay are especially obvious in the case of employee reactions to overtime work. In most companies, one finds a group of employees who are especially anxious to earn extra money through overtime and another group that actively avoids overtime work.

PROMOTIONS.   The ready availability of promotions administered according to a fair system contributes to job satisfaction. Ample opportunity for promotion is an important contributor to job satisfaction because promotions contain a number of valued signals about a person's self-worth. Some of these signals may be material (such as an accompanying raise) while others are of a social nature (recognition within the organization and increased prestige in the community). Of course, there are individual differences in what is seen to constitute a fair promotion system. Some individuals may prefer a strict seniority system, while others may wish for a system based strictly upon job performance. In addition, some people are more concerned with the opportunity for promotions than others. It is these people for whom fair and ample opportunities will contribute most to job satisfaction. Those individuals who are unwilling or unable to accept the extra work or responsibility that accompanies promotion will probably be less concerned with opportunities and fairness, and these factors will exert less influence on their job satisfaction.

PEOPLE.   It should not surprise you that friendly, considerate, good-natured superiors and co-workers contribute to job satisfaction. Individuals have an apparent need to affiliate with others, and this affiliation is most rewarding when these others are "nice" people. In this case, our criterion for job satisfaction is similar to our criterion for satisfaction in off-the-job relationships—we enjoy people who are easy to be around. There is, however, another aspect to interpersonal relationships on the job that contributes to job satisfaction. Specifically, we tend to be satisfied in the presence of people who help us attain job outcomes that we value. Such outcomes might include doing our work better or more easily, attaining a raise or promotion, or even staying alive. For example, a company of soldiers in battle might be less concerned with how friendly their commanding officer is than with how competently he is able to act to keep them from being overrun by the enemy. Similarly, an aggressive young executive might like a considerate boss, but prefer even more a boss who can clarify her work objectives and see that she is rewarded for attaining them. Similar analyses can be made in cases in which co-workers help us achieve our goals. The friendliness aspect of interpersonal relationships seems most important in lower level jobs with clear duties and various deadend jobs. As jobs become more complex, pay becomes tied to performance, or promotion opportunities increase, the ability of others to help us do our work well begins to contribute more to job satisfaction.

THE CONSEQUENCES OF JOB DISSATISFACTION

If you have to spend eight hours a day five days a week on the job, it would obviously be worthwhile for you to have favorable attitudes toward that job. Thus, job satisfaction is an attitude worthy of interest in and of itself. However, job satisfaction also has important personal and organizational consequences beyond mere happiness with the job. In this section we shall explore the nature of these consequences.

Physical Health and Life Span

Will job satisfaction contribute to a healthier, longer life? The tentative answer is yes. Several studies have shown that workers who describe their jobs as dissatisfying are prone to physical symptoms and complaints, ranging from headaches to heart disease.[16] One study showed fairly strong relationships between job dissatisfaction in various occupations and the incidence of death due to heart disease in those occupations.[17] Also, a researcher has demonstrated that satisfaction with work was a better predictor of length of life than physical condition or tobacco use.[18] Of course, this research is generally correlational in nature, and you will remember our discussion in Chapter 2 about the problems involved in interpreting such studies. For one thing, poor physical health may cause an individual to report dissatisfaction with his or her job, rather than the other way around. Also, some third variable (such as psychological disturbance) may lead to both poor health and job dissatisfaction. Despite these caveats, it would appear that job satisfaction may affect physical health. Such an outcome has important consequences for both the individual and the organization.

Mental Health and Off-the-Job Satisfaction

Can your job drive you crazy? Phrased more formally, can job dissatisfaction promote psychological disturbance? The opportunity to participate in satisfying work is often thought to contribute to psychological well-being. In fact, psychologists and psychiatrists frequently use the ability to attain and hold meaningful work as one criterion of adequate psychological adjustment. Although this question has not been very well researched, it would appear that more satisfied workers do tend to be psychologically healthier.[19] In addition, positive attitudes toward one's job are often associated with positive attitudes toward one's life in general.[20] That is, satisfied workers tend to report satisfaction with various nonwork aspects of their lives. Again, of course, the actual causality in these findings can be ambiguous. For example, it is not difficult to conceive of an individual who becomes psychologically disturbed because of off-the-job factors and *then* encounters problems on the job due to this disturbance, leading to dissatisfaction. However, to the extent that job satisfaction does contribute to mental health and general life satisfaction, this probably happens because of self-esteem. That is, people feel a sense of accomplishment and worth in performing a satisfying job, and this feeling spills over into their off-job life.

Absence from Work

Absenteeism is an expensive behavior in North America. One estimate pegs the annual U.S. cost at $30 billion and the Canadian cost at $8 billion.[21] On a smaller scale, one expert cites $1 million annually for a 1000-employee firm with a 5 percent absence rate.[22] Such costs are attributable to "sick" pay, lost productivity, chronic overstaffing to compensate for absentees, and so on. Many more days are lost to absenteeism than to strikes and other industrial disputes.

Is some of this absenteeism the product of job dissatisfaction? The research literature is fairly firm in the following conclusions:[23]

- Speaking generally, the association between job satisfaction and absenteeism is fairly small.

- The satisfaction facet that is the best predictor of absenteeism is the content of the work itself.

- Job satisfaction is a better predictor of how *often* employees are absent rather than how many *days* they are absent. In other words, it is more associated with frequency of absenteeism than time lost.

Why is the relationship between absenteeism and job satisfaction not stronger? After all, as we noted in Chapter 3, actions with unpleasant consequences are unlikely to be repeated. Thus, it seems that employees who dislike their jobs would be motivated to skip a lot of work. Earlier in the present chapter it was pointed out that the link between attitudes and behavior is not always strong, and the relationship between satisfaction and absence is an example of this. Several factors probably constrain the ability of many workers to convert their like or dislike of work into corresponding attendance patterns:

- Some absence is simply unavoidable because of illness, weather conditions, or other pressing matters. Thus, some very happy workers will occasionally be absent due to circumstances beyond their control.

- Opportunities for off-the-job satisfaction on a missed day may vary. Thus, you may love your job, but love skiing or sailing even more. In this case, you might skip work while a dissatisfied worker who has nothing better to do shows up.

- Some organizations have attendance control policies that can influence absence more than satisfaction does. In a company that refuses to pay workers for missed days (typical of many hourly paid situations), absence may be more related to economic needs than to dissatisfaction. The unhappy worker who absolutely needs money will probably show up for work. By the same token, dissatisfied and satisfied workers may be equally responsive to threats of dismissal and to threats of visits from the company nurse if they are absent. These various forms of pressure represent attempts to get employees to come to work whether or not they are satisfied.

■ On many jobs, it may be unclear to workers how much absenteeism is reasonable or sensible. With a lack of company guidelines, workers may look to the behavior of their peers for a norm to guide their behavior. This norm and its corresponding "absence culture" may have a stronger effect than the individual employee's satisfaction with his or her job.[24]

Research regarding the connection between job satisfaction and absence has some interesting implications for managing absenteeism. For one thing, general increases in job satisfaction will probably have little effect on absence levels unless this satisfaction stems mainly from a revision in job content (a topic we will consider in Chapter 7). In addition, a high frequency of short-term absence spells is probably a better indicator of an "attitude problem" than a few long spells of time lost. The latter pattern is more likely to reflect medical problems or family demands rather than job dissatisfaction.

Turnover

As used here, *turnover* refers to voluntary resignation from an organization. Turnover can be incredibly expensive for organizations. For example, it costs several thousand dollars to replace a nurse or a bank teller who resigns. As we move up the organizational hierarchy, or into technologically complex jobs, such costs escalate dramatically. For example, it costs hundreds of thousands of dollars to hire and train a single military fighter pilot. Thus, it is no wonder that turnover (failure to reenlist) has become an especially important problem for the armed forces. Estimates of turnover costs usually include the price of hiring, training, and developing to proficiency a replacement employee. Such figures probably underestimate the true costs of turnover, however, because they do not include intangible factors such as work group disruption or the loss of employees who informally acquire special skills and knowledge over time on a job. All of this would not be so bad if turnover were concentrated among poorer performers. Unfortunately, this is not always the case. In one study, 23 percent of scientists and engineers who left an organization were among the top 10 percent of performers.[25]

What is the relationship between job satisfaction and turnover? Research indicates a moderately strong connection.[26] That is, less satisfied workers are more likely to quit. Thus, you are probably more likely to withdraw from a disliked course than from one you enjoy. However, the relationship between the attitude (job satisfaction) and the behavior in question (turnover) is far from perfect. This probably happens because a number of steps intervene between being dissatisfied and actually leaving (Exhibit 5-4). At each of these steps, the dissatisfied individual may decide that it is too much trouble to proceed further or that resignation would be an unwise move. A few comments on some of the steps in the model shown in Exhibit 5-4 seem appropriate:[27]

EXHIBIT 5-4   **Decision process between job dissatisfaction and turnover.**

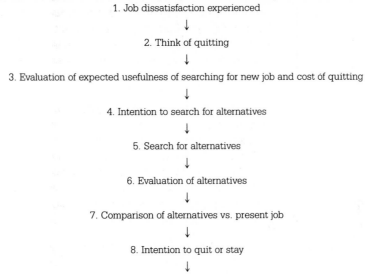

1. Job dissatisfaction experienced
↓
2. Think of quitting
↓
3. Evaluation of expected usefulness of searching for new job and cost of quitting
↓
4. Intention to search for alternatives
↓
5. Search for alternatives
↓
6. Evaluation of alternatives
↓
7. Comparison of alternatives vs. present job
↓
8. Intention to quit or stay
↓
9. Quit or stay

Source: From Mobley, W. H. (1977, April). Intermediate linkages in the relationship between job satisfaction and employee turnover. *Journal of Applied Psychology*, 62(2). Copyright 1977 by the American Psychological Association. Adapted by permission of the author.

Step 2: Certain individuals may be highly dissatisfied with their jobs but do not even think of quitting. Bad experiences with previous job searches or a poor self-image may not even permit *fantasies* about quitting.

Step 3: One key factor affecting this step is the labor market situation. Under conditions of high unemployment, the dissatisfied worker may evaluate the chances of finding another decent job at nearly zero. The cost of quitting also receives serious consideration here. Consider the senior professor who says, "I make too much money here to take another job elsewhere." You may hate a certain class, but have to remain in it because it is required for graduation.

Step 7: It is probably safe to assume that comparisons of alternative jobs with one's present job involve equity considerations. That is, the job seeker compares the inputs and outcomes of his or her present job with those that are anticipated on alternative jobs. If the comparison favors the alternative, the person will intend to resign.

Step 8: Substantial research indicates that stated intentions to quit are better predictors of turnover than is job satisfaction.[28] You will recall that one such study was described in Chapter 2. The reason for this should be clear from the process depicted in the model. Put simply, intentions to quit are "closer" to an actual behavior—quitting—than is job satisfaction. Such intentions take into account a number of factors that do not influence satisfaction, and they represent very specific attitudes about *quitting,* rather than more general attitudes about the job.

Performance

For many years, the literature targeted at practicing managers was filled with articles extolling the virtues of the human relations approach. In a nutshell, this approach suggested that considerate, humane supervision and a stated interest in the personal needs of employees was a useful way to manage. Such a management style was not advocated on sheerly humanitarian grounds, however. Each article usually indicated that such a style would pay off with increased performance on the part of the work force. Thus, human relations were seen as a good motivational strategy. For our purposes, the fact that this period of management history emphasized human relations (rather than designing more challenging work, for instance) is less important than its assumption about the relationship between satisfaction and performance. Specifically, the writers of that period suggested the following sequence:

GOOD HUMAN RELATIONS→JOB SATISFACTION→PERFORMANCE

That is, it was assumed that good human relations would lead to job satisfaction, and that satisfaction would in turn stimulate high performance. In discussing the causes of job satisfaction we have pointed out that certain human relations practices do lead to increased satisfaction. But, does satisfaction (however achieved) lead to high performance?

With reference to the quiz presented in Chapter 2, you will recall that satisfied workers are not generally much more productive than dissatisfied workers. In fact, a large body of research shows that the relationship between satisfaction and performance is positive, but usually very low and often inconsistent.[29] Why is this relationship between job attitudes and job behavior so low? Intuition suggests that we might work harder to pay back the organization for a satisfying job. However, intuition also suggests that we might be so busy enjoying our satisfying job that we have little *time* to be productive. For example, satisfying co-workers and a pleasant superior might lead us to devote more time to social interactions than to work. These contradictory intuitions provoke suspicion that the **"satisfaction causes performance" hypothesis** may be incorrect.

In recent years, the "satisfaction causes performance" hypothesis has been replaced by the so-called **"performance causes satisfaction" hypothesis.**[30] On the face of it, this viewpoint seems rather curious. How does performance lead to satisfaction? Specifically, performance would seem to lead to satisfaction when the performance is *followed by rewards.* That is:

PERFORMANCE→REWARDS→JOB SATISFACTION

For example, if you study hard for a midterm exam and are rewarded with a good grade, you should be satisfied with at least some aspects of the course. In this case your performance would be related to your satisfaction because the performance was rewarded. Similarly, if a supermarket manager increases his store's sales 30 percent (performance) and is then promoted to district manager (reward), this should increase job satisfaction. Again, in cases like this, performance and satisfaction should be fairly closely related. Now for a final crucial question: If performance does cause satisfaction, why do so many studies show a very low relationship between the two variables? Put very simply, many organizations do not do a very good job of tying rewards to performance. In many cases, especially high productivity is not followed by a promotion, extra pay, or assignment to a more interesting task. For example, you have probably experienced doing what you thought was a good job in a course only to receive a mediocre grade. It is doubtful that such an outcome will cause you to be happy with the course. In Chapters 6 and 7 we will consider in greater detail why organizations should attempt to link rewards to performance and why it is often difficult to do so. For the moment, it is sufficient to understand that simply increasing employees' satisfaction should not cause them to perform better.

USING ATTITUDE SURVEYS TO MEASURE JOB SATISFACTION AND EMPLOYEE CONCERNS

A good understanding of the determinants and consequences of job satisfaction can assist individual managers in improving the effectiveness of their work units. However, the potential financial impact of job dissatisfaction (in terms of health care costs, turnover costs, and poor labor relations) has prompted some organizations to take a formal interest in measuring and monitoring employee attitudes on a regular basis. Thus, the intuition of individual managers is supplemented with systematic data about the state of employee satisfaction. For most companies, "regular basis" usually means every couple of years, although greater frequency may be advisable. Printed questionnaires are the most common medium for such surveys, which may be prepackaged or custom tailored. Responses are anonymous, but employees are asked to provide enough information to summarize results by level, job, department, and so on. It is universally agreed that feedback of the results to employees is critical for gaining credibility (see Chapters 11 and 17).

To what uses can attitude surveys be put? One use is diagnosis of existing problems. For example, a survey may suggest that high turnover among engineers is due to boring work rather than low pay. Secondly, trends in repeated surveys can be used to predict future events such as increased turnover or unionization campaigns. Finally, repeated surveys can be used to evaluate the effectiveness of changes that have been made with the goal of increasing employee satisfaction.

A recent study asked human resources executives in the insurance industry their opinions about the use of attitude surveys.[31] As shown in Exhibit 5-5, the executives were in general agreement about the value of such surveys. However, only 16 percent of the insurance firms surveyed attitudes regularly! Perhaps concerns about survey interpretation or concentration on negative factors (noted in Exhibit 5-5) are responsible. Perhaps the human resources executives were unable to convince executives in other parts of their organizations of the value of surveys. For an example of a firm that does use surveys, see In–Focus 5-2.

EXHIBIT 5-5   **Opinions of insurance industry human resources executives about employee attitude surveys.**

Opinion	Agree	Disagree
1. Employees appreciate the opportunity to express their opinions and attitudes in an employee attitude survey.	98%	2%
2. Assessing employee attitudes is a waste of time.	5	95
3. Management should consider employee opinions and attitudes when formulating or changing company policies and practices.	98	2
4. Assessing employee opinions and attitudes is a good step toward developing methods to increase productivity.	93	7
5. Employee attitude surveys create more problems than they solve.	13	87
6. Employee attitude surveys can help management identify causes of labor problems (e.g., turnover, absenteeism).	94	6
7. Employee attitude surveys are too expensive and time-consuming	21	79
8. Employee attitude surveys are useful, even in companies that have good communication channels.	90	10
9. Attitude survey results are difficult to interpret.	51	49
10. Employee attitude surveys raise expectations on issues that management may not want or be able to address.	81	19
11. Conducting an attitude survey can be useful, even when a company has undergone a recent change.	88	12
12. Employee attitude surveys tend to focus more on the negative, rather than the positive, aspects of an organization.	59	41

Source: Neiner, A. G. (1985). Employee attitude surveys: Opinions and experiences of human resources executives. *The Industrial/Organizational Psychologist, 22* (3), 44–48, p. 46.

IN–FOCUS 5-2 EMPLOYEE ATTITUDE SURVEYS AT METROPOLITAN LIFE

The insurance company Metropolitan Life and its Affiliated Companies have been active sponsors of employee attitude surveys since the early 1970s. One major effort involved training 2000 supervisors, managers, and officers in survey-related skills. A key to success was the careful involvement of senior officers in charge (OIC) of major locations or departments. A comprehensive feedback and action planning process included:

1. **Local Management Responsibility** for addressing employee concerns, since most problems are local (usually at the unit level) and to create ownership of the process. The action planning process is bottom-up; this eliminates the question "What *do* these survey results mean?" Management doesn't have to spend hours speculating about alternative interpretations of the data. They don't agonize over the "truth." They simply ask employees "What did you mean when you said . . . ?"

2. **Feedback:**
   General Feedback from the OIC—A brief overview for all employees in a location, presented by the OIC. This demonstrates top management's involvement and responsiveness to employee concerns.
   Unit Reports—The immediate manager of a section (the smallest organizational unit in our company), in which at least six people respond to the survey, receives a computer report. This report compares their unit's results to those of the overall location/department.
   Unit Meetings—10-20 people from a unit meet for 2–4 hours; led by the unit's immediate manager. The unit's results are fed back and reasons for concerns are discussed. Specific action plans to address problems are developed; as much as possible, they reflect employee suggestions, but the manager has the final say. Plans are reviewed by the next level of management.

3. **Survey Utilization Workshop** for all first-level managers who conduct unit level feedback and action planning discussions. A full day, the workshop focuses on modeling non-defensiveness and encouraging specific input from employees on solutions to problems. Half-day workshops are held with senior managers and officers on their role in the process (support and follow-up).

4. **Executive Officer Reports**—To the executive, from each location/department OIC, on how problems have been addressed. This ensures continued involvement and support at top management levels.

5. **On-going Follow-up**—Results of actions are monitored by the unit manager and plans are fine-tuned, if necessary.

Source: Sherman, J. C. (1985). Survey survey: Management and employee reactions. *The Industrial/Organizational Psychologist, 22*(4), 33–35.

SUMMARY

■ In this chapter we have discussed the importance of attitudes and the impact that they have on organizational behavior. Attitudes are a function of what we think about the world (our beliefs) and how we feel about the world (our values). The fact that individuals have different learning histories means that they may develop different belief and value systems, and hence different attitudes. In theory, attitudes are especially important because they influence how we behave, although we have discussed several factors that reduce the correspondence between our attitudes and behaviors.

■ One method of attitude change is to attempt to change individuals' beliefs and values through persuasion. In general, this procedure works best when a credible, believable communicator requests a moderate degree of change from an audience that is not highly fixed in its beliefs and values. Cognitive dissonance theory suggests that attitude change occurs in cases such as this because the newly learned cognitions are inconsistent with previously held attitudes. Dissonance theory also suggests that attitudes can be changed by getting persons to enact desired behaviors that are incompatible with their attitudes.

■ Job satisfaction is an especially important attitude for organizations. Satisfaction is a function of the discrepancy between what individuals want from their jobs and what they perceive they obtain, taking into account equity or fairness. Factors such as challenging work, high pay, promotion opportunities, and friendly, helpful co-workers contribute to job satisfaction. Job satisfaction is important because it may promote physical and mental health and reduce expensive turnover. Satisfied workers are not necessarily much better performers because good performance may not lead to the acquisition of satisfying rewards. Regular attitude surveys can enable organizations to monitor employee satisfaction.

KEY CONCEPTS

Attitudes
Beliefs
Values
Communicators
Persuasion techniques
Audience
Theory of cognitive dissonance
Job satisfaction
Facet satisfaction
Overall satisfaction
Discrepancy theory

Equity theory
Inputs
Outcomes
"Satisfaction causes performance"
     hypothesis
"Performance causes satisfaction"
     hypothesis

DISCUSSION QUESTIONS

1. State several of your attitudes regarding school or work. What are the beliefs and values that underlie these attitudes? What are some of the behavioral outcomes of these attitudes? Are any of your behaviors inconsistent with these attitudes? Why?

2. The U.S. armed forces have been concerned with changing the attitudes of service personnel toward various racial and ethnic groups in order to improve working relationships. Given our discussion of attitude change, which factors would improve the success of such efforts at persuasion? How might the armed forces implement a behavior change program to foster attitude change?

3. Discuss the pros and cons of the argument, ''Organizations should do everything they can to enhance the job satisfaction of their employees.''

4. Using the model of the turnover process shown in Exhibit 5-4, explain why a very dissatisfied worker might not quit his or her job.

5. Use equity theory to explain why a dentist who earns $60,000 a year might be more dissatisfied with her job than a factory worker who earns $20,000.

6. Explain why workers who are very satisfied with their jobs may not be better performers than those who are less satisfied.

7. Discuss the pros and cons of using regular attitude surveys to monitor employee job satisfaction.

FOR FURTHER READING

Deutscher, I. (1973). *What we say/What we do.* Glenview, IL: Scott, Foresman.
> A really excellent exploration of the sometimes elusive connection between attitudes and behavior. Why do our deeds often contradict our words? The author attempts to provide some answers.

Mowday, R. T., Porter, L. W., & Steers, R. M. (1982). *Employee-organization linkages.* New York: Academic Press.
> Discusses the determinants, consequences, and management of organizational commitment, absenteeism, and turnover. Also looks at interrelationships among these important concepts.

Popovich, P., & Wanous, J. P. (1982). The realistic job preview as a persuasive communication. *Academy of Management Review, 7,* 570–578.
> Some companies have reduced turnover by providing job applicants with realistic previews of the nature of the jobs for which they are applying. The authors discuss how such previews can be conceived as examples of persuasive attitude change.

Rice, R. W., McFarlin, D. B., Hunt, R. G., & Near, J. P. (1985). Organizational work and the perceived quality of life: Toward a conceptual model. *Academy of Management Review, 10,* 296–310.
> Presents a detailed model of how worklife and attitudes toward worklife influence perceptions of one's overall quality of life.

Case Study

Striking Oil

Bruce Spiece frowned and stared out the window of his high-rise office. He had a problem. A *real* problem. In business school at SMU he had learned that the recognition of a problem was the first step in finding its solution. In this case, he wasn't so sure.

Spiece was the personnel director for Petrolin, a medium-size, Dallas-based oil company. The problem Spiece faced involved Petrolin's experienced earth scientists. Earth scientists are the professionals who do the "brain work" involved in discovering and extracting oil and gas from the depths of the earth. They include geologists, geophysicists, and petroleum engineers. Underlining the risky nature of oil exploration, Spiece half-jokingly described their work this way: "Geologists guess where the oil is, geophysicists guess what's between the surface and the oil, and petroleum engineers guess how to get the oil out. If they all guess right, we make profits."

With increased domestic oil exploration following the OPEC embargo of 1973, earth science graduates had become the "bonus babies" of the industry. New B.Sc.s in petroleum engineering were now receiving offers near $30,000, with graduates in geology and geophysics following close behind. Spiece's problem was not connected with the high demand for, and high salaries offered to, new graduates; rather, increasing turnover among Petrolin's experienced earth scientists was troubling him. In the past year, 15 percent of the company's earth scientists had resigned. Most were joining very small inde-

pendent oil companies. Virtually all of these resignees had been employees with five to fifteen years' experience, and constituted the very core of Petrolin's exploration staff.

Spiece knew that his problem was not unique. It had begun several years earlier with the major oil companies—the big, publicly traded firms such as Exxon, Amoco, Chevron, and Shell. The practical aspects of oil exploration and extraction are complex, and several years of experience are necessary before new graduates become full-fledged professionals. Thus, the majors, as well as medium-size firms such as Petrolin, provided training for earth scientists in the entire oil industry. Only the intermediate and major companies had the resources necessary to carry out this development. With the increase in domestic drilling following the oil embargo, many small independent oil companies had stepped up activities or entered the field. With no training resources and an immediate need for experienced earth scientists, these firms had resorted to "raiding" the majors and medium-size firms for seasoned personnel. Unfortunately, "veterans" were already in short supply—a slowdown in oil exploration in the 1960s had made the earth sciences relatively unattractive to university students at that time.

Some independents used "headhunting" agencies, and Spiece had heard horror stories of telephone calls echoing up and down the corridors of corporate geology departments as aggressive recruiters contacted one professional after another. Similarly, he knew that some headhunters became regulars at restaurants and cocktail lounges frequented by earth scientists, hoping to forge an "ac-

Source: Some material in this case is based on Alexander Stuart, "Manhunt in the Oil Fields," *Fortune,* October 6, 1980, 82–86.

cidental'' contact. As a result of this aggressive recruiting, all oil firms were experiencing an unacceptable level of turnover among experienced earth scientists. Just when the need for them was greatest, the experienced personnel of geology and engineering departments were being depleted, only to be made up with high-priced new graduates. Also, Spiece was convinced that some resignees were taking inside information about drilling prospects to the smaller competitors.

Why would an experienced earth scientist forsake the security, prestige, and large support staff of a major or intermediate oil company to join a small independent? Spiece recalled an exit interview he had conducted a week ago with Virginia Knox, a veteran Petrolin geologist who was moving to a small Houston independent. Knox had received her geology degree from an Oklahoma university in 1968 and started her career at Shell Oil. She had been at Petrolin since 1974. Spiece began by asking Virginia Knox why she was leaving Petrolin after eight successful years, hoping against hope to hear an answer he hadn't heard before.

"*Money,*" Virginia Knox responded, "money and opportunity. Look, Mr. Spiece, after fourteen years in the oil business I'm making $40,000 while you're bringing in bonus babies still wet behind the ears at $30,000. That just isn't right. The company I'm going to is paying me $50,000 and giving me a company car. In addition, I'll get a one percent override on everything I find."

Spiece cringed mentally at the word *override*. An override was a royalty paid on the gross revenues of any producing well developed by the geologist. Thus, Virginia Knox would receive one percent of the revenues of any oil she discovered for the independent. The independents had been using this incentive in their raiding efforts, and rumor was that some defectors from the larger firms had become millionaires due to overrides.

"I'm also excited by the work I'll be doing at the new company," continued Virginia Knox. "I'll be prospecting my *own* wells, with a two- or three-person team. Here at Petrolin we have dozens of geologists doing the same work I do, and it takes *forever* to get approval to drill."

Spiece understood Knox's point. The majors and intermediates tended to concentrate on the larger and more remote oil fields. Because drilling in such locations required substantial investment, several levels of management scrutinized drilling proposals very cautiously. The independents generally tended to stick to better-known territory, and geologists frequently took their proposals straight to the company president (usually a "shirt-sleeves" type) for consideration.

Spiece tried his best to discourage Virginia Knox's resignation.

"Look, Ms. Knox, I can understand some of the attraction you see in going to a small independent. But I think you should be aware of what you're in for. There's no support staff there, and you'll find yourself having to do routine work that you haven't done in years—the stuff our bonus babies do for you here. Also, in that environment you're going to stagnate professionally. Here, we've got a large staff with varied backgrounds, and people are coming in from the universities all the time. This keeps you fresh and current. And don't forget the pressure-cooker atmosphere at the independents. You're on call all the time, you're responsible for the prospects, and you can't take a vacation in the middle of a project. Here, you have others to rely on. And finally, don't expect any regular pay raises at the independent. They're generous up front, but stingy afterwards except for the override. And, personally, I think the value of overrides is rated too highly. You know as well as I do that only 10 percent of all prospects yield oil, and the independents are working smaller fields than we are here."

Virginia Knox had thanked Spiece for his advice and emphasized that she had nothing but the highest regard for Petrolin. But she insisted that her resignation was final.

Bruce Spiece continued to stare out his office window, wondering how turnover among the experienced Petrolin earth scientists could be reduced. Salary increases were not out of the question, but it was generally agreed that other employees would react negatively to such a move. Middle managers, marketing personnel, and employees who negotiated oil field leases were already incredulous of the salaries accorded to the bonus babies. For larger firms such as Petrolin, overrides were difficult to consider. Because such firms concentrated on bigger, more complex oil prospects, large teams of earth scientists worked together on exploration projects. With such teams, it was hard to decide exactly who deserved how much of a royalty on any given oil strike. Perhaps company cars or large cash bonuses based on exceptional individual performance would help to retain the experienced personnel. Spiece just wasn't sure.

■ ■ ■

1. *Describe* Virginia Knox's attitudes toward her job at the time of her resignation. Be specific as to job satisfaction facets.
2. Use discrepancy theory and equity theory to *explain* Virginia Knox's attitudes toward her job at the time of her resignation.

3. Not everyone who experiences job dissatisfaction actually quits his or her job. What factors contributed to Virginia's conversion of dissatisfaction into actual turnover?
4. How might the turnover problem at Petrolin have been prevented if the company had acted earlier?
5. Use your understanding of attitude change to explain why it would have been very difficult for Spiece to change Knox's mind during the exit interview.
6. What should Bruce Spiece do now?

REFERENCES

1. Jones, E. E., & Gerard, H. B. (1967). *Foundations of social psychology*. New York: Wiley, p. 158.
2. Spranger, E. (1928). *Types of men*. New York: Stechat.
3. Rokeach, M. (1973). *The nature of human values*. New York: Free Press.
4. England, G. W., & Lee, R. (1974). The relationship between managerial values and managerial success in the United States, Japan, India, and Australia. *Journal of Applied Psychology, 59,* 411–419.
5. The syllogistic relationship among beliefs, values, and attitudes is advocated by Jones & Gerard, 1967.
6. Readable summaries of this work can be found in Middlebrook, P. N. (1974). *Social psychology and modern life*. New York: Knopf; and Zimbardo, P. G., Ebbesen, E. B., & Maslach, C. (1972). *Influencing attitudes and changing behavior* (2nd ed.). Reading, MA: Addison-Wesley.
7. Festinger, L. (1957). *A theory of cognitive dissonance*. Stanford, CA: Stanford University Press.
8. Janis, I. L., & Mann, L. (1965). Effectiveness of emotional role-playing in modifying smoking habits and attitudes. *Journal of Experimental Research in Personality, 1,* 84–90; Culbertson, F. M. (1957). Modification of an emotionally held attitude through role-playing. *Journal of Abnormal and Social Psychology, 54,* 230–233.
9. Goldstein, A. P., & Sorcher, M. (1974). *Changing supervisor behavior*. New York: Pergamon.
10. Locke, E. A. (1976). The nature and causes of job satisfaction. In M. D. Dunnette (Ed.), *Handbook of industrial and organizational psychology*. Chicago: Rand McNally.
11. Smith, P. C., Kendall, L. M., & Hulin, C. L. (1969). *The measurement of satisfaction in work and retirement*. Chicago: Rand McNally.
12. Weiss, D. J., Dawis, R. V., England, G. W., & Lofquist, L. H. (1967). *Manual for the Minnesota satisfaction questionnaire: Minnesota studies in vocational rehabilitation*. Minneapolis: Vocational Psychology Research, University of Minnesota.
13. Locke, E. A. (1969). What is job satisfaction? *Organizational Behavior and Human Performance, 4,* 309–336.

14. Adams, J. S. (1973). Toward an understanding of inequity. *Journal of Abnormal and Social Psychology, 67*, 422–436.

15. This material draws upon Locke, 1976.

16. Locke, 1976.

17. Sales, S. M., & House, J. (1971). Job dissatisfaction as a possible risk factor in coronary heart disease. *Journal of Chronic Diseases, 23*, 861–873.

18. Palmore, E. (1969). Predicting longevity: A follow-up controlling for age. *The Gerontologist, 9*, 247–250.

19. Kavanagh, M. J., Hurst, M. W., & Rose, R. (1981). The relationship between job satisfaction and psychiatric health symptoms for air traffic controllers. *Personnel Psychology, 34*, 691–707; Jamal, M., & Mitchell, V. F. (1980). Work, nonwork and mental health: A model and a test. *Industrial Relations, 19*, 88–93.

20. See for example Schmidt, N., & Bedeian, A. G. (1982). A comparison of LISREL and two-stage least squares analysis of a hypothesized life-job satisfaction reciprocal relationship. *Journal of Applied Psychology, 67*, 806–817.

21. Steers, R. M., & Rhodes, S. R. (1984). Knowledge and speculation about absenteeism. In P. S. Goodman & R. S. Atkin (Eds.), *Absenteeism: New approaches to understanding, measuring, and managing employee absence.* San Francisco: Jossey-Bass.

22. Kempen, R. W. (1982). Absenteeism and tardiness. In L. W. Frederiksen (Ed.), *Handbook of organizational behavior management.* New York: Wiley.

23. Hackett, R. D., & Guion, R. M. (1985). A reevaluation of the absenteeism–job satisfaction relationship. *Organizational Behavior and Human Decision Processes, 35*, 340–381; Scott, D. D., & Taylor, G. S. (1985). An examination of conflicting findings on the relationship between job satisfaction and absenteeism: A meta-analysis. *Academy of Management Journal, 28*, 599–612.

24. Nicholson, N., & Johns, G. (1985). The absence culture and the psychological contract—Who's in control of absence? *Academy of Management Review, 10*, 397–407.

25. Farris, G. F. (1971). A predictive study of turnover. *Personnel Psychology, 24*, 311–328.

26. Steel, R. P., & Ovalle, N. K., 2d. (1984). A review and meta-analysis of research on the relationship between behavioral intentions and employee turnover. *Journal of Applied Psychology, 69*, 673–686.

27. In general, tests of aspects of the Mobley turnover model have been very supportive. See for example Mowday, R. T., Koberg, C. S., & McArthur, A. W. (1984). The psychology of the withdrawal process: A cross-validation test of Mobley's intermediate linkages model of turnover in two samples. *Academy of Management Journal, 27*, 79–94; Michaels, C. E., & Spector, P. E. (1982). Causes of employee turnover: A test of the Mobley, Griffeth, Hand, and Meglino model. *Journal of Applied Psychology, 67*, 53–59.

28. Steel & Ovalle, 1984.

29. Iaffaldano, M. T., & Muchinsky, P. M. (1985). Job satisfaction and job performance: A meta-analysis. *Psychological Bulletin, 97*, 251–273. For a more optimistic view see Petty, M. M., McGee, G. W., & Cavender, J. W. (1984). A meta-analysis of the relationships between individual job satisfaction and individual performance. *Academy of Management Review, 9*, 712–721.

30. Lawler, E. E., III. (1973). *Motivation in organizations.* Monterey, CA: Brooks/Cole.

31. Neiner, A. G. (1985). Employee attitude surveys: Opinions and experiences of human resources executives. *The Industrial/Organizational Psychologist, 22*(3), 44–48.

Chapter 6

Theories of Work Motivation

WHY DO *YOU* WORK?

Fred, Al, Tom, and Marilyn met for their usual Friday afternoon drinks at an establishment on Michigan Avenue near the Ford River Rouge plant in Dearborn, Michigan. Although they worked in different parts of the giant Ford complex, they had become friends through involvement in a sports league sponsored by the company. As usual, Fred began complaining, this time about his job.

"Man, I *hate* working. It's a good thing the assembly line keeps moving and the bosses are always on my tail, or I'd never get anything done. Been that way all my life. Give me a beer and a shade tree over any kind of work any time. If I could get me a little welfare, I'd quit in a minute. Too bad people have to work."

"Ah, you single guys," responded Tom, who was also on the line. "I've *gotta* work. I've got a wife and three kids to support. I admit I work for *money*, pure and simple. Offer me a buck and I'll follow you anywhere! Seriously, my philosophy is more work for more pay, and I'll take any job that provides the green stuff. Here's hoping the union gets us a good increase this time around," he said, raising his glass with a grin.

"Wait a minute," said Al. "I *like* my job. I have a real sense of accomplishment at the end of the day. Don't tell the company, but I'd even take a pay cut to keep doing the same kind of work. That job makes me feel good about myself, and I'll keep hustling for any company that gives me the chance to do it."

Tom and Fred protested in unison. Tom said, "Easy for you to say. You've got a trade, you're a machinist, and you're making a ton of money." Fred simply mumbled that anyone who *liked* work must be crazy.

Finally, Marilyn responded. "Fred, I don't see how you could sit around all day doing nothing. That would drive me batty! Sure, good pay and interesting work are nice, but I took this job to make some new friends. My husband makes a good salary, and I don't have to work, but I'd go insane cooped up at home all day. Working gives me an opportunity to get out and meet people."

Another round of drinks was ordered, and the debate continued.

Explicitly, the preceding discussion has to do with why the four Ford employees work. Implicitly, it also involves some notions about motivation on the job, that is, what makes people work "harder" or "better." As you can see, there is considerable variation in the philosophies of work held by the four employees. How correct are these philosophies? How useful are they for explaining work motivation? These are some of the questions that this chapter will explore.

First, we will examine some commonsense notions about why people work. Then we will define motivation and distinguish it from performance. After this, several popular theories of work motivation will be described and contrasted. Then a model that links motivation, performance, and job satisfaction will be presented. Finally, we will briefly explore a controversy about the compatibility of various forms of motivation.

WHY DO PEOPLE WORK?

Before we begin our formal discussion of motivation, we can profit from an exploration of a very basic issue—why do people work? An examination of some responses to this question will illustrate some themes that have concerned those who are interested in motivation at work. At the same time, the inconsistency of these responses should convince you of the need to develop and test comprehensive theories of work motivation.

At first glance, the answer to the question posed above may seem obvious to you: People work because _____ . In place of this blank, you have probably inserted a phrase such as "they have to," "they like to," "they want to earn money," "they want to meet people," and so on. In fact, these are the respective work philosophies espoused by Fred, Al, Tom, and Marilyn in the story that began the chapter. Let's examine some of the themes inherent in these commonsense explanations about why people work.

The "people work because they have to work" notion is illustrated by the Theory X view of people described by Douglas McGregor.[1] McGregor was a psychologist whose career spanned both private industry and the presidency of Antioch College. According to McGregor, **Theory X** (an arbitrarily coined label) includes assumptions that people generally dislike work, lack ambition, and will avoid responsibility if possible.

There are two prominent motivational themes underlying the assumption that people work because they have to work, as embodied in Theory X. One is that punishment, threat, and close supervision may be necessary to motivate individuals. Recall, for example, that in the story presented earlier, Fred said that he performed to the extent that the bosses were "on his tail." A second motivational theme underlying the notion that people work because they have to do so is that positive reinforcement (in the form of money) can serve as a powerful motivator. Thus, whether or not people like working, they can be induced to do so without explicit threat or punishment. Tom, the family man, voiced this point of view. Notice that both of these motivational themes assume that motivation is something that is "applied" to workers.

There is obviously a degree of truth in both themes. For example, the Nazis were able to make concentration camp prisoners contribute to the German war effort through force and intimidation. However, punishment and threat do little to explain why people continue to work after they are eligible for retirement, why people work for voluntary community organizations, or why entrepreneurs start their own businesses. Similarly, money is certainly an important commodity in our society, and people play lotteries, rob banks, show up for work, and change jobs with expectations that these efforts will be rewarded. On the other hand, if people work primarily for money, one is hard-pressed to explain why some people continue working after having won a lucrative lottery or why some millionaires continue to put in twelve-hour days at the office. Also, we are all familiar with individuals who have chosen jobs that paid lower than alternative offers. These contradictory observations suggest that the notion that people work because they have to work provides an incomplete basis for building a comprehensive theory of work motivation.

Now let's turn to the notion that "people work because they like to work," which seems diametrically opposed to the assumption that people work because they "have" to do so. This notion is illustrated by the Theory Y view of people, also described by Douglas McGregor.[2] **Theory Y** assumes that work is as natural as rest or play, and that workers will accept responsibility when self-control can be used to pursue valued objectives.

Like Theory X, Theory Y includes a theme that has relevance for work motivation. In assuming that work is as "natural" as rest or play, McGregor is arguing that work can be *inherently* motivating. That is, he assumes that people can apply their own motivators in the work setting which may be just as powerful as the close supervision or money which are applied by agents of the organization. This is seen in the use of the term *self*-control.

Obviously, there are some people, like Al in the story presented earlier, who are motivated by the fact that they really like their work. Perhaps the lottery winners and millionaires who continue to work fall into this category. However, if work is really as natural as rest or play, we would expect a substantial proportion of individuals to report that work is a central factor in their lives. In fact, this does not appear to be the case. Rather consistently, national surveys indicate that individuals are more concerned about their health, their family life, and their standard of living than they are about their jobs.[3] In addition, it would appear that many jobs in our society do not offer the self-control and valued objectives that McGregor associates with such a concern. Thus, once again, we see that the assumption that people work because they like to work is an inadequate basis for a comprehensive theory of work motivation.

Doubtless, some people work only because they have to do so and some work because they enjoy working. However, both everyday experience and research evidence suggest that both of these simple commonsense explanations are incomplete and in some sense inaccurate. Thus, comprehensive theories of work motivation are needed to guide our understanding of the complexity of work motives. The commonsense notions suggest some themes that such theories must confront.

For example, any useful theory of motivation should have something to say about those circumstances in which motivators are "applied to" workers, as well as those cases in which workers appear to be self-motivated. In addition, such a theory should attempt to specify the *conditions* under which either form of motivation might be more effective or more likely to occur.

WHAT IS MOTIVATION?

The term *motivation* is not easy to define. However, from an organization's perspective, when we speak of a person as being motivated we usually mean that the person works "hard," "keeps at" his or her work, and directs his or her behavior toward appropriate goals.

Basic Characteristics of Motivation

We can formalize the notions presented above into three basic characteristics of motivation.[4]

EFFORT.   The first aspect of motivation refers to the strength of the person's work-related behavior or the amount of *effort* the person exhibits on the job. Clearly, this involves different kinds of activities on different kinds of jobs. A loading dock worker might exhibit greater effort by carrying heavier crates, while a researcher might reveal greater effort by searching out an article in some obscure foreign technical journal. Both are exerting effort in a manner appropriate to their jobs.

PERSISTENCE.   The second characteristic of motivation refers to the *persistence* that individuals exhibit in applying effort to their work tasks. The organization would not be likely to think of the loading dock worker who stacks the heaviest crates for two hours and then goofs off for six hours as especially highly motivated. Similarly, the researcher who makes an important discovery early in her career and then rests on her laurels for five years would not be considered especially highly motivated. In each case, workers have not been persistent in the application of their effort.

DIRECTION.   Effort and persistence refer mainly to the quantity of work an individual will produce. Of equal importance is the quality of a person's work. Thus, the third characteristic of motivation refers to the *direction* of the person's work-related behavior. In other words, do workers channel persistent effort in a direction that benefits the organization? From the employer's point of view, motivated stockbrokers are expected to advise their clients of good investment opportunities, and motivated quality control inspectors are expected to discover defects and approve acceptable work. These correct decisions increase the probability that persistent effort is actually translated into accepted organizational outcomes.

To simplify matters, the preceding discussion has been presented from an organizational perspective, assuming that motivated individuals act to enhance organizational goals. Of course, you are aware that employees can be motivated to engage in many activities which are contrary to the goals of the organization. Thus, we can formally define **motivation** as the extent to which persistent effort is directed toward organizationally relevant outcomes. Such outcomes might include productivity, attendance, or creative job behaviors. Notice, however, that some organizationally relevant outcomes need not be good outcomes for the organization as a whole. Workers may be motivated to be absent, engage in strikes, or provoke sabotage. In these cases they are channeling their persistent effort in directions that are often times dysfunctional for the organization.

Extrinsic and Intrinsic Motivation

In our discussion of commonsense views about why people work, a distinction was noted concerning the source of motivation. Some views hold that workers are motivated by factors in the external environment (such as close supervision or pay) while others hold that people can in some sense be self-motivated without the application of these external factors. You may have experienced this distinction. As a worker, you may recall tasks that you enthusiastically performed simply for the sake of doing them and others that you performed only to keep your job or placate your boss.

Experts in organizational behavior have seen fit to distinguish between intrinsic and extrinsic motivation. At the outset, it should be emphasized that there is only weak consensus concerning the exact definitions of these concepts, and even weaker agreement about whether specific motivators should be labeled intrinsic or extrinsic.[5] However, the following definitions and examples seem to capture the distinction fairly well.

Intrinsic motivation stems from the direct relationship between the worker and the task, and is usually self-applied. Feelings of achievement, accomplishment, challenge, and competence derived from performing one's job are examples of intrinsic motivators, as is sheer interest in the job itself.

Extrinsic motivation stems from the work environment external to the task and is usually applied by someone other than the person being motivated. Pay, fringe benefits, company policies, and various forms of supervision are examples of extrinsic motivators.

Obviously, not all conceivable motivators can be packaged as neatly as these definitions suggest. For example, a promotion or a compliment may be applied by the boss but may also be a clear signal of achievement and competence. Thus, some potential motivators may have both extrinsic and intrinsic qualities.

Despite the fact that the distinction between intrinsic and extrinsic motivation is fuzzy, many theories of motivation seem to make the distinction. This will be demonstrated shortly. For an example of a person who is both intrinsically and extrinsically motivated, see the cartoon!

"I'll tell you why I want this job. I thrive on challenges. I like being stretched to my full capacity. I like solving problems. Also, my car is about to be repossessed."

Source: *Playboy*, May 1979, p. 247. Reproduced by Special Permission of PLAYBOY Magazine: Copyright © 1979 by PLAYBOY.

Motivation and Performance

At this point, you might well be saying, "Wait a minute. I know many people who are 'highly motivated' but just don't seem to perform well. They work long and hard, but they just don't measure up." This is certainly a sensible observation, and it points to the important distinction between motivation and performance. **Performance** can be defined as the extent to which an organizational member contributes to achieving the goals of the organization.

Some of the factors which contribute to individual performance in organizations are shown in Exhibit 6-1.[6] Notice that while motivation clearly contributes to performance, the relationship is not one to one, because a number of other factors intervene. Thus, it is certainly possible for performance to be low even when a person is highly motivated—low aptitude, weak skills, poor understanding of the task, or chance can damage the performance of the most highly motivated individual. Of course, an opposite effect is also conceivable. An individual with rather marginal motivation might "know the ropes" (understand the task) so well that some compensation occurs—what little effort the individual makes is expended very efficiently in terms of goal accomplishment. Also, a person with weak motivation might perform well due to some luck or chance factor that boosts performance. Thus, it is no wonder that workers sometimes complain that they receive lower performance ratings than colleagues who "don't work as hard."

To firm up your understanding of the relationships shown in Exhibit 6-1, consider the case of Ann Preston, an experienced draftsperson at the Connely Engineering Company. Ann had always received excellent performance ratings from her supervisor, Bill Martin. Martin attributed Ann's excellent performance to several factors. In addition to being highly motivated, Ann had good spatial abilities (the *aptitude* for visualizing in three dimensions), good technical school training (basic drafting *skills*), and understood the relationship between the draftsperson and the design engineer (*task understanding*). Based on her history of excellent performance, Bill nominated Ann to become his successor when he left Connely to take a job with another firm. Ann was even more motivated in her supervisory role than she had been in her drafting role. She began putting in longer hours and skipping coffee breaks, and she enrolled in a course in supervision at the local community college. Despite this high level of motivation, after several weeks it became clear that Ann's performance as drafting supervisor was less than satisfactory. Several interpersonal conflicts had developed in the drafting unit, and work was consistently behind schedule. Finally, Ann was demoted and replaced by an outside recruit. In summing up the situation, the vice-president of Connely said, "Ann really worked hard, but she wasn't very good at human relations. Furthermore, instead of organizing the work of the unit, she seemed to spend too much time looking over the shoulders of her subordinates, correcting their work. Finally,

EXHIBIT 6-1   **Factors contributing to individual job performance.**

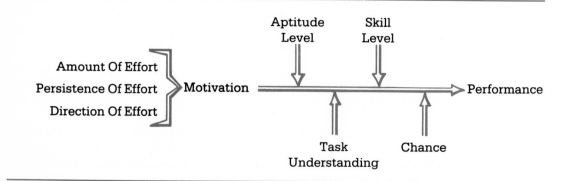

and this wasn't her fault, there's a slowdown in engineering work around here and there were rumors that some draftspersons would be laid off. I think this hurt the morale of the unit, and they took it out on her."

Using the language of Exhibit 6-1, Ann was well motivated, but lacked human relations skills, had a poor understanding of the supervisory job, and fell prey to circumstances beyond her control. Thus, her performance suffered in spite of her high motivation.

In this chapter we will concentrate on the motivational components of performance, rather than the other determinants shown in Exhibit 6-1. However, the moral here should be clear—motivation cannot be considered in isolation, and high motivation will not result in high performance if workers lack basic aptitudes and skills, don't understand their jobs, or encounter unavoidable obstacles over which they have no control. With this warning in mind, let's examine some theories of motivation.

NEED THEORIES OF WORK MOTIVATION

The first three theories of motivation to be considered are called **need theories.** These theories attempt to specify the kinds of needs people have and the conditions under which they will be motivated to satisfy these needs in an organizationally useful manner. Needs are physiological and psychological wants or desires that can be satisfied by acquiring certain incentives or achieving particular goals. It is the behavior stimulated by this acquisition process that reveals the motivational character of needs:

$$NEEDS \rightarrow BEHAVIOR \rightarrow INCENTIVES\ AND\ GOALS$$

Notice that need theories are concerned with *what* motivates workers (needs and their associated incentives or goals). They can be contrasted with *process theories* which are concerned with exactly *how* various factors motivate people. Need and process theories are complementary rather than contradictory. Thus, a need theory might contend that money can be an important motivator (what) and a process theory might explain the actual mechanics by which money motivates (how).[7]

In this section we will examine three prominent need theories of motivation and then explore their research support and managerial implications. In a following section we will consider two process theories.

Maslow's Hierarchy of Needs

Abraham Maslow was a psychologist who, over a number of years, developed and refined a general theory of human motivation.[8] According to Maslow, humans have five sets of needs that are arranged in a hierarchy, beginning with the most basic and compelling needs (see the left side of Exhibit 6-2):

EXHIBIT 6-2   **Relationship between Maslow and Alderfer need theories.**

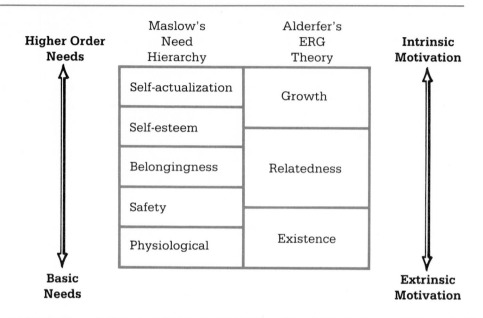

1. *Physiological needs.* These include those needs that must be satisfied for the person to survive, including food, water, oxygen, shelter, and so on. Organizational factors that might satisfy these needs include the minimum pay necessary for survival and working conditions that promote existence.

2. *Safety needs.* These include needs for security, stability, freedom from anxiety, and a structured and ordered environment. Organizational conditions that might meet these needs include safe working conditions, fair and sensible rules and regulations, job security, a comfortable work environment, pension and insurance plans, pay above the minimum needed for survival, freedom to unionize, and so on.

3. *Belongingness needs.* These include needs for social interaction, affection, love, companionship, and friendship. Organizational factors that might meet these needs include the opportunity to interact with others on the job, friendly and supportive supervision, opportunity for teamwork, opportunity to develop new social relationships, and so on.

4. *Esteem needs.* These include needs for feelings of adequacy, competence, independence, strength, and confidence, and the *deserved* appreciation and recognition of these characteristics by others. Organizational factors that might satisfy these needs include the opportunity to master tasks leading to feelings of achieve-

ment and responsibility. Also, awards, promotions, prestigious job titles, professional recognition, and the like may satisfy these needs when they are felt to be truly deserved.

5. *Self-actualization needs.* These needs are the most difficult to define. They involve the desire to develop one's true potential as an individual to the fullest extent and to express one's skills, talents, and emotions in a manner that is most personally fulfilling. Maslow suggests that self-actualizing people have clear perceptions of reality, accept themselves and others, and are independent, creative, and appreciative of the world around them. Organizational conditions that might provide self-actualization include absorbing jobs with the potential for creativity and growth as well as well as a relaxation of structure to permit self-development and personal progression.

Given the fact that individuals may harbor these needs, in what sense do they form the basis of a theory of motivation? That is, what exactly is the motivational premise of **Maslow's hierarchy of needs?** Put simply, the lowest-level unsatisfied need category has the greatest motivating potential. Thus, none of the needs is a "best" motivator; motivation depends upon the worker's position in the need hierarchy. According to Maslow, individuals are motivated to satisfy their physiological needs before they reveal an interest in safety needs, and safety must be satisfied before social needs become motivational, and so on. When a need is unsatisfied, it exerts a powerful effect on the individual's thinking and behavior, and this is the sense in which needs are motivational. However, when needs at a particular level of the hierarchy are satisfied, the individual turns his or her attention to the next higher level. Notice the clear implication here that *a satisfied need is no longer an effective motivator.* Once one has adequate physiological resources and feels safe and secure, one doesn't seek more of the factors that met these needs, but looks elsewhere for gratification. According to Maslow, the single exception to this rule involves self-actualization needs. He felt that these were "growth" needs which become stronger as they are gratified.

Individuals who are in the lower-level need categories (physiological, safety, and belongingness) seem to be most susceptible to extrinsic motivation, its exact form corresponding to the need which is most pressing. Notice, for example, that extrinsic threat and punishment might even prove to be effective stimuli for individuals who are fighting to satisfy their basic physiological needs. Such persons should show little interest in pleasant social relationships or interesting work if they are fighting to survive, and might endure strict control in exchange for the basics necessary for existence. As further evidence of the role of extrinsic motivation at lower levels of the need hierarchy, also observe that money and money substitutes (e.g., insurance and pension plans) figure heavily here. However, as individuals progress up the hierarchy, and higher-order needs (esteem and self-actualization) become prominent, intrinsic motivation comes into play. Here, organizational conditions must be arranged to permit individuals to "motivate themselves."

Alderfer's ERG Theory

Clayton Alderfer has developed another need-based theory called **ERG theory.**[9] It involves a streamlining of Maslow's need classifications and some different assumptions about the relationship between needs and motivation. The name ERG stems from Alderfer's compression of Maslow's five-category need system into three categories—existence, relatedness, and growth needs:

1. *Existence needs.* These are needs that are satisfied by some material substance or condition. As such, they correspond closely to Maslow's physiological needs and to those safety needs which are satisfied by material conditions rather than interpersonal relations. These include the need for food, shelter, pay, and safe working conditions.

2. *Relatedness needs.* These are needs that are satisfied by open communication and the exchange of thoughts and feelings with other organizational members. They correspond fairly closely to Maslow's belongingness needs and to those esteem needs involving feedback from others. However, Alderfer stresses that relatedness needs are satisfied by open, accurate, honest interaction rather than uncritical pleasantness.

3. *Growth needs.* These are needs that are fulfilled by strong personal involvement in the work setting. They involve the full utilization of one's skills and abilities and the creative development of new skills and abilities. Growth needs correspond to Maslow's need for self-actualization and some aspects of his esteem needs.

As you can see in Exhibit 6-2, Alderfer's need classification system does not represent a radical departure from that of Maslow. In addition, Alderfer agrees with Maslow that as lower level needs are satisfied, the desire to have higher level needs satisfied will increase. Thus, as existence needs are fulfilled, relatedness needs gain motivational power. Alderfer explains this by arguing that as more "concrete" needs are satisfied, energy can be directed toward satisfying less concrete needs. Finally, Alderfer agrees with Maslow that the least concrete needs, growth needs, become *more* compelling and *more* desired as they are fulfilled.

It is, of course, the differences between ERG theory and the need hierarchy that represent Alderfer's contribution to the understanding of motivation. First, unlike the need hierarchy, ERG theory does not assume that a lower level need *must* be gratified before a less concrete need becomes operative. Thus, ERG theory does not involve a rigid hierarchy of needs, and some individuals, due to background and experience, may seek relatedness or growth even though their existence needs are ungratified. Hence, ERG theory seems to account for a wide variety of individual differences in motive structure. Secondly, ERG theory assumes that if the higher-level needs are ungratified, individuals will increase their desire for the gratification of lower-level needs. Notice that this represents a *radical* departure from Maslow. According to Maslow, if esteem needs are strong but ungratified, a person will not revert to an interest in social needs, because these have necessarily already been gratified. (Remember, he argues that satisfied needs are not motivational). According to Alderfer, however, the frustration of higher order needs will lead workers to regress to a more concrete need category. For example, the office worker who is unable to establish rewarding social relationships with superiors or co-workers may increase his interest in fulfilling existence needs, perhaps by seeking a pay increase. Thus, according to Alderfer, an apparently satisfied need can act as a motivator by substituting for an unsatisfied need.

Given the preceding description of ERG theory, we can identify its two major motivational premises as follows: *The more lower level needs are gratified, the more higher level need satisfaction is desired;* and *the less higher level needs are gratified, the more lower level need satisfaction is desired.*

ERG theory is particularly interesting in its implications for extrinsic and intrinsic motivation. Obviously, extrinsic motivators are especially likely to satisfy existence and relatedness needs, while intrinsic motivators are especially likely to satisfy growth needs. Notice, however, that Alderfer contends that all three need categories can be operative at the same time. Thus, the opportunity to satisfy growth needs through stimulating and challenging work might prove motivational even though existence needs are not fully gratified. Similarly, extrinsic motivators can sometimes serve as substitutes for intrinsic motivators. For example, the person who is denied a job which provides for the satisfaction of growth needs may be responsive to an open, trusting, helpful supervisor.

McClelland's Theory of Needs

Harvard psychologist David McClelland has spent several decades studying the human need structure and its implications for motivation. According to McClelland, needs reflect relatively stable personality characteristics that are acquired through early life experiences and exposure to selected aspects of one's society. Unlike Maslow and Alderfer, McClelland has not been interested in specifying a hierarchical relationship among needs. Rather, he has been more concerned with the specific behavioral consequences of needs. In other words, under what conditions are certain needs likely to result in certain patterns of motivation? The three needs that have been most studied by McClelland have special relevance for organizational behavior—needs for achievement, affiliation, and power.[10]

Individuals high in **need for achievement** (*n* Ach) have a special desire to perform challenging tasks well. More specifically, they exhibit the following characteristics:

- *A preference for situations in which personal responsibility can be taken for outcomes.* Those high in *n* Ach do not prefer situations in which outcomes are determined by chance, because success in such situations does not provide an experience of achievement.

- *A tendency to set moderately difficult goals that provide for calculated risks.* Success with easy goals will provide little sense of achievement, while extremely difficult goals may never be reached. The calculation of successful risks is stimulating to the high *n* Ach person.

■   *A desire for performance feedback.* Such feedback permits individuals with high *n* Ach to modify their goal attainment strategies to ensure success and signals them when success has been reached.[11]

People high in *n* Ach are concerned with bettering their own performance or that of others. They are often concerned with innovation and long-term goal involvement. However, these things are not done to please others or to damage the interests of others. Rather, they are done because they are *intrinsically* satisfying. Thus, *n* Ach would appear to be an example of a growth or self-actualization need (see In–Focus 6-1).

People high in **need for affiliation** (*n* Aff) have a special desire to establish and maintain friendly, compatible interpersonal relationships. In other words, they like to like others, and they want others to like them! More specifically, they have an ability to learn social networks quickly and a tendency to communicate frequently with others, either face to face, by telephone, or by letter. Also, they prefer to avoid conflict and competition with others, and they sometimes exhibit strong conformity to the wishes of their friends. The *n* Aff motive is obviously an example of a belongingness or relatedness need.

People high in **need for power** (*n* Pow) desire to have a strong influence over others. In other words, they wish to make a significant impact or impression on them. People high in *n* Pow seek out social settings where they can be influential. When in small groups, they act in a "high profile" manner. There is some tendency for those high in *n* Pow to advocate risky positions. Also, some persons high in *n* Pow show a strong concern for personal prestige. The need for power is a complex need, because power can be used in a variety of ways, some of which serve the power-seeker and some of which serve other persons or the organization. However, *n* Pow seems to correspond most closely to Maslow's self-esteem need.

McClelland predicts that people should be motivated to seek out and perform well in jobs that match their needs. Thus, people with high *n* Ach should be strongly motivated by sales jobs or entrepreneurial positions, such as running a small business. Such jobs offer the feedback, personal responsibility, and opportunity to set goals noted above. People high in *n* Aff should be motivated by jobs such as social work or employee relations, because these jobs have as a primary task the establishment of good relations with others. Finally, high *n* Pow should result in high motivation on jobs that enable one to have a strong impact on others, jobs such as journalism and management. In fact, McClelland has found that the most effective managers have a low need for affiliation, a high need for power, and the ability to direct power toward organizational goals[12] (we will study this further in Chapter 13).

McClelland is careful to point out that there is not a one-to-one correspondence between a person's need structure and his or her behavior. Needs are only one determinant of behavior, and the person's values, habits, and skills, as well as environmental opportunities, are also influential. Thus, a person with high *n* Ach will not always exhibit higher motivation than a person with another need struc-

IN–FOCUS 6-1   CAN NEED FOR ACHIEVEMENT BE TRAINED?

Need for achievement is a relatively stable personality characteristic that is acquired through early life experiences. Nevertheless, David McClelland has shown that n Ach can be increased through training. He and his associates have developed programs that train businesspeople to act, talk, and think like high need achievers. In addition, they are trained to set moderately difficult but attainable goals and to seek the feedback needed to monitor their performance. These programs have been successful in increasing the achievement motivation of executives and owners of small businesses. In general, trained individuals engage in more business activity than untrained individuals, including starting new businesses and expanding existing premises and staff. Also, those trained tend to earn more money and promotions. One particularly interesting example occurred in India, where businesspeople in the city of Kakinada were trained in achievement motivation, while those in another city served as a control group. The Kakinadans were taught to write stories about pictures of people that reflected high needs for achievement, and they played a business simulation game that stimulated feelings of achievement. They were also introduced to successful entrepreneurs and were required to develop specific, concrete, moderate goals for their own businesses. Over a two-year period following the training, the Kakinadans engaged in more business activity than the control subjects, including creating twice as many new jobs. In fact, McClelland contends that the economic position of the entire city increased substantially as a result of the training.

Sources: McClelland, D. C. (1985). *Human motivation*. Glenview, IL: Scott, Foresman; McClelland, D. C., & Winter, D. G. (1969). *Motivating economic achievement*. New York: The Free Press.

ture. For example, a person with high n Aff might perform better than a person with high n Ach on a group task where high performance is the norm and friendship is contingent on good teamwork. Here, the need achiever's desire to set individual goals and take personal responsibility is constrained by the demands of the task.

Research Support for Need Theories

Measuring peoples' needs and the extent to which these needs are fulfilled has proven to be a difficult task. Thus, the need theories are not especially easy to test. Nevertheless, we can draw some tentative conclusions about their usefulness.

Maslow's need hierarchy suggests two main hypotheses. First, various specific needs should cluster into the five main need categories Maslow proposes. Second, as the needs in a given category are satisfied, they should become less important, while the needs in the adjacent higher need category should become more important. This second hypothesis captures the hierarchical and dynamic aspects of the theory. In general, research support for both of these hypotheses is weak or negative. This is probably a function of the rigidity of the theory, which suggests that most people experience the same needs in the same hierarchical order. However, in this research there is fair support for a more simple two-level need hierarchy comprising the needs toward the top and the bottom of Maslow's hierarchy.[13]

This latter finding provides some indirect encouragement for the compressed need hierarchy found in Alderfer's ERG theory. Several tests indicate fairly good support for many of the predictions generated by the theory, including its dynamic aspects. Particularly interesting is confirmation that the frustration of relatedness needs increases the strength of existence needs.[14] When it comes to hierarchies, the simplicity and flexibility of ERG theory seem to capture the human need structure better than the greater complexity and rigidity of Maslow's theory.

McClelland's need theory has generated a wealth of predictions about many aspects of human motivation. Recently, more and more of these predictions have been tested in organizational settings, and the results are generally supportive of the idea that particular needs are motivational when the work setting permits the satisfaction of these needs.[15] As noted in In–Focus 6-1, the theory has also stimulated some useful practical ideas about motivating economic achievement.

Managerial Implications of Need Theories

The need theories have some important things to say about managerial attempts to motivate workers.

The lack of support for the fairly rigid need hierarchy suggests that managers must be adept at evaluating the needs of individual employees and offering incentives or goals that correspond to these needs. Unfounded stereotypes about the needs of the "typical" worker and naive assumptions about the universality of need satisfaction are bound to reduce the effectiveness of chosen motivational strategies. Recall the story that began the chapter. Marilyn was interested in a job that provided her with a feeling of belongingness and enabled her to affiliate with others. Al, the machinist, was motivated by the opportunity to do a challenging job which enhanced his self-esteem and feelings of achievement. Observing these needs, it seems inadvisable to try to motivate Marilyn by promoting her to a job in which she is socially isolated or to transfer Al to a higher paying but boring job. Unfortunately, inattention to the needs of individual employees often leads to these kinds of motivational errors. The best salesperson may not make the best sales manager!

The need theories also serve the valuable function of calling to the attention of managers the existence of higher order needs (whatever specific label we apply to them). The recognition of these needs in many employees is important for two key reasons. First, you will recall from Chapter 1 that one of the basic conditions for organizational survival is the expression of some creative and innovative behavior on the part of members. Such behavior seems most likely to occur during the pursuit of higher-order need fulfillment, and ignorance of this factor may cause the demotivation of those who have the most to offer the organization. Secondly, observation and research evidence support Alderfer's idea that the frustration of higher order needs prompts demands for greater satisfaction of lower order needs. This can lead to a vicious motivational circle. That is, because the factors which gratify lower level needs are fairly easy to administer (e.g., pay and fringe benefits) management has grown to rely on them to motivate employees. In turn, some employees, deprived of higher-order need gratification, come to expect more and more of these extrinsic factors in exchange for their services. Thus, a circle of deprivation, regression, and temporary gratification continues at great cost to the organization.[16]

How can organizations take advantage of the intrinsic motivation inherent in strong higher order needs? First, such needs will fail to develop for most employees unless lower level needs are reasonably well gratified.[17] Thus, very poor pay, job insecurity, and unsafe working conditions will preoccupy most workers at the expense of higher order outcomes. Secondly, if basic needs are met, jobs can be "enriched" to be more stimulating and challenging and to provide feelings of responsibility and achievement. This will be discussed fully in the next chapter. Finally, organizations could pay more attention to designing career paths enabling interested workers to progress through a series of jobs that continue to challenge their higher order needs. In a similar vein, individual managers could assign tasks to subordinates with this goal in mind.

PROCESS THEORIES OF WORK MOTIVATION

In contrast to need theories of motivation, which concentrate upon *what* motivates persons, **process theories** concentrate upon *how* motivation occurs. In this section we will examine two important process theories, expectancy theory and equity theory.

Expectancy Theory

The basic idea underlying **expectancy theory** is the belief that motivation is determined by the outcomes that people expect to occur as a result of their actions on the job. Psychologist Victor Vroom is usually credited with developing the first complete version of expectancy theory to be applied to the work setting.[18] The basic components of Vroom's theory are shown in Exhibit 6-3:

- *Outcomes* are the consequences that may follow certain work behaviors. *First-level* outcomes are of particular interest to the organization, for example, high productivity versus average productivity (illustrated in Exhibit 6-3) or good attendance versus poor attendance. Expectancy theory is concerned with specifying how an employee might attempt to choose one first-level outcome instead of another. *Second-level* outcomes are consequences that follow the attainment of a particular first-level outcome. Contrasted with first-level outcomes, second-level outcomes are most personally relevant to the individual worker, and might involve amount of pay, sense of accomplishment, acceptance by peers, fatigue, and so on.

EXHIBIT 6-3 A hypothetical expectancy model (E = Expectancy, I = Instrumentality, V = Valence).

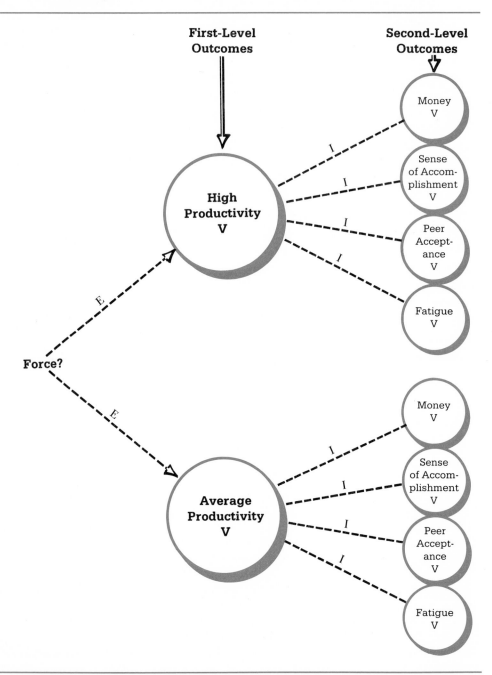

■ **Instrumentality** is the probability that a particular first-level outcome (such as high productivity) will be followed by a particular second-level outcome (such as pay). For example, a bank teller may figure that the odds are 50-50 (instrumentality = .5) that a good performance rating will result in a pay raise.

■ **Valence** is the expected value of outcomes, the extent to which they are attractive or unattractive to the individual. Thus, good pay, peer acceptance, the chance of being fired, or any other second-level outcome might be more or less attractive to particular workers. The valence of first-level outcomes is said by Vroom to be the sum of products of the associated second-level outcomes and their instrumentalities. That is, *the valence of a particular first-level outcome = Σ instrumentalities × second-level valences*. In other words, the valence of a first-level outcome depends upon the extent to which it leads to favorable second-level outcomes.

■ **Expectancy** is the probability that the worker can actually achieve a particular first-level outcome. For example, a machinist might be absolutely certain (expectancy = 1.0) that she can perform at an average level (producing 15 units a day) but less certain (expectancy = .6) that she can perform at a high level (producing 20 units a day).

■ *Force* is the end-product of the other components of the theory. It represents the relative degree of effort that will be directed toward various first-level outcomes. According to Vroom, the force directed toward a first-level outcome is a product of the valence of that outcome and the expectancy that it can be achieved. Thus, *force = first-level valence × expectancy*. An individual's effort can be expected to be directed toward the first-level outcome that has the largest force product. Notice that no matter how valent a particular first-level outcome might be, a person will not be motivated to achieve it if the expectancy of accomplishment approaches zero.

Believe it or not, the mechanics of expectancy theory can be distilled into a couple of simple sentences! In fact, these sentences nicely capture the premises of the theory: *People will be motivated to engage in those work activities that they find attractive and that they feel they can accomplish. The attractiveness of various work activities depends upon the extent to which they lead to favorable personal consequences.*

It is extremely important to understand that expectancy theory is based on the perceptual perspective of the individual worker. Thus, expectancies, valences, instrumentalities, and relevant second-level outcomes depend upon the perceptual system of the person whose motivation is being analyzed. For example, two workers performing the same job may attach different valences to money, differ in their perceptions of the instrumentality of performance for obtaining high pay, and differ in their expectations of being able to perform at a high level. Therefore, they would likely exhibit different patterns of motivation.

Although expectancy theory does not concern itself directly with the distinction between extrinsic and intrinsic motivators, it can handle any form of second-level outcome that has relevance for the person in question. Thus, some people might find second-level outcomes of an intrinsic nature, such as feeling good about performing a task well, positively valent. Others might find extrinsic outcomes such as high pay positively valent. Either intrinsic or extrinsic motivators should enhance motivation to the extent that they are highly valent, and to the extent that they reliably follow first-level outcomes which the individual feels able to achieve.

AN EXAMPLE. To firm up your understanding of expectancy theory, consider Tony Angelas, a middle manager in a firm that operates a chain of retail stores (Exhibit 6-4). Second-level outcomes which are relevant to him include the opportunity to obtain a raise and the chance to receive a promotion. The promotion is more highly valent to Tony than the raise (7 versus 5 on a scale of 10) because the promotion means more money *and* increased prestige. Tony figures that if he can perform at a very high level in the next few months the odds are six in ten that he will receive a raise. Thus, the instrumentality of high performance for obtaining a raise is .6. Promotions are harder to come by and Tony figures the odds at .3 if he performs well. The instrumentality of average performance for achieving these favorable second-level outcomes is a good bit lower (.2 for the raise and only .1 for the promotion). Recall that the valence of a first-level outcome is the sum of the products of second-level outcomes and their instrumentalities. Thus, the valence of high performance for Tony is $(5 \times .6) + (7 \times .3) = 5.1$. Similarly, the valence of average performance is $(5 \times .2) + (7 \times .1) = 1.7$. We can conclude that high performance is more valent for Tony than average performance.

Does this mean that Tony will necessarily try to perform at a high level in the next few months? To determine this we must take into account his expectancy that he can actually achieve the competing first-level outcomes. As shown in Exhibit 6-4, Tony is absolutely certain that he can perform at an average level (expectancy = 1.0), but much less certain (.3) that he can sustain high performance. Force is a product of these expectancies and the valence of their respective first-level outcomes. Thus, the force associated with high performance is $.3 \times 5.1 = 1.53$, while that associated with average performance is $1.0 \times 1.7 = 1.70$. As a result, although high performance is attractive to Tony, he will probably perform at an average level.

With all this complicated figuring you may be thinking "Look, would Tony really do all this calculation to decide his motivational strategy? Do people actually think this way?" The answer to these questions is probably no. Rather, the argument is that people *implicitly* take expectancy, valence, and instrumentality into account as they go about their daily business of being motivated. If you reflect for a moment on your behavior at work or school, you will realize that you have certain expectancies about what you can accomplish, the chances that these accomplishments will lead to certain other outcomes, and the value of these outcomes for you.

RESEARCH SUPPORT. Research tests of expectancy theory usually involve asking people in work settings to estimate the expectancy they have of achieving various first-level outcomes. In addition, they are requested to estimate the instru-

EXHIBIT 6-4 **Expectancy model for Tony Angelas (E = Expectancy, I = Instrumentality, V = Valence).**

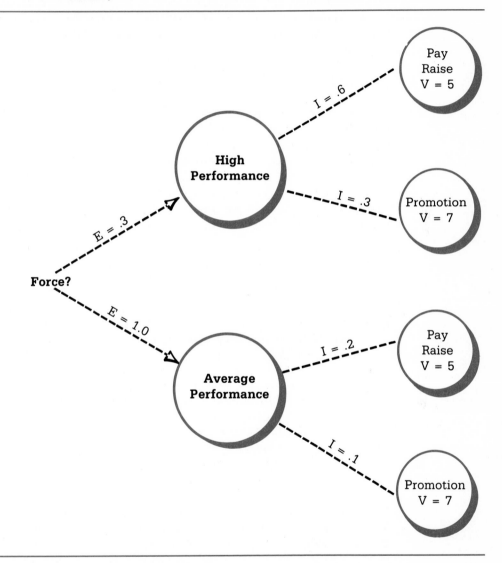

mentality connections between first- and second-level outcomes and to report the valence which various second-level outcomes have for them. Then, these estimates are combined as dictated by the theory to determine the extent to which they explain some behavior, such as effort expended on the job.

   In brief, such tests have provided moderately favorable support for expectancy theory.[19] In particular, there is especially good evidence that the valence of first-level outcomes depends upon the extent to which they lead to favorable second-level consequences. It must be recognized, however, that the sheer complicatedness of expectancy theory makes it difficult to test. For example, we have already suggested that people are not used to *thinking* in expectancy terminology. Thus, some research studies show that individuals have a difficult time discriminating between instrumentalities and second-level valences. Despite this and other technical problems, expectancy theory is generally well accepted by experts in motivation.

MANAGERIAL IMPLICATIONS.   The motivational practices suggested by expectancy theory involve "juggling the numbers" that individuals attach to expectancies, instrumentalities, and valences. One of the most basic things managers can do is ensure that their subordinates *expect* to be able to achieve first-level outcomes that are of interest to the organization. No matter how positively valent high productivity or good attendance may be, the force equation suggests that workers will not pursue these goals if expectancy is low. Low expectancies can take many forms, but a few examples will suffice to make the point:

■   Workers may feel that poor equipment, poor tools, or lazy co-workers impede their work progress.

■   Workers may not understand what is considered good performance or see how it can be achieved.

■   If performance is evaluated by a subjective supervisory rating, workers may see the process as capricious and arbitrary, not understanding how to obtain a good rating.

Although the specific solutions to these problems vary, expectancies can usually be enhanced by providing proper equipment and work facilities, demonstrating correct work procedures, carefully explaining how performance is evaluated, and listening to employee performance problems. The point of all this is to clarify the path to beneficial first-level outcomes.

Managers should also attempt to ensure that the paths between first- and second-level outcomes are clear. Employees should be convinced that first-level outcomes desired by the organization are clearly *instrumental* to obtaining positively valent second-level outcomes and avoiding negatively-valent outcomes. If a manager has a policy of recommending good performers for promotion, this policy should be spelled out. Similarly, if regular attendance is desired, the consequences of good and poor attendance should be clarified. To ensure that instrumentalities are strongly established, they should be clearly stated and then acted upon by the manager. Managers should also attempt to provide stimulating, challenging tasks for those who appear interested in such work. On such tasks, the instrumentality of good performance for feelings of achievement, accomplishment, and competence is almost necessarily high. The ready availability of intrinsic motivation in this case may reduce the need for the manager to constantly monitor and clarify instrumentalities.[20]

Obviously, it may be difficult for managers to change the valences that subordinates attach to second-level outcomes. Individual preferences for high pay, promotion, interesting work, and so on are probably the product of a long history of development and unlikely to change rapidly. However, managers would do well to analyze the preferences of particular subordinates and attempt to design individualized "motivational packages" to meet their needs. Of course, such packages must be perceived to be fair by all concerned. Let's examine another process theory that is concerned specifically with the motivational consequences of fairness.

Equity Theory

In Chapter 5 we discussed the role of **equity theory** in explaining job satisfaction. To review, the theory asserts that workers compare the inputs they invest in their jobs and the outcomes they receive against the inputs and outcomes of some other relevant person or group. When these ratios are equal, the worker should feel that a fair and equitable exchange exists with the employing organization. Such fair exchange should contribute to job satisfaction. When the ratios are unequal, inequity is perceived to exist and job dissatisfaction should be experienced, at least if the exchange puts the worker at a disadvantage vis-à-vis others.

But in what sense is equity theory a theory of motivation? Put simply, *individuals should be motivated to maintain an equitable exchange relationship.* Inequity is unpleasant and tension-producing, and persons should devote considerable energy to reducing inequity and achieving equity. What tactics can be used to do this? Psychologist J. Stacey Adams has suggested the following possibilities:

- Perceptually distort one's own inputs or outcomes
- Perceptually distort the inputs or outcomes of the comparison person or of the group
- Choose another comparison person or group
- Alter one's inputs or alter one's outcomes
- Leave the exchange relationship[21]

Notice that the first three tactics for reducing inequity are essentially psychological, while the latter two involve overt behavior.

AN EXAMPLE.   To clarify the motivational implications of equity theory, consider Terry, a middle manager in a consumer products company. He has five years work experience, an M.B.A. degree, and considers himself a good performer. His salary is $35,000 a year. Terry finds out that Maxine, a co-worker with whom he identifies closely, makes the same salary he does. However, she has only a Bachelor's degree and one year of experience, and he sees her performance as average rather than good. Thus, from Terry's perspective, the following outcome/input ratios exist:

TERRY		MAXINE
$35,000	‡	$35,000
Good performance, M.B.A., 5 years		Average performance, Bachelors, 1 year

In Terry's view, he is underpaid and should be experiencing inequity. What might he do to resolve this inequity? Psychologically, he might distort the outcomes he is receiving, rationalizing that he is due for a certain promotion which will bring his pay into line with his inputs. Behaviorally, he might try to increase his outcomes (by seeking an immediate raise) or reduce his inputs. Input reduction could include a decrease in work effort or perhaps excessive absenteeism. Finally, Terry might resign from the organization to take a more equitable job somewhere else.

Let's reverse the coin and assume that Maxine views the exchange relationship identically to Terry—same inputs, same outcomes, and so on. Notice that she too should be experiencing inequity, this time from relative overpayment. It doesn't take a genius to understand that Maxine would be unlikely to seek equity by marching into the boss's office and demanding a pay cut. However, she might well attempt to increase her inputs by working harder or enrolling in an M.B.A. program. Alternatively, she might distort her view of Terry's performance to make it seem closer to her own.

As this example implies, equity theory is somewhat vague about just when various inequity reduction strategies will be employed. However, it handles both intrinsic and extrinsic outcomes equally well when they are viewed as relevant to the exchange.

RESEARCH SUPPORT.   Most research on equity theory has been restricted to economic outcomes and has concentrated on the alteration of inputs and outcomes as a means of reducing inequity. In general, this research is very supportive of the theory when inequity occurs because of *underpayment*.[22] For example, when workers are underpaid on an hourly basis they tend to lower their inputs by producing less work. This brings inputs into line with (low) outcomes. Also, when workers are underpaid on a piecerate basis (e.g., paid $1 for each interview conducted) they tend to produce a high volume of low quality work. This enables them to raise their outcomes to achieve equity. Finally, there is also evidence that underpayment inequity leads to resignation. Presumably, some underpaid workers thus seek equity in another organizational setting.

The theory's predictions regarding *overpayment* inequity have received less support.[23] The theory suggests that such inequity can be reduced behaviorally by increasing inputs or by reducing one's outcomes. The weak support for these strategies suggests either that people tolerate overpayment more than underpayment or that they use perceptual distortion to reduce overpayment inequity.

MANAGERIAL IMPLICATIONS.   The most straightforward implication of equity theory is that perceived underpayment will have a variety of negative motivational consequences for the organization, including low productivity, low quality, and/or turnover (See In–Focus 6-2). On the other hand, attempting to solve organizational problems through overpayment (disguised bribery) may not have the intended motivational effect. The trick here is to strike an equitable balance.

But how can such a balance be struck? Managers must understand that feelings about equity stem from a *perceptual* social comparison process in which the worker "controls the equation." That is, employees decide what are considered relevant inputs, outcomes, and comparison persons, and management must be sensitive to these decisions. For example, offering the outcome of more interesting work may not redress inequity if pay is considered a more relevant outcome. Similarly, basing pay only on performance may not be perceived as equitable if employees consider seniority an important job input.

Understanding the role of comparison persons is especially crucial. The fact that the best engineer in the design department earns $2000 more than anyone else in the department may still lead to feelings of inequity if he compares his salary with that of more prosperous colleagues in *other* companies. Similarly, blue collar workers may experience inequity when they hear about the fantastic salaries being paid in exotic locations such as remote mining sites or the oil fields of the Middle East. However, they often ignore the inputs that may be mandated to achieve these high outcomes, such as separation from the family or high housing expenses. Awareness of the comparison persons chosen by workers may suggest strategies for reducing felt inequity. Perhaps the company will have to pay even more to retain its star engineer. Perhaps a detailed article in the company newsletter about remote employment will reduce felt inequity for the blue collar workers.

PUTTING IT ALL TOGETHER: THE PORTER-LAWLER MODEL

In this chapter, we have presented several theories of work motivation and attempted to distinguish between motivation and performance. In Chapter 5 we discussed the relationship between job performance and job satisfaction. At this point, it seems appropriate to review just how all of these concepts fit together. Psychologists Lyman Porter and Edward Lawler have devised an excellent model to portray these relationships (Exhibit 6-5).[24] Boxes 1 through 3 are simply a restatement of the expectancy theory of motivation. *Value of Reward* (Box 1) refers to the valence of second-level outcomes, while *Perceived Effort → Reward Probability* (Box 2) refers to perceptions of expectancy and instrumentality. Thus, an individual will exert effort on the job to the extent that this effort is expected to be followed by valued rewards.

Boxes 3 through 6 illustrate that high effort will be translated into good performance *if* the worker has traits and abilities relevant to the job, and *if* the worker understands his or her role in the organization (especially with regard to what the organization considers good performance). If these conditions are not met, high effort will not result in good performance. For example, consider a hospital nurse who exhibits tremendous effort but lacks compassion, doesn't know how to use a syringe, and is confused about the respective responsibilities of nurses,

IN–FOCUS 6-2 TWO-TIER WAGE CONTRACTS: INSTITUTIONALIZED INEQUITY?

"Equal pay for equal work" has long been a principle of labor contract negotiations endorsed by unions and generally conceded by employers. For both parties, the principle reflects an implicit understanding of equity theory—that workers who exhibit equivalent work inputs ("equal work") will expect equivalent work outcomes ("equal pay"). However, beginning in 1983, following several years of recession, many labor contracts were signed that squarely violated the "equal work for equal pay" principle. In essence, these contracts provide new employees with a much less lucrative salary structure than that enjoyed by existing employees. Thus, under a two-tier contract, new employees generally begin at a lower rate than their predecessors began at. In some cases, new employees can gradually achieve parity with experienced workers. In other cases, the wage discrepancy is permanent. For example, an American Airlines DC-10 pilot with high seniority could earn $127,900 in 1985. A new pilot hired that same year under a two-tier contract could only expect to earn half that amount.

What has been responsible for the reluctant acceptance by many unions of two-tier contracts? In general, such contracts have emerged where existing wage rates have been challenged by industry deregulation, foreign competition, or strong non-union competition. For example, new pilots were not the only employees to suffer the effects of airline deregulation. New American Airlines mechanics now require twelve years to achieve the top pay rate for their job classification, a progression that takes those hired earlier only two years. Similarly, flight attendants hired under the two-tier structure begin by making $222 less a month.

Strong non-union competition has also stimulated a host of two-tier contracts, especially in the retail food business. Supermarket chains such as Kroger, Safeway, and Giant Food have gone this route. For instance, new clerks at Giant Food stores in Baltimore begin at $5 an hour and can progress to almost $9 an hour. Those hired before the two-tier contract was in place started at almost $7 and progressed to over $11.

Equity theory predicts that a number of negative consequences should follow from the two-tier wage structure, even though it saves the organization money in the short run. Are the theory's predictions borne out? At first, new workers seem accepting of the two-tier system, apparently grateful for the job. However, as the theory predicts, those on the lower tier quickly develop dissatisfaction. As a Los Angeles supermarket clerk angrily put it, "It stinks—they're paying us lower wages for the same work. I can do just as much as an employee here for five years—and in the same amount of time."

Equity theory also predicts that one way to reduce underpayment inequity is to reduce inputs. Some senior flight attendants have reported that junior colleagues on the second tier have refused assigned tasks with the response, "You do it. You're making more." Such a situation has the potential to cause conflict among the new hires and the veterans, who may be experiencing some *overpayment* inequity.

Finally, equity theory predicts that, if feelings of inequity cannot be resolved on the job, the underpaid person may "leave the field." Indeed, Giant Food found that two thirds of its lower-tier employees quit during their first three months. At United Airlines, a costly strike resulted when a two-tier wage contract for pilots was proposed.

Source: Adapted from Ross, I. (1985, April 29). Employers win big in the move to two-tier contracts. *Fortune*, 82–92.

EXHIBIT 6-5   **The Porter-Lawler model.**

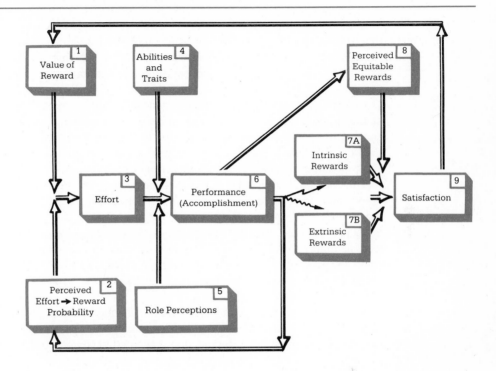

Source: From Porter, L. W., and Lawler, E. E., III (1968). *Managerial attitudes and performance.*
Homewood, IL: Richard D. Irwin, Inc. © Richard D. Irwin, Inc. Reprinted by permission.

doctors, and attendants. Clearly, such an individual will perform poorly in spite of high effort. It is at the link between effort and performance that observers frequently make judgments about the motivation of workers. Thus, our nurse might be judged by the head nurse as having "high" but "misdirected" motivation, because he or she is directing persistent effort in a way that doesn't help the hospital achieve its goals. You will see that this portion of the Porter-Lawler model is essentially a simplification of the relationships shown in Exhibit 6-1.

A particular level of performance (Box 6) will be followed by certain outcomes. To the extent that these are positively valent second-level outcomes, they can be considered *rewards* for good performance (Boxes 7A and 7B). In general, the connection between performance and the occurrence of *intrinsic* rewards should be strong and reliable, because such rewards are self-administered. For example, the nurse who assists several very sick patients back to health is almost certain to feel a sense of competence and achievement, because such feelings stem directly from the job. On the other hand, the connection between performance and *extrinsic* rewards may be much less reliable (note the wavy line in Exhibit 6-5), because the occurrence of such rewards depends on the actions of some organizational agent.

Thus, the head nurse may or may not recommend attendance at a nursing conference (an extrinsic fringe benefit) for the good performance.

The availability of intrinsic and extrinsic rewards affects job satisfaction (Box 9) to the extent that these rewards are seen as equitable (Box 8). You will recall that this relationship between job outcomes, equity, and job satisfaction was discussed in Chapter 5. Also recall that in Chapter 5 it was emphasized that job satisfaction does not lead to good performance. Rather, it was argued that *good performance leads to job satisfaction if that performance is rewarded.*

The feedback loop in the lower portion of the model indicates that the worker's actual experience with the connection between performance and rewards influences *future* expectations of the probability that effort will lead to reward. Thus, the worker whose effort is eventually rewarded uses this information to guide future effort expenditure. The feedback loop in the upper portion of the model suggests that the satisfaction derived from job rewards may influence the valence (anticipated value) of these rewards in the future. Sometimes, satisfaction may decrease the valence of a reward. For example, the person who is highly paid, and thus financially satisfied, may not see extra pay that can be achieved through overtime work as highly valent. On the other hand, satisfaction may increase the valence of some rewards. For example, Maslow argued that self-actualization is a growth need. This suggests that as the self-actualization need is satisfied, it should become more highly valent.

In summary, the Porter-Lawler model provides an excellent picture of the motivational process. It is entirely consistent with the process theories of motivation and the concept of job satisfaction presented in Chapter 5.

A FOOTNOTE: DO EXTRINSIC REWARDS DECREASE INTRINSIC MOTIVATION?

Frequently, when college students are asked what kind of job they would like to achieve following graduation, they respond, ''Give me an interesting job that pays well.'' Indeed, this may be the most commonly-held stereotype of a good job, and those who desire such a job would probably report that they would be motivated to perform the job especially well. Notice that there is an implicit assumption operating here—intrinsic motivators (in this case, interesting work) and extrinsic motivators (in this case, pay) ''add up'' to enhance motivation. Thus, from a motivational standpoint, a ''Superjob'' would be one which is especially high on both intrinsic and extrinsic motivation. Thus far in the chapter, little has been said about the possible **relationship between extrinsic and intrinsic motivation.** However, expectancy theory and the Porter-Lawler model suggest that if intrinsic outcomes and extrinsic outcomes are both highly valent, they should contribute to motivation in an additive fashion.

In recent years, a number of research studies have reached the conclusion that the availability of extrinsic motivators may reduce the intrinsic motivation stemming from the task itself.[25] At first, this may seem counterintuitive to you.

An "interesting job that pays well" is the most common stereotype of a motivating job.

However, many parents have observed that linking a monetary allowance to the completion of household chores may lead their children to denigrate work that was once enthusiastically performed. Similarly, many professors have noticed that a strong emphasis on grades seems to reduce students' motivation to engage in learning for its own sake. The notion here, then, is that when extrinsic rewards depend upon performance, the valence of intrinsic rewards decreases. A chief proponent of this view has suggested that making extrinsic rewards contingent upon performance makes individuals feel less competent and less in control of their own behavior.[26] That is, they come to believe that their performance is controlled by the environment, and that they only perform well because of the money. Thus, intrinsic motivation suffers.

Research tests of the effects of extrinsic rewards on intrinsic motivation have produced very mixed results—sometimes intrinsic motivation is reduced and sometimes it is not. Many of these tests have used students as subjects, and most have relied on rather artificial short-term tasks. One review concludes that intrinsic motivation is likely to suffer under these highly restrictive conditions. However, in more realistic settings where extrinsic rewards are seen as symbols of success and as signals of what to do to achieve future rewards, the hypothesis is less likely to be confirmed.[27] Thus, it is probably safe to assume that both kinds of rewards are compatible in enhancing motivation in actual work settings.

SUMMARY

■ Commonsense views about why people work were discussed, and it was concluded that such views provide an incomplete basis for a comprehensive theory of motivation. Motivation is the extent to which persistent effort is directed toward organizationally relevant outcomes. Intrinsic motivation stems from the direct relationship between the worker and the task and is usually self-applied. Extrinsic motivation stems from the environment surrounding the task and is applied by others. Performance is the extent to which an organization member contributes to achieving the goals of the organization. It is influenced by motivation but also by aptitudes, skills, task understanding, and chance factors.

■ Need theories propose that motivation will occur when employee behavior can be directed toward goals or incentives that satisfy personal wants or desires. The three need theories discussed were Maslow's need heirarchy, Alderfer's ERG theory, and McClelland's theory of needs for achievement, affiliation, and power. Maslow and Alderfer have concentrated on the hierarchical arrangement of needs and the distinction between intrinsic and extrinsic motivation. McClelland has focused on the conditions under which particular need patterns stimulate high motivation.

■ Process theories attempt to explain how motivation occurs rather than what specific factors are motivational. Expectancy theory argues that people will be motivated to engage in those work activities which they find attractive and which they feel they can accomplish. The attractiveness of these activities depends upon the extent to which they lead to favorable personal consequences. Equity theory states that workers compare the inputs they apply to their jobs and the outcomes they achieve from their jobs with the inputs and outcomes of others. When these outcome/input ratios are unequal, inequity exists, and workers will be motivated to restore equity. The Porter-Lawler model summarizes the relationships among the process theory variables and performance, rewards, and job satisfaction.

KEY CONCEPTS

Theory X versus Theory Y
Motivation
Intrinsic motivation
Extrinsic motivation
Performance
Need theories
Maslow's hierarchy of needs
ERG theory
Need for achievement

Need for affiliation
Need for power
Process theories
Expectancy theory
Instrumentality
Valence
Expectancy
Equity theory
Intrinsic/extrinsic relationship

DISCUSSION QUESTIONS

1. Many millionaires continue to work long, hard hours, sometimes even beyond the usual age of retirement. Use the ideas developed in the chapter to speculate about the reasons for this motivational pattern. Is the acquisition of wealth still a motivator for these individuals?

2. Discuss a time when you were highly motivated to perform well (at work, at school, in a sports contest) but performed poorly in spite of your high motivation. How do you know your motivation was really high? What factors interfered with good performance? What did you learn from this experience?

3. Use Maslow's hierarchy of needs and Alderfer's ERG theory to explain why assembly line workers and executive vice-presidents might be susceptible to different forms of motivation.

4. Do you feel that unions are more concerned with obtaining extrinsic rewards or intrinsic rewards for their members? What does ERG theory say about this?

5. Describe in detail a specific job where a person with high need for affiliation would be more motivated and perform better than a person with high need for achievement.

6. Colleen is high in need for achievement, Eugene is high in need for power, and Max is high in need for affiliation. They are thinking about starting a business partnership. To maximize the motivation of each, what business should they go into, and who should assume which roles or jobs?

7. Reconsider the case of Tony Angelas, which was used to illustrate expectancy theory. Imagine that you are Tony's boss and that you think he can be motivated to perform at a high level. Suppose you cannot modify second-level outcomes or their valences, but you can affect expectancies and instrumentalities. What would you do to motivate Tony? Prove that you have succeeded by recalculating the force equations to demonstrate that Tony will now perform at a high level.

8. Set up a hypothetical outcome/input equation that reveals inequity. Review the methods that might be used to reduce this particular case of inequity.

9. Using the Porter-Lawler model as a guide, design an ideal motivational system for a chain of food supermarkets. What would be the role of the supermarket managers in this system? What practical constraints would interfere with the operation of this ideal system?

10. Discuss the following assertion: Many organizations simply lack the time and resources to maximize the motivation of their employees. In many cases, energy could be better devoted to developing a new marketing plan or investing in better equipment rather than trying to motivate individual workers.

FOR FURTHER READING

Pinder, C. C. (1977). Concerning the application of human motivation theories in organizational settings. *Academy of Management Review, 2,* 384–397.

> Argues that the application of many motivational strategies may be unwise because they are based on motivation theories that lack clear support. Suggests that this is unethical and argues that even apparently successful strategies may have negative consequences for employees. See a reply to Pinder by Philip Bobko and Pinder's response in the October 1978 issue of the same journal.

Pinder, C. C. (1984). *Work motivation: Theory, issues, and applications.* Glenview, IL: Scott, Foresman.

> A comprehensive overview of various theories of work motivation and the applications they suggest. Careful coverage of the research support for each theory and application.

Steers, R. M., & Porter, L. W. (Eds.). (1987). *Motivation and work behavior* (4th ed.). New York: McGraw-Hill.

> A collection of useful articles on various aspects of motivation by well known authors.

Case Study

Phoenix or Ephemera?

Harry Moss was a group head in The Radar Detection Laboratory of Gideon and Trumpet, Inc., a large electronics producer. Harry's present concern was with one of the older employees in his group, Jo Enright. Harry's attempt to motivate Jo into productive work had seemed spectacularly, if briefly, successful. However, more recent events had given him pause. He recounted the following experience to the casewriter.

Harry Moss: I became Jo's supervisor about three-and-a-half years ago. Actually I had heard about him even before that. Jo was an enigma. He'd been with the company for 25 years and there were legends about what he had accomplished years ago. But nearly everyone agreed that he had shot his wad sometime early in his career. At any rate he was one of the most notoriously unproductive employees we had. That was three years ago.

I joined this group as a supervisor when I returned from our subsidiary in Belgium. We had a project that was top priority and the high hopes of our laboratory director were riding with us, which is not always an advantage. It was important to assemble a top-flight creative group. I forget how Jo came to be among them. I do remember the director objecting that he wasn't right for it. He hadn't received a

9-413-054 Phoenix or Ephemera
Copyright © 1967 by the President and Fellows of Harvard College. All names disguised. This case was made possible by the cooperation of a firm which remains anonymous. It was prepared by Charles Hampden-Turner under the direction of Charles D. Orth as a basis for class discussion rather than to illustrate either effective or ineffective handling of an administrative situation. Reprinted by permission of the Harvard Business School.

"star rating" for eight years. His last significant contributions was eighteen years ago. He was referred to as a "has-been." All this was discussed along with the possibility of transferring him to another division. I argued that we should give him a chance. I promised to support a decision to transfer him if things didn't work out.

I'd heard from other old-timers in the company that Jo's good work had mostly been done in collaboration with a senior man called Horrocks. He's dead now. Jo never did anything again after Horrocks retired. Somewhere in the back of my mind I was thinking that Jo might respond to a good working relationship. He had a long string of patents and awards when he was working with Horrocks. I got to thinking we might recapture it.

When you meet Jo, you'll see what I mean. He's kind of lethargic but very gracious and quite profound. You can't help feeling he has considerable potential. He's also very composed and reassuring—so much so that I just can't get mad at him. He's older than me and sometimes I feel he's wiser. He's a very good judge of people and I used to consult him on a lot of human problems—home, lab, social, all kinds. His advice was remarkably insightful and sort of *effortless*. That's the strongest impression I have about him. He's coasting along on a fraction of his potential power.

For years now there have been complaints about Jo's stock market dealings. You used to walk into the lab and likely as not Jo would be talking to his broker on the telephone. Rumour has it that he's made himself rich and isn't scared of being fired. People have frequently made sarcastic remarks in his presence about his hobby—and all his superiors have heard about it. Jo doesn't give the smallest sign that he ever hears criticism. I was told to crack down on his practice of issuing long instructions to Wall Street but I've refused. I'm not going to treat him like a baby. Anyway threatening him would not work and I wouldn't feel right doing it.

I decided to put Jo on the extremely important and central part of our project which was to obtain very high-frequency operation with diodes. We had not been able to use them at such high frequencies before and it was a challenge. During the next few days he would drop in to talk to me about this and that and quite soon he would start to talk about his work. I thought that this was an encouraging sign because generally speaking he eats lunch and talks informally to people outside the group whom he has known for a long time, and he doesn't discuss his work very much informally.

The more he talked to me about his ideas for the project the more excited he became and there was an animation in his voice which I had not heard before. When I told other people about his change of attitude they were rather dampening. "Oh he's had good ideas for a long time—only they never get implemented!" However, it was quite clear to me that he was implementing his ideas. He worked long hours with most intense concentration and every now and then he would burst into my office and tell me about it. We never heard from his broker during *that* time!

To make a long story short, in the weeks that followed he made a number of breakthroughs which have put us literally years ahead of the rest of the industry. It took everyone by surprise. People stopped and asked me, "What have you done with Jo? He's a changed man!" By the end of the year he'd got a pay raise, an award from the company, and had been presented with a prize by the industry at a banquet in Washington. That's the story.

Casewriter: Assuming that Jo's sudden creativity had something to do with your supervision, how do you behave differently from other supervisors?

Harry Moss: Well I have always had a respect for Jo that others lack. I admire his mind, his judgment of people and his ideas. I've always found him conversationally stimulating. For that reason I don't have to use any self-conscious supervisory techniques on him. I appreciate him and he knows it. I've always felt, though, that I have had to get the ball rolling between us. If we haven't seen each other for some time, it's I who will have to initiate and then he'll respond and keep coming back. But it's almost as if he needs winding up from time to time.

And then unlike some supervisors I come right out into the open and say what I think. I'm not afraid to ask him to help me and to admit that I need results. I'm a lot franker than most people and this sometimes gets me into trouble. Jo, I think, appreciates it. I like to think that I have empathy and rapport with people.

Casewriter: And how long did Jo's period of creativity last? Is he still a top-notch performer?

Harry Moss: That's another story in itself. I'm afraid we may have killed the spark. I shouldn't have let it happen.

What with the Vietnam war, basic research is being cut back and we are getting more and more of these "development" projects. You know, deadlines, guaranteed pay-off, close scheduling—the sort of thing development groups should be doing. One of these came up and Jo had just the experience needed for it. Moreover, the less creative people find it harder to avoid these assignments. Although Jo had improved out of all recognition in the last few months, there were many with better overall records who could be trusted to do basic research which would eventually pay off. You have to be *really* good to be left alone in this business.

I asked that Jo be left with my group. I was afraid his productiveness would not survive transfer to routine, highly supervised work. "It's only for a few months," I was told. "It's top priority." I hoped that if Jo, too, complained vigorously we might prevail. But Jo doesn't complain. He just shrugged, smiled and joined John Blair's group without a murmur of protest. I didn't see him for about three weeks, when I happened to pass through the room in which he was supposed to be working. There he was, hard at it, dictating instructions to his broker.

About eight months later my group was making disappointing progress on the work Jo had left and I began pulling strings to get him back. I was concerned about annoying John Blair. I needn't have worried. "You want him back—you can have him," said John. "He's done nothing for me except make a killing on the market. Why don't they send him to the financial division?"

I went to Jo and told him he was to rejoin my group. He nodded and smiled and moved again. I asked him to come and see me and really laid it on the line. "You've got the most fertile brain in this lab," I said. "I'm going to try and get you another raise—but that's only a fraction of what you could be making. You've got potential—we both know that."

He thanked me and left. He never said it was good to be back or that he enjoyed working with me, but he was his kind, obliging self. You know when people ask for his help, he will drop what he is doing and oblige them at once. No favor is too much trouble and he'll never complain. Perhaps that is why he gets moved around. We know there will be no unpleasantness. Lately I've been wondering whether at some level he doesn't resent it and if in the end we don't pay for it.

I wish I could say that now everything is rosy again and that we'd recaptured our former productive relationship but I'm not at all sure we have. It's been three months now since he came back. He's full of ideas when I talk to him but the results have not appeared. Perhaps he's storing them up. He does that sometimes. He did come up with some interesting results but they weren't related to our objectives and I had to tell him so. Perhaps I had it and I lost it, or perhaps it isn't connected with me at all. I wish I knew. I'm only sorry I let him be transferred.

The casewriter was later introduced to Jo Enright, a tall, white-haired man of about fifty years. He sat down in a chair opposite the casewriter. In contrast to several other people interviewed he seemed completely at ease from the first moment and never expressed any fears that his opinions could be used against him. Jo was asked about his recent creative resurgence after years in which he had been less active.

Jo Enright: Well it sometimes happens that by luck one finds oneself working in virgin territory, and it suddenly comes to you that what you are doing will affect millions of people. That's when I get excited. It's like opening up a frontier. Sometimes this will last for months or years and then it will dry up.

Casewriter: But can't you convince your supervisors to let you advance on a frontier for years on end?

Jo Enright: Yes and no. Sooner or later the administration will tend to get into a rut. They frequently fall into the error of thinking they can organize the process of discovery. They seem to think that if you repeat some motions that were successful in the past, then this will guarantee productiveness in the future. But that isn't usually true. If you know exactly what you are going to discover and how long it will take—then you are not really doing research at all. It's the unexpected things—and having the time to follow up the unexpected things that leads to really creative work.

But it's when you start following the unexpected that other people are likely to lose interest in you. I can't do creative work without some cross-fertilization of ideas. Your group has to care about your ideas and it must be flexible enough to turn aside from what was originally defined as the best procedure. But many groups go dead the moment anything gets complex or ambiguous. When I can't get people interested in the unusual results I feel like I'm banging my head against a wall. It's useless and it hurts.

In some ways it's like an aircraft trying to take off. When I first get an unusual idea I'm not always confident that I'm talking sense. Sometimes there is a key person who can give you that *early* understanding. If you get it this gives you momentum and you can "take off." The trouble is of course that you have to *earn* other people's attention. This means that if you get into a rut with uncongenial people or poor administrators, it can become harder and harder to win people's attention. They say, "Oh he's shot his wad!" Then, they give you all the routine assignments and the development stuff—and it's harder than ever to produce.

Casewriter: When you were transferred from Harry's group to John Blair's, was that bad?

Jo Enright: It was worse. It was a routine project. Your work is paced. There are a lot of little segments—all with deadlines for completion, and no time to follow up the interesting results. It wasn't John's fault.

Casewriter: Did you complain about being transferred?

Jo Enright: I didn't have very much information on what the transfer entailed. Had I known—I *might* have complained. [Laughs] I'm learning! For me, working is pushing unless you're discovering virgin territory. Then it's exciting and you get carried along.

Casewriter: How would you rate Harry Moss as a supervisor?

Jo Enright: The best thing about Harry is his flexibility. You can set goals jointly with him but if another lead appears, you can follow that. Harry's sound professionally, which means that when he understands an idea, that comprehension is significant for me. Some supervisors treat you as if you were babbling to yourself, and then you think, "Hell, forget it!" But when Harry reacts he's enthusiastic and he means it. He doesn't pretend to understand.

Casewriter: How often do these opportunities to work in virgin territory arise? For instance, prior to last year how long had it been since you were working in virgin territory?

Jo Enright: Oh, a long time. Fifteen years at least. Sometimes all the chips fall just right but more often they don't. In fact my recent work with high-frequency diodes was a development of the direction I was working in twenty years ago. Some of my best early work was similar to this. It was like rediscovering an old trail.

Casewriter: And where are you as of now? Back on the trail?

Jo Enright: [Shrugs] Perhaps, who knows? You can't force these things. I'm looking around. I have a number of interesting leads. These slack, interim periods come and go. The system gets hard and then suddenly shakes loose.

Casewriter: Can one struggle to get out of these interim periods?

Jo Enright: Maybe. Perhaps I don't struggle enough.

■ ■ ■

1. Discuss Jo's need structure.
2. When does Jo work effectively?
3. In expectancy theory terms, describe previous attempts to motivate Jo.
4. Is equity an issue in this case?
5. How good a boss is Harry?
6. What should Harry do now?

REFERENCES

1. McGregor, D. (1960). *The human side of enterprise*. New York: McGraw-Hill.
2. McGregor, 1960.
3. Kasl, S. (1978). Epidemiological contributions to the study of work stress. In C. L. Cooper & R. Payne (Eds.), *Stress at work*. New York: Wiley. Also see Dubin, R., Hedley, R. A., & Taveggia, T. C. (1976). Attachment to work. In R. Dubin (Ed.), *Handbook of work, organization, and society*. Chicago: Rand McNally.
4. Campbell, J. P., Dunnette, M. D., Lawler, E. E., III, & Weick, K. E., Jr. (1970). *Managerial behavior, performance, and effectiveness*. New York: McGraw-Hill. Also see Katerberg, R., & Blau, G. (1983). An examination of level and direction of effort and job performance. *Academy of Management Journal, 26*, 249–257.
5. Dyer, L., & Parker, D. F. (1975). Classifying outcomes in work motivation research: An examination of the intrinsic-extrinsic dichotomy. *Journal of Applied Psychology, 60*, 455–458. Also see Brief, A. P., & Aldag, R. J. (1977). The intrinsic-extrinsic dichotomy: Toward conceptual clarity. *Academy of Management Review, 2*, 496–500.
6. Based on Campbell, J. P., & Pritchard, R. D. (1976). Motivation theory in industrial and organizational psychology. In M. D. Dunnette (Ed.), *Handbook of industrial and organizational psychology*. Chicago: Rand McNally.
7. The distinction between need (content) and process theories was first made by Campbell et al., 1970.
8. Maslow, A. H. (1970). *Motivation and personality* (2nd ed.). New York: Harper and Row.
9. Alderfer, C. P. (1969). An empirical test of a new theory of human needs. *Organizational Behavior and Human Performance, 4*, 142–175. Also see Alderfer, C. P. (1972). *Existence, relatedness, and growth: Human needs in organizational settings*. New York: The Free Press.
10. McClelland, D. C. (1985). *Human motivation*. Glenview, IL: Scott, Foresman.
11. McClelland, D. C., & Winter, D. G. (1969). *Motivating economic achievement*. New York: The Free Press, 50–52.
12. McClelland, D. C., & Boyatzis, R. E. (1982). Leadership motive pattern and long-term success in management. *Journal of Applied Psychology, 67*, 737–743; McClelland, D. C., & Burnham, D. (1976, March–April). Power is the great motivator. *Harvard Business Review*, 159–166. However, need for power may not be the best motive pattern for managers of technical and professional people. See Cornelius, E. T., III, & Lane, F. B. (1984). The power motive and managerial success in a professionally oriented service industry organization. *Journal of Applied Psychology, 69*, 32–39.
13. Wahba, M. A., & Bridwell, L. G. (1976). Maslow reconsidered: A review of research on the need hierarchy theory. *Organizational Behavior and Human Performance, 15*, 212–240.
14. Schneider, B., & Alderfer, C. P. (1973). Three studies of measures of need satisfaction in organizations. *Administrative Science Quarterly, 18*, 498–505. Also see Alderfer, C. P., Kaplan, R. E., & Smith, K. K. (1974). The effect of relatedness need satisfaction on relatedness desires. *Administrative Science Quarterly, 19*, 507–532. For a disconfirming test see Rauschenberger, J., Schmitt, N., & Hunter, J. E. (1980). A test of the need hierarchy concept by a Markov model of change in need strength. *Administrative Science Quarterly, 25*, 654–670.
15. McClelland, 1985.
16. Herzberg, F. (1966). *Work and the nature of man*. Cleveland: World Publishing.

17. Lawler, E. E., III. (1973). *Motivation in work organizations*. Monterey, CA: Brooks/ Cole.

18. Vroom, V. H. (1964). *Work and motivation*. New York: Wiley.

19. Mitchell, T. R. (1974). Expectancy models of job satisfaction, occupational preference, and effort: A theoretical, methodological, and empirical appraisal. *Psychological Bulletin, 81,* 1053–1077. Also see Pinder, C. C. (1984). *Work motivation: Theory, issues, and applications*. Glenview, IL: Scott, Foresman.

20. A good discussion of how managers can strengthen expectancy and instrumentality relationships is presented by Strauss, G. (1977). Managerial practices. In J. R. Hackman & J. L. Suttle (Eds.), *Improving life at work: Behavioral science approaches to organizational change*. Glenview, IL: Scott, Foresman.

21. Adams, J. S. (1965). Injustice in social exchange. In L. Berkowitz (Ed.), *Advances in experimental social psychology* (Vol. 2). New York: Academic Press.

22. Carrell, M. R., & Dittrich, J. E. (1978). Equity theory: The recent literature, methodological considerations, and new directions. *Academy of Management Review, 3,* 202–210; Mowday, R. T. (1987). Equity theory predictions of behavior in organizations. In R. M. Steers & L. W. Porter (Eds.), *Motivation and work behavior* (4th ed.). New York: McGraw-Hill.

23. Carrell & Dittrich, 1978; Mowday, 1987.

24. Porter, L. W., & Lawler, E. E., III. (1968). *Managerial attitudes and performance*. Homewood, IL: Dorsey Press.

25. Deci, E. L. (1975). *Intrinsic motivation*. New York: Plenum Press. Also see Pritchard, R. D., Campbell, K. M., & Campbell, D. J. (1977). Effects of extrinsic financial rewards on intrinsic motivation. *Journal of Applied Psychology, 62,* 9–15.

26. Deci, Chapter 5. For another explanation see Mawhinney, T. C. (1979). Intrinsic x extrinsic work motivation: Perspectives from behaviorism. *Organizational Behavior and Human Performance, 24,* 411–440.

27. Guzzo, R. A. (1979). Types of rewards, cognitions, and work motivation. *Academy of Management Review, 4,* 75–86.

Chapter 7

Motivation in Practice

QUAD/GRAPHICS

Quad/Graphics is one of the largest magazine printers in the country. The company prints more than 100 magazines and catalogues, including *Newsweek, Playboy* and *Harper's*. Its president, Harry Quadracci, founded the company in 1972 with 10 others and a 20,000-square-foot plant with one press in Pewaukee, Wisconsin. It now boasts more than 1,800 employees, more than a million square feet in floor space, and new operations in Wisconsin and on the East Coast. The company has maintained a compound sales growth rate of 30-40 percent a year, though the industry average is less than 10 percent. Quad/Graphics makes its own ink and has a self-supporting trucking fleet.

Quad/Graphics' employees own 37 percent of the company through the Employee Stock Ownership Plan. But this is only the beginning of Quad/Graphics' efforts to make employees feel and act like owners. New workers have a mentor to school them in company culture. Performance is the key to success, they are told, and success is defined in terms of both job performance and personal satisfaction.

Each spring, Quadracci puts his managerial philosophy, his employees, and his company to the test. During the "Spring Fling," all managers take one day off for a special management retreat, leaving the company in the hands of the rank and file. Anything could go wrong, from a misplaced advertisement to a miscalculated ink hue on millions of magazine covers. The risk is worth it. "Responsibility should be shared," Quadracci says. "Our people shouldn't need me or anyone else to tell them what to do." This is "Theory Q"—management by walking away. Theory Q trains employees to be owners of the company.

Theory Q also trains managers to manage. Quadracci believes that the managerial function at any level is to coordinate, not control. Since Quadracci feels that "managers should be virtually indistinguishable from those they manage," Quad/Graphics has only three reporting levels.

The workweek at Quad/Graphics is short: just 36 hours in three days. Two shifts keep the presses going 24 hours a day. Institution of the three-day workweek increased productivity 20 percent and saved tremendous amounts in overtime pay.

These and other innovative management practices have earned Quad/Graphics numerous awards, including a spot in *The 100 Best Companies to Work for in America*. For Quad/Graphics' employee-partners, working at the company is its own reward, both financially and personally.

Source: Rosen, C., Klein, K. J., & Young, K. M. (1986, January). When employees share the profits. *Psychology Today,* 30–36, p. 34.

Notice the motivational strategies employed at Quad/Graphics—an economic incentive through stock ownership, job design that provides considerable independence, and a very unusual work schedule. In this chapter we will discuss four motivational techniques—money, job enrichment, goal setting, and modified working times. In each case, we will consider the practical problems involved in implementation. Also, we will be concerned with the impact of the motivational techniques on the **quality of working life** of organizational members; that is, to what extent do these techniques make the work experience more rewarding and fulfilling while avoiding stress and other negative personal consequences?

MONEY AS A MOTIVATOR

The money that workers receive in exchange for organizational membership is in reality a package made up of pay and various fringe benefits that have dollar values, such as insurance plans, sick leave, and vacation time. In this section, we shall be concerned with the motivational characteristics of pay for both production workers and white-collar personnel.

First, however, let us briefly consider what various motivation theories would suggest about the motivational properties of pay. According to Maslow and Alderfer, pay should prove especially motivational to those individuals who are characterized by strong lower-level needs. For these persons, pay can be exchanged for food, shelter, and other necessities of life. However, suppose you receive a healthy pay raise. Doubtless, this raise will enable you to purchase food and shelter, but it may also demonstrate that your boss cares about you, give you prestige among friends and family, and signal your competence as a worker. Thus, using need hierarchy terminology, pay may also function to satisfy social, esteem, and self-actualization needs. If pay has this capacity to fulfill a variety of needs, then it should have especially good potential to serve as a motivator. How can this potential be realized? Expectancy theory provides the clearest answer to this question. According to expectancy theory, if pay can satisfy a variety of needs it should be highly valent, and it should prove to be a good motivator to the extent that *good performance is instrumental to obtaining it*. The Porter-Lawler model and learning theory also support this assertion.

Let's now examine some methods of linking a person's pay to his or her performance.

Linking Pay to Performance on Production Jobs

The prototype of all schemes to link pay to performance on production jobs is piecerate. In its pure form, **piecerate** is set up so that individual workers are paid a certain sum of money for each unit of production completed. For example, sewing machine operators might be paid one dollar for each dress stitched together, or punch press operators might be paid a few cents for each piece of metal fabricated.

Even more common than pure piecerate is a system whereby workers are paid a basic hourly wage and paid a piecerate differential on top of this hourly wage. For example, a forge operator might be paid four dollars an hour plus ten cents for each unit produced. In some cases, of course, it is very difficult to measure the productivity of an individual worker because of the nature of the production process. Under these circumstances, group incentives are sometimes employed. For example, workers in a steel mill might be paid an hourly wage and a monthly bonus for each ton of steel produced over some minimum quota. These various schemes to link pay to performance on production jobs are called **wage incentive plans.**

In theory, compared with straight hourly pay, wage incentives should lead to greater motivation and consequent increases in productivity. From our brief discussion of piecerate in Chapter 3, you will recall that wage incentive systems approximate a fixed ratio schedule of reinforcement, while hourly pay approximates a fixed interval schedule. Learning theory indicates that the former should enhance productivity because workers can control the rate and the cumulative amount of reinforcement. Similarly, expectancy theory suggests that wage incentive plans should increase the instrumentality of good performance for the attainment of pay.

The predictions of learning theory and expectancy theory hold up in practice. The introduction of wage incentives is usually accompanied by substantial increases in productivity.[1] One review reports a median productivity improvement of 30 percent following the installation of piecerate pay, an increase not matched by goal setting or job enrichment.[2] Also, a study of four hundred manufacturing companies found that those with wage incentive plans achieved 43 to 64 percent greater productivity than those without such plans.[3] Given this evidence, you might expect that organizations would be establishing wage incentive plans right and left to stimulate the motivation of their employees. In fact, however, only about 26 percent of the American manufacturing work force is operating under some form of wage incentive.[4] What problems account for this relatively low utilization of a motivational system with proven results?

PROBLEMS WITH WAGE INCENTIVES.   In many cases, wage incentive systems are difficult to install because of technical considerations or psychological roadblocks on the part of both workers and management. It is sometimes argued that wage incentives can increase productivity at the expense of quality. While this may in some cases be true, it does not require particular ingenuity to devise a system to monitor and maintain quality. A more serious technical threat to the establishment of wage incentives exists when workers have differential opportunities to produce at a high level. If the supply of raw materials or the quality of production equipment varies from workplace to workplace, some workers will be at an unfair disadvantage under an incentive system (in expectancy theory terminology, workers will differ in the expectancy that they can produce at a high level). In addition, wage incentives that reward individual productivity may decrease cooperation among workers. For example, in order to maintain a high wage rate, machinists may hoard raw materials or refuse to engage in peripheral tasks such as keeping the shop clean or unloading supplies.

In some cases, the manner in which jobs are designed may make it very difficult to install wage incentives. On an assembly line, it is almost impossible to identify and reward individual contributions to productivity. As pointed out above, wage incentive systems can be designed to reward team productivity in such a circumstance. However, as the size of the team *increases,* the relationship between any individual's productivity and his or her pay *decreases.* For example, the impact of your productivity in a team of two is much greater than the impact of this productivity in a team of ten—as team size increases, the linkage between your performance and your pay is erased, removing the intended incentive effect.

A chief psychological impediment to the use of wage incentives may be the tendency for workers to restrict productivity under such systems (see the cartoon). This restriction is illustrated graphically in Exhibit 7-1. Under normal circumstances, without wage incentives, we can often expect productivity to be distributed in a ''bell-shaped'' manner—a few workers are especially low producers, a few are especially high producers, and most produce in the middle range. When wage incentives are introduced, however, workers may come to an informal agreement

"YOU NEW ON THE JOB?"

Source: Norris, Len (1984). *The best of Norris.* Toronto, Ontario: McClelland and Stewart Limited.

EXHIBIT 7-1   **Hypothetical productivity distributions, with and without wage incentives, when incentives promote restriction.**

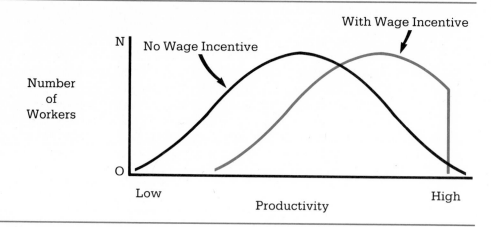

about what constitutes a fair day's work and artificially limit their output accordingly. In many cases, this **restriction of productivity** may decrease the expected benefits of the incentive system, as shown in the Exhibit.

Why does restriction often occur under wage incentive systems? Sometimes, it may happen because workers feel that increased productivity due to the incentive will lead to reductions in the work force. More frequently, however, employees may fear that if they produce at an especially high level the rate of payment will be reduced to cut labor costs. In the early days of industrialization, when unions were nonexistent or weak, this was especially likely to happen. Workers would be studied under normal circumstances by engineers, and a payment rate for each unit of productivity would be set by management. When the incentive system was introduced, workers would employ various legitimate shortcuts they had learned on the job to produce at a higher rate than expected. In response to this, management would simply change the rate to require more output for a given amount of pay! Stories of such rate-cutting are often passed down from one generation of workers to another in support of restricting output under incentive systems. As you might expect, restriction seems less likely when a climate of trust and a history of good relations exist between labor and management.

GAIN SHARING.   Many of the dysfunctional aspects of wage incentive systems stem from their concentration on individual-level performance as the basis for payment. In effect, workers become more concerned with their individual productivity (and pay) than they are with the overall performance of their department or unit. As a result, a number of group-level incentive plans have been proposed. In general, these plans are based on the assumption that the practical benefits of increased cooperation can offset the theoretical benefits of paying for individual performance. Profit sharing and stock option plans are examples of group incentives. However, their motivational impact may be limited because factors that control profit or stock prices (such as the condition of the general economy) may not be under the control of employees.

Gain-sharing plans are group incentive plans that are based on measurable cost reductions that are under the control of the work force—factors such as the cost of labor or materials and supplies used.[5] When measured costs decrease, a monthly bonus is paid according to a predetermined formula that shares this "gain" between employees and the firm. Gain-sharing plans have usually been installed using committees that include the participation of the workforce. This builds commitment for the formulas that are used to convert gains into bonuses. Also, most plans include all members of the work unit, including production people, managers, and support staff.

The most common gain-sharing plan is the Scanlon Plan, developed by union leader Joe Scanlon in the 1930s.[6] It has been used with apparent success by many small family-owned manufacturing firms. However, in recent years, many large corporations (e.g., General Electric, Motorola, Dana) have installed Scanlon-like gain-sharing plans in some manufacturing plants.[7] In general, productivity improvements following the introduction of Scanlon-type plans support the motivational impact of this group wage incentive.

QUALITY OF WORKING LIFE. We have established that wage incentive plans may serve as effective motivators, but what is their impact on the quality of working life of the individuals who operate under them? First, it should be obvious that a wage incentive plan that has any of the difficulties discussed above may promote feelings of inequity and induce conflict among organizational members. Secondly, North American unions have generally been opposed to wage incentive plans based on individual perfo mance, although they sometimes support group-based plans. Unionists often argue that plans such as piecerate may promote unhealthy competition among workers, lead to fatigue and accidents, and disadvantage older or less fit workers. Of course, individual incentives may undermine the notions of worker equality and the importance of seniority which are the very foundation of unionism. In summary, wage incentive systems must operate smoothly and be perceived as equitable by all relevant parties if they are not to have negative impact. Thus, such systems require very careful design and monitoring.

Linking Pay to Performance on White-Collar Jobs

Compared with production jobs, white-collar jobs (including clerical, professional, and managerial) frequently offer fewer objective performance criteria with which pay can be associated. To be sure, company presidents are often paid annual bonuses that are tied to the profitability of the firm, and salespeople are frequently paid commissions on sales. However, trustworthy objective indicators of individual performance for the majority of white-collar jobs are often difficult to find. For this reason (as pointed out in our discussion of perception) performance in many such jobs must be evaluated by the subjective judgment of the performer's superior.

Attempts to link pay to performance on white-collar jobs are often called **merit pay plans.** Just as straight piecerate is the prototype for most wage incentive plans, there is also a prototype for most merit pay plans: Periodically (usually yearly), managers are required to evaluate the performance of subordinates on some form of rating scales (such as those shown in Chapter 4) or by means of a written description of performance. Using these evaluations, the managers then recommend that some amount of merit pay be awarded to individuals over and above their basic salaries. This pay is usually incorporated into the subsequent year's salary checks.[8]

The theoretical justification for the use of merit pay to increase motivation is the same as that noted for the use of wage incentives on blue-collar production jobs—both learning theory and expectancy theory suggest that making rewards contingent upon performance should enhance motivation to perform at a high level. In addition, since the indicators of good performance may be unclear on some white-collar jobs (especially managerial jobs), merit pay can provide an especially tangible signal that an employee's performance is considered to be "on track" by the organization.

Again, theory seems to be an accurate predictor of reality. There is good evidence that individuals who see a strong link between rewards and performance tend to be better performers.[9] In addition, white-collar workers (especially managers) are particularly supportive of the notion that performance should be an important determinant of pay.[10] Thus, it should not be surprising that merit pay plans are employed with a much greater frequency than wage incentive plans. For example, a survey of 493 major companies revealed that 87 percent used some form of merit pay plan for salaried workers.[11]

At this point, we encounter a curiosity. Despite the facts that merit pay can stimulate effective performance, that substantial support exists for the idea of merit pay, and that most organizations claim to provide merit pay, it would appear that many such systems now in use are *ineffective.* Many individuals who supposedly work under such plans do not perceive a link between their job performance and their pay. Evidently, this is not simply the result of some perceptual aberration, because there is also evidence to suggest that pay is in fact *not* related to performance under some merit plans.[12] Adding more evidence of ineffectiveness are studies that track pay increases over time. For example, one study of managers showed that pay increases received in a given year were often uncorrelated with pay increases received in adjacent years.[13] From what we know about the consistency of human performance, such a result seems unlikely if organizations are truly tying pay to performance. It would seem that, in most organizations, seniority and job level account for more variation in pay than does performance.

PROBLEMS WITH MERIT PAY PLANS. One reason that many merit pay plans fail to achieve their intended effect is that managers may be unable or unwilling to discriminate between good performers and poor performers. In Chapter 4 it was pointed out that subjective evaluations of performance may be difficult to make and are often distorted by a number of perceptual errors. In the absence of performance rating systems designed to control these problems, managers may feel that the only fair response is to rate most employees as equal performers. Good rating systems are, evidently, rarely employed. In a survey of management performance evaluation systems, only 10 percent of the responding personnel executives deemed their systems as effective.[14] Even when managers feel capable of clearly discriminating between good and poor performers, they may be reluctant to do so. If the performance evaluation system does not assist the manager in giving feedback about his or her decisions to subordinates, the equalization strategy may be employed to prevent conflicts with them or among them. If there are true performance differences among subordinates, equalization overrewards poorer performers and underrewards better performers.

A second threat to the effectiveness of merit pay plans exists when merit increases are simply too small to be effective motivators. In this case, even if rewards are carefully tied to performance and managers do a good job of discriminating between more and less effective performers, the intended motivational effects of pay increases may not be realized. Ironically, some firms all but abandon merit when inflation soars or when they encounter economic difficulties. Just when high motivation is needed, the motivational impact of merit pay is removed. When merit pay makes up a substantial portion of the compensation package, however, extreme care has to be taken to ensure that the merit pay is tied to performance criteria that truly benefit the organization. Otherwise, employees may be motivated to earn their yearly bonus at the expense of long-term organizational goals (see In–Focus 7-1).

A final threat to the effectiveness of merit pay plans may be the extreme secrecy that surrounds salaries in most organizations. It has long been a principle of personnel management that salaries are confidential information, and employees who receive merit increases are frequently implored not to discuss these increases with their co-workers. Notice the implication of such secrecy for merit pay plans: Even if merit pay is fairly administered, contingent on performance, and generous, employees may remain ignorant of these facts because they have no way of comparing their own merit treatment with the treatment of others. In consequence, the motivational impact of a well-designed merit plan may be severely damaged. Rather incredibly, the great majority of organizations fail to inform employees about the average raise received by those doing similar work and fail to differentiate between merit pay and cost-of-living increases![15]

Given this extreme secrecy, you might expect that workers would profess profound ignorance about the salaries of other organizational members. In fact, this does not appear to be the case—in the absence of better information, employees are inclined to "invent" salaries for other members. Unfortunately, this invention seems to reduce both satisfaction and motivation. Specifically, several studies have shown that managers have a tendency to overestimate the pay of their subordinates and their peers and underestimate the pay of their superiors.[16] In general, these tendencies will reduce satisfaction with pay, damage perceptions of the linkage between performance and rewards, and reduce the valence of promotion to a higher level of management.

An interesting experiment examined the effects of pay disclosure on the performance and satisfaction of pharmaceutical salespeople who operated under a merit pay system:

At the time of a regularly scheduled district sales meeting, each of the 14 managers in the experimental group presented to his subordinates the new open salary administration program. The salesmen were given the individual low, overall average, and individual high merit raise amounts for the previous year. The raises ranged from no raise to $75 a month, with a company average of $43. Raises were classified according to district, region, and company increases in pay. Likewise, salary levels (low, average, and high) were given for salesmen on the basis of their years with the company (1 to 5; 5 to 10; 10 to 20; and more than 20 years). Specific individual names and base salaries were not disclosed to the salesmen. However, this information could be obtained from the supervisor. Each salesman's performance evaluation was also made available by the district manager for review by his other salesmen.[17]

After the pay disclosure was implemented, salespeople in the experimental group revealed significant increases in performance and satisfaction with pay. However, since performance consisted of supervisory ratings, it is possible that supervisors felt pressured to give better ratings under the open pay system, where their actions were open to scrutiny. This, of course, raises an important point. If performance evaluation systems are inadequate and poorly justified, a more open pay policy will simply expose the inadequacy of the merit system and lead managers to evaluate performance in a manner designed to reduce conflict. Unfortunately, this may be why most organizations maintain relative secrecy concerning pay.

QUALITY OF WORKING LIFE.   There is ample evidence to suggest that *well-conceived and implemented* merit pay plans could contribute to the quality of working life of white-collar personnel. As pointed out earlier, there is general support at this level for the notion that pay should be tied to performance. Also, there is evidence that those individuals who see a reliable connection between pay and performance tend to be more satisfied with their pay.[18] In a properly designed merit pay system, the Porter-Lawler model suggests that the following connections will be strong and reliable: Performance→reward→satisfaction. As a result of this connection, good performers should experience a sense of recognition and satisfaction which will encourage them to pursue their careers within the organization rather than seeking work elsewhere. Poor performers should experience dissatisfaction which may prompt them to seek work in an organization where they can more properly apply their skills. However, an effective merit pay system may provide some poor performers with the feedback necessary to correct their behavior and increase their performance. Overall, these conditions seem conducive to a high-quality work experience.

JOB DESIGN AS A MOTIVATOR

If the use of money as a motivator is primarily an attempt to capitalize on extrinsic motivation, current approaches to using job design as a motivator represent an attempt to capitalize on intrinsic motivation. Certainly, some tasks *seem* more intrinsically motivating than others. For example, an assembly line worker in an automobile plant who is poorly motivated on the job might go home and spend many highly motivated hours preparing his own racing car. Intrinsic motivation is apparent here. In essence, the current goal of job design is to discover the characteristics that make some tasks more motivating than others and to capture these characteristics in the design of jobs.

Traditional Views of Job Design

From the advent of the Industrial Revolution until the 1960s, the prevailing philosophy regarding the design of most nonmanagerial jobs was job simplification. The historical roots of job simplification are found in social, economic, and technological forces that existed even before the Industrial Revolution. This pre-industrial period was characterized by increasing urbanization and the growth of a free market economy which prompted a demand for manufactured goods. Thus, a division of labor within society occurred, and specialized industrial concerns, using newly developed machinery, emerged to meet this demand. With complex machinery and an uneducated, untrained work force, these organizations recognized that *specialization* was the key to efficient productivity. If the production of an object could be broken down into very basic, simple steps, even an uneducated and minimally trained worker could contribute his or her share by mastering one of these steps.

The zenith of job simplification occurred in the early 1900s when industrial engineer Frederick Winslow Taylor presented the industrial community with his principles of **Scientific Management.**[19] Rather than traditional ''rules of thumb'' for the design of jobs, Taylor advocated the use of careful study to determine the optimum degree of specialization and standardization. Also, he supported the development of written instructions to clearly define work procedures, and he encouraged supervisors to standardize workers' movements and rest pauses for maximum efficiency. Taylor even extended Scientific Management to the boss's job, advocating ''functional foremanship,'' whereby foremen would specialize in particular functions. For example, one foreman might become a specialist in training workers, while another might fulfill the role of a disciplinarian.

Intuitively, jobs designed according to the principles of Scientific Management do not seem intrinsically motivating. However, during the period sketched above, most managers' philosophies about why people work were probably confined to the assumption that ''people work because they have to work.'' Thus, it is not surprising that the motivational strategies used during this period consisted of close supervision and the use of piecerate pay. It would be a historical disservice to conclude that job simplification was unwelcomed by workers who were mostly nonunionized, uneducated, and fighting to fulfill their basic needs. Such simplification helped them to achieve a reasonable standard of living. However, in recent years, with a better-educated work force whose basic needs are fairly well met, behavioral scientists have begun to question the impact of job simplification on both performance and the quality of working life.

Job Scope and Motivation

Job scope can be defined as the breadth and depth of a job.[20] **Breadth** refers to the number of different activities performed on the job, while **depth** refers to the degree of discretion or control the worker has over how these tasks are performed. ''Broad'' jobs require workers to *do* a number of different tasks, while ''deep'' jobs emphasize freedom in *planning* how to do the work.

As shown in Exhibit 7-2, jobs which have great breadth *and* depth can be called high-scope jobs. The professor's job is a good example of a high-scope job. It is broad because it involves the performance of a number of different tasks, such as teaching, grading, doing research, writing, and participating in committees. It is also deep because there is considerable discretion in how these tasks are performed. In general, professors have a fair amount of freedom to choose a particular teaching style, grading format, and research area. Similarly, management jobs are high-scope jobs. Managers perform a wide variety of activities (supervision, training, performance evaluation, report writing, etc.), and have some discretion over how these activities are accomplished.

The classic example of a low-scope job is the traditional assembly line job. This job is both "shallow" and "narrow" in the sense that a single task (such as bolting on car wheels) is performed repetitively and ritually, with no discretion as to method. Traditional views of job design were attempts to construct low-scope jobs in which workers specialized in a single task.

Occasionally, jobs are encountered which involve high breadth but little depth, or vice versa. For motivational purposes, these jobs can also be considered relatively low in scope. For example, a utility worker on an assembly line fills in for absent workers on various parts of the line. While this job involves the performance

EXHIBIT 7-2   **Job scope as a function of job depth and job breadth.**

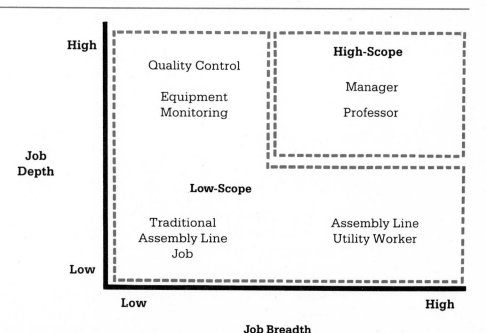

of a number of tasks, it involves little discretion as to when or how the tasks are performed. On the other hand, some jobs involve a fair amount of discretion over a single, narrowly defined task. For example, quality control inspectors perform a single, repetitive task, but they may be required to exercise a fair degree of judgment in performing this task. Similarly, workers who monitor the performance of equipment (such as in a nuclear power plant) may perform a single task but again be required to exercise considerable discretion when a problem arises.

The motivational theories discussed in the previous chapter suggest that high-scope jobs (*both* broad and deep) should provide more intrinsic motivation than low-scope jobs. Maslow's need hierarchy and the ERG theory both seem to indicate that higher-order needs can be fulfilled by the opportunity to perform high-scope jobs. Expectancy theory suggests that high scope jobs can provide intrinsic motivation *if* the outcomes derived from such jobs are positively valent. This is an important qualification. As we shall see shortly, not everyone is enthusiastic about high-scope jobs.

The Job Characteristics Model

The concept of job scope provides an easy-to-understand introduction to why some jobs seem more intrinsically motivating than others. However, the concepts of breadth and depth are more descriptive than scientific. A more rigorous delineation of the motivational properties of jobs is found in the Job Characteristics Model developed by J. Richard Hackman and Greg Oldham (Exhibit 7-3).[21] As you can observe, the Job Characteristics Model proposes that there are several "core" job characteristics that have a certain psychological impact upon workers. In turn, the psychological states induced by the nature of the job lead to certain outcomes that are relevant to the worker and the organization. Finally, several other factors (moderators) influence the extent to which these relationships hold true.

Let's look more closely at the major parts of this model.

CORE JOB CHARACTERISTICS.   The Job Characteristics Model shows that there are five core job characteristics that have particularly strong potential to affect worker motivation—skill variety, task identity, task significance, autonomy, and job feedback. These characteristics are defined in Exhibit 7-4. In general, higher levels of these characteristics should lead to the favorable outcomes shown in Exhibit 7-3. Notice that **skill variety** corresponds fairly closely to the notion of job breadth discussed earlier, while **autonomy** corresponds to job depth. However, Hackman and Oldham recognized that one could have a high degree of control over a variety of skills that were perceived as meaningless or fragmented. Thus, the concepts of **task significance** and **task identity** are introduced. In addition, they recognized that **feedback** regarding one's performance is also essential for high intrinsic motivation.

Hackman and Oldham have developed a questionnaire called the Job Diagnostic Survey (JDS) to measure the core characteristics of jobs. The JDS requires

EXHIBIT 7-3   **The Job Characteristics Model.**

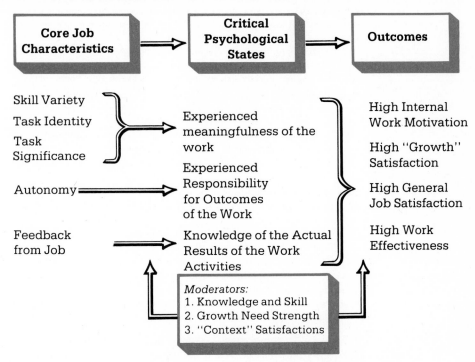

Source: Hackman, J. R., & Oldham, G. R. (1980). *Work redesign*. Reading, MA: Addison-Wesley. Copyright © 1980 by Addison-Wesley Publishing Company. Figure 4.6. Reprinted with permission.

job incumbents to report the amount of the various core characteristics contained in their jobs. From these reports, profiles can be constructed to compare the motivational properties of various jobs. For example, Exhibit 7-5 shows JDS profiles for lower level managers in a certain company (collected by your author) and those for keypunchers in another firm (reported by Hackman and Oldham). While the managers perform a full range of managerial duties, the keypunchers perform a highly regulated job—anonymous work from various departments is assigned to them by a supervisor and their output is verified for accuracy by others. Not surprisingly, the JDS profiles reveal that the managerial jobs are consistently higher on the core characteristics than the keypunching jobs.

According to Hackman and Oldham, an overall measure of the **motivating potential** of a job can be calculated by the following formula:

$$\text{Motivating potential score} = \left[\frac{\text{Skill variety} + \text{Task identity} + \text{Task significance}}{3} \right] \times \text{Autonomy} \times \text{Job feedback}$$

EXHIBIT 7-4   **Core job characteristics and examples.**

---

1. **Skill variety:** The degree to which a job requires a variety of different activities in carrying out the work, involving the use of a number of different skills and talents of the person.

   High variety: The owner-operator of a garage who does electrical repair, rebuilds engines, does body work, and interacts with customers.

   Low variety: A body shop worker who sprays paint eight hours a day.

2. **Task identity:** The degree to which a job requires completion of a "whole" and identifiable piece of work, that is, doing a job from beginning to end with a visible outcome.

   High identity: A cabinet maker who designs a piece of furniture, selects the wood, builds the object, and finishes it to perfection.

   Low identity: A worker in a furniture factory who operates a lathe solely to make table legs.

3. **Task significance:** The degree to which the job has a substantial impact on the lives of other people, whether those people are in the immediate organization or in the world at large.

   High significance: Nursing the sick in a hospital intensive care unit.

   Low significance: Sweeping hospital floors.

4. **Autonomy:** The degree to which the job provides substantial freedom, independence, and discretion to the individual in scheduling the work and in determining the procedures to be used in carrying it out.

   High autonomy: A telephone installer who schedules his or her own work for the day, makes visits without supervision, and decides on the most effective techniques for a particular installation.

   Low autonomy: A telephone operator who must handle calls as they come according to a routine, highly specified procedure.

5. **Job feedback:** The degree to which carrying out the work activities required by the job provides the individual with direct and clear information about the effectiveness of his or her performance.

   High feedback: An electronics factory worker who assembles a radio and then tests it to determine if it operates properly.

   Low feedback: An electronics factory worker who assembles a radio and then routes it to a quality control inspector who tests it for proper operation and makes needed adjustments.

Source: Definitions from Hackman, J. R., & Oldham, G. R. (1980). The properties of motivating jobs. *Work redesign.* Reading, MA: Addison-Wesley. Copyright © 1980 by Addison-Wesley Publishing Company, Reading, Massachusetts. Reprinted by permission.

Since the JDS measures the job characteristics on 7-point scales, a motivating potential score could theoretically range from 1 to 343. For example, the motivating potential score for the keypunchers' jobs shown in Exhibit 7-5 is 20, while that for the managers' jobs is 159. The average motivating potential score for 6930 employees on 876 jobs has been calculated at 128.[22]

CRITICAL PSYCHOLOGICAL STATES.   Why should jobs which are higher on the core characteristics be intrinsically motivating? What is their psychological

EXHIBIT 7-5   **Levels of core job characteristics for managers and keypunchers.**

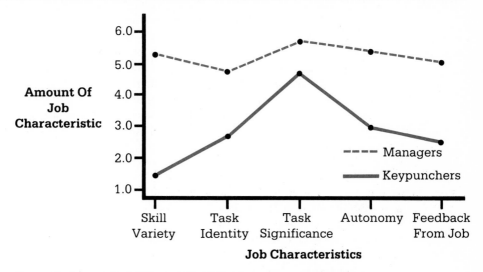

Source: Hackman, J. R., & Oldham, G. R. (1980). *Work redesign.* Reading, MA: Addison-Wesley. Copyright © 1980 by Addison-Wesley Publishing Company. Figure 6.2. Reprinted with permission. (Managers' data collected by the author.)

impact? Hackman and Oldham argue that work will be intrinsically motivating when it is perceived as *meaningful,* when the worker feels *responsible* for the outcomes of the work, and when the worker has *knowledge* about his or her work progress. As shown in Exhibit 7-3, the Job Characteristics Model proposes that the core job characteristics affect meaningfulness, responsibility, and knowledge of results in a systematic manner. When an individual uses a variety of skills to do a "whole" job that is perceived as significant to others, the work should be perceived as meaningful. When a person has autonomy to organize and perform the job as he or she sees fit, the person should feel personally responsible for the outcome of the work. Finally, when the job provides feedback about performance, the worker will have knowledge of the results of this opportunity to exercise responsibility.

OUTCOMES.   The presence of the critical psychological states should lead to a number of outcomes that are relevant to both the individual and the organization. Chief among these is high intrinsic motivation. When the worker is truly in control of a challenging job that provides good feedback about performance, the key prerequisites for intrinsic motivation are present. The relationship between work and the worker is emphasized, and the worker is able to draw motivation from the job itself. This should result in high-quality productivity. By the same token, such a state of affairs should lead workers to report satisfaction with higher order needs (growth needs) and general satisfaction with the job itself. This may lead to reduced absenteeism and turnover.

MODERATORS.   Hackman and Oldham recognize that jobs that are high in motivating potential may not *always* lead to favorable outcomes. Thus, as shown in Exhibit 7-3, they propose certain moderator or contingency variables (Chapter 1) that intervene between job characteristics and outcomes. One of these is the job-relevant knowledge and skill of the worker. Put simply, workers with weak knowledge and skills should not respond favorably to jobs that are high in motivating potential, since such jobs will prove too demanding. Another proposed moderator is **growth need strength,** which refers to the extent to which workers desire to achieve higher order need satisfaction by performing their jobs. It is argued that those with high growth needs should be most responsive to challenging work. Finally, Hackman and Oldham argue that workers who are dissatisfied with the **context factors** surrounding the job (such as pay, supervision, and company policy) will be less responsive to challenging work than those who are reasonably satisfied with context factors.

RESEARCH SUPPORT.   Tests of the Job Characteristics Model have usually required workers to describe their jobs by means of the Job Diagnostic Survey and then measured their reactions to these jobs via a variety of techniques. Although there is some discrepancy regarding the relative importance of the various core characteristics, these tests have generally been very supportive of the basic prediction of the model—workers tend to respond more favorably to jobs that are higher in motivating potential. Also as predicted by the model, workers high in growth need strength respond most favorably.[23] However, there is contradictory evidence regarding the role of context satisfaction in influencing reactions to job characteristics.[24]

Job Enrichment

Job enrichment is the attempt to design jobs to enhance intrinsic motivation and the quality of working life. In general, enrichment involves increasing the motivating potential of jobs via the arrangement of their core characteristics. There are no hard and fast rules for the enrichment of jobs. Specific enrichment procedures depend upon a careful diagnosis of the work to be accomplished, the available technology, and the organizational context in which enrichment is to take place. However, many job enrichment schemes involve one or more of the following techniques:[25]

■   *Combining tasks.* This involves assigning tasks that might be performed by different workers to a single individual. For example, in a furniture factory, a lathe operator, an assembler, a sander, and a stainer might become four "chair makers"; each worker would then do all four tasks. Such a strategy should increase the variety of skills employed and may contribute to task identity as each worker approaches doing a unified job from start to finish.

■   *Establishing external client relationships.* This involves putting workers in touch with those outside the organization who depend upon their products or services. For example, automobile mechanics who work in large dealer-ships could be permitted to discuss service problems with customers before and after repairs are effected, rather than relying on the service manager to do this. Such a strategy may involve the use of new (interpersonal) skills, increase the identity and significance of the job, and increase feedback about one's performance.

■   *Establishing internal client relationships.* This involves putting workers in touch with people who depend upon their products or services within the organization. For example, billers and expediters in a manufacturing firm might be assigned permanently to certain salespersons, rather than working on any salesperson's order as it comes in. The advantages are similar to those mentioned for establishing external client relationships.

■   *Reducing supervision or reliance on others.* The goal here is to increase autonomy and control over one's own work. For example, clerical employees might be permitted to check their own work for errors instead of having someone else do it. Similarly, workers might be allowed to order needed supplies or contract for outside services up to some dollar amount without obtaining permission.

■   *Forming work teams.* This can be used as an alternative to a sequence of "small" jobs performed by individual workers when a product or service is too large or complex for one person to complete alone. For example, social workers with particular skills might operate as a true team to assist a partic-ular client, rather than passing the client from person to person. Similarly, stable teams can be formed to construct an entire product, such as a car or boat, in lieu of an assembly-line approach. Such approaches should lead to the formal and informal development of a variety of skills and increase the identity of the job.

■   *Making feedback more direct.* This technique is usually used in conjunction with other job design aspects that permit workers to be identified with their "own" product or service. For example, an electronics firm might have as-semblers "sign" their output on a tag which includes an address and toll-free phone number. If problems are encountered, customers contact the assembler directly. In Sweden, workers who build trucks by team assembly are responsible for service and warranty work on "their" trucks which are sold locally.

For an example of a job with reduced supervision and direct feedback see In–Focus 7-2. In the next sections we will explore some actual applications of job enrichment and then look at some problems associated with the technique.

Examples of Job Enrichment

As pointed out earlier, the exact techniques used to enrich jobs vary with the nature of the organization and its particular products or services. Thus, in this section we will examine enrichment exercises that were carried out in two very different organizational environments—one involving the mass production of automobiles in Sweden and the other office jobs in the United States.

VOLVO. Volvo is a large Swedish producer of cars, buses, trucks, and industrial equipment. In the late 1960s Volvo was beset by serious labor problems—wildcat strikes occurred, turnover was running about 40 percent a year, 20 percent of the work force was absent on a given day, and recruiting was very difficult. With the encouragement of a new president, Pehr Gyllenhammar, Volvo decided to build a new car assembly plant at Kalmar designed around enriched jobs. There is no assembly line at Kalmar. Rather, partially assembled cars move around the plant on self-propelled electric carriers, guided by a central computer and an electric track.

Cars at Kalmar are assembled by twenty-five permanent groups of about fifteen workers. Each group is responsible for installing all of a particular assembly, such as the electrical system, the interior, or wheel and brake units. The group is free to decide how to divide up and schedule its work, as long as it completes so many assemblies each day. When a car arrives at the group's permanent "workshop," the computer can be overridden and the carrier stopped. If any group detects a problem, such as scratched paint, it can automatically send the car back to the appropriate work station for corrections. The group also inspects its own work. After about every three workshops, more sophisticated quality control procedures are performed. A computer immediately informs the group when a problem has been detected, and its memory system tells the group how the problem was solved in the past. In addition, the computer informs the group when error-free performance is occurring. Each assembly group is responsible for initiating the contacts necessary to secure its own supplies and parts from a storage core.

Notice the techniques that have been implemented to enrich the assembly jobs at Kalmar: Permanent *work teams* perform a *combined series of tasks* that have a logical identity. Since the teams plan, organize, and inspect their own work, *supervision and reliance on others are reduced*. Obtaining their own parts and supplies *enhances internal client relationships*. Finally, self-inspection and the more sophisticated computer inspection *make feedback more direct*.

The Kalmar plant represents a remarkable achievement in enriching jobs that might seem to lack the potential for such treatment. Attitude surveys indicate that workers have responded very favorably to Kalmar. Absence and turnover are reported to be lower than at conventional plants, while productivity is equivalent.[26]

AT&T. American Telephone and Telegraph and its former associated companies in the Bell System have shown that job enrichment can also work on this side of the Atlantic. Beginning in 1964, these organizations were involved in an ongoing series of enrichment exercises.

The first job to be enriched was that of stockholder correspondent in the AT&T Treasury Department. This job involves dealing with queries and complaints from AT&T stockholders by mail or telephone. Since many of these issues can be quite complex, the work force consisted mostly of college graduates. Ironically, although interactions with stockholders are important and sensitive, the correspondent's job had been designed as a glorified clerical job—after correspondents had researched the problem in question, they composed a form letter response which was verified and signed by their supervisors. Job dissatisfaction was high among the correspondents and this dissatisfaction was reflected in a high rate of costly turnover. In addition, quality measures indicated an unacceptable level of errors and delays in responses. Gradually, a number of changes were introduced to the correspondent's job with the goal of enhancing its motivating potential. As you can see, these changes involved combining tasks, increasing teamwork, reducing supervision, and indirectly enhancing the external client relationship:

- *Subject-matter experts were appointed within each unit for other members of the unit to consult with before seeking supervisory help.*

- *Correspondents were told to sign their own names to letters from the very first day on the job after training.*

- *The work of the more experienced correspondents was looked over less frequently by supervisors, and this was done at each correspondent's desk.*

- *Production was discussed, but only in general terms: "A full day's work is expected," for example.*

- *Outgoing work went directly to the mail room without crossing the supervisor's desk.*

- *All correspondents were told they would be held fully accountable for quality of work.*

- *Correspondents were encouraged to answer letters in a more personalized way, avoiding the previous form letter approach.*[27]

In general, these changes would seem to affect each of the five core job characteristics, and the results were highly favorable. Compared with control groups, job satisfaction increased, while absence and turnover decreased.[28] In addition, the quality of performance rose and more promotions were made from among the correspondents whose jobs had been enriched, presumably because they were now better able to demonstrate their skills and responsibility to management.

Numerous other enrichment attempts were made by AT&T and the former Bell System on jobs as diverse as service representatives, toll and information operators, telephone installers, keypunchers, and equipment engineers. While some of these attempts were more successful than others, AT&T, like Volvo, has shown strong commitment to the goal of making work more challenging and rewarding.

Problems With Job Enrichment

Despite the theoretical attractiveness of job enrichment as a motivational strategy, and despite the fact that many organizations have experimented with such schemes, practical attempts at enrichment may encounter a number of difficult problems.

First, put simply, some workers do not *desire* enriched jobs. Almost by definition, enrichment places greater demands upon workers, and some may not relish this extra responsibility. In such cases, enrichment should lead to nothing but trouble. Finding out who is ready for enrichment could be accomplished by measuring the growth need strength of the work force. Also, some research suggests that organizations might do well to simply ask workers directly whether they would prefer to participate in job enrichment.[29] The results of this approach will be most trustworthy when workers feel absolutely free to decline the invitation and when they have a clear picture of what an enriched job will be like.

Even when workers have no basic objections to enrichment in theory, they may lack the skills and competence necessary to perform enriched jobs effectively. Thus, for some poorly educated work forces, enrichment may entail substantial training costs. In addition, it may be very difficult to train workers in certain skills required by enriched jobs, such as social skills. For example, part of the job enrichment scheme at a Philips television manufacturing plant in Holland required TV assemblers to initiate contacts with high-status staff members in other departments when problems were encountered. This is an example of the establishment of an internal client relationship, and many workers found this job requirement threatening.[30]

Occasionally, workers who experience job enrichment may ask that greater extrinsic rewards, such as pay, accompany their redesigned jobs. Most frequently, this desire is probably prompted by the fact that such jobs require the development of new skills and entail greater responsibility. For example, one enrichment exercise for clerical jobs in a U.S. government agency encountered this reaction.[31] Sometimes, such requests may be motivated by the wish to share in the financial benefits of a successful enrichment exercise. In one documented case, workers with radically enriched jobs in a General Foods dog food plant in Topeka sought a financial bonus that they based on the system's success.[32]

Generally, it is safe to say that North American unions have been less than enthusiastic about job enrichment. As one union leader has said:

> If you want to enrich the job, enrich the paycheck. . . . If you want to enrich the job, do something about the nerve-shattering noise, the heat, the fumes. . . . Worker dissatisfaction diminishes with age. And that's because older workers have accrued more of the kinds of job enrichment that unions have fought for—better wages, shorter hours, vested pensions, a right to have a say in their working conditions, the right to be promoted on the basis of seniority, and all the rest. That's the kind of job enrichment that unions believe in.[33]

While this statement may represent an extreme position, it is certain that interesting work has not been one of the traditional union bargaining issues. In fact, almost all attempts at job redesign must confront labor contracts that segment and specialize work (see In–Focus 7-3). This is ironic, since unionists have seldom been fans of Taylor's Scientific Management!

Another problem with job enrichment may occur when it is effected without a careful diagnosis of the needs of the organization and the particular jobs in question. Some enrichment attempts may be half-hearted tactical exercises that really don't increase the motivating potential of the job adequately. An especially likely error here is increasing job breadth (variety) while leaving the other crucial core characteristics unchanged. Thus, workers are simply given *more* boring, fragmented, routine tasks to do, such as bolting intake manifolds *and* carburetors onto engines. On the other side of the coin, in their zeal to use enrichment as a cure-all, organizations may attempt to enrich jobs which are already perceived as "too rich" by their incumbents:

> "When I read this stuff on job enrichment it makes me shake my head. My job is already too enriched for me or anyone else. Every day I'm being called on to make decisions I'm not prepared to make. I don't have enough time and I've got too many things to do. It's frustrating to be spread so thin."[34]

Even when enrichment schemes are carefully implemented to truly enhance the motivating potential of deserving jobs, they may fail because of their unanticipated impact on other jobs or other parts of the organizational system. A key problem here may involve the supervisors of the workers whose jobs have been enriched. By definition, enrichment involves increasing the autonomy of employees. Unfortunately, such a change may "disenrich" the boss's job, a consequence that is hardly calculated to facilitate the smooth implementation of the job redesign. Some organizations have responded to this problem by effectively doing away with direct supervision of workers performing enriched jobs. More likely, however, is the use of the supervisor as a trainer and developer of individuals on enriched jobs. Enrichment increases the need for this supervisory function in most cases.

In summary, although job enrichment has the potential to increase motivation and enhance the quality of working life, there are many obstacles to the effective implementation of enrichment. It is simply not a strategy that can be casually adopted and expected to take care of itself.

GOAL SETTING AS A MOTIVATOR

As pointed out in Chapter 1, one of the basic characteristics of all organizations is that they have goals. In Chapter 6, individual performance was defined as the extent to which a member contributes to the attainment of these goals. Thus, if acceptable performance is to be achieved by employees, some method of translating organizational goals into individual goals must be implemented.

Unfortunately, there is ample reason to believe that personal performance goals may be vague or nonexistent for many organizational members. Employees frequently report that their role in the organization is unclear or that they don't really know what their boss expects of them. Even in cases where performance goals would seem to be obvious because of the nature of the task (e.g., filling packing crates to the maximum to avoid excessive freight charges) employees may be ignorant of their current performance. This suggests that the implicit performance goals simply aren't making an impression.

The notion of **goal setting** as a motivator has been around for a long time. However, theoretical developments and some very practical research demonstrations have begun to suggest just when and how goal setting can be effective.[35]

What Kinds of Goals Are Motivational?

A large body of evidence suggests that goals are most motivational when they are *specific, challenging,* and *accepted* by organizational members. In addition, *feedback* about progress toward goal attainment should be provided.[36] Let's examine each of these characteristics in turn.

Specific goals are goals that specify an exact level of achievement to be accomplished in a particular time frame. For example, "I will enroll in five courses next semester and achieve a *B* or better in each course" is a specific goal. Similarly, "I will increase my net sales by 20 percent in the coming business quarter" is a specific goal. On the other hand, "I will do my best" is not a specific goal, since level of achievement and time frame are both vague.

Obviously, specific goals will not motivate effective performance if the goals are especially easy to achieve. However, goal challenge is a much more personal matter than goal specificity, since it depends upon the experience and basic skills of the organizational member. One thing is certain, however—when goals become so difficult that they are perceived as *impossible* to achieve, the goals will lose their potential to motivate. Thus, goal challenge is best when pegged to the competence of individual workers and increased as the particular task is mastered. One practical way to do this is to base initial goals upon past performance. For example, an academic counselor might encourage a *D* student to set a goal of achieving *C*s in the coming semester and encourage a *C* student to set a goal of achieving *B*s. Similarly, a sales manager might ask a new salesperson to try to increase his sales by 5 percent in the next quarter and ask an experienced salesperson to try to increase her sales by 10 percent.

Finally, specific, challenging goals must be accepted by the individual if the goals are to have effective motivational properties. In a sense, goals really aren't goals unless they are consciously accepted. In the next section we will discuss some factors that affect goal acceptance.

Just why should specific, challenging, accepted goals, in and of themselves, serve as effective motivators? First, in expectancy theory terms, goal specificity may strengthen both expectancy and instrumentality connections. The individual now has a clear picture of a first-level outcome to which effort should be directed and greater certainty about the consequences of achieving this outcome. Turning to goal challenge, the need theories of motivation suggest that feelings of achievement, competence, and esteem should accompany the mastery of a challenging goal. In addition, certain motivational side effects may accompany goal setting. For one thing, workers may compete with their own "best record" and set even higher goals. For example, the typist who sets and achieves a goal of typing thirty pages on Monday may set a goal of thirty-two pages on Tuesday. In addition, in some goal-setting situations, workers may informally compete among themselves to outdo each other. Again, this may stimulate individual workers to set more challenging personal goals.

Specific, challenging, accepted goals have the most beneficial effect when they are accompanied by ongoing feedback that enables the person to compare current performance with the goal. Having set a goal, the typist who keeps a running log of pages typed should perform better than one who is unaware of his or her progress.

Enhancing Goal Acceptance

It has probably not escaped you that the requirements for goal challenge and goal acceptance seem potentially incompatible. After all, you might be quite amenable to accepting an easy goal but balk at accepting a "toughie." Thus, it is important to consider some of the factors that might affect the acceptance of challenging, specific goals.

It seems reasonable that organizational members should be more accepting of goals that are set with their participation rather than simply handed down from their superior. Sensible as this sounds, the research evidence on the effects of participation is very mixed—sometimes participation in goal setting increases performance and sometimes it doesn't.[37] If goal acceptance is a potential *problem,* participation may prove beneficial.[28] When a climate of distrust between superiors and subordinates exists, or when participation provides information that assists in the establishment of fair, realistic goals, then it should facilitate performance. On the other hand, when subordinates trust their boss, and when the boss has a good understanding of the capability of the subordinates, participation may be quite unnecessary for acceptance. It is interesting to note that participation has been shown to increase performance by increasing the *difficulty* of the goals which are adopted.[39] This may occur because participation induces competition or a feeling of team spirit among members of the work unit which leads them to exceed the goal expectations of the supervisor.

Will the promise of extrinsic rewards (such as money) for goal accomplishment increase the acceptance of goals? Probably, although there is little field research on this issue. However, there is plenty of evidence that goal setting has led to performance increases *without* the introduction of monetary incentives for goal accomplishment. One reason for this may be the fact that many "ambitious" goals involve no more than doing the job as it was designed to be done in the first place. For example, encouraging employees to pack crates or load trucks to within 5 percent of their maximum capacity doesn't really involve a greater expenditure of effort or more work. It simply requires more attention to detail. Finally, goal setting should be compatible with any systems to tie pay to performance which already exist for the job in question, such as wage incentives, commissions, or merit pay.

There is considerable agreement about one factor that will *reduce* the acceptance of specific, challenging performance goals. When supervisors behave in a coercive manner to encourage goal accomplishment, commitment to the goal should be badly damaged. For goal setting to work properly, supervisors must demonstrate a desire to assist employees in goal accomplishment and behave supportively if failure occurs, even adjusting the goal downward if it proves to be unrealistically high. Threat and punishment in response to failure will be extremely counterproductive.[40]

Goal setting has led to increased performance on a wide variety of tasks, including servicing drink machines, keypunching, selling, cutting trees, and typing. Studies reveal that the positive results of goal setting are not a "flash in the pan"—they persist over a long enough time to have practical value.[41] For a detailed example of goal setting see In–Focus 7-4.

Management by Objectives

In the bare-bones form presented above, goal setting is just that—a specific, challenging goal is established in order to solve a particular performance problem.

In this basic form, goal setting is rather lacking in the potential to assist in employee development over time. No particular provisions are made for counseling employees in goal accomplishment or for changing goals in some systematic manner as the need arises. It may also occur to you that certain jobs require the simultaneous accomplishment of *several* goals, and that superiors and subordinates may differ in the importance attached to these goals or disagree about how goal accomplishment can be evaluated. This is particularly likely in the more complex jobs that exist at higher levels in the organization, such as management jobs and staff jobs (e.g., the personnel department or the research and development department).

Management by Objectives (MBO) is an elaborate, systematic, ongoing management program that is designed to facilitate goal establishment, goal accomplishment, and employee development.[42] The objectives in MBO are simply another label for goals. In a well-designed MBO program, objectives for the organization as a whole are developed by top management and diffused down through the organization by the MBO process. In this manner, organizational objectives are translated into specific behavioral objectives for individual members. Our primary focus here is with the nature of the interaction between superiors and individual subordinates in an MBO program. Although there are many variations on the MBO theme, most superior-subordinate interactions share the following similarities:

1. The superior meets with individual subordinates to develop and agree upon subordinate objectives for the coming months. These objectives usually involve both current job performance and personal development that may prepare the subordinate to perform other tasks or seek promotion. The objectives are made as specific as possible and quantified, if feasible, to assist in subsequent evaluation of accomplishment. Time frames for accomplishment are specified, and the objectives may be given priority according to their agreed-upon importance. The methods to be used to achieve the objectives may or may not be discussed. Objectives, time frames, and priorities are put in writing.

2. Periodic meetings are held to monitor subordinate progress in achieving objectives. During these meetings, objectives can be modified if new needs or problems are encountered.

3. An appraisal meeting is held to evaluate the extent to which the agreed-upon objectives have been achieved. Special emphasis is placed upon diagnosing the reasons for success or failure so that the meeting serves as a learning experience for both parties.

4. The MBO cycle is repeated.

An example of a simple MBO objectives form is shown in Exhibit 7-6. Plant manager John Atkins has met with company president F. W. Crawford and agreed upon eight objectives for the coming months. Notice that these objectives are

EXHIBIT 7-6   **A simple format for recording objectives in an MBO program.**

Manager's job title

John Atkins	7/2	PLANT MANAGER
Prepared by the Manager	Date	Managerial Job Objectives
F. W. Crawford	7/2	PRESIDENT
Reviewed by His Supervisor	Date	Supervisor's Job Title

Statement of Objectives	Priority	Dead-line	Outcomes or Results
1. To Increase Deliveries to 98% of All Scheduled Delivery Dates	A	6/31	
2. To Reduce Waste and Spoilage to 3% of All Raw Materials Used	A	6/31	
3. To Reduce Lost Time Due to Accidents to 100 Man-Days/Year	B	2/1	
4. To Reduce Operating Cost to 10% Below Budget	A	1/15	
5. To Install a Quality Control Radioisotope System at a Cost of Less Than $53,000	A	3/15	
6. To Improve Production Scheduling and Preventative Maintenance so as to Increase Machine Utilization Time to 95% of Capacity	B	10/1	
7. To Complete the UCLA Executive Program This Year	A	6/31	
8. To Teach a Production Management Course in University Extension	B	6/31	

Source: Adapted from Raia, A. P. (1974). *Managing by objectives.* Glenview, IL: Scott, Foresman, © 1974, p. 60. Reprinted by permission.

specific and in most cases quantified. Objectives 7 and 8 are personal development objectives, while the others are performance objectives. The objectives have been given ''A'' priority or ''B'' priority (column 2) and a specific deadline for accomplishment (column 3). In his own role as a manager, Atkins would probably use some of these objectives as a basis for establishing the objectives of *his* subordinates. Thus, objectives 1 through 6 would become the basis of even more specific goals for the production manager, the shipping manager, and the personnel manager who report to Atkins. In this manner, the MBO program diffuses a ''goal mentality'' tnroughout the organization.

Although many organizations have implemented MBO programs, careful tests of the impact of these exercises on employee performance have been rare. Further, the more sophisticated research studies tend to be less complimentary of the effectiveness of MBO. Still, the weight of the evidence seems to indicate that when MBO programs are properly established and administered they can have a positive effect on performance.[43]

Experience and research indicate that a number of factors may be associated with the failure of MBO programs. For one thing, MBO is an elaborate, difficult, time-consuming process, and its implementation must have the full support of top management. If such support is absent, managers at lower levels simply go through the motions of practicing MBO. At the very least, this reaction will lead to the haphazard specification of objectives and thus subvert the very core of MBO, goal setting. A frequent symptom of this degeneration is the complaint that MBO is "just a bunch of paperwork." Indeed, at this stage, it is! Even with the best of intentions, setting specific, quantified objectives may be a difficult process. This may lead to an overemphasis on measurable objectives at the expense of more qualitative objectives. For example, it may be much easier to agree on production goals than on goals that involve subordinate development, although both may be equally important. Finally, even if reasonable objectives are established, MBO can still be subverted if the performance review becomes an exercise in browbeating or punishing subordinates for failure to achieve objectives.[44]

Goal Setting and Quality of Working Life

By now, you should be able to anticipate the argument—goal setting exercises, whether simple or elaborate, have the potential to enhance the quality of working life if they are *properly managed.* Clear, specific performance goals should reduce role ambiguity and stress and thus promote a high quality work experience. By the same token, achieving challenging goals should promote feelings of competence and self-reliance among many employees. It should be clear, however, that goal setting programs place very special demands upon supervisory personnel. Even in simple goal-setting exercises, a proper level of challenge must be identified, unavoidable obstacles to performance must be recognized, and the necessity for subordinate participation must be accurately gauged. More elaborate programs, such as MBO, compound these demands. If employees perceive that goals are too difficult, arbitrary, or unachievable through no fault of their own, they will experience dissatisfaction and resentment.

MODIFIED WORKING TIMES AS MOTIVATORS

Most North Americans work a five-day, forty-hour week. Furthermore, they are usually required to do this work within a fixed set of hours—e.g., the "nine-to-five grind." Recently, some organizations have begun to experiment with modifications of these traditional working times. Although sometimes prompted in part by general social concerns (such as saving energy or reducing traffic during rush hours), these experiments are primarily of interest because of their potential impact on motivation and the quality of working life.

One alternative to traditional working time is **flex-time,** which was first introduced on a large scale in Europe. In its most simple and common form, workers are required to report for work on each working day and work a given number of hours. However, the times at which they arrive and leave are flexible, as long as they are present during certain core times. For example, employees might be permitted to begin their day anytime after 7 A.M. and work until 6 P.M., as long as they put in eight hours and are present during the core time of 9:15 until noon and 2 until 4:15 (Exhibit 7-7). Other systems permit employees to tally hours on a weekly

EXHIBIT 7-7   An example of a flex-time schedule.

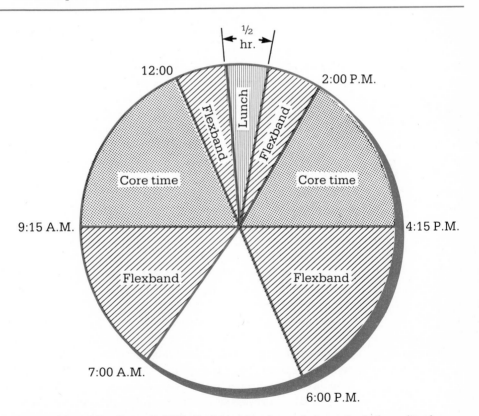

Source: Adapted from Ronen, S. (1981). *Flexible working hours: An innovation in the quality of work life.* New York: McGraw-Hill, p. 42.

or monthly basis, although they are still usually required to be present during the core time of each working day.[45]

A second alternative to traditional working time is the **compressed work-week.** This system compresses the hours worked each week into fewer days. The most common compressed workweek is the 4-40 system, in which employees work four ten-hour days each week rather than the traditional five eight-hour days. Thus, the organization or department may operate Monday through Thursday or Tuesday through Friday, although rotation schemes that keep the organization open five days a week are also employed.[46]

It should be obvious that there are certain technical constraints to the implementation of modified working times. When jobs are highly interdependent, such as on an assembly line, flex-time becomes an unlikely strategy. To cite an even more extreme example, we simply can't have members of a hospital operating room team showing up for work whenever it suits them! In addition, flex-time may lead to problems in achieving adequate supervisory coverage. For these reasons, it should not surprise you that flex-time has been implemented most frequently in office environments. For instance, in a bank, the core hours might be when the bank is open to the public.

Technical roadblocks to the implementation of the 4-40 workweek include the possibility of reduced customer service and the negative effects of fatigue which may accompany longer working days. The latter problem may be especially acute when the work is strenuous and may be magnified if employees use their extra day off to ''moonlight'' on another job.

Despite these technical limitations, what are the supposed advantages of modified working times? First, it should be clear that the theories of motivation discussed in the last chapter would suggest few *direct* performance benefits. That is, simply manipulating the hours of work should not motivate employees to produce more work or higher quality work. However, modified working hours may have both direct and indirect effects upon other work behaviors and on the quality of working life of employees. For example, both flex-time and the 4-40 workweek may reduce absenteeism because they permit workers greater freedom to take care of personal business or family matters during what had been working time. In addition, the 4-40 schedule reduces commuting costs by 20 percent, while flexible working hours may connote a degree of prestige and trust usually reserved for executives and professionals. Such consequences may increase job satisfaction, reducing turnover and making it easier to recruit new employees.

Although flex-time has generally been limited to white-collar personnel, it has been applied in a variety of organizations, including insurance companies (Prudential), financial institutions (Canada Trust, Boston's State Street Bank), and government offices (many U.S. states, Canadian and U.S. civil service). Although the quality of the research on flex-time varies, a number of conclusions can be drawn.[47] First, employees who work under flex-time almost always prefer the system to fixed hours. In addition, work attitudes generally become more positive, and employers report minimal abuse of the arrangement. When measured, absenteeism and tardiness have often shown decreases following the introduction of flex-time, and first-line supervisors and managers are usually positively inclined toward the system. Interestingly, slight productivity gains are often reported under flex-time, probably due to better use of scarce resources or equipment rather than increased motivation. As an extreme example, a computer-programming group that shared a computer system increased its productivity 24 percent following the introduction of flex-time (a clear improvement over several control groups). Flex-time evidently gave more programmers more access time to the computer each work day.[48]

While solid evidence regarding the effects of the four-day week is rare, a couple of tentative conclusions stand out.[49] First, workers who have experienced the four-day system seem to *like* it. Sometimes this liking is accompanied by increased job satisfaction, but the effect may be short-lived.[50] In many cases, the impact of the compressed workweek may be better for family life than for work life. Secondly, workers have often reported an increase in fatigue following the introduction of the compressed week. This may be responsible for the uneven impact of the system on absenteeism, sometimes decreasing it and sometimes not. Potential gains in attendance may be nullified as workers take an occasional day off to recuperate from fatigue.[51] Finally, the more sophisticated research studies do not report lasting changes in productivity due to the short workweek.[52]

In conclusion, research has shown some positive outcomes and very few negative attitudinal or motivational effects stemming from flex-time or the compressed workweek. Furthermore, their general popularity among the work force makes the systems good recruiting tools for attracting competent workers.

A FOOTNOTE: A GENERAL MOTIVATIONAL PRINCIPLE

If it is possible to distill a general principle of motivation from our discussion of motivational strategies, it is the following: *A motivator will only motivate if it is valued by the person to be motivated and contingent upon good performance.* This principle is perfectly congruent with learning theory and with the process and need theories of motivation. Furthermore, it applies whether the motivator in question is money or the feelings derived from performing an interesting job or achieving a challenging goal. There is a simple corollary to this principle: *Motivational systems must be properly implemented and managed.* Tying trivial amounts of money to performance, giving all employees the same amount of merit pay, pretending to enrich jobs, or setting unrealistic goals simply subverts the motivational principle. As if this were not bad enough, such tactical errors may be perceived by employees as patronizing or grossly unfair and thus have a severe negative impact on their quality of working life. Such an outcome is unlikely to make it easy to attract and retain a competent and committed work force. Thus, while there is evidence that each of the strategies discussed in this chapter can increase motivation and/or enhance the quality of the work experience, there is plenty of room for error in their installation.

Some Caveats Concerning Motivational Strategies

Several warnings are in order regarding the general implementation of motivational strategies. The first involves the selection of a particular strategy, the second involves initial judgments about its effectiveness, and the third involves observations about effectiveness over some time period.

INDIVIDUAL DIFFERENCES.   It is convenient to assume that many people are interested in the opportunity to earn more money, do interesting work, accomplish challenging goals, and set their own working hours. Indeed, *some* people must be interested in these factors, or it is unlikely that the motivational strategies discussed in this chapter would have ever been proposed. Clearly, however, people differ in the outcomes they seek from their jobs. Some portions of the work force may object to tying pay to performance and others may feel severely threatened by more complex jobs or the imposition of challenging performance goals. Such individual preferences must be considered when designing a motivational program.

HAWTHORNE EFFECTS.   You will recall from Chapter 2 that Hawthorne effects are short-lived motivational effects that can occur when workers receive special attention in the course of a research study or intervention by management. The Hawthorne effect might infringe on motivational strategies in two ways. First, some strategies may be introduced on a small scale in an experimental manner. This is especially true of job enrichment, where special workers may be selected to take part and given extra training and privileges. If they repay this kindness with favorable performance, the actual motivational properties of the redesigned jobs may be obscured. Clearly, such a reaction will not persist when the enrichment program is expanded. In addition, certain motivational programs involve increases in supervisory attention by their very nature. This is particularly the case with merit pay plans and MBO. Again, such programs may stimulate effective performance when initiated but begin to flounder when the novelty of increased attention wears off.

ADAPTATION.   Even when motivation programs respect initial worker needs and have true motivational properties, they may lose these properties over time because the work outcomes derived from the program become less valent as the needs to which they correspond are fulfilled. Thus, in a sense, workers may "adapt out" of the motivational system. This seems especially likely in the case of extrinsic motivators. For example, tying pay to performance may cease to be an effective motivator when the material needs which pay fulfills are largely satisfied. This could also occur for intrinsic motivators. For example, an enriched job may lose its motivating potential when it is fully mastered. Thus, motivational systems may atrophy over time, especially for a stable work force.

In summary, motivational programs should be adopted with some concern for the individual differences within the work force. When implemented, they should initially be monitored for Hawthorne effects and then monitored over time for adaptation effects.

SUMMARY

- In this chapter we have discussed four strategies that have been employed to increase the motivation of organizational members. Money should be most effective as a motivator when it is made contingent upon performance. Schemes to link pay to performance on production jobs are called wage incentive plans. Piecerate, in which workers are paid a certain amount of money for each item produced, is the prototype of all wage incentive plans. In general, wage incentives have been shown to increase productivity, but their introduction may be accompanied by a number of problems, one of which is the restriction of production. Attempts to link pay to performance on white-collar jobs are called merit pay plans. Evidence suggests that many merit pay plans are less effective than they could be because merit pay is inadequate, performance ratings are mistrusted, or extreme secrecy about pay levels prevails.

- Recent views advocate increasing the scope (breadth and depth) of jobs to capitalize on their inherent motivational properties, as opposed to the job simplification of the past. The Job Characteristics Model, proposed by Hackman and Oldham, suggests that jobs have five core characteristics that affect their motivating potential: skill variety, task identity, task significance, autonomy, and feedback. When jobs are high in these characteristics, favorable motivational and attitudinal consequences should occur. Job enrichment involves designing jobs to enhance intrinsic motivation and the quality of working life. Some specific enrichment techniques include combining tasks, establishing client relationships, reducing supervision and reliance on others, forming work teams, and making feedback more direct.

- Goal setting can be an effective motivator when goals are specific, challenging, and acceptable to workers. In some cases, acceptance may be facilitated by participation in goal setting and by financial incentives for goal attainment, but freedom from coercion and punishment seems to be the key factor in achieving goal acceptance. Management by Objectives (MBO) is an elaborate goal-setting and evaluation process typically used for management jobs.

- Some organizations have adopted modified working times such as flex-time or the compressed workweek with expectations of motivational benefits. Although these schemes should have little effect on productivity, they have the potential to reduce absence and turnover and enhance the quality of working life. Where adopted, both schemes have usually proved acceptable to workers and management.

KEY CONCEPTS

Quality of working life   Gain-sharing plans
Piecerate   Merit pay plans
Wage incentive plans   Scientific Management
Restriction of productivity   Job scope

Job breadth

Job depth

Skill variety

Task identity

Task significance

Autonomy

Feedback

Motivating potential

Growth need strength

Context factors

Job enrichment

Goal setting

Management by Objectives (MBO)

Flex-time

Compressed workweek

DISCUSSION QUESTIONS

1.   Describe some jobs for which you think it would be difficult to link pay to performance. What is there about these jobs which provokes this difficulty?

2.   Imagine two insurance companies that have merit pay plans for salaried white-collar personnel. In one organization the plan truly rewards good performers, while in the other it does not. Both companies decide to make salaries completely public. What will be the consequences of such a change for each company? (Be specific, using concepts such as expectancy, instrumentality, job satisfaction, and turnover.)

3.   You are, of course, familiar with the annual lists of the world's ten worst-dressed women or the ten worst movies. Here's a new one: A job enrichment consultant has developed a list of the ten worst jobs which includes a highway toll collector, pool typist, bank guard, and automatic elevator operator. Use the five core job characteristics to describe each of these jobs. Could any of these jobs be enriched? How? Which should be completely automated? Can you add some jobs to the list?

4.   Hackman and Oldham state that context dissatisfaction may detract from the motivational properties of an enriched job. Use Maslow's Need Hierarchy to explain this statement.

5.   Some have argued that the jobs of the President of the United States and the Prime Minister of Canada are "too big" for one person to perform adequately. This probably means that the jobs are perceived as having too much scope or being too enriched. Use the Job Characteristics Model to explore the accuracy of this contention.

6.   Debate the following statements: Of all the motivational techniques discussed in this chapter, goal setting is the simplest to implement. Goal setting is no more than doing what a good manager should be doing anyway.

7.   Imagine an office setting in which a change to either a four-day week or flex-time would appear to be equally feasible to introduce. What would be the pros and cons of each system? How would factors such as the nature of the business, the age of the work force, or the average commuting distance affect the choice of systems?

8. Debate the following proposition: The motivational strategies discussed in this chapter are manipulative and unethical, and they put too much pressure on the work force.

FOR FURTHER READING

Greiner, J. M., et al. (1981). *Productivity and motivation: A review of state and local government initiatives*. Washington: The Urban Institute Press.
    Reports comprehensively on the successes and failures encountered in introducing motivational techniques in the public sector. Major sections on monetary incentives, goal setting, performance appraisal, and job enrichment.

Griffin, R. W. (1982). *Task design: An integrative approach*. Glenview, IL: Scott, Foresman.
    A comprehensive look at the design of jobs. Relates job design to organizational design, technology, group processes, and leader behavior.

Locke, E. A. (1982). The ideas of Frederick W. Taylor: An evaluation. *Academy of Management Review, 7*, 14–24.
    Evaluates Taylor's Scientific Management in light of contemporary understanding of motivation and productivity. Concludes that Taylor's views were essentially correct and that he is underappreciated by current observers.

Case Study

FAB Sweets Limited

ORGANIZATIONAL SETTING

FAB Sweets Limited is a manufacturer of high quality sweets [candies]. The company is a medium-sized, family-owned, partially unionized and highly successful confectionery producer in the north of England. The case study is set within a single department in the factory where acute problems were experienced.

BACKGROUND TO THE CASE

The department (hereafter called 'HB') produces and packs over 40 lines of hard-boiled sweets on a batch-production system. It is organized in two adjacent areas, one for production staffed by men and one for packing staffed by women. The areas are separated by a physical barrier, allowing the packing room to be air conditioned and protected from the humidity resulting from production. Management believed this was necessary to stop the sweets from sweating (thus sticking to their wrappers) during storage. Each room has a chargehand and a supervisor who reports to the departmental manager, who himself is responsible to the factory manager. In total 37 people work in the department (25 in production, 12 in packing), the majority of whom are skilled employees. Training takes place on the job, and it normally takes two years to acquire the skills necessary to complete all the production tasks. Figure 1 presents

Source: Case prepared by Kemp, N., Clegg, C., & Wall, T. (1985). In Clegg, C., Kemp, N., & Legge, K. (Eds). *Case studies in organizational behaviour.* London: Harper & Row.

an outline of the physical layout of the department and the work flow.

The production process is essentially quite simple. Raw materials, principally sugar, are boiled to a set temperature, with 'cooking time' varying from line to line. The resulting batches are worked on by employees who fold and manipulate them so as to create the required texture, while adding coloring and favorings ('slabbing' and 'mixing'). Different batches are molded together to create the flavor mixes and patterns required ('make up'). The batch, which by now is quite cool, is then extruded through a machine which cuts it into sweets of individual size. Some products at this stage are automatically wrapped and then passed by conveyor belt to the packing room where they are inspected, bagged, and boxed ready for dispatch to retail and wholesale outlets. Other products progress unwrapped into the packing room where they are fed into a wrapping machine, inspected, bagged and dispatched. Several different product lines can be produced at the same time. The most skilled and critical tasks occur early in the process; these include 'cooking' mixtures for different products and 'make up' (e.g., for striped mints). These skills are gradually learned until the operator is able to 'feel' the correct finish for each of the 40 lines. All the tasks are highly interdependent such that any one individual's performance affects the ease with which the next person down the line can successfully achieve his/her part of the production process. Although the work appears quite simple and the management of the process straightforward, the department neverthe-

EXHIBIT 1   **The HB department: physical layout and work flow.**

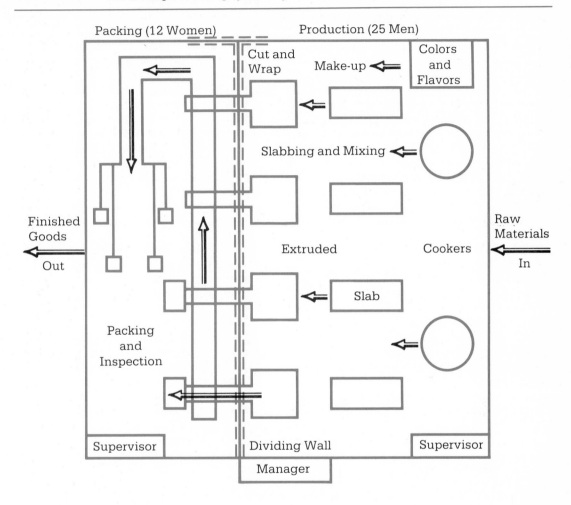

less experienced acute problems. These are outlined below.

THE PROBLEM

In objective terms the problems in HB were manifest in a high level of labor turnover, six new managers in eight years, production which consistently fell below targets based on work study standards, and high levels of scrap. The department was known as the worst in the factory and its problems were vari-

ously characterized in terms of 'attitude', 'atmosphere' and 'climate'. Moreover, employees had few decision-making responsibilities, low motivation, low job satisfaction, and received little information on their performance. Finally there were interpersonal problems between the employees in the production and packing rooms, between the two supervisors, and also among the operators, and there were a number of dissatisfactions relating to grading and payment levels.

EXPERIENCE OF THE METHOD
OF WORKING

To understand how HB works and how people experienced their work it is necessary to recognize the strong drive throughout the organization for production. Departmental managers are judged primarily in terms of their production levels (against targets) and the efficiency (against work study standards) at which they perform. In HB this pressure was transmitted to the two supervisors. In practice, production levels were the number of batches of sweets processed, and efficiency was the ratio of batches produced to hours used by direct labor.

The production supervisor responded to the pressure for production in a number of ways. First, in an attempt to maximize production, he always allocated people to the jobs at which they performed best. He also determined the cooker speeds. In effect, this set the pace of work for both production and packing. Buffer stocks were not possible in production because the sweets needed processing before they cooled down. If he was falling behind his target, the supervisor responded by speeding up the pace of work. In addition, he regarded his job purely in terms of processing batches, and ignored problems in the packing room which may in fact have resulted directly from his actions or from those of his staff. The supervisory role thus involved allocating people to tasks, setting machine speeds (and hence the pace of work), organizing reliefs and breaks, monitoring hygiene, safety and quality standards, maintaining discipline and recording data for the management information systems. The chargehand undertook these responsibilities in the absence of a supervisor, spending the rest of his time on production.

The men in production complained that they were bored with always doing the same jobs, especially as some were physically harder than others (for example, 'slabbing' involved manual manipulation of batches of up to 50 kilograms). Several claimed that their greater efforts should receive financial recognition. Furthermore, this rigidity of task allocation was in direct conflict with the grading system which was designed to encourage flexibility. To be on the top rate of pay in the department, an operator had to be capable of performing all the skills for all the lines, and hence be able to cover any job. Training schedules matched this. In practice, however, people rarely used more than one or two of their skills.

The others decayed through disuse. All the staff recognized that the grading system was at odds with how the department actually worked and tended to be dissatisfied with both. The production supervisor's strict control over the pace of work also proved suboptimal in other ways. For example, he sometimes pushed the pace to a level regarded as impossible by the staff. Whether this was true or self-fulfilling is a moot point—the net result was an increase in the level of scrap. Also he ignored the wishes of the staff to work less hard in the afternoon when they were tired: again scrap resulted. In addition the feeling was widespread among the men in production that management and supervision organized the work badly and would do better if they took advice from the shop floor. Their own perceived lack of control over the job led them to abrogate responsibility when things went wrong ("We told them so!!"). And finally, although the processes of production were highly interdependent, operators adopted an insular perspective and the necessary cooperation between workers was rarely evident, and then only on the basis of personal favors between friends.

The equivalent pressure on the packing supervisor was to pack the sweets efficiently. As her section could pack no more than was produced, her only manipulable variable was hours worked. Thus to increase her efficiency she could only transfer the packers to 'other work' within her room (e.g. cleaning) or to another department.

The packers for their part resented being asked to work flat out when HB was busy, only to be moved elsewhere when things were slacker. As described above, their own work flow was basically controlled by the speed at which the men were producing. When in difficulty, direct appeals to the men to slow down were unsuccessful and so they channeled their complaints through their supervisor. Because of the insular perspective adopted by the production supervisor (in rational support of his own targets), her approaches were usually ignored ("It's my job to produce sweets"), and the resulting intersupervisory conflict took up much of the departmental manager's time. In addition the packing room was very crowded and interpersonal conflicts were common.

Finally, production problems throughout the factory were created by seasonal peaks and troughs in the market demand for sweets. These 'busy' and 'slack' periods differed between production departments. In order to cope with market demands the production planning department transferred staff, on a temporary basis, between production departments. In HB this typically meant that, when they were busy, 'unskilled' employees were drafted in to help, whereas when demand was low HB employees were transferred to other departments where they were usually given the worst jobs. Both of these solutions were resented by the employees in HB.

This description of the department is completed when one recognizes the complications involved in scheduling over 40 product lines through complex machinery, all of it over 10 years old. In fact breakdowns and interruptions to smooth working were common. The effects of these on the possible levels of production were poorly understood and in any case few operators were aware of their targets or of their subsequent performance. More immediately the breakdowns were a source of continual conflict between the department and the maintenance engineers responsible to an engineering manager. The department laid the blame on poor maintenance, the engineers on abuse or lack of care by production workers in handling the machinery. Much management time was spent in negotiating 'blame' for breakdowns and time allowances resulting since this affected efficiency figures. Not surprisingly, perhaps, the factory-wide image of the department was very poor on almost all counts, and its status was low.

PARTICIPANTS' DIAGNOSES OF THE PROBLEMS

Shopfloor employees, chargehands, supervisors, the department manager and senior management were agreed that much was wrong in HB. However, there was no coherent view of the causes and what should be done to make improvements. Many shopfloor employees placed the blame on supervision and management for their lack of technical and planning expertise, and their low consideration for subordinates. The production supervisor favored a solution in terms of ''getting rid of the trouble-makers,'' by transferring or sacking his nominated culprits. The department manager wanted to introduce a senior supervisor to handle the conflicts between the production and packing supervisors and further support the pressure for production. The factory manager thought the way work was organized and managed might be at the core of the difficulties.

■ ■ ■

1. Use expectancy theory and equity theory (Chapter 6) to analyze the general motivational climate in the HB department.
2. Discuss the specific role of money, job design, and goal setting as they relate to the problems experienced in the HB department.
3. What should be done by management to improve the motivation and quality of working life in the HB department? Be specific, and cover major issues as well as supporting details.
4. In light of the above, evaluate the solutions proposed by the shopfloor employees, the production supervisor, the department manager, and the factory manager.

REFERENCES

1. For reviews see Lawler, E. E., III. (1971). *Pay and organizational effectiveness: A psychological view.* New York: McGraw-Hill, and Chung, K. H. (1977). *Motivational theories and practices.* Columbus, OH: Grid.
2. Locke, E. A., Feren, D. B., McCaleb, V. M., Shaw, K. N., & Denny, A. T. (1980). The relative effectiveness of four methods of motivating employee performance. In K. D. Duncan, M. M. Gruneberg, & D. Wallis (Eds.), *Changes in working life.* London: Wiley.
3. Fein, M. (1973, September). Work measurement and wage incentives. *Industrial Engineering,* 49–51.
4. Fein, M. (1976). Motivation for work. In R. Dubin (Ed.), *Handbook of work, organization, and society.* Chicago: Rand McNally.

5.   Lawler, E. E., III. (1981). *Pay and organizational development.* Reading, MA: Addison-Wesley.

6.   Lesieur, F. G. (Ed.). (1958). *The Scanlon plan.* Cambridge, MA: M.I.T. Press.

7.   Lawler, E. E. (1984). Whatever happened to incentive pay? *New Management, 1*(4), 37–41.

8.   Bureau of National Affairs. (1974). *Management performance appraisal programs.* BNA Personnel Policies Forum survey no. 104.

9.   Lawler, 1971.

10. Lawler, 1971; Nash, A., & Carrol, S. (1975). *The management of compensation.* Monterey, CA: Brooks/Cole.

11. Weeks, D. A. (1976). *Compensating employees: Lessons of the 1970's.* New York: The Conference Board.

12. Lawler, 1971; Ungson, G. R., & Steers, R. M. (1984). Motivation and politics in executive compensation. *Academy of Management Review, 9,* 313–323.

13. Haire, M., Ghiselli, E. E., & Gordon, M. E. (1967). A psychological study of pay. *Journal of Applied Psychology Monograph, 51,* (Whole No. 636).

14. Bureau of National Affairs, 1974. Also see De Vries, D. L., & McCall, M. W., Jr. (1976, January). *Performance appraisal: Is it tax time again?* Paper presented at the Center for Creative Leadership, Greensboro, NC.

15. Weeks, 1976.

16. Lawler, E. E., III (1972). Secrecy and the need to know. In H. L. Tosi, R. J. House, & M. D. Dunnette (Eds.), *Managerial motivation and compensation.* East Lansing, MI: Michigan State University Press.

17. Futrell, C. M., & Jenkins, O. C. (1978). Pay secrecy versus pay disclosure for salesmen: A longitudinal study. *Journal of Marketing Research, 15,* 214–219, p. 215.

18. Penner, D. D. (1966). *A study of the causes and consequences of salary satisfaction.* Crotonville, NY: General Electric Behavioral Research Service; Lawler, E. E. (1966). Managers' attitudes toward how their pay is and should be determined. *Journal of Applied Psychology, 50,* 273–279.

19. Taylor, F. W. (1967). *The principles of scientific management.* New York: Norton.

20. This discussion draws upon Gibson, J. L., Ivancevich, J. M., & Donnelly, J. H., Jr. (1985). *Organizations* (5th ed.). Plano, TX: Business Publications.

21. Hackman, J. R., & Oldham, G. R. (1980). *Work redesign.* Reading, MA: Addison-Wesley.

22. Oldham, G. R., Hackman, J. R., & Stepina, L. P. (1979). Norms for the job diagnostic survey. *JSAS Catalog of Selected Documents in Psychology, 9,* 14. (Ms. No. 1819).

23. Loher, B. T., Noe, R. A., Moeller, N. L., & Fitzgerald, M. P. (1985). A meta-analysis of the relation of job characteristics to job satisfaction. *Journal of Applied Psychology, 70,* 280–289.

24. For a supporting study see Oldham, G. R., Hackman, J. R., & Pearce, J. L. (1976). Conditions under which employees respond favorably to enriched work. *Journal of Applied Psychology, 61,* 395–403. For negative evidence see Katerberg, R., Jr., Hom, P. W., & Hulin, C. L. (1979). Effects of job complexity on the reactions of part-time employees. *Organizational Behavior and Human Performance, 24,* 317–332.

25. This section draws in part on Hackman & Oldham, 1980.

26. The description of Volvo's job enrichment efforts draws on Dowling, W. F. (1973, Autumn). Job redesign on the assembly line: Farewell to the blue-collar blues? *Organizational Dynamics,* 51–67; Gyllenhammar, P. G. (1977). *People at work.* Reading, MA: Addison-Wesley; Walton, R. E. (1977). Successful strategies for diffusing work innovations. *Journal of Contemporary Business, 6,* 1–22.

27. Ford, R. N. (1969). *Motivation through the work itself.* New York: American Management Association, pp. 29–30. Other description in this section also relies upon Ford.

28. Job enrichment has proven fairly effective in reducing turnover. See McEvoy, G., & Cascio, W. F. (1985). Strategies for reducing employee turnover: A meta-analysis. *Journal of Applied Psychology, 70,* 342–353.

29. Cherrington, D. J., & England, J. L. (1980). The desire for an enriched job as a moderator of the enrichment-satisfaction relationship. *Organizational Behavior and Human Performance, 25,* 139–159.

30. Dowling, 1973.

31. Locke, E. A., Sirota, D., & Wolfson, A. D. (1976). An experimental case study of the successes and failures of job enrichment in a government agency. *Journal of Applied Psychology, 61,* 701–711.

32. Stonewalling plant democracy. (1977, March 28). *Business Week.*

33. Winpisinger, W. (1973, February). Job satisfaction: A union response. *AFL-CIO American Federationist,* pp. 8–10.

34. Cherrington & England, 1980, p. 156.

35. The best developed theoretical position is that of Locke, E. A. (1968). Toward a theory of task motivation and incentives. *Organizational Behavior and Human Performance, 3,* 157–189.

36. Locke, E. A., Shaw, K. N., Saari, L. M., & Latham, G. P. (1981). Goal setting and task performance: 1969–1980. *Psychological Bulletin, 90,* 125–152.

37. Locke et al., 1981.

38. See Erez, M., Earley, P. C., & Hulin, C. L. (1985). The impact of participation on goal acceptance and performance: A two-step model. *Academy of Management Journal, 28,* 50–66.

39. Latham, G. P., Mitchell, T. R., & Dosset, D. L. (1978). The importance of participative goal setting and anticipated rewards on goal difficulty and job performance. *Journal of Applied Psychology, 63,* 163–171; Saari, L. M., & Latham, G. P. (1979). The effects of holding goal difficulty constant on assigned and participatively set goals. *Academy of Management Journal, 22,* 163–168.

40. For a dicsussion of this issue, see Saari & Latham, 1979.

41. Latham, G. P., & Locke, E. A. (1979, Autumn). Goal setting—a motivational technique that works. *Organizational Dynamics,* 68–80.

42. Good descriptions of MBO programs can be found in Raia, A. P. (1974). *Managing by objectives.* Glenview, IL: Scott, Foresman; Odione, G. S. (1965). *Management by objectives.* New York: Pitman.

43. Kondrasuk, J. N. (1981). Studies in MBO effectiveness. *Academy of Management Review, 6,* 419–430.

44. For discussions of these and other problems with MBO see Pringle, C. D., & Longenecker, J. G. (1982). The ethics of MBO. *Academy of Management Review, 7,* 305–312; Levinson, H. (1979, July–August). Management by whose objectives. *Harvard Business Review,* 125–134; McConkey, D. D. (1972, October). 20 ways to kill management by objectives. *Management Review,* 4–13.

45. See Ronen, S. (1984). *Alternative work schedules: Selecting, implementing, and evaluating.* Homewood, IL: Dow Jones-Irwin; Ronen, S. (1981). *Flexible working hours: An innovation in the quality of work life.* New York: McGraw-Hill; Nollen, S. D. (1982). *New work schedules in practice: Managing time in a changing society.* New York: Van Nostrand Reinhold.

46. See Ronen, 1984, and Nollen, 1982.

47. Ronen, 1981 and 1984; Golembiewski, R. T, & Proehl, C. W. (1978). A survey of the empirical literature on flexible workhours: Character and consequences of a major innovation. *Academy of Management Review, 3,* 837–853.
48. Ralston, D. A., Anthony, W. P., & Gustafson, D. J. (1985). Employees may love flextime, but what does it do to the organization's productivity? *Journal of Applied Psychology, 70,* 272–279.
49. Ronen, 1984; Ronen, S., & Primps, S. B. (1981). The compressed work week as organizational change: Behavioral and attitudinal outcomes. *Academy of Management Review, 6,* 61–74.
50. Ivancevich, J. M., & Lyon, H. L. (1977). The shortened workweek: A field experiment. *Journal of Applied Psychology, 62,* 34–37.
51. Johns, G. (1987). Understanding and managing absence from work. In S. L. Dolan & R. S. Schuller (Eds.), *Canadian readings in personnel and human resource management.* St Paul, MN: West.
52. Ivancevich & Lyon, 1977; Calvasina, E. J., & Boxx, W. R. (1975). Efficiency of workers on the four-day workweek. *Academy of Management Journal, 18,* 604–610; Goodale, J. G., & Aagaard, A. K. (1975). Factors relating to varying reactions to the 4-day workweek. *Journal of Applied Psychology, 60,* 33–38.

Part Three

Social Behavior and Organizational Processes

Chapter 8

Group Formation and Structure

TRITON COMPUTERS

Like many small computers of the time, the first Triton was designed and constructed in a California garage. The brainchild of three young engineers, Triton succeeded where many others had failed. Although Triton never became an Apple or an IBM, it became a strong factor in the burgeoning personal computer market of the 1980s.

The first Triton was a crude device, really just a circuit board for the growing ranks of dedicated computer hobbyists. The three engineers, Max Bart, Ali Sharma, and Wayne Griggs, were employed full time by established electronics and computer firms. Over many evenings and weekends in Max Bart's garage, they managed to design and build the first Triton prototype. The work was difficult and frustrating, but the men worked as a closely knit team to solve the problems they encountered. With the prototype, Bart scoured the mushrooming electronics and computer stores of the region and finally obtained orders for one hundred of the Triton computers. After much difficulty, financing was secured, and Max, Ali, and Wayne built the hundred computers in record time on a crude "assembly line" in the garage. They felt just great.

Over the next several months, Max, Ali, and Wayne set about designing a prototype for a real personal computer. At the same time, plans had been laid for establishing a real company. Finally, the men quit their jobs, pooled their personal savings, and with the help of some venture capital, acquired small premises in a local industrial park. Several other computer experts and technicians were hired, and work began in earnest.

The atmosphere at Triton was informal and exciting. Although there were no set working hours, most of the people put in 12- to 14-hour days and could be found at Triton well into the evening. There were no formal job descriptions, and everyone was welcome to contribute ideas and labor to the various aspects of the project. A couple of new employees found this lack of structure not to their liking and quit, but they were replaced by people who functioned well. Everyone dressed casually in jeans and t-shirts, and there were no private offices, just a "bull pen" of terminals and drawing boards which were decorated with posters and cartoons.

As the design of the Triton personal computer was finalized, things at Triton began to change. An M.B.A. was brought in to handle finance, and another was brought in to assist Max Bart, who had now assumed the role of marketer and outside spokesperson. Bart was seen more frequently in a suit, and a separate office was designed so that he could entertain visitors in a more formal atmosphere. A production crew was hired, and Wayne Griggs took over their management. Ali Sharma was formally named head of design, and he set to work with his staff fine-tuning future models of the personal computer.

A year after the successful introduction of the Triton personal computer, Max Bart was interviewed about the company's future.

"A key problem is maintaining a team spirit in design and in production," Bart said. "As you get bigger, that's hard to do. In design, a lot of what we do now involves developing the existing product. Some people don't find that challenging. In production, we've got a large staff, and it's hard to get such a large group excited about shipping computers. In the old days, we were all equals here. Now, some are more equal than others, and that can't be helped. Maybe it was more fun slaving away back in the garage."

Shortly after this interview, Wayne Griggs quit his job at Triton to take a design job at a small start-up computer firm. "I just decided I'm a computer designer, not a production manager," he told Bart and Sharma.

The Triton Computer story illustrates how a small group of dedicated entrepreneurs developed into an organization made up of several larger groups. What accounted for the enthusiasm and success of the initial group of three, and why does Max Bart fear for future enthusiasm and success? Was the division of labor and status among Triton members as inevitable as Bart suggests? What happens when groups make incompatible demands on people? These are some of the questions we will try to answer in this chapter.

First, we will define the term *group* and discuss the nature of formal groups and informal groups in organizations. After this, the reasons for group formation will be presented. Finally, we will consider how groups differ from one another structurally and explore the consequences of these differences.

WHAT IS A GROUP?

The word *group* is used rather casually in everyday discourse—special-interest group, ethnic group, and so on. However, for behavioral scientists, a **group** consists of two or more people interacting interdependently to achieve a common goal.

Interaction is the most basic aspect of a group—it suggests to us who is in the group and who is not. The interaction of group members need not be face-to-face and it need not be verbal. For example, astronauts in a space shuttle and Mission Control personnel in Houston form a group by virtue of radio communication, even though they are separated by thousands of miles of space. Also, the primitive group that forms to pass water buckets to fight a fire need not speak to meet the requirement of interaction. Interdependence simply means that group members rely to some degree upon each other to accomplish goals. Ten individuals who independently throw buckets of water on a fire do not constitute a true group. Finally, all groups have one or more goals that their members seek to achieve. These goals can range from having fun, to marketing a new product, to achieving world peace.

Group memberships are very important for two reasons. First, groups exert a tremendous influence *upon us.* They are the social mechanisms by which we acquire many beliefs, values, attitudes, and behaviors. For example, membership in work groups provides us with information about how satisfied we should be with our jobs ("This is a lousy job, isn't it?") and how hard we should work ("Look, we only turn out fifty widgets a day here"). In many cases, the influence provided by these social cues may be as potent or more potent than the "objective" cues provided by the job itself.

Group membership is also important because groups provide a context in which *we* are able to exert influence upon *others.* These others can include the members of the group or persons outside of the group who are affected by its activities. This opportunity for influence can often lead to considerable feelings of self-esteem and power.

Let's have a look at two categories of groups that form in organizations.

FORMAL VERSUS INFORMAL GROUPS

For the purposes of organizational behavior, groups can be characterized most usefully as formal and informal.

Formal Groups

Formal work groups are groups that are established by the organization to facilitate the achievement of organizational goals. They are intentionally designed to channel individual effort in an appropriate direction. The most common formal group consists of a superior and the subordinates who report to that superior. In a manufacturing company, one such group might consist of a production manager and the six shift supervisors who report to him. In turn, the shift supervisors head work groups composed of themselves and their respective subordinates. Thus, the hierarchy of most organizations is a series of formal interlocked work groups.

Other types of formal work groups include task forces and committees. Task forces are temporary groups that are formed to achieve particular goals or to solve particular problems, such as suggesting productivity improvements. Committees are usually permanent groups that handle recurrent assignments outside of the usual work group structures. For example, a firm may have a standing committee on equal employment opportunity.

Informal Groups

It is safe to say that early writers about management and organization felt that their work was done when they had described an organization's formal groups. After all, such groups had management's seal of approval and could be illustrated in black and white on an organizational chart. What more was there to say about grouping? In fact, you probably recognize how incomplete this view is. In addition to formal groups sanctioned by management to achieve organizational goals, informal grouping occurs in all organizations. **Informal groups** are groups that emerge naturally in response to the common interests of organizational members. They are seldom sanctioned by the organization, and their membership often cuts across formal groups. Common interests that frequently promote the development of informal groups include self-defense, work assistance, and friendship.[1]

In many cases, there is indeed strength in numbers, and organizational members often develop informal groups to defend themselves against real or perceived threat or inequity. Thus, workers may band together to request a change in overtime allocation procedures, demand the reinstatement of a dismissed co-worker, or call attention to unsafe working conditions. Sometimes, informal groups emerge to assist individuals in the performance of their jobs. For example, a health teacher in a public school might seek the informal cooperation of the school nurse in developing instructional aids for his students. Finally, the most frequent common interest which leads to informal group formation in organizations is simple friendship.

The development of informal groups is a natural consequence of formal organization for work purposes. As such, there is nothing intrinsically good or bad about the existence of such groups. Informal groups formed for self-defense may prove to be a thorn in the side of an organization, but they may also point out legitimate inequities that can easily be resolved rather than left to fester. Similarly, informal alliances that assist workers in accomplishing their jobs are so common that if by magic they were suddenly dissolved it is unlikely that many organizations could function properly. Finally, informal grouping based upon simple friendship may enhance formal task cooperation and promote job satisfaction. Conversely, we have all observed situations in which co-workers were so busy being friends that they had little time to get any work accomplished.

In summary, the mere existence of informal groups tells us little about the impact of these groups on organizational functioning. As we shall see in this chapter and the next, this impact depends upon additional characteristics of the informal group in question.

FACTORS INFLUENCING GROUP FORMATION AND MAINTENANCE

What factors determine the probability that a random collection of individuals will assume and maintain the characteristics of a group? Although some tentative answers to this question have been suggested above, in this section we will explore the issue more systematically. In the case of formal groups, we are interested in the conditions which lead organizations to form such groups. In the case of informal groups, we are concerned with the factors that prompt their emergence in the formal work setting.

Opportunity For Interaction

Let's first consider informal groups. I once had a job in a very large steel mill that required me to travel throughout the plant. I noticed that a particular locomotive engineer was very friendly with the personnel who worked in a particular production unit. Since this unit did not receive rail service, I wondered how this relationship had been formed. On the other hand, in another part of the mill, I was amazed to learn that two people who worked within twenty feet of each other were barely acquainted, even though they had worked side by side for two years. What accounted for these differences in informal grouping?

Opportunity for interaction increases the probability of group formation. When people are able to interact with one another they are able to recognize that they may have common goals that can be achieved through dependence on each other. A key factor that influences opportunity for interaction is *proximity* or physical distance. Other things equal, individuals who are physically close to each other over a period of time are more likely to develop mutual attraction and form a group.[2] I finally found out how the engineer had been included in the friendship group at the production unit. There was a rail siding adjacent to the unit where the engineer would kill time between runs. Occasionally, he would saunter over to the unit coffee machine. Thus, his physical proximity to the production workers led to interaction which resulted in his being included in their informal friendship group.

Sometimes, the relationship between physical distance and interaction is overridden by what might be called *psychological distance*. That is, certain factors increase or decrease the *perceived* or *apparent* distance between coworkers, thus affecting interaction appropriately. One of these factors is *social position*. Consider a department in which secretaries and managers are situated equidistantly throughout an office complex. Their differences in social position in this setting may affect psychological distance, and it would not be surprising to see managers and secretaries develop informal groups among "their own kind." Psychological distance can also be influenced by *architectural barriers*. For example, a crucially situated opaque wall or glass barrier may decrease interaction above and beyond what could be expected on the basis of mere distance between individuals. I finally discovered why the two mill employees who worked within twenty feet of each other showed no signs of informal grouping: The work area was so noisy that interaction was nearly impossible! Again, psychological distance overruled physical distance.

Turning to formal groups, managers know that groups will only become and remain true groups if their members are able to interact to a necessary degree. Therefore, means of interaction are routinely "designed into" formal groups, most often by locating the members in close physical approximation. Organizations are also adept at using conference calls and face-to-face meetings to reduce physical or psychological distance which might exist between group members.

Potential For Goal Accomplishment

Even when individuals have ample opportunity for interaction, group relationships will fail to develop or persist if they lack the potential to facilitate goal accomplishment. The goals of groups can be divided into physical goals, intellectual goals, and social-emotional goals.

PHYSICAL GOALS. Physical goals reveal the most obvious motive for group formation and maintenance. One person acting alone simply can't build a skyscraper or put out a large fire. One side effect of using groups to accomplish physical goals is the **social facilitation effect.** This is the tendency for persons to perform simple, well-learned tasks more vigorously in the presence of others than when they are alone.[3] Thus a jackhammer operator on a road crew should cut more pavement in the presence of colleagues than when working alone. Thus, group membership may have both direct and indirect effects on goal accomplishment, the former through multiplication of effort and the latter by social facilitation.

INTELLECTUAL GOALS. The potential to accomplish intellectual goals through joint effort is also a factor in the formation of groups. Corresponding to the notion that "two heads are better than one," groups are often organized to accomplish problem-solving and decision-making tasks, such as determining political strategies, designing bridges, or judging loan applicants. In some cases, group effort is *necessary* to accomplish an intellectual goal. For example, it is impossible for one person to master the range of intellectual skills necessary to design a complex computer. In other cases, group effort may be unnecessary to achieve an intellectual goal, but may be used to provide fresh ideas or gain commitment to a chosen alternative. For instance, a good structural engineer may be able to design a workable bridge without assistance, but a design team may provide a more creative, elegant solution and convince team members of its adequacy.

SOCIAL-EMOTIONAL GOALS. The opportunity to achieve social-emotional goals also influences group formation. These are goals which are associated with needs in the middle categories of Maslow's Hierarchy—safety, belongingness, and self-esteem. The case regarding *belongingness* was presented earlier. Most people have strong needs to affiliate with others, and the formation of informal friendship groups enables them to achieve this goal.

At the *safety* level, there is plenty of evidence that group formation is likely when the environment becomes stressful or threatening.[4] This can be seen in times of natural disaster, when neighbors who never speak to each other form effective groups to rescue and shelter the unfortunate. In organizations, informal grouping in response to stress and threat can be seen in the formation of strike committees and the development of drives toward unionization. The classic example, however, is the formation of close, intimate friendship groups among military personnel during wartime.[5]

It is tempting to assume that people gravitate to groups in times of stress simply out of sheer fright. Further reflection, however, suggests more rational motives. For one thing, stressful situations are novel and confusing, and those encountering stress may be unsure of just how they should be responding—that is, what emotions are appropriate. When this occurs, affiliation with others in the same fix may provide some useful clues ("The enemy is coming over the hill at dawn, but my friends seem calm, so I'll be calm too.")[6] In addition, informal grouping in response to stress provides a social structure for actually *combatting* the source of stress. For example, employees threatened by a rumored plant closure may band together to get the facts and to lobby their congressional representative for assistance.

Another social-emotional goal which group membership may achieve is attainment of *self-esteem*. In many cases, such membership enables those who are included in the group to feel good about themselves by virtue of the group's power or prestige.

Social-emotional goals may also play a part in formal group development. For example, a bank president may insist that all loan applications over $100,000 be reviewed by a *group* of bank officers to provide a degree of psychological security in case a bad decision is made. Similarly, organizations are adept at using special titles and uniforms to enhance the self-esteem and identity of work groups. Just ask Green Berets, SWAT members, and Ranger recruits about their units.

Personal Characteristics of Members

In addition to opportunity for interaction and goal attainment, do the personal characteristics of individuals contribute to group formation and maintenance? Put another way, do "birds of a feather flock together"? Or, do "opposites attract"? We have already established that specific common interests in achieving physical, intellectual, and social-emotional goals often prompt group formation. However, a question still remains as to whether more abstract characteristics, such as attitudes and personality traits, influence grouping.

The evidence with regard to attitudes is fairly clear-cut—people tend to be attracted to those who share similar attitudes, especially when these attitudes are relevant to the social setting in which they meet.[7] Thus, just as liberals and conservatives are attracted to "their own kind," workers who are dissatisfied with their jobs may be attracted to each other and prefer to work together.

The evidence regarding personality traits and group formation is more complex. First, as with attitudes, there is some support for the similarity hypothesis.[8] Thus, salespeople who are high need achievers may be especially interested in interacting with similar others. However, in the domain of personality there is also evidence that opposites attract.[9] For example, dominant individuals may seek the company of submissive individuals and vice versa.

Attitudes and personality traits may also be relevant to the formation and maintenance of formal groups. Managers often use judgments about personality or attitudes to assign similar members to particular groups on the assumption that compatibility will exist. Of course, groups may also be staffed to take advantage of *differences* in attitudes and personality among members. Consider a task force formed by a company to investigate the development of new products. The chairperson may seek a tight-fisted, practical accountant to offset an impulsive, creative marketing representative. The skills of one are expected to complement those of the other.

GROUP STRUCTURE AND ITS CONSEQUENCES

As a member of at least several groups, you are no doubt aware that groups frequently seem to differ from one another. The differences that are most obvious may include the way members interact with one another, how members feel about the group, and how the group performs. It is often possible to trace these differences in interaction, feelings, and performance back to how the group is organized.

Group structure refers to the characteristics of the stable social organization of groups. As such, it refers to the way a group "looks" to a behavioral scientist or the way the group is "put together." The most basic structural characteristic along which groups vary is size. Other structural characteristics involve the expectations members have about each other's behavior (norms), agreements about "who does what" in the group (roles), the rewards and prestige allocated to various group members (status), and how attractive the group is to its members (cohesiveness).

Group Size

Of one thing we can be certain—the smallest possible group consists of two persons, such as that made up of a superior and a particular subordinate. It is possible to engage in a lot of theoretical nit-picking about just what constitutes an upper limit on group size. However, given the definition of *group* presented earlier, it would seem that congressional or parliamentary size (three to four hundred members) is somewhere close to this limit. In practice, most work groups, including task forces and committees, usually have between three and twenty members.

SIZE AND PARTICIPATION.   As group size increases, the time available for verbal participation by each member decreases. (See the cartoon for an example!) For example, assuming equal participation, a two-person task force that meets for one hour allows each member one half hour of input. If this task force were composed of four members, each would only have fifteen minutes of input. This analysis assumes ideal conditions. In fact, as groups get larger, time for participation is lessened even more by the sheer mechanics of deciding "who should participate when about what." In addition, there is evidence that *inhibition* regarding participation increases among many group members as group size increases.[10] As you may know, popular surveys show that fears about speaking in front of groups frequently top the fear list. Thus, the assumption of equal participation becomes less valid as group size gets bigger.

SIZE AND SATISFACTION.   The more the merrier? In theory, yes. On an informal level, larger groups provide more opportunities for members to encounter friends who share their attitudes or meet their social needs. For example, in a three-person work group, each member is confronted with two friendship possibilities, while in a seven-person work group six such possibilities exist. In fact, however, members of larger groups rather consistently report less satisfaction with group membership than those who find themselves in smaller groups.[11] What accounts for this apparent contradiction?

For one thing, as opportunities for friendship increase, the chance to work on and develop these opportunities may decrease due to the sheer time and energy

"I believe the gentleman over there had his hand up first."

Drawing by Richter; © 1978 The New Yorker Magazine, Inc. Reprinted by permission.

required. In addition, larger groups, in incorporating more members with different viewpoints, may prompt conflict and dissension which work against member satisfaction. Turning to formal task requirements, we have already pointed out that participation decreases with size. To the extent that such participation is valued, dissatisfaction should again be the outcome. Finally, in larger groups, individual members can identify less easily with the success and accomplishments of the group. For example, a particular member of a four-person cancer research team should be able to identify *his* or *her* contributions to a research breakthrough more easily than can a member of a twenty-person team.

SIZE AND PERFORMANCE. Participation and satisfaction aside, do large groups perform tasks better than small groups? This question has great relevance to practical organizational decisions: How many people should a bank assign to evaluate loan applications? How many carpenters should a construction company assign to build a garage? If a school system decides to implement team teaching, how big should the teams be? The answers to these and similar questions depend upon the exact task to be accomplished and upon just what we mean by good performance.[12]

Some tasks are **additive tasks.** This means that potential performance can be predicted by adding the performances of individual group members together. For example, moving a heavy stone is an additive task, and the potential productivity of a group of laborers can be estimated by summing the forces which they are able to exert. Similarly, building a garage is an additive task, and potential speed of construction can be estimated by adding the efforts of individual carpenters. Thus, for additive tasks, the potential performance of the group increases with group size.

Some tasks are **disjunctive.** This means that the potential performance of the group depends on the performance of its *best member*. For example, suppose that a research team is looking for a single error in a complicated computer program. In this case, the performance of the team may hinge upon its containing at least one bright, attentive, logical individual. Obviously, the potential performance of groups doing disjunctive tasks also increases with group size, because the probability that the group includes a superior performer is greater.

The term "potential performance" is used consistently in the preceding two paragraphs for the following reason: As groups performing tasks get bigger, they tend to suffer from *process losses*.[13] Process losses involve performance difficulties that stem from the problems of organizing and coordinating larger groups. For one thing, in larger groups, members may feel more anonymous and less responsible. In this case, they may feel more freedom to "goof off" and "let Joe do it." Also, even with good intentions, problems of communication and decision making increase with size—imagine fifty carpenters trying to build a house. Thus, actual performance = potential performance − process losses. These points are summarized in Exhibit 8-1. As you can see in part (a), both potential performance and process losses increase with group size for additive and disjunctive tasks. The net effect is shown in part (b), which demonstrates that actual performance increases with size up to a point and then falls off. Part (c) shows that the *average* performance of group members decreases as size gets bigger. Thus, up to a point, larger groups may perform better as groups, but their individual members should be less efficient.

One other kind of task should be noted. **Conjunctive tasks** are those where the performance of the group is limited by its *poorest performer*. For example, an assembly line operation is limited by its weakest link. Also, if team teaching is employed to train workers how to perform a complicated, sequential job, one poor teacher in the sequence will severely damage the effectiveness of the team. Both the potential and actual performance of conjunctive tasks should decrease as group size increases, because the probability of including a weak link in the group goes up.

In summary, for additive and disjunctive tasks, larger groups may perform better up to a point, but at increasing costs to the efficiency of individual members. By any standard, performance on purely conjunctive tasks should decrease as group size increases. At Triton Computers, Max Bart feared the negative impact of increasing group size.

EXHIBIT 8-1   **Relationships among group size, productivity, and process losses.**

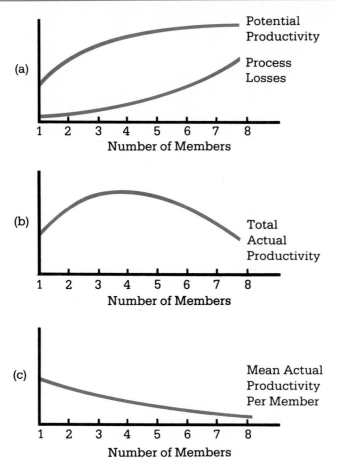

Source: From Steiner, I. D. (1972). *Group process and productivity.* New York: Academic Press, p. 96. Copyright © 1972, by Academic Press, Inc.

Group Norms

Social **norms** are expectations that members of social units have regarding the behavior of others. As such, they are codes of conduct that specify what ought and ought not to be done or standards against which the appropriateness of behavior is evaluated. Some norms are supported by society as a whole ("Thou shalt not kill"), while others are peculiar to particular portions of society (e.g., the white middle class) or to individual small groups (e.g., the billing office staff at XYZ Company).

It is impossible to overestimate the pervasiveness with which norms regulate our behavior. Many habits that we have acquired, such as brushing our teeth x times a day, are in fact the product of socal norms. As this example indicates, much normative influence is unconscious, and we are often only aware of such influence in special circumstances, such as when we see children struggling to master adult norms or foreigners sparring with the norms of our culture. We also become conscious of norms when we encounter ones that seem to conflict ("Get ahead," but "Don't step on others") or when we enter new social situations. For instance, the first day on a new job, workers frequently search for cues about what is considered proper office etiquette: Should I call the boss "mister"? Can I smoke in the presence of clients?

NORM DEVELOPMENT.   *Why* do norms develop? The most important function served by norms is to provide regularity and predictability to behavior. This consistency provides important psychological security and permits us to carry out our daily business with minimal disruption.

What do norms develop *about*? Norms are developed to regulate behaviors that are considered at least marginally important to their supporters. For example, managers are more likely to adopt norms regarding the performance and attendance of subordinates than norms concerning how offices are personalized and decorated. In general, less deviation is accepted from norms that concern more important behaviors. Stealing from a co-worker's locker will probably result in ostracism, while failing to assist her on the job may not. Some norms involve behaviors that are considered so important that they are stated as formal rules and/or backed by laws which specify penalties for violation. For example, the law specifies strict penalties for violating the "thou shalt not kill" norm. However, formal rules and laws should not be confused with social norms. Alcohol prohibition and the 55 mile-an-hour speed limit are examples of laws that have had little normative support among the public.

How do norms develop? In short, a norm develops from the shared attitudes of at least some of its supporters (Exhibit 8-2).[14] As we discussed in Chapter 5, individuals develop attitudes as a function of a related belief and value. In many cases, their attitudes affect their behavior. When the members of a group *share* related beliefs and values we can expect them to share consequent attitudes. These shared attitudes then form the basis for norms. For example, the sequence for a work group performing under piecerate might go something like this:

"If we produce too much, management will cut the pay rate." *(Shared belief)*
"Economic loss is bad." *(Shared value)*
"Therefore, high production is bad." *(Shared attitude)*
"We should limit productivity." *(Norm)*
Productivity is limited. *(Behavior)*

Recall that individuals can hold personal, idiosyncratic attitudes toward some person or activity. On the other hand, it really doesn't make sense to talk about "my personal norm." Norms are *collectively* held expectations, depending upon

---

EXHIBIT 8-2   **Individual attitude development and social norm development.**

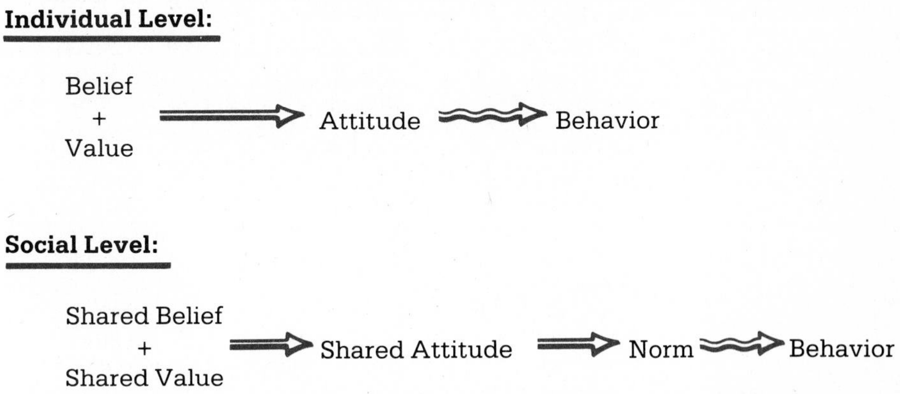

Individual Level:

Belief
+   =====⟹ Attitude ⟿ Behavior
Value

Social Level:

Shared Belief
+   =====⟹ Shared Attitude =====⟹ Norm ⟿ Behavior
Shared Value

---

two or more people for their existence. However, norms can be targeted at a single individual. For example, work groups frequently develop agreed-upon expectations about how their bosses should behave.

Why do individuals tend to comply with norms? Much compliance occurs simply because the norm corresponds to privately held attitudes. This is the case with true supporters of the norm. In addition, even when norms support trivial social niceties (such as when to shake hands or when to look serious), they often save time and prevent social confusion. Most interesting, however, is the case in which individuals comply with norms that *go against* their privately held attitudes and opinions (see In–Focus 8-1). For example, couples without religious convictions frequently get married in religious services, and male workers who hate neckties often wear them to work. In short, groups have an extraordinary range of rewards and punishments available to induce conformity to norms. In the next chapter, we will examine the process of conformity in detail.

SOME TYPICAL NORMS.   Specifying a typical list of organizational norms is something like trying to describe the typical pattern of snowflakes. In an organization of any size, an incredibly complex pattern of norms may exist across formal groups, informal groups, and levels in the hierarchy. Nevertheless, there are some classes of norms that seem to crop up in most organizations to affect the behavior of members. They include the following:

- *Loyalty norms.* Groups and organizations frequently attempt to exact a strong degree of commitment and loyalty from their members. In the military, these norms are formalized with specific sanctions to be applied to traitors and deserters. In most other cases, loyalty norms tend to be informal. Managers frequently perceive that they must work late, come in on weekends, and

IN–FOCUS 8-1 COCKPIT NORMS THREATEN AIR SAFETY

In 1982, subsequent to an accident in which an aircraft struck a bridge shortly after takeoff and crashed into the Potomac River, the National Transportation Safety Board ruled that the captain of that aircraft did not react to the copilot's repeated, subtle advisories that all was not normal during the takeoff. Moreover, in recommending that pilot training include "considerations for command decision, resource management, role performance, and assertiveness," the Board implied that the copilot's lack of assertiveness (possibly induced by the inherent role structure of the cockpit) may have been a causal factor.

Apparently, the reluctance to question captains or assume control is not an isolated problem. In an investigation conducted by Harper, Kidera, and Cullen at a major air carrier, captains feigned subtle incapacitation at a predetermined point during final approach in simulator trials characterized by poor weather and visibility. In that study, approximately 25% of these simulated flights "hit the ground" because, for some reason, the first officers did not take control.

Much of the normative structure of professional pilots is well established, having evolved during a time when aviation was not routine and the dangers of flight were considerable. These conditions fostered, largely through self-selection processes, a pilot profile that has been characterized by Tom Wolfe as "the right stuff." An individual who typifies the right stuff is generally described as a highly goal-oriented, extremely self-reliant, macho, decisive person.

Despite the fact that the aviation environment has changed considerably, these norms are ubiquitous, and an attempt is being made to alter the normative structure of the flightcrew in some training programs. One method employed in an effort to correct certain ineffective task performance strategies is the use of videotape feedback and diagnosis of task-specific behaviors. In one program, crews are asked to fly a full-mission simulation that is videotaped from start to finish. Following these simulated flights, crewmembers view the tape with an instructor and discuss such aspects of the group process as the effects of interpersonal styles, the appropriate delegation of responsibility, and how the role structure can inhibit the input of subordinate flight crewmembers.

In the United States, the labor pool is weighted heavily with pilots whose formative years were spent in high-performance, single-seat, military aircraft. It has been suggested that pilots with this type of experience may bring an individualistic emphasis to the air carrier cockpit and that learning team member skills can only be accomplished slowly and painfully. One obvious solution would be the selection of individuals for the position of airline pilot who possess the skills associated with good leadership or team function.

By changing the norms of the group and reinforcing the importance of coordinated performance, the malady some refer to as "captainitis" may begin to subside, and subordinate crewmembers may find it easier to have sufficient input into the group process.

Source: Abridged from Foushee, H. C. (1984). Dyads and triads at 35,000 feet. *American Psychologist, 39,* 885–893. Reprinted by permission.

accept transfers to other cities in order to prove their loyalty to the company and to their peers.[15] Despite official policy, police officers may refuse to "squeal" on fellow officers who commit brutality or accept favors.

- *Dress norms.* Social norms frequently dictate the kind of clothing worn to work. Again, formal norms tend to be invoked by military and quasi-military organizations, which support polished buttons and razor-edged creases. Of course, sometimes normative expectations from above confront informal counternorms from below. A certain pub popular with university students required its waiters to wear ties. They did so—usually with jeans and hunting shirts! Even when there are no dress codes, social norms are remarkably effective in dictating who should wear what on the job:

  Managers of whatever sex were likely to present a tailored, conservative appearance. . . . (Nonmanagers), on the other hand, were likely to be dressed much less "professionally." "You can tell the professional women from the secretaries by their shoes," one person reported. "The professionals wear pumps; the secretaries wear four-inch wedgies."[16]

- *Reward allocation norms.* There are at least four norms that might dictate how rewards such as pay, promotions, and informal favors could be allocated in organizations:

  —Equity—reward according to inputs such as effort, performance, or seniority
  —Equality—reward everyone equally
  —Reciprocity—reward people the way they reward you
  —Social responsibility—reward those who truly need the reward[17]

  Officially, of course, most organizations tend to stress allocation according to some combination of equity and equality norms—give employees what they deserve, but no favoritism. However, further normative forces may come into play in reward allocation. In the last chapter it was mentioned that managers often equalize pay increases awarded to subordinates under merit pay plans. In this case, equality subverts equity. If overtime is awarded according to seniority (equity) or randomly (equality), a work group may invoke a social responsibility norm to insist that a financially needy co-worker be given special consideration. Finally, the reciprocity norm is frequently invoked, especially among managers. Those who rise in rank may feel they owe special favors to those who sponsored their progress.

- *Performance norms.* The performance of organizational members may be as much a function of social expectations as it is of inherent ability, personal motivation, or technology.[18] Work groups provide their members with potent cues about what is judged to be an appropriate level of performance, and new group members are alert for these cues: Is it OK to take a break now? Under what circumstances can I be absent from work without being punished? Of course, the official organizational norms sent to subordinates by managers usually favor high performance. However, work groups often establish their own informal performance norms, such as those that restrict productivity under a piecerate pay system (Chapter 7).[19]

In the early days of Triton Computers, obvious norms included dressing casually, working long hours, and helping others with their projects.

Roles

In addition to size and norms, roles constitute another characteristic of group structure. **Roles** are positions in a group that have attached to them a set of expected behaviors. Thus, in a sense, roles represent "packages" of norms that apply to particular group members. As implied in the previous section, many norms apply to all group members in order to be sure that they engage in *similar* behaviors (such as restricting productivity or dressing a certain way). However, the development of roles is indicative of the fact that group members may also be required to act *differently* from one another. For example, in a committee meeting, not every member is required to function as a secretary or a chairperson, and these become specific roles fulfilled by particular people.

In organizations, we find two basic kinds of roles. First, we can identify designated or **assigned roles.** These are roles formally prescribed by an organization as a means of dividing labor and responsibility. In general, assigned roles indicate "who does what" and "who can tell others what to do." In a manufacturing organization, labels that might be applied to formal roles include president, engineer, machinist, manager, and subordinate. In a university, such labels might include department chairperson, professor, and student. In addition to assigned roles, we invariably see the development of **emergent roles.** These are roles that develop naturally to meet the social-emotional needs of group members or to assist in formal job accomplishment. The class clown and the office gossip fulfill emergent social-emotional roles, while an "old pro" may emerge to assist new group members learn their jobs. Other emergent roles may be assumed by informal leaders or scapegoats who are the targets of group hostility.

ROLE ASSUMPTION.   The assumption of roles may be particularly easy or excruciatingly difficult. Let's first consider the ease of role assumption. Over time, many social experiences are designed to prepare individuals to assume subsequent roles. In all cultures, children gradually undergo a series of social experiences (e.g., part-time jobs and increasingly later curfews) designed to ease their transition into the adult role. When such experiences are unavailable, role assumption is much more difficult. For example, teenagers are usually ill-prepared for the parenthood role.

The assumption of assigned roles in organizations is also carefully managed. Twenty-five-year-old M.B.A. graduates are not expected to assume the role of company vice-president. Rather, they may be carefully groomed by the organization for many years, experiencing a series of intermediate roles before getting a chance at the "big one." Similarly, raw recruits learn to assume the role of master electrician through a lengthy apprenticeship. When such individuals finally achieve these work roles, they look like naturals.

On the other hand, individuals may encounter difficulties in the assumption of roles. In this regard, it is instructive to contrast real-life roles with those played by actors in films and plays. Peter Sellers excepted, actors are fortunate in that they usually only act one role at a time. The real world is a lot more complicated, because we must simultaneously fulfill the requirements of a number of roles. For example, most managerial role incumbents must also fulfill a subordinate role vis-à-vis their bosses. In addition, actors are fortunate to have a script and an attentive director. As we shall see, some organizational roles lack a clear script and careful direction. Finally, actors can reject roles that don't suit their personalities or career plans. This option may be less likely for many organizational roles. Now, let's consider these matters more systematically.

ROLE AMBIGUITY.   **Role ambiguity** exists when the goals of one's job or the methods of performing it are unclear. Ambiguity may be characterized by confusion about how performance is evaluated, how good performance can be achieved, or what the limits of one's authority and responsibility are.

Exhibit 8-3 shows a model of the process involved in assuming an organizational role. As you can see, certain organizational factors lead role senders (such as managers) to develop role expectations and "send" roles to focal persons (such as subordinates). Presumably, the focal person "receives" the role and then tries to engage in behavior to fulfill the role. Attributes of the focal person (such as personality traits) and interpersonal factors (such as how well the sender and receiver get along) may influence how the role is developed, sent, received, and translated into behavior.

In portraying the complexity of the role assumption process, this model reveals a variety of elements that can lead to ambiguity:

- *Organizational factors.* Some roles seem inherently ambiguous because of their function in the organization. For example, middle management roles may fail to provide the "big picture" that upper management roles do or do not require the attention to supervision necessary in lower management roles. Thus, two factors that can contribute to role clarity are absent. Similarly, staff specialists who have the role of advising managers or generating information may find their jobs unclear. The theoretical physicist charged by a communications firm to "generate new knowledge" may feel uncertain about the direction her work should take or the criteria that will be used to evaluate its worth.

- *The role sender.* Role senders may have unclear expectations of a focal person. A male sales manager who obtains his first female salesperson may vacillate about her exact role requirements—should he expect her to have dinner with male customers and "go out with the boys" after sales meetings? Even when the sender has specific role expectations, they may be ineffectively sent to

EXHIBIT 8-3   **A model of the role assumption process.**

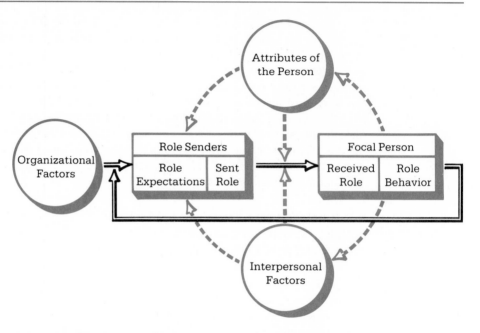

Source: From Katz, D., et al. (1966, 1978). *The social psychology of organizations.* New York: Wiley, p. 196. Copyright © 1966, 1978, by John Wiley & Sons, Inc. Reprinted by permission.

the focal person. A weak orientation session, vague performance reviews, or inconsistent feedback and discipline may send ambiguous role messages to subordinates.

■ *The focal person.* Even role expectations that are clearly developed and sent may not be fully digested by the focal person. This is especially true when he or she is new to the role. Ambiguity tends to decrease as length of time in the job role increases.[20]

What are the practical consequences of role ambiguity? The most frequent outcomes appear to be job dissatisfaction, reduced organizational commitment, tension, anxiety, and intentions to quit.[21] In fact, you will recall that at Triton Computers, several employees found the ambiguity of the unstructured roles not to their liking and quit. It must be emphasized, however, that few workers would prefer a perfectly clear role stemming from repetitive job duties, close supervision, and a myriad of rules and regulations. Rather, it is probably *unnecessary* ambiguity stemming from the role sender which causes the most problems. Finally, some individuals cope with ambiguity better than others. For example, one study of military and civil service personnel found that high need achievers were more likely than low need achievers to respond with dissatisfaction to role ambiguity.[22]

ROLE CONFLICT. **Role conflict** exists when an individual is faced with incompatible role expectations. Conflict can be distinguished from ambiguity in that role expectations may be crystal clear but incompatible in the sense that they are mutually exclusive, can't be fulfilled simultaneously, or don't suit the role occupant. However, some forms of conflict are associated with ambiguity (see In–Focus 8-2). Since expectations can be incompatible for various reasons, it is useful to distinguish among several forms of role conflict:

■ **Intra-sender role conflict** occurs when a single role sender provides incompatible role expectations to the role occupant. For example, a manager may tell a subordinate to take it easy and not work so hard while delivering yet another batch of reports that requires immediate attention. This form of role conflict seems especially likely to also provoke ambiguity.

■ If two or more role senders differ in their expectations for a role occupant, **inter-sender role conflict** may develop. Boundary role occupants who straddle the boundary between the organization and its clients or customers are especially likely to encounter this form of conflict. Salespeople, police officers, and teachers may face very different sets of demands from those inside and those outside of the organization. For example, a school principal may insist that teachers treat children equally, while a parent may insist on special treatment for his Sally. Inter-sender conflict can also stem exclusively from within the organization. The classic example here is the first-level supervisor, who serves as the interface between "management" and "the workers." From above, the supervisor may be pressured to get the work out and keep the troops in line. From below, he or she may be encouraged to behave in a considerate and friendly manner. Finally, inter-sender role conflict can stem exclusively from senders outside of the organization. A police chief may have to contend with community groups that desire law and order and those which assert that police officers exercise too much power.

■ Especially if we include roles external to the organization, organizational members necessarily play several roles at the same time. Often, the expectations inherent in these several roles are incompatible, and **inter-role conflict** results.[23] One person, for example, might fulfill the roles of a functional expert in marketing, head of the market research group, subordinate to the vice-president of marketing, and member of a product development task force. As a member of the task force, this individual might have to contribute to plans that go against the best interests of her research group. To complicate matters, she also fulfills a number of roles outside of the organization, including wife, mother, daughter, daughter-in-law, and so on. This is obviously a busy person, and competing demands for *time* are a frequent symptom of inter-role conflict.

■ Even when role demands are clear and otherwise congruent, they may be incompatible with the personality or skills of the role occupant—thus, **person-role conflict.**[24] As shown in Exhibit 8-3, the received role must be converted into adequate role behavior, and some individuals may simply be unwilling or unable to effect this conversion. It is reasonable to assume that much person-role conflict is precluded by self-selection. That is, people will normally try to avoid assuming roles with which they are personally incompatible. However, an employee may still end up in a role for which he or she is unsuited. At Triton Computers, you will recall that computer designer Wayne Griggs experienced person-role conflict when he was required to work as production manager.

As with role ambiguity, the most consistent consequences of role conflict are dissatisfaction, stress reactions, lowered organizational commitment, and turnover intentions.[25]

Status

One janitor to another:

> You should see the executive bathrooms on my end of the building! Amazing! Marble sinks, gold-plated spigots, thick carpeting, shoe shine machines, bottles of cologne. Wanna dry your hands? They got a choice of hot air, regular towels, or paper towels. That's class! Always nice and tidy, not like the locker room where *you* work.

Status is the rank, or social position, or prestige accorded to group members. Put another way, it represents the group's *evaluation* of a member. Just *what* is evaluated depends on the status system in question. However, when a status system works smoothly, the group will exhibit clear norms about who should be awarded more or less status.

The above example illustrates three curiosities about status. First, status, like beauty, is in the eye of the beholder. Secondly, we often obtain our own status from a connection (however removed) with those who have more. Finally, we are extremely adept at detecting (or inventing) differences in status when they can benefit us. However, as we shall see, status is not one person's fantasy. Rather, it is another characteristic of *social* structure which depends upon some degree of agreement among group members about who has it and who doesn't.

FORMAL STATUS SYSTEMS.   All organizations have both formal and informal status systems. Since formal systems are most obvious to observers, let's begin there. The **formal status system** represents management's attempt to publicly identify those persons who have more status than others. It is so obvious because this identification is implemented by the application of **status symbols** which are tangible indicators of status. As shown in Exhibit 8-4, status symbols may include titles, particular working relationships, the pay package, the work schedule, and the physical working environment. Just what are the criteria for achieving formal

---

EXHIBIT 8-4   **Some status symbols of the formal status system.**

Titles

   Director
   Manager
   Chief
   Head
   Senior

Relationships

   Work for an important individual
   Job requires you to work with high-ranking organizational members
   Work in a critical group or on an important assignment

Pay and Fringe Benefits

   Expense account
   Liberal travel opportunities
   Reserved parking space with your name on it
   Company-paid car
   Key to executive washroom

Work Schedule

   Day work rather than evening or shift
   Freedom from punching a time clock
   Freedom to come and go as one pleases

Work Location

   Large office
   Large desk with high-back chair
   Low noise level
   Protected from easy access by several secretaries

Source: Robbins, S. P. (1979). *Organizational behavior: Concepts and controversies.* Englewood Cliffs, NJ: Prentice-Hall, p. 187. © 1979. Reprinted by permission of Prentice-Hall, Inc., Englewood Cliffs, N.J.

---

organizational status? One criterion is often seniority in one's work group. Employees who have been with the group longer may acquire the privilege of choosing steady daylight work or a more favorable office location. Even more important than seniority, however, is one's assigned role in the organization, one's job. Because they perform different jobs, secretaries, laborers, supervisors, and executives acquire different statuses. Organizations often go to great pains to ensure that status symbols are appropriately tied to assigned roles, as this description of telephone allocation at Western Electric indicates:

> As the junior manager moves up through the ranks, he will usually first have a Touch-Tone desk set. He will then progressively move up to a colored Touch-Tone desk set, a Touch-Tone set with a "hands free" device, a Touch-Tone telephone with a set of programmed cards to insert that dial the desired number; an electronic preset dialing system requiring only the touch of one button to dial a specific number; and—for the president and executive vice-presidents—a Picturephone.[26]

Why do organizations go to all this trouble to differentiate status? For one thing, status and the symbols connected to it serve as powerful magnets to induce members to aspire to higher organizational positions (recall Maslow's need for esteem). Secondly, status differentiation reinforces the authority hierarchy in work groups and in the organization as a whole, since people *pay attention* to high status individuals. At Triton Computers, Max Bart's suits and private office served as a symbol of his growing status to both Triton employees and outsiders.

The differences in formal status that exist within organizations usually carry over to the evaluation of the status of occupations by the public at large. Thus, doctors have more prestige than nurses in the community, just as they do in the hospital. Exhibit 8-5 summarizes ratings of occupational prestige obtained from a number of cross-national surveys. In general, surveys of this nature show remarkable stability over time and good agreement across various societies. In addition, people who themselves differ in status tend to agree very closely in their ratings of the prestige of various occupations.[27] Thus, status judgments of the public at large are influenced by some of the same factors that indirectly lead to formal status differences in organizations—the skill, training, and education of the persons being judged.

INFORMAL STATUS SYSTEMS.   In addition to formal status systems, we can detect **informal status systems** in organizations. Such systems are not well advertised, and they may lack the conspicuous symbols and systematic support usually accorded to the formal system. Nevertheless, they can operate just as effectively. Sometimes, job performance may be a basis for the acquisition of informal status. The "power hitters" on a baseball team or the "cool heads" in a hospital emergency unit may be highly evaluated by co-workers for their ability to assist in task accomplishment. Some managers who perform well early in their careers are identified as "fast trackers" and given special job assignments that correspond to their elevated status. Just as frequently, though, informal status is linked to factors other than job performance. Blacks and women may be accorded

EXHIBIT 8-5   **Standard prestige scores for various occupations.**

78 College and university teachers; physicians
72 Architects; lawyers
70 Dentists
69 Chemists
67 Bank officers and financial managers
66 Psychologists; airplane pilots; chemical and mechanical engineers
63 Controllers and treasurers
62 Accountants
60 Clergymen; economists
57 Elementary school teachers
56 Stock and bond salesmen; painters and sculptors
55 Office managers; draftsmen
54 Librarians; registered nurses
52 Sales managers (non-retail); actors
51 Computer programmers
50 Radio and television announcers; airline stewardesses
49 Real estate agents and brokers
48 Bank tellers
45 Musicians and composers
44 Insurance agents, brokers, and underwriters
43 Automobile mechanics
40 Farmers; policemen and detectives
39 Foremen
38 Receptionists
37 Air traffic controllers
34 Funeral directors
33 Mail carriers; truck drivers
31 File clerks
23 Bartenders; waiters
22 Garage workers and gas station attendants
14 Newsboys
13 Garbage collectors

Note: Scores can range from 92 to −2. They are derived from studies of occupational prestige carried out in many countries around the world and applied to the 1970 U.S. Census Detailed Occupational Classifications. This is why some labels are sex-typed.

Source: From Donald J. Treiman, *Occupational prestige in comparative perspective,* pp. 306–315. Copyright © 1977 by Academic Press, Inc. Reprinted by permission.

low status in spite of good performance. Also, some jobs may be informally perceived as glamor jobs, elevating the status of their occupants. In an industrial supply firm these may be sales positions, and in a high technology firm they may be engineering positions. Of course reality may follow fiction as employees are promoted into management positions from these glamor jobs and accorded *formal* status. Finally, even the most apparently irrelevant nonwork associations may contribute to informal status on the job. Consider this interaction among three machine operators:

The "professor theme" was the cream of verbal interaction. It involved George's connection with higher learning. His daughter had married the son of a professor who instructed in one of the local colleges. The professor theme was not in the strictest sense a conversation piece. When the subject came up, George did all the talking. The two Jewish operators remained silent as they listened with deep respect, if not actual awe, to George's accounts. . . . I came to the conclusion that it was the professor connection . . . which provided the fount of George's superior status in the group.[28]

As we said earlier, status is in the eye of the beholder!

CONSEQUENCES OF STATUS.   What are the consequences of status differences in groups and organizations? One of the most obvious is the manner in which individuals who differ in status address each other.[29] Social units develop clear norms about such matters, and the violation of these norms can lead to considerable confusion and embarrassment. Mr. Jennings, the president of a large firm, may address his secretary as "Marie," but Ms. Garcia must address him as "Mr. Jennings," not "Bob." Of course, such norms depend upon the social setting. A doctor and nurse who are well acquainted may use first names when alone, but the nurse may revert to the title "Doctor" when others are present.

Status affects communication in ways other than form of address. For one thing, most persons desire to communicate with those at their own status level or higher, rather than those below them.[30] The result is a tendency for communication to move up the status hierarchy. Thus, people at each level of a group's status hierarchy could be expected to direct more comments toward their peers and "betters" than would be directed downward. Why does this occur? Perhaps equals and those of higher status are perceived as attractive, and if they are not seen as attractive they are perceived as powerful. In either case, we may try to enhance our *own* status by interacting with them. (Recall George and "the professor," and observe the popularity of the star on a Little League team).

Status also affects the *amount* of communication engaged in by various group members and their influence in group affairs. As you might guess, higher status members do more talking and have more influence.[31] Some of the most convincing evidence comes from studies of jury deliberations, in which jurors with higher social status (such as managers and professionals) participate more and have more effect on the verdict.[32] Thus, if the plant superintendent, the production manager, and a production supervisor make the rounds on an assembly line, we can offer a pretty good guess about who will do the most talking. The relationship of status to amount of communication and influence probably stems from several factors. First, since high status members are *targets* of a lot of communication, they have a disproportionate opportunity to respond. Secondly, high-status group members may be perceived as more knowledgeable about the issue at hand (even if they aren't). Also, awareness of one's high status may promote self-confidence and assertiveness, leading one to contribute ideas more forcefully.

Finally, who should conform more readily to group norms, high status members or low status members? In the next chapter we shall consider this important issue.

GROUP COHESIVENESS

You will recall from the story that began the chapter that the founders of Triton Computers worked in the early days as a closely knit team. That is a casual description of a characteristic known more formally as **group cohesiveness.** Cohesive groups are those that are especially attractive to their members. Because of this attractiveness, members are especially desirous of staying in the group, and tend to describe the group in favorable terms.

The arch-stereotype of a cohesive group is the major league baseball team that begins September looking like a good bet to win its division and get into the World Series. On the field we see well-oiled, precision teamwork. In the clubhouse, all is sweetness and joviality, and interviewed players tell the world how fine it is to be playing with "a great bunch of guys."

Two initial points about cohesiveness are worth noting. First, cohesiveness is a relative, rather than absolute, property of groups. While some groups are more cohesive than others, there is no objective line between cohesive and noncohesive groups. Thus, we will use the adjective *cohesive* to refer to groups that are more attractive than average for their members. Secondly, cohesiveness is an informal, emergent group process. However, the manager who clearly understands why cohesiveness occurs may be able to affect the extent to which it develops in a work unit.

Factors Influencing Cohesiveness

What makes some groups more cohesive than others? There is probably no single factor that will make a particular group highly cohesive. Rather, a number of factors in combination contribute to cohesiveness.

THREAT AND COMPETITION.   Earlier we pointed out that groups often form to accomplish social-emotional goals. Thus, any factor which increases the importance of these goals for the group should promote cohesiveness. External threat to the survival of the group has been shown to increase cohesiveness in a wide variety of situations.[33] In this case, the social-emotional goal of *safety* is accentuated. As an example, consider the wrangling, uncoordinated corporate board of directors that quickly forms a united front in the face of a takeover bid. Honest competition with another group can also promote cohesiveness.[34] In this case, the social-emotional goal of *self-esteem* is on the line for the groups in question. Obviously, this is the case with the World Series contenders mentioned earlier.

Why do groups often become more cohesive in response to threat or competition? They probably feel a need to improve communication and coordination, so that they can better cope with the situation at hand. The group is now perceived as more attractive because it is seen as capable of doing what has to be done to ward off threat or to win. There are, of course, limits to this. Under *extreme* threat or very *unbalanced* competition, increased cohesiveness will serve little purpose. For example, the partners in a firm faced with certain financial disaster would be unlikely to exhibit cohesiveness because it would do nothing to combat the severe threat.

SUCCESS.   It should come as no surprise that a group becomes more attractive to its members when it has successfully accomplished some important goal, such as defending itself against threat or winning a prize.[35] By the same token, cohesiveness should decrease after failure, although there may be "misery loves company" exceptions. The situation for competition is shown graphically in Exhibit 8-6. Fit-Rite Jeans owns two small clothing stores (A and B) in a large city. In order to boost sales, it holds a contest between the two stores, offering $150 worth of merchandise to each employee of the store achieving the highest sales during the next business quarter. Before the competition begins, the staffs of the two stores are equally cohesive. As suggested above, as the competition begins, both groups become more cohesive. The members become more cooperative with each other, and in each store there is much talk about "we" versus "them." At the end of the quarter, store A wins the prize and becomes yet more cohesive. The group is especially attractive to its members because it has succeeded in the attainment of a desired goal. On the other hand, cohesiveness plummets in losing store B— the group has become less attractive to its members.

In general, the accomplishment of any goal that the group feels is important should facilitate cohesiveness—even if the goal is only having fun or establishing a friendly work atmosphere.

EXHIBIT 8-6   Competition, success, and cohesiveness.

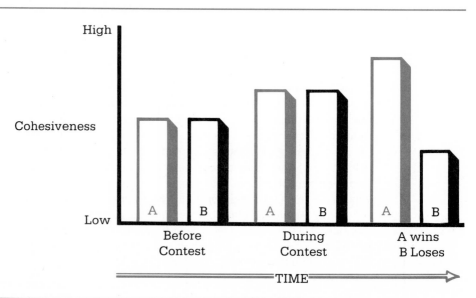

SIMILARITY OF MEMBERS.   Earlier it was pointed out that similarity of attitudes tends to increase the attraction between individuals and thus promotes group formation. A logical extension of this would suggest that similarity of attitudes among group members would increase cohesiveness and that, furthermore, similar background characterisics such as race, age, and education might do the same. In fact, this appears to be true when the group's primary goal is that of creating a friendly interpersonal climate. However, if the group is especially interested in accomplishing some particular task, its success in performing the task will usually outweigh member similarity in determining cohesiveness.[36] For example, one study found no relationship between cohesiveness and similarity of age or education for industrial work groups.[37] Similarly, another study found that the cohesiveness of groups composed of black and white southern soldiers was dependent upon successful task accomplishment rather than racial composition.[38]

SIZE.   Other things equal, bigger groups should have a more difficult time becoming and staying cohesive. In general, such groups should have a more difficult time agreeing on goals and more problems communicating and coordinating effort to achieve these goals. Earlier it was pointed out that large groups frequently divide into subgroups. Clearly, such subgrouping is contrary to the cohesiveness of the larger group. There is, however, a potential exception to this rule. A larger group may exhibit high cohesiveness if its very size aids in goal accomplishment. For example, a large coalition of dissatisfied workers may threaten a wildcat strike if its demands are not met. In this case, size may promote cohesiveness because it enhances chances for success.

TOUGHNESS OF INITIATION.   Despite its rigorous admissions policies, the Harvard Business School doesn't lack applicants. Similarly, exclusive yacht and golf clubs may have waiting lists for membership extending several years into the future. All of this suggests that groups that are tough to get into should be more attractive than those that are easy to join. Indeed, one study of university fraternities showed that those that had more rigorous "hazing" practices for potential members tended to be more cohesive.[39] This effect is well known in the military, where rigorous physical training and stressful "survival schools" may precede entry into elite units such as the Special Forces or the Rangers. Of course, there may be an element of dissonance operating here. Having worked so hard to join a group, new members may be psychologically compelled to find the group attractive.

Consequences of Cohesiveness

From the previous section, it should be clear that managers (or group members) may be able to influence the level of cohesiveness of work groups by inducing competition or threat, varying group size or composition, or manipulating membership requirements. The question remains, however, as to whether *more* or *less* cohesiveness is a desirable group property. This, of course, depends on the consequences of group cohesiveness and who is doing the judging.

MORE PARTICIPATION IN GROUP AFFAIRS.   Because cohesive groups are attractive to their membership, members should be especially motivated to participate (in several senses of the word) in group affairs. For one thing, because members wish to remain in the group, voluntary turnover from cohesive groups should be low. For another, members like being with each other; therefore, absence should be lower than that exhibited by less cohesive groups. During the Fit-Rite sales contest, for example, we might expect casual absence in both stores to drop as the sales staff become more reliant on each other to achieve their goal. In a third sense, participation should be reflected in a high degree of communication within the group as members strive to cooperate with and assist each other. In addition, this communication may well be of a more friendly and supportive nature, depending on the key goals of the group.[40]

MORE CONFORMITY.   Because they are so attractive and coordinated, cohesive groups are well equipped to supply information, rewards, and punishment to individual members. These factors take on special significance when they are administered by those who hold a special interest for us. Thus, highly cohesive groups are in a superb position to induce conformity to group norms because ''they have so much to offer.''

Members of cohesive groups should be especially motivated to engage in activities that will *keep* the group cohesive. Chief among these activities is applying pressure to deviants to get them to comply with group norms. Cohesive groups react to deviants by increasing the amount of communication directed at these individuals.[41] Presumably, such communication may contain information to help the deviant ''see the light,'' as well as veiled threats about what might happen if he or she doesn't. Over time, if such communication is ineffective in inducing conformity, it tends to decrease. This is a signal that the group has isolated the deviant member in order to maintain cohesiveness among the majority.

MORE SUCCESS.   Above it was pointed out that successful goal accomplishment contributes to group cohesiveness. In line with the old saying that nothing succeeds like success, it is also true that cohesiveness contributes to group success—in general, cohesive groups are good at achieving their goals. Thus, there is a reciprocal relationship between success and cohesiveness:

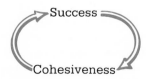

Success

Cohesiveness

Why are cohesive groups effective at goal accomplishment? Probably because of the other consequences of cohesiveness noted above. A high degree of participation and communication, coupled with active conformity to group norms, should ensure a high degree of agreement about the goals to be pursued and the methods to be used to achieve these goals. Thus, coordinated effort pays dividends to the group.

Now for a very important question: Since cohesiveness contributes to goal accomplishment, should managers attempt to increase the cohesiveness of work groups by juggling the factors that influence cohesiveness? To answer this question, it must be emphasized that cohesive groups are especially effective at accomplishing *their own* goals. If these goals happen to correspond with those of the organization, increased cohesiveness may have substantial benefits with regard to group performance. If not, organizational effectiveness may be threatened. For example, during the Vietnam War, cohesive units of American soldiers occasionally united to defy a command to move into dangerous territory. In this case, the goals of the cohesive GIs (to remain safe and secure) did not correspond to those of the military brass (to pursue the enemy). Your own value system will tell you who was right and wrong here. However, from the Army command's perspective, this was a case in which cohesiveness threatened organizational effectiveness.

Studies of industrial work groups have contributed to our understanding of the consequences of cohesiveness with regard to the productivity of individual group members. In particular, one large-scale study reached the following conclusions:

- In highly cohesive groups, the productivity of individual group members tends to be fairly similar to that of other members. In less cohesive groups there is more variation in productivity.

- Highly cohesive groups tend to be *more* or *less* productive than less cohesive groups.[42]

These two facts are shown graphically in Exhibit 8-7. The lower variability of productivity in more cohesive groups stems from the power of such groups to induce conformity. To the extent that work groups have productivity norms, more cohesive groups should be better able to enforce them. Furthermore, if cohesive groups accept organizational norms regarding productivity they should be highly productive. If cohesive groups reject such norms they are especially effective in limiting productivity.

The moral here should be clear: Cohesive groups tend to be successful in accomplishing what they wish to accomplish. In a good labor relations climate, group cohesiveness should contribute to high productivity. If the climate is marked by tension and disagreement, cohesive groups may effectively pursue goals that result in low productivity.

To return to the story at the beginning of the chapter, early adversity, common interests, and early success led to high cohesiveness among the founders of Triton Computers. This in turn stimulated the successful introduction of the personal

EXHIBIT 8-7   **Hypothetical productivity curves for groups varying in cohesiveness.**

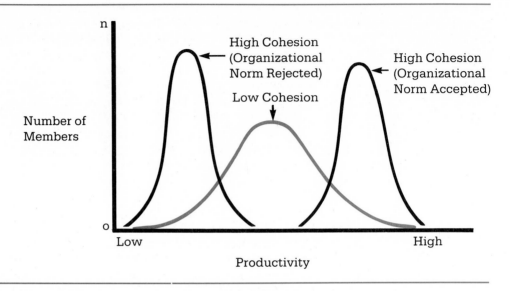

computer. However, growth, turnover, and the addition of less committed members now threaten cohesiveness.

SUMMARY

■ A group consists of two or more people interacting interdependently to achieve a common goal. Formal groups are the basis of any organization. However, informal groups also develop to satisfy friendship needs, aid in task accomplishment, and provide self-defense.

■ The formation and maintenance of groups depends upon opportunity for interaction, potential for goal accomplishment, and the personal character-istics of members. Opportunity for interaction is enhanced by physical and psychological proximity. The goals that groups attempt to accomplish can be divided into physical, intellectual, and social-emotional goals. Individuals with similar attitudes tend to be attracted to each other, while persons with both similar and opposite personalities may be attracted.

■ As groups get bigger they provide less opportunity for member satisfaction. When tasks are additive (performance depends upon the addition of individ-ual effort) or disjunctive (performance depends upon that of the best member) larger groups should perform better than smaller groups if process losses due to poor coordination and communication can be avoided. When tasks are conjunctive (performance is limited by the weakest member), performance decreases as the group gets bigger because the chance of adding a weak member increases.

■ Norms are expectations that group members have about each other's behavior. They provide consistency to behavior and develop as a function of shared attitudes. In organizations, both formal and informal norms often develop to control loyalty, dress, reward allocation, and performance.

■ Roles are positions in a group which have associated with them a set of expected behaviors. Assigned roles are formally designated by the organization to accomplish work. Emergent roles develop to meet the informal needs of organizational members. Role ambiguity refers to a lack of clarity of job goals or methods. Role conflict exists when an individual is faced with incompatible role expectations, and it can take four forms: intra-sender, inter-sender, inter-role, and person-role. Both ambiguity and conflict have been shown to provoke job dissatisfaction, tension, anxiety, and lowered commitment.

■ Status is the rank or prestige accorded to group members by the group. Formal status systems are designed by the organization to reinforce the authority hierarchy and reward progression up the hierarchy. In practice, this involves allocating status symbols to individuals on the basis of seniority and formal organizational roles. Informal status systems also operate in organizations, though they may lack conspicuous status symbols. Higher status members are usually addressed more formally, communicate more, and have more influence than lower status members.

■ Cohesive groups are especially attractive to their members. Threat, competition, success, and small size contribute to cohesiveness, as does a tough initiation into the group. The consequences of cohesiveness include increased participation in group affairs, improved communication, and increased conformity. Cohesive groups are especially effective in accomplishing their own goals, which may or may not be those of the organization.

KEY CONCEPTS

Group	Role ambiguity
Formal work groups	Role conflict
Informal groups	Intra-sender conflict
Social facilitation effect	Inter-sender conflict
Group structure	Inter-role conflict
Additive tasks	Person-role conflict
Disjunctive tasks	Status
Conjunctive tasks	Formal status system
Norms	Status symbols
Roles	Informal status system
Assigned roles	Group cohesiveness
Emergent roles	

DISCUSSION QUESTIONS

1. Pick a group of which you are a member. Why did this group form, and why does it continue to persist as a group? Consider the issues of proximity, potential for goal accomplishment, and the personal characteristics of members.

2. Give an example of an observation you have made of attraction and group formation under stress. What functions did the formation of this group serve? Did it remain intact when and if the stress was removed? Does stress always lead to group formation? Consider the behavior that might occur on a rapidly sinking ship before answering.

3. Consider a large office in an insurance firm which consists of clerks, typists, and claims processors. Suppose that several informal friendship groups have formed on the basis of proximity and attitude similarity. Discuss the potential pros and cons of these groups for the organization. Does the existence of such informal groups make special demands upon office managers? Should organizations try to prevent the development of such groups?

4. Suppose that a group of United Nations representatives from various countries forms to draft a resolution regarding world hunger. Does this appear to be an additive, disjunctive, or conjunctive task? What kinds of process losses would such a group be likely to suffer? Can you offer a prediction about the size of this group and its performance?

5. State several norms that exist in your classroom or in your work group. What functions do these norms serve? What are the shared attitudes that underlie these norms? How are the norms enforced?

6. Describe some work roles which seem inherently ambiguous because of organizational factors. Describe some factors which cause professors or supervisors to send ambiguous role messages to students or subordinates.

7. Mark Allen, a representative for an international engineering company, is a very religious person and an elder in his church. Mark's direct superior has instructed him to use "any legal means" to sell a large construction project to a South American government. The vice-president of international operations has informed Mark that he can offer a generous "kickback" to government officials to clinch the deal, although such practices are illegal. Discuss the three kinds of role conflict Mark is experiencing.

8. Some organizations have made concerted efforts to do away with many of the status symbols associated with differences in organizational rank. All employees park in the same lot, eat in the same dining room, and have similar offices and privileges. Discuss the pros and cons of such a strategy. How might such a change affect organizational communications?

9. You are an executive in a consumer products corporation. The president assigns you to form a task force to develop new marketing strategies for the organization. You are permitted to choose its members. What things would you do to make this group as cohesive as possible?

10. Discuss the dangers of group cohesiveness for the group itself and for the organization of which the group is a part.

FOR FURTHER READING

Albanese, R., & Van Fleet, D. D. (1985). Rational behavior in groups: The free-riding tendency. *Academy of Management Review, 10,* 244–255.

> Discusses free riding, a form of process loss in which the members of larger groups reduce their efforts. Covers management implications.

Feldman, D. C. (1984). The development and enforcement of group norms. *Academy of Management Review, 9,* 47–53.

> Argues that norms develop to ensure group survival, increase predictability, avoid embarrassment, or underline the group's central values.

Goodman, P. S., & Associates (1986). *Designing effective work groups.* San Francisco: Jossey-Bass.

> Eleven chapters discuss many aspects of work groups that have an impact on their effectiveness. Presents many new insights on group effectiveness.

Greenhaus, J. H., & Beutell, N. J. (1985). Sources of conflict between work and family roles. *Academy of Management Review, 10,* 76–88.

> Is there inherent conflict between work and family roles? The authors review the causes of this form of inter-role conflict.

Case Study

Doubling Up

Linda Rosen first heard of the walkout at the automobile assembly plant while listening to her car radio. The brief news report suggested that a walkout had occurred because several workers had received disciplinary suspensions. That evening, as Rosen listened to a radio talk show, the issue became clearer. The workers had been suspended because they had been "doubling up" against the wishes of management.

Rosen didn't need to listen carefully to understand what doubling up meant. She had worked one summer during college on an assembly line in a furniture factory, and had occasionally doubled up on that job. Doubling up, she knew, referred to doing one's own job on the assembly line as well as the job of an adjacent co-worker on the line. At the furniture factory, for example, her usual job was installing desk drawers in the frames of desks. The next job on the line was installing the legs on one side of the desk. Sometimes, Rosen would spell the next assembler by doing the legs as well. It required some hustling, but it could be done. Rosen knew that doubling up was common on assembly lines, but temporary and casual. One might spell a fellow worker so he or she could go for a soda or to the washroom, but nothing more.

The workers who called in to the radio station indicated that a very different form of doubling up was occurring at the automobile plant. They had evidently been trying to *institutionalize* doubling up by doing it for an entire shift! As near as Rosen could make out, one worker would double up for a half an hour and then rest for an equivalent period while his

or her "partner" did both workers' jobs. This had been going on for several months before the crackdown occurred. Several of the callers took pains to point out that money was not an issue in the walkout.

As a freelance journalist, Rosen saw the raw material for an interesting article. The next morning she made some phone calls. Rosen's first stop was the local union hall, where several of the suspended workers, eager for publicity, had agreed to talk with her. Al Kobal's comments were typical.

"Look," Kobal said, "we double up because of the boredom and pressure of the line. They run a car through my work station every thirty-odd *seconds*. What kind of a life is that to lead eight hours a day? I do one job, installing a left taillight over and over again. I'm supposed to do every other car, so that gives me a little more than a minute to do the work. On my job, this is how we double up. Me and the guy who does the right taillight do the lights on *every* car instead of every other car for a half-hour. The other two guys relax, read, or whatever. They usually stick around so that they can give us a hand if we fall behind, get a stripped screw, or whatever. Then they spell us for a half hour while we rest. I read about 'job redesign' in the paper all the time. Well, this is grass-roots job redesign!"

Ike Davis, another worker, explained how doubling up was accomplished at his work station.

"I usually install windshield-wiper motors," said Davis. "It's a four-bolt operation, using an air wrench. The next person on the line installs the upper radiator hose with two clamps. When we double up, I do both jobs for about a half hour, then she takes over. I do a motor, then follow the car to the next station, where I catch the hose. Quality is good because we really have to pay attention and because we don't want any trouble. If the company has quality problems it's because of bad design or bad sup-

---

Source: This case is based on incidents that occurred at the General Motors plant at Lordstown, Ohio, in 1971 and 1972. For further information see "Lordstown—Searching for a Better Way of Work" by Bennett Kremen, *New York Times*, September 9, 1973, section 3, pages 1 and 4.

pliers, not bad assembly. About 10 percent of the bolts I get for the wiper motors are defective."

The following day Rosen obtained an appointment with a production manager to get the company's point of view. Before the interview, the manager's assistant took Rosen on a brief tour of the assembly line area, where work had resumed even though the doubling-up dispute had not been resolved. Rosen noted that the garb of the assembly workers ranged from standard work clothes to the jeans and T-shirts favored by the younger workers. Everyone was drenched in sweat due to the high heat, and Rosen had to shout at the assistant to be heard over the din. The area had the smell of oil and burnt metal so common to heavy industrial operations. The tour completed, Rosen was grateful for the quiet, air-conditioned isolation of the production manager's office. The manager, dressed in a white shirt and tie, summarized his position.

"We pay our assembly workers to put in an eight-hour day and we pay them well. When they double up, they're taking home eight hours worth of pay for four hours work. On top of this, they tell us the line moves too fast. Now both of these things can't be true simultaneously. That is, the line can't be moving too fast if they have time to double up. Furthermore, the hustling that doubling up requires threatens worker safety. Some day, there'll be a serious accident and we'll be blamed. And the quality index of this plant isn't what it should be. Doubling up leads to missing bolts and screws and so on, and our customers and dealers don't deserve that. We believe that our industrial engineers have designed the work in this plant for maximum efficiency—one worker for one job."

Later in the day Rosen had a chance to talk to several production supervisors about doubling up. The meeting had been arranged by the production manager. Rosen was especially interested to hear the views of the supervisors, since they were the management representatives who were closest to the action.

"I absolutely forbid doubling up," said one supervisor. "When those folks are being spelled by their buddies they wander all over the plant. We can never find them when we need them. It's my job to assign work, and the company says no doubling up. If the workers get away with it my authority is undermined, and it's hard to know what they'll want next. If I can't tell my workers what jobs to do, I've got no

function here. I try to do what I'm told by management."

Rosen had heard from the workers that some supervisors tolerated or even encouraged doubling up. In response to her query, one supervisor admitted to putting up with the practice.

"Look," he said, "I honestly feel that the quality of the work and the safety aspect are improved when my people double up. At least they pay attention instead of working in a daydream! And allowing them to do it sure reduces tension on the line, if you know what I mean. I treat them right and they treat me right. *I'm* the one who takes the heat from management if quality falls off and we get a lot of bad inspection tickets. Ever hear of sabotage on the line? Well, it happens, and I don't want it to happen in my area."

Finally, Rosen called the international union to learn its position. The results weren't surprising. The union condemned the walkout and said that doubling up was an issue for local negotiations. Rosen understood the latter response. The fact that workers who doubled up could relax for half the shift didn't provide ammunition for the union's constant campaign against line speed-ups. It just didn't look good.

Linda Rosen knew she would be able to write a fascinating article.

■   ■   ■

1. Discuss the doubling-up process in terms of informal, emergent group activity. What goals did doubling up accomplish for the workers?
2. Al Kobal said that the workers were engaged in job redesign. Did doubling up affect the scope or motivating potential of the assembly line jobs? Justify your answer.
3. Do production supervisors in the assembly plant experience particular kinds of role conflict when confronted by subordinates who double up? Explain your answer.
4. How do the dynamics of group cohesiveness apply to this case?
5. Imagine that you are the top manager of the assembly plant. You view your job as one of getting out a high volume of quality production while maintaining good labor-management relations and safe working conditions. What would you do to resolve the doubling-up problem?

REFERENCES

1. For a more detailed analysis of the motives for informal group formation see Tichy, N. (1973). An analysis of clique formation and structure in organizations. *Administrative Science Quarterly, 18,* 194–208.

2. For a brief review see Kahn, A., & McGaughey, T. A. (1977). Distance and liking: When moving close produces increased liking. *Sociometry, 40,* 138–144.

3. Zajonc, R. B. (1965). Social facilitation. *Science, 149,* 269–274; Bond, C. F., Jr., & Titus, L. J. (1983). Social facilitation: A meta-analysis of 241 studies. *Psychological Bulletin, 94,* 265–292.

4. Stein, A. (1976). Conflict and cohesion: A review of the literature. *Journal of Conflict Resolution, 20,* 143–172.

5. For a World War II perspective, see Shils, E. A. (1950). Primary groups in the American army. In R. K. Merton & P. F. Lazarsfeld (Eds.), *Continuities in social research: Studies in scope and method of the "American Soldier."* Glencoe, IL: Free Press. Such grouping had a different character in Vietnam. See Moskos, C. C., Jr. (1970). *The American enlisted man.* New York: Russell Sage Foundation.

6. Schachter, S. (1959). *The psychology of affiliation.* Stanford, CA: Stanford University Press.

7. Byrne, D. (1969). Attitudes and attraction. In L. Berkowitz (Ed.), *Advances in experimental social psychology* (Vol. 4). New York: Academic Press.

8. Shaw, M. E. (1981). *Group dynamics: The psychology of small group behavior* (3rd ed.) New York: McGraw-Hill.

9. Jones, E. E., & Gerard, H. B. (1967). *Foundations of social psychology.* New York: Wiley.

10. Hare, A. P. (1976). *A handbook of small group research.* New York: The Free Press; Shaw, 1981.

11. Hare, 1976; Shaw, 1981.

12. The following discussion relies upon Steiner, I. D. (1972). *Group process and productivity.* New York: Academic Press.

13. Steiner, 1972; Hill, G. W. (1982). Group versus individual performance: Are n + 1 heads better than one? *Psychological Bulletin, 91,* 517–539.

14. For an example of the social process by which this sharing may be negotiated in a new group see Bettenhausen, K., & Murnighan, J. K. (1985). The emergence of norms in competitive decision-making groups. *Administrative Science Quarterly, 30,* 350–372.

15. For a good discussion of this, see Kanter, R. M. (1977). *Men and women of the corporation.* New York: Basic Books, pp. 63–67.

16. Kanter, 1977, p. 37.

17. Leventhal, G. S. (1976). The distribution of rewards and resources in groups and organizations. In L. Berkowitz & E. Walster (Eds.), *Advances in experimental social psychology* (Vol. 9). New York: Academic Press.

18. See Mitchell, T. R., Rothman, M., & Liden, R. C. (1985). Effects of normative information on task performance. *Journal of Applied Psychology, 70,* 48–55.

19. See Roy, D. (1952). Quota restriction and goldbricking in a machine shop. *American Journal of Sociology, 57,* 426–442.

20. Jackson, S. E., & Schuler, R. S. (1985). A meta-analysis and conceptual critique of research on role ambiguity and role conflict in work settings. *Organizational Behavior and Human Decision Processes, 36,* 16–78.

21. Jackson & Schuler, 1985.

22. Johnson, T. W., & Stinson, J. E. (1975). Role ambiguity, role conflict, and satisfaction: Moderating effect of individual differences. *Journal of Applied Psychology, 60,* 329–333.

23. Cooke, R. A., & Rousseau, D. M. (1984). Stress and strain from family roles and work-role expectations. *Journal of Applied Psychology, 69,* 252–260; Beutell, N. J., & Greenhaus, J. H. (1983). Integration of home and nonhome roles: Women's conflict and coping behavior. *Journal of Applied Psychology, 68,* 43–48.

24. See Latack, J. C. (1981). Person/role conflict: Holland's model extended to role-stress research, stress management, and career development. *Academy of Management Review, 6,* 89–103.

25. Jackson & Schuler, 1985.

26. Robbins, S. P. (1978). *Personnel: The management of human resources.* Englewood Cliffs, NJ: Prentice-Hall, p. 294.

27. Treiman, D. J. (1977). *Occupational prestige in comparative perspective.* New York: Academic Press.

28. Roy, D. F. (1960). "Banana time": Job satisfaction and informal interaction. *Human Organization, 18,* 158–169, p. 164.

29. Ervin-Tripp, S. M. (1969). Sociolinguistics. In L. Berkowitz (Ed.), *Advances in experimental social psychology* (Vol. 4). New York: Academic Press.

30. Shaw, 1981.

31. Berger, J., Cohen, B. P., & Zelditch, M., Jr. (1972). Status characteristics and social interaction. *American Sociological Review, 37,* 241–255.

32. Strodbeck, F. L., James, R. M., & Hawkins, C. (1957). Social status in jury deliberations. *American Sociological Review, 22,* 713–719.

33. Stein, 1976.

34. Cartwright, D. (1968). The nature of group cohesiveness. In D. Cartwright & A. Zander (Eds.), *Group dynamics* (3rd ed.). New York: Harper & Row.

35. Lott, A., & Lott, B. (1965). Group cohesiveness as interpersonal attraction: A review of relationships with antecedent and consequent variables. *Psychological Bulletin, 64,* 259–309.

36. Anderson, A. B. (1975). Combined effects of interpersonal attraction and goal-path clarity on the cohesiveness of task-oriented groups. *Journal of Personality and Social Psychology, 31,* 68–75. Also see Cartwright, 1968.

37. Seashore, S. (1954). *Group cohesiveness in the industrial workgroup.* Ann Arbor, MI: Institute for Social Research.

38. Blanchard, F. A., Adelman, L., & Cook, S. W. (1975). Effect of group success and failure upon interpersonal attraction in cooperating interracial groups. *Journal of Personality and Social Psychology, 31,* 1020–1030.

39. Walker, M. (1968). Organizational type, rites of incorporation, and group solidarity: A study of fraternity hell week. *Dissertation Abstracts, 29,* (2-A), 689–690. Also see Aronson, E., & Mills, J. (1959). The effects of severity of initiation on liking for a group. *Journal of Abnormal and Social Psychology, 59,* 177–181.

40. Cartwright, 1968; Shaw, 1981.

41. Schacter, S. (1951). Deviation, rejection, and communication. *Journal of Abnormal and Social Psychology, 46,* 190–207.

42. Seashore, 1954. Also see Stogdill, R. M. (1972). Group productivity, drive, and cohesiveness. *Organizational Behavior and Human Performance, 8,* 26–43.

Chapter 9

Social Influence, Socialization, and Culture

LEARNING THE ROPES

Sue Dittmer and Eve Polanksi had been employed by Consolidated Nuclear Industries for almost two years. Both had Master's degrees in nuclear engineering and had been hired upon graduation when CNI had obtained a lucrative contract to design a series of nuclear power plants for a major New England power company. They had become part of the twelve-member Monitoring and Containment Task Force, which was concerned with part of the design of the safety systems for the nuclear reactor. This involved the arrangement and installation of certain monitoring devices and emergency systems and, most important, the design of the hydraulic cooling system for the reactor core.

The task force was a cohesive group, and this generally provided a pleasant working environment with little dissension or tension. The team was elite and success-oriented, and team members could be relied upon to help each other out when necessary. However, there was some price to be paid for this cohesiveness. Because they had been hired at almost the same time, Sue and Eve had learned the ropes at CNI together. Since there was no formal training or orientation, this learning was basically an informal process, but it was nevertheless very potent. Quickly, both had learned that rookie members of the design team were expected to follow the party line and defer to more experienced team members in design matters. Signals to this effect were subtle but effective. Doing an assigned task quickly and accurately was praised by other members of the staff, but innovative ideas or questions about design parameters were met with responses of detached amusement by more experienced team members. This certainly wasn't the kind of collaborative atmosphere that the women had been led to expect from their university training!

Although this situation was frustrating, both engineers were aware that it was surely temporary. During the two years they had been there, they had observed that team members who conformed to the group's expectations gradually got the autonomy to suggest design features and develop initial plans.

Most recently, Sue and Eve had been involved with a series of computer simulations used to test the effectiveness of the cooling system design.

Although they were unaware of each other's thoughts, both had perceived a disturbing trend to these tests. The first had indicated a clear meltdown of the reactor core, showing that the cooling system wasn't properly designed. After several minor design features were changed, simulations were again run. Each time, as the data indicated that a meltdown was imminent, Max Schmidt, the head of the task force, ordered the test to be terminated. Finally, by reprogramming the simulation to involve an extremely unlikely emergency scenario, they had managed to get a clean run indicating that the safety system would work.

The next day, Sue and Eve had lunch together. After some strained small talk, Eve got to the point.

"Sue, those simulations were dummied up. That cooling system doesn't work worth a damn."

Sue responded, "Eve, I'm glad you feel this way too. I was beginning to think those tests were my personal fantasy or nightmare. But what can we do? Tomorrow at the group meeting Max is sure to push for the approval of the design. The brass is on him to act fast, and I can't see anyone arguing with him."

"Neither can I," said Eve. "Once they make a decision, the experienced people stick together."

The next day, the group meeting began as expected. Max argued for the approval of the safety design that included the suspect cooling system. When he asked for comments, all were vaguely supportive. Finally, Bob Daniels spoke up. Daniels, an older man, was highly respected as the best engineer on the task force.

"Look, people," said Daniels quietly, "the emperor has no clothes. That cooling system wouldn't chill my beer, let alone prevent a meltdown. Let's stop kidding ourselves."

Quickly, the tide turned as other group members expressed some doubts about the design and the tests. Soon, the group had generated some new design ideas and decided who would work on what. It was agreed that the brass would just have to wait for a good design.

Sue and Eve exchanged smiles and looked relieved.

This story raises a number of interesting questions. Exactly how did Sue and Eve learn the ways of the group? Why did Bob Daniels have the courage to protest the faulty design? Why did the others finally support him? These are the kinds of questions we will probe in this chapter.

First, we will examine the general issue of social influence in organizations. Then we will discuss different motives for conformity to norms and the various factors that influence such conformity. After this, we will explore how new members learn the ways of the organization. Finally, we will examine the overall social environment of organizations as expressed in their cultures.

SOCIAL INFLUENCE IN ORGANIZATIONS

In the previous chapter, it was pointed out that groups exert influence over the attitudes and behavior of their individual members. As a result of social influence, people often feel or act differently than they would as independent operators. In the story that began the chapter, Sue and Eve were somehow induced to keep innovative ideas and doubts about design matters to themselves, even though they found the situation frustrating. What accounts for such influence? in short, in many social settings, and especially in groups, persons are highly *dependent* upon others. This dependence sets the stage for influence to occur.

Information Dependence

We are frequently dependent upon others for information about the adequacy and appropriateness of our behavior, thoughts, and feelings. How satisfying is this job of mine? How nice is our boss? How much work should I take home to do over the weekend? Should we protest the bad design at the meeting? Objective, concrete answers to such questions may be hard to come by. Thus, we must often rely upon information provided by others. In turn, this **information dependence** gives others the opportunity to influence our thoughts, feelings, and actions via the signals they send to us.[1]

Social comparison theory suggests that individuals are often motivated to compare their own thoughts, feelings, and actions with those of others as a means of acquiring information about their adequacy.[2] In one well-known series of studies designed to explore this hypothesis, students volunteered to participate in an experiment concerning the effects of electric shock on physiological functioning. Some were led to believe that they would receive very painful shocks, a condition that was reinforced by the presence of a forbidding "shock generator." Others were led to expect very mild tingling shocks and reassured that the experience would not be harmful. While the equipment was being readied the volunteers were given the option of waiting with someone else or alone. Actually, no shocks were delivered, and when the subjects had made their choice, the experiment was over. In sum, 63 percent of those who expected nasty shocks chose to wait with others, while only 33 percent of those who expected mild shocks chose to do so.[3] Subsequent studies suggested that those in the high threat condition wished to wait with others to obtain *information* about how they should be feeling and behaving in a threatening situation.

Some people are more in need of information than others. In the shock studies, those who faced more frightening prospects were more motivated to seek information. In general, novel, threatening, or confusing settings should increase information dependence. As you can imagine, as new members of the Monitoring and Containment Task Force, Sue and Eve were especially tuned in to information conveyed by the more experienced members, not to mention each other.

Some people are better *sources* of information than others. In the shock studies, those in the threatening condition did not wish to wait with just anyone. Rather, they revealed this tendency only when the potential company was about to undergo the same experience. As this illustrates, *peers* are often a preferred source of information. Thus, in deciding how satisfying your job is, you would be especially likely to rely on the impressions of your co-workers. Similarly, Sue and Eve relied on each other in exploring their feelings about the faulty simulations. In other cases, we may seek information from *experts* rather than peers. An expert is simply someone who we perceive to be especially knowledgeable about the situation at hand. For this reason, Bob Daniels served as an important source of information for the CNI design team.

In summary, groups often influence members via the information they provide about important issues. Social comparison theory indicates that group members are especially susceptible to this information. The effects of social comparison can be very strong, often exerting as much or more influence over others as objective reality (see In–Focus 9-1).[4]

Effect Dependence

As if group members were not busy enough tuning in to information provided by the group, they must also be sensitive to the rewards and punishments the group has at its disposal. Thus, individuals are dependent upon the *effects* of their behavior as determined by the rewards and punishments provided by others. **Effect dependence** actually involves two complementary processes. First, the group frequently has a vested interest in how individual members think and act because such matters can affect the goal attainment of the group. Secondly, the member frequently desires the approval of the group. In combination, these circumstances promote effect dependence.

In organizational settings there are plenty of effects available to keep individual members "under the influence." Superiors typically have a fair array of rewards and punishments available, including promotions, raises, and the assignment of more or less favorable tasks. At the informal level, the variety of such effects available for use by co-workers is staggering. Cooperative behavior may be rewarded with praise, friendship, and a helping hand on the job. Lack of cooperation may result in nagging, harassment, name calling, social isolation, and even physical punishment. Perhaps Sue and Eve were lucky to only experience detached amusement in response to their questions about task force designs!

CONFORMITY: SOCIAL INFLUENCE IN ACTION

One of the most obvious consequences of information and effect dependence is the tendency for group members to conform to the norms that have been established by the group. In the last chapter we discussed the development and function of such norms, but we have postponed the discussion of why norms are supported until now. Put simply, much of the information and many of the effects upon which group members are dependent are oriented toward enforcing group norms.

Motives for Conformity

It may occur to you that **conformity** is a rather general term. After all, the fact that Roman Catholic priests conform to the norms of the Church hierarchy seems rather different from the case in which convicts conform to norms established by prison officials. Clearly, the motives for conformity differ in these two cases. What is needed, then, is some system to classify different motives for conformity.[5]

COMPLIANCE.   **Compliance** is the simplest, most direct motive for conformity to group norms. It occurs because a member wishes to acquire rewards from the group and avoid punishment. As such, it primarily involves effect dependence. Although the complying individual adjusts his or her behavior to the norm, he or she does not really subscribe to the beliefs, values, and attitudes that underlie the norm. Most convicts conform to formal prison norms out of compliance. Similarly, very young children behave themselves only because of external forces.

IDENTIFICATION.   Conformity may also occur because an individual finds other supporters of the norm attractive. In this case, the individual identifies with these supporters and sees himself or herself as similar to them. Although there are elements of effect dependence here, information dependence is especially important—if someone is basically similar to you, then you will be motivated to rely on them for information about how to think and act. **Identification** as a motive for conformity is often revealed by an imitation process in which established members serve as models for the behavior of others. For example, a newly promoted executive may attempt to dress and talk like her successful, admired boss. Similarly, as children get older they may be motivated to behave themselves because such behavior corresponds to that of an admired parent with whom they are beginning to identify.

INTERNALIZATION.   Some conformity to norms occurs because individuals have truly and wholly accepted the beliefs, values, and attitudes that underlie the norm. As such, **internalization** of the norm has happened, and conformity occurs because it is seen as *right,* not because it achieves rewards, avoids punishment, or pleases others. That is, conformity is due to internal, rather than external, forces. In general, we expect that most religious leaders conform to the norms of their religion for this reason. Similarly, the career army officer may come to support the strict discipline of the military because it seems right and proper, not simply because such discipline is supported by colleagues.

In organizations, it may occur to you that some of these motives are more likely to exist than others. We shall discuss this issue shortly.

Experiments in Conformity

The various motives for conformity can be illustrated by two well-known studies of the conformity process. In turn, we can use these studies to illustrate the conditions under which conformity is more or less likely to occur.

THE ASCH STUDY.   In a study by Solomon Asch, subjects were led to believe that they were participating in an experiment on visual perception.[6] They were seated last in a row of seven to nine other individuals and exposed to lines of the type shown in Exhibit 9-1. The object was to indicate which of the three comparison lines was equal in length to the standard line. Judgments were given successively, and the subject was the last to respond. On the first two trials, things went smoothly, and all of the people agreed as to which line matched the standard. On the third trial an amazing thing happened. The first person to respond gave a clearly inaccurate answer, and this response was also given by the others. Quickly, it was the subject's turn to respond. What would you do? As you may have guessed,

EXHIBIT 9-1   **Which comparison line matches the standard? The Asch conformity study task.**

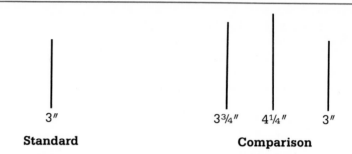

3″	3¾″ 4¼″ 3″
Standard	**Comparison**

Source: From Asch, S. A. (1956). Studies of independence and conformity: A minority of one against a unanimous majority. *Psychological Monographs: General and Applied,* Vol. 70, No. 9, Whole No. 416, p. 7. Copyright 1956 by the American Psychological Association. Adapted by permission of the author.

the other persons in the row were confederates of the experimenter, and this was a study in conformity rather than perception. Over a number of trials, the confederates communicated a ''false norm'' several times. Conformity to this false norm occurred about one-third of the time, by subjects that had remarkably varied degrees of independence.

In this study, why was there so much conformity to the false norm? Clearly, the perceptual task was very easy; control subjects who performed the task alone made few errors in judgment. When asked why they had yielded, most subjects said something to the effect that ''I knew they were wrong, but I gave in anyway.'' The majority of the subjects did not believe that the false norm was correct, but they doubted both the majority's perceptions and their own capacities to judge, and were torn in conflicting directions. Evidently they were in a state of effect dependence, anticipating rejection or other punishment by the others if they disagreed.

THE SHERIF STUDY.   Research by Muzafer Sherif was also explained to the participants as an exercise in visual perception. What they were required to do was to estimate the amount of movement of a point of light in a darkened room. In fact, the light was absolutely stationary. However, in this situation, observers invariably report some movement. This phenomenon is called the autokinetic (self-movement) effect, and it is due to certain physiological processes. Because there is no frame of reference in a completely dark environment, individuals usually give widely differing estimates of the distance the light has ''moved.''

First, Sherif tested subjects individually to determine their estimates without social influence. Then, subjects were assembled into groups of two or three and asked to judge the movement over a series of trials. On each trial, they made simultaneous judgments. The results were clear-cut. Over the series of trials, the estimates of the movement of the group members tended to *converge*. Gradually, those who initially reported large movements decreased their estimates, and vice versa—in other words, a compromise was reached. Sherif argued that this convergence represented the development of a norm to which group members conformed.[7]

Notice that the situation here is very different from that in the Asch line study. This is clearly an ambiguous situation, and the subjects are in certain need of information. Thus, minimally, it would appear that identification occurred among group members. The case here is not so much that they found each other attractive as that they recognized each other as equally bemused. In such cases, we often rely upon others for information about how to think or act. In fact, it would appear that the compromise norm was frequently *internalized* as representing correct information. When subjects were tested alone after the group experience, they tended to respond with the group-established norm. Amazingly, this effect has been shown to persist a whole year after the group interaction.[8]

It is important to recognize that there are many decision tasks facing existing groups that have elements in common with the Asch and Sherif experimental situations. For example, imagine the negotiating committee of a trade union that is trying to decide whether to accept a company contract offer. Each member offers a successive opinion about the course of action to be taken. If the first three unionists all favor acceptance, will the fourth be willing to offer a contrary view? (Asch situation). Similarly, consider three partners who own a restaurant who are trying to decide if they should expand their premises during an uncertain economic climate. Initially, one favors no expansion, one favors a large expansion, and one falls in the middle (Sherif situation). Will they compromise on a medium-sized expansion? To answer questions of this nature, we must explore the variables that influence degree of conformity.

Factors Influencing Conformity

What determines the extent to which a particular group member will be likely to conform to group norms? Put simply, factors that increase or decrease information and effect dependence should influence the extent of conformity of individual group members.

PUBLICITY. In the Asch setting, one obvious way to reduce the conformity of the naive subject to the false norm is to permit the subject to render opinions about line length in secret. Such a condition reduces effect dependence. For example, suppose an executive group has two equally strong informal norms—not cheating on expense accounts and not leaving the office before six o'clock. Other things equal, an executive who disagrees with both norms would be more likely to comply with the leaving-time norm than the cheating norm because violation of the former would be more obvious. In some piecerate pay situations where groups have developed norms to restrict productivity, workers will lie about their own output to prevent pressure from their coworkers.

SIZE OF THE OPPOSITION.   Any tendency to "go along with the crowd" is enhanced when the "crowd" is bigger, because a large opposition contains more sources of information and more sources of reward and punishment. In the Asch setting, subjects are less likely to conform to the false norm when confronting only one or two others, as opposed to seven or eight.[9] Research on jury size shows that smaller juries tend to render less consistent verdicts than larger juries.[10] This may stem in part from the fact that dissenters in small juries feel freer to stand their ground. (For a related view on the judicial perspective, see the cartoon!)

DISSENSION.   Imagine that, in the Asch setting, the naive subject finds that he or she has a "partner in crime" somewhere earlier in the lineup; that is, someone who also rejects the false norm and gives correct responses. As you might guess, such a condition strongly reduces the subject's tendency to conform. Recall, for example, the story that began the chapter. In the design meeting all parties publicly agreed that the flawed design was acceptable until Bob Daniels spoke against it. Quickly, support for the design faded. Dissenters provide alternative sources of information to the group consensus and change potential reward and punishment patterns.

THE ISSUE AT HAND.   In the Asch routine, it is possible to increase the naive subject's tendency to conform to the false norm by making the stimulus lines more nearly equal in length. In general, difficult, ambiguous issues increase the tendency toward conformity to group norms. For example, suppose four sales managers are asked to nominate one of their subordinates for promotion to manager. The subordinates are usually on the road, and there has been little opportunity to observe their managerial abilities. If for some reason three of the managers favor a particular candidate, it should be difficult for the fourth to dissent, since the choice is difficult and ambiguous.

Other things equal, issues that are directly relevant to a group's goal accomplishment are also likely to prompt high conformity. For example, suppose a college

"Well, heck! If all you smart cookies agree, who am I to dissent?"

Source: Drawing by Handelsman; © 1972 The New Yorker Magazine, Inc. Reprinted by permission.

history department is interested in increasing its national reputation so that it can hire well-known scholars. In this case, we should see more conformity to a norm that insists on a high publication rate than to a norm that favors conservative tweed clothing.

STATUS.   The relationship between status in the group and conformity is complex but easy to understand. If nonconformity occurs, it should usually occur among two classes of persons—high status members, or low status members who have been actively rejected by the group (the latter have often been socially isolated or serve as scapegoats). High status members have often *achieved* their high status because they have generally conformed to group norms. Thus, on an issue chosen at random, it is often safe to predict conformity from such a person. However, high status members also receive **idiosyncrasy credits** from the group because of their history of conformity. This means that having paid their dues to the group, they are permitted to occasionally deviate without fear of censure.[11] This was exactly the case with Bob Daniels at CNI. A full-fledged high status member of the task force (by virtue of his seniority and engineering expertise), Daniels exercised his idiosyncrasy credit to speak against the bad design. He simply wasn't effect dependent in this case. On the other hand, low status isolates and scapegoats have already rejected the group as a source of information and suffered the negative effects of doing so. Thus, they have little to gain by conforming in a particular case. Finally, low status members who are striving to become fully integrated into the group (usually *new* members) should reveal a strong tendency to conform, since they are both effect and information dependent. Thus, Sue Dittmer and Eve Polanski were afraid to speak up about the badly designed cooling system (Exhibit 9-2).

EXHIBIT 9-2   **Status, idiosyncrasy credits, and conformity.**

Status	Idiosyncrasy Credits?	Use Credits?	Conform?
High	Yes	Yes	No
		No	Yes
Low (Rejected Member)	No	Can't	No
Low (New Member)	No	Can't	Yes

The Subtle Power of Compliance

In many of the examples given in the previous section, especially those dealing with increased effect dependence, it is obvious that the doubting group member is motivated to conform only in the *compliance* mode. That is, he or she really doesn't support the belief, value, and attitude structure underlying the norm, but conforms simply to avoid trouble or obtain rewards. Of course, this happens all the time. Individuals without religious beliefs or values may agree to be married in a church service to please others. Similarly, a bank teller may verify that a small check being cashed by a familiar customer is covered by sufficient funds, even though he feels the whole process is a waste of time. These examples of compliance seem trivial enough, but as we shall now see, a little compliance can go a long way, in at least two senses.

First, consider the **foot-in-the-door phenemenon,** named for a well-known technique used by door-to-door salespeople. This concept refers to the tendency for compliance with a fairly minor request to prime persons to be receptive to more demanding requests.[12] For instance, suppose an employee asks a co-worker to "punch out" for him one day so he can leave work early. The co-worker reluctantly complies. The following week, the employee asks the co-worker to punch in for him in the morning for the next three days because his car is in the shop and he must take a late bus to work. According to the "foot" phenomenon, the co-worker should be more likely to comply with this more demanding request than he would be if he had not first complied with the less demanding request. Why does the "foot" phenomenon occur? Probably because the initial compliance slightly changes the complier's self-image vis-á-vis the other person ("I punched out for him. I'm a helpful person to him.") Confronted with a more demanding request, the complier then needs to maintain this self-image. Let the innocent complier beware!

Over time, the effects of compliance may be even more powerful and more subtle. Specifically, the compliant individual is necessarily *doing* something which is contrary to the way he or she *thinks* or *feels*. As pointed out in our discussion of attitudes in Chapter 5, such a situation is highly dissonant and arouses a certain tension in the individual. Now one way to reduce this dissonance is to cease conformity. However, this may require the person to adopt an isolate or scapegoat role, equally unpleasant prospects. The other method of reducing dissonance is to gradually accept the beliefs, values, and attitudes that support the norm in question. In practice, how might this occur?

Consider Joan, an idealistic graduate of a college social work program who acquires a job with a social services agency. Joan loves helping people, but hates the bureaucratic red tape and reams of paper work necessary to accomplish this goal. However, to acquire the approval of her boss and co-workers, and to avoid trouble, she follows the rules to the letter of the law. This is pure compliance. Over time, however, Joan begins to *identify* with her boss and more experienced co-workers because they are in the enviable position of controlling those very rewards and punishments that are so important to her. Obviously, if she is to *be* one of them, she must begin to think and feel like them. Finally, Joan is promoted to a supervisory position partly because she is so cooperative. Breaking in a new social worker, Joan is heard to say, "Our rules and forms are very important. You don't understand now, but you will." The metamorphosis is complete—Joan has *internalized* the beliefs and values that support the bureaucratic norms of her agency.

Although this story is slightly dramatized, the point it makes is accurate—simple compliance can set the stage for more complete involvement with organizational norms and roles.

SOCIALIZATION: GETTING (SOME) CONFORMITY FROM MEMBERS

The story of Joan the social worker in the previous section describes how one individual was socialized into a particular organization. **Socialization** is the process by which people learn the norms and roles necessary to function in a group or organization. As we shall see, some of this process may occur before membership formally begins. Furthermore, socialization is an ongoing process by virtue of continuous interaction with others in the workplace. However, there is good reason to believe that socialization is most potent during certain periods of membership transition, such as when one is promoted or assigned to a new work group, and especially when one joins a new organization.[13]

Stages of Socialization

Since organizational socialization is an ongoing process, it is useful to divide this process into three stages.[14] One of these stages occurs before entry, another immediately follows entry, and the last occurs after one has been a member for some period of time. In a sense, the first two stages represent hurdles for achieving passage into the third stage (see Exhibit 9-3).

ANTICIPATORY SOCIALIZATION.   A considerable amount of socialization may occur even before a person becomes a member of a particular organization. This process is called anticipatory socialization. Some anticipatory socialization involves a formal process of skill and attitude acquisition, such as that which might occur by attending university. Other anticipatory socialization may be informal, such as that acquired through a series of summer jobs or even by watching the portrayal of organizational life in television shows and movies. As we shall see shortly, organizations vary in the extent to which they encourage anticipatory socialization in advance of entry. Also, we shall see that not all anticipatory socialization is accurate and useful for the new member.

ACCOMMODATION.   In the accommodation stage the new recruit, armed with some expectations about organizational life, encounters the day-to-day reality of

EXHIBIT 9-3   **Stages of organizational socialization.**

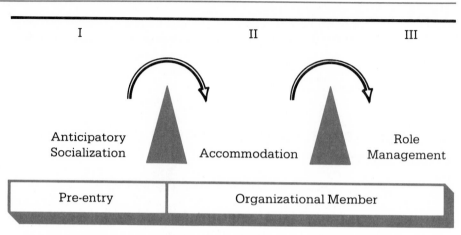

Source: Based on Feldman, D. D. (1976). A contingency theory of socialization. *Administrative Science Quarterly, 21,* 433–452. Reprinted by permission.

this life. Formal aspects of this stage may include orientation programs, training programs, and rotation through various parts of the organization. Informal aspects include getting to know and understand the style and personality of one's boss and co-workers. At this stage, the organization and its experienced members are looking for an acceptable degree of conformity to organizational norms and the gradual acquisition of appropriate role behavior. Recruits, on the other hand, are interested in having their personal needs and expectations fulfilled. If accommodation is reached, the recruit will have complied with critical organizational norms and may begin to identify with experienced organizational members.

ROLE MANAGEMENT.   Having survived the accommodation process and acquired basic role behaviors, the member's attention shifts to fine-tuning and actively managing his or her role in the organization. He or she may be expected to exercise some idiosyncrasy credits and modify the role to better serve the organization. This may require forming connections outside the immediate work group. And the organizational member must confront balancing the now-familiar organizational role with nonwork roles and family demands. Each of these experiences provides additional socialization to the role occupant, who may begin to internalize the norms and values that are prominent in the organization.

Now that we have seen a basic sketch of how socialization proceeds, let's look in greater detail at some of the key issues in the process.

The Naive New Member

People seldom join organizations without expectations about what membership will be like. In fact, it is just such expectations that lead them to choose one career or job over another. Management majors have some expectations about what they will be doing when they become management trainees in the Ajax Company. Similarly, even eighteen-year-old army recruits have notions about what military life will be like.

Research indicates that many expectations that are held by entering organizational members are inaccurate and often unrealistically high.[15] In one study of telephone operators, for example, expectations about the nature of the job were obtained before employment commenced and perceptions of the actual job were obtained shortly after. The results indicated that many perceptions were less favorable than expectations. A similar result occurred for students entering a Master of Business Administration program.[16] Such changes, which are fairly common, give support to the notion that socialization has an important impact on new organizational members.[17]

Why do new members often have unrealistic expectations about the organizations they join? To some extent, occupational stereotypes such as those discussed in Chapter 4 may be responsible. Such stereotypes are often communicated by the media. For example, a person entering nurses' training may have gained some expectations about hospital life from watching *General Hospital.* Those of us who teach may also be guilty of communicating stereotypes. After four years of study, the new management trainee at Ajax may be dismayed to find that the emphasis is on *trainee* rather than *management!* Finally, unrealistic expectations may also stem from overzealous recruits who paint rosy pictures in order to attract job candidates to the organization. Taken together, these factors demonstrate the need for socialization.

The Dilemmas of Socialization

Individuals enter organizations with a unique set of skills, interests, and attitudes. This fact of life poses interesting dilemmas for both the individual and the organization.

On one hand, new members wish to maintain their individual identity and self-respect by retaining their unique qualities and building upon them. On the other hand, they are also anxious to learn the ropes of the organization and use these unique qualities in a manner acceptable to peers and superiors. The organization and its experienced members also face a similar dilemma. On one hand, new members must to some extent be encouraged to support the norms and role requirements of the organization. Without this support, organizational goals will be impossible to achieve, because the firm or institution simply won't be *organized.* On the other hand, complete and total allegiance to existing norms and role requirements will render the organization dinosaurlike, unable to adapt to a changing environment. In this case, creative and innovative behaviors on the part of individual members are stifled, and existing norms and roles take on a life of their own. In Chapter 1, you learned that two very basic conditions for organizational survival are reliable role behavior *and* creative, innovative activity.

These, then, are the dilemmas of socialization: How should individuals react to socialization practices? And how can organizations socialize members to an adequate extent without frustrating them or stifling their uniqueness?

From the individual's viewpoint, many persons simply avoid joining organizations whose socialization practices are incompatible with their needs. Of course, this may be tricky business given the inaccurate perceptions of organizational practices held by many outsiders. Finding themselves at the mercy of socialization that doesn't meet their needs, individuals may effect a compromise or decide to seek employment elsewhere.

Organizations attempt to solve *their* socialization dilemmas by tailoring socialization practices to their particular needs. Intuitively, this seems reasonable. Somehow, the making of a priest seems different from the making of a stockbroker! Let's now turn to the different schemes various organizations employ to meet their particular needs.

Methods of Socialization

For various jobs, organizations differ in terms of *who* does the socializing, *how* it is done, and *how much* is done. In turn, these differences affect the job behavior of those who are socialized.

RELIANCE ON EXTERNAL AGENTS.   Organizations differ in the extent to which they make use of *other* organizations to help socialize their members. For example, hospitals do not develop experienced cardiologists from scratch. Rather, they depend on medical schools to socialize potential doctors in the basic role requirements of being a physician. Similarly, business firms rely upon university business schools to send them recruits who think and act in a businesslike manner. In this way, a fair degree of anticipatory socialization may exist before a person joins an organization. On the other hand, organizations such as police forces, the military, and religious institutions are less likely to rely upon external socializers. Police academies, boot camps, and seminaries are set up as extensions of these organizations to aid in socialization.

It appears that organizations that handle their own socialization are especially interested in maintaining the continuity and stability of job behaviors over a period of time. Conversely, those which rely on external agencies to perform anticipatory socialization are oriented toward maintaining the potential for creative, innovative behavior on the part of members—there is less "inbreeding." Of course, reliance on external agents may present problems. The engineer who is socialized in university courses to respect design elegance may find it difficult to accept cost restrictions when employed by an engineering firm. Similarly, Sue and Eve were disappointed that their design ideas did not receive a warm reception from the task force. For these reasons, organizations that rely heavily upon external socialization always supplement it with formal training and orientation or informal on-the-job training. Sue and Eve experienced the latter.

COLLECTIVE VERSUS INDIVIDUAL.   A collective socialization strategy or an individual strategy may be employed.[18] In the collective case, a number of new or aspiring members are socialized as a group, going through the same experiences and facing the same challenges. Army boot camps, fraternity pledge classes, and training classes for salespeople and airline attendants are examples. Under an individual system, socialization is tailor-made for each new member. Simple on-the-job training and apprenticeship to develop skilled craftspersons constitute individual socialization.

Collective socialization is often used to promote organizational loyalty, esprit de corps, and uniformity of behavior among those being socialized. This last characteristic is often very important. No matter where they are in the world, soldiers know who to salute and how to do it. Similarly, air passengers need not expect any surprises from cabin attendants due to the attendants' collective socialization. Collective socialization is especially effective in inducing uniform behavior because there are so many models present who are undergoing the same experience. In addition, those being socialized may pressure each other to toe the line and "do things right." Thus, in collective socialization, one's peers prove to be especially potent sources of information.

Under individual socialization, new members are more likely to take on the particular characteristics and style of their socializers. Thus, two newly hired real estate agents who receive on-the-job training from their bosses may soon think and act more like their bosses than like each other. As you can see, uniformity is less likely under individual socialization.

It must be mentioned that collective socialization is always followed up by individual socialization as the member joins his or her regular work unit. For example, rookie police officers are routinely partnered with more experienced officers. At this point, they will begin to develop some individuality in the style with which they perform their jobs.

DEBASEMENT AND HAZING.   Organizations frequently put new members through a series of experiences designed to humble them and strip away some of their initial self-confidence. These experiences are called **debasement** (or, informally, hazing). Often, debasement is seen as a way of testing the commitment of new members and correcting for faulty anticipatory socialization. Having been humbled and stripped of preconceptions, members are then seen as ready to learn the norms of the organization. Some debasement experiences are formal and planned (see In–Focus 9-2). An extreme example is the rough treatment and shaved heads experienced by Marine Corps recruits. However, many successful business firms also apply debasement to new college graduates:

> This may sound like brainwashing or boot camp, but it usually just takes the form of pouring on more work than the newcomer can possibly do. IBM and Morgan Guaranty socialize with training programs in which, to quote one participant, "You work every

night until 2 A.M. on your own material, and then help others." Proctor & Gamble achieves the same result with what might be called upending experiences—requiring a recent college graduate to color in a map of sales territories, for example. The message is clear: while you may be accomplished in many respects, you are in kindergarten as far as what you know about this organization.[19]

Not all debasement experiences are formally designed. The immediate work group may take it upon itself to test the new member through informal hazing (see In–Focus 9-3). For example, the newly hired engineer may be asked to explain the plans for an impossible or "nonsense" electrical circuit. Similarly the rookie cop may be sent in alone to shake down a bar frequented by unfriendly bikers. Often such experiences are designed to illustrate how group members must depend upon each other.

Debasement experiences most commonly occur in entry-level jobs, whether blue-collar or white-collar. A new executive vice-president would be unlikely to suffer debasement unless he or she was entering a hostile environment.

EXTENT OF SOCIALIZATION. Under some circumstances, organizations are pretty much willing to make do with what they get in terms of recruits. That is, they attempt to build upon the characteristics the person brings into the setting rather than attempting radical socialization. Many volunteer organizations such as charities and community groups are like this, since they have little power over recruits. Similarly, if a university physics department hires a prominent but eccentric physicist, socialization will probably consist of showing her the library and the computer center and hoping she will win the Nobel Prize soon! At the other extreme, some organizations have as their goal the radical socialization of members, hoping to strip them of old beliefs, values, and attitudes and get them to internalize new ones. Whether they are successful or not, prisons, mental hospitals, and religious orders have this orientation toward inmates, patients, and novitiates. Of course, most organizations fall between these extremes, and try to exact a degree of conformity needed to regulate behavior while permitting necessary innovation.[20]

Realistic Job Previews

It was noted earlier that new organizational members often harbor unrealistically inflated expectations about what their jobs will be like. When the job is actually begun, it fails to live up to these expectations, "reality shock" is experienced, and job dissatisfaction results. As a consequence, costly turnover is most likely to occur among newer employees who are unable to survive the discrepancy between expectations and reality. For the organization, this sequence of events represents a failure of socialization.

Obviously, organizations cannot control all sources of unrealistic job expectations, such as those provided by television shows and glorified occupational stereotypes. However, they *can* control those generated during the recruiting process by providing job applicants with realistic job previews. **Realistic job previews** provide a balanced, realistic picture of the positive and negative aspects of the job to job applicants.[21] Thus, they provide "corrective action" to expectations at the anticipatory socialization stage. Exhibit 9-4 compares the realistic job preview process with the traditional preview process that often sets expectations too high by ignoring the negative aspects of the job.

How are realistic job previews designed and conducted? Generally, experienced employees and personnel officers are interviewed to obtain their views on the positive and negative aspects of the job. Then, these views are incorporated

IN–FOCUS 9-3 HAZING AS A FORM OF SOCIALIZATION

SAN DIEGO—Hazing is often thought of as a fact of life at college fraternities or in the armed services.

But hazing in the workplace?

"There isn't a human group anywhere that doesn't require a rite of passage, whether it's the medieval guild or corporate America," said Natasha Josefowitz, professor of management at San Diego State University's College of Business Administration.

She says hazing occurs to some degree in all kinds of work situations and in almost every industry.

Blue-collar hazing tends to be more physical, the white-collar variety more verbal.

Mostly, the hazing is directed at the newest employees as a way of making them prove they "fit" before they're accepted.

But it's also directed at new bosses and people who have just received promotions, as well.

Much of hazing is good-natured, intended to give the "victim" a mildly hard time.

But sometimes it gets violent, nasty or prolonged.

Women and minorities—anyone who's "different," says Josefowitz—often are hazed more severely or for longer periods of time than others. When hazing is sexual, it's harassment.

Both men and women haze, but men are more active and more used to it, says Josefowitz. Women haze by exclusion or gossip.

Josefowitz says hazing falls into three categories—teaching, testing and teasing.

Teaching shows people their place in the office pecking order, by giving the newcomer less desirable tasks or work shifts, or by exclusion, by not inviting him or her to lunch or by leaving the new worker out of conversations.

Testing measures various attributes, such as loyalty or competence.

The oldtimers deliberately goof off to see if the newcomer will tell; or the oldtimers will give the newcomer a difficult or unexplained task to see how it is handled.

Teasing, says Josefowitz, "doesn't seem to have a specific purpose, except to have fun."

This category includes pranks, such as sending the person to buy striped paint or to a non-existent address.

"They test how the person will take it," said Josefowitz. "The response is supposed to be good-natured."

But if you're not hazed, says Josefowitz, watch out.

You're probably being discriminated against, because you're not getting an opportunity to prove yourself.

Source: Hazing fellow workers is part of our survival. (1983, Oct. 22). *The Gazette* (Montreal).

EXHIBIT 9-4   **Traditional and realistic job previews compared.**

Traditional Procedures	**Realistic Procedures**
Set initial job expectations too high	Set job expectations realistically
Job is typically viewed as attractive	Job may or may not be attractive, depending on individual's needs
High rate of job offer acceptance	Some accept, some reject job offer
Work experience disconfirms expectations	Work experience confirms expectations
Dissatisfaction and realization that job not matched to needs	Satisfaction; needs matched to job
Low job survival, dissatisfaction, frequent thoughts of quitting	High job survival, satisfaction, infrequent thoughts of quitting

Source: Wanous, J. P. (1975, July-August). Tell it like it is at realistic job previews. *Personnel,* 50–60. © 1975 American Management Association, New York. All rights reserved.

into booklets or videotape presentations for applicants.[22] For example, a video presentation might involve interviews with job incumbents discussing the pros and cons of their jobs. Realistic previews have been designed for jobs as diverse as telephone operator, life insurance salesperson, Marine Corps recruit, and supermarket worker. Exhibit 9-5 shows the elements of a realistic preview for bank tellers that was conducted using booklets.

Realistic job previews have been shown to be effective in reducing turnover. What is less clear is exactly why this reduction occurs. Reduced expectations and increased job satisfaction are part of the answer. Less clear is whether or not realistic previews cause those who are not cut out for the job to withdraw from the application process.[23] Although the turnover reductions from realistic previews are small, they can result in substantial financial savings for organizations.[24]

| EXHIBIT 9-5 | **Elements covered in a realistic job preview for bank tellers.** |

Topic	Job Preview Coverage
Training	Training described
	Final exam at the end of training mentioned
	Failure rate during training reported
Work	Banking transactions described
	Accuracy important and it is checked daily
	Working under pressure, e.g., Mondays & Fridays
	Manager schedules work 1 week in advance
	Working on your feet
	Working may become routine and repetitive
Customers	Courtesy is always required
	Rude customers encountered
Career opportunities	Promotion criteria specified
	Average promotion rates for each job given
	How to move into branch management (college degree needed)
Compensation	Pay rates specified
	Employee benefits described
	How pay increases are determined
Summary of major points	Summary included—½ page long, titled "It's not for everyone"

Source: Adapted from Dean, R. A., & Wanous, J. P. (1984). Effects of realistic job previews on hiring bank tellers. *Journal of Applied Psychology, 69,* 61–68.

The Power of Socialization

Socialization can be a powerful process, even overcoming cultural boundaries in the case of multinational corporations:

> It was in Brussels, at the annual ITT [International Telephone and Telegraph] barbecue for managers from all over the world, that I first felt the full impact. . . . Belgian waiters were cooking steaks and sweet corn on the charcoal grills, while the polyglot managers queued up docilely with their plates. . . . It was not immediately easy to tell the Europeans from the Americans, except perhaps by the shoes and trousers, for the Europeans, too—whether Swedish, Greek, or even French—had a hail-fellow style and spoke fluent American, joshing and reminiscing about old times in Copenhagen and Rio. I soon had a sense of being enveloped by the company, by its rites, customs, and arcane organogram, of being swept right away from Brussels, or Europe, or anywhere.[25]

ORGANIZATIONAL CULTURE

The last several pages have been concerned with socialization into an organization. To a large degree, the course that socialization takes depends on the culture of the organization. Let's examine culture, a concept that has rapidly gained the attention of both researchers and practicing managers.

What Is Organizational Culture?

At the outset, it can be said that organizational culture is not the easiest concept to define. Informally, culture might be thought of as an organization's style, atmosphere, or personality. This style, atmosphere, or personality is most obvious when we contrast what it must be like to work in various organizations such as IBM, U.S. Steel, the Bank of America, the U.S. Marine Corps, or the New York Yankees. Even from their mention in the popular press, we can imagine that these organizations provide very different work environments. Thus, culture provides uniqueness and social identity to organizations.

More formally, **organizational culture** consists of the shared beliefs, values, and assumptions that exist in an organization.[26] In turn, these shared beliefs, values, and assumptions determine the norms that develop and the patterns of behavior that emerge from these norms. The term *shared* does not necessarily mean that members are in close agreement on these matters, although they may well be. Rather, it means that they have been uniformly exposed to them and have some minimum common understanding of them. Several other characteristics of culture can be noted:

- Culture represents a true "way of life" for organizational members, who often take its influence for granted. Frequently, an organization's culture only becomes obvious when contrasted with that of other organizations or when it undergoes changes.

- Because culture involves basic assumptions, values, and beliefs, it tends to be fairly stable over time. In addition, once a culture is well-established, it can persist despite turnover among organizational personnel, providing social continuity.

- The content of a culture can involve matters that are internal to the organization or external. Internally, a culture might support innovation, risk taking, or secrecy of information. Externally, a culture might support "putting the customer first" or behaving unethically toward competitors.

It is important to note that culture is truly a social variable, reflecting yet another aspect of the kind of social influence that we have been discussing in this chapter. Thus, culture is not simply an automatic consequence of an organization's technology, products, or size. For example, there is some tendency for organizations to become more bureaucratic as they get larger. However, the culture of a particular large organization might support an informal, nonbureaucratic atmosphere.

Can an organization have several cultures? The answer is yes. Often unique subcultures develop that reflect departmental differences or differences in occupation or training. A researcher who studied Silicon Valley computer companies found that technical and professional employees divided into "hardware types" and "software types." In turn, hardware types subdivided into engineers and technicians and software types into software engineers and computer scientists. Each group was seen to have its own values, beliefs, and assumptions about how to design computer systems.[27] Effective organizations will develop an overarching culture that manages such divisions. For instance, a widely shared norm may exist that in effect says, "We fight like hell until a final design is chosen, and then we all pull together."

The "Strong Culture" Concept

Some cultures have more impact on the behavior of organizational members than others. In a **strong culture,** the beliefs, values, and assumptions that make up the culture are both intense and pervasive across the organization.[28] In other words, the beliefs, values, and assumptions are strongly supported by the majority of members, even cutting across any subcultures that might exist. Thus, the strong culture provides great consensus concerning "what the organization is about" or what it stands for. In weak cultures, on the other hand, beliefs, values, and assumptions are less strongly ingrained and/or less widely shared across the organization. Weak cultures are thus fragmented and less impactful on organizational members. For example, In–Focus 8-2 revealed the weak, fragmented culture that existed at Atari. All organizations can be said to have a culture, although it may be hard to detect the details of weak cultures.

In order to firm up your understanding of strong cultures, let's consider thumbnail sketches of three organizations that are generally agreed to have strong cultures:[29]

- *Procter & Gamble.* This Cincinnati-based consumer products giant markets everything from Crest toothpaste to Pampers. Known for fanatical attention to product quality and consumer tastes. Also known for rigorous selection practices and inducing healthy competition among its brand managers.

- *IBM.* Every employee at this computer giant knows and understands the company's complete devotion to customer service. This is backed by knowledge that extensive training and education are an ongoing way of life at IBM. Strong attention to details, right down to the clothing worn by company representatives.

- *3M.* This Minneapolis-based company produces tape, adhesives, abrasives, and building materials. Known for its extreme dedication to product innovation. Employees are rewarded for creativity and risk taking to this end, and failure is accepted as part of the game.

Three points are worth emphasizing about these examples of strong cultures. First, an organization need not be big to have a strong culture. If its members agree strongly about certain beliefs, values, and assumptions, a small business, school, or social service agency can have a strong culture. Second, strong cultures do not necessarily result in blind conformity. For example, the strong culture at 3M supports and rewards *non*conformity in the form of innovation and creativity. Finally, Procter & Gamble, IBM, and 3M are obviously successful organizations. Do strong cultures always result in organizational success?

Assets and Liabilities of Strong Cultures

Ever since the publication of the immensely popular book *In Search of Excellence,* observers have been interested in the possible advantages for organizational effectiveness that might result from having a strong culture.[30] In this book, Thomas Peters and Robert Waterman list what they claim are the best run, most innovative American companies, firms such as Hewlett-Packard, Texas Instruments, Eastman Kodak, Revlon, DuPont, and the three discussed above. They then go on to cite the common characteristics that these firms share (Exhibit 9-6), many of which contribute to a strong culture. For instance, ''stick to the knitting'' (point 6 in the Exhibit) means that successful firms have generally limited their business to areas with which they are familiar, allowing them to concentrate on core values (point 5), including staying close to the customer (point 2). Similarly, they argue that successful firms are loose (point 8) in granting employees autonomy (point 3) but tight when it comes to reinforcing core values.

Both the companies chosen and the characteristics noted by Peters and Waterman have received some criticism. However, there is growing consensus that strong cultures contribute to organizational success *when the culture supports the mission, goals, and strategy of the organization.*[31] In this case a strong common culture should ease communication and coordination and provide a means for dealing with conflict when it arises.

On the other side of the coin, strong cultures can prove to be a liability under certain circumstances. First, the mission, goals, or strategy of an organization may

---

EXHIBIT 9-6   **Characteristics of excellent organizations according to Peters and Waterman.**

---

1. A bias for action.
2. Close to the customer.
3. Autonomy and entrepreneurship.
4. Productivity through people.
5. Hands-on, value driven.
6. Stick to the knitting.
7. Simple form, lean staff.
8. Simultaneous loose-tight properties.

Source: Peters, T. J., & Waterman, R. H., Jr. (1982). *In search of excellence: Lessons from America's best-run companies.* New York: Harper & Row.

change, and the strong culture that supported past success may not suit the new order. Later, we will examine how deregulation in the telecommunications industry challenged the strong traditional culture of AT&T.

Secondly, strong cultures can mix as badly as oil and water when a merger or acquisition pushes two of them together under the same corporate banner. Both General Electric and Xerox, large organizations with strong cultures of their own, had interesting experiences when they acquired small high-technology Silicon Valley companies with unique cultures:

> So Versatec retained its first-come, first-served parking lot, its volleyball courts, its raucous Halloween party, its pension and health plans, its cookies and coffee on silver trays outside the chief executive's office, and the freewheeling, egalitarian attitudes that go along with these things.
>
> In the early days Xerox kept sending in its helpful minions. First came the security men, munificently offering to install the corporate badge system at Versatec headquarters. Zaphiropoulos fed them coffee and cookies and patiently explained that though doubtless his company would someday embrace badges gratefully, now was too soon. Later came the facilities department, offering to oversee the construction of Versatec's second building and refusing to take no for an answer. Zaphiropoulos bowed to necessity but served notice not to interfere again by ignoring the bill that later arrived.[32]

Finally, some strong cultures can threaten organizational effectiveness simply because the cultures are in some sense pathological.[33] Such cultures may be based on beliefs, values, and assumptions that support infighting, secrecy, and paranoia, pursuits that hardly leave time for doing business. Here's an example of an unsuccessful semiconductor firm whose culture exhibited considerable paranoia:

> The two founders took all kinds of precautions to prevent their ideas from being stolen. They fragmented jobs and processes so that only a few key people in the company really understood the products. They rarely subcontracted work. And they paid employees very high salaries to give them an incentive to stay with the firm. These three precautions combined to make Paratech's costs among the highest in the industry.[34]

Contributors to the Culture

How are cultures built and maintained? In this section we consider two key factors that contribute to the foundation and continuation of organizational cultures.

THE FOUNDER'S ROLE.   It is certainly possible for cultures to emerge over time without the guidance of a key individual. However, it is remarkable how many cultures, especially strong cultures, reflect the values of an organization's founder.[35] The imprint of Ray Kroc on McDonald's, T. J. Watson on IBM, and Steven Jobs on Apple Computer is obvious. As we shall note shortly, such imprint is often kept alive through a series of stories about the founders which is passed on to successive generations of new employees. This provides continuing reinforcement for the firm's core values. In a similar vein, it is usually agreed that the organization's culture is strongly shaped by top management. The culture will usually begin to emulate what top management "pays attention to." Sometimes, the culture begun by the founder can cause conflict when top management wishes to see an organization change directions. At Apple Computer, Steven Jobs nurtured a culture based on new technology and new products—innovation was everything. When this strategy was perceived by top management to be damaging profits, a series of controls and changes was introduced by management that led to Jobs's resignation as chairman.[36]

SOCIALIZATION.   The precise nature of the socialization process is a key contributor to the culture that emerges in an organization, because socialization is the means by which the culture's beliefs, values, and assumptions are learned. Weak or fragmented cultures often feature haphazard selection and a nearly random series of job assignments that fail to present the new hire with a coherent set of experiences. On the other hand, Richard Pascale of Stanford University notes that organizations with strong cultures go to great pains to expose employees to a careful step-by-step socialization process (Exhibit 9-7):[37]

■   *Step 1.* New employees are carefully selected to obtain those who will be able to adapt to the existing culture, and realistic job previews are provided to allow candidates to deselect themselves. As an example, Pascale cites Procter & Gamble's series of individual interviews, group interviews, and tests for brand management positions.

■   *Step 2.* Debasement and hazing are used to provoke humility in new hires so that they are open to the norms of the organization.

■   *Step 3.* Employees are trained "in the trenches" so that they begin to master one of the core areas of the organization. For example, even experienced M.B.A.s will be required to start on the bottom of the professional ladder to assure that they understand how *this* organization works.

■   *Step 4.* The reward and promotion system is carefully used to reinforce those employees who perform well in areas that support the goals of the organization.

■   *Step 5.* Again and again, the culture's core beliefs, values, and assumptions are asserted to provide guidance for member behavior. This is done to emphasize that the personal sacrifices required by the socialization process have a true purpose.

■   *Step 6.* Members are exposed to folklore about the organization, stories that reinforce the nature of the culture. We examine this in more detail below.

■   *Step 7.* Role models who are consistent with the culture are identified as "fast-trackers" to serve as tangible examples to imitate.

Pascale is careful to note that it is the *consistency* among these steps and their mutually reinforcing properties that make for a strong culture.

EXHIBIT 9-7   **Socialization steps in strong cultures.**

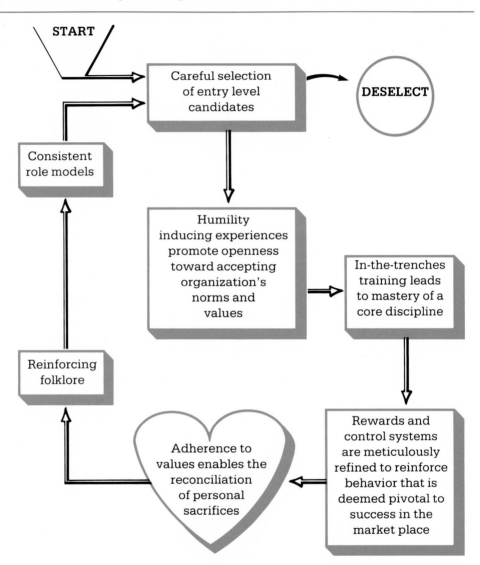

Source: Pascale, R. (1985, Winter). The paradox of "corporate culture": Reconciling ourselves to socialization. *California Management Review*, 26–41. Reprinted by permission.

Diagnosing a Culture

Earlier it was noted that culture represents a "way of life" for organizational members. Even when the culture is strong, this way of life may be difficult for uninitiated outsiders to read and understand. One way to grasp a culture is to examine the symbols, rituals, and stories that characterize the organization's way of life. For insiders, these symbols, rituals, and stories are mechanisms that teach and reinforce the culture.

SYMBOLS. At IBM, the sayings "IBM means service" and "respect for the individual" are seen and heard again and again. Observers generally concede that these sayings have a powerful symbolic impact on employees because the organization tries to live by them. On the other hand, consider the corrupt police force that has "Integrity and Honor" painted on the sides of all its squad cars. Here, the corrupt culture is reinforced by the irony of the motto. Porsche Managing Director Peter Schutz was asked why his company is involved in auto racing. After citing the publicity and product development benefits of racing, Schutz noted its symbolic cultural function:

> Probably the most important dimension, though, from my point of view, is the contribution that racing makes to our corporate culture. The racing activity is highly visible, and it has a couple of characteristics that I find extremely valuable in achieving the kind of quality we want. One of them is the concept that work has to be ready on time. You have to develop a critical path and plan all of your material flow. Whether you do this formally or informally, you have to get your arms around the vital dimensions of the project. And, of course, it introduces the idea that you work until the job is done, not until it's quitting time. Our racing team would never think of going home just because it's evening. If there's a race the next day, the car has to be finished. And that gets transferred to other areas of the company. It becomes part of the fiber of the entire company.[38]

RITUALS. Observers have noted how rites, rituals, and ceremonies may convey the essence of a culture.[39] For example, at Tandem, a California computer company, Friday afternoon "beer busts" are a regular ritual. The beer busts reinforce a "work hard, play hard" atmosphere and reaffirm the idea that weekly conflicts can be forgotten. At Mary Kay Cosmetics, elaborate "seminars" with the flavor of a Hollywood premiere combined with a revival meeting are used to make the sales force feel good about themselves and the company. Pink Cadillacs and other extravagant sales awards reinforce the cultural imperative that any Mary Kay woman can be successful. Rituals need not be so exotic to send a cultural message. In some companies, the annual performance review is seen as an act of feedback and development. In others, it may be viewed as an exercise in punishment and debasement.

STORIES. As noted above, the folklore of organizations as expressed in stories about past organizational events is a common aspect of culture. These stories, told repeatedly to successive generations of new employees, are evidently meant to communicate "how things work," whether they are true, false, or a bit of both. Anyone who has spent much time in a particular organization is familiar with such stories, and they often appear to reflect the uniqueness of organizational cultures. However, research indicates that a few common themes may underlie many organizational stories:

- Is the big boss human?
- Can the little person rise to the top?
- Will I get fired?
- Will the organization help me when I have to move?
- How will the boss react to mistakes?
- How will the organization deal with obstacles?[40]

Issues of equality, security, and control underlie the stories that pursue these themes. Also, such stories often have a "good" version, where things turn out well, and a "bad" version where things go sour. For example, there is a story that Ray Kroc, McDonald's founder, cancelled a franchise after finding a single fly in the restaurant.[41] This is an example of a sour ending to a "how will the boss react to mistakes?" story. Whether the story is true or not, its retelling is indicative of one of the core values of the McDonald's culture—a fanatical dedication to clean premises.

AT&T—A Culture in Transition

To conclude our discussion of culture, let's examine an organization that has undergone a radical cultural transition in recent years.[42] On January 1, 1984, AT&T was required by a U.S. Justice Department Consent Decree to divest itself of its local telephone company operations. This was one of a long series of deregulation changes that forced the former monopoly to confront a new competitive marketplace. The "physical" consequences of the consent decree were impressive in themselves, as the work force was reduced considerably, and millions of dollars in assets were sold. Equally important, however, was the change that was required in AT&T's culture.

Prior to the years leading up to the divestiture, AT&T had a strong corporate culture based on providing universal telephone service at a reasonable price. The core values were oriented toward excellent service, and stories are told with pride about the dedication of Bell System staff to keeping the lines open. To support this mission, cultural emphasis was placed on loyalty, lifetime careers, and promotion from within. Since it was a monopoly, product development could proceed slowly, and aggressive salesmanship was not necessary.

With deregulation, AT&T was required to change its mission to include the development and sale of innovative communications products and services. A new culture that was supportive of this mission would have to be grounded on entrepreneurship, fast decision making, and creative risk taking. To accomplish this, the company has given increased power to the marketing function and taken increased pains to tie rewards to individual performance. Sales personnel have been placed on commissions, and service personnel have been given more autonomy in doing their jobs. The changes have been supported by information campaigns in which top management regularly asserts the need for a new culture at AT&T.

Some AT&T employees enjoy the new ''action'' and the increased job autonomy offered by the cultural change. Others, however, have expressed anxiety and uncertainty regarding the changed way of life that the new culture requires. Some worry that the service ethic will be sacrificed for the sales ethic. As we noted earlier, strong cultures can be difficult to change. And as we have noted throughout the chapter, social influence has a strong impact on organizational members.

SUMMARY

- There are two basic forms of social dependence. Information dependence means that we rely upon others for information about how we should think, feel, and act. Effect dependence means that we rely on rewards and punishments provided by others. Both contribute to conformity to norms.

- There are several motives for conformity. One is compliance, where conformity occurs mainly to achieve rewards and avoid punishment. It is mostly indicative of effect dependence. Another motive for conformity is identification with other group members. Here, the person sees himself or herself as similar to them and relies upon them for information. Finally, conformity may be motivated by the internalization of norms, and the person is no longer conforming simply because of social dependence.

- Conformity to norms is most likely when others will be aware of deviance, when the opposition is big and unanimous, and when the issue at hand is ambiguous or important to the group. High-status group members have generally achieved their status by conformity to group norms. However, they may deviate on a particular issue by exercising idiosyncrasy credits which they have built up by previous conformity. Low-status members who are new to the group are especially likely to exhibit conformity, while those who have been rejected by the group have nothing to gain by conformity.

- Conformity due to simple compliance can have strong long-term effects. The foot-in-the-door phenomenon suggests that complying with minor requests sets the stage for conformity to more demanding requests. In addition, the person who complies with norms simply to gain rewards or avoid punishment may feel dissonance, since the behavior does not correspond to private attitudes. One way to reduce this dissonance is to adopt the belief and value structure underlying the norm.

- Organizational members learn norm and role requirements through stages of socialization. Some organizations rely on other organizations to do a certain amount of anticipatory socialization, while others handle the process themselves. Some rely on collective socialization, in which new members learn the ropes as a group, while others socialize new members on an individual basis. Debasement and hazing may be used to test the stuff of new members. Also, realistic job previews can be used to cope with initial unrealistic expectations.

- Organizational culture consists of the shared beliefs, values, and assumptions that exist in an organization. Strong cultures can be an asset when they support the mission and strategy of the organization, but they can pose problems when change is necessary. The organization's founder and its socialization process can be strong contributors to the shape of the culture, which is often revealed by symbols, rituals, and stories.

KEY CONCEPTS

Information dependence
Social comparison theory
Effect dependence
Conformity
Compliance
Identification
Internalization

Idiosyncrasy credits
Foot-in-the-door phenomenon
Socialization
Debasement
Realistic job previews
Organizational culture
Strong culture

DISCUSSION QUESTIONS

1. Compare and contrast information dependence with effect dependence. Under which conditions should persons be especially information-dependent? Under which conditions should persons be especially effect-dependent?

2. Describe an instance of conformity which you have observed in an organizational setting. Was this incident motivated by compliance, identification, or internalization? Were the results beneficial for the organization? Were they beneficial to the individual involved?

3. Imagine that a large organization is charged with making illegal financial contributions to a political campaign. What are the situational factors that might prompt executives to conform to such organizational norms at the expense of societal norms that stand against such behavior?

4. Consider the case that began the chapter. How could Sue and Eve use the foot-in-the-door technique to get more challenging job assignments?

5.   Consider how you were socialized into the college or university where you are taking your organizational behavior course. Did you have some unrealistic expectations? Where did your expectations come from? What outside experiences prepared you for college or university? Are you experiencing collective or individual socialization? What is the extent of socialization required by most colleges and universities?

6.   Contrast the socialization process used by the army with that employed by the typical business firm. Why do they differ?

7.   What are the pros and cons of providing realistic job previews for a job that is objectively pretty bad?

8.   Imagine that you are starting a new business in the retail trade. You are strongly oriented toward providing excellent customer service. What could you do to nurture a strong organizational culture that would support such a mission?

9.   Discuss the advantages and disadvantages of developing a strong organizational culture.

FOR FURTHER READING

Kiesler, C. A., & Kiesler, S. B. (1969). *Conformity*. Reading, MA: Addison-Wesley.
A small paperback concerned with the general issue of conformity. Especially valuable is the authors' exploration of the factors that separate simple compliance with norms from private acceptance of the belief and value structure that underlies norms.

Moritz, M. (1984). *The little kingdom: The private story of Apple Computer*. New York: William Morrow.
An unauthorized account of the genesis and growth of Apple Computer. A wonderful portrait of the development and transition of a corporate culture.

Sathe, V. (1985). *Culture and related corporate realities*. Homewood, IL: Richard D. Irwin.
Text, cases, and readings concerned with the establishment and change of corporate cultures. Includes some interesting cases.

Case Study

The White-shirt Rule

A consultant had been hired by a large insurance company to study its work flow and office procedures. She began by interviewing a large number of head office personnel to determine their perceptions of the current working arrangements. During the course of her interviews the consultant noticed an interesting phenomenon—all of the men in the firm, from clerks to upper level managers, were wearing white dress shirts. Over a period of several days she scanned the offices for a striped or pastel shirt, but none was to be found. After two weeks, the consultant interviewed the president of the company. At the end of the interview, out of curiosity, she asked him about the "white-shirt rule" that appeared to exist in the firm.

"White-shirt rule?" he said. "Nonsense, no way. Just so male employees wear dress shirts and ties, the color or pattern of the shirt doesn't matter. I've always worn white shirts myself. There *do* seem to be a lot of white shirts around here, though!"

In the days that followed, the consultant probed the white-shirt mystery as she continued her interviews. All employees reported that they had never seen the "white-shirt rule" in writing. Most recalled that they had learned the requirement shortly after they joined the company. Some had learned by sim-

ple observation, while others had been informed by helpful co-workers or bosses. One new manager reported that he had been informed of the rule by a tactful but concerned *subordinate*.

At the end of the job, the consultant concluded that there was really no white-shirt rule, except in the minds of the employees.

■ ■ ■

1. What functions does the "white-shirt rule" serve in the insurance company?
2. Do organizational members follow the "white-shirt rule" due to information dependence, effect dependence, or both? Explain your answer.
3. How do you think the "white-shirt rule" began? How might it have spread across the organization?
4. Who might be likely to deviate from the "white-shirt rule"? That is, who might wear another color or pattern of shirt to work?
5. What clues does the "white-shirt rule" provide about the culture of the insurance company?
6. Can you think of other informal organizational norms that are similar to the "white-shirt rule"?

Case Study

Foster Creek Post Office

The United States Post Office in Foster Creek, New York, is a small first-class office serving a suburban community of 11,000. Normally, the post office employs eleven people—a postmaster, an assistant postmaster, six carriers (including one parcel-post truck driver), and three clerks.

Each postal employee's job requirements are minutely subdivided and explicitly prescribed by the *Post Office Manual*—a large two-volume publication of the U.S. Post Office Department in Washington, D.C. There is a "suggested" rate per minute and/or day for sorting and delivering letters of which every postal employee is well aware. The work is highly prescribed, routine, and repetitive, with little basis for the development of individual initiative. Although each man contrives a few little tricks (which he may or may not pass along to his fellow workers) for easing his *own* work load, there is little incentive for a postal employee to attempt to improve any part of the mail delivery system *as a whole*. Each man performs pretty much as he is expected to perform (nothing more or less). Roger, the assistant postmaster, clearly verbalized this attitude, "The inspectors can't get us if we go by the book [manual]."

The irregular, unannounced visits by the district postal inspectors arouse a strange fear in *all* employees at the Foster Creek Post Office. Although each of the 11 employees is fairly well acquainted with the inspectors, there is something disturbing about the presence of a man whose recommendations may

This case was written under the supervision of Alvar O. Elbing. Names of people and places have been disguised. Source: From Elbing, A. O. (1970). *Behavioral decisions in organizations*. Glenview, IL: Scott, Foresman. Copyright © 1970 by Scott, Foresman and Company. Reprinted by permission.

mean the loss of your job. The security of their position in the post office is highly valued by employees of Foster Creek, some of whom are no longer young and must provide for their families. It is customary, therefore, to see an entire post office staff snap to attention and work harder at the arrival, or possibility of arrival, of a postal inspector.

Larry, the Foster Creek postmaster, had a philosophy regarding the affairs of his office which was: "Keep the patrons and the inspectors happy." Outside of this requirement and an additional one which made it imperative that each employee punch in and off the time clock at the exact appointed time (this requirement was primarily for the ease of bookkeeping), each man could do his job pretty much as he wished. The clerks reported at 6 A.M. to sort the day's mail into different stacks for the carriers who arrived at 7 A.M. The carriers then "cased" (further sorting according to street and number) their letters and usually were "on the road" by 9 A.M. They were required to be back in the office at 3:30 P.M. if possible, for further casing, and at 5 P.M. all the carriers went home.

In the summer months when the mail is relatively light and the weather is clear, each carrier easily finishes his route (including time allowed for a half-hour lunch break) by 1:30 P.M. It is standard procedure for the men to relax at home for two hours before reporting back in at 3:30 P.M. In the winter, on the other hand, with snow piled high in the yards, each carrier can no longer take the shorter route across the yards, and the men often finish long after 3:30 P.M. Larry is well aware of this procedure and says: "It all balances out, and in the hot summer they can use the extra hours to take it easy."

At 3:30 P.M. (or so) the day's big social event takes

place at the post office. With the cry of "Flip for Cokes," all the employees except Jane, the one female clerk, match dimes to see who will be the day's loser and provide cokes for the others. This daily gaming is one of the many examples of the free and frequent sociability which exists among the ten male employees. Although the office's formal organization is detailed by postal regulations (see Exhibit 1), owing to the similar socioeconomic status and interests of the employees, the post office atmosphere is very relaxed and informal (see Exhibit 2). Many of the men bowl together; they go to the same church; and they often attend high school graduations and funerals affecting the families of their co-workers.

On payday (every Friday) each of the ten male employees contributes 50 cents of his paycheck to "the fund." This fund is used for coffee and donuts, to provide sick employees with flowers and "get-well" cards, and to purchase a ham to be shared at work during Christmas time.

Other important parts of each day are the regular morning and afternoon conversations. In the morning the talk invariably turns to news items in the morning's paper. In addition, the men often talk about "those politicians in Washington" and the possibility of a postal pay raise. In the afternoons the men relate any interesting experiences from the day's rounds. These experiences range from dog bites to coffee with an attractive female patron.

In general the 11 employees of the Foster Creek Post Office enjoyed their work. They comprised a close-knit team doing similar and somewhat distasteful work, but as George, a senior carrier, put it, "We get good steady pay; and it's a lot easier than digging ditches."

In mid-June 1968, Larry filed a request for a

EXHIBIT 1   **Foster Creek Post Office formal organization.**

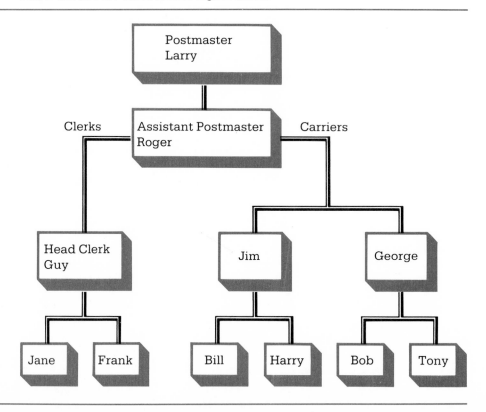

carrier to replace a regular Foster Creek carrier who had died suddenly. At 7 A.M. on Monday, July 8th, Harry reported for work as a permanent replacement.

Harry was a tall skinny man with thinning hair, long fingers, and wire-rimmed eyeglasses. He appeared to be in his fifties. He seemed nervous and shy, and when Larry introduced him to the Foster Creek regulars, Harry stared at the floor and said only "Hi!" Initial opinions of this new carrier were mixed. Jim, another senior carrier, probably best expressed the employees' sentiments when he said: "He's not too friendly—yet—he's probably a little nervous here—but, *man,* can he case mail!"

Harry was an excellent caser. For 27 years he had been a clerk in the main post office. The attitudes and work environment in big city post offices differ markedly from those in smaller offices (as Larry was quick to point out when any of Foster Creek's employees complained). In the city post offices, where competition for the few available positions is extremely keen, a man must not only be very competent but must follow the postal regulations *to the letter.* As Harry said quietly to Roger upon his arrival at Foster Creek, "Things were just too pushy in the city. And besides, my wife and I wanted to move out here in the country to have a house and garden of our own to take care of."

Harry had a well-kept and attractive house and garden. It was apparent that Harry loved to take care of his lawn and garden, because he spent all day Sunday working on it. As a member of the Foster Creek Building and Loan Association, Larry knew that Harry had purchased the property with cash.

On Wednesday, Harry's third day at work, the opinions regarding Harry had become more concrete. As Jim said: "Harry's strange. He thinks he's better than all of us, coming from that city office. He never talks to us or says anything about himself. All

---

EXHIBIT 2   **Foster Creek Post Office informal organization.**

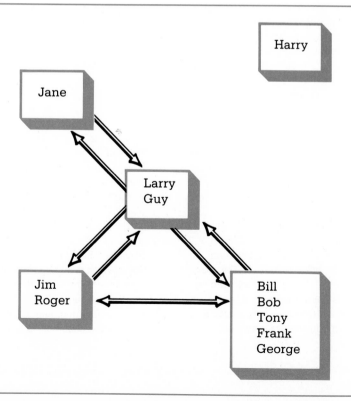

he does is stand there and case mail, but *man,* is he fast at that!''

The first real problem arose on the fourth day. Harry had learned his route well enough so that he, too, was able to finish by 1:30 P.M. His ability to case and ''tie out'' (gathering the mail in leather straps) his mail so quickly put him on the road by 8:30 in the morning—ahead of the other four carriers.

On this Thursday afternoon Harry reported back to the post office at 1:15, having finished his entire route. Upon seeing this, Roger's first reaction was to say, ''Go home and have some lunch, Harry. Relax at home for a little while.''

Harry replied, ''I've had my lunch. There are letters on my case. I've got to do them now. I've got to do my job.'' Having said this, he began to case the several hundred letters which had piled up since the morning. He finished these quickly and then went on and cased all the mail which was lying on the other four carriers' cases. When the four regular carriers returned at 3:30 P.M., they were, to say the least, surprised.

Bill, the youngest and least energetic of the carriers, thanked Harry. However, Jim and George in particular were very angry. They grumbled about having a ''newcomer'' interfere with his ''city tricks'' and ''fancy casing.'' They were especially angry that Harry had violated the 3:30 rule. They were determined that he would not be the one who would make them lose their precious privileges, and they complained to Larry about Harry. The postmaster told Harry to case only his own mail and to take it easy when walking his route in the future.

The next day, Friday, was payday. Each man contributed his share to ''the fund.'' Harry refused. ''I don't drink coffee,'' was his only answer. No one pushed the matter further, although discontent over Harry had developed among all the employees.

As the next week passed by, Harry appeared to sink into an even deeper shell. He punched in at 7 A.M. and punched out at 5 P.M. In between, he neither looked at nor spoke to any of the other employees. He continued to report back into the office before 3:30, case all his own mail, and then sit on the stool in front of his case reading magazines. Larry was worried primarily about Harry's exposure

to the public as he sat at his case reading, and so on Friday of Harry's second week, Harry's and Bill's cases were switched to move Harry out of the public eye.

When each of the carriers reported in on Friday afternoon, Bill was told that his case was moved so as to give him more room to handle his quickly growing route (which, in part, was true). Harry said nothing about the switch but went straight to work in his new location.

During Harry's third week at the post office, Larry began to worry even more about his behavior. Although the carrier was hidden from the public now, a postal inspector could catch Harry reading at his case very easily.

On Thursday, July 18th, Larry's worst fears were realized. An inspector came to the Foster Creek Post Office. As he walked in, Harry was sitting quietly at his case, reading as usual. The inspector looked at Harry, then at Larry.

Larry explained that Harry had an easier route than the other carriers. Because of this and his ability as a caser, Harry was able to finish his route more easily. Larry pointed out that he did not know what to say to the carrier, for he had finished all his *required* work. The inspector suggested that Larry readjust the routes to give Harry more houses to deliver and more mail to case. This was attempted but Jim, George, and Tony reacted unfavorably.

■ ■ ■

1. Discuss the norms that regulate behavior in the Foster Creek Post Office.
2. Describe the socialization process at Foster Creek Post Office. Would it differ for an inexperienced recruit?
3. Discuss Harry's lack of conformity to the norms of the Foster Creek Post Office. Why doesn't he conform? Who might conform to such norms?
4. Describe the culture of the Foster Creek Post Office. What is its impact on worker performance? How does it seem to differ from the culture of big city post offices?
5. What, if anything, should Larry have done differently? What should he do now?

REFERENCES

1. The terms information dependence and effect dependence are used by Jones, E. E., & Gerard, H. B. (1967). *Foundations of social psychology.* New York: Wiley.
2. Festinger, L. (1954). A theory of social comparison processes. *Human Relations, 7,* 117–140.
3. Schacter, S. (1959). *The psychology of affiliation.* Stanford, CA: Stanford University Press.
4. For a review of social influence effects on perceptions of task design see Thomas, J., & Griffin, R. (1983). The social information processing model of task design: A review of the literature. *Academy of Management Review, 8,* 672–682.
5. Kelman, H. C. (1961). Processes of opinion change. *Public Opinion Quarterly, 25,* 57–78.
6. Asch, S. E. (1952). *Social psychology.* Englewood Cliffs, NJ: Prentice-Hall.
7. Sherif, M. (1935). A study of some social factors in perception. *Archives of Psychology, 27,* No. 187.
8. Rohrer, J., Baron, S., Hoffman, E., & Swander, D. (1954). The stability of autokinetic judgments. *Journal of Abnormal and Social Psychology, 49,* 595–597.
9. Asch, 1952; Gerard, H., Wilhelmy, R., & Connolley, E. (1968). Conformity and group size. *Journal of Personality and Social Psychology, 8,* 79–82.
10. Saks, M. J. (1977). *Jury verdicts.* Lexington, MA: Heath.
11. Hollander, E. P. (1958). Conformity, status, and idiosyncrasy credit. *Psychological Review, 65,* 117–127; Hollander, E. P. (1964). *Leaders, groups, and influence.* New York: Oxford University Press.
12. Freedman, J. L., & Fraser, S. C. (1966). Compliance without pressure: The foot-in-the-door technique. *Journal of Personality and Social Psychology, 4,* 195–202; Seligman, C., Bush, M., & Kirsch, K. (1976). Relationship between compliance in the foot-in-the-door paradigm and size of the first request. *Journal of Personality and Social Psychology, 33,* 517–520.
13. Van Maanen, J., & Schein, E. H. (1979). Toward a theory of organizational socialization. *Research in Organizational Behavior, 1,* 209–264.
14. Feldman, D. C. (1976). A contingency theory of socialization. *Administrative Science Quarterly, 21,* 433–452.
15. Wanous, J. P. (1980). *Organizational entry: Recruitment, selection, and socialization of newcomers.* Reading, MA: Addison-Wesley.
16. Wanous, J. P. (1976). Organizational entry: From naive expectations to realistic beliefs. *Journal of Applied Psychology, 61,* 22–29.
17. For other such studies see Van Maanen, J., & Schein, E. H. (1977). Career development. In J. R. Hackman & J. L. Suttle (Eds.), *Improving life at work: Behavioral science approaches to organizational change.* Glenview, IL: Scott, Foresman.
18. Van Maanen & Schein, 1979.
19. Pascale, R. (1984, May 28). Fitting new employees into the company culture. *Fortune,* 28–43, p. 30.
20. This discussion draws upon Van Maanen & Schein, 1979, but differs in detail.
21. Wanous, 1980.
22. Wanous, 1980.
23. Premack, S. L., & Wanous, J. P. (1985). A meta-analysis of realistic job preview experiments. *Journal of Applied Psychology, 70,* 706–719.

24. Premack & Wanous, 1985; McEvoy, G. M., & Cascio, W. F. (1985). Strategies for reducing employee turnover: A meta-analysis. *Journal of Applied Psychology, 70,* 342–353.
25. Sampson, A. (1973). *The sovereign state of ITT.* Greenwich, CT: Fawcett, pp. 13–14.
26. For a more complete discussion of various definitions, theories, and concepts of culture see Smircich, L. (1983). Concepts of culture and organizational analysis. *Administrative Science Quarterly, 28,* 339–358; Schein, E. H. (1985). *Organizational culture and leadership.* San Francisco: Jossey-Bass; Allaire, Y., & Firsirotu, M. E. (1984). Theories of organizational culture. *Organization Studies, 5,* 193–226.
27. Gregory, K. L. (1983). Native-view paradigms: Multiple cultures and culture conflicts in organizations. *Administrative Science Quarterly, 28,* 359–376.
28. Kilmann, R., Saxton, M. J., & Serpa, R. (1986, Winter). Issues in understanding and changing culture. *California Management Review,* 87–94; Deal, T. E., & Kennedy, A. A. (1982). *Corporate cultures: The rites and rituals of corporate life.* Reading, MA: Addison-Wesley.
29. These sketches are drawn in part from Peters, T. J., & Waterman, R. H., Jr. (1982). *In search of excellence: Lessons from America's best-run companies.* New York: Harper & Row.
30. Peters & Waterman, 1982.
31. Lorsch, J. W. (1986, Winter). Managing culture: The invisible barrier to strategic change. *California Management Review,* 95–109.
32. Magnet, M. (1984, November 12). Acquiring without smothering. *Fortune,* 22–30, p. 28.
33. Kets de Vries, M. F. R., & Miller, D. (1984). *The neurotic organization: Diagnosing and changing counterproductive styles of management.* San Francisco: Jossey-Bass.
34. Kets de Vries, M. F. R., & Miller, D. (1984, October). Unstable at the top. *Psychology Today,* 26–34, p. 32.
35. See Schein, 1985.
36. Uttal, B. (1985, August 5). Behind the fall of Steve Jobs. *Fortune,* 20–24.
37. Pascale, R. (1985, Winter). The paradox of "corporate culture": Reconciling ourselves to socialization. *California Management Review,* 26–41; Pascale, 1984.
38. Gumpert, D. E. (1986, March–April). Porsche on nichemanship. *Harvard Business Review,* 98–106, p. 100.
39. Trice, H. M., & Beyer, J. M. (1984). Studying organizational cultures through rites and ceremonials. *Academy of Management Review, 9,* 653–669.
40. Martin, J., Feldman, M. S., Hatch, M. J., & Sitkin, S. B. (1983). The uniqueness paradox in organizational stories. *Administrative Science Quarterly, 28,* 438–453.
41. Peters, T., & Austin, N. (1985). *A passion for excellence: The leadership difference.* New York: Random House.
42. The following draws on Tunstall, W. C. (1986, Winter). The breakup of the Bell System: A case study in culture transformation. *California Management Review,* 110–124; Main, J. (1984, December 24). Waking up at AT&T: There's life after culture shock. *Fortune,* 66–74.

Chapter 10

Leadership

ELECTROCO

Electroco is a small electronics design and manufacturing firm located south of San Francisco which is concerned with the application of sophisticated silicon technology to everyday devices such as police radar units, automotive ignition systems, and children's toys. Last April, as a result of resignations, Electroco acquired two new managers. Both were having their problems.

Bernie Reiman had enlisted in the army straight out of high school and remained there for seven years, rising to the rank of sergeant. Seeking a career change, he then enrolled in a local community college and earned an Associate degree in industrial supervision. Bernie was hired as a production supervisor at Electroco because the president was impressed by his combination of army experience and academic credentials.

The jobs Bernie supervised were routine and boring, consisting of the assembly of various small electronic units. Most of the jobs could be learned in a few days. Despite this, the work force performed well and exhibited little turnover and absence. Based on his army experience, Bernie made a conscious effort to remain aloof from his subordinates and not involve himself personally with them. To impress the production manager, Bernie monitored productivity carefully and spent most of his time on the shop floor, observing his workers, making suggestions, and giving advice.

Evidently, something was wrong with these tactics. In the months following Bernie's hiring, productivity fell, several workers resigned, and absenteeism increased. Several workers were heard mumbling, ''I wish he'd stay off my back and let me do my work.''

At the other end of the Electroco complex a different kind of leadership problem had developed. Dr. Charles Hackett had been appointed as head of the research and development group, which consisted of sixteen engineers who were electronics specialists. This group experimented with sophisticated silicon electronics, and their findings were then passed to a design team for adaptation to practical problems. The jobs were challenging, although their goals were often vague. Hackett had been hired away from his position as chairman of the electrical engineering department at a California university. His Ph.D. in solid state electronics and his leadership experience as department chairman had convinced Electroco's president that he was the right man to head the R & D group.

Quickly, Hackett had decided that he could manage the R & D group the way he had run his university department. First, he got to know all of the engineers on a friendly personal basis and assured them that they could come to him if they had problems. He insisted that they were all professional equals. Then, he retired to his office, where he spent most of his time reading scientific and technical journals. "After all," he thought, "these people have advanced degrees. They know what to do."

During the next several months, two of Hackett's engineers resigned. Frequent quarrels broke out about who was supposed to be doing what work. Worst of all, Hackett discovered that two engineers had been working independently on the same research problem for over a month. Neither engineer was aware of what the other had been doing.

Ironically, Bernie Reiman and Charles Hackett responded to their problems in the same way—both decided to involve their subordinates in decision making about their jobs. However, Bernie failed, while Charles acted successfully.

Considerable problems often occurred on the production line when a change of products was made. There was usually great confusion, and productivity often remained low for some time following the change. Since a change was coming up, Reiman told his subordinates to develop a plan for easing the transition. They worked hard and came up with a plan for phasing out the current product line while simultaneously starting up the new line. The plan was for several workers to gradually train others on the new assemblies. Bernie thought the idea was great, and he took it to his boss, the production manager. The production manager thought it was great too, except for one problem—the components for the new production run wouldn't be available until the last minute. The phase-in plan was impossible. When Bernie told his unit about this, morale sank even lower. The workers felt cheated.

Charles Hackett was more fortunate when he asked his subordinates for suggestions. The engineers proposed regular team meetings and a peer review system to work out and monitor research assignments. In addition, they requested that Charles meet with each engineer every two weeks to go over his or her progress and to provide clear feedback. Charles readily agreed, and within a month things were operating smoothly.

Meanwhile, Electroco's president was debating whether to fire Bernie Reiman. Also, he was wondering whether a consultant could use psychological tests to choose leaders with the proper personality.

This story poses several questions of practical importance. Why weren't Bernie and Charles able to translate their previously acquired leadership skills to their new jobs? Why didn't Bernie's directive approach work on the production job? Why didn't Charles' easy-going approach work on the R & D job? Why did the involvement of subordinates in decision making work for Charles but not for Bernie? Could personality tests have been used to choose good leaders in these situations? These are the kinds of questions we will attempt to answer in this chapter.

First, we will define leadership and consider the possibility that special leadership traits can be identified. After this, we will explore how leaders emerge in groups. Next, we will examine the consequences of various leadership behaviors and examine two theories suggesting that effective leadership depends upon the nature of the work situation. Following this is a discussion of leadership strategies that involve subordinates in decision making. We will conclude by critically evaluating the importance of leadership in organizations.

WHAT IS LEADERSHIP?

We see the headlines all the time:

- *Senator Charges Leadership Crisis in Executive Branch*
- *Strong Leadership Boosts Leadbottom Mines Productivity*
- *Rookie Quarterback Demonstrates Leadership in Big Game*
- *Union Leadership Says No to Contract Offer*

Although the meaning of such headlines poses no mysteries for us as newspaper readers, we can gain some understanding of the essence of leadership by examining the common notion underlying each one. Basically, they say:

- The senator feels the president isn't exerting enough influence.
- Leadbottom Mines executives influenced their work force to work harder and produce more.
- The quarterback influenced other team members to perform well.
- Influential union members vetoed the contract offer.

In other words, **leadership** occurs when particular individuals exert influence upon others in an organizational context. Thus, while the senator thinks the president isn't doing enough leading, financial observers feel that Leadbottom executives are doing a good job of leading. Effective leadership involves exerting influence in a way that achieves the organization's goals by enhancing the productivity and satisfaction of the work force.

In theory, *any* organizational member can exert influence on other members, thus engaging in leadership. In practice, though, some members are in a better position to be leaders than others. Individuals with titles such as manager, executive, supervisor, and department head occupy formal or assigned leadership roles

(Chapter 8). As part of these roles they are *expected* to influence others, and they are given specific authority to direct subordinates. At Electroco, Bernie Reiman (production supervisor) and Charles Hackett (head of R & D) occupied formal leadership roles. The presence of a formal leadership role is no guarantee that any leading will be done (see In–Focus 10-1). Some managers and supervisors may fail to exert any influence on others. These people will usually be judged as ineffective leaders. Thus, leadership involves going beyond formal role requirements to influence others.

Individuals may also emerge to occupy informal leadership roles. Since informal leaders do not have formal authority, they must rely on being well liked or being perceived as highly skilled in order to exert influence. In this chapter, we will concentrate on formal leadership, although we will consider informal leadership as well.

Leadership involves status differences as well as role differences, and leaders are almost always granted higher status than those who serve as followers. Thus, there is generally no shortage of candidates who aspire to leadership roles. But who is actually likely to become a leader?

THE (SOMEWHAT ELUSIVE) SEARCH FOR LEADERSHIP TRAITS

Throughout history, social observers have been fascinated by obvious examples of successful interpersonal influence, whether the consequences of this influence were good, bad, or mixed. Individuals such as Henry Ford, Martin Luther King, Jr., Ralph Nader, and Joan of Arc have been analyzed and reanalyzed to discover what made them leaders and what set them apart from less successful leaders. The implicit assumption here is that those who become leaders and do a good job of it possess a special set of traits which distinguish them from the masses of followers. While such a position has been advocated by philosophers and the popular media for centuries, trait theories of leadership did not receive serious scientific attention until the 1900s.

Research on Leadership Traits

During World War I the U.S. military recognized that it had a leadership problem. Never before had such a massive war effort been mounted, and able officers were in short supply. Thus, the search for leadership traits that might be useful in identifying potential officers began. Following the war, and continuing through World War II, this interest expanded to include searching for leadership traits in populations as diverse as school children and business executives. Some studies tried to differentiate traits of leaders and followers, while others were a search for traits that predicted leader effectiveness or separated lower-level leaders from higher-level leaders.[1]

IN–FOCUS 10-1   IS THERE A LEADERSHIP CRISIS IN THE WORKPLACE?

With almost daily reports about terrorism in the Middle East, nuclear prolif-eration and economic protectionism, it is easy to see the crisis of political leadership in the world today. Much less appreciated is the leadership crisis that is closer to most of us and affects almost all of us directly and daily—the leadership crisis in the workplace.

Of course, many people see a small part of it—at the top of work organi-zations. Here, sometimes painfully visible examples exist of senior manage-ment teams in certain companies and institutions failing to adapt to new competitive environments, to changing technologies or to global markets. If only we had more Iacoccas, people sigh.

But we often fail to recognize that the problem at the top is only a small part of the leadership crisis today.

Millions of technical, professional and managerial jobs today require much more than technical competence and professional expertise. They also require leadership. That is, they ask job incumbents to get things done in a complex social milieu, which requires influencing a large and diverse group of people (bosses, subordinates, peers, customers and others), despite lack-ing much or any formal control over them, and despite a general disinclina-tion to cooperate.

The consequence of this leadership crisis is prosaic but potentially le-thal—things get bogged down. Good ideas go unrecognized or simply never get carried out. Conflicts get blown out of proportion and lead to bureau-cratic infighting, parochial politics and destructive power struggles. As a result, corporations often react slowly and ineptly to competition or changing customer preferences. And, Government agencies seem, at times, hardly to react at all.

The crisis has many roots. The entire educational system contributes significantly. It is not designed to produce leadership in any quantity.

If that sounds excessively harsh, stop and think for a moment about the implicit message about ''work'' that gets drummed into students' heads from kindergarten through graduate school. Work (a student's job) means performing some task or tasks largely by oneself, even though this is often done with other people present.

Because the needed tools are supplied, goals and rules clearly specified and the grading of performance ''objective,'' securing cooperation from others is not an important issue. (It is even sometimes discouraged as ''cheating''.) Leadership is usually needed only in extracurricular activities, which are neither required nor graded. From kindergarten through graduate school, one can get excellent performance appraisals and yearly promotions, and yet learn virtually nothing about leading others.

When you put a person who has been an individual contributor for 25 or 30 years into a job that demands leadership, what usually happens is quite predictable. The person focuses on the technical aspect of the job and does poorly in getting the group to function at its full potential.

Jobs that demand leadership are usually not impossible, even the tough-est of them. But preparing people to assume them will require an entirely different approach from educational institutions and employers, one that em-phasizes that jobs are not just made up of separate tasks but include rela-tionships that must be managed and people who must be led.

Source: Abridged from Kotter, J. P. (1985, October 20). Why business has so few lead-ers. *The New York Times*. Copyright © 1985 by The New York Times Company. Reprinted by permission.

Just what is a trait, anyway? **Traits** are personal characteristics of the individual, including physical characteristics, social background, intellectual ability, personality, task orientation, and social skills. Exhibit 10-1 lists just a few examples of the dozens of traits that have been investigated in the study of leadership.

You will recall that the president of Electroco wondered if personality tests could be used to select better leaders. Similarly, the sergeant shown in the cartoon evidently embraces the trait theory of leadership. But are traits associated with the assumption or the successful performance of leadership?

A cautious assessment would indicate that the results of the trait approach have been disappointing. Hundreds of studies suggest that many traits are unassociated with leadership, while others are inconsistently or weakly related. However, a somewhat more liberal and selective view of this work suggests that several traits are frequently (though still weakly) associated with the assumption or performance of leadership duties.[2]

Intelligence	Energy
Education	Self-confidence
Social status	Dominance
Participativeness	Need for achievement

EXHIBIT 10-1   Examples of traits investigated in leadership studies.

Physical Characteristics	Social Background	Intellectual Ability
Energy	Education	Intelligence
Age	Social status	Judgment
Height	Mobility	Verbal fluency
Weight		Problem solving

Personality	Task Orientation	Social Skills
Dominance	Achievement need	Administrative ability
Aggressiveness	Responsibility need	Cooperativeness
Self-confidence	Initiative	Popularity
Originality		Interpersonal competence
Stress tolerance		Participativeness
Emotional balance		Tact

Source: From Stogdill, R. M. (1974). *Handbook of leadership.* New York: Free Press. Copyright © 1974 by The Free Press, a Division of Macmillan Publishing Co., Inc. Adapted with permission of Macmillan Publishing Co., Inc.

As you would expect, leaders (or more successful leaders) tend to be higher than average on these dimensions. However, the *usefulness* of such findings is open to some question.

Problems with the Trait Approach

Even though some traits appear to be related to leadership, there are several reasons for the trait approach not being the best means of understanding and improving leadership.

In many cases, it is difficult to determine whether traits make the leader, or the opportunity for leadership produces the traits. For example, do dominant individuals tend to become leaders, or do employees become more dominant *after* they successfully occupy leadership roles? This distinction is important. If the former is true, we might wish to seek out dominant people and appoint them to leadership roles. If the latter is true, this strategy will be unproductive.

Even if we know that dominance, intelligence, or tallness are associated with effective leadership, we have few clues about what dominant or intelligent or tall people *do* to influence others successfully. As a result, we have no information about how to train and develop leaders and no way to diagnose failures of leadership.

The most crucial problem of the trait approach to leadership is its failure to take into account the *situation* in which leadership occurs. Intuitively, it seems reasonable that top executives and first-level supervisors might require different traits to be successful. Similarly, physical prowess may be useful in directing a logging crew but irrelevant to managing a team of scientists.

A series of studies of military officers found that leader intelligence (a trait) was associated with effective performance when a good relationship existed between the leader and his superior officer. However, when the relationship between the two was stressful, amount of experience in the role was a better predictor of performance than intelligence.[3] This suggests that leaders can only *use* high intelligence effectively in certain situations. Neglecting to include such situational factors may be responsible for the weak relationships between traits and leadership.

LESSONS FROM EMERGENT LEADERSHIP

The trait approach is mainly concerned with what leaders *bring* to a group setting. Discouragement with this approach gradually promoted an interest in what leaders *do* in group settings. Of particular concern were the behaviors in which certain group members engage that cause them to *become* leaders. As we shall see, this study of **emergent leadership** gives us some good clues about what formally assigned or appointed leaders must do to be effective.

Imagine that a grass-roots organization has assembled to support the election of a local politician to the state legislature. In response to a newspaper ad, thirty individuals show up, all of whom admire Jonathan Greed, the aspiring candidate. The self-appointed chairperson begins the meeting and asks for volunteers for various subcommittees. The publicity subcommittee sounds interesting, so you volunteer and find yourself with six other volunteers, none of whom knows each other. Your assigned goal is to develop an effective public relations campaign for Greed. From experience you are aware that someone will emerge to become the leader of this group. Who will it be?

Without even seeing your group interact, we can make a pretty good guess as to who will become the leader. Quite simply, it will be the person who *talks* the most, as long as he or she does not antagonize the group. Remember, leadership is a form of influence, and one important way to influence the group is by speaking a lot. What would the "big talker" talk about? Probably about planning strategy, getting organized, dividing labor, and so on—things to get the task at hand accomplished. Social psychologists often call such a leader a **task leader** because he or she is most concerned with accomplishing the task at hand.

Suppose I also ask the group members who they *liked* the most in the group. Usually, there will be a fair amount of agreement, and the nominated person might be called the **social-emotional leader.** Social-emotional influence is more subtle than task influence, and it involves reducing tension, patching up disagreements, settling arguments, and maintaining morale.

In many cases, the task and social-emotional leadership roles are performed by the same group member.[4] In some instances, though, two separate leaders emerge to fill these roles. When this happens, these two leaders usually get along well with each other and respect each other's complementary skills.[5] In fact, for better or worse, in the typical North American family, the father often assumes the task role and the mother the social-emotional role.

Such emergence of two leadership roles has been noted again and again in a wide variety of groups. This suggests that task and social-emotional leadership are two important functions that must occur in groups. On one hand, the group must be structured and organized to accomplish its tasks. On the other hand, the group must stick together and function well as a social unit, or the best structure and organization will be useless. Thus, in general, leaders must be concerned with both the social-emotional and task functions. Furthermore, organizations almost never appoint *two* formal leaders to a work group. Thus, the formal appointed leader must often be concerned with juggling the demands of two distinct roles.

There is an important qualifier to the preceding paragraph. It should be obvious that task and social-emotional functions are both especially important in the case of newly developing groups. However, for mature, ongoing groups one leadership role may be more important than the other. For example, if group members have learned to get along well with each other, the social-emotional role may decrease in importance. Also, the two leadership roles may be differentially important in different situations. Suppose a team of geologists is doing a routine series of mineral prospecting studies in a humid, bug-infested jungle. In this case, its leader may be most concerned with monitoring morale and reducing tensions provoked by the uncomfortable conditions. If the team is attacked by hostile natives, task leadership should become more important—a defense must be mounted and a plan for retreat developed.

THE BEHAVIOR OF ASSIGNED LEADERS

We turn now to the behavior of assigned or appointed leaders, as opposed to emergent leaders. What are the crucial behaviors engaged in by such leaders, and how do these behaviors influence subordinate performance and satisfaction? In other words, is there a particular *leadership style* that is more effective than other possible styles? In the case that began the chapter, Bernie Reiman and Charles Hackett exhibited different leadership styles. Are such differences important?

Consideration and Initiating Structure

The most involved, systematic study of leadership to date was begun at Ohio State University in the late 1940s. The Ohio State researchers began by having subordinates describe their superiors along a number of behavioral dimensions. Statistical analyses of these descriptions revealed that they boiled down to two basic kinds of behavior—consideration and initiating structure.

Consideration involves the extent to which the leader is approachable and shows personal concern for subordinates. The considerate leader is seen as friendly, egalitarian, and protective of group welfare. Obviously, consideration is related to the social-emotional function discovered in studies of emergent leadership. As you will recall, Charles Hackett adopted a considerate leadership style at Electroco.

Initiating structure involves the degree to which the leader concentrates on group goal attainment. The structuring leader stresses standard procedures, schedules the work to be done, and assigns subordinates to particular tasks. Clearly, initiating structure is related to the task function revealed in studies of emergent leadership. At Electroco, Bernie Reiman based his leadership style on initiating structure.

Theoretically, consideration and initiating structure are not incompatible. Presumably, a leader could be high, low, or average on one or both dimensions. Given our earlier discussion of emergent leadership functions, you might assume that a leader who is high on both dimensions would be the most effective. In the next section we shall consider this possibility.

The Consequences of Consideration and Structure

The association between leader consideration, leader initiating structure, and subordinate responses has been the subject of hundreds of research studies. At first glance, the results of these studies seem confusing and often contradictory.[6] Sometimes consideration seems to promote satisfaction or high performance, and sometimes it does not. Sometimes structure prompts satisfaction or performance, and sometimes it does not. However, when we consider the particular *situation* in which the leader finds himself or herself, a clearer picture emerges:

- When subordinates are under a high degree of pressure due to deadlines, unclear tasks, or external threat, initiating structure increases satisfaction and performance. (Soldiers stranded behind enemy lines should perform better under directive leadership.)

- When the task itself is intrinsically satisfying, the need for high consideration and high structure is generally reduced. (The teacher who really enjoys teaching should be able to function with less social-emotional support and less direction from the principal.)

- When the goals and methods of performing the job are very clear and certain, consideration should promote subordinate satisfaction while structure should promote dissatisfaction. (The job of garbage collection is clear in goals and methods. Here, subordinates should appreciate social support but view excessive structure as redundant and unnecessary.)

- When subordinates lack knowledge as to how to perform a job, or the job itself has vague goals or methods, consideration becomes less important, while initiating structure takes on additional importance. (The new astronaut recruit should appreciate direction in learning a complex, unfamiliar job.)[7]

As you can see from the above propositions, the effects of consideration and initiating structure depend upon characteristics of the task, the subordinate, and the setting in which work is performed. Thus, the leader high in both consideration and structure will not always perform better than other types of leaders.[8] In some cases, one type of behavior or the other may be unhelpful or even damaging to subordinate performance or satisfaction.

You should now be able to understand why Bernie Reiman and Charles Hackett had leadership troubles at Electroco. Bernie attempted to use a high degree of initiating structure in supervising jobs that were routine and easily learned, and his subordinates resented this leadership style. Charles, on the other hand, relied on a considerate approach to supervise jobs that were complex and had unclear goals. His subordinates craved direction, but he was not providing it.

Leader Reward and Punishment Behaviors

Consideration and initiating structure are the leader behaviors that have received the greatest attention from behavioral scientists. However, assigned leaders can do other things besides initiate structure and be considerate. For example, a leader might set goals for subordinate performance, redesign jobs to better suit subordinate needs, or assign subordinates to particular tasks in which they are likely to be effective.[9] From previous chapters, it should be clear that these behaviors will prove effective when they are pursued in an intelligent and systematic way.

Two additional leader behaviors that have been the focus of research are leader reward behavior and leader punishment behavior. **Leader reward behavior** involves providing subordinates with compliments, tangible benefits, and deserved special treatment. When such rewards *are made contingent on performance,* subordinates perform at a high level and experience job satisfaction.[10] Under such leadership, subordinates have a clear picture of what is expected of them, and they understand that positive outcomes will occur if they achieve these expectations. Put another way, contingent rewards serve as positive reinforcers (Chapter 3) for desired subordinate responses.

Leader punishment behavior involves the use of reprimands or unfavorable task assignments and the active withholding of raises, promotions, and other rewards (see our cartoon). Compared with reward behavior, the consequences of leader punishment are much less favorable.[11] At best, punishment seems to have little impact on satisfaction or productivity. At worst, when punishment is per-

Al, do whatever you have to do to increase productivity. Threaten, cajole, fire at will. Have fun.

Robert Weber, Valan Associates

ceived as random and not contingent on subordinate behavior, subordinates react with great dissatisfaction. You will recall from Chapter 3 that punishment is extremely difficult to use effectively, and these results seem to prove the point.

Leaders vary considerably in their access to reward opportunities, and this in turn may affect their tendency to resort to punishment. At lower organizational levels, leaders often exert little control over promotion opportunities or salary decisions. Also, they may have so many subordinates that individualized rewards are difficult to administer. Finally, rigid technologies at lower organizational levels (such as assembly lines) may prohibit leaders from redesigning jobs or giving subordinates favorable task assignments. Limited by time, technology, or an absence of tangible rewards, supervisors may resort to searching for negative behavior and punishing it.[12] Organizations that want supervisors to be effective leaders must ensure that they have the tools to do so!

Leader Behavior: An Evaluation

The study of leader behavior represents an improvement over the trait approach, since it is concerned specifically with what leaders actually *do* in their leadership roles. However, the traditional exploration of leader behavior is not without its weaknesses.

In this section, we have been speaking as if certain leader behaviors *cause* subordinate satisfaction or performance. Doubtless, this is often true. However, the reverse is also possible. That is, subordinates who exhibit a particular level of satisfaction or performance may themselves cause the leader to act in certain ways.[13] For example, computer programmers who are especially productive may cause their supervisor to be considerate, rather than the other way around. The point here, of course, is that leadership involves *interaction* between leaders and followers, and both parties have the capability to influence each other. Leadership styles that appear to be effective may sometimes be the results, rather than the causes, of subordinate behavior.

Another problem of the traditional behavioral approach to leadership has been its neglect of the situation in which leadership occurs. In this regard, the behavioral approach is guilty of the sins of the trait approach. However, as we observed in discussing consideration and initiating structure, it is possible to identify certain situations in which one combination of leader behaviors is more effective than another. We now turn to two theories of leadership that take the situation into account.

SITUATIONAL THEORIES OF LEADERSHIP

We have referred to the potential impact of the situation on leadership effectiveness several times. Specifically, *situation* refers to the *setting* in which influence attempts occur. This setting includes the nature of the subordinates being led, the nature of the task they are performing, and characteristics of the organization. The two leadership theories that follow consider situational variables that seem especially likely to influence leadership effectiveness.

Fiedler's Contingency Theory

Fred Fiedler of the University of Washington has spent over two decades developing and refining a situational theory of leadership called **Contingency Theory.**[14] This name stems from the notion that the association between *leadership orientation* and *group effectiveness* is contingent upon (depends upon) the extent to which the *situation is favorable* for the exertion of influence. In other words, some situations are more favorable for leadership than others, and these situations require different orientations on the part of the leader. Let's examine some aspects of this theory.

LEADERSHIP ORIENTATION. Fiedler has measured leadership orientation by having leaders describe their **Least Preferred Co-Worker (LPC).** This person may be a current or past co-worker. In either case, it is someone with whom the leader has had a difficult time getting the job done. To obtain an LPC score, the troublesome co-worker is described on eighteen scales of the following nature:

$$\text{PLEASANT} : \underset{8}{\_} : \underset{7}{\_} : \underset{6}{\_} : \underset{5}{\_} : \underset{4}{\_} : \underset{3}{\_} : \underset{2}{\_} : \underset{1}{\_} : \text{UNPLEASANT}$$

$$\text{FRIENDLY} : \underset{8}{\_} : \underset{7}{\_} : \underset{6}{\_} : \underset{5}{\_} : \underset{4}{\_} : \underset{3}{\_} : \underset{2}{\_} : \underset{1}{\_} : \text{UNFRIENDLY}$$

The leader who describes the LPC relatively favorably (a high LPC score) can be considered *relationship* oriented. That is, despite the fact that LPC is or was difficult to work with, the leader can still find positive qualities in him or her. On the other hand, the leader who describes the LPC unfavorably (a low LPC score) can be considered *task* oriented. This person allows the low task competence of the LPC to color his or her views of the personal qualities of the LPC ("If he's no good at the job, then he's not good, period.")

Fiedler has argued that the LPC score reveals a personality trait that reflects the leader's motivational structure. High LPC leaders are motivated to maintain interpersonal relations, while low LPC leaders are motivated to accomplish the task. Despite the apparent similarity, the LPC score is *not* a measure of consideration or initiating structure. These are observed *behaviors,* while the LPC score is evidently an *attitude* of the leader toward work relationships.

SITUATIONAL FAVORABLENESS. Situational favorableness is the "contingency" part of Contingency Theory. That is, it specifies when a particular LPC orientation should contribute most to group effectiveness. According to Fiedler, a favorable leadership situation exists when the leader has a high degree of control and when the results of this control are very predictable. Factors affecting situational favorableness, in order of importance, are:

1. *Leader-member relations.* When the relationship between the leader and the group members is good, the leader is in a favorable situation to exert influence. Loyal, supportive subordinates should trust the leader and follow his or her directives with little complaint. A poor relationship should damage the leader's influence and even lead to insubordination or sabotage.

2. *Task structure.* When the task at hand is highly structured, the leader should be able to exert considerable influence on the group. Clear goals, clear procedures to achieve these goals, and straightforward performance measures enable the leader to set performance standards and hold subordinates responsible ("Fill ten of these crates an hour"). When the task is unstructured ("Devise a plan to improve the quality of life in our city") the leader may be in a poor position to evaluate subordinate work or to prove that her approach is superior to that of the group.

3. *Position power.* Position power is formal authority to tell others what to do that is granted by the organization. The more position power held by the leader the more favorable the leadership situation. In general, committee chairpersons and leaders in volunteer organizations have weak position power. Managers, supervisors, and military officers have strong position power.

In summary, the situation is most favorable for leadership when leader-member relations are good, the task is structured, and the leader has strong position power—for example, a well-liked army sergeant who is in charge of servicing jeeps in the base motor pool. The situation is least favorable when leader-member relations are poor, the task is unstructured, and the leader has weak position power—for instance, the disliked chairperson of a voluntary homeowner's association who is trying to get agreement on a list of community improvement projects.

THE CONTINGENCY MODEL.   Under what conditions is one leadership orientation more effective than another? As shown in Exhibit 10-2, the various possible combinations of situational factors can be arranged into eight octants which form a continuum of favorability. The model indicates that a task orientation (low LPC) is most effective when the leadership situation is very favorable (octants I, II, and III) *or* when it is very unfavorable (octant VIII). On the other hand, a relationship orientation (high LPC) is most effective in conditions of medium favorability (octants IV, V, VI, and VII). Why is this so? In essence, Fiedler argues that leaders can "get away" with a task orientation when the situation is favorable—subordinates are "ready" to be influenced. Conversely, when the situation is very unfavorable for leadership, task orientation is necessary to get anything accomplished. In conditions of medium favorability, the boss is faced with some combination of an unclear task or a poor relationship with subordinates. Here, a relationship orientation will help to make the best of a situation that is stress-provoking but not impossibly bad.

EVIDENCE AND CRITICISM.   The conclusions about leadership effectiveness shown in Exhibit 10-2 are derived from many studies summarized by Fiedler.[15]

EXHIBIT 10-2   **Predictions of leader effectiveness from Fiedler's Contingency Theory of leadership.**

Favorableness	High ⟵⟶ Low							
Leader-Member Relations	Good				Poor			
Task Structure	Structured		Unstructured		Structured		Unstructured	
Position Power	Strong	Weak	Strong	Weak	Strong	Weak	Strong	Weak
	I	II	III	IV	V	VI	VII	VIII
Most Effective Leader Orientation	Task				Relationship			Task

However, the Contingency Theory has been subjected to as much debate as any theory in organizational behavior.[16] Critics have argued that Fiedler has applied questionable statistical techniques, and the results of laboratory studies have not always matched those found in natural settings. Also, Fiedler's explanation for the superior performance of high LPC leaders in the middle octants is not especially convincing, and the exact meaning of the LPC score is one of the great mysteries of organizational behavior. It does not seem to be correlated with other personality measures or predictive of specific leader behavior. It now appears that a major source of the many inconsistent findings regarding Contingency Theory is the small sample sizes used in many of the studies. Advances in correcting for this problem statistically have led recent reviewers to conclude that there is reasonable support for the theory.[17] However, Fiedler's prescription for task leadership in octant II (good relations, structured task, weak position power) seems contradicted by the evidence, suggesting that the theory needs some adjustment.

Despite the controversy, Fred Fiedler's contribution to our understanding of leadership should not be underestimated. The Contingency Theory was the first theory of leadership to take the role of the situation seriously. Let's now examine another such theory.

House's Path-Goal Theory

Robert House of the University of Toronto has proposed a situational theory of leadership called Path-Goal Theory.[18] Unlike Fiedler's Contingency Theory, which relies on the somewhat ambiguous LPC trait, **Path-Goal Theory** is concerned with the situations under which various leader *behaviors* are most effective.

THE THEORY.   Why did House choose the name Path-Goal for his theory? According to House, the most important activities of leaders are those that clarify the paths to various goals of interest to subordinates. Such goals might include a promotion, a sense of accomplishment, or a pleasant work climate. In turn, the opportunity to achieve such goals should promote job satisfaction, leader acceptance, and high effort. Thus, *the effective leader forms a connection between subordinate goals and organizational goals.*

In order to provide *job satisfaction* and *leader acceptance,* House argues that leader behavior must be perceived as immediately satisfying or as leading to future satisfaction. Leader behavior that is seen as unnecessary or unhelpful will be resented. In order to promote subordinate *effort,* House contends that leaders must make rewards dependent on performance and ensure that subordinates have a clear picture of how these rewards can be achieved. To do this, the leader may have to provide support through direction, guidance, and coaching. For example, the bank teller who wishes to be promoted to supervisor should exhibit superior effort when his boss promises a recommendation contingent on good work and explains carefully how he can do better on his current job.

LEADER BEHAVIOR.   Path-Goal Theory is concerned with four specific kinds of leader behavior. These include:

- *Directive behavior.* Directive leaders schedule work, maintain performance standards, and let subordinates know what is expected of them. This behavior is essentially identical to initiating structure.

- *Supportive behavior.* Supportive leaders are friendly, approachable, and concerned with pleasant interpersonal relationships. This behavior is essentially identical to consideration.

- *Participative behavior.* Participative leaders consult with subordinates about work-related matters and consider their opinions.

- *Achievement-oriented behavior.* Achievement-oriented leaders encourage subordinates to exert high effort and strive for a high level of goal accomplishment. They express confidence that these goals can be reached.

According to Path-Goal Theory, the effectiveness of each set of behaviors depends upon the situation which the leader encounters.

SITUATIONAL FACTORS.   Path-Goal Theory has concerned itself with two primary classes of situational factors—subordinate characteristics and environmental factors. Exhibit 10-3 illustrates the role of these situational factors in the theory. Put simply, the impact of leader behavior on subordinate satisfaction, effort, and accceptance of the leader depends upon the nature of the subordinates and the work environment. Let's consider these two situational factors in turn, along with some of the theory's predictions.

EXHIBIT 10-3   **The Path-Goal Theory of leadership.**

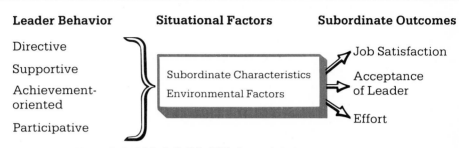

Source: From House, R. J., & Mitchell, T. R. (1974, Autumn). Path-goal theory of leadership. *Journal of Contemporary Business*, University of Washington/Vol. 3, No. 4, p. 89. Copyright 1974 by the Graduate School of Business Administration, University of Washington. Reprinted by permission.

According to the theory, different types of subordinates need or prefer different forms of leadership. For example:

■ Subordinates who are high need achievers (Chapter 6) should work well under achievement-oriented leadership.

■ Subordinates who prefer being told what to do should respond best to a directive leadership style.

■ When subordinates feel that they have rather low task abilities, they should appreciate directive leadership and coaching behavior. When they feel quite capable to perform the task, such behaviors will be viewed as unnecessary and irritating.

As you can observe from these examples, leaders may have to tailor their behavior to the needs, abilities, and personalities of individual employees.

Also according to the theory the effectiveness of leadership behavior depends upon the particular work environment. For example:

■ When tasks are clear and routine, directive leadership should be perceived as a redundant and unnecessary imposition. This should reduce satisfaction and acceptance of the leader. Similarly, participative leadership would not seem to be useful when tasks are clear, since there is little in which to participate. Obviously, such tasks are most common at lower organizational levels.

■ When tasks are challenging but ambiguous, both directive and participative leadership should be appreciated by subordinates. Such styles should clarify the path to good performance and demonstrate that the leader is concerned with helping subordinates do a good job. Obviously, such tasks are most common at higher organizational levels.

■   Frustrating, dissatisfying jobs should increase subordinate appreciation of supportive behavior. To some degree, such support should compensate for a disliked job, although it should probably do little to increase effort.

As you can see from these examples of environmental factors, effective leadership should *take advantage of* the motivating and satisfying aspects of jobs while *offsetting or compensating for* those job aspects which demotivate or dissatisfy. You will recall that Bernie Reiman chose a directive leadership style, even though the assembly jobs he supervised were routine and clear and his subordinates were very competent. Not surprisingly, they viewed this direction as unnecessary and responded with dissatisfaction. On the other hand, Charles Hackett tried to be supportive in supervising challenging, ambiguous research jobs. His subordinates needed direction in order to clarify the path to task accomplishment, but he did not realize this. This provoked dissatisfaction and lowered the performance of the Research and Development unit.

EVIDENCE AND CRITICISM.   In general, there is some research support for most of the situational propositions discussed above. In particular, there is substantial evidence that supportive or considerate leader behavior is most beneficial in supervising routine, frustrating, or dissatisfying jobs and that directive or structuring leader behavior is most effective on ambiguous, less structured jobs.[19]

Although the Path-Goal Theory has not been subjected to a serious degree of criticism, one point does deserve mention. The theory appears to work better in predicting subordinate job satisfaction and acceptance of the leader than in predicting subordinate performance.[20] This may be due in part to the difficulty of *measuring* performance accurately. However, the theory itself may be at fault here. For example, while employees performing clear, routine jobs may be grateful for supportive leadership, directive leadership may be necessary to get any work done, since the task itself doesn't seem inherently motivating.

PARTICIPATIVE LEADERSHIP: INVOLVING SUBORDINATES IN DECISIONS

In the discussion of Path-Goal Theory, the issue of participative leadership was raised. Because this is such an important topic, it is appropriate to devote further attention to participation.

What is Participation?

At a very general level, **participative leadership** means involving subordinates in making work-related decisions. The term *involving* is intentionally broad. Participation is not a fixed or absolute property, but a relative concept. This is illustrated in Exhibit 10-4. Here, we see that leaders can vary in the extent to which

EXHIBIT 10-4   Subordinate participation in decision making can vary.

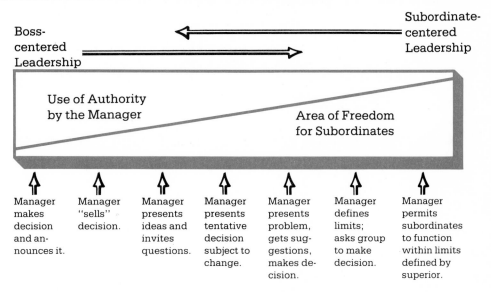

| Manager makes decision and announces it. | Manager "sells" decision. | Manager presents ideas and invites questions. | Manager presents tentative decision subject to change. | Manager presents problem, gets suggestions, makes decision. | Manager defines limits; asks group to make decision. | Manager permits subordinates to function within limits defined by superior. |

Source: Reprinted by permission of the Harvard Business Review. An exhibit from "How To Choose a Leadership Pattern" by Robert Tannenbaum and Warren H. Schmidt (March/April 1958). Copyright © 1958 by the President and Fellows of Harvard College; all rights reserved.

they involve subordinates in decision making. Minimally, participation involves obtaining subordinate opinions before making a decision oneself. Maximally, it allows subordinates to make their own decisions within agreed-upon limits. As the "area of freedom" on the part of subordinates increases, the leader is behaving in a more participative manner. There is, however, an upper limit to the area of subordinate freedom available under participation. Participative leadership should not be confused with the *abdication* of leadership, which is almost always ineffective.

The kind of participation with which we are concerned here might be called *direct* and *informal*. That is, the leader voluntarily implements participation on an informal level and deals directly and personally with subordinates. This style of participation can be contrasted with *indirect, formal* participation, in which some workers are elected to represent their peers in formal negotiations with management. Indirect, formal participation is seen most frequently in union-management negotiations, and in the work councils that have been established in some European countries.[21]

Direct, informal participation can involve individual subordinates or the entire group of subordinates that reports to the leader. Logic suggests that some problems are more conducive to the individual approach, while others are more conducive to the group approach. For example, participation on an individual basis might work best when setting performance goals for particular subordinates, planning subordinate development, or dealing with problem employees. On the other hand, the leader might involve the entire work group in decision making when determining vacation schedules, arranging for telephone coverage during lunch hour, or deciding how to allocate scarce resources such as travel money or secretarial help. As these examples suggest, the choice of an individual or group participation strategy should be tailored to specific situations.

Potential Advantages of Participative Leadership

Just why might participation be a useful leadership technique? What are its potential advantages?

MOTIVATION.   Participation may increase the motivation of subordinates.[22] In some cases, participation permits them to contribute to the establishment of work goals and to decide how these goals can be accomplished. For example, suppose that, early in the spring quarter, a university department chairperson projects that she will have some budget money remaining at the end of the academic year. She informs her department members, and they decide to use the money to fund a trip to a professional conference in New Orleans for the three professors who have the best student evaluations at the end of the quarter. Here, participation has clarified the path toward a valued goal, and the professors should be motivated to perform well in the classroom.

It may also occur to you that participation can increase intrinsic motivation by enriching subordinates' jobs. In Chapter 7 you learned that enriched jobs include high task variety and increased subordinate autonomy. Participation adds some variety to the job and promotes autonomy by increasing the "area of freedom" (Exhibit 10-4).

QUALITY.   An old saying argues that "two heads are better than one." While this is not always true, there do seem to be many cases when "two heads" (participation) lead to higher quality decisions than the leader could make alone.[23] In particular, this is most likely when subordinates have special *knowledge* to contribute to the decision. For example, when subordinates are in direct contact with clients while the leader is not, they should be the first to detect service problems. Salespeople for an office supply company will be the first to hear complaints about quality control problems. Similarly, desk clerks at city hall will be the first to find out that citizens are unable to understand the city's new building permit forms. A participative leadership style will increase the chances that such problems will be detected and corrected.

In many research and engineering departments, it is common for the professional subordinates to have technical knowledge superior to that of their boss. This occurs either because the boss is not a professional or because the boss's knowledge has become outdated. Under these conditions, participation in technical matters should enhance the quality of decisions.

ACCEPTANCE.   Even when participation does not promote motivation or increase the quality of decisions, it may increase the subordinates' acceptance of decisions. This is especially likely when issues of *fairness* are involved.[24] For example, consider the problems of scheduling vacations or scheduling telephone coverage during lunch hours. Here, the leader could probably make high quality decisions without involving subordinates. However, the decisions might be totally unacceptable to the employees because they are perceived as unfair. Involving subordinates in decision making could result in solutions of equal quality which do not provoke dissatisfaction. Public commitment and ego involvement probably contribute to the acceptance of such decisions.

Potential Problems of Participative Leadership

You have no doubt caught on to the fact that every issue in organizational behavior has two sides. Consider the potential difficulties of participation.

TIME AND ENERGY.   Participation isn't a state of mind. It involves specific behaviors on the part of the leader (soliciting ideas, calling meetings) and these behaviors use time and energy. When a quick decision is needed, participation isn't an appropriate leadership strategy. The hospital emergency room isn't the place to implement participation on a continuous basis!

JEALOUSY.   When participation works well, it may provide the participators with benefits that provoke jealousy on the part of subordinates who do not experience this leadership style. For example, consider the department chairperson in a university who implemented participation to allocate the department's yearly budget. Department members made creative decisions which left a substantial balance for travel to conferences in exotic locations. Members of other departments that had not had the advantages of participation responded with envy and jealousy.

LOSS OF POWER.   Some leaders feel that a participative style will reduce their power and influence. Sometimes, they respond by asking subordinates to make trivial decisions of the ''what color shall we paint the lounge'' type. Clearly, the consequences of such decisions (for motivation, quality, and acceptance) are near zero.

LACK OF RECEPTIVITY OR KNOWLEDGE.   Subordinates may not be receptive to participation. When the leader is distrusted, or when a poor labor climate exists, they may resent ''having to do management's work.'' There is also evidence that certain personality characteristics may cause subordinates to reject participative leadership.[25] Even when receptive, subordinates may lack the knowledge to contribute effectively to decisions. Usually, this occurs because they are unaware of *external constraints* on their decisions. For example, consider the case of the toy factory with the following production process:

PARTS MADE → PARTS PAINTED → TOYS ASSEMBLED

In this factory, participation among the paint crew led them to establish elevated production levels that led to problems for the parts makers and toy assemblers. Management was forced to take control of production levels, and most of the painters quit![26]

Our discussion of the advantages and problems of participation should clarify what happened to Bernie Reiman and Charles Hackett in the story that began the chapter. Bernie's subordinates came up with a sensible solution to the problem of introducing a new product line. Unfortunately, they lacked knowledge of the "big picture," which dictated that their solution was impossible to implement. On the other hand, Charles Hackett's R & D engineers had the expertise to identify their problems while avoiding external constraints. They used participation to come up with solutions that *took advantage of further participation* (team meetings, peer reviews, and frequent consultation with Hackett). These solutions clarified paths to valued goals for the engineers.

A Situational Model of Participation

How can leaders capitalize upon the potential advantages of participation while avoiding its pitfalls? Victor Vroom and Philip Yetton have developed a model which attempts to specify in a practical manner when participation should be used and to what extent it should be used.

Vroom and Yetton begin with the recognition that there are various degrees of participation that can be exhibited by the leader. For issues involving the entire work group, the following range of behaviors is plausible (A stands for autocratic, C for consultative, and G for group):

AI. You solve the problem or make the decision yourself, using information available to you at the time.

AII. You obtain the necessary information from your subordinates, then decide the solution to the problem yourself. You may or may not tell your subordinates what the problem is in getting the information from them. The role played by your subordinates in making the decision is clearly one of providing the necessary information to you, rather than generating or evaluating alternative solutions.

CI. You share the problem with the relevant subordinates individually, getting their ideas and suggestions without bringing them together as a group. Then you make the decision, which may or may not reflect your subordinates' influence.

CII. You share the problem with your subordinates as a group, obtaining their collective ideas and suggestions. Then you make the decision, which may or may not reflect your subordinates' influence.

GII. You share the problem with your subordinates as a group. Together you generate and evaluate alternatives and attempt to reach agreement (consensus) on a solution. Your role is much like that of chairman. You do not try to influence the group to adopt "your" solution, and you are willing to accept and implement any solution which has the support of the entire group.[27]

Which of these behaviors is most effective? According to Vroom and Yetton, this depends on the situation or problem at hand. In general, the leader's goal should be to make high-quality, acceptable decisions without undue delay. To do this, he or she must consider questions A through G shown in Exhibit 10-5. Notice that these questions consider factors such as the knowledge possessed by the leader and the group, the importance of subordinate acceptance, and the potential for conflict.

Exhibit 10-5 presents a decision tree prescribing the degree of participation that may be employed in response to various problems. By tracing a problem through the tree, the administrator encounters the prescribed technique. For some problem types (2, 5, 6a, 9, 11, and 12) only one technique will protect decision quality and acceptance. For the remaining problem types, a "feasible set" of several techniques is available. Here, the manager pressed for time would use the most autocratic technique available, while one who wished to foster participation might sacrifice time for a more subordinate-oriented technique. In–Focus 10-2 illustrates how the model is applied to a problem.

There is growing research support for the validity of the Vroom and Yetton model in that successful managerial decisions are more likely than unsuccessful decisions to follow the model's prescriptions.[28] All in all, the model is useful in sensitizing managers to the proper degree of participation to use in solving various problems.

Does Participation Work?

Now we come to the bottom line—does participative leadership result in beneficial outcomes? There is substantial evidence that employees who have the opportunity to participate in work-related decisions report more job satisfaction than those who do not. Thus, most workers seem to *prefer* a participative work environment. However, the positive effects of participation on productivity are open to some question. For participation to be translated into higher productivity, it would appear that certain facilitating conditions must exist. Specifically, participation should work best when subordinates feel favorable toward it, when they are intelligent and knowledgeable about the issue at hand, and when the task is complex enough to make participation useful.[29] In general, these conditions are incorporated into the Vroom and Yetton model. Like any other leadership strategy, the usefulness of

EXHIBIT 10-5   **The Vroom and Yetton decision tree for participative leadership.**

A. Does the problem possess a quality requirement?
B. Do I have sufficient information to make a high-quality decision?
C. Is the problem structured?
D. Is acceptance of the decision by subordinates important for effective implementation?
E. If I were to make the decision by myself, am I reasonably certain that it would be accepted by my subordinates?
F. Do subordinates share the organizational goals to be attained in solving this problem?
G. Is conflict among subordinates likely in preferred solutions?

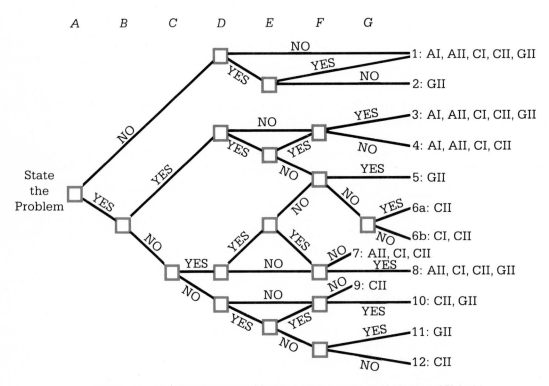

Reprinted from LEADERSHIP AND DECISION-MAKING by Victor H. Vroom and Philip W. Yetton by permission of the University of Pittsburgh Press. © 1973 by University of Pittsburgh Press.

IN–FOCUS 10-2 HOW THE VROOM AND YETTON MODEL OF PARTICIPATION WORKS

Here is a case that illustrates how the Vroom and Yetton model works. Read the case and trace the analysis through the decision tree. Vroom and Yetton have used such cases to train managers in decision-making skills.

You are on the division manager's staff and work on a wide variety of problems of both administrative and technical nature. You have been given the assignment of developing a universal method to be used in each of the five plants in the division for manually reading equipment registers, recording the readings, and transmitting the scorings to a centralized information system. All plants are located in a relatively small geographical region.

Until now there has been a high error rate in the reading and/or transmittal of the data. Some locations have considerably higher error rates than others, and the methods used to record and transmit the data vary between plants. It is probable, therefore, that part of the error variance is a function of specific local conditions rather than anything else, and this will complicate the establishment of any system common to all plants. You have the information on error rates but no information on the local practices that generate these errors or on the local conditions that necessitate the different practices.

Everyone would benefit from an improvement in the quality of the data, as it is used in a number of important decisions. Your contacts with the plants are through the quality-control supervisors who are responsible for collecting the data. They are a conscientious group committed to doing their jobs well, but they are highly sensitive to interference on the part of higher management in their own operations. Any solution that does not receive the active support of the various plant supervisors is unlikely to reduce the error rate significantly.

Analysis

Question A (Quality requirement?) = yes
Question B (Does leader have information?) = no
Question C (Is the problem structured?) = no
Question D (Is acceptance critical?) = yes
Question E (Will subordinates accept leader's decision?) = no
Question F (Do subordinates share organizational goals?) = yes
Conclusion: Use GII

Source: Vroom, V. H., and Yetton, P. W. (1973). *Leadership and decision-making.* Pittsburgh: University of Pittsburgh Press, pp. 43–44.

participation depends upon the constraints of the situation. In Chapter 12 we will consider group decision making, a topic that has additional relevance for participation.

DOES LEADERSHIP MATTER?

Does leadership really *matter?* That is, does it have a strong influence on the effectiveness of organizations? This may seem like an incredible question after having devoted so many pages to consideration, initiating structure, situational influence, and participation. However, as you have seen, the study of leadership, despite its great volume, has not produced perfect agreement about what constitutes effective leadership. Perhaps we are tilting at windmills. Maybe leadership just isn't important to organizations. Let's examine the pros and cons of this issue.

Pros (Leadership Matters)

The notion that leadership is important rests mainly on the premise that special influence is necessary to get things done because organizations aren't and can't be designed perfectly and completely. You have probably experienced this phenomenon. The university financial office can't give you a refund until it is okayed by the registrar. The registrar can't okay the refund until it is approved by the professor. And the professor just went on sabbatical to Tasmania! *Here's* a case where leadership is necessary! In other words, schools, hospitals, and business firms exhibit many loose ends or gaps that can only be dealt with by effective leadership. More specifically:

- Organizations do not have a rule or policy for every contingency. (The boss decides whether a particular absence is legitimate or illegitimate).
- Someone must coordinate between the groups making up the organization. (If two hospital departments have sensible budget requests, the budget director must decide who gets what while trying to keep both departments reasonably satisfied.)
- Organizational environments change, and someone must be responsive to this change. (If the economy takes a downturn, some members of the firm must convince others what the firm's response should be.)
- Organizational members differ in their needs and goals. (A sensitive manager may be able to motivate one employee with challenging work assignments and another with the promise of a raise in pay.)[30]

Conditions of this nature suggest that there is considerable *latitude* for leadership actions which can help or hinder the organization in achieving its goals. That is, the incomplete or imperfect design of organizations provides an environment where influence can be *exercised.*[31] For an example, see In–Focus 10-3.

Cons (Leadership Doesn't Matter)

The notion that leadership isn't so important rests mainly on the premise that a number of factors conspire to constrain the influence that individuals in leadership roles might have. In other words, the potential for influence is inhibited, and the leader's latitude is more apparent than real. One author has argued that the following factors limit leader impact:[32]

- In most organizations, rigid selection and promotion policies dictate that those who achieve leadership positions have very similar leadership styles.

IN–FOCUS 10-3   DOES LEE IACOCCA HAVE CHARISMA?

Professor Robert House of the University of Toronto has studied the characteristics of leaders who are described as having charisma, a term stemming from a Greek word meaning favored or gifted. Charismatic leaders have been portrayed throughout history as having personal qualities that enable them to have extraordinary influence over followers. In a sense, they are "superleaders" who command strong loyalty and devotion. In turn, this loyalty and devotion inspires enthusiastic, emotional dedication toward the leader's chosen mission. Charismatic leaders inspire trust in followers, who come to identify with the values, goals, and behavior of the leader.

House notes that charismatic leaders exhibit high self-confidence, dominance, and a strong conviction in their own beliefs. They act to create an impression of personal success and accomplishment. They hold high expectations for follower performance while at the same time expressing confidence in followers' capabilities. This enhances the self-esteem of the followers. The goals set by charismatic leaders often have a moral or ideological flavor to them. In addition, charismatic leaders often emerge to articulate the feelings of followers in times of stress or discord. If these feelings go against an existing power structure, the leader may be perceived as especially courageous.

Some political leaders have exhibited charisma, and House cites Winston Churchill, Martin Luther King, and Gandhi as examples. But can charisma be seen in the business world? Let's consider Lee Iacocca, dubbed by *Time* as "America's hottest new folk hero." When Iacocca took over the helm at Chrysler Corporation in 1979 the company's financial plight was so serious that many observers felt that it would not survive. Iacocca obtained federal loan guarantees against strong resistance and championed radical changes in marketing and management, and by 1984 Chrysler achieved a year of record-breaking profits.

But did charismatic leadership help Iacocca turn Chrysler around? Many observers think so. During the years of rebuilding , Iacocca exhibited resolute confidence in himself and in his employees. This confidence was played out publicly in a series of television commercials in which Iacocca starred ("If you can find a better car, buy it!"). The moral and ideological goal of defeating unfair foreign competition and preserving American manufacturing dominance was undisguised in his public speeches, hitting the right chord with the Chrysler work force and the public at large. Iacocca boldly and bluntly advocated import quotas against strong resistance from the federal administration. When the turnaround finally occurred, he gave tangible expression to his confidence in the workforce by awarding every one of Chrysler's 100,000 employees a $500 bonus.

During this period, Iacocca was being touted as a potential presidential candidate and receiving literally thousands of requests to make speeches. But it is the warm, enthusiastic reception that Iacocca received from groups of dealers and assembly line workers that reveals the likelihood of his charisma. Mobbed and cheered by well-wishers, it was clear that they shared with Iacocca the vision that had saved their jobs.

Sources: House, R. J. (1977). A 1976 theory of charismatic leadership. In J. E. Hunt & L. L. Larson (Eds.), *Leadership: The cutting edge.* Carbondale, IL: Southern Illinois University Press; Andersen, K. (1985, April 1). A spunky tycoon turned superstar. *Time,* 24–34; Flax, S. (1985, January 7). Can Chrysler keep rolling along? *Fortune,* 34– 39.

(If all the managers in a government office behave similarly they should have similar influence—one manager is easily replaceable by another who should be equally effective.)

■ The freedom of leaders is severely constrained by the demands of others. (A supervisor may fear to reward a good performer with a special work assignment because other subordinates will be jealous or claim favoritism.)

■ The leader's performance can be strongly affected by external factors beyond his or her control. (The best boss in the company may not be able to overcome subordinates' resentment of the dirty, boring work required by a particular technology.)

Obviously, the argument that leadership matters and the position that leadership doesn't matter both sound pretty rational. This suggests that both positions may be true under certain circumstances. Let's examine what these circumstances might be.

Leadership Neutralizers and Substitutes

Some interesting ideas have been proposed in response to the dilemma of whether leadership matters.[33] First, it has been argued that certain subordinate, task, and organizational characteristics can serve as **neutralizers of leadership.** When these factors are present in the work setting, the opportunities for leaders to exercise influence are reduced. In this case, then, leadership might not "matter" because the leader's influence attempts are stymied. When such factors are not present, the leader may have an important effect on subordinate satisfaction and performance. For example, consider the following situations:

> Martin is a petroleum engineer for a major oil company. He is a troubleshooter who deals with company problems around the world, and he is constantly "on the go." He sees his boss about every two months. Martin is very interested in his job, and he doesn't care about what performance rating or merit raise he receives.

> Shawn is a management trainee in a large insurance company. Her office is beside that of her boss, and she consults with him about ten times a day. Shawn hopes to obtain a good performance rating so that she can receive a lucrative promotion.

Obviously, Shawn's boss is in a better position to exercise influence than Martin's boss. The latter's leadership potential is to some extent neutralized by the fact that he seldom sees Martin and because Martin is unresponsive to the rewards he can provide.

Going a step further, some neutralizers of leadership may actually serve as **substitutes for leadership.** In other words, some subordinate, task, and organizational characteristics might operate to make leadership unnecessary or redundant. While simple neutralizers reduce the *effectiveness* of leadership attempts, substitutes reduce the *necessity* for leadership. For example, consider these situations:

A group of ten welders and riveters is assembling a large natural gas pipeline. All of them are highly experienced, and they work well together as a friendly, cohesive unit. Their task is clear and unambiguous—assemble fifty yards of pipe each day.

A group of computer experts has decided to start a new company to design and market software packages. Although they are all technical experts, they know nothing about financing their venture or marketing their proposed products. There is much disagreement about how to establish the new enterprise and how to choose which software to develop.

In which of these situations does leadership seem more necessary? For the pipe crew, the straightforwardness of the task at hand and the friendly, cooperative working relationships could well serve as substitutes for active, formal leadership. We would not be surprised to see the crew work well if the boss called in sick for several days. On the other hand, the proposed computer firm is begging for leadership. Its goals are unclear, and its founders are unlikely to reach an easy agreement. There are no substitutes for leadership here.

Exhibit 10-6 summarizes a number of potential neutralizers of leadership. In some cases, these neutralizers can also serve as substitutes. In the first example discussed above (Martin versus Shawn) indifference toward rewards and spatial distance were presented as simple neutralizers. These factors reduce the impact

EXHIBIT 10-6   **Neutralizers of leadership.**

Neutralizing Characteristics	Will neutralize considerate or social-emotional leadership	Will neutralize initiating structure or task leadership
Of Subordinate		
Ability, experience, knowledge		X
Professional orientation	X	X
Indifference toward rewards	X	X
Of Task		
Routine and clear		X
Provides its own feedback		X
Intrinsically satisfying	X	
Of Organization		
Inflexible rules and procedures		X
Cohesive work groups	X	X
Spatial distance between leader and subordinate	X	X

From Kerr, S., & Jermier, J. M. (1978). Substitutes for leadership: Their meaning and measurement. *Organizational behavior and human performance, 22,* p. 378. Copyright © 1978 by Academic Press, Inc. Reprinted by permission.

of leadership, but they do not reduce the need for leadership. In the second example, a clear task, experienced workers, and a cohesive work group served as substitutes for formal leadership for the pipe crew. The computer group did not have the advantages of these substitutes. Notice that some factors neutralize social-emotional influence, some neutralize task influence, and some neutralize both. For example, highly experienced, knowledgeable subordinates may need little task leadership, but they still require social-emotional support from the leader.

In summary, it would appear that leadership "matters" most when neutralizers and substitutes are not present in subordinates' skills and attitudes, task design, or the organizational design. When neutralizers and substitutes are present, the impact of formal leadership is reduced.[34]

SUMMARY

■ Leadership occurs when an individual exerts influence upon others in an organizational context. Early studies of leadership were concerned with identifying physical, psychological, and intellectual traits that might predict leader effectiveness. While some traits appear weakly related to leadership capacity, there are no traits that guarantee leadership across various situations.

■ Studies of emergent leadership have identified two important leadership functions—the task function and the social-emotional function. The former involves helping the group achieve its goals through planning and organizing, while the latter involves resolving disputes and maintaining a pleasant group environment. Explorations of the behavior of assigned leaders have concentrated on initiating structure and consideration, which are similar to task behavior and social-emotional behavior. The effectiveness of consideration and structure depends upon the nature of the task and the subordinates. Leader reward behavior is probably a more foolproof strategy than leader punishment behavior.

■ Two situational theories of leadership were discussed. Fiedler's Contingency Theory suggests that different leadership orientations are necessary depending upon the favorableness of the situation for the leader. Favorableness depends upon the structure of the task, the position power of the leader, and the satisfactoriness of the relationship between the leader and the group. Fiedler argues that task-oriented leaders perform best in situations that are either very favorable or very unfavorable. Relationship-oriented leaders are said to perform best in situations of medium favorability. House's Path-Goal Theory suggests that leaders will be most effective when they are able to clarify the paths to various subordinate goals that are also of interest to the organization. According to House, the effectiveness of directive, supportive, participative, and achievement-oriented behavior depends upon the nature of the subordinates and the characteristics of the work environment.

■ Participative leader behavior involves subordinates in work decisions. Participation may increase subordinate motivation and lead to higher quality and more acceptable decisions. The Vroom and Yetton model specifies how much participation should be used for various kinds of decisions. Participation works best when subordinates are desirous of participation, when they are intelligent and knowledgeable, and when the task is reasonably complex.

■ Leadership is most important when few neutralizers or substitutes for leadership exist. Neutralizers are factors that make leadership attempts less effective, and substitutes are factors that can act in place of leader influence.

KEY CONCEPTS

Leadership
Traits
Emergent leadership
Task leader
Social-emotional leader
Consideration
Initiating structure
Leader reward behavior

Leader punishment behavior
Fiedler's Contingency Theory
Least Preferred Co-Worker (LPC)
House's Path-Goal Theory
Participative leadership
Neutralizers of leadership
Substitutes for leadership

DISCUSSION QUESTIONS

1. Name a physical, intellectual, or personality trait that might be associated with effective leadership and defend your position. Then, discuss a situation in which this trait might *not* be associated with effective leadership.

2. Discuss a case of emergent leadership you have observed. Why did the person in question emerge as a leader? Did he or she fulfill the task role, the social-emotional role, or both?

3. Contrast the relative merits of consideration and initiating structure in the following leadership situations: Running the daily operations of a branch bank; commanding an army unit under enemy fire; supervising a group of college students who are performing a hot, dirty, boring summer job. Use House's Path-Goal Theory to support your arguments.

4. Fred Fiedler argues that leader LPC is difficult to change and that situations should be "engineered" to fit the leader's LPC orientation. Suppose that a relationship-oriented (high LPC) person finds herself assigned to a situation with poor leader-member relations, an unstructured task, and weak position power. What could she do to make the situation more favorable for her relationship-oriented leadership?

5. Describe a situation that would be ideal for having subordinates participate in a work-related decision. Discuss the subordinates, the problem, and the

setting. Describe a situation in which participative decision making would be an especially unwise leadership strategy. Why is this so?

6. Discuss the pros and cons of the following statement: Even when a manager can make an adequate decision on his or her own, the manager should attempt to involve subordinates in the decision.

7. Distinguish between neutralizers of leadership and substitutes for leadership. Give an example of each.

8. Julio is an extremely experienced salesperson of sophisticated electronic equipment. He has an M.Sc. in electrical engineering and is on the road eleven months a year. He really enjoys his job, and he is extremely interested in the high commissions the job offers. Discuss Julio's situation from the perspective of neutralizers of and substitutes for the leadership of his sales manager.

FOR FURTHER READING

Flax, S. (1984, August 6). The toughest bosses in America. *Fortune,* 18–23.
   Profiles the leadership style of ten of America's senior executives who are reputed to be among the toughest bosses. Discusses subordinate reactions and examines the effectiveness of such a style. Also follows up on the "terrible ten" who were chosen four years earlier.

Meindl, J. R., Ehrlich, S. B., & Dukerich, J. M. (1985). The romance of leadership. *Administrative Science Quarterly, 30,* 78–102.
   Reports three archival studies and three experiments designed to explore suppositions people hold about leadership. Concludes that a romanticized view of leadership causes us to believe that leaders have more control than they really do over what happens in organizations.

Yukl, G. A. (1981). *Leadership in organizations.* Englewood Cliffs, NJ: Prentice-Hall.
   Looks at the theory and practice of leadership with a special emphasis on leadership effectiveness. Covers traits, behaviors, situational factors, and participation in detail.

Case Study

801st Air Transport Unit

The United Nations Emergency Force (U.N.E.F.) was formed to ensure peace and stability in the Middle East. Its formation was a direct result of the 1956 Arab-Israeli war. In order to develop this peacekeeping force, the United Nations turned to a more neutral world power, Canada, for assistance. Canada responded by contributing a number of military units, including the 801st Air Transport Unit. The 801st was attached to U.N.E.F. in the early stages of the peace-keeping mission between Israel and Egypt. In 1964 it consisted of sixty members and was stationed in the Sinai Desert, nine miles from the coastal city of El Arish. The 801st was responsible for providing air transport, air reconnaissance, and border patrols for U.N.E.F.

During this period, the Canadian government froze the budget of the armed forces. As purchases of advanced equipment began absorbing the larger portion of the financial resources, personnel strength was reduced from 125,000 to 85,000. Small units, in locations far from Ottawa headquarters, found replacement personnel difficult to secure. This was particularly noticeable in the 801st, which seldom had more than two-thirds of its authorized strength. Furthermore, the effective personnel strength was hampered because new members had to be trained and conditioned for life in the desert.

The 801st was located in an extremely isolated area. Only one road through the desert ran near the unit, and it was controlled by the Egyptian Army. Use of the road depended on the goodwill of the military commander of the Sinai Desert, General

Source: Prepared by John Goodwin. Reprinted by permission.

Hassin. Seldom did the unit have visitors, as the road was frequently closed by military maneuvers or sand storms. The one steady, welcome "visitor" they had was an aircraft from Canada, which arrived on every second Tuesday with supplies and mail from home.

The isolated location of the 801st worked many hardships. For example, it was the last unit to receive supplies and food rations; a fifty-mile drive through the desert was necessary to obtain the unit's food allocation. The unit knew that it was receiving the least desirable of the food issue. Since refrigeration and storage were limited, dried beef and hardtack biscuits were often the menu of the day. Also, the men lived in tents, most of which were only minimally successful in keeping the shifting sand out of everything. The outside temperature of 130 degrees during the daytime made living under canvas virtually unbearable. Bedbugs and scorpions added to the discomfort.

Working conditions were arduous for the men. The extreme heat dictated that their flying be done in the early morning and in the early evening prior to darkness. Ideally, the aircrew worked either the morning or the evening shift; however, lack of personnel normally resulted in the same people covering both shifts. Flights were made seven days a week. Aircraft maintenance and repairs took place during the heat of the day when the metal skin absorbed sufficient heat to fry an egg or blister a hand. Canvas shades were put up to allow the ground crew to repair and service the planes.

The crew of the 801st was well aware that all other U.N.E.F. units lived and worked under much better conditions than did they. Visits to other units brought back reports of how others were working and living. The Canadian Army contingent in Rafah was housed in permanent buildings with modern plumbing, while the headquarters people in Gaza lived in villas.

Six pilots and three navigators, hand picked for their competence and professionalism, made up the aircrew group assigned to the 801st. Each aircrew officer held the top air transport command rating and had logged six to ten thousand hours of flying time. Further, each group member had flown all over the world, was a career officer, and had put in approximately ten years of service. These extremely capable and resourceful aircrew members took great pride in their ability to carry out an operation without a hitch. They considered themselves professionals in the complex game of flying.

The aircrew formed a closely knit group, and an aircrew replacement would be welcomed with great warmth and friendliness. One of the group would volunteer to indoctrinate the new arrival into the whys and wherefores of desert life, thus easing the transition period. Most of these replacements were previously acquainted with one or more of the present group members.

The aircrew usually could be found in the operations tent, where electric fans, a drink cooler, and other niceties had been garnered from unknown sources by the operations officer, Captain Rob Riley. In this and other respects the aircrew had considerable influence on the activities of the whole unit. Riley had also managed to arrange the exclusive use of a stretch of beach for the entire unit. The operations vehicle made frequent trips to the beach as a dip in the Mediterranean Sea became a daily ritual. Each evening was show time at the unit's outdoor theatre. There was always a full house, regardless of the movie, but the choicest section of seats was always discreetly reserved for the aircrew. A well-stocked bar, perpetual card games, and letter writing rounded out the unit's off-hours diversions.

The United Nations pay was seventy-five cents a day. Laundry and barber facilities were provided at no cost. A small post exchange sold toilet articles and cigarettes at minimal cost. In addition, each member was entitled to twenty-one extra days of leave while serving in the desert. Few of the members used this allotment of leave because of the extra work load it would put on the other group members.

As an alternative, the operations officer had succeeded in instituting one four-day "training trip" each quarter year. This trip was formally deemed "essential" for the aircrew to maintain their proficiency. The training trip involved flying across the Mediterranean into southern European countries, thus allowing each member to escape from the desert at least once during his tour of duty. Arrangements were made by the aircrew to allow ground crew members, on United Nations leave, to participate in these trips.

Besides their regular tasks of daily scheduled transport, border patrol, and air reconnaissance flights, the flying duties of the 801st included nonscheduled special transport flights ordered by U.N.E.F. headquarters (as well as the special training trips). It was not difficult to get members of the aircrew to make an extra flight of any kind, as they preferred the "wild blue yonder" to being earthbound.

The possibility of stopping overnight in Cairo, Alexandria, or Beirut made special flights the "plums" of the flying jobs. The seating capacity of the unit's C47 transports was reported as twenty-one rather than twenty-two by operations officer Riley to U.N.E.F. headquarters (contrary to the standard operating procedures of the United Nations and of the Canadian Air Force regarding full aircraft utilization). A "godfather" system of awarding the unreported seat as a prize was instituted. The seat either went to a selected ground crew member for his own use or to one of the section officers for allocation. An example of how the seat was awarded involved Corporal Simms. A radio repairman, Simms, through diligence and extra effort, rewired a radio in time to allow an airplane to depart and successfully complete its assigned mission.

Rusty Hanson had joined the Air Force in 1942 and received his pilot's wings in January 1943. Subsequently, he was transferred to Air Navigation School as a line pilot assigned to flying with student navigators. For the next twelve years his flying and administrative tours were interspersed. In 1955, Major Hanson was "flying a desk" in Air Force headquarters, where for the next eight years he was selectively moved from one administrative position to another. In April 1963, Hanson was given the temporary rank of lieutenant colonel and was des-

EXHIBIT 1   **Organization chart—801st Air Transport Unit.**

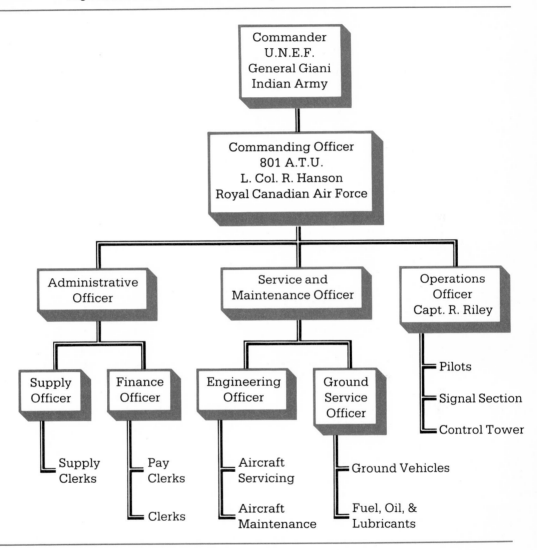

ignated commanding officer of the 801st. After a four-month flying refresher course, he proceeded to his new command. At this time his pilot log book recorded less than one thousand hours. Although confident of his administrative abilities, Hanson knew he was no crack pilot. And he knew little about the 801st other than the fact that it had received a U.N.E.F. citation for outstanding effectiveness and efficiency under its previous commanding officer.

When his transport landed at the 801st camp, Hanson was immediately struck by the very unmilitary garb worn by the aircrew and ground crew members. A typical ''uniform'' consisted of desert boots (obtained in the local Arab market), shorts cut down from khaki issue trousers, a T-shirt, and a flying jacket. The blue beret, a symbol of United Nations affiliation, was common to all—either worn on the head or protruding from the back pocket.

When he had been with the unit a few days, Hanson learned of the "training trips" to southern Europe and the "phantom" seat that was allocated on the C47s.

Rusty Hanson's innermost desire was to have his first command appraised as highly successful. A high rating would result in his temporary rank being made permanent. Hanson wondered what he should do about the curious practices at the 801st.

■ ■ ■

1. Discuss the informal norms, roles, status hierarchy, and degree of cohesiveness that have developed in the 801st Air Transport Unit.

2. What kind of role conflict does Lieutenant Colonel Rusty Hanson experience when he arrives at the 801st unit?
3. Are there factors in the setting of the 801st that might neutralize Hanson's attempts at leadership? Are there substitutes for leadership in this setting? Does "leadership matter" at the 801st?
4. Use House's Path-Goal Theory to analyze the leadership situation confronting Rusty Hanson. Which leadership style does the theory suggest?
5. Use Fiedler's Contingency Theory to analyze the leadership situation confronting Rusty Hanson. Which leadership style does the theory suggest?

Exercise

Leadership Style

Below are three cases in which a leader confronts a problem that requires a decision to be made. After reading each case, use your intuition to decide which of Vroom and Yetton's five decision strategies (AI, AII, CI, CII, GII) the leader should use. Then, reread each case and trace its characteristics through the decision tree shown in Exhibit 10-5. Did your intuitive answers differ from those provided by the decision tree analysis? If so, what factors led to the difference?

CASE I

You are general foreman in charge of a large gang laying an oil pipeline. It is now necessary to estimate your expected rate of progress in order to schedule material deliveries to the next field site.

You know the nature of the terrain you will be traveling and have the historical data needed to compute the mean and variance in the rate of speed over that type of terrain. Given these two variables it is a simple matter to calculate the earliest and latest times at which materials and support facilities will be needed at the next site. It is important that your estimate be reasonably accurate. Underestimates result in idle foremen and workers, and an overestimate results in tying up materials for a period of time before they are to be used.

Progress has been good and your five foremen and other members of the gang stand to receive substantial bonuses if the project is completed ahead of schedule.

Source of Cases: Vroom, V. H., & Yetton, P. W. (1973). *Leadership and decision-making.* Pittsburgh: University of Pittsburgh Press. © 1973 by University of Pittsburgh Press.

CASE II

You are supervising the work of twelve engineers. Their formal training and work experience are very similar, permitting you to use them interchangeably on projects. Yesterday, your manager informed you that a request had been received from an overseas affiliate for four engineers to go abroad on extended loan for a period of six to eight months. For a number of reasons he argued, and you agreed, that this request should be met from your group.

All your engineers are capable of handling this assignment, and, from the standpoint of present and future projects, there is no particular reason why any one should be retained over any other. The problem is somewhat complicated by the fact that the overseas assignment is in what is generally regarded in the company as an undesirable location.

CASE III

You are the head of a staff unit reporting to the vice-president of finance. He has asked you to provide a report on the firm's current portfolio including recommendations for changes in the selection criteria currently employed. Doubts have been raised about the efficiency of the existing system in the current market conditions, and there is considerable dissatisfaction with prevailing rates of return.

You plan to write the report, but at the moment you are quite perplexed about the approach to take. Your own specialty is the bond market, and it is clear to you that a detailed knowledge of the equity market, which you lack, would greatly enhance the value of the report. Fortunately, four members of your staff are specialists in different segments of the equity market. Together they possess a vast amount of knowledge about the intricacies of investment. However, they seldom agree on the best way to achieve anything when it comes to the stock market. While they are obviously conscientious as well as knowledgeable, they have major differences when it comes to investment philosophy and strategy.

You have six weeks before the report is due. You have already begun to familiarize yourself with the firm's current portfolio and have been provided by management with a specific set of constraints that any portfolio must satisfy. Your immediate problem is to come up with some alternatives to the firm's present practices and select the most promising for detailed analysis in your report.

REFERENCES

1. Bass, B. M. (1981). *Stogdill's handbook of leadership: A survey of research* (rev. ed.). New York: Free Press.
2. This list is derived from Bass, 1981, and House, R. J., & Baetz, M. L. (1979). Leadership: Some empirical generalizations and new research directions. *Research in Organizational Behavior, 1,* 341–423.
3. Fiedler, F. E., Potter, E. A., III, Zais, M. M., & Knowlton, W. A, Jr. (1979). Organizational stress and the use and misuse of managerial intelligence and experience. *Journal of Applied Psychology, 64,* 635–647; Potter, E. H., III, & Fiedler, F. E. (1981). The utilization of staff member intelligence and experience under high and low stress. *Academy of Management Journal, 24,* 361–376.

4. Lewis, G. H. (1972). Role differentiation. *American Sociological Review, 37*, 424–434.

5. Bales, R. F., & Slater, P. E. (1955). Role differentiation in small decision-making groups. In T. Parsons, et al. (Eds.), *Family, socialization, and interaction process.* Glencoe, IL: Free Press; Slater, P. E. (1955). Role differentiation in small groups. *American Sociological Review, 20,* 300–310.

6. For a pessimistic review see Korman, A. K. (1966). ''Consideration,'' ''initiating structure,'' and organizational criteria—A review. *Personnel Psychology, 19,* 349–361. For an optimistic update see Kerr, S., & Schriesheim, C. (1974). Consideration, initiating structure, and organizational criteria—An update of Korman's 1966 review. *Personnel Psychology, 27,* 555–568.

7. Kerr, S., Schriesheim, C. A., Murphy, C. J., & Stogdill, R. M. (1974). Toward a contingency theory of leadership based upon the consideration and initiating structure literature. *Organizational Behavior and Human Performance, 12,* 62–82.

8. For a review of the evidence see Filley, A. C., House, R. J., & Kerr, S. (1976). *Managerial process and organizational behavior* (2nd ed.). Glenview, IL: Scott, Foresman. Also see Larson, L. L., Hunt, J. G., & Osborn, R. N. (1976). The great hi-hi leader behavior myth: A lesson from Occam's razor. *Academy of Management Journal, 19,* 628–641.

9. Oldham, G. R. (1976). The motivational strategies used by supervisors: Relationships to effectiveness indicators. *Organizational Behavior and Human Performance, 15,* 66–86.

10. Ashour, A. S., & Johns, G. (1983). Leader influence through operant principles: A theoretical and methodological framework. *Human Relations, 36,* 603–626; Podsakoff, P. M., & Schriesheim, C. A. (1984). Leader reward and punishment behavior: A review of the literature. In D. F. Ray (Ed.), *Southern Management Association Proceedings,* 12–14.

11. Ashour & Johns, 1983; Podsakoff & Schriesheim, 1984.

12. Ashour & Johns, 1983. Also see Podsakoff, P. M. (1982). Determinants of a supervisor's use of rewards and punishments: A literature review and suggestions for further research. *Organizational Behavior and Human Performance, 29,* 58–83.

13. For a review of evidence see Kerr & Schriesheim, 1974.

14. Fiedler, F. E. (1967). *A theory of leadership effectiveness.* New York: McGraw-Hill; Fiedler, F. E., & Chemers, M. M. (1974). *Leadership and effective management.* Glenview, IL: Scott, Foresman; Fiedler, F. E. (1978). The contingency model and the dynamics of the leadership process. In L. Berkowitz (Ed.), *Advances in experimental social psychology* (Vol. 11). New York: Academic Press.

15. For a summary see Fiedler, 1978.

16. See Ashour, A. S. (1973). The contingency model of leader effectiveness: An evaluation. *Organizational Behavior and Human Performance, 9,* 339–355; Graen, G. B., Alvares, D., Orris, J. B., & Martella, J. A. (1970). The contingency model of leadership effectiveness: Antecedent and evidential results. *Psychological Bulletin, 74,* 285–296.

17. Peters, L. H., Hartke, D. D., & Pohlmann, J. T. (1985). Fiedler's contingency theory of leadership: An application of the meta-analysis procedures of Schmidt and Hunter. *Psychological Bulletin, 97,* 274–285; Strube, M. J., & Garcia, J. E. (1981). A meta-analytic investigation of Fiedler's contingency model of leadership effectiveness. *Psychological Bulletin, 90,* 307–321.

18. The best descriptions of the theory can be found in House, R. J., & Dessler, G. (1974). The path-goal theory of leadership: Some post hoc and a priori tests. In J. G. Hunt & L. L. Larson (Eds.), *Contingency approaches to leadership.* Carbondale, IL: Southern Illinois University Press; House, R. J., & Mitchell, T. R. (1974, Autumn). Path-goal

theory of leadership. *Journal of Contemporary Business,* 81–97; Filley, House, & Kerr, 1976.

19.   House & Dessler, 1974; House & Mitchell, 1974; Filley, House, & Kerr, 1976.

20.   See, for example, Greene, C. N. (1979). Questions of causation in the path-goal theory of leadership. *Academy of Management Journal, 22,* 22–41; Griffin, R. W. (1980). Relationships among individual, task design, and leader behavior variables. *Academy of Management Journal, 23,* 665–683.

21.   Locke, E. A., & Schweiger, D. A. (1979). Participation in decision making: One more look. *Research in Organizational Behavior, 1,* 265–339.

22.   Mitchell, T. R. (1973). Motivation and participation: An integration. *Academy of Management Journal, 16,* 160–179.

23.   Maier, N. R. F. (1973). *Psychology in industrial organizations* (4th ed.). Boston: Houghton Mifflin; Maier, N. R. F. (1970). *Problem solving and creativity in individuals and groups.* Belmont, CA: Brooks/Cole.

24.   Maier, 1970; 1973.

25.   House & Baetz, 1979.

26.   Strauss, G. (1955). Group dynamics and intergroup relations. In W. F. Whyte, *Money and motivation.* New York: Harper & Row.

27.   Vroom, V. H., & Yetton, P. W. (1973). *Leadership and decision-making.* Pittsburgh: University of Pittsburgh Press, p. 13.

28.   Vroom, V. H., & Jago, A. G. (1978). On the validity of the Vroom/Yetton model. *Journal of Applied Psychology, 63,* 151–162; Jago, A. G., & Vroom, V. H., (1980). An evaluation of two alternatives to the Vroom/Yetton normative model. *Academy of Management Journal, 23,* 347–355; Field, R. H. G. (1982). A test of the Vroom-Yetton normative model of leadership. *Journal of Applied Psychology, 67,* 523–532.

29.   Good reviews of the work on participation can be found in Filley, House, & Kerr, 1976, and Locke & Schweiger, 1979.

30.   Adapted from Katz, D., & Kahn, R. L. (1978). *The social psychology of organizations* (2nd ed.). New York: Wiley.

31.   For a review of the evidence that concludes that leadership matters see House & Baetz, 1979.

32.   Pfeffer, J. (1977). The ambiguity of leadership. *Academy of Management Review, 2,* 104–112. Pfeffer also cites evidence that leadership is less important than other organizational factors.

33.   Kerr, S. (1977). Substitutes for leadership: Some implications for organizational design. *Organizational and Administrative Sciences, 8,* 135–146; Kerr, S., & Jermier, J. M. (1978). Substitutes for leadership: Their meaning and measurement. *Organizational Behavior and Human Performance, 22,* 375–403.

34.   Sheridan, J. E., Vredenburgh, D. J., & Abelson, M. A. (1984). Contextual model of leadership influence in hospital units. *Academy of Management Journal, 27,* 57–78; Howell, J. P., & Dorfman, P. W. (1981). Substitutes for leadership: Test of a construct. *Academy of Management Journal, 24,* 714–728.

Chapter 11

Communication

This incident is interesting because it illustrates a communication breakdown caused by an earlier series of communication events. Otis went outside of approved channels of communication to help his clients. Myra found out about it through her own informal channels. Otis somehow felt that Myra wasn't interested in his work problems, even though she said she was. Both avoided communicating bad news to each other.

In this chapter we shall explore these and other aspects of communication in organizations. First, communication will be defined, a model of the communication process will be presented, and the importance of communication will be illustrated. Then two hypothetical extreme forms that organizational communication could take will be discussed. An exploration of the reality of organizational communication will explain why these extremes are not achieved. After this, superior-subordinate communication, communication and technical innovation, the "grapevine," and the verbal and nonverbal language of work will be investigated. Finally, several means of improving communication will be evaluated.

WHAT IS COMMUNICATION?

Communication is the process by which information is exchanged between a sender and a receiver. This seductively simple definition is broad enough to cover a wide variety of information exchanges. For example, the wall thermostat and the furnace in your house are constantly engaged in communication. The thermostat (sender) tells the furnace (receiver) how hot it should run. In turn, the furnace (sender) gives the thermostat (receiver) feedback about how hot it is running. This ongoing exchange of information contributes to your comfort.

The kind of communication we are concerned with in this chapter is *interpersonal* communication—the exchange of information between people. The most simple prototype for interpersonal communication is a one-on-one exchange between two individuals. Exhibit 11-1 presents a model of the interpersonal communication process and an example of a communication episode between a purchasing manager and her assistant. As you can see, the sender must **encode** his or her thoughts into some form that can be *transmitted* to the receiver. In this case, the manager has chosen to encode her thoughts in writing and transmit them via electronic mail. Alternatively, the manager could have encoded her thoughts in speech and transmitted them via a tape recording or face-to-face. The assistant, as a receiver, must *perceive* the message and accurately **decode** it to achieve accurate understanding. In this case, the assistant uses a parts catalog to decode the meaning of an "A-40." In order to provide *feedback* the assistant might send the manager a copy of the order form for the flange bolts. Such feedback involves yet another communication episode which tells the original sender that her message has been received and understood.

This simple communication model is valuable because it points out the complexity of the communication process and demonstrates a number of points at which errors can occur. Such errors lead to a lack of correspondence between the

EXHIBIT 11-1   **A model of the communication process and an example.**

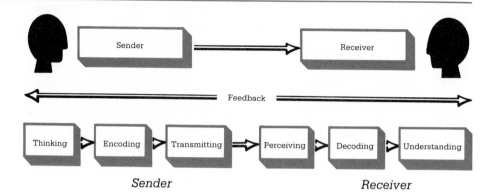

Thinking:
Purchasing manager says to herself, "I think we're getting short on A-40s."

Encoding:
Keyboards memo to assistant instructing him to order A-40s.

Transmitting:
Sends memo through electronic mail.

Perceiving:
Assistant reads memo.

Decoding:
Checks parts catalog to find out what an A-40 is.

Understanding:
Realizes that he must place an order for flange bolts.

Source: From Glueck, W. F. (1980). *Management,* Second Edition. New York: Holt, Rinehart and Winston. Copyright © 1980 by the Dryden Press, a division of Holt, Rinehart and Winston, Publishers. Reprinted by permission of Holt, Rinehart and Winston, CBS College Publishing.

sender's initial thoughts and the receiver's understanding of the intended message. A slip of the finger on the keyboard may lead to improper encoding. A poor electronic mail system may lead to ineffective transmission. An outdated parts catalog may result in inaccurate decoding.

THE IMPORTANCE OF COMMUNICATION

The importance of communication for effective organizational functioning can be illustrated in two ways. First, we can consider the relationship between communication and the topics covered earlier in the book. Then, we can explore how much time organizational members spend communicating.

Think back to our discussion of the nature of organizations in Chapter 1. There, we defined organizations as social inventions for accomplishing goals through group effort. Obviously, organizational goals will not be accomplished if they are inadequately communicated to the individuals and groups that comprise the organization—members will work at cross-purposes. Going a step further, in

Chapter 8 we defined groups as people interacting interdependently to achieve a common goal. The interaction referred to in this definition is a form of communication. Thus, at the most basic level, organizations wouldn't *be* organizations without communication among their members.

Less abstractly, it should be clear to you that *every* chapter in the book so far has been concerned implicitly with the exchange of information among organizational members. For example, the application of reinforcement and punishment (Chapter 3) is a form of communication because these stimuli contain important information. By the same token, our discussion of perceiving the motives of others in Chapter 4 described how we try to decode the social cues which they provide. In addition, our discussions of attitude change (Chapter 5), motivation (Chapter 6), and socialization (Chapter 9) revealed that these processes are often accomplished through interpersonal communication. Thus, communication is necessary for organizational effectiveness.

The importance of communication is also revealed by analyses of how organizational members spend their time at work. Careful studies of production workers indicate that they participate in between sixteen and forty-six communication episodes per hour.[1] Even the low figure of sixteen works out to one episode every four minutes. As we move up the organization's hierarchy, it is evident that more and more time is spent communicating. For first-level supervisors of production jobs, various studies show that 20 to 50 percent of the boss's time at work is spent in verbal communication. When communication through paperwork is added, these figures increase to between 29 and 64 percent.[2] Moving to middle and upper management, we find that from 66 to 89 percent of managers' time is spent in verbal (face-to-face and telephone) communication.[3] Since these figures exclude other forms of communication (such as reading and writing letters, memos, and reports) it is obvious that the content of many managerial jobs is composed almost exclusively of communication tasks.

In summary, communication is important because it defines the nature of organizations, because it is a part of so many important organizational processes, and because it comprises so much of the time usage of organizational members.

HYPOTHETICAL EXTREME FORMS OF ORGANIZATIONAL COMMUNICATION

In order to understand some of the basic issues involved in communication in organizations, let's consider two hypothetical extreme forms that such communication could take. As we shall see, the reality of organizational communication falls somewhere between these extremes. To do this, we will examine Blake Plastics, a hypothetical designer and producer of high-impact plastic products. A partial organizational chart for Blake is shown in Exhibit 11-2. Imagine that Blake has seventy members in total.

EXHIBIT 11-2   Partial organizational chart for Blake Plastics.

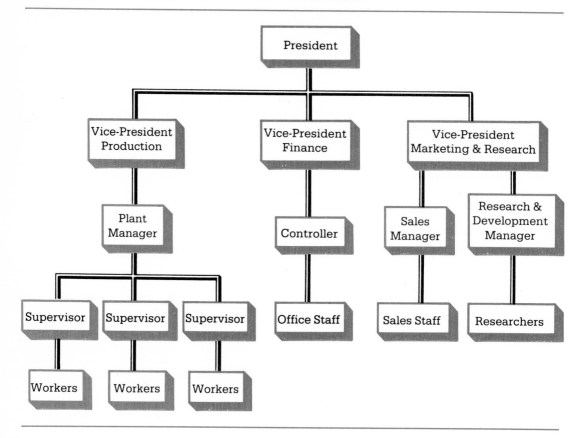

All-Channel Communication

At one extreme, each employee at Blake could in theory communicate with any of sixty-nine other members, for a staggering total of 2,415 potential communication channels!* In fact, of course, this **all-channel communication** doesn't happen. For one thing, organizations are *designed* in part to discourage the completely free flow of information. This is one thing that separates an organization from a random collection of individuals. For example, if a salesperson receives evidence from a client that a particular product has flaws, he or she would not be encouraged to enter the plant and complain directly to the mold operator who produced the product. Rather, there are "proper channels" that should be observed. Secondly, many organizational members may be *disinterested* in communicating with other

---

*The relevant formula here is $N(N-1)/2$, where N equals the number of organizational members.

members and even be unaware of their existence. For instance, a production worker may not know what a controller is, or who the controller is, even though the controller signs his paycheck! In summary, considerably less than Blake's 2,415 potential communication channels would actually be used.

Strict Chain of Command

Now let's consider the other extreme. The lines on Blake's organizational chart represent lines of authority and reporting relationships. For example, a vice-president has authority over the plant manager, who has authority over the production supervisors, and so on. Conversely, production workers report to their supervisors, who report to the plant manager, and so on. In theory, organizational communication could stick to this strict **chain of command.** Under this system, three necessary forms of communication can be accomplished:

- **Downward communication.** This is communication that flows from the top of the organization toward the bottom. For example, the vice-president of production might instruct the plant manager to gear up for manufacturing a new product. In turn, the plant manager would provide specifics to supervisors, who would instruct the production workers accordingly.

- **Upward communication.** This form of communication flows from the bottom of the organization toward the top. For instance, a research engineer might conceive a new plastic formula with unique properties. She might then pass this on to the research and development manager who would then inform the relevant vice-president.

- **Horizontal communication.** This is communication that occurs between departments or functional units, usually as a means of coordinating effort. Within a strict chain of command, such communication would flow up to and then down from a *common superior.* For example, suppose a salesperson gets an idea for a new product from a customer. To get this idea to the research staff, it would have to be transmitted up to and down from the vice-president of marketing and research, the common superior for these departments.

Clearly, a lot of organizational communication does follow the formal lines of authority shown on organizational charts. This is especially true with regard to the examples of upward and downward communication given above—directives and instructions usually pass downward through the chain of command, and ideas and suggestions pass upward. However, the reality of organizational communication suggests that the formal chain of command provides an underestimate of all the channels of communication that actually exist in organizations. Thus, the communication channels in any organization fall somewhere between the theoretical maximum of all-channel communication and the severely limited number prescribed by strict chain of command.

THE REALITY OF ORGANIZATIONAL COMMUNICATION

There are two major reasons why a formal chain of command is an underestimation of the number of communication channels within organizations.

Informal Communication

The chain of command obviously fails to consider *informal* communication between members. In previous chapters we discussed in some detail how informal inter-action helps people accomplish their jobs more effectively. Within a particular work group, it helps employees coordinate their work efforts. Thus, two researchers in Blake's research and development unit may make an informal agreement to review each other's calculations and written reports before they are submitted to the boss. Similarly, the research and development manager may meet the plant manager on the golf course and ask if any problems have been encountered in introducing a new product line. Of course, not all informal communication benefits the organi-zation. An informal grapevine may spread unsavory, inaccurate rumors across the organization. We will discuss this process shortly.

The Chain of Command is Often Ineffective

The formal chain of command also underestimates the number of communication channels that exist in organizations because managers recognize that sticking strictly to the chain is often ineffective. **Effective communication** occurs when the right people receive the right information in a timely manner. If any of these three conditions is violated, a particular communication episode is ineffective. In the story that began the chapter, Otis Roberts felt that communicating with the police through formal channels would be ineffective because it would not be timely.

Getting the right information to the right people is often inhibited by filtering. **Filtering** is the tendency for a message to be watered down or stopped altogether at some point during transmission, and it is something of a double-edged sword. On one hand, employees are *supposed* to filter information. For example, production workers are not expected to inform their bosses of every trivial event which occurs on the job. Similarly, vice-presidents are not expected to communicate every detail of the management of the company clear to the shop floor. On the other side of the coin, overzealous filtering will preclude the right people from getting the right information, and the organization will suffer accordingly. Upward filtering often occurs because subordinates are afraid that their boss will use the information against them. Downward filtering is often due to time pressures or simple lack of attention to detail, but more sinister motives may be at work. As the old saying goes, ''information is power,'' and some managers may filter downward communi-cations to maintain an edge on their subordinates. For example, a manager who feels that an up-and-coming subordinate may be promoted over her may filter crucial information to make the subordinate look bad at a staff meeting. The performance review at Tri-City Social Services indicated that both Myra and Otis had been filtering information.

Obviously, the potential for filtering increases with the number of links in the communication chain. For this reason, many organizations establish channels in addition to those revealed in the formal chain of command. For instance, many managers establish an **open door policy** in which any organizational member below them can communicate directly without going through the chain. Such a policy should decrease the upward filtering of sensitive information if subordinates trust the system. To prevent downward filtering, many organizations attempt to communicate directly with potential receivers, bypassing the chain of command. For example, the president of Blake Plastics might use the public address system to accurately inform employees about intended layoffs. Research has shown that certain types of information are more likely to be filtered than are others, thus indicating the selective need for alternative channels of communication. For example, information concerned directly with production may pass down through the hierarchy relatively intact, while that concerned with nonproduction matters (such as a change in the parking regulations) may be subjected to considerable filtering.[4]

The need for effective horizontal communication between departments probably provides the best example of why communication channels are established outside the formal chain of command. Returning to Blake Plastics, suppose the plant manager has an idea for cutting costs by modifying the construction of a particular product. Such an idea should be evaluated by the research and development manager and passed on to the research staff for detailed tests. Following the strict chain of command, this message would pass through the following sequence: Plant Manager → Vice-President Production → President → Vice-President Marketing and Research → Research and Development Manager. Obviously, this form of transmission is very inefficient. The large number of links in the chain increases the probability of filtering, and even if the message remains unfiltered, transmission time may be prohibitive. For this reason, many organizations form semiformal "bridges" or "gangplanks" between horizontal functions that need coordination.[5] At Blake, the plant manager would probably be encouraged to consult directly with the research and development manager.

In summary, informal communication and the recognition of filtering and time constraints guarantee that organizations will develop channels of communication beyond the strict chain of command. However, these channels will seldom approximate the total number available. Now, let's examine several aspects of organizational communication in detail.

SUPERIOR-SUBORDINATE COMMUNICATION

Superior-subordinate communication consists of the one-to-one exchange of information between a boss and a subordinate. As such, it represents a key element in upward and downward communication in organizations. Ideally, such exchange should enable the boss to instruct the subordinate in proper task performance, clarify reward contingencies, and provide social-emotional support. In addition, it should permit the subordinate to ask questions about his or her work role and make suggestions that may further the goals of the company or institution. As the story which began the chapter illustrated, such ideals may be difficult to achieve.

A survey of 32,000 employees in the U.S. and Canada asked them to rank their preferred and current sources of organizational information. As shown in Exhibit 11-3, the immediate supervisor was the actual source *and* the preferred source of most information.[6] In addition, perceptions that supervisors are good communicators tend to be correlated positively with organizational performance.[7] Thus, any organization would wish to establish good superior-subordinate communication.

How Good Is It?

The extent to which superiors and subordinates agree about work-related matters and are sensitive to each other's point of view is one index of good communication. Although the parties may "agree to disagree" about certain matters, extreme and persistent perceptual differences are problematic. Research has indicated that superiors and subordinates may differ in their perceptions of the following matters:

■   How subordinates should and do allocate time

■   How long it takes to learn a job

EXHIBIT 11-3   **Preferred and current sources of information about organizational issues.**

Preferred Ranking	Sources of Information	Current Ranking
1	My immediate supervisor	1
2	Small group meetings	4
3	Top executives	11
4	Employee handbook/other brochures	3
5	Local employee publication	8
6	Orientation program	12
7	Organization-wide employee publication	6
8	Annual state-of-the-business report	7
9	Bulletin boards	5
10	Upward communication program	14
11	The union	9
12	Mass meetings	10
13	Audiovisual programs	15
14	Mass media	13
15	The grapevine	2

Source: Foltz, R. G., (1985). Communication in contemporary organizations. In C. Reuss & D. Silvis (Eds.), *Inside organizational communication* (2nd ed.). New York: Longman, p. 10. Reprinted by permission.

- The importance subordinates attach to pay
- The amount of authority the subordinate has
- The subordinate's skills and abilities
- The subordinate's performance and obstacles to good performance
- The superior's leadership style[8]

Perceptual differences of this nature suggest a lack of openness in communication which may contribute to much role conflict and ambiguity, especially on the part of subordinates. In addition, there is substantial evidence that a lack of openness in communication promotes subordinate dissatisfaction.[9]

Inhibiting Factors

What are the factors that contribute to communication problems between superiors and subordinates?

CONFLICTING ROLE DEMANDS.   In the previous chapter we noted that the leadership role requires superiors to attend to both task and social-emotional functions. That is, the boss must simultaneously direct and control the subordinate's work *and* be attentive to the emotional needs and desires of the subordinate. Many superiors have difficulties balancing these two role demands. For example, imagine the following memo from a sales manager to one of the company's younger sales representatives:

> I would like to congratulate you on being named Sales Rep of the Month for March. You can be very proud of this achievement. I now look forward to your increased contribution to our sales efforts, and I hope you can begin to bring some new accounts into the company. After all, new accounts are the key to our success.

In congratulating the young sales rep and in suggesting that he increase his performance in the future, the manager tries to take care of social-emotional business and task business in one memo. Unfortunately, the sales rep may be greatly offended by this communication episode, feeling that it slights his achievement and implies that he has not been pulling his weight in the company. In this case, two separate communiques, one dealing with congratulations and the other with the performance directive, would probably be more effective. Given misunderstandings of this nature, it is not surprising that superiors and subordinates often differ in their descriptions of the superior's leadership style.[10]

THE MUM EFFECT.   Another factor inhibiting effective superior-subordinate communication is the **mum effect.** This distinctive term refers to the tendency to avoid communicating unfavorable news to others.[11] Evidently, people would rather "keep mum" than convey bad news that may provoke negative reactions on the part of the receiver (see the cartoon). For example, physicians are often reluctant to inform patients or their families of the existence of terminal illness. At Tri-City

"Have a good vacation. I've decided not to give you your bad news until you get back."

Social Services, Otis Roberts kept mum about his unorthodox work procedures, while Myra Greenfield kept mum about her objections to them.

As the example involving the physician illustrates, the sender need not be *responsible* for the bad news in order for the mum effect to occur. For instance, a structural engineer may be reluctant to tell her boss that cracks have been discovered in the foundation of a building even though a subcontractor was responsible for the faulty work. It should be obvious, though, that the mum effect is probably even more likely when the sender *is* responsible for the bad news. For example, the nurse who mistakenly administers an incorrect drug dosage may be very reluctant to inform the head nurse of her error. Research has shown that subordinates with strong aspirations for upward mobility are especially likely to encounter communication difficulties with their bosses.[12] This may be due in part to the mum effect—those who desire to impress their bosses to achieve a promotion have strong motives to withhold bad news.[13]

As the story that began the chapter illustrates, the mum effect does not apply only to subordinates. The boss may be reluctant to transmit bad news downward.

In my research in one organization, I found that subordinates who had good performance ratings were more likely to be informed of those ratings than subordinates who had bad ratings. Managers evidently avoided communicating bad news for which they were partly responsible, since they themselves had done the performance ratings. Given this state of affairs, it is not surprising that managers and their subordinates often differ in their perceptions of subordinate performance.[14]

STATUS EFFECTS. A third factor that may inhibit superior-subordinate communication is the tendency for superiors to *devalue* communication with their subordinates. In Chapter 8 it was pointed out that the status of group members affects communication patterns—people reveal a clear desire to communicate with those of a similar or higher status, rather than those of a lower status. From this, it follows that necessary communications with those of lower status, such as one's subordinates, may be viewed negatively. In an interesting study designed to test this proposal, managers were asked to record every communication episode they engaged in during a week at work.[15] In addition to specifying the method of communication and identifying the other party, they were asked to report their attitude toward each episode on scales of the following nature:

Valuable	⊢┼┼┼┼┼┤	Worthless
Dissatisfying	⊢┼┼┼┼┼┤	Satisfying
Boring	⊢┼┼┼┼┼┤	Interesting
Precise	⊢┼┼┼┼┼┤	Vague

The results indicated a clear tendency for the managers to react more favorably to episodes with higher-status organizational members than to those involving their subordinates. It is reasonable to expect that subordinates catch on to such negative reactions and begin to withhold information, a situation that contributes to poor communication.

TIME. A final factor that may lead to poor superior-subordinate communication is the simple constraint of time. This is especially true at lower organizational levels. You will recall that we concluded that first level supervisors spend between 20 and 50 percent of their working time in verbal communication. Furthermore, these studies reveal that most of this time is spent communicating with subordinates. Now, on the face of it, this seems pretty generous—subordinates may receive up to 50 percent of the boss's time on the job. However, there is a catch here. It must be remembered that many first-level supervisors may have more than twenty subordinates reporting to them. Thus, simple division indicates that *each* subordinate may receive less than 1 percent of the boss's total time on the job each day. Indeed, three studies have indicated that superior-subordinate communication on production jobs averages only *four minutes* a day![16] Thus, it is entirely possible that Otis Roberts was correct when he said that Myra Greenfield didn't seem to have much time for her subordinates.

COMMUNICATION AND TECHNICAL INNOVATION

In recent years, it has become increasingly apparent that communication plays a critical role in an organization's ability to develop innovative products and services. With increasing competition, innovation in scientific and technical areas has become especially important. Thus, considerable interest has developed in how new information of a scientific and technical nature gets into organizations and how this information is communicated within the organization. Much research shows that such communication is critical to the successful performance of project teams and research and development units.[17]

Communication requirements vary according to the nature of projects.[18] Providing technical services to other functions or fine-tuning existing products or services places a high premium on good internal communications with other departments such as sales or production. At the other extreme, basic research places a high premium on external communication with others involved in similar work. Between these extremes, there are many developmental projects that require the "translation" of external information to meet specific project needs and the communication of this information to project members. You might expect that this process would be accomplished via a rather formal network of journal articles, technical reports, and internal memoranda. In fact, technical personnel are more likely to be exposed to new information via informal oral communication networks in which key personnel import the information, translate it for local use, and disseminate it to project members.

Who are these key personnel? They are sometimes called information boundary spanners or **gatekeepers.** Such persons tend to have well developed communication networks with other professionals outside the organization *and* with the professionals on their own team or project. Thus, they are in key positions to both receive and transmit new technical information. Also, they are perceived as highly competent and a good source of new ideas.[19] Furthermore, they have an innovative orientation, they read extensively, and they can tolerate ambiguity.[20] It is important to note that gatekeeping is essentially an informal, emergent role, as many gatekeepers are not in supervisory positions.

One especially interesting line of research suggests just how important communication is to the performance of research and development project groups.[21] This research found that groups with members who had worked together a short time or a long time engaged in less communication (within the group, within the organization, and externally) than groups that had medium longevity. In turn, performance mirrored communication, with the high-communicating medium-longevity groups being the best performers (Exhibit 11-4). Evidently, when groups are new, it takes time for members to decide on what information is required and to forge the appropriate communication networks. When groups get "old" they may get comfortable and isolate themselves from critical sources of feedback. It should be emphasized that it is the age of the *group* that is at issue here, not the age of the workers or their tenure in the organization.

EXHIBIT 11-4 **Group longevity, communication, and performance of research and development groups.**

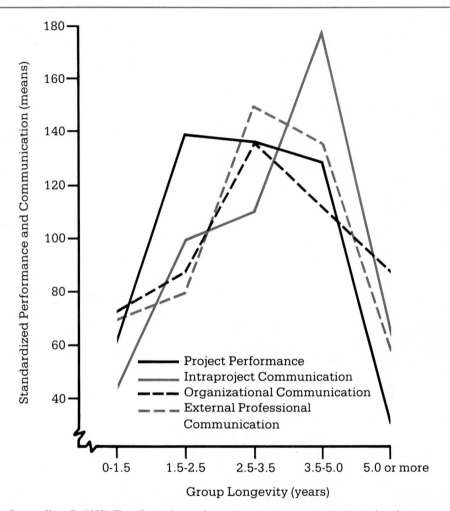

Source: Katz, R. (1982). The effects of group longevity on project communication and performance. *Administrative Science Quarterly, 27*, 81–104, p. 96.

THE GRAPEVINE

Just inside the gate of a steel mill there was a large sign which read "*X* days without a major accident." The sign was revised each day to impress upon the work force the importance of safe working practices. A zero posted on the sign caught one's attention immediately, since this meant that a serious accident or fatality had just occurred. Seeing a zero upon entering the mill, workers seldom took more than five minutes to find someone who knew the details. While the victim's name might be unknown, the location and nature of the accident were always accurate, even though the mill was very large and the accident had often occurred on the previous shift. How did this information get around so quickly? It travelled through the "grapevine." In the story that began the chapter, Myra found out about Otis's "midnight ride" to the police station through the grapevine.

Characteristics of the Grapevine

The **grapevine** is the informal communication network that exists in any organization. As such, the grapevine often cuts across formal lines of communication that are recognized by management. Observation suggests several distinguishing features of grapevine systems:

■ We generally think of the grapevine as communicating information by word of mouth. However, written notes and telex messages may contribute to the transmission of information. For example, a telex operator in the New York office may tell the Zurich office that the chairman's wife just had a baby.

■ Organizations often have several grapevine systems, some of which may be loosely coordinated. For instance, a secretary who is part of the "office grapevine" may communicate information to a mail carrier who passes it on to the "warehouse grapevine."

■ The grapevine may transmit information relevant to the performance of the organization as well as personal gossip. Many times, it is difficult to distinguish between the two: "You won't *believe* who just got fired!"

How accurate is the grapevine? One expert concludes that at least 75 percent of the noncontroversial organizationally-related information carried by the grapevine is correct.[22] Personal information and emotionally charged information are more likely to be distorted.

Grapevine information does not run through organizations in a neat chain in which person A tells only person B who tells only person C, etc. Neither does it sweep across the organization like a tidal wave, with each sender telling six or seven others, who each in turn transmit the information to six or seven *other* members. Rather, only a proportion of those who receive grapevine news pass it on, with the net effect that more "know" than "tell."[23]

Who Participates in the Grapevine?

Just who is likely to tell? That is, who is likely to be a transmitter of grapevine information? Personality characteristics may play a role. For instance, extroverts may be more likely to pass on information than introverts. Similarly, those who lack self-esteem may pass on information that gives them a personal advantage.

The nature of the information may also influence who chooses to pass it on. In a hospital, the news that a doctor has obtained a substantial cancer research grant may follow a very different path from news involving his affair with a nurse!

Finally, it is obvious that the *physical* location of organizational members is related to their opportunity to both receive and transmit news via the "vine." Occupants of work stations that receive a lot of traffic are good candidates to be grapevine transmitters. A warm control room in a cold plant or an air-conditioned computer room in a sweltering factory may provide their occupants with a steady stream of potential receivers for juicy information. On the other side of the coin, jobs that require movement throughout the organization also give their holders much opportunity to serve as grapevine transmitters. Mail carriers and maintenance personnel are good examples. Or, consider the daily arrival of the man who picked up the production of an isolated group of factory workers:

> The arrival . . . was always a noisy one, like the arrival of a daily passenger train in an isolated small town. Interaction attained a quick peak of intensity to crowd into a few minutes all communications necessary and otherwise. . . . News items would be dropped, some of serious import, such as reports of accomplished or impending layoffs in the various plants of the company, or of gains or losses in orders for company products. Most of the news items, however, involved bits of information on plant employees told in a light vein.[24]

Pros and Cons of the Grapevine

Is the grapevine desirable from the organization's point of view or not? As the above quotation illustrates, it can keep employees informed about important organizational matters such as job security. In some organizations management is so notoriously lax at this that the grapevine is a regular substitute for formal communication. The grapevine can also provide a test of employee reactions to proposed changes without making formal commitments. Managers have been known to "leak" ideas (such as a change to a four-day workweek) to the grapevine in order to probe their potential acceptance. Finally, participation in the grapevine may add a little interest and diversion to the work setting. In this context, it is simply part of the informal grouping system discussed in Chapter 8.

The grapevine can become a real problem for the organization when it becomes a constant pipeline for rumors. A **rumor** is an unverified belief that is in general circulation.[25] The key word here is unverified—although it is possible for a rumor to be true, it is not likely to *remain* true as it runs through the grapevine (see the cartoon). Because the information cannot be verified as accurate, rumors are susceptible to severe distortion as they are passed from person to person.

The distortion of rumors can take two forms. Some rumors seem to get longer and more complex as each sender adds his or her "two cents' worth." Other rumors are simplified through retelling, enhancing ease of communication. When this occurs, unfamiliar, difficult-to-remember details will usually be omitted, while

Source: Drawing by Ziegler, © 1972 *The New Yorker*.
Reprinted by permission.

interesting, dynamic details will be embellished. For example, a rumor that begins as:

> Paul Jones was laid off because of the installation of that new automated casting machine. They think he'll be back on another job soon.

may end up as:

> Word is that automation will cost a lot of jobs around here. Some guys are already gone.

Rumors seem to spread fastest and farthest when the information is especially ambiguous, when the content of the rumor is important to those involved, and when the recipient is emotionally aroused.[26] Thus, the rumor about Paul Jones would probably circulate most widely among production workers rather than office personnel, and it would probably be more potent if the economic climate of the community was bad.

THE VERBAL LANGUAGE OF WORK

A friend of mine had just moved into a new neighborhood. In casual conversation with a neighbor he mentioned that he was "writing a book on OB." She replied with some enthusiasm, "Oh, that's great. My husband's in obstetrics too!" My friend, of course, is a management professor who was writing an organizational behavior book. The neighbor's husband was a physician who specialized in delivering babies.

Every student knows what it means to do a little "cramming" in the "caf" before an exam. Although this phrase may sound vaguely obscene to the uninitiated listener, it reveals how circumstances shape our language and how we often take this shaping for granted. In many jobs, occupations, and organizations we see the development of a specialized language or **jargon** that associates use to communicate with each other. Thus, OB means organizational behavior to management professors and obstetrics to physicians.

Dr. Rosabeth Moss Kanter, in studying a large corporation, discovered its attempt to foster COMVOC, or "common vocabulary," among its managers.[27] Here, the goal was to facilitate communication among employees who were often geographically separated, unknown to each other, and "meeting" impersonally through telex or memo. COMVOC provided a common basis for interaction among virtual strangers. In addition, managers developed their own informal supplements to COMVOC. Upward mobility, an especially important topic in the corporation, was reflected in multiple labels for the same concept:

Fast trackers	One performers
High fliers	Boy (girl) wonders
Superstars	Water walkers

While jargon is an efficient means of communicating with peers and provides a touch of status to those who have mastered it, it can also serve as a *barrier* to communicating with others. For example, local jargon may serve as a barrier to clear communication between departments such as sales and engineering. New organizational members may find the use of jargon especially intimidating and confusing. For instance, consider the fledgling computer scientist who found himself assigned to a project group to develop a new computer:

> A *canard* was anything false, usually a wrongheaded notion entertained by some other group or company; things could be done in ways that created *no muss, no fuss,* that were *quick and dirty,* that were *clean. Fundamentals* were the source of all right thinking, and weighty sentences often began with the adverb *fundamentally,* while *realistically* prefaced many flights of fancy. There was talk of *wars, shootouts, hired guns* and people who *shot from the hip.* The *win* was the object of all this sport and *the big win* was something that could be achieved by *maximizing* the smaller one.[28]

A second serious problem with the use of jargon is the communication barrier that it presents to those *outside* of the organization or profession. This is particularly true when the jargon is designed *for* those on the outside. As an example, consider In–Focus 11-1, which points out how the jargon used by business school professors reduces their effectiveness in communicating with business practitioners. Of course, business commits its own sins in this area (see In–Focus 11-2). Consider the language of the corporate takeover, with its greenmail, poison pills, and white knights! Kanter, the researcher who studied COMVOC in a large corporation, found that wives of male executives could generate a total of 103 unfamiliar terms and phrases used by their husbands in relation to work![29] Such a situation may contribute to a poor understanding of what the spouse does at work and how work can make such heavy demands on family life.

THE NONVERBAL LANGUAGE OF WORK

Have you ever come away from a conversation having heard one thing yet believing the opposite of what was said? Professors frequently hear students say that they understand a concept but somehow know that they don't. Students often hear professors say, "Come up to my office any time," but somehow know that they don't mean it. In the case that began the chapter, Otis Roberts reported that he didn't feel welcome in his boss's office despite what she said. How can we account for these messages we receive in spite of the word we hear? The answer is often nonverbal communication.

Nonverbal communication refers to the transmission of messages by some medium other than speech or writing. As indicated above, nonverbal messages can be very powerful in that they often convey "the real stuff" while words serve as a smoke screen. Raised eyebrows, an emphatic shrug, or an abrupt departure can communicate a lot of information with great economy. The minutes of dramatic meetings (or even verbatim transcripts) can make for extremely boring reading

IN–FOCUS 11-2 BIZSPEAK

The men who run the Montreal-based Provigo Inc. are so smart they've turned it into Canada's second-biggest food distributor, next only to the Weston-Loblaw group, but they are also so beef-witted they contaminate their lavish annual report with businessbabble.

How can it be that men so tough and able they can run a company with annual revenues of more than $4 billion are at the same time so silly they can sign their names to a document that calls sports gear *leisure articles* and boasts an *operating entity* to establish *home improvement centers?* Ordinary folk will recognize these as hardware stores. The ordinary folk are the targets of Provigo's new *customer reception philosophy,* which may just have something to do with courtesy.

I don't know how the president of Volkswagen of America talks during stud poker at a fishing lodge, but when sales of the Volkswagen Rabbit fell 44 percent in one year, he advised the world, "We have some flexibility in the months ahead of reformulating the configuration of the product line to a combination that better suits the competitive situation." Not to worry.

The Quaker State Oil Refining Corp. has urged the press to quit calling it a mere oil company. Like gas stations which have taken to calling their gas jockeys *petroleum transfer engineers,* Quaker Oil believes in using words as the fuel of fake upward mobility. From now on, please, Quaker State is a "customer marketing company serving the automotive aftermarket."

Surely you'd have to go to a special school to learn to write this sort of palaver: "One of the biggest technical problems now is the current negative advance-decline breadth divergence." That's from a report by a big American firm of stockbrokers, and it reminds me that when the price of gold fell to shoelace-level a Toronto broker authoritatively observed, "The gold market has not been responding conveniently."

Would you buy stocks and bonds from fellows who write things like that? For that matter, would you buy a used car from a dealer who sells *preowned* or, worse, *experienced* vehicles? Would you buy a new Cadillac Brougham simply because a Cadillac vice-president calls the model "the most heavily contented car we have"?

If your car breaks down, will you be prepared to have it towed not to a repair shop but to *Customer Engineering?* Is it time to scrap the heap? Be warned, junkyards may be hard to find. They're being replaced by *auto dismantlers* and *recyclers,* who sell *predismantled, previously owned parts.*

Source: Bruce, H. Bizspeak: Tough talk in private, pseudobabble in public. © Harry Bruce, published by arrangement with Bella Pomar Agency, Inc.

because they are stripped of nonverbal cues. These examples involve the transmission of information by so-called body language. Below we consider body language and the manipulation of objects as major forms of nonverbal communication.

Body Language

Body language is nonverbal communication that occurs by means of the sender's bodily motions and facial expressions or the sender's physical location in relation to the receiver.[30] Although a variety of information can be communicated via body language, two important messages involve the extent to which the sender likes and is interested in the receiver, and the sender's views concerning the relative status of the sender and the receiver.

In general, senders communicate liking and interest in the receiver when they:

- Position themselves physically close to the receiver
- Touch the receiver during the interaction
- Maintain eye contact with the receiver
- Lean forward during the interaction
- Direct the torso toward the receiver[31]

As you can see, each of these behaviors demonstrates that the sender has genuine consideration for the receiver's point of view.

Senders who feel themselves to be of higher status than the receiver act more *relaxed* than those who perceive themselves to be of lower status. Relaxation is demonstrated by:

- The casual, asymmetrical placement of arms and legs
- A reclining, nonerect seating position
- A lack of fidgeting and nervous activity[32]

In other words, the greater the difference in relaxation between two parties, the more they communicate a status differential to each other.

As indicated earlier, when a contradiction exists between verbal behavior and body language we tend to rely more heavily upon the information transmitted via body language. For example, the boss who claims to be interested in a subordinate's problem while positioning herself across the room, failing to maintain eye contact, and orienting her body away from the subordinate will doubtless signal a true lack of interest.

One area where body language has been shown to have an impact is on the outcome of employment interview decisions. Employment interviewers are usually faced with applicants who are motivated to make a good verbal impression. Thus, in accord with the idea that "the body doesn't lie," interviewers may consciously or unconsciously turn their attention to nonverbal cues on the assumption that they are less likely to be censored than verbal cues. Research has shown that nonverbal behaviors such as smiling, gesturing, and maintaining eye contact have a favorable impact on interviewers when they are not overdone.[33] However, it is unlikely that such body language can overcome bad credentials or poor verbal performance.[34] Rather, increased body language may give the edge to applicants who are otherwise equally well qualified. Remember, in an employment interview, it's not just what you say, but also what you do!

Props, Artifacts, and Costumes

In addition to the use of body language, nonverbal communication can also occur through the use of various *objects* such as props, artifacts, and costumes. Consider the spontaneous use of a handy prop to make a nonverbal point:

> I have observed a plant superintendent in a concrete-block plant who absentmindedly picked up a small piece of broken brick while talking to the foreman. As soon as he had left, the foreman ordered a half-hour of overtime for the entire crew to clean up the plant. Nothing had been actually said about it.[35]

Most of us are probably less creative than the superintendent, and thus tend to do our communicating with less transient objects. For example, consider the manner in which people decorate and arrange their offices. Does this tell visitors anything about the occupant? Does it communicate any useful information? One observer thinks so:

> The more a person does influence his own surroundings, however, through decoration, personal artifacts, rearrangement, bringing in his own furniture, and the like, the more data he provides about who he is. A visitor can then get information fairly quickly about similarities and differences between himself and the occupant of the place. This can help in establishing a new relationship, since it provides more data about what realistic expectations the visitor may have of the occupant, and it may stimulate the visitor to disclose more information about himself than he would if they were in some anonymous place, starting from zero information.[36]

If personalization of one's office does communicate something about the personality of the occupant, another observer suggests that, in the company she studied, secretaries were more open than their bosses:

> Secretaries added a personal touch to Industrial Supply Corporation workplaces. Professional and managerial offices tended to be austere: generally uniform in size and coloring, and unadorned except for a few family snapshots or discrete artworks. . . . But secretaries' desks were surrounded by splashes of color, displays of special events, signs of individuality and taste of the residents: postcards from friends' or bosses' travels pasted on walls, newspaper cartoons, large posters with funny captions, huge computer printouts that formed the names of the secretaries in gothic letters.[37]

Does careful research confirm these observations of the decor and arrangement of offices transmitting nonverbal information? The answer is yes. One typical study found that students would feel more welcome and comfortable in professors' offices when the office was 1) tidy, 2) decorated with posters and plants, and 3) the desk was against the wall instead of between the student and the professor.[38] A neat office evidently signaled that the prof was well organized and had time to talk to them. Perhaps personal decoration signaled, "I'm human." When the desk was against the wall, a tangible barrier between the parties was removed. Other research has shown that persons who arrange their desks and visitors' chairs in an open and inviting manner are more outgoing and internally controlled.[39] Thus, it appears that visitor responses to variations in office decor may have some validity.

Frequently, the first few minutes of plays and movies have no dialogue. Despite this lack of verbal communication, we often learn much about the actors by means of the costumes they wear. In the right setting, proper costumes send clear messages—"I'm a stuffy English butler;" "I'm a damsel in distress;" "I'm a tough gangster." It stands to reason that the costumes worn by people in organizational settings also send nonverbal communications.

Does clothing communicate? "Wardrobe engineer" John T. Molloy is convinced that the clothing worn by organizational members sends clear signals about their competence, seriousness, and promotability. That is, receivers unconsciously attach certain stereotyped meanings to various clothing, and then treat the wearer accordingly. For example, Molloy insists that a black raincoat is the kiss of death for an aspiring male executive. He claims that black raincoats signal "lower middle class," while beige raincoats lead to "executive" treatment both inside and outside of the firm. For the same reason, Molloy strongly vetoes sweaters for women executives. Molloy stresses that proper clothing will not make up for a lack of ambition, intelligence, and savvy. Rather, he argues that the wrong clothing will prevent these qualities from being detected. To this end, he prescribes detailed "business uniforms," the men's built around a conservative suit and the women's around a skirted suit and blouse.[40] The popularity of such thinking is revealed by a rise in the number of image consultants who help aspiring executives to "dress for success" (see In–Focus 11-3).

Research is beginning to reveal that clothing does indeed communicate.[41] Even at the ages of ten to twelve, children associate various brand names of jeans with different personality characteristics of the wearer! Such effects persist in adulthood, where research simulations have shown that more masculinely dressed and groomed women are more likely to be selected for executive jobs (see In–Focus 11-4). However, one study shows that there may be a point at which women's dress becomes "too masculine" and thus damages their prospects.[42] Observers note that women's clothing styles have been of special research interest because there is less clear consensus about just how female executives should dress.

If clothing does indeed communicate, it may do so in part because of the impact it has on the wearer's own self-image. Proper clothing may enhance self-esteem and self-confidence to a noticeable degree. One study contrived to have some student job applicants appear for an interview in street clothes, while others had time to dress in more appropriate formal interview gear. Those who wore more formal clothes felt that they had made a better impression on the interviewer. They also asked for a starting salary that was $4,000 higher than the job seekers who wore street clothes![43]

IMPROVING ORGANIZATIONAL COMMUNICATION

Thus far, we have discussed a variety of barriers to effective communication in organizations. In this section we shall discuss some relatively straightforward techniques that have been proposed to improve communication. More complex

IN–FOCUS 11-3 CONSULTANTS POLISH IMAGES

Underneath that overweight, stuttering, bumbling, scuffed-shoe exterior there may be someone with intelligence, wit, competence and true competitive ability. But who knows unless the exterior reveals the interior? And so an industry has come along dedicated to making men and women look good on the job so they can perhaps rise to top management posts in their companies.

The operative word of this business is image, and the practitioners call themselves image consultants. First seen a decade ago, they are now multiplying like reflections off a ballroom mirror. The *Directory of Personal Image Consultants* lists 256 firms, vs. only 36 in 1978. Their projected sales this year: $20 million.

The stylemakers offer to shape, polish and crease almost all aspects of a person to achieve success in the corridors of corporate power. Emily Cho of New York City, who wrote *Looking, Working, Living Terrific 24 Hours a Day,* is one of the industry's top consultants. She specializes in helping women assemble a complete business wardrobe.

At fees that can hit $225 an hour, the specialists try to create a complete image—from corporate hairstyle to speech—for the ambitious man or woman who is still a few tantalizing rungs from the top. Self-styled "wardrobe engineers" advise men to discard cheap ties and reject anything in polyester. Women executives are cautioned to button up at the collar and resist the current custom of walking into the office in running shoes.

Honing one's social small-talk skills is also urged. For those with no interests outside their jobs, *Image Impact for Men,* a new book, has succinct advice: "Develop some." Readers are advised that a person's face must be carefully controlled: let positive feelings show, but reveal negative ones selectively. The complete executive commands a "repertoire of effective facial expressions," writes James G. Gray, a consultant in Washington.

The advisers offer "personal public relations" guidance on looking and acting like an expert in a particular field. Clients are even taught how to stand for success. John T. Molloy, one of the most successful imagemakers, says that the "power stance" is with arms hanging down, feet apart, almost in a military fashion.

The image business, though, is having a few image problems of its own. The field is attracting unqualified amateurs, and some consultants are trying to keep out tacky practitioners. Says Andrea Reynolds, managing director of the two-year-old Professional Image Consultants Association International: "It's making a lot of us angry. People lacking training are giving consulting advice that is incomplete, inaccurate and sometimes damaging." The group sets standards for imagemakers, including at least some advanced education in such fields as marketing, fashion design and communications.

After a few sessions with consultants, presto! the door to the executive suite should swing wide open. Right? Well, no. Basics still matter. In *Live for Success,* Molloy reports that of 1,000 men and women interviewed, nearly all agreed that success depends more on energy than image. All the image consulting in the world cannot help the true corporate loser. Nor can it cure incompetence. Nonetheless, Molloy found that most people believe that speaking, moving and dressing correctly are critical to getting ahead. The office slob remains so at his or her peril.

Source: DeMott, John S. as reported by Richard Bruns/New York. (1985, April 8). *Time.* Reprinted by permission.

IN–FOCUS 11-4 DOES CLOTHING MAKE THE (EXECUTIVE) WOMAN?

Sandra Forsythe, Mary Frances Drake, and Charles E. Cox were interested in how a female job applicant's clothing might influence a simulated hiring decision. Personnel administrators viewed videotapes of potential applicants and rated their acceptability for a management position. Below are pictures of four applicants from their study. First, rank order the applicants in terms of how acceptable you feel they are for a management position. Then, rank order them in terms of the degree of masculinity exhibited by their clothing. To compare your rankings with those found in the research, see the end of the references to this chapter.

Costume 1

Costume 2

Costume 3

Costume 4

Source: Forsythe, S., Drake, M. F., & Cox, C. E. (1985). Influence of applicant's dress on interviewer's selection decision. *Journal of Applied Psychology, 70,* 374–378.

techniques will be considered in Chapter 13 (with regard to conflict reduction) and Chapter 17 (with regard to organizational development).

Exit Interviews

Exit interviews are interviews conducted with resigning or dismissed employees in order to gain useful information about problems affecting those who remain employed. As such, they represent an attempt to improve upward communication. The interviews are traditionally conducted by a management representative, the person's immediate superior, or someone from the personnel department.

In theory, exit interviews should provide some frank information about the work situation that those remaining might be afraid to report for fear of reprisal. In fact, they don't appear to accomplish this goal. Several studies have demonstrated that reasons for resignation given in traditional exit interviews do not correspond to those given in follow-ups by researchers.[44] Since those provided to researchers tend to be more negative, it can be concluded that resigning employees hide their true feelings so as not to "burn their bridges" with management. Clearly, traditional exit interviews provide a poor source of upward communication.

Employee Surveys and Survey Feedback

In contrast to exit interviews, surveys of the attitudes and opinions of current employees can provide a useful means of upward communication. Since surveys are usually conducted with questionnaires that provide for anonymous responses, employees should feel free to voice their genuine views. A good **employee survey** contains questions that reliably tap employee concerns and also provide information that is useful for practical purposes. Survey specialists must summarize (encode) results in a manner easily decoded by management. Surveys are especially useful when they are administered periodically. In this case, managers can detect changes in employee feelings that may deserve attention. For example, a radical decrease in satisfaction with pay might be a precursor of labor troubles and signal needed revision of the compensation package.

When survey results are fed back to employees, along with management responses and any plans for changes, downward communication should be enhanced. Survey feedback shows workers that their comments have been heard and considered by management. Plans for changes in response to survey concerns indicate a commitment to two-way communication.[45]

Suggestion Systems, Query Systems, and Hotlines

Suggestion systems are designed to enhance upward communication by soliciting ideas for improved work operations from nonmanagerial employees. They represent a formal attempt to encourage useful ideas and prevent their filtering through the chain of command. The simplest example of a suggestion system involves the use of a suggestion box into which employees put written ideas for improvements (usually anonymously). This simple system is usually not very effective, since there is no tangible incentive for making a submission and no clear mechanism to show that a submission has been considered.

Much better are programs that *reward* employees for suggestions actually adopted and provide feedback as to how each suggestion was evaluated. For simple suggestions a flat fee is usually paid (perhaps $100). For complex suggestions of a technical nature that may result in substantial savings to the firm, a percentage of the anticipated savings is often awarded (perhaps several thousand dollars). An example of such a suggestion might be how to perform machinery maintenance without costly long-term shutdowns. When strong publicity is given to the adopted suggestions (such as explaining them in the organization's employee newsletter) downward communication is also enhanced, since employees receive information about the kind of innovations desired.

Related to suggestion systems are *query systems* that provide a formal means of answering questions employees may have about the organization. These systems foster two-way communication and are most effective when questions and answers are widely disseminated. Many organizations have a column of questions and answers in their employee newsletters, the content ranging from questions about benefits to the firm's stock performance. Many libraries have adopted a similar system to answer queries from users about library services. One provides "Library Dialogue" forms that are routed to the library official most qualified to respond. Most completed forms and responses are then posted in a prominent location in the library so that others may learn from the dialogue.

Many organizations have adopted *telephone hotlines* to further communication. Some are actually query systems in that employees can call in for answers to their questions. For example, AT&T developed a "Let's Talk" program to answer employee questions about the impact of its antitrust divestiture, and C&P Telephone Companies has an interactive system to handle queries about equal employment opportunity and affirmative action. More common are hotlines that use a news format to present company information. (See In–Focus 11-5). News may be presented live at prearranged times or recorded for 24-hour availability. Such hotlines prove especially valuable at times of crisis such as storms, strikes, and so on.[46]

Managing Gatekeepers

Earlier in the chapter, when we discussed the communication of innovative technical information, the role of gatekeepers was stressed. Gatekeepers, you will recall, span organizational boundaries to import technical information from the environment and disseminate it among project or team members. Traditionally, the gatekeeper role has been emergent and informal, but it is possible that organizations could do a better job of actively encouraging and managing this role among those

IN–FOCUS 11-5   SOUTHERN COMPANY SERVICES' TELEPHONE HOTLINE

"This is 'Southern Today' for Friday, June the third. On Wall Street yesterday, Southern Company stock closed at. . . ."

Thus begins a typical morning edition of "Southern Today," Southern Company Services' telephone newsline program for more than 3,000 employees in Atlanta and Birmingham. Getting timely news and information to the employees is a primary objective of the program. On many days, the message is updated three times; whenever news is happening fast, the message may be changed five or six times.

Subject matter included in the program ranges from the latest development in a rate-case hearing to announcements on meetings, executive promotions and cost controls. Southern Company Services provides technical and professional services to five other firms within the Southern electric system, so many of the news items are selected from major events as they occur at each of those companies. Union contracts, energy sales, bond offerings, plant operating status, state legislation, regulatory actions and construction updates are among the subjects included in the program. "Southern Today" also keeps employees informed about national issues affecting electric utilities—for example, acid rain, nuclear power safety, nuclear waste disposal, new regulations and tax legislation.

News is gathered from a variety of sources: editors at other system companies, industry associations, local newspapers, Dow Jones News Wire, UPI and AP newswires, *USA Today* and a number of contacts within and outside the organization. When appropriate, an executive may be contacted for comment on a local, regional or national event.

One staff member researches, writes and produces the program daily. Scripts must be written in crisp broadcast style and the message delivered in a professional broadcast manner. The length of most reports is limited to less than two minutes.

Effectiveness of the program is measured by the number of calls and through biennial surveys. On average, more than 400 calls are recorded daily, and well over 1,000 calls may be received on "hot" news days. The most recent employee survey rated "Southern Today" as one of the company's most believable and effective programs.

Source: Taft, W. F. (1985). Bulletin boards, exhibits, hotlines. In C. Reuss & D. Silvis (Eds). *Inside organizational communication* (2nd ed.), New York: Longman, pp. 185–186. Reprinted by permission.

professionals who are capable of building strong internal and external information networks. Internal connections can be managed by providing potential gatekeepers with in-house training, transfers, and varied job assignments.[47] *Fortune* magazine noted a common trend among innovative corporations:

> People in different disciplines are simply not allowed to remain in isolation. Business units are kept small in part to throw engineers, marketers, and finance experts together into the sort of tight groups most often found in start-up companies. Where the interaction fails to arise naturally, it is engineered: all of these companies require their workers to spend a great deal of time at meetings where information is shared and plans are discussed.[48]

Along these same lines, one study found that the actual physical location of gatekeepers was important to their ability to function as such. The authors suggested the clustering of offices and use of common lounge areas as a means of facilitating technical communication.[49] Equal thought could be devoted to the design of electronic communication media.

Finally, in order to facilitate external communication, potential gatekeepers could be provided with more generous telephone allowances and travel allowances to encourage attendance at seminars, short courses, and professional meetings. Also, the promotion of gatekeepers will provide a clear signal of the organization's intent to reward those technical personnel who have cultivated special communication skills.[50]

Supervisor Training

Is good communication a mysterious inherited art, or can bosses be trained to communicate more effectively with subordinates? The evidence suggests that proper training can improve the communication skills of supervisors. Notice the specific use of the word *skills* here. Vague lectures about the importance of good communication simply don't tell supervisors *how* to communicate better. However, isolating specific communication skills and giving the boss an opportunity to practice these skills should have positive effects. The supervisor who has confidence in how to handle delicate matters should be better able to handle the balance between social-emotional and task demands.

Effective training programs usually present videotaped models correctly handling a typical communication problem. Supervisors then role-play the problem and are reinforced by the trainers when they exhibit effective skills. At General Electric, for example, typical communication problems addressed with this kind of training have included discussing undesirable work habits, reviewing work performance, discussing salary changes, and dealing with subordinate-initiated discussions.[51]

It might seem that training of this nature is essentially focused on downward communication. However, there is much evidence that the disclosure of one's attitudes and feelings promotes reciprocity on the part of the receiver. Thus, the boss who can communicate effectively downward can expect increased upward communication in return.[52]

A FOOTNOTE: LET'S NOT BLAME EVERYTHING ON COMMUNICATION

"What we have here is a failure to communicate." As you are no doubt aware, it is fashionable to blame a variety of social problems on poor communication—everything from teenage pregnancies to the questionable quality of television programming. Not surprisingly, it is also fashionable to emphasize the role of communication in creating problems in businesses, schools, and hospitals. There is a strong element of truth in this, and a fair proportion of this chapter has been devoted to discussing such problems. In this concluding section the dangers of overglorifying the role of communication will be emphasized.

First, *more* communication is not always *better* communication. Communication takes time, and endless meetings and conferences designed to improve communication may simply result in reduced productivity. Putting warring parties together so that they can "work things out" may simply enable them to take better shots at each other. In addition, interviews with workers often suggest that the workers perform best and are most satisfied when their bosses leave them alone. To repeat, effective communication involves getting the right information to the right people on time, and the right information does not always mean more information.

Secondly, communication difficulties are often the symptoms or results of organizational problems rather than the causes. Attempts to correct symptoms without identifying causes may prove ineffective. The sales staff may claim that it "just can't communicate" with the production staff to obtain fast deliveries to customers. Careful listening and frequent meetings between the two departments may not alter the fact that these groups essentially see themselves as serving different masters (internal management versus external purchasers).

Finally, we all have some tendency to use the term *communication problem* as if it really explained something. Such easy labeling often obscures the fact that such problems are *specific* difficulties with specific solutions. Correcting a problem due to lack of subordinate trust may require a different strategy from correcting one due to lack of supervisory feedback to the subordinate.

SUMMARY

■ Communication is the process by which information is exchanged between a sender and a receiver. Organizational members (especially managers) spend a considerable portion of their time communicating. Effective communication involves getting the right information to the right people in a timely manner.

■ In theory, any organizational member could communicate with any other in a totally random fashion. At the other extreme, communication could follow the strict chain of command. Both of these hypothetical extremes are unrealistic. All-channel communication is discouraged by the organization, while the chain of command fails to account for informal communication and may be extremely ineffective. This ineffectiveness stems from filtering and the long time it may take for information to pass through the chain.

■ Superior-subordinate communication is frequently ineffective. The superior may have difficulty balancing task and social-emotional demands, and both superiors and subordinates may be reluctant to inform each other of bad news (the mum effect). Also, superiors may devalue communicating with subordinates or simply not have enough time to spend interacting with them.

■ For organizations to remain competitive, innovative technical information must be imported from the environment and diffused within the organization. This is accomplished by personnel called gatekeepers.

■ The grapevine is the organization's informal communication network. Only a portion of those who receive grapevine information pass it on. Key physical locations or jobs that require movement around the organization encourage certain members to pass on information. The grapevine may be useful to the organization, and it often transmits information accurately. However, it becomes problematic when rumors (unverified beliefs) circulate.

■ Verbal language that is tailored to the needs of a particular occupation or organization is known as jargon. While jargon aids communication between experienced associates, it can often prove confusing for new organizational members and those outside the organization. Nonverbal communication involves the transmission of messages by a medium other than speech or writing. One major form is body language, which involves body movement or the placement of the body in relation to the receiver. Much body language is subtle and automatic, communicating factors such as liking, interest, and status differences. Other forms of nonverbal communication involve office decoration, office arrangement, and the clothing worn at work.

■ Traditional exit interviews do little to enhance communication, while employee surveys and survey feedback, suggestion and query systems, and supervisor training may be useful in improving communication. Also, gatekeepers could be better managed in most organizations.

KEY CONCEPTS

Communication
Encode
Decode
All-channel communication
Chain of command
Downward communication
Upward communication
Horizontal communication
Effective communication
Filtering
Open door policy
Mum effect
Gatekeepers
Grapevine
Rumor
Jargon

Nonverbal communication
Body language
Exit interviews
Employee surveys
Suggestion systems

DISCUSSION QUESTIONS

1. Using Exhibit 11-1 as a guide, describe a communication episode you have observed in an organization. Who were the sender and receiver?

2. It was pointed out that effective communication involves getting the right information to the right person on time. Was the episode you described in question 1 effective? Why or why not?

3. Why does the proportion of working time devoted to communication increase as we move up the hierarchy of the organization?

4. Describe or invent a situation in which communicating strictly by the chain of command would be very ineffective.

5. "It is very difficult to establish good superior-subordinate communication." What evidence would support this position?

6. Discuss the pros and cons of the existence of the grapevine in organizations. Suppose an organization wanted to "kill" the grapevine. How easy do you think this would be?

7. Interview someone who performs a job with which you are unfamiliar. Make a list of the unusual language or jargon used on this job and define the terminology. Why was this jargon developed?

8. Discuss a case in which you heard one message communicated verbally and "saw" another transmitted nonverbally. What was the content of each message? Which one did you believe?

9. Under what conditions might body language or clothing have a strong communicative effect? When might the effect be weaker?

10. What qualities would the ideal gatekeeper possess to facilitate the communication of technical information in his or her firm?

FOR FURTHER READING

Baskin, O. W., & Aronoff, C. E. (1980). *Interpersonal communication in organizations*. Glenview, IL: Scott, Foresman.
> A basic introduction to communication in organizations which includes the role of communication in decision making and instituting organizational change.

Luthans, F., & Larsen, J. K. (1986). How managers really communicate. *Human Relations, 39,* 161–178.
> Presents an observational study of the communication behavior of 120 managers. Reports how much time was spent communicating to whom about what. Develops an interesting model of managerial communication.

Steele, F. (1975). *The open organization*. Reading, MA: Addison-Wesley.
> An excellent and unconventional discussion of the reasons for secrecy and poor communication in organizations. Advocates increased disclosure to overcome a range of traditional organizational taboos.

Case Study

ADCO Pharmacy

The events occurred in the Crescent Street branch of a large pharmacy chain called ADCO. "Pharmacy" was perhaps a misnomer, since the stores, in addition to drugs, sold everything from expensive perfumes to magazines to snack foods to motor oil to household cleaning products. The Crescent Street store was staffed by a manager, an assistant manager, a pharmacist, and a large crew of young workers, most of whom were college students who worked part-time.

Mr. Rollins, the manager of the store, was fifty-two years old and had been with ADCO for sixteen years, managing stores in a number of locations as the chain grew with the demand for larger self-service drug emporiums. Mr. Rollins always prided himself with concern for customer opinion, and he tried to be a visible and helpful manager despite the fact that the store was large and essentially self-service in nature. Besides this important public relations function, his major tasks were ordering drugs and other goods and working with the pharmacist to ensure the security of the prescription drug stock.

Cindy Nellis has been the assistant manager at the Crescent Street branch for two years. Twenty-four years old and a part-time student, her job primarily involved maintaining the work schedule for the rest of the staff and deploying them on various tasks throughout the store. This was a critical function. The profits stemming from the dispensing of prescription drugs were fairly constant, since they were under the sole control of the pharmacist. However, the overall profitability of the store was highly dependent upon the efficient deployment and motivation of the rest of the staff, since the operation was fairly labor intensive.

The mostly student staff at ADCO unpacked received goods, priced them, and stocked the shelves.

In addition, they engaged in "housekeeping" and the operation of the cash registers. Although the work was far from exciting, the store received a large amount of student traffic, and it was often possible to say "hello" to one's friends and chat for a few minutes while one worked. In addition, most of the staff enjoyed listening to FM 95 ("The Big Five") as they worked. The hard rock station was played over the store's public address system and was audible in all parts of the store, as all ADCO stores employed some kind of background music. Cindy Nellis had long ago taken informal control of the "sounds," tuning in FM 95 every morning to "keep the staff awake." Quite by coincidence, the ADCO chain featured frequent advertisements and promotions on the station. During the day, it was not uncommon for the student help to be seen mouthing the words to popular rock tunes or snapping their fingers as they worked in time to the music.

One day, Mrs. Zima, a senior citizen and long-time patron of the store, in to refill a medical prescription, accosted Mr. Rollins and complained that "the music is so loud I can't think." Mr. Rollins expressed concern and told her that everything would be taken care of. At the end of the day he saw Cindy Nellis and told her that there had been customer complaints about the rock music and that she should from now on tune the radio to another station, an "easy listening" station that he occasionally listened to at home.

The next morning, Cindy found the station after some searching (she had never heard of it before). Within fifteen minutes, the student staff began to complain about the music to Cindy, who informed them that they would just have to accept the change. During the week, the complaints continued, and Cindy found that she had to begin supervising much more closely than usual. Twice, she had to "hustle employees up" when she found them lounging around rather than pricing goods or stacking shelves. Both took the opportunity to complain yet again about the music, citing boredom for their lax performance. Once, Cindy had to stop a loud bickering match between two employees who had always gotten along well together. During a break, several employees speculated that Mr. Rollins didn't like rock music because his nephew had been in trouble with the police over drugs. Whether the music was as bad as the employees said or not, Cindy became convinced that it was damaging productivity. Besides, she thought, ADCO didn't even advertise on the easy listening station.

About two weeks after the radio station had been switched, Mr. Rollins asked Cindy to see him in his office.

"Cindy," he said, "I think you've lost control of the staff. Housekeeping has gone from bad to worse, the shelves just aren't being stocked effectively, and we have conflict that we've never had before. And sales are down, too. What's going on? You know I'm always open to suggestions."

Cindy wondered whether Mr. Rollins would believe that the problems were due to radio music.

■ ■ ■

1. How effective is communication at the Crescent Street branch of ADCO? Cite specific examples where ineffective communication occurred.
2. Is there evidence of the mum effect in the case?
3. Most of the communication occurred via the store's formal chain of command. Was this appropriate?
4. Is Cindy correct? Is radio music the problem?
5. How should Mr. Rollins and Cindy Nellis resolve the current state of affairs?

Exercise

Bay City Police Department

GENERAL INSTRUCTIONS

This is a role-playing exercise. DO NOT READ THE ROLES GIVEN BELOW UNTIL ASSIGNED TO DO SO BY YOUR INSTRUCTOR! In the exercise, you will be asked to play a member of the Bay City Police Department, either a sergeant or one of the sergeant's patrol officers. In role playing, assume the facts and attitudes supplied by the role. When things come up that are not included in the role, act in accordance with your feelings and the way things might happen in the real world of work. It is best to read your role carefully and then not consult your role during the role-playing.

When the role-playing begins, assume that Sergeant Royce has called patrol officers Davis and Ellis to the duty watch office. Royce will begin the discussion.

ROLE FOR PATROL OFFICERS RON DAVIS AND JAN ELLIS

At the time, it had seemed like a pretty routine piece of police work. Yesterday, when you were on radio patrol, you were dispatched to a "disturbance at the university." When you arrived in front of the administration building, Davis driving, the nature of the disturbance became obvious. Two factions of students had been picketing the administration building trying to influence the university's policy regarding defense research. From the signs, it looked like the "pros" were made up of defense hawks, supporters of academic freedom, and students who feared losing research funding. The "antis" seemed to base their position on moral grounds. The leaders of each faction were taking tentative swings at each other, and the mood of the crowd (about two hundred people) was turning nasty.

You both bolted out of the patrol car and headed for the leaders. Ron isolated the head of the pros and Jan isolated the head of the antis. After a little quiet talk and a few jokes by both of you, a compromise regarding the area in front of the stairs to the administration building was arranged so that both groups could have space to circulate without violating each other's territory. The leaders shook hands, you both got a cheer from the crowd, and the demonstration continued peacefully. A TV 6 news crew had been on hand the whole time, but neither of you paid much attention.

Last night, to your surprise, the whole university episode, including the cheering, appeared on the TV 6 evening news. Linda Smith, the TV 6 reporter, generally had a reputation on the force for being anti-police. However, in the university story, she praised the "fast and sensible" response of the officers. In an interview clip, the head of campus security voiced the same sentiment.

On meeting outside the locker rooms today, you congratulated each other on the slick police work yesterday. Most of the other officers in the squad saw the TV 6 news report last night. Although they are teasing you about being TV stars, you know they are really saying "nice work."

Just after the morning briefing, you are told that Sergeant Royce wants to see you before you go out on patrol. You both wonder what's up, while secretly hoping for a commendation.

ROLE FOR SERGEANT AL ROYCE

For a long time now, the management of the Bay City Police Department has been concerned about the appearance and public demeanor of its uniformed police officers. A particular issue has involved the wearing of hats while on duty. Traditionally, most police departments have required officers to wear their uniform hats at all times to maintain a neat appearance, convey authority, and make themselves visible to other officers in a crowd. A few years ago, rules were relaxed in Bay City to permit officers to remove their hats while riding in their patrol cars. However, it is department policy that hats be worn when officers are outside the cruiser. About two months ago, the Chief sent down an order reminding patrol personnel in no uncertain terms about the hat rule. Evidently, on a hot summer night at the county fair, he had seen two rookies manning the department information booth with their hats off. This event prompted the order.

Last night on the TV 6 news, you saw two of the officers in your squad, Ron Davis and Jan Ellis, dealing with some trouble at a demonstration down at the university. Of course, you knew about this incident from the duty reports, but you were surprised to see it on television all the same. The film clip showed Davis and Ellis arriving on the scene in their car and charging out without their hats on. For two or three minutes, Davis and Ellis were shown in living color violating department dress rules. You don't know whether the Chief saw the TV news, but you figure you had better talk to Davis and Ellis about this right now and straighten things out. Rules are rules, and police officers have to have respect for discipline!

DISCUSSION QUESTIONS

1. What happened in your group?
2. Patrol officers, how did you feel in this situation?
3. Sergeants, how did you feel in this situation?
4. How should this situation have been handled by Sergeant Royce?

REFERENCES

1. Meissner, M. (1976). The language of work. In R. Dubin (Ed.), *Handbook of work, organization, and society.* Chicago: Rand McNally.

2. Meissner, 1976.

3. Mintzberg, H. (1973). *The nature of managerial work.* New York: Harper & Row.

4. Davis, K. (1968). Success of chain-of-command oral communication in a manufacturing management group. *Academy of Management Journal, 11,* 379–387.

5. Fayol, H. (1916/1949). *General and industrial management* (trans. by C. Storrs). New York: Pitman.

6. Foltz, R. G. (1985). Communication in contemporary organizations. In C. Reuss & D. Silvis (Eds.), *Inside organizational communication* (2nd ed.). New York: Longman.

7. Snyder, R. A., & Morris, J. H. (1984). Organizational communication and performance. *Journal of Applied Psychology, 69,* 461–465.

8. From an unpublished review by the author. Some studies are cited in Jablin, F. M. (1979). Superior-subordinate communication: The state of the art. *Psychological Bulletin, 86,* 1201–1222.

9. Jablin, 1979.

10. Mitchell, T. R. (1970). The construct validity of three dimensions of leadership research. *Journal of Social Psychology, 80,* 89–94; Jago, A. G., & Vroom, V. H. (1975). Perceptions of leadership style: Superior and subordinate descriptions of decision-making behavior. *Organizational and Administrative Sciences, 6,* 103–120.

11. Tesser, A., & Rosen, S. (1975). The reluctance to transmit bad news. In L. Berkowitz (Ed.), *Advances in experimental social psychology* (Vol. 8). New York: Academic Press.

12. Read, W. (1962). Upward communication in industrial hierarchies. *Human Relations, 15,* 3–16; For related studies see Jablin, 1979.

13. Evidence that subordinates tend to suppress communicating negative news to the boss can be found in O'Reilly, C. A., & Roberts, K. H. (1974). Information filtration in organizations: Three experiments. *Organizational Behavior and Human Performance, 11,* 253–265.

14. Thornton, G. C., III. (1980). Psychometric properties of self-appraisals of job performance. *Personnel Psychology, 33,* 263–271.

15. Lawler, E. E., III, Porter, L. W., & Tennenbaum, A. (1968). Managers' attitudes toward interaction episodes. *Journal of Applied Psychology, 52,* 432–439. For a similar study with similar results see Whitely, W. (1984). An exploratory study of managers' reactions to properties of verbal communication. *Personnel Psychology, 37,* 41–59.

16. Reviewed by Meissner, 1976.

17. Katz, R. (1982). The effects of group longevity on project communication and performance. *Administrative Science Quarterly, 27,* 81–104.

18. Katz, 1982.

19. Tushman, M. L., & Scanlan, T. J. (1981). Characteristics and external orientations of boundary spanning individuals. *Academy of Management Journal, 24,* 83–98; Tushman, M. L., & Scanlan, T. J. (1981). Boundary spanning individuals: Their role in information transfer and their antecedents. *Academy of Management Journal, 24,* 289–305.

20. Keller, R. T., & Holland, W. E. (1983). Communicators and innovators in research and development organizations. *Academy of Management Journal, 26,* 742–749.

21. Katz, 1982.

22. Davis, K. (1977). *Human behavior at work* (5th ed.). New York: McGraw-Hill.

23. Davis, K. (1953). Management communication and the grapevine. *Harvard Business Review, 31*(5), 43–49; Sutton, H., & Porter, L. W. (1968). A study of the grapevine in a governmental organization. *Personnel Psychology, 21,* 223–230.

24. Roy, D. F. (1960). "Banana time": Job satisfaction and informal interaction. *Human Organization, 18,* 158–168, p. 162.

25. Rosnow, R. L. (1980). Psychology of rumor reconsidered. *Psychological Bulletin, 87,* 578–591.

26. However, as Rosnow, 1980, points out, the evidence for these conditions is sparse. Specifically, rumors might *become* important because they are rumors, rather than the other way around.

27. Kanter, R. M. (1977). *Men and women of the corporation.* New York: Basic Books.

28. Kidder, T. (1981). *The soul of a new machine.* Boston: Little, Brown, p. 46.

29. Kanter, 1977.

30. For reviews see Heslin, R., & Patterson, M. L. (1982). *Nonverbal behavior and social psychology.* New York: Plenum; Harper, R. G., Wiens, A. N., & Matarazzo, J. D. (1978). *Nonverbal communication: The state of the art.* New York: Wiley.

31. Mehrabian, A. (1972). *Nonverbal communication.* Chicago: Aldine-Atherton.

32. Mehrabian, 1972.

33. Edinger, J. A., & Patterson, M. L. (1983). Nonverbal involvement and social control. *Psychological Bulletin, 93,* 30–56.

34. Rasmussen, K. G., Jr. (1984). Nonverbal behavior, verbal behavior, resume credentials, and selection interview outcomes. *Journal of Applied Psychology, 69,* 551–556.

35. Meissner, 1976, p. 244.

36. Steele, F. I. (1973). *Physical settings and organizational development.* Reading, MA: Addison-Wesley.

37. Kanter, 1977, p. 69.

38. Campbell, D. E. (1979). Interior office design and visitor response. *Journal of Applied Psychology, 64,* 648–653. For a replication see Morrow, P. C., & McElroy, J. C. (1981). Interior office design and visitor response: A constructive replication. *Journal of Applied Psychology, 66,* 646–650.

39. McElroy, J. C., Morrow, P. C., & Ackerman, R. J. (1983). Personality and interior office design: Exploring the accuracy of visitor attributions. *Journal of Applied Psychology, 68,* 541–544.

40. Molloy, J. T. (1975). *Dress for success.* New York: Warner; Molloy, J. T. (1977). *The woman's dress for success book.* Chicago: Follett.

41. Solomon, M. R. (1986, April). Dress for effect. *Psychology Today,* 20–28; Solomon, M. R. (Ed.). (1985). *The psychology of fashion.* New York: Lexington.

42. Forsythe, S., Drake, M. F., & Cox, C. E. (1985). Influence of applicant's dress on interviewer's selection decisions. *Journal of Applied Psychology, 70,* 374–378.

43. Solomon, 1986.

44. Lefkowitz, J., & Katz, M. L. (1969). Validity of exit interviews. *Personnel Psychology, 22,* 445–456; Hinrichs, J. R. (1975). Measurement of reasons for resignation of professionals: Questionnaire versus company and consultant exit interviews. *Journal of Applied Psychology, 60,* 530–532.

45. For a good description of how to develop and use organizational surveys see Dunham, R. B., & Smith, F. J. (1979). *Organizational surveys.* Glenview, IL: Scott, Foresman.

46. Taft, W. F. (1985). Bulletin boards, exhibits, hotlines. In C. Reuss & D. Silvis (Eds.). *Inside organizational communication* (2nd ed.). New York: Longman.

47.   Tushman & Scanlan, 1981.

48.   Sherman, S. P. (1984, October 15). Eight big masters of innovation. *Fortune,* 66–84, p. 72.

49.   Keller & Holland, 1983.

50.   Tushman & Scanlan, 1981.

51.   Burnaska, R. (1976). The effects of behavior modeling training upon managers' behaviors and employees' perceptions. *Personnel Psychology, 29,* 329–335.

52.   Capella, J. N. (1981). Mutual influence in expressive behavior: Adult-adult and infant-adult dyadic interaction. *Psychological Bulletin, 89,* 101–132.

With regard to In–Focus 11-4, the researchers found that independent judges ranked the costumes as follows from least masculine to most masculine: 1, 2, 3, 4. In terms of hiring recommendations, costume 3 was favored, costumes 2 and 4 were rated essentially equally, and costume 1 came last.

Chapter 12

Decision Making

JUST LIKE MATT

Barbara Lane's bedside phone rang at 3:21 A.M. She answered groggily, and it took several moments for the news to sink in. Matt Klein was dead, killed in a car accident on his way home from a party. Barbara was chairperson of the board of directors of Glamor International, an East Coast chain of retail clothing stores. Matt Klein had been Glamor's successful president for eight years.

Guiding her Mercedes through the morning rush hour, Barbara reflected that it would be a problem to find a good replacement for Matt. He had been a real "hands on" executive, doing much of the important fashion buying personally. He spoke French fluently and was well acquainted with the customs and business practices of the Far East. Thus, his frequent buying trips to France, Hong Kong, and Taiwan had always been very successful. To Barbara, the issue was clear: Find a replacement just like Matt.

When she arrived at the office, Barbara called the members of the board and advised them of her intended course of action. She would call several headhunting agencies with experience in the fashion trade and have them screen applicants. Also, she would consult with several executives she knew in the industry.

Within two weeks, twelve candidates for the job had been identified. Barbara had their résumés and dossiers copied and sent by courier to the board members. A meeting was called for the next day to decide who would be interviewed by the board. Although many members found the lengthy file too much to digest in one evening, none mentioned this.

Barbara opened the meeting with a short, pointed speech. "Ladies and gentlemen, the obvious problem we face here is finding a new president who is as similar as possible to our able former president, Matt Klein. We must present a united front in this matter. We have worked together well in the past, and I know I can count on your total support. Now, let me tell you who I think the best candidate is. . . ."

There had been no objections to her suggestion. A week later, the board interviewed Roger Nesmith, an executive with a large New York department store. Nesmith had been a head fashion buyer for the store and had experience in France and the Far East. After the interview, Barbara spoke.

"I suggest we go with this man. He has experience in France and the Far East, and our competitors aren't waiting around for us to make a decision."

One board member protested that several other candidates should be interviewed, but he was quickly chastised by two other members for being too cautious. A vote was taken, and Roger Nesmith assumed the presidency of Glamor International.

A year later, Glamor was in trouble. Sales were down, and it was clear that Nesmith had poor judgment about which fashions would prove popular.

After a meeting to discuss the sales problem, several of the board members reminisced about Nesmith's selection. One said, "I knew all along that he wasn't the best candidate, but I thought everyone else felt differently." Another said "Don't blame yourself. Those headhunting agencies are worthless."

Why did the board make a faulty decision? Did they have enough information? Did they have too much information? Was finding a replacement just like Matt Klein the real problem? Why wasn't there more discussion during the meetings? Why didn't they interview more candidates? These are the kinds of questions we will attempt to answer in this chapter.

First, decision making will be defined and a model of a rational decision-making process will be presented. As we work through this model we shall be especially concerned with the practical limitations of rationality. Then, the types of problems requiring organizational decisions will be discussed. After this, the use of groups to make decisions will be investigated. Finally, some techniques to improve decision making will be evaluated.

WHAT IS DECISION MAKING?

Consider the following questions that might arise in a variety of organizational settings:

- How much inventory should our store carry?
- Where should the proposed community mental health center go?
- Should I remain on this job or accept another?
- How many classes of Philosophy 200 should our department offer next semester?
- Should our bank grant this loan?
- What type of ammunition should our city police force use?
- Should our diplomats attend the summit conference?

Common sense tells us that questions such as these have something to do with decision making. Specifically, they suggest that someone is going to have to do some decision making in order to provide answers!

Decision making is the process of developing a commitment to some course of action.[1] Three things are noteworthy about this definition. First, decision making involves making a *choice* among several action alternatives—the store can carry more or less inventory, and the city council can choose hollow point or solid bullets. Secondly, decision making is a *process* that involves more than simply the final choice among alternatives—if the worker mentioned above decides to accept the offer of a new job, we want to know *how* this decision was reached. Finally, the "commitment" mentioned in the definition usually involves some commitment of *resources* such as time, money, or personnel—if the store carries a large inventory it will tie up cash; if the chairperson of Philosophy offers too many introductory classes he may have no one available to teach a graduate seminar. As a consequence, incorrect decisions may be very costly to the organization.

In addition to conceiving of decision making as the commitment of resources, we can also describe it as a process of problem solving.[2] A **problem** exists when a gap is perceived between some existing state and some desired state. For example, the chairperson of the Philosophy department may observe that there is a projected increase in university enrollment for the upcoming year, and that his course schedule is not completed (existing state). In addition, he may wish to adequately service the new students with Philosophy 200 classes and at the same time satisfy his Dean with a timely, sensible schedule (desired state). In this case, the decision-making process involves the perception of the existing state, the conception of the desired state, and the steps the chairperson takes to move from one state to the other. At Glamor International, the board had a problem—how to fill an empty position (existing state) with a good candidate (desired state).

It should be clear that decision making is at the heart of the correct application of many of the topics we have discussed thus far in the book. Choosing a correct motivational strategy for subordinates or deciding on the proper degree of participation to utilize depends upon a careful process of decision making.

THE COMPLEAT DECISION MAKER—A RATIONAL DECISION-MAKING MODEL

Exhibit 12-1 presents a model of the decision process that might be used by a rational decision maker. When a problem is identified a search for information is begun. This information clarifies the nature of the problem and suggests alternative solutions. These are carefully evaluated, and the best is chosen for implementation. The implemented solution is then monitored over time to assure its immediate and continued effectiveness. If difficulties occur at any point in the process, repetition or recycling may be effected.

It may occur to you that we have not yet determined exactly what is meant by a "rational" decision maker. Before we discuss the specific steps of the model in detail, let's contrast two forms of rationality.

Perfect Versus Bounded Rationality

The prototype for **perfect rationality** is the familiar Economic Person (formerly Economic Man) whom we meet in the first chapter of most introductory textbooks in economics. Economic Person is the perfect cool, calculating decision maker. More specifically, he or she:

- Can gather information about problems and solutions without cost and is thus completely informed

- Is perfectly logical—if solution A is preferred over solution B, and B is preferred over C, then A is necessarily preferable to C

- Has only one criterion for decision making—economic gain

While Economic Person is useful for theoretical purposes, the perfectly rational characteristics embodied in Economic Person do not exist in real decision makers. This point has been recognized by Nobel Prize winner Herbert Simon.

EXHIBIT 12-1   **The rational decision-making process.**

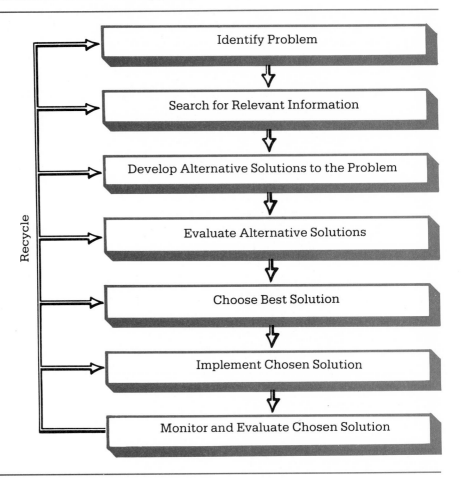

Simon suggests that administrators exhibit **bounded rationality** rather than perfect rationality.[3] That is, while they try to act rationally, they are limited in their capacity to acquire and process information. In addition, time constraints and political considerations (such as the need to please others in the organization) act as bounds to rationality.

Now let's examine the steps in the decision-making process, contrasting how they are handled with perfect rationality and bounded rationality.

Problem Identification

You will recall that a problem exists when a gap occurs between existing and desired conditions. Such gaps may be signaled by dissatisfied customers or vigilant superiors or subordinates. Similarly, the press may contain articles about legislation or ads for competing products that signal difficulties for the organization. The perfectly rational decision maker, infinitely sensitive and completely informed, should be a great problem identifier. Bounded rationality, however, may lead to difficulties in problem identification:

- *Perceptual defense.* In Chapter 4 we pointed out that the perceptual system may act to defend the perceiver against unpleasant perceptions. As a consequence, problems in one's own work domain may go undetected. For example, a marketing manager may fail to identify a sales problem even though she is sensitive to problems outside her area of responsibility (e.g., production).

- *Problem defined in terms of solution.* This form of jumping to conclusions effectively short-circuits the rational decision-making process. In the story that began the chapter, Barbara Lane defined Glamor's problem in terms of a solution—find a replacement "just like Matt." This may have led her to look for similarities and overlook differences. When Coca-Cola changed its time-honored formula to produce the "new" Coke, it appears that its market share problem was prematurely defined in terms of a particular solution—we need to change our existing product (see In–Focus 12-1).

- *Problem diagnosed in terms of symptoms.* "What we have here is a morale problem." While this may be true, a concentration on surface symptoms will provide the decision maker with few clues about an adequate solution. The *real* problem here involves the *cause* of the morale problem. Low morale due to poor pay suggests different solutions than does low morale due to boring work.[4]

Information Search

Once a problem is identified, Exhibit 12-1 indicates that a search for information is instigated. This information search may clarify the nature or extent of the problem and begin to suggest alternative solutions. Again, our perfectly rational Economic Person is in good shape at this second stage of the decision-making process. He or she has free and instantaneous access to all information necessary to clarify the problem and develop alternative solutions. Bounded rationality, however, presents a different picture. Information search may be slow and costly. For example, the executive who has a vague suspicion that a morale problem exists may have to decide whether to order a costly and time-consuming attitude survey. If this survey indicates dissatisfaction with pay, he may then have to decide whether to authorize another costly and time-consuming survey of the pay rates provided by competitors (decisions, decisions, decisions!) At Glamor International Barbara Lane screened many résumés, but seemed to limit her interest to candidates with experience in France and the Far East.

Of course, surveys, company records, and input from others are not the only sources of information available to the decision maker. Decision makers frequently

IN—FOCUS 12-1 THE NEW COKE—BRILLIANT DECISION OR MARKETING FIASCO?

In the spring of 1985, the Coca-Cola Company of Atlanta made a surprising announcement. After ninety-nine years of sales success, it intended to change the formula of "The Real Thing," its principal soft drink, Coca-Cola. Dubbed the "new" Coke, the revised product was to be sweeter and less filling than traditional Coke, whose exact formula has been a well-guarded secret since its inception. The change was made in response to arch-rival Pepsi-Cola's increasing share of supermarket sales and its aggressive "taste test" advertising campaigns.

The decision to change the Coke formula was based on marketing research. Blind taste comparisons gave the new Coke a slight edge over Pepsi. However, when subjects were told the identity of new Coke, the lead over Pepsi was substantial. Coke executives interpreted this as public acceptance for the change and decided to mount a publicity campaign rather than make the change secretly. In retrospect, subjects may have been reacting positively to convey their sophistication to the researchers. Also in retrospect, it is clear that the taste tests failed to capture brand loyalty and dedication to the Coke tradition.

A consumer backlash followed the introduction of the new Coke. Consumers were seen hoarding supplies of the traditional Coke and joining protest groups. A class action suit was threatened by retailers whose sales might be damaged. Within weeks, with sales below expectations and under pressure from local bottlers, Coca-Cola management announced the introduction of another "new" product—the old coke, now labeled Coke Classic! The two products would now be marketed simultaneously.

Some observers praised Coke's decision making, citing its fast reintroduction of Coke Classic and its presence in both the youth market and the more traditional market. Most observers, however, called the episode a blunder and a disaster. Local bottlers are severely limited in the number of product lines they can run, and retail shelf space and soda fountain outlets have limited capacity. Increased advertising costs were also cited. Only time (and sales) will tell whether the series of decisions was correct.

Sources: DeMott, J. S. (1985, May 6). Fiddling with the real thing. *Business Week,* 38–40; Fierman, J. (1985, May 27). How Coke decided a new taste was it. *Fortune,* 80; Kilman, S. (1985, July 11). Coca-Cola Co. to bring back its old Coke. *Wall Street Journal.*

rely on their own *memory* to provide information—"Have I ever encountered a problem like this before? How did we solve it?" Here, the bounds of rationality again intrude. Specifically, we are most likely to recall events that happened *frequently* in the past, or *unusual* or *exotic* events.[5] While such events may prove irrelevant in the context of the current problem, we nonetheless rely on our past experience. The manager who remembers, "Every time we went to an outside supplier for parts we got burned," may be ignoring the uniqueness of her current problem.

While the bounds of rationality often force us to make decisions with incomplete or imperfect information, *too much* information may also damage the quality of decisions. Consider the following example, attributed to former General Motors executive John Z. De Lorean:

About the same time, I was suddenly inundated with tons of paperwork, the likes of which I had never seen as an executive before or since. There were literally 600 to 700 pages a day to be read and processed. Some of it was important material, such as performance reports from the divisions. Most of it, however, was unimportant to this level of management—like a lease agreement to be signed for a new Buick zone office in St. Louis. As with Terrell's assignments, most of these matters should have stopped somewhere far down the line. But somehow these matters were ending up on The Fourteenth Floor.[6]

And you think your course assignments are heavy! The condition described by De Lorean is called information overload. **Information overload** involves the reception of more information than is necessary to make effective decisions.

As you might guess, information overload may lead to errors, omissions, delays, and cut corners.[7] In addition, decision makers facing overload often attempt to use all of the information at hand, then get confused and permit low quality information or irrelevant information to influence their decisions.[8] Perhaps you have experienced this when writing a term paper—trying to incorporate too many references and too many viewpoints into a short paper can lead to a confusing, low-quality end product. Or consider the executive who receives crucial sales data in a package of information that also includes leasing costs, production figures, and overtime payments. Trying to incorporate this additional information into what would have been a simple decision may reduce the effectiveness of the decision. Again, more isn't necessarily better.

However, decision makers seem to *think* that more is better. In one study, even though information overload resulted in lower-quality decisions, overloaded decision makers were more *satisfied* than those who did not experience overload.[9] Why is this so? For one thing, even if decisions do not improve with additional information, *confidence* in the decisions may increase ("I did the best I could"). Secondly, decision makers may fear being "kept in the dark" and associate the possession of information with power.

One review draws the following conclusions about information gathering and use:[10]

- Much information that is gathered has little decision relevance.

- Much information that is used to justify a decision is collected and interpreted *after* the decision has been made.

- Much requested information is not used in making the decision for which it was requested.

- Regardless of the information available, more information is requested.

- Complaints occur that not enough information is available to make a decision even though available information is ignored.

In conclusion, although good information improves decisions, organizational members are often motivated to obtain more information than is necessary for adequate decisions.

Alternative Development, Evaluation, and Choice

Perfectly informed or not, the decision maker can now list alternative solutions to the problem, examine the solutions, and choose the best one. For the perfectly rational, totally informed, ideal decision maker, this is easy—he or she:

■ Can conceive of all alternatives

■ Knows the ultimate value of each alternative

■ Knows the probability that each alternative will work

In this case, the decision maker can exhibit **maximization**—that is, he or she can choose the alternative with the greatest expected value. Consider a simple example:

	Ultimate Value	Probability	Expected Value
Alternative 1	$100,000 Profit	.4	$40,000 Profit
Alternative 2	$ 60,000 Profit	.8	$48,000 Profit

Here, the expected value of each alternative is calculated by multiplying its ultimate value by its probability. In this case, the perfectly rational decision maker would choose to implement the second alternative.

Unfortunately, things do not go so smoothly for the decision maker working under bounded rationality. All alternative solutions are not known, and the decision maker may be ignorant of the ultimate values and probabilities of success of those which are known:

> A colleague and I were talking after having accepted our first jobs. Contemplating the misery of moving, we discussed whether to send our libraries to either our respective university offices, or to our new homes (wherever those might be). We noted that there was no way to intelligently make this choice, for the information necessary to make it would not even exist until several months after the decision was finalized. That is, *we could not know* what our offices or homes would be like until we had moved and arranged these matters, but we needed to make the choice months before the event could occur.[11]

Obviously, the new professors lacked adequate information to make a wise decision. However, there is strong evidence that humans are poor intuitive statisticians even when they have adequate experience with some event. People are particularly bad at revising probability estimates as they acquire information.[12] For example, an employment interviewer might screen hundreds of applicants without learning that source of referral (saw ad in newspaper, heard about job from friend, etc.) is associated with different probabilities of good job performance.

Finally, the perfectly rational decision maker can evaluate alternative solutions against a single criterion—economic gain. The decision maker who is bounded by reality may have to factor in other criteria as well, such as the political acceptability of the solution to other organizational members—will the boss like it? Since these additional criteria have their own values and probabilities, the decision-making task increases in complexity.

The bottom line here is that the decision maker working under bounded rationality frequently "satisfices" rather than maximizes.[13] **Satisficing** means that the decision maker establishes an adequate level of acceptability for a solution and then screens solutions until one that exceeds this level is found. When this occurs, evaluation of alternatives ceases and the solution is chosen for implementation. For instance, the personnel manager who feels that absenteeism has become too high may choose a somewhat arbitrary acceptable level (e.g., the rate one year earlier), then accept the first solution that seems likely to achieve this level. Few organizations seek to *maximize* attendance.

Solution Implementation

When a decision is made to choose a particular solution to a problem, the solution must be implemented. The perfectly rational decision maker will have factored any possible implementation problems into his or her choice of solutions. Of course, the bounded decision maker will attempt to do the same when estimating probabilities of success. However, in organizations, decision makers are often dependent upon others to implement their decisions, and it may be difficult to anticipate their ability or motivation to do so. The French architect Roger Taillibert conceived a brilliant technical and aesthetic solution for the design of Montreal's Olympic Stadium. Unfortunately, the design was so complex that Quebec construction workers encountered tremendous problems in getting the stadium built on time. These unanticipated implementation problems contributed to extreme cost overruns.

Solution Evaluation

When time comes to evaluate the implemented solution, the decision maker is effectively examining the possibility that a new problem has occurred: Does the (new) existing state match the desired state? Has the decision been effective? For all the reasons stated previously, the perfectly rational decision maker should be able to evaluate the effectiveness of the decision with calm, objective detachment. Again, however, the bounded decision maker may encounter problems at this stage of the process.

There is substantial evidence that people tend to be overconfident about the adequacy of their decisions.[14] This suggests that substantial dissonance may be aroused when a decision turns out to be faulty. One way to prevent such dissonance is to avoid careful tests of the adequacy of the decision. As a result, many organizations are notoriously lax when it comes to evaluating the effectiveness of expensive training programs or advertising campaigns. If the bad news cannot be avoided, the erring decision maker may devote his or her energy to trying to justify the faulty decision.[15]

The justification of faulty decisions is best seen in the irrational treatment of sunk costs. **Sunk costs** are permanent losses of resources incurred as the result of a decision.[16] The key word here is "permanent." Since these resources have been lost (sunk) due to a past decision, they should not enter into future decisions. Despite this, people often "throw good resources after bad," acting as if sunk costs can be recouped. This process is termed **escalation of commitment** to a course of action, where the escalation involves devoting more and more resources to actions implied by the decision.[17] For example, suppose an executive authorizes the purchase of several microcomputers in order to improve office productivity. The machines turn out to be very unreliable, and they are frequently out of commission for repair. Perfect rationality suggests admitting to a mistake here. However, the executive may authorize an order for more machines from the same manufacturer to "prove" he was right all along, hoping to recoup sunk costs with improved productivity from an even greater number of machines.

Dissonance reduction is not the only reason that escalation of commitment to a faulty decision may occur. In addition, a social norm that favors *consistent* behavior by administrators may be at work.[18] Changing one's mind and reversing previous decisions may be perceived as a sign of weakness, a fate to be avoided at all costs.

Escalation of commitment is sometimes observed even when the current decision maker is not responsible for previous sunk costs. For example, politicians may continue an expensive unnecessary public works project even though it was begun by a previous political administration. Here, dissonance reduction and the appearance of consistency are irrelevant, and some other causes of escalation are suggested. For one thing, decision makers may be motivated not to appear wasteful.[19] ("Even though the airport construction is way over budget and flight traffic doesn't justify a new airport, let's finish the thing. Otherwise, the taxpayers will think we've squandered their money.") Also, escalation of commitment may be due to the way decision makers frame the problem once some resources have been sunk. Rather than seeing the savings involved in reversing the decision, the problem may be framed as a decision between a sure loss of x dollars (which have been sunk) and an uncertain loss of x + y dollars (maybe the additional investment will succeed). Research shows that when problems are framed this way, people tend to avoid the certain loss and go with the riskier choice, which in this case involves escalation.[20]

One interesting example of escalation of commitment and an inability to write off sunk costs involved the epic western film *Heaven's Gate*. Writer-director Michael Cimino initially proposed to United Artists that the film would cost $7.5 million. By the time production began, this figure had increased to $10 million. Production was behind schedule from the very first week, and Cimino was spending $200,000 a day. At this rate, the projected cost of the film would be close to $50 million, and the film would have had to do better than almost any movie ever made to break even! United Artists finally capped production costs at over three times the initial estimate and ordered Cimino to construct a commercial product from the thousands of feet of film he had shot. *Heaven's Gate* turned out to be one of the biggest box office flops in movie history.[21]

The careful evaluation of decisions is also inhibited by faulty hindsight. **Hindsight** refers to the tendency to review the decision-making process we used in order to find out what we did right (in the case of success) or wrong (in the case of failure). While hindsight can prove useful, it is also open to some serious errors.

The classic example of hindsight involves the armchair quarterback who "knew" that a chancy intercepted pass in the first quarter was unnecessary because the team won the game anyway! The armchair critic is exhibiting the **knew-it-all-along effect.** This is the tendency to assume after the fact that we knew all along what the outcome of a decision would be. In effect, our faulty memory adjusts the probabilities we estimated before making the decision to correspond to what actually happened.[22] This can prove quite dangerous. The money manager who consciously makes a very risky investment which turns out to be successful may revise his memory to assume that the decision was a sure thing. The next time, the now-confident investor may not be so lucky!

Another form of faulty hindsight is **beneffectance,** the tendency to take personal responsibility for successful decision outcomes while denying responsibility for unsuccessful outcomes.[23] Thus, when things work out well, it is because *we* made a careful, logical decision. When things go poorly, some unexpected *external* factor messed up our sensible decision! For example, students are very willing to take responsibility for good grades, while bad grades are attributed to poor teaching or a heavy course load. Similarly, the marketing manager who approves an advertising campaign resulting in increased sales will assume that she planned the campaign properly. A downturn in sales may be attributed to the poor economy or the unanticipated actions of a competitor. Some beneffectance may reflect conscious excuse-making. Much of it, however, probably reflects an unconscious search for additional information when poor decision outcomes occur.

When the board members at Glamor International realized they had chosen the wrong person as president they exhibited both hindsight and beneffectance. They knew all along that headhunting agencies couldn't be trusted.

Rational Decision Making—A Summary

It is difficult to argue against the use of the rational decision-making model portrayed in Exhibit 12-1. In fact, there is evidence that people often go through these processes when making complex decisions. For example, studies of occupational choice reveal that people search out information about the rewards of various occupations and the probabilities that they can get a job in these occupations. Then, they pursue the occupation with the greatest expected rewards.[24] Our discussion of bounded rationality simply suggests that such decisions will be far from perfect. At every stage of the rational decision-making process the bounds on rationality present difficulties of which the decision maker should be aware.[25] Exhibit 12-2 summarizes the operation of perfect and bounded rationality at each stage of the decision process.

EXHIBIT 12-2 **Perfectly rational decision making contrasted with bounded rationality.**

Stage	Perfect Rationality	Bounded Rationality
Problem Identification	Easy, accurate perception of gaps which constitute problems	Perceptual defense; jump to solutions; attention to symptoms rather than problems
Information Search	Free; fast; right amount obtained	Slow; costly; reliance on flawed memory; obtain too little or too much
Development of Alternative Solutions	Can conceive of all	All not known
Evaluation of Alternative Solutions	Ultimate value of each known; probability of each known; only criterion is economic gain	Potential ignorance of or miscalculation of values and probabilities; criteria include political factors
Solution Choice	Maximizes	Satisfices
Solution Implementation	Considered in evaluation of alternatives	May be difficult due to reliance on others
Solution Evaluation	Objective, according to previous steps	May involve justification, escalation to recover sunk costs, faulty hindsight

TYPES OF PROBLEMS

It probably doesn't surprise you that people try to behave rationally and analytically when making a decision such as choosing a career. This is obviously a tough decision with important consequences. For many, in fact, it is literally a once-in-a-lifetime decision and not something one gets a lot of practice at. In contrast, it has probably occurred to you that many decisions appear to be made almost automatically, as if they made themselves. In many of these cases it may even be difficult to believe that a true "decision" has been made—the dentist reaches quickly and confidently for a particular drill; the clerk routes the invoice to shipping without a thought.

This discussion suggests that the elaborate rational decision-making model presented earlier applies more to some problems than to others. Let's contrast two kinds of problems encountered in organizations.

Well-Structured Problems

For **well-structured problems,** the existing state is clear, the desired state is clear, and how to get from one state to the other is fairly obvious.[26] Intuitively, these problems are simple and their solutions arouse little controversy. This is because such problems are repetitive and familiar. Here are some examples:

■ Assistant bank manager—Which of these ten automobile loan applications should I approve?

■ Brewmaster—How much hops should I put in the batch of beer?

■ Typist—Should this go on a letterhead or memo paper?

■ Merchant—Is it time to re-order garden hoses?

■ Welfare officer—How much assistance should this client receive?

■ Truckdriver—How much weight should I carry?

Because decision making takes time and is prone to error, organizations (and individuals) attempt to program the decision making for well-structured problems. A **program** is simply a standardized way of solving a problem. As such, programs short-circuit the rational decision making process by enabling the decision maker to go directly from problem identification to solution.

Programs usually go under labels such as *rules, routines, standard operating procedures, rules of thumb,* and so on. Sometimes, they come from experience and exist only ''in the head.'' For example, the merchant may have a rule of thumb that says to order more hoses when inventory drops below fifty in the summer or ten in the winter. Other programs are more formal. You are probably aware that routine loan applications are ''scored'' by banks according to a fixed formula which takes into account income, debt, previous credit, and so on. Similarly, the welfare officer will score applicants for assistance according to family size, other sources of income, etc. Some programs exist in the form of straightforward rules—''Truck-drivers will always carry between 85 and 95 percent of legal weight.''

It should be mentioned that people often bring programs with them when they join organizations. This is because they have been socialized by education or previous training to solve problems in particular ways. The experienced welder comes to the organization knowing which welding rods should be used to join particular kinds of metal. The business school graduate takes her first job knowing how to interpret a routine financial statement.

Many of the problems encountered in organizations are well-structured, and programmed decision making provides a useful means of solving these problems. However, programs are only as good as the hopefully rational decision-making process which led to the adoption of the program in the first place. In computer terminology, ''garbage in'' will result in ''garbage out.'' Another difficulty with decision programs is their tendency to persist even when problem conditions change. Decision makers thus continue to use programs even when they become ineffective.

These difficulties of programmed decision making are seen in the hiring procedures used by many firms in the 1950s and 1960s. In order to solve the recurrent problem of choosing workers for lower level jobs, many companies used batteries of selection tests. Such testing is a form of programmed decision making. Unfortunately, some firms adopted such tests without actually determining if they were valid predictors of job performance (garbage in—garbage out). To complicate matters, the tests might have discriminated unfairly against minority applicants. Despite this, many firms persisted to use their tests in the face of strong Equal Employment Opportunity Commission guidelines introduced in the 1970s. A number of costly lawsuits resulted from this persistence of inadequate decision programs.

Ill-Structured Problems

The extreme example of an **ill-structured problem** is one where the existing and desired states are unclear, and the method of getting to the desired state (even if clarified) is unknown. For example, a vice-president of marketing may have a vague feeling that the sales of a particular product are too low. However, she may lack precise information about the product's market share (existing state) and the market share of its most successful competitor (ideal state). In addition, she may be unaware of exactly how to increase the sales of this particular product.

Ill-structured problems are generally unique. That is, they are unusual and have not been encountered before. In addition, they tend to be complex, and they involve a high degree of uncertainty. As a result, they frequently arouse controversy and conflict among those who are interested in the decision. Although the choice of a new president at Glamor was an ill-structured problem, controversy was suppressed. Other examples of ill-structured problems:

- Should we vaccinate the population against a new flu strain when the vaccination may have some bad side effects?
- Should a risky attempt to rescue political hostages be implemented?
- In which part of the country should we build a new plant?
- A new surgery procedure could save this patient, but not much is known about the technique. Should I try it?

It should be obvious that ill-structured problems such as these cannot be solved with programmed decisions. Rather, the decision makers must resort to **nonprogrammed decision making.** This simply means that they are likely to try to implement the full rational decision making model shown in Exhibit 12-1. Clearly, though, ill-structured problems test the bounds of rationality very severely. They involve much uncertainty, and they may stimulate strong political considerations.

As illustrated in Exhibit 12-3, there is a tendency for more ill-structured problems to be encountered as one moves up the hierarchy of an organization. Consequently, more nonprogrammed decision making is necessary at higher levels. This isn't especially surprising. Those in the upper ranks are paid more and given more status partially because they are expected to be able to make tough decisions. At lower organizational levels we find more well-structured problems and greater reliance on programmed decision making. Of course, there are exceptions to this

---

EXHIBIT 12-3 **Problem types and decision strategies at different organizational levels.**

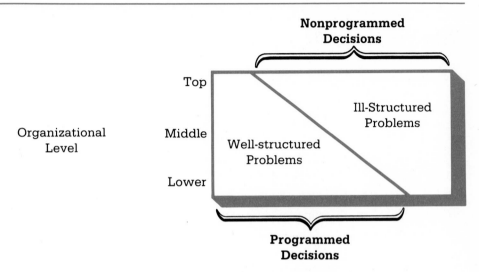

Source: From Donnelly, J. H., Jr., et al. (1978). *Fundamentals of management* (3rd. ed.). Plano, Tx: Business Publication, Inc., p. 347. © Business Publications, Inc. Reprinted by permission.

---

general rule. The president of a small firm may scan sales data and order needed adjustments in production according to a routine rule of thumb. Conversely, a janitor may discover a broken water pipe and act in a nonprogrammed manner to solve the problem.

Because ill-structured problems involve complexity, uncertainty, and potential controversy, organizations often rely upon groups rather than individuals to provide solutions. Let's examine group decision making.

GROUP DECISION MAKING

Odds are, the book you are now reading was chosen by a group. A study revealed that "departmental committees, not individual faculty members, are making more and more of the decisions about which textbooks to adopt for college classes."[27] This is especially true in public colleges and universities.

Many, many organizational decisions are made by groups rather than individuals. If you reconsider the examples of ill-structured problems noted in the previous section, you will see how unlikely it would be for them to be solved by a lone decision maker. Presidents are usually chosen by boards of directors. The surgeon considering an unproven operating technique will voluntarily consult with colleagues, and his or her hospital probably has a formal review committee for such procedures.

In this section we shall consider the advantages and problems of group decision making.

Why Use Groups?

There are a number of reasons for groups being employed to make organizational decisions.

DECISION QUALITY.   It is often argued that groups can make higher quality decisions than individuals. There are three assumptions to this argument:

- Groups are *more vigilant* than individuals—more people are scanning the environment.
- Groups can *generate more ideas* than individuals.
- Groups can *evaluate ideas better* than individuals.

A reexamination of the decision process shown in Exhibit 12-1 indicates why these should be valuable characteristics.

At the problem identification and information search stages, vigilance is especially advantageous. A problem missed by some group members may be identified by others. For example, a member of the board of directors may notice a short article in an obscure business publication that has great relevance for the firm. In searching for information to clarify the problem suggested in the article, other members of the board may possess unique information that proves useful.

When it comes to developing alternative solutions, more people should literally have more ideas, if only because someone remembers something others have forgotten. In addition, members with different backgrounds and experiences may bring different perspectives to the problem. This is why undergraduate students, graduate students, faculty, and administrators are often included on university task forces to improve the library or develop a course evaluation system. Finally, in listening to each other's ideas, group members may combine information to develop unique solutions that no single member could conceive (see the cartoon).

When it comes to evaluating solutions and choosing the best one, groups have the advantage of checks and balances. That is, an extreme position or incorrect notion held by one member should be offset by the pooled judgments of the rest of the group.

In summary, these characteristics suggest that groups *should* make higher quality decisions than individuals. Shortly, we will see if they actually do so.

DECISION ACCEPTANCE.   As pointed out in our discussion of participative leadership in Chapter 10, groups are often used to make decisions on the premise that a decision made this way will be more acceptable to those involved. Again, there are several assumptions underlying this premise:

- People wish to be involved in decisions that will affect them.
- People will better understand a decision in which they participated.

"It's been moved and seconded, then, that we are greater
than the sum of the individual parts."

Source: Drawing by D. Reilly. © 1985 The New Yorker Magazine, Inc.
Reprinted by permission.

- People will be more committed to a decision in which they invested personal time and energy.

- In addition to achieving a high quality decision, people prefer decisions that correspond to their personal values.

The role of values in decision acceptance is illustrated by a controversy that erupted in Denver. The Denver Police Department wished to replace its standard handgun ammunition with hollow point bullets, which it claimed provided greater "stopping power." Many individual citizens and community groups protested, claiming that hollow point ammunition caused greater injury to suspects and innocent bystanders because of its tendency to fragment on impact. Outside decision experts had the City Council, the Mayor, and interested citizens and community groups rate the importance of three criteria to be used in selecting ammunition—stopping power, injury to suspects, and injury to bystanders. The City Council decided that a good compromise could be made between the various factions by assigning equal weight to each criterion. Then, outside ballistics experts were asked to evaluate types of bullets according to these same criteria. A bullet that had greater stopping power than the conventional ammunition but did not result in greater injury to suspects or bystanders was identified and chosen. The decision was acceptable to all parties because it reflected their diverse values.[28]

It should be noted that the acceptability of group decisions is especially useful in dealing with a problem described earlier—getting the decision implemented. If decision makers truly understand the decision and feel committed to it, they should be willing to follow through and see that it is carried out.

DIFFUSION OF RESPONSIBILITY.   High quality and acceptance are sensible reasons for using groups to make decisions. As you may recall from Chapter 10, a somewhat less admirable reason to employ groups is to **diffuse responsibility** across the members in case the decision turns out poorly. In this case, each member of the group will share part of the burden of the negative consequences, and no one person will be singled out for punishment. Of course, when this happens individual group members often "abandon ship" and exhibit biased hindsight— "I knew all along that the bid was too high to be accepted, but they made me go along with them."

Do Groups Actually Make Higher Quality Decisions Than Individuals?

The discussion in the first part of the previous section suggested that groups *should* make higher quality decisions than individuals. But *do* they? Is the frequent use of groups to make decisions warranted by evidence? The answer is yes. One review concludes that *"groups usually produce more and better solutions to problems than do individuals working alone."*[29] Another concludes that group performance is superior to that of the average individual in the group.[30]

As you might suspect, this conclusion may be qualified by the exact nature of the problem and the composition of the group. More specifically, groups should perform better than individuals when:

- The group members differ in relevant skills and abilities, as long as they don't differ so much that conflict occurs
- Some division of labor can occur
- Memory for facts is an important issue
- Individual judgments can be averaged to arrive at a group position[31]

To consolidate your understanding of these conditions, consider a situation that should favor group decision making: A small construction company wishes to bid on a contract to build an apartment complex. The president, the controller, a construction boss, and an engineer work together to formulate the bid. Since they have diverse backgrounds and skills, they divide the task initially. The president reviews recent bids on similar projects in the community; the controller gets estimates on materials costs; the engineer and boss review the blueprints. During this process, each racks his brain to recall lessons learned from making previous bids. Finally, they put their information together, and each member voices an opinion about what the bid should be. The president decides to average these opinions to arrive at the actual bid.

Disadvantages of Group Decision Making

Although groups have the ability to develop high quality, acceptable decisions, there are a number of potential disadvantages to group decision making.

TIME.   Groups seldom work quickly or efficiently when compared to individuals. This is because of the process losses (Chapter 8) involved in discussion, debate, and coordination. The time problem increases with group size. When the speed of arriving at a solution to a problem is a prime factor, the use of groups should be avoided.

ESCALATION OF DEMANDS.   Participation in group decisions can be a rewarding experience. In a sense, such participation may constitute a form of job enrichment. Thus, the opportunity to incorporate one's own values into an acceptable decision may escalate demands for participation in other decisions that are not suitable for a group approach.

CONFLICT.   Many times, participants in group decisions have their own personal axes to grind or their own resources to protect. When this occurs, decision quality may take a back seat to political wrangling and infighting. In the example about the construction company presented earlier, the construction boss may see it to his advantage to overestimate the size of the crew required to build the apartments. On the other hand, the controller may make it his personal crusade to pare labor costs. A simple compromise between these two extreme points of view may not result in the highest quality decision.

GROUPTHINK.   In retrospect, have you ever been involved in a group decision that you knew was a "loser" but that you felt unable to protest? Perhaps you thought you were the only one who had doubts about the chosen course of action. Perhaps you tried to speak up, but others criticized you for not being on the team. Maybe you found yourself searching for information to confirm that the decision was correct and ignoring evidence that the decision was bad. What was happening? Were you suffering from some strange form of possession? Mind control?

In Chapters 8 and 9 we discussed the processes of conformity and cohesiveness in groups. As you might expect, these processes can have a strong influence on the kinds of decisions that groups make. The most extreme influence is seen in the occurrence of groupthink. **Groupthink** happens when group pressures lead to reduced mental efficiency, poor testing of reality, and lax moral judgments.[32] It tends to occur in highly cohesive groups which stress unanimous acceptance of the decision over the quality of the decision.

Not all cohesive groups exhibit groupthink. Rather, there appear to be some special conditions associated with its occurrence. Psychologist Irving Janis has provided a detailed list of symptoms:

- *Illusion of invulnerability.* Members are overconfident and willing to assume great risks. They ignore obvious danger signals.

- *Rationalization.* Problems and counterarguments that can't be ignored are ''rationalized away.''

- *Illusion of morality.* The decisions adopted by the group are not only perceived as sensible, they are also perceived as *morally* correct.

- *Stereotypes of outsiders.* The group constructs unfavorable stereotypes of those outside the group who are the targets of their decisions.

- *Pressure for conformity.* Members pressure each other to fall into line and conform with the group's views.

- *Self-censorship.* Members convince themselves to avoid voicing opinions contrary to the group.

- *Illusion of unanimity.* Members perceive that unanimous support exists for the chosen course of action.

- *Mindguards.* Some group members may adopt the role of ''protecting'' the group from information that goes against its decisions.[33]

Obviously, victims of groupthink are operating in an atmosphere of unreality which should lead to low-quality decisions. As an example, Janis cites the disastrous Cuban Bay of Pigs invasion which was planned by President Kennedy and his advisors during the early 1960s. All of the above symptoms of groupthink were present during the planning sessions: State Department doubts about the invasion were ignored and rationalized; the Cuban army was stereotyped as ineffective; various advisors subsequently reported having censored their own doubts. Janis also describes similar examples from the Vietnam era.

You may be tempted to assume that groupthink is peculiar to group decision making in government and military settings. However, evidence suggests that it frequently occurs in the business world. The design and marketing of the ill-fated Edsel automobile have been attributed to groupthink. Similarly, individuals as diverse as Wall Street investors and corporate price fixers have been described as succumbing to its pressures.[34] In the story that began the chapter, groupthink was exhibited. Controversy was stifled as the board members quickly agreed to the choice of a new Glamor president.[35]

Shortly, we shall consider some techniques for improving decision making in organizations. You will notice that some of these techniques should help prevent groupthink.

How Do Groups Handle Risk?

Almost by definition, problems suitable for group decision making involve some degree of risk and uncertainty. This raises a very important question: Do groups make decisions that are more or less risky than individuals? Or, will the degree of risk assumed by the group simply equal the average risk preferred by its individual members? The answer here is obviously important. Consider the following scenarios:

> An accident has just occurred at a nuclear power plant. Several corrections exist, ranging from expensive and safe to low-cost but risky. On the way to an emergency meeting, each nuclear engineer formulates an opinion about what should be done. But what will the group decide?

> A company has been sued for $10 million in a product liability case. A conservative strategy indicates settling out of court. A riskier strategy suggests going to court and fighting the case. Each top executive has a private opinion about the matter. But what will they decide when they meet together?

Conventional wisdom provides few clear predictions about what the groups of engineers and executives will decide to do. On one hand, it is sometimes argued that groups will make riskier decisions than individuals because there is security in numbers. That is, diffusion of responsibility for a bad decision encourages the group to take greater chances. On the other hand, it is often argued that groups are cautious, with the members checking and balancing each other so much that a conservative outcome is sure to occur. Just contrast the committee-laden civil service with the swashbuckling style of independent operators such as Ted Turner and the Hunt brothers of Texas!

Given this contradiction of common sense, the history of research into group decision making and risk is both interesting and instructive. In 1961, a student at the Massachusetts Institute of Technology reported in a Master's thesis that he had discovered clear evidence of a **risky shift** in decision making.[36] Participants in the research were asked to review hypothetical cases involving risk, such as those involving career choices or investment decisions. As individuals, they recommended a course of action. Then they were formed into groups, and the groups discussed each case and came to a joint decision. In general, the groups tended to advise riskier courses of action than the average risk initially advocated by their members. This is the risky shift. As studies were conducted to explore the reasons for its causes, things got more complicated. For some groups and some decisions, **conservative shifts** were observed. In other words, groups came to decisions that were *less* risky than those of the individual members before interaction.

It is now clear that both risky and conservative shifts are possible, and they occur in a wide variety of real settings, including investment and purchasing decisions. But what determines which kind of shift occurs? A key factor appears to be the initial positions of the group members before they discuss the problem. This is illustrated in Exhibit 12-4. As you can see, when group members are

EXHIBIT 12-4   **The dynamics of risky and conservative shifts for two groups.**

Position of Group Members Before Discussion:

Most   Medium   Most
Conservative   Risk   Risky
Alternative   Alternative

Position of Group Members After Discussion:

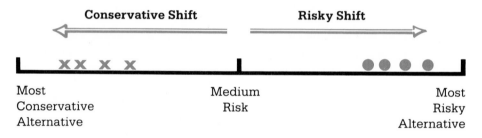

Most   Medium   Most
Conservative   Risk   Risky
Alternative   Alternative

somewhat conservative before interaction (the x's), they tend to exhibit a conservative shift when they discuss the problem. When group members are somewhat
risky initially (the ●'s), they exhibit a risky shift after discussion. In other words,
group discussion seems to polarize or exaggerate the initial position of the group.[37]
Returning to the nuclear accident, if the engineers initially prefer a somewhat
conservative solution, they should adopt an even more conservative strategy during
the meeting.

Why do risky and conservative shifts occur when groups make decisions?
Evidence seems to indicate three main factors:

■   Group discussion generates ideas and arguments that individual members
    haven't considered before. This information naturally favors the members'
    initial tendency toward risk or toward conservatism. Since discussion pro-
    vides ''more'' and ''better'' reasons for the initial tendency, the tendency
    ends up being exaggerated.

■   Group members try to present themselves as basically similar to other mem-
    bers, but ''even better.'' Thus, they try to one-up others in discussion by
    adopting a slightly more extreme version of the group's initial stance.

■ When the group's initial position is somewhat risky, diffusion of responsibility may contribute to a risky shift. The consequences of a bad decision can be distributed over the group.[38]

In summary, administrators should be aware of the tendency for group interaction to polarize initial risk levels. If this polarization results from the sensible exchange of information, it may actually improve the group's decision. However, if it results from one-upmanship or diffusion of responsibility, it may lead to low-quality decisions.

IMPROVING DECISION MAKING IN ORGANIZATIONS

It stands to reason that organizational decision making can be improved if decision makers can be encouraged to approximate more closely the rational decision-making model shown in Exhibit 12-1. This should help preclude the various biases and errors we have alluded to throughout the chapter. Each of the following techniques has this goal.

Training Discussion Leaders

When group decision making is utilized, an appointed leader often convenes the group and guides the discussion. The actions of this leader can "make or break" the decision. On one hand, if the leader behaves autocratically, trying to "sell" a preconceived decision, the advantages of using a group are obliterated and decision acceptance may suffer. If the leader fails to exert *any* influence, however, the group may develop a low-quality solution which does not meet the needs of the organization. One expert has argued that discussion leaders should be trained to develop the following skills:

■ State the problem in a nondefensive, objective manner. Do not suggest solutions or preferences.

■ Supply essential facts and clarify any constraints on solutions (e.g., "We can't spend more than $5000").

■ Draw out all group members. Prevent domination by one person and protect members from being attacked or severely criticized.

■ Wait out pauses. Don't make suggestions or ask leading questions.

■ Ask stimulating questions that move the discussion forward.

■ Summarize and clarify at several points to mark progress.[39]

Notice that these skills are not vague attitudes, but specific behaviors. Thus, they are subject to training and practice. There is good evidence that this training can be accomplished through role-playing, and that it can increase the quality and acceptance of group decisions.[40]

Stimulating and Managing Controversy

Full-blown conflict among organizational members is hardly conducive to good decision making. Information is certain to be withheld, and personal or group goals will take precedence over developing a decision that solves organizational problems. On the other hand, a complete lack of controversy may be equally damaging, since alternative points of view that may be very relevant to the issue at hand will never surface. Such a lack of controversy is partially responsible for the groupthink effect, and it also contributes to many cases of escalation of commitment to flawed courses of action. For example, it is now clear that stifled controversy played a part in the disastrous launch of the space shuttle Challenger (In-Focus 12-2).

Research shows that controversy can be stimulated in decision-making groups by incorporating members with diverse ideas and backgrounds, forming subgroups to "tear the problem apart," and establishing norms that favor the open sharing of information.[41] However, these tactics must be managed carefully to ensure that open conflict does not result. The discussion skills covered in the previous section can help here. In addition, one expert suggests that the following climate be maintained:[42]

■ Decision makers should continually emphasize that "we are all in this together" and that cooperation is necessary.

■ Even though their ideas are disputed, decision makers should continue to feel that they are competent persons.

■ Decision makers should try to influence each other rather than dominate each other.

One interesting method of controversy stimulation is the appointment of a **devil's advocate** to challenge existing plans and strategies. The advocate's role is to challenge the weaknesses of the plan or strategy and state why it should not be adopted. For example, a bank might be considering offering an interest-paying checking account plan. Details to be decided include interest rate, required minimum balance, and so on. A committee might be assigned to develop a position paper. Before a decision is made, someone would be assigned to read the paper and "tear it apart," noting potential weaknesses. Thus, a decision is made in full recognition of the pros and cons of the plan.

Evidence indicates that the controversy promoted by the devil's advocate improves decision quality.[43] However, to be effective, the advocate must present his or her views in an objective, unemotional manner.

Brainstorming

Brainstorming is the "brain child" of a Madison Avenue advertising executive.[44] Its major purpose is to increase the number of creative solution alternatives to problems. Thus, **brainstorming** focuses on the *generation* of ideas rather than

IN–FOCUS 12-2 SPACE SHUTTLE DECISION MAKING FLAWED

On January 28, 1986, a clear, bright day, the space shuttle *Challenger* exploded little more than a minute after lift-off from the Kennedy Space Center in Florida. All seven of its crew were killed. Not surprisingly, early news coverage focused on the possible technical reasons for the disaster. In quick order, with the help of video replays of the explosion, attention was directed toward the giant solid rocket boosters that served to propel the shuttle off the launch pad. Speculation, later confirmed, suggested that the synthetic O-ring seals that separated the booster segments had failed, causing the uncontrolled explosion. It had been unusually cold on the launch pad that morning, and the seals did not respond well to low temperatures.

Even before these technical flaws were confirmed, attention began to shift to the behavioral aspects of the launch. Who actually approved the launch? And weren't there any warnings about the problematic seals? The answers to these and other questions were provided several months later by a presidential committee into the *Challenger* disaster that was chaired by former Secretary of State William Rogers. The commission concluded that "there was a serious flaw in the decision-making process" used by NASA.

An especially conspicuous aspect of the decision-making process was the suppression of controversial information that might have contributed to a delay of the fatal launch and even a rethink of shuttle design. It is now clear that engineers at Morton Thiokol, the producer of the boosters, had expressed fears about the integrity of the O-rings to their management for some time, but this information was evidently not passed on to NASA. NASA itself had detected O-ring erosion in previous flights but did not order a suspension of launches, and top NASA management claimed it had never heard of the seal problem. The night before the launch, cold weather was expected, and a telephone conference was held to discuss its probable effects. Morton Thiokol engineers strongly opposed the launch. However, Thiokol managers, pressured by NASA flight managers at the Marshall Space Flight Center in Alabama, finally agreed to sign off on the launch. Since Thiokol "agreed" to the flight, top NASA management was never informed of the controversy.

Observers noted that the safety consciousness of the earlier space program had been replaced by schedule consciousness as NASA attempted to demonstrate the commercial capabilities of the shuttle. Reports surfaced that astronauts who dissented from this line were pressured by NASA to keep their thoughts to themselves.

Sources: Magnuson, E. (1986, March 10). "A serious deficiency." *Time*, 42–44; Marbach, W. D. (1986, February 10). What went wrong? *Newsweek*, 32–34; various articles, *New York Times*, June 10, 1986.

the *evaluation* of ideas. If a large number of ideas can be generated, the chance of obtaining a truly creative solution is increased.

Brainstorming was originally conceived as a group technique. It was assumed that in generating ideas, group members could feed off of each other's suggestions and be stimulated to offer more creative solutions. In order to ensure this, the group is encouraged to operate in a free-wheeling, off-the-wall manner.

No ideas should be considered too extreme or unusual to be voiced. In addition, no criticism of ideas should be offered, as this may inhibit useful lines of thinking. For instance, an advertising agency might convene a group to generate names for a new toothpaste or soft drink (as in our cartoon). Similarly, a government agency might convene a group to generate possible solutions for welfare fraud.

Brainstorming has not fulfilled its creative promise. Research has shown rather conclusively that individuals working alone tend to generate more ideas than when in groups. In other words, four people working independently (and encouraged to be creative and nonevaluative) will usually generate more ideas than the same four people working as a team.[45] Evidently conformity asserts itself even under brainstorming conditions—members feel constrained, get in a rut, or allow an ineffective person to dominate the proceedings.

Nominal Group Technique

The fact that nominal (in name only) brainstorming groups generate more ideas than interacting brainstorming groups gave rise to the **nominal group technique**

"On second thought, let's not take another crack at it."

Source: Drawing by Drucker; © 1977 The New Yorker Magazine, Inc. Reprinted by permission.

(NGT) of decision making. Unlike brainstorming, NGT is concerned with both the generation of ideas and the evaluation of these ideas:

> Imagine a meeting room in which seven to ten individuals are sitting around a table in full view of each other; however, at the beginning of the meeting they do not speak to each other. Instead, each individual is writing ideas on a pad of paper in front of him or her. At the end of five to ten minutes, a structured sharing of ideas takes place. Each individual, in round-robin fashion, presents one idea from his or her private list. A recorder writes that idea on a flip chart in full view of other members. There is still no discussion at this point of the meeting—only the recording of privately narrated ideas. Round-robin listing continues until all members indicate they have no further ideas to share.
>
> Discussion follows during the next phase of the meeting; however, it is structured so that each idea receives attention before independent voting. This is accomplished by asking for clarification, or stating support or nonsupport of each idea listed on the flip chart. Independent voting then takes place. Each member privately, in writing, selects priorities by rank-ordering (or rating). The group decision is the mathematically pooled outcome of the individual votes.[46]

As you can observe, NGT carefully separates the generation of ideas from their evaluation. Ideas are generated nominally (without interaction) to prevent inhibition and conformity. Evaluation permits interaction and discussion, but it occurs in a fairly structured manner to be sure each idea gets adequate attention.

NGT has been used in a variety of organizational settings, including business and the health care field. Its chief disadvantage would seem to be the time and resources required to assemble the group for face-to-face interaction. The Delphi technique was developed in part to overcome this problem.

The Delphi Technique

The **Delphi technique** of decision making was developed at the Rand Corporation to forecast changes in technology. Its name derives from the future-telling of the famous Greek Delphic Oracle.[47] Unlike NGT, the Delphi process relies solely upon a nominal group—participants do not engage in face-to-face interaction. Thus, it is possible to poll a large number of experts without assembling them in the same place at the same time. It should be emphasized that these experts do not actually make a final decision; rather, they provide information for organizational decision makers (see In–Focus 12-3).

The heart of Delphi is a series of questionnaires mailed to respondents. Minimally, two waves of questionnaires would be used, but more are not unusual. The first questionnaire is usually general in nature and permits free responses to the problem. For example, suppose the vice-president of personnel of a large multibranch corporation wishes to evaluate and improve the firm's Management by Objectives program. A random sample of managers who have worked with MBO might be identified and sent an initial questionnaire asking them to list the strengths and weaknesses of the program. The personnel staff would collate the responses and develop a second questionnaire that might share these responses and ask for suggested improvements. A final questionnaire might then be sent asking respondents to rate or rank each improvement. The staff would then merge the ratings or rankings mathematically and present them to the vice-president for consideration.

A chief disadvantage of Delphi is the rather lengthy time frame involved in the questionnaire phases (Exhibit 12-5). In addition, its effectiveness depends upon the writing skills of the respondents and their interest in the problem, since they must work on their own rather than as part of an actual group. Despite these problems, Delphi is an efficient method of pooling a large number of expert judgments while avoiding the problems of conformity and domination that can occur in interacting groups.

EXHIBIT 12-5 **The plan for a typical Delphi exercise.**

Activities	Estimated Minimum Time for Accomplishment
1) Develop the Delphi question	½ day
2) Select and contact respondents	2 days
3) Select sample size	½ day
4) Develop Questionnaire #1 and test	1 day
a. Type and send out	1 day
b. Response time	5 days
c. Reminder time	3 days
5) Analysis of Questionnaire #1	½ day
6) Develop Questionnaire #2 and test	2 days
a. Type and send out	1 day
b. Response time	5 days
c. Reminder time	3 days
7) Analysis of Questionnaire #2	1 day
8) Develop Questionnaire #3 and test	2 days
a. Type and send out	1 day
b. Response time	5 days
c. Reminder time	3 days
9) Analysis of Questionnaire #3	1 day
10) Prepare a final report	4 days
a.. Type report and send out	1 day
b. Prepare respondents' report	1 day
c. Type report and send out	1 day
Total estimated minimum time	44½ days

Source: Delbecq, A. L., Van de Ven, A. H., & Gustafson, D. *Group techniques for program planning.* Glenview, IL: Scott, Foresman. Copyright © 1975 Scott, Foresman. Reprinted by permission.

SUMMARY

- Decision making is the process of developing a commitment to some course of action. Alternatively, it is a problem solving process. A problem exists when a gap is perceived between some existing state and some desired state.

- Rational decision making involves 1) problem identification, 2) information search, 3) development of alternative solutions, 4) evaluation of alternatives, 5) choice of best alternative, 6) implementation, and 7) ongoing evaluation of the implemented alternative. The imaginary perfectly rational decision maker has free and easy access to all relevant information, can process it accurately, and has a single ultimate goal—economic maximization. Real decision makers must suffer with bounded rationality. They do not have free and easy access to information, and the human mind has limited information processing capacity. In addition, time constraints and political considerations can outweigh anticipated economic gain. As a result, bounded decision makers usually satisfice (choose a solution which is "good enough") rather than maximize. The bounds of rationality intrude at each stage of the decision-making process. For example, perceptual defense, faulty hindsight, attempts to recover sunk costs, and information overload may damage the quality of decisions.

■   Some problems are well structured. This means that existing and desired states are clear, as is the means of getting from one state to the other. Well-structured problems are often solved with programs, which simply standardize solutions. Programmed decision making is effective as long as the program is developed rationally, and as long as conditions do not change.

■   Ill-structured problems involve some combination of an unclear existing state, an unclear desired state, or unclear methods of getting from one state to the other. They tend to be unique and nonrecurrent, and they require nonprogrammed decision making, in which the rational model comes into play.

■   It is often assumed that groups can make higher quality decisions than individuals because of their vigilance and their potential capacity to generate and evaluate more ideas. Also, group members may accept more readily a decision in which they have been involved. Given the proper problem, groups will frequently make higher quality decisions than individuals. However, using groups takes a lot of time, may lead to demands for greater participation, and provoke conflict. In addition, highly cohesive groups may fall prey to groupthink, in which social pressures to conform to a particular decision outweigh rationality. Groups may also make decisions which are more risky or conservative than individuals.

■   Attempts to improve decision making have involved training discussion leaders, stimulating controversy, brainstorming, the nominal group technique, and the Delphi technique.

KEY CONCEPTS

Decision making	Well-structured problems
Problem	Program
Perfect rationality	Ill-structured problems
Bounded rationality	Nonprogrammed decision making
Information overload	Diffusion of responsibility
Maximization	Groupthink
Satisficing	Risky shift
Sunk costs	Conservative shift
Escalation of commitment	Devil's advocate
Hindsight	Brainstorming
Knew-it-all-along effect	Nominal group technique
Beneffectance	Delphi technique

DISCUSSION QUESTIONS

1. Why can any example of decision making be considered an exercise in problem solving? Give an example of a decision-making episode you have observed and illustrate how it solved a problem. What kinds of resources did the decision commit?

2. The director of an urban hospital feels that there is a turnover problem among the hospital's nurses. About 25 percent of the staff resigns each year, leading to high replacement costs and disruption of services. Use the decision model shown in Exhibit 12-1 to explore how the director might proceed to solve this problem. Discuss probable bounds to the rationality of the director's decision.

3. Debate the following: Business schools spend too much time teaching students to be maximizers. What they should do is teach students how to be more effective satisficers.

4. Describe a decision-making episode (in school, work, or personal life) in which you experienced information overload. How did you respond to this overload? Did it affect the quality of your decision?

5. Many universities must register thousands of students for courses each semester. Is this a well-structured problem or an ill-structured problem? Does it require programmed decisions or nonprogrammed decisions? Elaborate.

6. An auditing team fails to detect a case of embezzlement which has gone on for several months at a bank. How might the team members use hindsight to justify their faulty decisions?

7. A very cohesive planning group for a major oil company is about to develop a long-range strategic plan. The head of the unit is aware of the groupthink problem and wishes to prevent it. What steps should she take?

8. Discuss the implications of diffusion of responsibility, risky shift, and conservative shift for the members of a parole board.

9. What are the similarities and differences of the nominal group technique and the Delphi technique? What are the comparative advantages and disadvantages?

10. Discuss the reasons why decision makers might continue to commit resources to a failing course of action.

FOR FURTHER READING

Isenberg, D. J. (1984, November–December). How senior managers think. *Harvard Business Review,* 81–90.

> Reports an intensive study of how senior managers think and what they think about. Discusses how they combine intuition with rationality.

Maier, N. R. F. (1963). *Problem-solving discussions and conferences: Leadership methods and skills.* New York: McGraw-Hill.

A practical examination of the leadership of decision-making groups. Chapters include advice on problem location, problem presentation, conduct of discussion, and how to reach decisions. A "how to do it" book by a respected researcher.

Schwenk, C. (1986). Information, cognitive biases, and commitment to a course of action. *Academy of Management Review, 11,* 298–310.
Discusses how managers might actually use decision-making biases such as those discussed in the chapter to make others committed to a course of action. Covers creating colorful information, stimulating confidence, and "entrapping" others in the course of action.

Taylor, R. N. (1984). *Behavioral decision making.* Glenview, IL: Scott, Foresman.
Concentrates on how decisions are made and how decisions can be improved given the biases and limitations of human decision makers. Good chapters on complex decision problems and uncertain decision problems.

Case Study

Eastern Province Light and Power Company

I work as a Systems and a Procedures Analyst for the Eastern Province Light and Power Company. The Systems and Procedures Department analyzes corporate policies, procedures, forms, equipment, and methods to simplify and standardize operations. We apply "organized common sense" to develop new practices and to improve old ones.

Requests for analysis of organizational problems are submitted to the Systems and Procedures Department by persons of department head or higher status. Our manager places projects in line for consideration and assigns them to an analyst on the basis of availability; projects are accepted and assigned on the "fifo" (first in-first out) method. Projects must undergo analysis, design, and implementation before a change in procedure is realized. What follows is a description of a problem assigned to me. I am in the midst of investigating it right now.

THE PROBLEM

For some time, management had been concerned with the inventory carrying charges that accrue when material is stored in company warehouses. Not only is there a cost attached to carrying inventory for future use, but there are additional related costs such as labor to handle the inventory, warehouse usage in terms of square feet taken up in storage, and clerical time used to account for materials flow-

Source: Hampton, D. R. (1981). *Contemporary management.* New York: McGraw-Hill. Reprinted by permission.

ing into and out of inventory. One type of material stored is office supplies—pens, writing pads, forms, stationery, envelopes, and dozens of similar items. A desire to reduce the costs of storing these items prompted the head of the Department of Purchasing and Material Control to submit a request for study by Systems and Procedures.

The request came in the required written form. It described the current procedures, estimated their costs, and invited us to explore ways of changing the procedures to reduce costs. In brief, at the time the study request was submitted, purchases of office supplies were made through eleven vendors. The items were stored in a common warehouse area and disbursed to using departments as requested. As is customary, I convened a meeting of the requesting manager and others who seemed most directly involved in the problem.

THE FIRST MEETING

I opened the meeting by summarizing the present procedures for purchasing and storing office supplies and the estimated costs associated with these problems. I explained that we were meeting to explore ways of reducing these costs. I suggested we might try to generate as many ideas as we could without being too critical of them and then proceed to narrow the list by criticizing and eliminating the ideas with obvious weaknesses.

Just as soon as I finished my opening remarks, the head of Purchasing and Material Control said that we should conduct a "pilot study" in which we contract with one of the regular vendors to supply each using department directly, eliminating company storage of any inventory. The vendor would continue to sell us whatever we usually purchased from it, but sell and deliver the items to various departments, instead of to our central purchasing group. A pilot study with one vendor would indicate how such a system would work with all vendors of office supplies. If it worked well we could handle all office supplies this way.

She went on to explain that she had already spoken to the Vice President to whom she (and, through intermediate levels, the rest of us) reported and that he recognized the potential savings that would result. She also said that she had gone over the idea with the Supervisor of Stores (who reported to her) and that he agreed. She wanted to know how long it would take me to carry out the pilot study. I looked at a few faces to see if anybody would say anything, but nobody did. I said I didn't know. She said, "Let's meet in a week when you've come up with a proposal." The meeting ended without anything else of any real substance being said.

I felt completely frustrated. She was the highest-ranking person in the meeting. She had said what she wanted and, if her stature wasn't enough, she had invoked the image of the Vice President being in agreement with her. Nobody, including me, had said diddly boo. No idea other than hers was even mentioned and no comments were made about hers.

I decided that I would work as hard as I could to study the problem and her proposed pilot study before the next meeting and come prepared to give the whole thing a critical review.

BETWEEN MEETINGS

I talked to my boss about my feeling that it seemed as though I was expected to "rubber-stamp" the pilot study idea. I said I wished he would come to the next meeting. I also said that I wanted to talk to some people close to the problem, some clerks in Stores, some vendors, and some buyers in Purchasing to see if I could come up with any good ideas or find any problems in the pilot study area. He told me to learn all I could and that he would come to the next meeting.

My experience with other studies had taught me that sometimes the people closest to the work had expertise to contribute, so I found one Stores clerk, two buyers, and two vendor sales representatives to talk to. Nobody had spoken to any of them about the pilot study and the general plan it was meant to test. This surprised me a little. Each one of these people had some interesting things to say about the proposed new way of handling office supplies. A buyer, for example, thought it would be chaotic to have seventeen different departments ordering the same items. She thought we might also lose out on some quantity discounts. She said it would mean seventeen times the paperwork. A vendor said he didn't think any vendor would like the idea because it would increase the number of contacts necessary to sell the amount that could be sold now through one contact—the buyer in the Purchasing Department. A Stores clerk said it might be risky to depend upon a vendor to maintain inventories at adequate levels. He said, "What if a vendor failed to supply us with, say, enough mark-sensing tools for our meter readers one month, thereby causing them to be unable to complete their task and our company to be unable to get its monthly billings out on time?"

THE SECOND MEETING

Armed with careful notes, I came to the next meeting prepared to discuss these and other criticisms. One of the Stores clerks had even agreed to attend so that I could call upon him for comments. But when I looked around the conference room, everyone was there except the Stores clerk. The Head of Purchasing and Material Control said she had talked to the clerk and could convey any of his ideas so she had told him it wasn't necessary for him to come.

I pointed out that the Stores clerk had raised a question about the company's ability to control inventory. He had said that we now have physical control of inventory, but the proposal involved making ourselves dependent on the vendor's maintaining adequate inventory. The Head of Purchasing and Material Control said, "Not to worry. It will be in the vendor's own interest to keep us well supplied." No one, including my boss, said anything.

I brought up the subject of selecting a vendor to participate in the pilot study. My boss mentioned that I had told him some vendors might object to the scheme because the additional contacts would increase their costs of sales. The Head of Purchasing and Material Control said, "Any vendor would be interested in doing business with a company as big as Eastern Province Light and Power." No further comments were made.

I mentioned that it was the practice of the Systems and Procedures staff to estimate independently the costs and benefits of any project before undertaking it and also to have Internal Auditing review the proposal. I said we would need to go ahead with those steps. I asked the Head of Purchasing and Material Control to give me the name of somebody in her area I should contact to get the costs of the present system. She said that it really didn't seem necessary to go through all the usual steps in this case since she had already submitted an estimate. Besides, it was only going to be a pilot study. She said, "I think we can all agree on that and just move ahead now with the designation of a vendor." She looked around the table and nobody said anything. She said, "Fine. Let's use Moore Business Forms." Nobody said anything. She then said to me, "OK, let's get back together after you've lined things up."

■ ■ ■

1. Is the inventory problem faced by Eastern Province Light and Power Company ill-structured or well-structured?
2. Use the rational decision-making model shown in Exhibit 12-1 to describe and evaluate the decision-making process described in the case. Contrast the decision style of the Systems and Procedures analyst with that of the head of the Department of Purchasing and Material Control.
3. Discuss the group dynamics illustrated in the case. Did groupthink occur?
4. Suppose the results of the pilot study are mixed and uncertain. What might happen?
5. Why is the head of Purchasing and Material Control acting the way she is acting?
6. What should the Systems and Procedures Analyst do now?

Exercise

The New Truck Dilemma

PREPARATION FOR ROLE-PLAYING

The instructor will:
1. Read general instructions to class as a whole.
2. Place data regarding name, length of service, and make and age of truck on chalkboard for ready reference by all.
3. Divide class into groups of six. Any remaining members should be asked to join one of the groups and serve as observers.
4. Assign roles to each group by handing out slips with the names Walt Marshall, Denise, Sal, Rhonda, John, and Wilma. Ask each person to read his or her own role only. Instructions should not be consulted once role-playing is begun.

Source: Adapted from Maier, N. R. F. (1973). *Psychology in industrial organizations* (4th ed.). Boston: Houghton Mifflin.

5. Ask the Walt Marshalls to stand up when they have completed reading their instructions.
6. When all Walt Marshalls are standing, ask that each crew member display conspicuously the slip of paper with his or her role name so that Walt can tell who is who.

THE ROLE-PLAYING PROCESS

1. The instructor will start the role-playing with a statement such as the following: "Walt Marshall has asked his crew to wait in his office. He is out now. Apparently he wants to discuss something with the crew. When Walt sits down that will mean he has returned. What you say to each other is entirely up to you. Are you ready? All Walt Marshalls please sit down."
2. Role-playing proceeds for twenty-five to thirty minutes. Most groups reach agreement during this interval.

COLLECTION OF RESULTS

1. Each supervisor in turn reports his or her crew's solution. The instructor summarizes on the chalkboard by listing the initials of each repairperson and indicating with arrows which truck goes to whom.
2. A tabulation should be made of the number of persons getting a different truck, the crew members considering the solution unfair, and the supervisor's evaluation of the solution.

DISCUSSION OF RESULTS

1. Comparison of solutions will reveal differences in the number of persons getting a different truck, who gets the new one, the number dissatisfied, etc. Discuss why the same facts yield different outcomes.
2. The quality of the solution can be measured by the trucks retained. Highest quality would require the poorest truck (Wilma's) to be discarded. Evaluate the quality of the solutions achieved.
3. Acceptance is indicated by the low number of dissatisfied repairpersons. Evaluate solutions achieved on this dimension.
4. List problems that are similar to the new truck problem. See how widely the group will generalize.

GENERAL INSTRUCTIONS

This is a role-playing exercise. DO NOT READ THE ROLES GIVEN BELOW UNTIL ASSIGNED TO DO SO BY YOUR INSTRUCTOR!

Assume that you are a repairperson for a large utility. Each day you drive to various locations in the city to do repair work. Each of you drives a small truck and you take pride in keeping it looking good. You have a possessive feeling about your truck and like to keep it in good running order. Naturally, you'd like to have a new truck too, because a new truck gives you a feeling of pride.

Here are some facts about the trucks and the crew that reports to Walt Marshall, the supervisor of repairs:

Denise—17 years with the company, has a 2-year-old Ford
Sal—   11 years with the company, has a 5-year-old Dodge
Rhonda—10 years with the company, has a 4-year-old Ford
John—   5 years with the company, has a 3-year-old Ford
Wilma— 3 years with the company, has a 5-year-old Chevrolet

Most of you do all of your driving in the city, but Rhonda and John cover the jobs in the suburbs.

You will be one of the persons mentioned above and will be given some further individual instructions. In acting your part in role-playing, accept the facts as well as assume the attitude supplied in your specific role. From this point on let your feelings develop in accordance with the events that transpire in the role-playing process. When facts or events arise that are not covered by the roles, make up things which are consistent with the way it might be in a real-life situation.

When the role-playing begins, assume that Walt Marshall called the crew into the repair office.

Role for Walt Marshall, Supervisor

You are the supervisor of a repair crew, each of whom drives a small service truck to and from various jobs. Every so often you get a new truck to exchange for an old one, and you have the problem of deciding to which one of your crew you should give the new truck. Often there are hard feelings because each person seems to feel entitled to the new truck, so you have a tough time being fair. As a matter of fact, it usually turns out that whatever you decide, most of the crew consider wrong. You now have to face the issue again because a new truck has just been allocated to you for assignment. The new truck is a Chevrolet.

In order to handle this problem you have decided to put the decision up to the crew themselves. You will tell them about the new truck and will put the problem in terms of what would be the fairest way to assign the truck. *Don't take a position yourself, because you want to do what the crew thinks is most fair.* However, be sure that the group reaches a decision.

Role for Denise

When a new Chevrolet truck becomes available, you think you should get it because you have most seniority and don't like your present truck. Your own car is a Chevrolet, and you prefer a Chevrolet truck such as you drove before you got the Ford.

Role for Sal

You feel you deserve a new truck. Your present truck is old, and since the more senior crew member has a fairly new truck, you should get the next one. You have taken excellent care of your present Dodge and have kept it looking like new. People deserve to be rewarded if they treat a company truck like their own.

Role for Rhonda

You have to do more driving than most of the other crew because you work in the suburbs. You have a fairly old truck and feel you should have a new one because you do so much driving.

Role for John

The heater in your present truck is inadequate. Since Wilma backed into the door of your truck it has never been repaired to fit right. The door lets in too much cold air, and you attribute your frequent colds to this. You want a warm truck since you have a good deal of driving to do. As long as it has good tires, brakes, and is comfortable you don't care about its make.

Role for Wilma

You have the poorest truck in the crew. It is five years old, and before you got it, it had been in a bad wreck. It has never been good, and you've put up with it for three years. It's about time you got a good truck to drive, and you feel the next one should be yours. You have a good accident record. The only accident you had was when you sprung the door of John's truck when he opened it as you backed out of the garage. You hope the new truck is a Ford since you prefer to drive one.

REFERENCES

1. Mintzberg, H. (1979). *The structuring of organizations.* Englewood Cliffs, NJ: Prentice-Hall.
2. MacCrimmon, K. R., & Taylor, R. N. (1976). Decision making and problem solving. In M. D. Dunnette (Ed.), *Handbook of industrial and organizational psychology.* Chicago: Rand McNally.
3. Simon, H. A. (1957). *Administrative behavior* (2nd ed.). New York: Free Press.
4. The latter two difficulties are discussed by Huber, G. P., (1980). *Managerial decision making.* Glenview, IL: Scott, Foresman. For further discussion of problem identification see Kiesler, S., & Sproull, L. (1982). Managerial response to changing environments: Perspectives on problem sensing from social cognition. *Administrative Science Quarterly, 27,* 548–570.
5. Tversky, A., & Kahneman, D. (1973). Availability: A heuristic for judging frequency and probability. *Cognitive Psychology, 5,* 207–232. Also see Taylor, S. E., and Fiske, S. T. (1978). Salience, attention, and attribution: Top of the head phenomena. In L. Berkowitz (Ed.)., *Advances in experimental social psychology* (Vol. 11). New York: Academic Press.
6. Wright, P. J. (1979). *On a clear day you can see General Motors.* New York: Avon, p. 27.
7. Miller, J. G. (1960). Information input, overload, and psychopathology. *American Journal of Psychiatry, 116,* 695–704.
8. Manis, M., Fichman, M., & Platt, M. (1978). Cognitive integration and referential communication: Effects of information quality and quantity in message decoding. *Organizational Behavior and Human Performance, 22,* 417–430; Troutman, C. M., & Shanteau, J. (1977). Inferences based on nondiagnostic information. *Organizational Behavior and Human Performance, 19,* 43–55.
9. O'Reilly, C. A., III. (1980). Individuals and information overload in organizations: Is more necessarily better? *Academy of Management Journal, 23,* 684–696.
10. Feldman, M. S., & March, J. G. (1981). Information in organizations as signal and symbol. *Administrative Science Quarterly, 26,* 171–186.
11. Bonoma, T. V. (1977). Business decision making: Marketing implications. In M. F. Kaplan & S. Schwartz (Eds.), *Human judgment and decision processes in applied settings.* New York: Academic Press.
12. MacCrimmon & Taylor, 1976.
13. Simon, H. A. (1957). *Models of man.* New York: Wiley; Cyert, R. M., & March, J. G. (1963). *A behavioral theory of the firm.* Englewood Cliffs, NJ: Prentice-Hall.
14. Slovic, P., Fischhoff, B., & Lichtenstein, S. (1977). Behavioral decision theory. *Annual Review of Psychology, 28,* 1–39.

15. Staw, B. M. (1980). Rationality and justification in organizational life. *Research in Organizational Behavior, 2,* 45–80.

16. For a detailed treatment and other perspectives see Northcraft, G. B., & Wolf, G. (1984). Dollars, sense, and sunk costs: A life cycle model of resource allocation decisions. *Academy of Management Review, 9,* 225–234.

17. Staw, B. M. (1981). The escalation of commitment to a course of action. *Academy of Management Review, 6,* 577–587.

18. Staw, 1981. For the limitations on this view see Knight, P. A. (1984). Heroism versus competence: Competing explanations for the effects of experimenting and consistent management. *Organizational Behavior and Human Performance, 33,* 307–322.

19. Arkes, H. R., & Blumer, C. (1985). The psychology of sunk cost. *Organizational Behavior and Human Decision Processes, 35,* 124–140.

20. Whyte, G. (1986). Escalating commitment to a course of action: A reinterpretation. *Academy of Management Review, 11,* 311–321.

21. Bach, S. (1985). *Final cut: Dreams and disaster in the making of Heaven's Gate.* New York: Morrow.

22. Fischhoff, B. (1975). Hindsight ≠ foresight: The effect of outcome knowledge on judgment under uncertainty. *Journal of Experimental Psychology: Human Perceptual Performance, 1,* 288–299; Fischhoff, B., & Beyth, R. (1975). ''I knew it would happen''—Remembered probabilities of once-future things. *Organizational Behavior and Human Performance, 13,* 1–16.

23. Greenwald, A. G. (1980). The totalitarian ego: Fabrication and revision of personal history. *American Psychologist, 35,* 603–618.

24. Mitchell, T. R., & Beach, L. R. Expectancy theory, decision theory, and occupational preference and choice. In Kaplan & Schwartz, 1977.

25. To see just how infrequently the full rational model is applied to complex organizational decisions, see Nutt, P. C. (1984). Types of organizational decision processes. *Administrative Science Quarterly, 29,* 414–450.

26. MacCrimmon & Taylor, 1976.

27. Watkins, B. T. (1980, April 28). More decisions on purchasing textbooks now made by committees, survey shows. *Chronicle of Higher Education,* 1–4, p. 1.

28. Hammond, K. R., Rohrbaugh, J., Mumpower, J., & Adelman, L. Social judgment theory: Applications in policy formation. In Kaplan & Schwartz, 1977.

29. Shaw, M. E. (1981). *Group dynamics* (3rd. ed.). New York: McGraw-Hill, p. 78.

30. Hill, G. W. (1982). Group versus individual performance: Are n + 1 heads better than one? *Psychological Bulletin, 91,* 517–539.

31. Shaw, 1981; Davis, J. H.. (1969). *Group performance.* Reading, MA: Addison-Wesley.

32. Janis, I. L. (1972). *Victims of groupthink.* Boston: Houghton Mifflin.

33. Janis, 1972.

34. Huseman, R. C., & Driver, R. W. (1979). Groupthink: Implications for small-group decision making in business. In R. Huseman & A. B. Carroll (Eds.), *Readings in organizational behavior: Dimensions of management actions.* Boston: Allyn and Bacon.

35. Experimental tests of groupthink have produced mixed results. For a review and study see Moorhead, G., & Montanari, J. R. (1986). An empirical investigation of the groupthink phenomenon. *Human Relations, 39,* 399–410.

36. Stoner, J. A. F. (1961). *A comparison of individual and group decisions involving risk.* Unpublished master's thesis. School of Industrial Management, Massachusetts Institute of Technology.

37.   Lamm, H., & Myers, D. G. (1978). Group-induced polarization of attitudes and behavior. In L. Berkowitz (Ed.), *Advances in experimental social psychology* (Vol. 11). New York: Academic Press.

38.   Lamm & Myers, 1978.

39.   Maier, N. R. F. (1973). *Psychology in industrial organizations* (4th ed.). Boston: Houghton Mifflin.

40.   Maier, N. R. F. (1970). *Problem solving and creativity in individuals and groups.* Belmont, CA: Brooks/Cole.

41.   Tjosvold, D. (1985). Implications of controversy research for management. *Journal of Management, 11*(3), 21–37.

42.   Tjosvold, 1985.

43.   Schwenk, C. R. (1984). Devil's advocacy in managerial decision-making. *Journal of Management Studies, 21,* 153–168. For a recent study see Schweiger, D. M., Sandberg, W. R., & Ragan, J. W. (1986). Group approaches for improving strategic decision making: A comparative analysis of dialectical inquiry, devil's advocacy, and consensus. *Academy of Management Journal, 29,* 51–71.

44.   Osborn, A. F. (1957). *Applied imagination.* New York: Scribners.

45.   For an example see Madsen, D. B., & Finger, J. R., Jr. (1978). Comparison of a written feedback procedure, group brainstorming, and individual brainstorming. *Journal of Applied Psychology, 63,* 120–123.

46.   Delbecq, A. L., Van de Ven, A. H., & Gustafson, D. H. (1975). *Group techniques for program planning.* Glenview, IL: Scott, Foresman, p. 8.

47.   Delbecq et al., 1975.

Chapter 13

Power, Politics, and Conflict

MARY CUNNINGHAM

In 1977 Mary Cunningham entered the Harvard Business School. Two years later, at age twenty-seven, she graduated and proceeded to exhibit one of the fastest starts to a business career ever seen in North America. Faced with a variety of job offers, she accepted a position as executive assistant to William Agee, chairman of Bendix Corporation. In this job, she wrote his speeches and prepared testimony for him to offer in hearings in Washington. A year later Ms. Cunningham was promoted to vice-president for corporate and public affairs and headed up a task force to review the firm's North American automotive supplies activities. Three months after this she was again promoted, this time to vice-president for strategic planning. Two months later, Cunningham resigned from Bendix. Her resignation followed an extraordinary meeting of 600 employees in which Agee denied that her rapid advancement was due to personal involvement with him.

What accounted for the rise and fall of Mary Cunningham? As for the rise, there is no doubt that she was extremely bright and highly motivated to obtain power. In addition, Agee took a strong interest in her career development, admiring her expertise. They were clearly kindred spirits. At best, critics attributed her rise to unwarranted favoritism on the part of Agee. At worst, they hinted at an affair.

Several factors probably accounted for the ill will toward Cunningham. For one thing, some executives did not share Agee's view about Cunningham's expertise, especially in the automotive parts field. Some felt that her task force report yielded little new information. In addition, some managers were angered that Cunningham had not consulted them in the preparation of the report, and some senior executives were upset that she had been promoted over them. Finally, Cunningham had become closely identified with Agee's plan to move Bendix away from automobile parts and into high technology. Although most executives agreed that this change was necessary, some may have feared the rapid redistribution of power that was occurring.

Mary Cunningham survived a vote of confidence from the board of directors but resigned because the controversy had reduced her effectiveness within the company. Shortly thereafter, she took a planning position at Seagrams. Sometime later, Agee himself was forced out of Bendix. Eventually, Cunningham and Agee married and set up a consulting firm.[1]

This true story illustrates the main themes of this chapter—power, politics, and conflict. First, power will be defined and the bases of individual power will be discussed. Then we shall examine how organizational members get power and who seeks power. After this we shall explore how organizational subunits, such as particular departments, obtain power. Organizational politics will be defined, and the relationship of politics to power will be explored. The final topic of the chapter is conflict. The causes and results of conflict will be examined and the pros and cons of conflict will be considered. Finally, some methods of managing conflict are discussed.

SEE NO EVIL, HEAR NO EVIL, SPEAK NO EVIL— A PROLOGUE

"But no matter how we're going to word it, to the manager of Corporate Services our recommendation is going to say that he has done a lousy job. And naturally he is resisting. He is resisting because he thinks he's got some power. Not he himself but someone higher up; he's got contacts. And we think we've got some power; and we've got people who can bring some influence to bear upon this question. It isn't a matter of who is right; it's who's got the power. And a lot of times the support is not because our facts are 100 per cent correct, but because some guy likes what we're doing. Or he likes the individuals. Or he thinks, politically speaking, he should back us. And right now, politically speaking, it's going to be favorable for some big guy to back us because of the slump in the economy—see?"[2]

We see! We see! And somehow we *know* that many organizational decisions do not depend upon who is "100 per cent correct." Rather, as the speaker insists, decisions often depend upon power dynamics and political considerations. And, as he implies, this often promotes organizational conflict.

Until fairly recently, power, politics, and conflict were not considered polite topics for coverage in organizational behavior textbooks. At best, they were seen as irrational, and at worst, as evil. Now, though, theorists and researchers have begun to recognize what managers have known all along—that power, politics, and conflict are *natural* expressions of life in organizations. They often develop as a rational response to a complex set of needs and goals, and their expression may be beneficial rather than evil.

WHAT IS POWER?

Power is the capacity to influence others who are in a state of dependence. Several points about this definition deserve elaboration. First, notice that power is the *capacity* to influence the behavior of others. Power is not always exercised.[3] For example, most professors hold a great degree of potential power over students in terms of grades, assignment load, and the ability to embarrass students in class. Under normal circumstances, only a small amount of this power is actually used.

Secondly, the fact that the target of power is dependent upon the power-holder does not imply that a poor relationship exists between the two. For instance, your best friend has power to influence your behavior and attitudes because you are dependent upon him or her for friendly reactions and social support. Presumably, you can exert reciprocal influence for similar reasons.

Third, power can flow in any direction in an organization. Often, members at higher organizational levels have more power than those at lower levels. However, in specific cases, reversals can occur. For example, the janitor who finds the president in a compromising position with a secretary may find himself in a powerful position if the president wishes to maintain his reputation in the organization!

Finally, power is a broad concept that applies to both individuals and groups. On one hand, an individual production manager may exert considerable influence over the supervisors who report to him. On the other, the marketing department at XYZ Foods may be the most powerful department in the company, able to get its way more often than other departments. But from where do the production manager and the marketing department obtain their power? In the following sections this issue is explored. First, we will consider individual bases of power and how they are obtained. Then we will examine how organizational subunits (such as the marketing department) obtain power.

THE BASES OF INDIVIDUAL POWER

If you wanted to marshal some power to influence others in your organization, where would you get it? Put simply, power can be found in the *position* you occupy in the organization or the *resources* you are able to command. The first base of power to be discussed, legitimate power, is dependent upon one's position or job. The other bases (reward, coercive, referent, and expert power) involve the control of important resources. If other organizational members do not respect your position or value the resources you command, they will not be dependent on you, and you will lack power to influence them.[4]

Legitimate Power

Legitimate power derives from a person's position or job in the organization. It constitutes the organization's judgment about who is formally permitted to influence whom, and it is often called authority. As we move up the organization's hierarchy we find that members possess more and more legitimate power. In theory, organizational equals (e.g., all vice-presidents) have equal legitimate power. Of course, some people are more likely than others to *invoke* their legitimate power— "Look, *I'm* the boss around here." (See the cartoon.)

Organizations differ greatly in the extent to which they emphasize and reinforce legitimate power. At one extreme is the U.S. Army, which has many levels of command, differentiating uniforms, and rituals (e.g., salutes), all designed to emphasize legitimate power. On the other hand, the academic hierarchy of

Source: *Psychology Today,* August 1986, p. 10.
Reprinted by permission.

universities tends to downplay differences in the legitimate power of lecturers, professors, chairpersons, and deans.

When legitimate power works, it does so because people have been socialized to accept its influence. Experiences with parents, teachers, and law enforcement officials cause members to enter organizations with a degree of readiness to submit to (and exercise) legitimate power. In fact, studies consistently show that industrial workers cite legitimate power as a major reason for following their supervisors' directives, even across various cultures.[5]

Reward Power

Reward power exists when the powerholder can exert influence by providing positive outcomes and preventing negative outcomes. In general, it corresponds to the concept of positive reinforcement discussed in Chapter 3. Reward power is often used to back up legitimate power. That is, managers and supervisors are given the chance to recommend raises, do performance evaluations, and assign preferred tasks to subordinates. Of course, *any* organizational member can attempt to exert influence over others with praise, compliments, and flattery, which also constitute rewards.

Coercive Power

Coercive power is available when the powerholder can exert influence by the use of punishment and threat. Like reward power, it is often used as a support for legitimate power. Supervisors and managers may be permitted to dock pay, assign unfavorable tasks, or block promotions. Despite a strong civil service system, even U.S. government agencies provide their executives with plenty of coercive power:

> Some agencies have a Siberia—an unpleasant or professionally unproductive duty station, to which rebellious employees may be reassigned. Faced with Siberia, an employee may, of course, resign, but even if he accepts exile, he is effectively removed from the position in which he caused difficulty.
>
> "You'd be surprised how many resignations we had when people discovered they had been reassigned to Anchorage," said one former Federal Aeronautics Administration official.[6]

Of course, coercive power is not perfectly correlated with legitimate power. Lower level organizational members can also apply their share of coercion. For example, work-to-rule campaigns, designed to slow productivity by adhering religiously to organizational procedures, may be employed. Cohesive work groups are especially skillful at enforcing such campaigns.

In Chapter 3 it was pointed out that the use of punishment to control behavior is very problematic because of emotional side effects. Thus, it is not surprising that the use of coercive power by managers is often associated with workgroup ineffectiveness.[7]

Referent Power

Referent power exists when the powerholder is *well liked* by others. It is not surprising that we are readily influenced by those we like. We are prone to consider their points of view, ignore their failures, and seek their approval. In fact, it is often highly dissonant to hold a point of view that is discrepant from that held by someone we like.[8]

Referent power is especially potent for two reasons. First, it stems from *identification* with the powerholder. Thus, it seems to represent a truer or deeper base of power than reward or coercion, which may stimulate mere compliance to achieve rewards or avoid punishment. Secondly, *anyone* in the organization may be well liked, irrespective of their other bases of power. Thus, referent power is available to everyone from the janitor to the president.

Friendly interpersonal relations often permit influence to be extended across the organization, outside of the usual channels of legitimate authority, reward, and coercion. For example, a production manager who becomes friendly with the design engineer through participation in a task force may later use this contact to ask for a favor in solving a production problem.

Expert Power

A person has **expert power** when he or she has special expertise that is valued by the organization. In any circumstance, we tend to be influenced by experts or by those who are known to perform their jobs well. However, the more crucial and unusual this expertise, the greater the expert power available. Thus, expert power corresponds to difficulty of replacement. Consider the business school that has one highly published professor who is an internationally known scholar and past presidential cabinet member. Such a person would obviously be difficult to replace, and should have much greater expert power than an unpublished lecturer.

One of the most fascinating aspects of expert power occurs when it is accrued by lower level organizational members. Many secretaries have acquired expert power through long experience in dealing with clients, keeping records, or sparring with the bureaucracy. Frequently, they have been around longer than those they serve. In this case, it is not unusual for bosses to create special titles and develop new job classifications to reward their expertise and prevent their resignation.

Expert power is especially likely to exist for lower level members in scientific and technical areas. Consider the solid-state physicist who has just completed her Ph.D. dissertation on a topic of particular interest to her new employer. Although new to the firm, she may have considerable expert power. Put simply, she *knows* more than her boss, whose scientific knowledge in this area is now outdated. At the Bendix Corporation, some executives granted Mary Cunningham expert power while others did not. William Agee marvelled at her expertise, but some others felt that she had little understanding of the automotive supplies area.

Studies show that expert power is a valuable asset for managers. Of all the bases of power, expertise is most consistently associated with subordinate effectiveness.[9]

In–Focus 13-1 shows how the introduction of computers affects power bases.

HOW DO INDIVIDUALS OBTAIN POWER?

Now that we have discussed the individual bases of power, we can turn to the issue of how people *get* power. That is, how do organizational members obtain promotions to positions of legitimate power, demonstrate their expertise, and get others to like them? And how do they acquire the ability to provide others with rewards and punishment? Rosabeth Moss Kanter, an organizational sociologist, has provided some succinct answers—Do the right things, and cultivate the right people.[10]

Doing the Right Things

We would hope that most organizational members do the "right thing" most of the time. However, according to Kanter, some activities are "righter" than others for

IN–FOCUS 13-1   COMPUTER POWER

Peter Nulty and Stephen E. Frantzich have both examined how increased computerization has influenced the power structure of organizations. Nulty has looked at how the proliferation of small personal computers affects managers and executives in the private sector:

David Dell, vice president of the Diebold Group, a management consulting firm, estimates that 17% of the nation's managers and 13% of top executives now have hands-on-the-keyboard access to computers. He estimates that FORTUNE 500 companies with annual sales of $1 billion or more now have 200 to 500 personal computers in operation, and that the number will increase tenfold by 1990.

Nulty expects that the proliferation of personal computers has the potential to increase the power of individual managers by making them less dependent on the company's large mainframe computer, by making them less dependent on their peers, and by increasing their ability to check up on subordinates:

Managers who would like to have the company mainframe programmed to answer their pet questions at the drop of a hat soon discover, says Levy of IDC, that the hat takes forever to hit the ground: the average backlog for programming new applications on corporate mainframes is two years. The payroll department's latest scheme inevitably takes priority, and besides, the head of data processing isn't sure that he wants anyone mucking around in the electronic sanctum sanctorum.

But the political change goes beyond this. Corporate America has traditionally placed great emphasis on teamwork, with each member of the team supplying a piece of the puzzle to a manager-captain who fits all the pieces together to make a decision. Now, using a personal computer, one person working alone can frequently solve a problem. As one executive puts it, "I feel master of my destiny at last."

In the long run, however, Nulty notes that the large amounts of data generated by personal computers may expose the detailed operations of the department or firm to more and more company members at all levels. When this happens, individual executives will find the power they hold due to information diminished.

Stephen E. Frantzich has studied the gradual increase in the use of computers in the United States Congress. Computer technology is available to the Congress as a whole to monitor and track ongoing legislation, schedule committee meetings, perform bibliographic searches, access commercial data bases, retrieve budget information, and perform econometric analyses. In addition, many House and Senate members have computerized their own offices to build specialized mailing lists, enhance communications with constituents, send electronic mail around the Hill, and manage personal schedules and files.

What are the implications of this increased computerization for the Congressional power structure? Information is an especially critical source of power in Congress. Traditionally, information has been acquired by chairing important committees and having easy access to key government officials, activities which are the province of high-seniority Congress members. In turn, these experienced members of Congress have used their control over information to exact loyalty and conformity from newer members. Frantzich speculates that computerization will "democratize" access to information, making it more readily available to all representatives and senators.

Sources: Nulty, P. (1984, September 3). How personal computers change managers' lives. *Fortune*, 38–48. © 1984, Time Inc. All rights reserved; Frantzich, S. E. (1982). *Computers in Congress: The politics of information.* Beverly Hills, CA: Sage. Reprinted by permission.

obtaining power. She argues that activities lead to power when they are extraordinary, highly visible, and especially relevant to the solution of organizational problems.

EXTRAORDINARY ACTIVITIES.   Excellent performance of a routine job may not be enough to obtain power. This is especially true in the management and professional ranks, where one is generally expected to demonstrate a high level of competence. What is needed to obtain power, according to Kanter, is excellent performance in *unusual* or *nonroutine* activities. In the large company she studied, these activities included occupying new positions, managing substantial changes, and taking great risks. For example, consider the business school professor who establishes and directs a new M.B.A. program. This is a risky major change which involves the occupancy of a new position. If successful, the professor should acquire substantial power in the school.

VISIBLE ACTIVITIES.   Extraordinary activities will fail to generate power if no one knows about them. This is a special problem in large, geographically dispersed organizations. The manager who successfully "turns around" the Peoria plant may go unrecognized by executives in New York. Those with an interest in power are especially good at identifying visible activities and publicizing them. The successful marketing executive whose philosophy is profiled in *Fortune* will reap the benefits of power. Similarly, the innovative surgeon whose techniques are reported in the *New England Journal of Medicine* will enhance her influence in the hospital.

RELEVANT ACTIVITIES.   Extraordinary, visible work may fail to generate power if no one cares. If the work is not seen as relevant to the solution of important organizational problems, it will not add to one's influence. The English professor who wins two Pulitzer prizes will probably not accrue much power if his small college is financially strapped and hurting for students. The same may apply to an innovative personnel manager in a company fighting for survival. Neither is seen as contributing to the solution of pressing organizational problems. As we shall see shortly, being in the right place at the right time is crucial to the acquisition of power. In another college or company, these extraordinary, visible activities might generate considerable influence.

At Bendix, Mary Cunningham's activities were perceived by some as extraordinary, visible, and relevant. Running the special task force was an important, visible job because the company was rethinking its heavy involvement in the automotive field.

Cultivating the Right People

An old saying advises "It's not what you know, it's *who* you know." In reference to power in organizations, there is probably more than a grain of truth to the latter part of this statement. Developing informal relationships with the right people (especially when coupled with doing the right things) can prove a useful means of acquiring power. Dr. Kanter suggests that the right people can include organizational subordinates, peers, and superiors. To these we might add certain crucial outsiders.

OUTSIDERS.   Establishing good relationships with key people outside of one's organization can lead to increased power within the organization. Sometimes this power is merely a reflection of the status of the outsider, but all the same it may add to one's internal influence. The assistant director of a hospital who is friendly with the president of the American Medical Association may find herself holding power by association. Cultivating outsiders may also contribute to more tangible sources of power. Organizational members who are on the boards of directors of other companies may acquire critical information about business conditions that they can use in their own firms. The purchasing agent who develops good relations with suppliers may be able to "work wonders" when shortages exist, thus adding to his power base. The tendency for business leaders to cultivate relationships with Senate and House members is no accident!

SUBORDINATES.   At first blush, it may seem unlikely that power can be enhanced by cultivating relationships with subordinates. However, as Kanter notes, influence can be accrued by being closely identified with certain up-and-coming subordinates—"I taught her everything she knows." In academics, some professors are better known for the brilliant Ph.D. students they have supervised than for their own published work. Of course, there is also the possibility that an outstanding subordinate will one day become one's boss! Having cultivated the relationship earlier, one may then be rewarded with special influence.

Cultivating subordinate interests can also provide power when a manager can demonstrate that he or she is backed by a cohesive team. The research director who can oppose a policy change by honestly insisting that, "My people won't stand for this," knows that there is strength in numbers.

PEERS.   Cultivating good relationships with peers is mainly a means of ensuring that nothing gets in the way of one's *future* acquisition of power. As one moves up through the ranks, favors can be asked of former associates, and fears of being "stabbed in the back" for a past misdeed are precluded. Organizations often reward good "team players" with promotions on the assumption that they have demonstrated good interpersonal skills. For instance, the military sometimes uses peer ratings as an input in promotion decisions.

SUPERIORS.   Liaisons with key superiors probably represent the best way of obtaining power through cultivating others. Such superiors are often called mentors or sponsors because of the special interest they show in a promising subordinate. Mentors can provide power in several ways. Obviously, it is useful to be identified as a protégé of someone higher in the organization. More concretely, mentors can provide special information and useful introductions to other "right people."

It is often argued that mentors are especially important for women junior executives because of the general lack of female role models at higher organizational ranks. It is absolutely clear that Mary Cunningham acquired power at Bendix because William Agee served as her mentor. Her story also points out a common problem with the mentor-protégé relationship—some organizational members may attack the protégé as an indirect means of damaging his or her mentor. We will discuss mentorship in more detail in a later chapter.

WHO WANTS POWER?

Who wants power? At first glance, the answer would seem to be *everybody*. After all, it is both convenient and rewarding to be able to exert influence over others. Power whisks celebrities to the front of movie lines, gets rock stars the best restaurant tables, and enables executives to shape organizations in their own image. Actually, there are considerable individual differences in the extent to which persons pursue and enjoy power. On television talk shows we occasionally see celebrities recount considerable embarrassment over the unwarranted power that public recognition brings.

Earlier it was indicated that power is often considered a manifestation of evil. This is due in no small part to the image of power seekers that has historically been portrayed by some psychologists and political scientists. Several aspects of this image are strikingly similar:

- Power seekers are neurotics who are covering up feelings of inferiority.
- Power seekers are striving to compensate for childhood deprivation.
- Power seekers are substituting power for lack of affection.[11]

There can be little doubt that these characteristics do apply to some power seekers. Underlying this negative image of power seeking is the idea that some power seekers feel weak and resort primarily to coercive power to cover up, compensate for, or substitute for this weakness.[12] Power is sought for its own sake and used irresponsibly to hurt others. Adolf Hitler comes to mind as an extreme example.

But can power be used responsibly to influence others? Harvard psychologist David McClelland says yes. In Chapter 6 we discussed McClelland's research on need for power (*n* Pow). You will recall that *n* Pow is defined as the need to have strong influence over others. This need is a reliable personality characteristic—some people have more *n* Pow than others.[13] In "pure" form, those high in *n* Pow conform to the negative stereotype depicted above—they are rude, sexually exploitive, abusive of alcohol, and show a great concern with status symbols. However, when *n* Pow is used in a responsible and controlled manner, these negative properties are not observed. Specifically, McClelland argues that the most effective managers:

- Have high *n* Pow
- Use their power to achieve organizational goals

■   Adopt a participative or "coaching" leadership style

■   Are relatively unconcerned with how much others like them

McClelland calls such managers *institutional managers,* because they use their power for the good of the institution rather than for self-aggrandizement. They refrain from coercive leadership but don't play favorites, since they aren't worried about being well liked. His research reveals that institutional managers are more effective than *personal power managers* who use their power for personal gain, and *affiliative managers,* who are more concerned with being liked than with exercising power. Exhibit 13-1 shows that institutional managers are generally

---

EXHIBIT 13-1   **Responses of subordinates of managers with different motive profiles.**

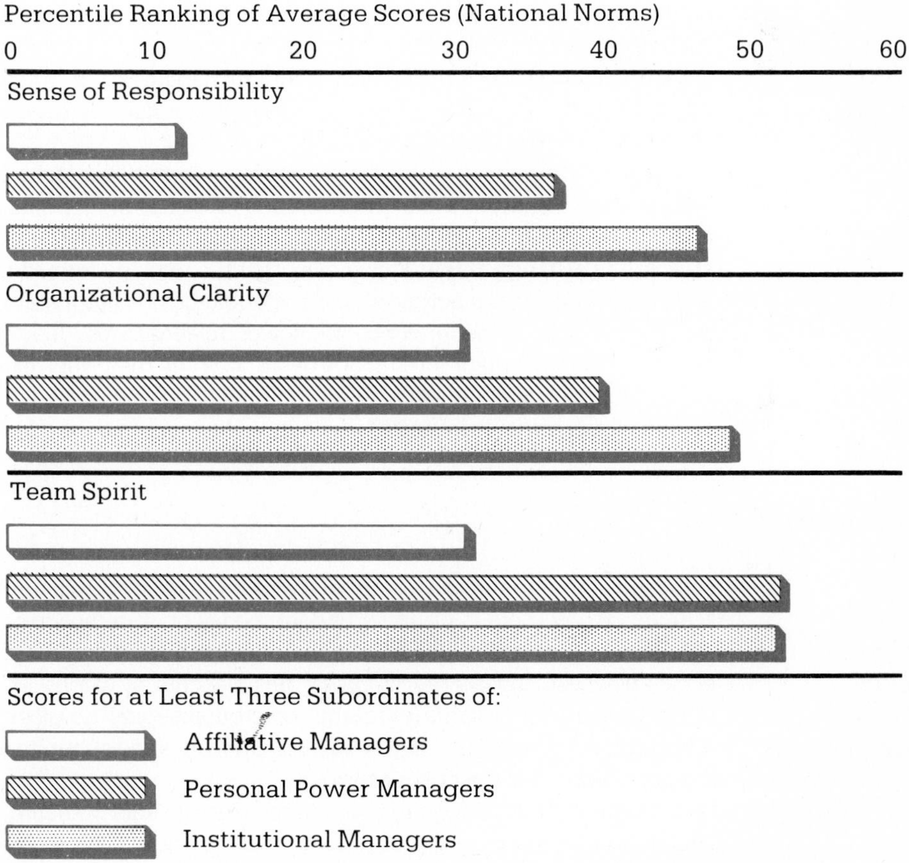

Percentile Ranking of Average Scores (National Norms)

| 0 | 10 | 20 | 30 | 40 | 50 | 60 |

Sense of Responsibility

Organizational Clarity

Team Spirit

Scores for at Least Three Subordinates of:

☐   Affiliative Managers

▨   Personal Power Managers

▨   Institutional Managers

Source: Reprinted by permission of the *Harvard Business Review.* An exhibit from "Power Is the Great Motivator" by David C. McClelland and David H. Burnham (March/April 1976). Copyright © 1976 by the President and Fellows of Harvard College; all rights reserved.

superior in giving subordinates a sense of responsibility, clarifying organizational priorities, and instilling team spirit.[14]

In summary, we conclude that the need for power can be a useful asset for organizational members as long as it is not a neurotic expression of perceived weakness.

CONTROLLING STRATEGIC CONTINGENCIES— HOW SUBUNITS OBTAIN POWER

Thus far we have been concerned with the bases of *individual* power and how individual organizational members obtain influence. In this section we shift our concern to **subunit power.** Most straightforwardly, the term *subunit* applies to organizational departments. In a business firm these departments might include production, marketing, finance, research, and personnel. In a university they might include personnel, registration, records, maintenance, and the various academic departments (e.g., history, chemistry, and management). In some cases, subunits could also refer to particular jobs, such as those held by intensive care nurses, mechanics, or mail carriers.

How do organizational subunits acquire power? That is, how do they achieve influence that enables them to grow in size, get a bigger share of the budget, obtain better facilities, and have greater impact on decisions? In short, they control **strategic contingencies.** This means that the work performed by *other* subunits is contingent upon the activities and performance of a key subunit. Again, we see the critical role of *dependence* in power relationships. If some subunits are dependent upon others for smooth operations (or their very existence) they are susceptible to influence. We turn now to the conditions under which subunits can control strategic contingencies.

Scarcity

Differences in subunit power are likely to be magnified when resources become scarce.[15] When there is plenty of budget money or office space or support staff for all subunits they will seldom waste their energies jockeying for power. If cutbacks occur, however, differences in power will become apparent. For example, well-funded quality of worklife programs or organizational development efforts may disappear when economic setbacks occur, because the subunits that control them are not essential to the firm's existence.

Subunits tend to acquire power when they are able to *secure* scarce resources which are important to the organization as a whole. One study of a large state university found that the power of academic departments was associated with their ability to obtain funds through consulting contracts and research grants. This mastery over economic resources was more crucial to their power than was the number of undergraduates taught by the department.[16]

Uncertainty

Organizations detest the unknown. Unanticipated events wreak havoc with financial commitments, long-range plans, and tomorrow's operations. The basic sources of uncertainty exist mainly in the organization's environment—government policies may change, sources of supply and demand may dry up, or the economy may take an unanticipated turn. It stands to reason that the subunits most capable of coping with uncertainty will tend to acquire power.[17] In a sense, these subunits are able to protect the others from serious problems. By the same token, uncertainty promotes confusion which permits *changes* in power priorities as the organizational environment changes:

> The most power goes to those people in those functions that provide greater control over what the organization finds currently problematic: sales and marketing people when markets are competitive; production experts when materials are scarce and demand is high; personnel or labor relations specialists when labor is scarce; lawyers, lobbyists, and external relations specialists when government regulations impinge; finance and accounting types when business is bad and money tight. There is a turning to those elements of the system that seem to have the power to create more certainty in the face of dependency, to generate a more advantageous position for the organization.[18]

A dramatic example of a shift in subunit power has occurred for the personnel or human resource departments of large corporations during the past twenty years. For many years, the personnel function in most organizations had relatively little power. However, beginning in the 1970s, increased government intervention into personnel policies began. This was especially true in the area of employment discrimination, where legislation provoked considerable uncertainty. In coming to the rescue, personnel departments acquired a long-awaited measure of power. Currently, the uncertainty provoked by downsizing, new technology, and mergers and acquisitions has continued the trend (In–Focus 13-2).

Centrality

Other things equal, subunits whose activities are most central to the work flow of the organization should acquire more power than those whose activities are more peripheral.[19] A subunit's activities can be central in at least three senses. First, they may influence the work of most other subunits. The finance or accounting department is a good example here—its authority to approve expenses and make payments affects every other department in the firm.

Centrality also exists when a subunit has an especially crucial impact on the quantity or quality of the organization's key product or service. This is one reason for the traditional low power of personnel departments—their activities are fairly remote from the primary goals of the organization. Similarly, a production department should have more power than a research and development department that only "fine tunes" existing products.

Finally, a subunit's activities are more central when their impact is more immediate. As an example, consider a large city government that includes a fire department, a police department, and a public works department. The impact of a lapse in fire or police services will be felt more immediately than a lapse in street repairs. This gives the former departments more potential for power acquisition.

Substitutability

A subunit will have relatively little power if its activities can be performed by others inside or outside of the organization. If the subunit's staff is nonsubstitutable, however, it may acquire substantial power.[20] One crucial factor here is the labor market for the specialty performed by the subunit. A change in the labor market may result in a change in the subunit's influence:

> In the 1950s, when there were relatively few engineers to service an expanding American economy, engineers had great prestige and power. They could force employers to provide them with large salaries and benefits, by threatening to withhold their services. By the early 1970s, however, many persons had become engineers and consequently the bargaining power of engineers with employers was practically nil.[21]

If the labor market is constant, subunits whose staffs are highly trained in technical areas tend to be less substitutable than those which involve minimal technical expertise. For example, consider the large telephone company that makes extensive use of a computerized management information system. The department in charge of this system may acquire considerable power because its computer analysts perform specialized work that can't be done by others in the company. On the other hand, if telephone operators go on strike, management personnel can substitute for them by handling the phones.

Finally, if work can be contracted out, the power of the subunit that usually performs these activities is reduced. Typical examples include temporary office help, off-premises data entry, and contracted maintenance and laboratory services. The subunits that control these activities often lack power because the threat of "going outside" can be used to counter their influence attempts.

ORGANIZATIONAL POLITICS—USING AND ABUSING POWER

In previous pages use of the terms *politics* or *political* has been avoided in describing the acquisition and use of power. This is because not all uses of power constitute politics.

The Basics of Organizational Politics

"**Organizational politics** is the management of influence to obtain ends not sanctioned by the organization or to obtain sanctioned ends through nonsanctioned influence means."[22] From the organization's standpoint, politics may involve some abuse of power, either in the way it is enacted (means) or in the outcomes to which it is directed (ends).

Three preliminary points should be made about organizational politics. First, political activity typically involves placing self-interest before organizational interests. Means or ends that suit the politician rather than the organization are adopted. Notice, however, that political activities can have beneficial outcomes for the organization even though these outcomes are achieved by nonsanctioned tactics. Secondly, political activity is self-conscious and intentional. This separates politics from ignorance, stupidity, or lack of experience with approved means and ends. Finally, we can conceive of politics as either individual activity or subunit activity. In some cases, a single organizational member may act politically; in others, an entire department may be politicized.

We can explore organizational politics using the means/ends matrix shown in Exhibit 13-2. It is the association between influence means and influence ends that determines whether activities are political and whether these activities benefit the organization.

I. *Sanctioned means/sanctioned ends.* Here, power is used routinely to pursue agreed-upon goals. Familiar, accepted means of influence are employed to achieve sanctioned outcomes. For example, a manager agrees to recommend a

EXHIBIT 13-2   **The dimensions of organizational politics.**

Influence Means	Influence Ends	
	Organizationally Sanctioned	Not Sanctioned by Organization
Organizationally Sanctioned	Non-Political Job Behavior I	Organizationally Dysfunctional II Political Behavior
Not Sanctioned by Organization	Political Behavior III Potentially Functional to the Organization	IV Organizationally Dysfunctional Political Behavior

Source: from Mayes, B. T., & Allen, R. T. (1977, October) Conceptual notes—Toward a definition of organizational politics, *The Academy of Management Review,* Vol. 2, No. 4, p. 675. © 1977 by the Academy of Management. Reprinted by permission.

raise for a subordinate if she increases her net sales 30 percent in the next six months. There is nothing political about this.

II. *Sanctioned means/nonsanctioned ends.* In this case, acceptable means of influence are abused to pursue goals that are not approved by the organization. For instance, a head nurse agrees to assign a subordinate nurse to a more favorable job if the nurse agrees not to report the superior for stealing medical supplies. While job assignment is often a sanctioned means of influence, covering up theft is not a sanctioned end. This is dysfunctional political behavior.

III. *Nonsanctioned means/sanctioned ends.* Here, ends that are useful for the organization are pursued through questionable means. For example, a commercial artist is vying with a co-worker to have his proposal accepted for an advertising campaign. Feeling his proposal is truly better, the artist takes the account executive to dinner, flatters him, and subtly discredits the co-worker's proposal. Currying favor and discrediting others are seldom approved methods of influence. However, if the proposal is really superior the consequences may be beneficial for the firm. This is obviously a gray area of politics. At Bendix, some observers felt that Mary Cunningham acted politically in not consulting key managers about her task force report. Still, it appears she had the firm's interests at heart.

IV. *Nonsanctioned means/nonsanctioned ends.* This quadrant may exemplify the most flagrant abuse of power, since disapproved tactics are used to pursue disapproved outcomes. For example, to increase his personal power, the head of an already overstaffed legal department wishes to increase its size. He intends to hire several of his friends in the process. To do this he falsifies work load documents and promises special service to the accounting department in exchange for the support of its manager.

We have all seen cases in which politics have been played out publicly in order to "teach someone a lesson." More frequently, though, politicians are motivated to conceal their activities with a "cover story" or "smoke screen" designed to make them appear legitimate.[23] Such a tactic will increase the odds of success and avoid punishment from superiors. A common strategy is to cover nonsanctioned means and ends with a cloak of rationality:

> The head of a research unit requests permission to review another research group's proposal in case she can add information to improve the project. Her covert intent is to maintain her current power which will be endangered if the other research group carries out the project. Using her informational power base, her covert means are to introduce irrelevant information and pose further questions. If she sufficiently confuses the issues, she can discredit the research group and prevent the project from being carried out. She covers these covert intents and means with the overt ones of improving the project and reviewing its content.[24]

Do political activities occur under particular conditions or in particular locations in organizations? Some tentative conclusions include the following:

- Managers report that most political maneuvering occurs among middle and upper management levels rather than at lower levels.

- Some subunits are more prone to politicking than others. Clear goals and routine tasks (e.g., production) may provoke less political activity than vague goals and complex tasks (e.g., research and development).

- Some issues are more likely than others to stimulate political activity. Budget allocation, reorganization, and personnel changes are likely to be the subjects of politicking. Setting performance standards and purchasing equipment are not.

- In general, scarce resources, uncertainty, and important issues provoke political behavior.[25]

Machiavellianism—The Harder Side of Politics

Have you ever known people in an organization or another social setting who had the following characteristics?

- Act very much in their own self-interest, even at the expense of others

- Cool and calculating, especially when others get emotional

- High self-esteem and self-confidence

- Form alliances with powerful people to achieve their goals

These are some of the characteristics of individuals who are high on a personality dimension known as Machiavellianism. **Machiavellianism** is a set of beliefs about human nature, morality, and the permissibility of using various tactics to achieve one's ends. The term derives from the sixteenth-century writings of the Italian civil servant Niccolo Machiavelli, who was concerned with how people achieve social influence and the ability to manipulate others. Psychologists have suggested that the degree of an individual's endorsement of the beliefs expressed by Machiavelli is representative of a stable psychological trait.

Compared with "low Machs," "high Machs" are more likely to advocate the use of lying and deceit to achieve desired goals and to argue that morality can be compromised to fit the situation in question. In addition, high Machs assume that many people are excessively gullible and do not know what is best for themselves. Thus, in interpersonal situations, the high Mach acts in an exceedingly practical manner, assuming that the ends justify the means. Not surprisingly, high Machs tend to be convincing liars and good at "psyching out" competitors by creating diversions. Furthermore, they are quite willing to form coalitions with others to outmaneuver or defeat those who get in their way.[26] In summary, high Machs are likely to be enthusiastic organizational politicians.[27]

This discussion of the Machiavellian personality trait probably raises two questions on your part. First, you might wonder, do high Machs feel *guilty* about the social tactics that they utilize? The answer would appear to be no. Since they are cool and calculating, rather than emotional, high Machs seem to be able to insulate themselves from the negative social consequences of their tactics. Secondly, you might wonder how *successful* high Machs are at manipulating others and why such manipulation would be tolerated by others. After all, the characteristics detailed above are hardly likely to win a popularity contest, and you might assume that targets of a high Mach's tactics would vigorously resist manipulation by such a person. Again, the high Mach's rationality seems to provide an answer to this question. Put simply, it appears that high Machs are able to accurately identify those situations where their favored tactics will work. Such situations have the following characteristics:

- The high Mach can deal with those to be influenced face-to-face.
- The interaction occurs under fairly emotional circumstances.
- The situation is fairly unstructured, with few guidelines for appropriate forms of interaction.[28]

In combination, these characteristics reveal a situation in which the high Mach can use his or her tactics because others are distracted by emotion. High Machs, by remaining calm and rational, can create a social structure that facilitates their personal goals at the expense of others. Thus, it would appear that high Machs are especially skilled at getting their way when power vacuums or novel situations confront a group, department, or organization. For example, imagine a small family-run manufacturing company whose president dies suddenly, and no special plans for succession have been made. In this power vacuum, a high Mach vice-president would have an excellent chance of manipulating the choice of a new president. The situation is novel, emotion-provoking, and unstructured, since no guidelines for succession exist. In addition, the decision-making body would be small enough for face-to-face influence and coalition formation.

Networking—The Softer Side of Politics

Only a small proportion of the population has the personality profile characteristic of the hardball Machiavellian politician. Despite this, political influence is often necessary to enable organizational members to achieve their goals, especially if these goals involve some degree of change or innovation. Thus, a more common and more subtle form of political behavior involves networking. **Networking** can be defined as establishing good relations with key organizational members and/or outsiders in order to accomplish one's goals. If these goals are beneficial to the organization, we can describe networking as functional political behavior. In essence, networking involves developing informal social contacts that can be used to enlist the cooperation of others when their support is necessary. Upper-level managers often establish very large political networks both inside and outside of the organization (see Exhibit 13-3). Lower-level organizational members might have a more restricted network, but the principle remains the same.

Some networking is a function of one's location in the organization's work flow and formal communication channels.[29] A key location provides the opportunity to interact with and establish influence over others. However, individuals can also pursue networking more aggressively. One study of general managers found that they used face-to-face encounters and informal small talk to bolster their political networks. They also did favors for others and stressed the obligations of others to them. Personnel were hired, fired, and transferred to bolster a workable network, and the managers forged connections *among* network members to create a climate conducive to goal accomplishment.[30]

The influence acquired by establishing a strong political network has great advantages for managers. Research shows that active networkers tend to be rated better performers and achieve more frequent promotions.[31]

In summary, politics, like power, is a natural occurrence in all organizations. Whether or not politics is functional for the organization depends upon which ends are pursued and which influence means are used.

CONFLICT BETWEEN INDIVIDUALS OR SUBUNITS

It is nearly impossible to discuss power and politics without considering conflict. For one thing, political maneuvering and the exercise of power are two of the many causes of conflict in organizations. Furthermore, power plays and politics often result as individuals or groups attempt to cope with conflict. In this chapter we are concerned with interpersonal conflict—conflict between persons or groups.

What Is Interpersonal Conflict?

Interpersonal conflict is a process of antagonism that occurs when one person or organizational subunit frustrates the goal attainment of another. Notice that

EXHIBIT 13-3   A typical general manager's network.

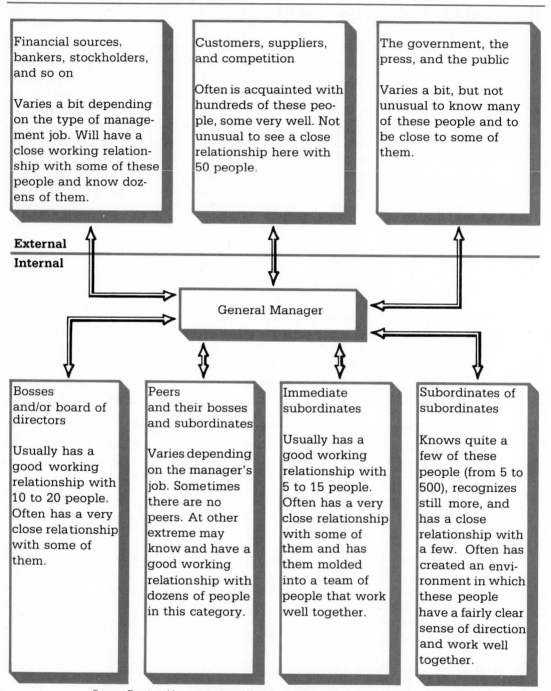

Financial sources, bankers, stockholders, and so on

Varies a bit depending on the type of management job. Will have a close working relationship with some of these people and know dozens of them.

Customers, suppliers, and competition

Often is acquainted with hundreds of these people, some very well. Not unusual to see a close relationship here with 50 people.

The government, the press, and the public

Varies a bit, but not unusual to know many of these people and to be close to some of them.

External

Internal

General Manager

Bosses and/or board of directors

Usually has a good working relationship with 10 to 20 people. Often has a very close relationship with some of them.

Peers and their bosses and subordinates

Varies depending on the manager's job. Sometimes there are no peers. At other extreme may know and have a good working relationship with dozens of people in this category.

Immediate subordinates

Usually has a good working relationship with 5 to 15 people. Often has a very close relationship with some of them and has them molded into a team of people that work well together.

Subordinates of subordinates

Knows quite a few of these people (from 5 to 500), recognizes still more, and has a close relationship with a few. Often has created an environment in which these people have a fairly clear sense of direction and work well together.

Source: Reprinted by permission of the *Harvard Business Review*. An exhibit from "What Effective General Managers Really Do," by John P. Kotter (November/December 1982). Copyright © 1982 by the President and Fellows of Harvard College; all rights reserved.

conflict can exist between individuals or between groups. The curator of a museum may be in conflict with the director over the purchase of a particular work of art. Likewise, the entire curatorial staff may be in conflict with the financial staff over cutbacks in acquisition funds.

Conflict involves the joint occurrence of antagonism and blocked goals. Antagonism may involve both attitudes and behaviors. As for attitudes, the conflicting parties may develop a dislike for each other, see each other as unreasonable, and develop negative stereotypes of their opposites. (''Those scientists should get out of the laboratory once in a while.'') Antagonistic behaviors may include name calling, sabotage, or even physical aggression. Frustrated goals often indicate that mutual assistance between the conflicting parties is low. Rather than aiding each other in goal attainment, each party views its loss as the other's gain. Thus, conflict is characterized by high antagonism and low mutual assistance.

Conflict, Collaboration, and Competition

It is useful to contrast conflict with two other processes of interaction, collaboration and competition (Exhibit 13-4). **Collaboration** exists when mutual assistance is high and antagonism is low. For instance, carpenters and electricians on a construction site may consult frequently to be sure that their work is sequenced in an optimal manner. Such collaboration should help both groups accomplish their work and prevent antagonism. As we shall see, organizations often attempt to stimulate collaboration to prevent or reduce conflict.

Competition exists when both mutual assistance and antagonism are low. Here, each party sees its loss as the other's gain, but this does not result in destructive attitudes or behavior. Sport probably provides the purest example of a competitive relationship. Although each tennis set or football game can have only one winner, and the opponents certainly don't attempt to help each other, hostility is the exception rather than the rule. Likewise, sales reps may compete for a quarterly sales prize without antagonism. Experience indicates that competitive relationships are delicate. When either party decides not to ''play by the rules,'' antagonism develops and competition deteriorates into conflict.[32] We have all seen ''bad blood'' develop between sports teams.

EXHIBIT 13-4   Relationships among conflict, competition, and collaboration.

	Conflict	Competition	Collaboration
Mutual Assistance	Low	Low	High
Antagonism	High	Low	Low

Since conflict is a process, we might expect to see it progress through a series of stages. We will consider the conflict process once some causes of conflict have been identified.

CAUSES OF ORGANIZATIONAL CONFLICT

It is possible to isolate a number of factors that contribute to organizational conflict. You should keep in mind that some of these factors may occur in combination.[33]

Interdependence

When individuals or subunits are mutually dependent upon each other to accomplish *their own* goals, the potential for conflict exists. For example, the sales staff is dependent upon the production department for the timely delivery of high-quality products. This is the only way sales can maintain the good will of its customers. On the other hand, production depends upon the sales staff to provide routine orders with adequate lead times. Custom-tailored emergency orders will wreak havoc with production schedules and make the production department look bad. In contrast, the sales staff and the office maintenance staff are not highly interdependent. Salespeople are on the road a lot and should not make great demands on maintenance. Conversely, a dirty office probably won't lose a sale!

Interdependence can set the stage for conflict for two reasons. First, it necessitates interaction between the parties so that they can coordinate their interests. Conflict will not develop if the parties can "go it alone." Secondly, as indicated at the beginning of the chapter, interdependence implies that each party has some *power* over the other. It is relatively easy for one side or the other to abuse its power and create antagonism.

It must be emphasized that interdependence does not *always* lead to conflict. In fact, it often provides a good basis for collaboration through mutual assistance. Whether or not interdependence prompts conflict depends upon the presence of other conditions which we will now consider.

Differences in Power, Status, and Culture

Conflict can erupt when parties differ significantly in power, status, or culture.

POWER.   If dependence is not mutual, but one way, the potential for conflict increases. If party A needs the collaboration of party B to accomplish its goals, but B does not need A's assistance, antagonism may develop. B has power over A, and A has nothing with which to bargain. A good example is the quality control system in many factories. Production workers may be highly dependent upon inspectors to approve their work, but this dependence is not reciprocated. The inspectors may have a separate boss, their own office, and their own circle of friends (other inspectors). In this case, production workers may begin to treat inspectors with hostility, one of the symptoms of conflict.

STATUS.   Status differences provide little impetus for conflict when those of lower status are dependent upon those of higher status. This is the way organizations are supposed to work, and most members are socialized to expect it. However, because of the design of the work, there are occasions when those with technically lower status find themselves giving orders to, or controlling the tasks of, higher-status persons. The restaurant business provides a good example. In many restaurants, lower status waiters and waitresses give orders and initiate queries to higher-status cooks or chefs. The latter may come to resent this reversal of usual lines of influence.[34] The advent of the ''electronic office'' may have led to similar kinds of conflict. As secretaries master the complexities of electronic word processing, they find themselves having to educate executives about the capabilities and limitations of such systems. Some executives are defensive about this reversal of roles.

At Bendix, it is reasonable to expect that some older male executives resented taking orders from twenty-nine-year-old Mary Cunningham.

CULTURE.   In Chapter 9 we discussed the concept of organizational culture, defining it as consisting of shared beliefs, values, and assumptions within an organization. When two or more very different cultures develop in an organization, the clash in beliefs, values, and assumptions may result in overt conflict. For example, hospital administrators who develop a strong culture centered on efficiency and cost-effectiveness may find themselves in conflict with physicians who share a strong culture based on providing excellent patient care at any cost. A telling case of cultural conflict occurred when Apple Computer expanded and hired professionals away from several companies with their own strong cultures:

> The newcomers brought their own strands and strains. During the first couple of years Apple recruited heavily from Hewlett-Packard, National Semiconductor, and Intel, and the habits and differences in style among these companies were reflected in Cupertino. There was a general friction between the rough and tough ways of the semiconductor men (there were few women) and the people who made computers, calculators, and instruments at Hewlett-Packard. . . . Some of the Hewlett-Packard men began to see themselves as civilizing influences and were horrified at the uncouth rough-and-tumble practices of the brutes from the semiconductor industry. . . . Many of the men from National Semiconductor and other stern backgrounds harbored a similar contempt for the Hewlett-Packard recruits. They came to look on them as prissy fusspots. They didn't question their professionalism; they just seemed to feel that they were too professional.[35]

Ambiguity

Ambiguous goals, jurisdictions, or performance criteria may lead to conflict. Under such ambiguity the formal and informal rules that govern interaction break down.

In addition, it may be difficult to accurately assign praise for good outcomes or blame for bad outcomes when it is hard to see who was responsible for what. For example, if sales drop following the introduction of a "new and improved" product, the design group may blame the marketing department for a poor advertising campaign. In response, the marketers may claim that the "improved" product is actually inferior to the old product. Obviously, it may be difficult to marshal evidence to prove who is correct.

Ambiguous jurisdictions are often revealed when new programs are introduced. This is a common occurrence in universities. For instance, the division of continuing education may initiate series of management development seminars that compete with those offered by the business school. Likewise, the political science department may wish to establish a master's degree in applied politics similar to a degree offered by the school of public administration. In both cases, charges of "poaching" are almost certain to occur.

Ambiguous performance criteria are a frequent cause of conflict between superiors and subordinates. The basic scientist who is charged by a chemical company to "discover new knowledge" may react negatively when her boss informs her that her work is inadequate. This rather open-ended assignment is susceptible to a variety of interpretations.

At Bendix Corporation, ambiguity occurred as the company shifted into the high technology field and changed its organizational structure. This promoted conflict, some of which affected William Agee and Mary Cunningham.

Scarcity

Earlier, it was pointed out that differences in power are magnified when resources become scarce. This does not occur without a battle, however, and conflict often surfaces in the process of power jockeying. Limited budget money, secretarial support, or computer time can contribute to conflict. Consider the company that installs a new computer which is to be used for administrative and research purposes. At first, there is plenty of computer time and space for both uses. However, as both factions make more and more use of the computer, access becomes a problem. Conflict may erupt at this point.

Scarcity has a way of turning latent or disguised conflict into overt conflict. Two scientists who don't get along very well may be able to put up a peaceful front until a reduction in laboratory space provokes each to protect his domain.

In conclusion, interdependence, ambiguity, scarcity, and differences in power, status, and culture can contribute to conflict. See if you can see these factors at work in In–Focus 13-3.

THE CONFLICT PROCESS

Earlier, it was pointed out that conflict is a process. This means that a number of events occur when one or more of the causes of conflict noted above takes effect.

We will assume here that the conflict in question occurs between groups, such as organizational departments. However, much of this is also relevant to conflict between individuals. Specifically, when conflict begins we often see the following events transpire:

- "Winning" the conflict becomes more important than developing a good solution to the problem at hand.

- The parties begin to conceal information from each other, or to pass distorted information.

- Each group becomes more cohesive. Deviants who speak of conciliation are punished, and strict conformity is expected.

- Contact with the opposite party is discouraged except under formalized, restricted conditions.

- While the opposite party is negatively stereotyped, the image of one's own position is boosted.

- On each side, more aggressive persons who are skilled at engaging in conflict may emerge as leaders.[36]

You can certainly see the difficulty here. What begins as a problem of inter-dependence, ambiguity, or scarcity quickly escalates to the point that the conflict process *itself* becomes an additional problem. The elements of this process then work against the achievement of a peaceful solution. The conflict continues to cycle "on its own steam."

IS ALL CONFLICT BAD?

In everyday life, there has traditionally been an emphasis on the negative, dysfunctional aspects of conflict. This is not difficult to understand. Discord between parents and children, severe labor strife, and international disputes are unpleasant experiences. To some degree, this emphasis on the negative aspects of conflict is also characteristic of thinking in the area of organizational behavior. Recently, though, there has been growing awareness of the potential *benefits* of organizational conflict.

Further reflection on the conflict process presented above demonstrates why it is often dysfunctional for both the organization and its members. From the organization's standpoint, conflict may waste an excessive amount of time and energy, diverting people from their jobs. In fact, parties may collaborate briefly to conceal their conflict from organizational agents so that they can continue to fight without censure! In general, the excessive self-interest that characterizes conflict seems to work against the very reason organizations are formed. From the individual's perspective, severe conflict may lead to stress. Pressures for conformity and the spectre of "losing" may take a personal toll.

The argument that conflict can be functional rests mainly on the idea that it promotes necessary organizational change. One advocate of this position puts it this way:

$$\text{CONFLICT} \rightarrow \text{CHANGE} \rightarrow \text{ADAPTATION} \rightarrow \text{SURVIVAL}[37]$$

In other words, for organizations to survive they must adapt to their environments. This requires changes in strategy that may be stimulated through conflict. For example, consider the museum that relies heavily upon government funding and consistently mounts exhibits that are appreciated only by "true connoisseurs" of art. Under a severe funding cutback, the museum can survive only if it begins to mount more popular exhibits. Such a change may only occur after much conflict within the board of directors.

Just how does conflict promote change? For one thing, it may bring into consideration new ideas which would not be offered without conflict. In trying to "one up" the opponent, one of the parties may develop a unique idea that the other can't fail to appreciate. In a related way, conflict may promote change because each party begins to monitor the other's performance more carefully. This search for weaknesses means that it is more difficult to hide errors and problems from the rest of the organization. Such errors and problems (e.g., a failure to make deliveries on time) may be a signal that changes are necessary. Finally, conflict may promote useful change by signaling that a redistribution of power is necessary. Consider the personnel department which must battle with managers to get antidiscrimination programs implemented. This conflict may be a clue that some change is due in power priorities.[38]

The conclusion we can draw is that some conflict is functional and some is dysfunctional. This indicates that conflict in organizations must be properly *managed*.

CONFLICT MANAGEMENT STRATEGIES

The previous section suggests that there are circumstances when conflict should be resolved and others when conflict should be stimulated. Let's examine these two basic conflict management strategies in turn.

Conflict Resolution

A large number of strategies for interpersonal **conflict resolution** have been suggested.[39] Although each may be effective in certain situations, several have little to recommend them because they fail to get at the *source* of the conflict. For example, a manager may issue a directive for warring parties to cease conflict or make a slightly more sophisticated attempt to smooth over conflict by emphasizing common interests. In each case, the source of the conflict remains, and the parties may simply respond by concealing or disguising their conflict behaviors.

Other resolution strategies have the potential to be effective but may be very difficult to implement. For example, the conflicting parties can attempt to withdraw from each other, effectively avoiding further hostile behavior. Unfortunately, this option is seldom available because interdependence and required interaction caused the conflict in the first place! Also, if a conflict is prompted by the demand for scarce resources, the manager can attempt to expand these resources. Again, however, this reasonable idea may be impossible to implement.

Several other resolution strategies seem to have the potential to affect the sources of conflict while not involving severe problems of implementation. These include compromise, problem solving, and the introduction of superordinate goals.

COMPROMISE.   **Compromise** is a form of "horse trading" in which each party gives up something with the expectation that it will receive something in exchange. In effect, its goal is to establish *rules of exchange* to resolve conflict. Thus, compromise can be an effective means of resolving conflict stimulated by scarce resources. On the other hand, it should not be useful for resolving conflicts that stem from power asymmetry, because the weaker party has little to offer the stronger party. Effective compromises are obviously highly dependent on the bargaining skills and the good will of the bargainers.[40]

Compromise might be used to resolve the traditional conflict that can develop between sales and production. The sales manager and the production superintendent might be asked to develop a set of guidelines for salespeople to use in making promises to customers. These guidelines could include provisions for volume of merchandise, delivery lead times, and custom-tailored orders.

PROBLEM SOLVING.   Problem solving is an attempt to move from conflict to collaboration. It differs from compromise in that the parties are encouraged to *integrate* their needs so that both are fully satisfied. There is no assumption that something must be lost in the process. Rather, it is assumed that the solution to the conflict problem will leave each party in better condition. Problem solving probably works best when the conflict is not intense and when each party has information that is useful to the other. In addition, one expert suggests that several beliefs are helpful in stimulating problem solving:

- A mutually acceptable decision is desirable.
- Differences of opinion are valuable.
- People are essentially equals despite differences in knowledge, attitudes, and status.
- Others can be trusted.
- The other party has the ability to continue the conflict but has chosen to attempt collaboration.[41]

Obviously, an effective problem-solving effort may take time and practice to develop. However, its success should be self-reinforcing. Research evidence suggests that cooperation through problem solving frequently enhances productivity and achievement.[42]

SUPERORDINATE GOALS.   Superordinate goals are attractive outcomes that can only be achieved by collaboration.[43] Neither party to a conflict can attain the goal on its own. In a sense, superordinate goals require a problem-solving orientation. However, their introduction may be especially useful when conflict is so extreme that the parties use normal problem-solving meetings only as an excuse to attack each other.

An excellent example of the imposition of a superordinate goal occurred in the Chrysler Corporation in 1980. With the prospect of bankruptcy and massive unemployment looming large, the United Auto Workers and Chrysler management collaborated on developing a scheme for keeping the company afloat. On a different scale, a feud between police detectives and uniformed officers might be put aside to pool information to solve a series of murders.

You will observe that a superordinate goal does not really change the underlying cause of the conflict. However, research suggests that the conflict may remain resolved even after the goal is achieved. In addition, the failure to achieve a superordinate goal does not seem to make the existing conflict worse.[44]

Conflict Stimulation

Earlier, it was pointed out that conflict may be necessary to cause needed changes in the organization. This suggests that there are times when administrators will wish to *stimulate* conflict rather than reduce it. The implicit assumption here is that the strategy of **conflict stimulation** will result in changes that benefit the organization.

How does the manager know when some conflict might be a good thing? One signal is the existence of a "friendly rut," in which peaceful relationships take precedence over organizational goals. Another signal is seen when parties that should be interacting closely have chosen to withdraw from each other to avoid overt conflict. A third signal occurs when conflict is suppressed or downplayed by denying differences, ignoring controversy, and exaggerating points of agreement.[45]

The idea of intentionally stimulating conflict has received little research attention. However, logic suggests that the causes of conflict discussed earlier could be manipulated by managers to achieve change.[46] A few examples will suffice to make the point:

■ *Scarcity.* The president and the controller of a manufacturing company felt that the budgets allocated to various departments were not a good reflection of changing priorities. They introduced a zero-base budget that required all departments to justify their needs regardless of past allocations. Since the departments were required to compete for a scarce resource, considerable conflict developed. It was agreed that this conflict helped promote needed changes in funding emphasis.

■ *Status differences.* The dean of a business school appointed a low-status assistant professor as director of a lethargic M.B.A. program. The "old guard" professors who staffed the program resented having to answer to the new director. In order to assert their superiority, they suggested a series of changes that revitalized the program.

■ *Ambiguity.* The director of a medical research laboratory was very unhappy with the lack of coordination among the lab's research projects. The position of assistant director was opening up because of a retirement, and the director gave contradictory, ambiguous signals about who might be promoted to the job. This led to conflict, which magnified the lack of coordination so much that the researchers held a series of meetings to resolve the problem.

SUMMARY

■ Power is the capacity to influence others who are in a state of dependence. Individuals have power by virtue of their position in the organization (legitimate power) or by virtue of the resources they command (reward, coercion, friendship, or expertise).

■ Organizational members can obtain power by doing the right things and cultivating the right people. Activities that lead to power acquisition need to be extraordinary, visible, and relevant to the needs of the organization. People to be cultivated include outsiders, subordinates, peers, and superiors. Managers with high need for power are effective when they use this power to achieve organizational goals.

■ Organizational subunits obtain power by controlling strategic contingencies. This means that they are able to affect events critical to *other* subunits. Thus, departments that can obtain resources for the organization will acquire power. Similarly, subunits gain power when they are able to reduce uncertainty for the organization, when their function is central to the work flow, and when their tasks can't be performed by other subunits or outside contractors.

■ Organizational politics occurs when influence means not sanctioned by the organization are used or when nonsanctioned ends are pursued. The pursuit of nonsanctioned ends is always dysfunctional, but the organization may benefit when nonsanctioned means are used to achieve approved goals. Machiavellian tactics represent an extreme form of politics, while networking represents a subtle form.

■ Interpersonal conflict is a process of antagonism that occurs when one person or subunit frustrates the goal attainment of another. Causes of conflict include high interdependence, ambiguous jurisdictions, scarce resources, and differences in power, status, and culture.

■ Conflict management includes both resolution and stimulation. One resolution tactic is compromise, in which each party agrees to make a sacrifice in exchange for some benefit. Another is problem solving, in which both parties work to effect a solution that meets their needs with no sacrifice. Finally, superordinate goals that are attractive but not obtainable without collaboration may be introduced.

■ Conflict stimulation generally involves manipulating those factors that are known to cause conflict. This might involve making resources less available or increasing ambiguity.

KEY CONCEPTS

Power	Networking
Legitimate power	Interpersonal conflict
Reward power	Collaboration
Coercive power	Competition
Referent power	Conflict resolution
Expert power	Compromise
Subunit power	Problem solving
Strategic contingencies	Superordinate goals
Organizational politics	Conflict stimulation
Machiavellianism	

DISCUSSION QUESTIONS

1. Contrast the bases of power available to an army sergeant with those available to the president of a voluntary community association. How would these differences in power bases affect their influence tactics?

2. Are the bases of individual power easily substitutable for each other? Are they equally effective? For example, can coercive power substitute for expert power?

3. Present a profile of someone who acquires power in an organization. What activities does he or she pursue? What relationships does he or she cultivate?

4. Imagine that you are on a committee at work or in a group working on a project at school that includes a "high Mach" member. What could you do to neutralize the high Mach's attempts to manipulate the group?

5. Discuss the conditions under which the following subunits of an organization might gain or lose power: Legal department; research and development unit; public relations department. Use the concepts of scarcity, uncertainty, centrality, and substitutability in your answers.

6. Differentiate between power and politics. Give an example of the use of power that is not political.

7. It has been said that, "Politics is a way of life in organizations." Do your agree? Is political activity necessary for organizations to function?

8. Suppose two accounting majors are hired right out of college by an accounting firm. Being in a new and unfamiliar environment, they quickly develop a collaborative relationship, helping each other with work assignments and so on. What factors could turn this collaboration into competition? What factors could turn the competition into open conflict?

9. The manager of a fast food restaurant observes that conflict among the staff is damaging service. How might he or she implement a superordinate goal to reduce this conflict?

10. Describe a situation you have observed where conflict stimulation had a beneficial outcome. How was the conflict stimulated? Why was the conflict ultimately beneficial?

FOR FURTHER READING

Allen, R. W., & Porter, L. W. (Eds.) (1983). *Organizational influence processes*. Glenview, IL: Scott, Foresman.

    A collection of articles on power and politics in organizations. Separate sections on upward influence, downward influence, and lateral influence.

Cobb, A. T. (1984). An episodic model of power: Toward an integration of theory and research. *Academy of Management Review, 9*, 482–493.

    Presents a model that examines the operation of power over a period of time. Moves from antecedent conditions to the power episode to the aftermath of the episode.

Cunningham, M. (with F. Schumer). (1985). *Powerplay: What really happened at Bendix.* New York: Fawcett.

> Mary Cunningham's own story about the case that began the chapter. Filled with examples of power, politics, and conflict.

Special section. (1978, Winter). Conflict and the collaborative ethic. *California Management Review,* 56–95.

> Contains six overview articles about conflict in organizations. Covers definitions, resolution, stimulation, and the relation of conflict to other organizational processes.

Case Study

Managing the Marketing Department

Richard Walsh's first career had been that of a researcher for a small Midwestern market research firm. He had begun this job with a fresh M.B.A. degree, dividing his time between working long hours, getting married, and beginning a family. At the research firm Walsh was recognized as bright and competent, but he was also seen as somewhat arrogant and egotistical. Walsh liked to flaunt his intellect, and he frequently strung multisyllabic words together as if he were an Oxford University don. He prided himself on keeping up with the latest marketing research techniques emanating from the top universities, and he frequently gave rambling lectures about the virtues or vices of some new technique to the perplexed staff of the firm.

At the age of thirty-seven Richard Walsh made a radical career change. Selling the family home, he and his family moved to the East Coast, and he enrolled in a Ph.D. program at a university with a reasonable reputation. The move had been carefully planned, and the family lived in a small rented apartment and conserved resources to support Richard's endeavor. As a graduate student he was perceived as fairly intelligent, but argumentative. After three and one half years Walsh received his Ph.D. degree and took a job as an assistant professor at Collins College. He felt that he could have gone to a much more prestigious school, but he told friends that his wife and children really wanted to return to the Midwest. "Besides, I'll build that place into a powerhouse or else move on to Stanford," he laughed.

When Richard arrived at Collins College, the dean of the business school immediately appointed him coordinator of the marketing area. At the time, faculty at Collins were organized by teaching areas and not separated into formal departments. There were only two other marketing professors, both older individuals who did not hold Ph.D.s, and the dean was eager to put Ph.D.s in the coordination positions to take advantage of their more recent university experience for curriculum development. Both of Walsh's senior colleagues were happy to be relieved of the coordination job, since it cut into their consulting time, and were very supportive of their new colleague.

Richard took to the coordinator's job with relish. He updated many course descriptions and introduced two new courses in his specialty, marketing research. In addition, he revised the scheduling of the marketing courses, taking pains to incorporate the time preferences of his two senior colleagues. Richard quickly acquired a reputation as an effective if long-winded speaker at faculty meetings, where he showed an impressive command of the language. During his first three years at Collins his prestige among the faculty was aided considerably by the publication of several works from his Ph.D. dissertation. Two of these were technical notes in prestigious marketing journals and the other was a monograph put out by an obscure New York publisher. Since the publication efforts of Collins faculty were almost nil, this activity was noticed. Privately, Richard's two marketing colleagues described the monograph as brilliant, although both admitted they really didn't understand it very well.

Richard's fourth year at Collins was an important one for him. He was promoted to associate professor, received tenure, and was appointed chairperson of the newly formed marketing department. The business school at Collins was going to be expanded, and the dean felt that formal departments would be necessary as the school grew in size. Richard's appointment was enthusiastically supported by his two older colleagues, who had consistently deferred to his judgment during his years as coordinator.

The key task of the new department chairpersons was to hire additional faculty and to make decisions about the renewal of their contracts. Previously, these tasks had been performed directly by the dean. The dean was particularly interested in increasing the research and publication output of the business school, and Richard readily agreed. "After all," he said, "I'm the only person around here publishing in the top journals. We need more of that."

During the next few years, Collins's chairpersons were generally successful in recruiting new faculty. Most departments hired new Ph.D.s or individuals in the very last stages of their doctoral dissertations. Although they were not from exceptional schools, most turned out to be good teachers and active researchers and publishers. Gradually, the reputation of the Collins business school was increasing.

In the marketing department, Richard Walsh employed a somewhat different recruiting strategy. He tended to hire Ph.D. students who were in the very early phases of their dissertations. They were usually from the better schools, and Richard said that they had great potential for building an "intellectual core" in the department. His senior marketing colleagues agreed. When someone asked Richard how he managed to attract people from the better schools to the relatively modest Collins campus he replied that he looked for those who were "poverty stricken." "You'd be surprised what a job offer will do to a poor graduate student with a whole dissertation to complete," he grinned.

Some of the new marketing faculty complained that their teaching loads were heavier than they had expected, and that Richard had been vague about this when they were being recruited. In the other departments new recruits were given a reprieve from committees so that they could devote their time to getting their teaching and research off to a good start. Richard, on the other hand, assigned new recruits to several committees so that they could "get the feel of the college."

Over the years, successive new recruits in marketing experienced considerable difficulty in completing their dissertations. Although some surreptitiously looked for jobs elsewhere, they soon learned that it was difficult to obtain another position without

having finished their Ph.D.s. Richard was very sympathetic to their difficulties, and he frequently recounted the privations he and his family had endured during his graduate study. In addition, he was always willing to provide frank and lengthy critiques of the dissertation work they had accomplished.

New recruits were hired under two-year contracts, and a decision was made early in the second year as to whether they would be renewed for another two years. Although the chairpersons had the final say in this matter, it was standard practice in all departments to convene a department meeting to evaluate those up for renewal and to vote on renewal decisions. At the first renewal meeting for each candidate, Richard spoke forcefully in favor of contract renewal, citing his or her "great potential." Consistently, the two senior members agreed with Richard, as did the junior members (who were often in the same boat as the person on whom they were voting). Thus, over the years, first renewals occurred in spite of incomplete dissertations.

Second renewal decisions were made early in a faculty member's fourth year at Collins. By this time, most had completed their dissertations or were very close to doing so. Richard's approach to second renewal decisions varied considerably from that used in first renewal decisions. Typically, he began second-renewal meetings with an eloquent speech about maintaining the quality of the department and increasing its research and publication efforts. "After all," he said, "we don't want to end up granting tenure to someone who will never publish anything." Invariably, those up for renewal had achieved no publications, and Richard spoke against their renewal. His senior colleagues always agreed, as did all of the junior members who were awaiting their own first renewal decisions. This group consistently carried the vote, and no junior member lasted more than four years in the Collins marketing department.

Jack Ross, dean of the school of business at Collins, sat in his office and wondered what to do about the marketing department. During his reign as dean, Ross felt that he had generally been successful in increasing the quality of the school. However, he had gradually come to see the marketing department as a weak link in the chain. Although marketing had hired some promising people, turnover was high because of nonrenewals, and publication productivity was low. Even Richard Walsh hadn't published anything since his success years ago.

Recently, a delegation of the other chairpersons had complained to Ross that their departments were not receiving enough travel money to cover the presentation of research papers at learned conferences. They had implied (though not said directly) that the marketing department received too much travel money. Ross knew that almost all of marketing's travel allocation was spent by Richard Walsh, who frequently attended conferences for recruiting purposes. However, the dean had begun to wonder about Walsh's recruiting strategy. For years, he had been unable to hire anyone in his own specialty, marketing research, even though another person in this area was desperately needed. Furthermore, Walsh never seemed to follow up on leads provided by the dean for experienced, well-published marketing professors who might be attracted to Collins.

Jack Ross worried about what he should say to Richard Walsh.

■ ■ ■

1. Is power an issue in *Managing the Marketing Department?* If so, who has power over whom?
2. What bases of individual power does Richard Walsh command?
3. How did Richard Walsh acquire the power he holds?
4. Why did Richard Walsh engage in his unique hiring and contract renewal strategy? What are his motives? Is he a Machiavellian?
5. Is there evidence of organizational politics in the case? Defend your answer.
6. Is conflict an issue in this case? Explain your answer.
7. What should Dean Ross do about the marketing department?

REFERENCES

1. This case is based on two sources: Bernstein, P. B. (1980, November 3). Upheaval at Bendix. *Fortune,* 48–56; Sheehy, G. (1980, October 30). Gossip undoes top corporate woman. *The Gazette* (Montreal), p. 45.

2. Cohen, P. (1973). *The gospel according to the Harvard Business School.* New York: Penguin, p. 302.

3. Provan, K. G. (1980). Recognizing, measuring, and interpreting the potential/enacted power distinction in organizational research. *Academy of Management Review, 5,* 549–559.

4. These descriptions of bases of power were developed by French, J. R. P., Jr., & Raven, B. (1959). In D. Cartwright (Ed.), *Studies in social power.* Ann Arbor, MI: Institute for Social Research.

5. Student, K. R. (1968). Supervisory influence and work group performance. *Journal of Applied Psychology, 52,* 188–194; Tannenbaum, A. S. (1974). *Hierarchy in organizations.* San Francisco: Jossey-Bass.

6. Vaughn, R. (1975). *The spoiled system.* New York: Charterhouse, p. 19.

7. Student, 1968; Bachman, J. G., Bowers, D. G., & Marcus, P. M. (1968). Bases of supervisory power: A comparative study in five organizational settings. In A. S. Tannenbaum (Ed.), *Control in organizations.* New York: McGraw-Hill.

8. Heider, F. (1958). *The psychology of interpersonal relations.* New York: Wiley.

9. Student, 1968; Bachman et al., 1968.

10. The following is based upon Kanter, R. M. (1977). *Men and women of the corporation.* New York: Basic Books.

11. Kipnis, D. (1976). *The powerholders.* Chicago: University of Chicago Press.

12. Some observers, such as Kipnis (1976), feel that all power seekers are motivated by some form of perceived weakness. I disagree.

13. McClelland, D.C. (1975). *Power: The inner experience*. New York: Irvington.
14. McClelland, D. C., & Burnham, D. H. (1976, March–April). Power is the great motivator. *Harvard Business Review*, 100–110.
15. Salancik, G. R., & Pfeffer, J. (1977, Winter). Who gets power—and how they hold on to it: A strategic contingency model of power. *Organizational Dynamics, 3*, 3–21.
16. Salancik, G. R., & Pfeffer, J. (1974). The bases and use of power in organizational decision making: The case of a university. *Administrative Science Quarterly, 19*, 453–473. Also see Pfeffer, J., & Moore, W. L. (1980). Power in university budgeting: A replication and extension. *Administrative Science Quarterly, 25*, 637–653. For conditions under which the power thesis breaks down see Schick, A. G., Birch, J. B., & Tripp, R. E. (1986). Authority and power in university decision making: The case of a university personnel budget. *Canadian Journal of Administrative Sciences, 3*, 41–64.
17. Hickson, D. J., Hinings, C. R., Lee, C. A., Schneck, R. E., & Pennings, J. M. (1971). A strategic contingency theory of intraorganizational power. *Administrative Science Quarterly, 16*, 216–229; For support of this theory see Hinings, C. R., Hickson, D. J., Pennings, J. M., & Schneck, R. E. (1974). Structural conditions of intraorganizational power. *Administrative Science Quarterly, 19*, 22–44; Saunders, C. S., & Scamell, R. (1982). Intraorganizational distributions of power: Replication research. *Academy of Management Journal, 25*, 192–200; Hambrick, D.C. (1981). Environment, strategy, and power within top management teams. *Administrative Science Quarterly, 26*, 253–276.
18. Kanter, 1977, pp. 170–171.
19. Hickson et al., 1971; Hinings et al., 1974.
20. Hickson et al., 1971; Hinings et al., 1974. Saunders & Scamell, 1982.
21. Kipnis, 1976, p. 159.
22. Mayes, B. T., & Allen, R. W. (1977). Toward a definition of organizational politics. *Academy of Management Review, 2*, 672–678, p. 675.
23. Porter, L. W., Allen, R. W., & Angle, H. L. (1981). The politics of upward influence in organizations. *Research in Organizational Behavior, 3*, 109–149.
24. Schein, V. E., (1977). Individual power and political behaviors in organizations: An inadequately explored reality. *Academy of Management Review, 2*, 64–72, p. 67.
25. Porter et al., 1981; Madison, D. L., Allen, R. W., Porter, L. W., Renwick, P. A., & Mayes, B. T. (1980). Organizational politics: An exploration of managers' perceptions. *Human Relations, 33*, 79–100.
26. Geis, F., & Christie, R. (1970). Overview of experimental research. In R. Christie & F. Geis (Eds.), *Studies in Machiavellianism*. New York: Academic Press.
27. See Ralston, D. A. (1985). Employee ingratiation: The role of management. *Academy of Management Review, 10*, 477–487.
28. Geis & Christie, 1970.
29. Brass, D. J. (1984). Being in the right place: A structural analysis of individual influence in an organization. *Administrative Science Quarterly, 29*, 518–539.
30. Kotter, J. P. (1982). *The general managers*. New York: Free Press.
31. Kotter, 1982; Luthans, F., Rosenkrantz, S. A., & Hennessey, H. W. (1985). What do successful managers really do? An observation study of managerial activities. *Journal of Applied Behavioral Science, 21*, 255–270.
32. For a discussion of the relationship between rules and conflict see Thomas, K. (1976). Conflict and conflict management. In M. D. Dunnette (Ed.), *Handbook of industrial and organizational psychology*. Chicago: Rand McNally. Also see Katz, D., & Kahn, R. L. (1978). *The social psychology of organizations* (2nd ed.). New York: Wiley.

33. This section relies heavily on Walton, R.E., & Dutton, J. M. (1969). The management of interdepartmental conflict: A model and review. *Administrative Science Quarterly, 14,* 73–84.

34. See Whyte, W. F. (1948). *Human relations in the restaurant industry.* New York: McGraw-Hill.

35. Moritz, M. (1984). *The little kingdom: The private story of Apple Computer.* New York: Morrow, pp. 246–247.

36. See Sherif, M. (1966). *In common predicament: Social psychology of intergroup conflict and cooperation.* Boston: Houghton Mifflin; Blake, R. R., Shepard, H. A., & Mouton, J. S. (1964). *Managing intergroup conflict in industry.* Houston: Gulf; Walton, R. E. (1966). Theory of conflict in lateral organizational relationships. In J. R. Lawrence (Ed.), *Operational research and the social sciences.* London: Tavistock.

37. Robbins, S. P. (1974). *Managing organizational conflict: A nontraditional approach.* Englewood Cliffs, NJ: Prentice-Hall, p. 20.

38. For other advantages of conflict see Thomas, 1976.

39. See Robbins, 1974, and Filley, A. C. (1975). *Interpersonal conflict resolution.* Glenview, IL: Scott, Foresman.

40. For a review of bargaining tactics see MacCrimmon, K. R., & Taylor, R. N. Decision making and problem solving, in Dunnette, 1976. Also see Bazerman, M. H., & Lewicki, R. J. (Eds.) (1983). *Negotiating in organizations.* Beverly Hills, CA: Sage.

41. Filley, 1975.

42. Johnson, D. W., Maruyama, G., Johnson, R., Nelson, D., & Skon, L. (1981). Effects of cooperative, competitive, and individualistic goal structures on achievement: A meta-analysis. *Psychological Bulletin, 89,* 47–62.

43. Sherif, 1966.

44. Hunger, J. D., & Stern, L. W. (1976). An assessment of the functionality of the superordinate goal in reducing conflict. *Academy of Management Journal, 19,* 591–605.

45. Brown, L. D. (1983). *Managing conflict at organizational interfaces.* Reading, MA: Addison-Wesley.

46. Robbins, 1974; Also see Brown, 1983.

Chapter 14

Stress

ALAN WINDSOR

At the age of twenty-eight, Alan Windsor graduated from a prestigious Eastern university with a Master of Business Administration degree. As one of the best students majoring in marketing, Alan received a number of job offers from the nation's top advertising agencies, and after much deliberation he chose a position in New York City. For a period of two years Alan directed a number of marketing research studies and contributed many successful ideas to various account executives' advertising plans. Because of his excellent performance, Alan was offered a position as an account executive. Although he enjoyed the technical aspects of market research, he realized that the account executive job was the "fast track" through the organization and he accepted it. More than anything, Alan wanted to succeed in the new position. The following months proved both painful and educational for Alan. Put simply, he was an exceedingly *shy* individual who found it difficult to establish new interpersonal relationships. When Alan had first started with the organization, his co-workers and superiors had noticed this quality, but it seemed to wear off as he became acquainted with the staff. However, the account executive job required him to entertain potential clients and sell them on his ideas, and this proved very difficult. Most problematic were the crucial presentations of a completed advertising campaign proposal to "strangers" from a client organization. In these meetings, Alan stuttered badly and was generally unconvincing. Although the proposals were considered technically excellent by Ann Howe, Alan's superior, she was convinced that his inability to establish rapport with clients was responsible for his failure to land several important accounts. This situation was very threatening for Alan, who became more and more hostile toward his support personnel, often blaming them for the failure of his proposals. Alan eventually resigned to accept a marketing research position with a major producer of food products. During the job interview, he had been happy to learn that the new position would require a fairly narrow and stable range of interactions solely within the company.

Alan Windsor accepted a new assignment that was incompatible with his personality and experienced considerable stress as a result. In this chapter we will explore the phenomenon of stress in organizations. First, a model of a stress episode will be presented and dissected in some detail. Particular attention will be paid to the causes of stress at various points in organizations and to the consequences stress can have for the individual and the organization. Finally, some strategies for reducing organizational stress will be considered.

STRESS IN ORGANIZATIONS—A PROLOGUE

It is easy to imagine situations that must surely prove stressful for organizational members. Hockey players battling for the Stanley Cup, the White House staff during the Irangate scandal, and personnel working in power plants during nuclear accidents have obviously been exposed to elevated levels of tension. However, these dramatic cases should not obscure the fact that stress is part of the everyday routine of organizations. We often experience stress-provoking situations outside of organizations, and it would be naive to assume that things are different behind organizational walls. In fact, many individuals are employed by organizations primarily for their ability to respond effectively to stressful conditions. Police officers, fire fighters, and hospital emergency room personnel all seem to occupy positions that are thought of as stressful. Even apparently routine jobs can provide stress when the routine becomes unbearable or when a minor change in the routine is implemented. Some teachers may experience stress when required to teach the same course year after year, while others may experience stress when asked to teach a new course. (See In–Focus 14-1).

A MODEL OF ORGANIZATIONAL STRESS

The story that began the chapter provides an example of a typical stress episode that can serve as a prototype for our subsequent discussion. We can divide this episode into three key stages:

1. Alan Windsor assumed a new position in the advertising agency that was incompatible with his personality (*stressor*).

2. Alan was unable to achieve his goal of performing well as an account executive and experienced considerable anxiety (*stress*).

3. Alan blamed his support staff for his problem but set out to find a job that was compatible with his personality (*stress reactions*).

A model of a stress episode is shown in Exhibit 14-1.

Stressors

Stressors are environmental events or conditions that have the potential to induce stress. As we shall see shortly, organizational stressors might include the nature of a person's job, the organizational setting in which the job is performed, and the people encountered at work. In Alan Windsor's case, the job itself proved to be the key stressor. The requirement for him to interact with clients was the beginning of his problem. There are probably some conditions which would prove stressful for just about everyone. These include things like extreme heat, extreme cold, isolation, or the presence of hostile others. More interesting is the fact that the individual personality often determines the extent to which a potential stressor becomes a real stressor and actually induces stress. Thus, Alan's shyness led him to *interpret* his new position as stress-provoking. Evidently, the same job requirements did not serve as stressors for other account executives with different personality makeups.

Stress

Stress is a psychological reaction to the demands inherent in a stressor that has the potential to make a person feel tense or anxious, because the person does not feel capable of coping with these demands.[1] As we shall see shortly, stress can be

EXHIBIT 14-1   **Model of a stress episode.**

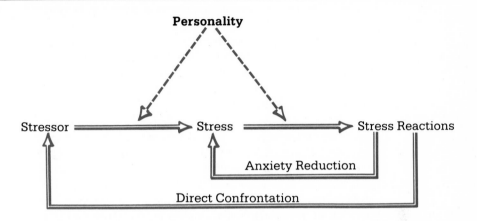

divided into feelings of frustration and conflict. Although Alan Windsor probably experienced both forms of stress, the key one would appear to be frustration, the blocking of an important goal. He wanted to be successful in fulfilling the demands of his new job, but he felt incapable of doing so.

It should be understood that stress is not intrinsically bad. All individuals require a certain level of stimulation from their environment, and moderate levels of stress can serve this function. In fact, one would wonder about the perceptual accuracy of a person who *never* experienced frustration or conflict. On the other hand, stress does become a problem when it leads to especially high levels of anxiety and tension. People reveal individual differences in their ability to *tolerate* stress. Despite his shyness, Alan Windsor had a high need for achievement, and this need evidently led to great anxiety in response to his frustration. An equally frustrated individual with lower need for achievement might have been much less anxious.

Stress Reactions

Stress reactions are the behavioral, psychological, and physiological consequences of stress. Some of these reactions are essentially passive responses over which the individual has little direct control, such as elevated blood pressure or the development of stomach ulcers. Other reactions are active attempts to *cope* with some previous aspect of the stress episode. Exhibit 14-1 indicates that stress reactions that involve coping attempts might be directed toward dealing directly with the stressor or simply reducing the anxiety generated by stress. In general, the former strategy has more potential for effectiveness than the latter because the chances of the stress episode being *terminated* are increased.[2] The executive under extreme pressure to complete a difficult report by Friday will do well to work on the report. This activity confronts the stressor directly, and it should terminate the stress episode. On the other hand, "throwing a drunk" may temporarily reduce anxiety, but it would not end the stress episode—the report is still due by Friday. Again, notice that personality characteristics often intervene between the experience of stress and the enactment of stress reactions. For example, individuals who usually feel that self-initiative, personal actions, and free will determine their behavior tend to confront stressors directly. Those who habitually feel that fate, luck, and chance determine what happens to them are more prone to simple anxiety-reduction strategies.[3]

You will observe that Alan Windsor used a mixed coping strategy for dealing with the stress episode he encountered. Blaming his support staff probably temporarily reduced his anxiety and made him feel a little better. Seeking out and accepting a new job directly confronted the stressor (the account executive job requirements) and terminated the stress cycle. Later we will discuss a number of stress reactions typical of organizational stress episodes.

Often, reactions that are useful for the individual in dealing with a stress episode may be very costly to the organization. The individual who is conveniently absent from work on the day of a difficult inventory check may prevent personal stress but leave the organization short-handed (provoking stress in others). This simple example shows that organizations should be interested in the stress that individual employees experience. Stress is *motivational,* and the organization will not always benefit from the reactions that stress motivates.

Personality and Stress

In the previous sections we have noted in a general sense how personality can intervene to influence the extent to which stressors lead to actual stress. We have also seen how personality may affect which stress reactions are exhibited in response to stress. A question remains, however, as to whether there is any particular type of personality that is especially likely to experience stress and to exhibit negative reactions to it. In recent years, physicians, psychologists, and management scholars have developed an interest in one such personality type, that defined by the Type A behavior pattern.

Interest in the Type A behavior pattern began when physicians noticed that many sufferers of coronary heart disease, especially those who developed the disease relatively young, tended to exhibit a distinctive pattern of behaviors and emotions.[4] This pattern of behaviors and emotions contributed to heart disease even when cigarette smoking, cholesterol level, and elevated blood pressure were accounted for. Individuals who exhibit the **Type A behavior pattern** tend to be aggressive and ambitious. Their hostility is easily aroused, and they feel a great sense of time urgency. They are impatient, competitive, and preoccupied with their work. The Type A individual is often contrasted with the Type B, who does not exhibit these extreme characteristics. Close to half of the urban population seems prone to the Type A behavior pattern. Although more men than women are

Type As, the negative effects of the Type A personality are equivalent for men and women.[5] Research suggests that the Type A pattern may have its beginnings in childhood (see the cartoon).[6]

Is stress a key factor in the Type A equation? In other words, is the elevated heart disease seen in Type As a physiological reaction to stress? The answer seems to be yes. Compared to Type B individuals, Type As report heavier workloads, longer work hours, and more conflicting work demands.[7] Whether or not these reports are accurate, we will see later that such factors turn out to be potent stressors. Thus, Type As either encounter more stressful situations than Type Bs, or they perceive themselves as doing so. In turn, Type As are likely to exhibit adverse physiological reactions in response to stress. These include elevated blood pressure, elevated heart rate, and modified blood chemistry. Frustrating, difficult, or competitive events are especially likely to prompt these adverse reactions. In addition, Type As perform better than Type Bs in situations that call for persistence, endurance, or speed. They can ignore fatigue and distraction to accomplish their goals. Type As seem to have a strong need to control their work environment. This is doubtless a full-time task that stimulates

You're a Type A just like your father.

Source: *Psychology Today,* May 1986, p. 12.

their feelings of time urgency and leads them to overextend themselves physically.[8]

The Type A behavior pattern has some interesting ramifications. For one thing, Type As do not generally report more tension, anxiety, or job dissatisfaction than Type Bs, even though they do report more of the stressors noted earlier.[9] Thus, Type As may be unaware of the impact that work stress has on them. To complicate matters, many work organizations reward the very behaviors that Type A persons favor—achievement orientation, long work hours, and extreme work involvement. Thus, it is not surprising that Type A individuals as a group tend to reach higher organizational levels and achieve higher occupational success than Type Bs. The message here is that organizations may be unintentionally threatening to health and well-being of their best performers. This is another example of why the study of work stress is important.

BASIC FORMS OF STRESS

Earlier it was pointed out that there are two basic forms of stress—frustration and conflict. Both of these forms of stress are preliminary psychological reactions to environmental stressors, determined in part by the individual's personality. Although they will be discussed separately, it should be understood that both forms of stress often occur in a single stress episode.

Frustration

Frustration occurs when progress toward some important goal is blocked. We are sometimes frustrated in our attempts to achieve a promotion, to get subordinates (or superiors!) to act according to our wishes, or to get to work on time on a snowy morning. Frustration commonly occurs due to delays, lacks, losses, and failure.[10]

DELAYS.   Even when goals are eventually achievable, many people react to the delay of achievement with frustration. Almost by design, organizations frequently delay the prompt and easy completion of task assignments by specific individuals for the good of the organization as a whole. Your typing may have to wait until that of a colleague's is completed. One salesperson's order may have to be filled before another's. These routine delays are often accompanied by more serious delays such as those involved in career progression. Every organization has a ''pecking order'' which requires members to ''pay their dues'' before achieving promotion. Many well-equipped college graduates are dismayed that their academic credentials do not speed them up through the organization at the pace they had anticipated.

LACKS.   Individuals often lack the physical, personal, or interpersonal resources necessary to achieve their goals.[11] The manager of an understaffed department may find it impossible to make the unit function effectively during busy periods. Similarly, the manager who lacks the intellect or training to understand the newer computer systems may feel frustrated and threatened by the inability to master this aspect of the job. You will recall that Alan Windsor lacked the interpersonal skills he needed in order to perform well as an account executive.

LOSSES.   Sometimes organizational members lose a skill or resource that leads to the frustration of their attempts to achieve an important goal. More than one executive has been badly frustrated by the resignation of an invaluable assistant or secretary. Sometimes professionals who assume administrative positions gradually lose their currency with professional issues. Many university deans report that their work load stemming from their administrative duties prevents them from keeping up with the literature in their academic specialty.

FAILURE.   Organizations provide plenty of opportunities to achieve success, but they also provide equal opportunity for failure. Even if they overcome delays, lacks, and losses, members are often frustrated in attempts to achieve their goals. The most obvious cases of failure are those that other organizational members notice. A late report, a lost client, a poor performance rating, or the inability to achieve a promotion all represent failure that someone else in the organization has observed. In addition, employees often set personal, covert goals which, when not achieved, can be equally frustrating. The person who resolved to obtain a university degree by evening study may find this goal impossible to accomplish if he or she has a heavy work schedule requiring much travel.

Intrapersonal Conflict

Intrapersonal conflict occurs when an individual is confronted with incompatible goals or action tendencies or a single goal that has both positive and negative features. As we shall see, conflict involves indecision, and indecision can be anxiety-producing.

APPROACH-AVOIDANCE CONFLICT.   Approach-avoidance conflicts involve a single goal or action tendency that has positive and negative features. The positive features of the goal attract the individual while the negative features of the goal repel the individual. Imagine that a manager is instructed by the vice-president of international operations to offer a bribe to an official of a foreign government to ensure that the organization's products are purchased by the government. The manager suspects that he may be promoted if he successfully accomplishes the sale, but has doubts about the morality of the action:

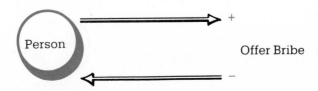

Person   Offer Bribe

In this case, the prospects of promotion are attractive but the thoughts of committing an immoral act are not, and the manager should experience severe conflict. Examples of approach-avoidance conflicts abound in organizations—Should I quit my job? Shall I tell my boss what I think of his proposal? Should our company make this investment?

MULTIPLE APPROACH-AVOIDANCE CONFLICT. **Multiple approach-avoidance conflicts** involve two or more goals or action tendencies, each of which has positive and negative features. Consider a computer analyst for a large bank who has just been offered a promotion to a managerial position. The promotion offers a higher salary, which is attractive, but also involves greater responsibility, which is threatening. At the same time, the analyst is offered a job in a new computer consulting firm that will provide a very high salary, but the job will lack security, since consulting is a risky business venture:

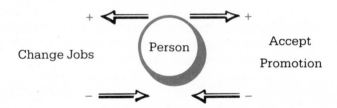

Obviously the analyst is in a bind. Changing jobs involves taking a risk *and* turning one's back on a sure promotion with good salary. Accepting the promotion involves dealing with the pressures that face a manager *and* turning down a very high salary for doing a familiar job. Multiple approach-avoidance conflicts are common in organizations—Should we purchase a tried-and-true piece of equipment which may become outdated or a "state of the art" model which may be unreliable? Should I crack down on my subordinates to show my boss I'm a tough manager, or should I act considerately to keep the office running smoothly and risk offending the boss?

AVOIDANCE-AVOIDANCE CONFLICT. **Avoidance-avoidance conflicts** involve two or more goals or action tendencies, each of which is repugnant to the individual. For example, consider the insurance executive whose company decides to move its head office from a relatively small city in the Midwest to New York City. The executive is given the choice of moving to New York or assuming a position at the main West Coast office in San Francisco. She and her spouse are well integrated into the Midwestern community, having lived there for many years. The husband has a good job there and they have three children in school:

Move to
San Francisco   — ⟹ Person ⟸ —   Move to
New York

In this case the executive is faced with an especially unpalatable decision, since both moves are seen as involving totally negative consequences. It should be clear that such avoidance-avoidance conflicts are especially likely to arouse anxiety, because the individual is "trapped between the devil and the deep blue sea." Many conflicts that occur in organizational life have avoidance-avoidance qualities—Which of two equally inexperienced subordinates should I assign to this job? Which piece of bad news should I tell the boss first?

STRESSORS IN ORGANIZATIONAL LIFE

In the previous section on the basic forms of stress, several examples of stress-provoking situations were given. In this section we will examine potential stressors more systematically. Scientific interest in work-related stress has developed only recently. Thus, we are uncertain about exactly which work-related conditions have the most potential to induce frustration and conflict. However, intuition suggests that some stressors can affect almost everyone in any organization, while others seem especially likely to affect persons performing particular roles in organizations. First, we will examine some role-specific stressors and then some more general stressors.

Executive and Managerial Stressors

Executives and managers make key organizational decisions and direct the work of others. In these capacities, they seem to experience special forms of stress.

ROLE OVERLOAD. **Role overload** occurs when too many tasks must be performed in too short a time period. Research indicates that role overload is an especially common stressor for management.[12] In Chapter 2, Henry Mintzberg's observational study of managers was discussed. Mintzberg summarizes his findings in the following way:

> My own study of chief executives found no break in the pace of activity during office hours. The mail (average of 36 pieces per day), telephone calls (average of 5 per day), and meetings (average of 8) accounted for almost every minute from the moment these men entered their offices in the morning until they departed in the evenings. A true break seldom occurred. Coffee was taken during meetings, and lunchtime was almost always devoted to formal or informal meetings. When free time appeared, ever present subordinates quickly usurped it.
>
> Thus the work of managing an organization may be described as taxing. The quantity of work to be done, or that the manager chooses to do, during the day is substantial and the pace is unrelenting. After hours, the chief executive (and probably many other managers as well) appears to be able to escape neither from an environment that recognizes the power and status of his position nor from his own mind, which has been well trained to search continually for new information.[13]

Mintzberg argues that the open-ended nature of the managerial job is responsible for this heavy and protracted work load. Management is an ongoing *process,* and there are few signposts to signify that a task is complete and that rest and relaxation are permitted. Even when managers truly enjoy confronting their heavy work load, they are often frustrated by their inability to contemplate or to perfect some strategy. "When can I get some time to *think* around here?" is a frequently heard complaint. In addition, the heavy work load may frustrate the executive's attempt to develop other skills and interests. Many a project such as a partially restored vintage automobile or a partly build summer cottage languish while organizational fires are fought. Especially when coupled with frequent moves or excessive travel demands, heavy work load often provokes conflict between the manager's role as an organizational member and his or her role as a spouse or parent. Such role conflicts can be especially stressful because they involve incompatible demands made by parties who are both important to the executive. They are a form of multiple approach-avoidance conflict, since the rewards for complying with one party involve negative consequences from the other party. Thus, role overload may provoke stress while at the same time preventing the executive from enjoying the pleasures of life which can reduce stress. Some executives even ignore threats to their health in combatting role overload:

> Ray Brant, vice-president for human relations at National Semiconductor, contracted a rare blood disease that had to be treated with intravenous medication twenty-four hours a day. The disease required hospitalization, but Brant talked his way out of that because of his heavy workload. The semiconductor executive carried his intravenous bottle and pump with him to business meetings and arranged his car so the medication pumped as he drove. "If I backed off work for six weeks, I'd be too far offstream when I came back," he said.[14]

See In–Focus 14-2 for another perspective on role overload.

HEAVY RESPONSIBILITY.   The work load of the executive is not only heavy, but it can have extremely important consequences for the organization and its members. The president of a company may have the final say on the implementation of a million-dollar marketing plan. Similarly, a vice-president of labor relations may be in charge of a negotiation strategy that could either result in labor peace or a protracted and bitter strike. These "make-or-break" responsibilities may confront executives with severe cases of multiple approach-avoidance conflict, since each of several strategies will have pros and cons and a decision must be made with incomplete information. To complicate matters, the personal consequences of an incorrect decision can be staggering. For example, the courts have fined or even jailed executives who have engaged in illegal activities on behalf of their organizations. Clearly, the anticipation of imprisonment for an incorrect business decision falls into the stressor category! (See In–Focus 14-3.) Finally, it should be noted that executives are responsible for people, as well as things, and this influence over the future of others has the potential to induce stress. The executive who must terminate the operation of an unprofitable plant, putting many out of work, or the

IN–FOCUS 14-2   STRESS IN SILICON VALLEY

Silicon Valley, located in Santa Clara County, south of San Francisco, is the microelectronics and high technology center of North America. Laser technology, video games, and microprocessors were conceived and developed here in an entrepreneurial atmosphere that provides an exciting and rewarding work environment for many. However, *Newsweek* has reported on the stressful side-effects of the Silicon Valley culture:

A 1,509-person survey of Silicon Valley attitudes, published this week by the San Jose Mercury News, reveals a work-obsessed culture in which workweeks of 50 hours or more are standard and where more than a third of the residents admit that job stress damages their home life. Fully two-thirds describe the scene as "thrilling" and say they do not want to leave. A separate study, now being completed for Santa Clara County by economist Richard Carlson, indicates that even though Silicon Valley has achieved the limits of what is considered to be normal growth, it continues to expand.

Workaholics: The fever to get rich has induced a daunting level of workaholism. In the Mercury News survey, nearly half worked more than 40 hours a week, 17 percent more than 50. "It extends all the way down to secretaries," says Judith Larsen, a social scientist who studies the valley. "Almost everyone knows someone who is rich because they worked a lot. It motivates a kind of greed in people, because wealth is possible—it's not based on fantasy." Those long hours, says Larsen, erode personal relationships. Santa Clara County consistently posts one of the highest divorce rates in the nation. And in Larsen's studies, parents report little time to spend with children. "But," notes Larsen, "the kids don't have much time to spend with parents either. They have highly structured lives, with soccer or gymnastics or computer club. Almost like little models of their parents."

'Sting': Like the old frontier, Silicon Valley tends to encourage a freewheeling style. There is also outright lawlessness. "The currency of Silicon Valley is cocaine," says San Jose Police Chief Joseph McNamara. He describes a company celebration where a top executive passed around a sugar bowl of cocaine, and San Jose police investigators recently found one company of 400 employees "where almost everyone was on drugs." Many executives seem unwilling to face the problem. "Management," McNamara charges, "is either oblivious or part of it." But there are signs that some companies are starting to take the situation more seriously. IBM is now giving urinalysis tests to prospective employees.

Source: Abridged from Rogers, M., with Sandza, R. (1985, February 25). Trouble in the valley. *Newsweek*, 92–94. Reprinted by permission.

manager who must fire a subordinate, putting one out of work, may experience guilt and tension.[15]

Professional Stressors

Professionals are individuals who have acquired highly specialized training in a particular area of expertise. They typically subscribe to a particular set of beliefs, values, and attitudes regarding their work and are members of a professional organization that sets standards for training and disciplining its members. Scientists, engineers, accountants, psychologists, doctors, lawyers, and teachers are among those individuals who are often considered professionals. Like managers, professionals are sometimes exposed to a particular set of stressors.

IN—FOCUS 14-3   (UNINSURED) STRESS IN THE BOARDROOM

Serving on boards of directors at some companies was once a pleasant, undemanding hobby for business biggies. The directorships offered short hours, fine camaraderie, handsome pay and hardly any tough decisions. "Sitting on a board as little as 15 years ago was almost like going to a men's club," says Arjay Miller, former president of Ford and the current director of nine companies. "The chairman put his buddies on the board."

These days the director's job has become much tougher. Reason: stockholders and Government regulators, notably the Securities and Exchange Commission, have begun taking directors to task for failing to perform their duties properly. In a landmark decision last week, the Delaware Supreme Court ruled that ten former directors of Trans Union, a railroad-equipment leasing company, were financially liable for selling their company too hastily in 1980. A lawsuit filed on behalf of 10,000 shareholders claimed that the directors spent just two hours considering a purchase offer of $55 a share, or $688 million in total, while the company may have been worth as much as $70 a share. The ten directors could be held personally liable for the difference. In another stunning decision last December, the Federal Deposit Insurance Corporation fired nine directors at Chicago's Continental Illinois Bank, holding them partly to blame for the institution's near collapse in September.*

■   ■   ■

Managers and Directors, already beset as never before by hostile takeover bids and shareholder suits, now face another anxiety: skyrocketing renewal rates for the insurance that protects them should they be sued—as one in five is. Some companies are likely to find that adequate insurance for directors and officers isn't available at any price.

The Wyatt Co., an insurance industry consulting firm, estimates that new lawsuits against directors have jumped 20% since 1982 after having leveled off for several years before that. Some of the new lawsuits have been costly. Last fall, a group of insurance companies ponied up $25 million to settle a shareholder suit against former directors and officers of Wickes Cos., a California retailer that went bankrupt in 1982; shareholders charged that the company issued false financial statements before it went under.

Some insurance companies have responded by dropping directors-and-officers policies entirely. Those still offering the policies are reducing the amount of coverage they will sell to a single company and are continuing to raise prices. "Any buyer who thinks the cost of his insurance will only double is a dreamer," says Robin A. G. Jackson, a director of Merrett Syndicates, the leading directors-and-officers insurer at Lloyd's of London. "In my view, putting the prices up 300% or 400% would only just be adequate."**

*Source: Koepp, S. (1985, February 11). On the boards. *Time*, p. 59.
**Source: Newport, J. P., Jr. (1985, March 18). Protecting directors suddenly gets costly. *Fortune*, p. 61. Reprinted by permission.
Both are abridgments.

PROFESSION VERSUS ORGANIZATION. One stressor that professionals often confront is contradictory demands from the employing organization and their profession. These contradictory demands lead to a form of role conflict in which one's role as a professional is at odds with one's role as an employee. In general, when professionals are employed by organizations that specialize in the professional service, such conflicts are rare. Accountants who work in public accounting firms and lawyers who work in law firms find themselves in an organizational environment that supports their professional values. However, when the professional is employed by an organization that does not offer the professional's service as its main product, role conflict may develop. For example, the accountant who is the controller of a manufacturing firm may experience stress when asked by the president to institute some questionable bookkeeping practices. Similarly, the scientist who values "knowledge for its own sake" may encounter stress when required by an electronics firm to terminate an interesting basic research project for a more practical investigation of some specific problem. In both cases, the organization and the profession can be characterized as competing for the *loyalty* of the professional. For instance, one study of scientists and managers in an aerospace company found that only 15 percent of the scientists identified with their organization more than their profession. In contrast, 68 percent of the managers studied identified most strongly with the organization.[16]

LACK OF AUTHORITY. Even though professionals in a nonprofessional-oriented organization have the power of special knowledge in their area of expertise, they frequently lack formal authority to implement decisions and influence organizational policy. This happens because professionals are usually found in staff jobs where they generate information on which managers take action. As such, they serve in essentially advisory roles. Speaking of scientists, one writer has said:

> Since the scientist enters the organization at the lower end of the hierarchy, he finds his immediate group subordinated to several decision-making and coordinating echelons. When the upper echelons generate policies that disrupt his work or change its direction, he often reacts with irritation and frustration.[17]

The irritation and frustration to which this writer refers also stem from the fact that professionals must consistently "sell" their ideas to those organizational members who have the authority to implement them. For example, industrial psychologists who work as personnel specialists for large organizations must frequently find a department or divisional manager who is willing to sponsor their ideas for a new motivational scheme or performance evaluation plan. This puts the specialist in the potentially stressful position of having to convince the busy manager to devote substantial time and resources to a plan of action that may have an unclear or delayed payoff. If lack of authority were not problematic enough in inducing stress, it can be compounded by the fact that professionals are frequently supervised by nonprofessional personnel. The psychologists referred to above may report to a Director of Human Resources who is not a psychologist. Similarly, the lawyers who work in the claims department of an insurance firm may report to a manager who is not a lawyer. This condition may lead to poor communication and a lack of support for professionals even *within* their own organizational units.

Operative Level Stressors

Operatives are individuals who occupy nonprofessional and nonmanagerial positions in organizations. In a manufacturing organization, operatives perform the work on the shop floor and range from skilled craftspersons to unskilled laborers. As is the case with other organizational roles, the occupants of operative positions are sometimes exposed to a special set of stressors.

POOR PHYSICAL WORKING CONDITIONS.   Operative level employees are more likely than managers and professionals to be exposed to physically unpleasant and even dangerous working conditions. Although social sensibility and the actions of unions have improved working conditions over the years, many employees must still face excessive heat, cold, noise, pollution, and the chance of accidents. A spot welder in an automobile assembly plant had this to say about his job:

> I don't know if you've heard of plant pollution. It's really terrible. Especially where I work, you have the sparks and smoke. . . . If you don't turn the fans down, the smoke'll come right up. . . . I usually go outside to get a breath of fresh air. The further you are from the front door the worse it is. You can cut the heat with a knife, especially when it gets up in the nineties. You get them carbon monoxide fumes, it's just hell.[18]

Speaking about the stress involved in maintaining safe working conditions, a crane operator reported:

> It's not so much the physical, it's the mental. When you're working on a tunnel and you're down in a hole two hundred feet, you use hand signals. You can't see these. You have to have something else that's your eyes. There has been men dropped and such because some fellow gave the wrong signal. . . . The average crane operator lives to be fifty-five years old. They don't live the best sort of life. There's a lot of tension. We've had an awful lot of people have had heart attacks.[19]

POOR JOB DESIGN.   We have all heard stories about individuals with master's degrees who drive taxicabs for a living. In fact, the educational level of the North American work force has risen consistently over the years. This rise in educational level has been accompanied by greater expectations of interesting work and a greater desire for influence over work-related decisions.[20] These changes have been paralleled by an increase in the proportion of white-collar jobs, especially in the public sector and service industries. However, many of these jobs, as well as traditional lower level blue-collar jobs, do not offer challenge and opportunity commensurate with the education and skills of their incumbents.[21] While bad job design can provoke stress at any organizational level (executive role overload is an example) lower-level blue- and white-collar jobs are particular culprits. It may seem paradoxical that jobs that are too simple or not challenging enough can act as stressors.

However, monotony and boredom can prove extremely frustrating to individuals who see themselves as capable of handling more complex tasks.

Jobs that make high demands on workers while giving them little control over workplace decisions seem especially prone to produce stress and negative stress reactions.[22] High demands might include a hectic work pace, excessive workload, or limited time to accomplish tasks. Lack of control involves limited decision latitude and authority. Jobs that often involve high demand and little control include telephone operators, nurse's aides, assembly line workers, and garment stitchers. As shown in Exhibit 14-2, these jobs fall into a zone of increased

EXHIBIT 14-2   **Heart disease risk among males.**

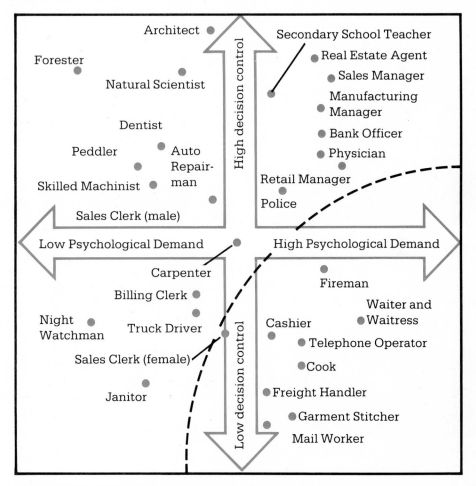

Note: High-risk occupations are to the right of the dotted line.
Source: Nelson, B. (1983, April 3). Bosses face less risk than bossed. *New York Times*, Section E, p. 16

risk for heart disease (the area to the right of the dotted line). Stress may be partially responsible for this elevated risk.

Boundary Role Stressors

Boundary roles are positions in which organizational members are required to interact with members of other organizations or with the public. As such, boundary roles exist at the executive, professional, and operative levels of organizations. For example, a vice-president of public relations is responsible for representing his or her company to the public, while the vice-president of labor relations is responsible for interacting with a variety of union organizations. In the professional domain, a medical doctor who works for a pharmaceutical company may be required to represent the company before a congressional committee. At the operative level, receptionists, salespeople, and installers often interact with the public or representatives of other organizations.

There is evidence suggesting that occupants of boundary role positions are especially likely to experience stress as they straddle the imaginary boundary between the organization and its environment.[23] This is yet another form of role conflict in which one's role as an organizational member may be incompatible with the demands made by the public or other organizations. For example, the presidential press secretary is responsible for presenting the White House position on various matters to the public. This involves providing a limited amount of select information to the press corps, who consistently demand more and "juicier" information. This presents the press secretary with a stress-provoking dilemma. If he provides further information to the press corps the administration will be displeased; if he "stonewalls," the reporters will be unhappy.

A classic case of boundary role stress involves salespeople, especially those who sell to other organizations such as wholesalers and retailers. In extreme cases, these buyers desire fast delivery of a large quantity of custom-tailored products. The salesperson may be tempted to "offer the moon," but is at the same time aware that such an order may place a severe strain on his or her organization's production facilities. Thus, the salesperson is faced with the dilemma of doing his or her primary job (selling) while protecting another function (production) from unreasonable demands that may result in a broken delivery contract.

A particular form of stress experienced by some boundary role occupants is burnout. **Burnout** is an extreme form of emotional pressure stemming mostly from interactions with other people.[24] Frequently, these other people are organizational clients who are themselves experiencing severe problems. Thus, teachers, nurses, social workers, and police are especially likely candidates for burnout. The symptoms of burnout include:

- *Physical exhaustion*. The person lacks energy and feels tired. Frequently, daytime tiredness is accompanied by inability to sleep at night.
- *Emotional exhaustion*. The person feels depressed, helpless, and hopeless.

IN–FOCUS 14-4 POLICE OFFICERS EXPERIENCE BURNOUT

At a meeting of the American Psychological Association, a panel was convened to discuss the role of stress and burnout in policing. These are some observations of the panel:

Contrary to the machismo stereotype, panel members said, most police officers choose the profession out of altruism. Then they find themselves rejected or ignored by members of the very community they tried to help. They begin to identify with the criminals and underworld characters who inhabit the shady streets they patrol and the cesspools that are their beats.

Wracked with guilt over the loss of idealism, they become burned out after only a few years of swing shifts and long stretches of boredom which they know may explode at any moment into violence and danger. They are vulnerable prey to alcoholism and deviant sex, and pay with broken marriages and delinquent children.

Panel members enumerated the stress factors that plague the front line police officer: rotating shifts, boredom, isolation, poor equipment, constant temptation, rigid compartmentalization and poor communication within departments, and most damaging, public apathy and hostility.

Herbert J. Freudenberger, in private practice in New York City, counsels a number of officers, who have said that the work "gets to them" in as little as three years. As they perceive that the idealism with which they enter the profession does not match reality, they begin to display the physical and emotional signs of burn-out: headaches, chest pains, insomnia, bursts of anger, cynicism, resentfulness, and subtle paranoia.

Eventually, Freudenberger said, they begin to identify with other inhabitants of the "cesspool" in which they work. This is particularly true of the vice squad. When he has police officers and "mafioso types" together in group therapy, "I find they are very much alike. They become buddies."

Because police form such a closed community, it is much more difficult for psychologists as outsiders to gain their trust.

One successful solution has been peer counseling, using either officers with similar problems or those who seem particularly adept at counseling others.

Source: Abridged from Fisher, K. (1982, October). Psychology meets the Prince of the City. *APA Monitor*, p. 15. Reprinted by permission.

■ *Mental exhaustion.* The person develops negative attitudes toward work and life. Frequently, he or she develops impatience with others and reacts cynically toward their problems.

Burnout seems most common among those who entered their jobs with especially high ideals. Their expectations of being able to "change the world" are badly frustrated when they encounter the reality shock of troubled clients (who are often perceived as unappreciative) and the inability of the organization to help them. Teachers get fed up with being disciplinarians, nurses get upset when patients die, and police officers get depressed when they must constantly deal with the "losers" of society[25] (see In–Focus 14-4).

What are the consequences of burnout? Some individuals bravely pursue a new occupation, often experiencing guilt about not having been able to cope in the old one. Others stay in the same occupation but seek a new job. For instance, the burned-out nurse may go into nursing education to avoid contact with sick patients. In a related vein, some persons pursue administrative careers in their profession, attempting to "climb above" the source of their difficulties. These persons often set cynical examples for idealistic subordinates. Finally, some persons stay in their jobs and become part of the legion of "deadwood" collecting their paychecks but doing little to contribute to the mission of the organization. Many "good bureaucrats" seem to choose this route.

Some General Stressors

To conclude our discussion of stressors that are encountered in organizational life, we will consider some stressors that are probably experienced equally by occupants of executive, professional, operative, and boundary roles.

JOB INSECURITY.   Secure employment is an important goal for almost everyone, and stress may be encountered when secure employment is threatened. At the operative level, unionization has provided a degree of employment security for many, but the vagaries of the economy and the threat of automation hang heavy over many workers. Among professionals, a curious paradox exists. In many cases, the very specialization that enables them to obtain satisfactory jobs becomes a millstone whenever social or economic forces change. For example, aerospace scientists and engineers have long been prey to the boom and bust nature of their industry. When layoffs occur, they are often perceived as overqualified or too specialized to easily obtain jobs in related industries. Another source of insecurity for many professionals is the ease with which one's knowledge of a particular field can become obsolete. Especially in highly technical fields such as science, the undergraduate's knowledge of today may be the Ph.D.'s knowledge of yesterday. Finally, job insecurity does not escape the executive suite. Recent pressures for corporate performance have made cost cutting a top priority for many companies. One of the surest ways to cut costs in the short run is to reduce executive positions and thus reduce the total management payroll. Many top corporations, including Union Carbide and DuPont, have greatly thinned their executive ranks in recent years.

ROLE AMBIGUITY.   We have already noted how role conflict, having to deal with incompatible role expectations, can provoke stress. There is also substantial evidence that role ambiguity can provoke stress.[26] From Chapter 8, you will recall that role ambiguity exists when the goals of one's job, or the methods of performing the job, are unclear. Such a lack of direction can prove stressful, especially for persons who are low in their tolerance for such ambiguity. Almost by definition, many managerial and executive jobs seem prone to ambiguity. For example, the president of a manufacturing firm may be instructed by the board of directors to increase profits and cut costs. While this goal seems clear enough, the means by which it can be achieved may be unclear. This ambiguity can be devastating, especially when the organization is doing poorly and no strategy seems to improve things. In general, jobs that are lower in the organization seem clearer in method and may have less intrinsic role ambiguity. However, even at lower levels, ambiguity can exist when supervision is weak or inconsistent in its demands and direction. Severe stress can be encountered when one is told to do one thing one minute and something contradictory the next. Often, both the task and the boss can contribute to role ambiguity. A former copywriter in an advertising agency described a typical assignment this way:

> I would go to the boss and he'd tell me what he wanted. I'd go back to my room and try to write it, and get mad and break pencils and pound on the wall. Then finish it and take it in to him, and change it and change it, and then I'd go back and write it over again and take it in to him and he'd change it again, and I'd take it back. This would happen thirty or forty times and then we'd move to another man. He'd put his feet on the desk and change it again.[27]

INTERPERSONAL INCOMPATIBILITY.   So-called "personality clashes" are unpleasant enough outside of organizations to provoke a considerable degree of stress. When such unpleasantries occur within an organizational context, they would seem to have the potential to induce even more stress. For one thing, outside of the organization, one can often simply cease interaction with the disliked person. This option is frequently unavailable when people are working together. Secondly, the stress stemming from incompatibility can have substantial spillover in an organization. That is, not only is the incompatibility stress-provoking in and of itself, but it can create further stress by interfering with perceived or actual job performance. A personality clash with the boss may lead the boss to give the subordinate a poor performance rating, only exacerbating the subordinate's stress. In addition, the subordinate may spend so much time complaining about the boss or trying to "mend fences" that his or her actual performance suffers. Clearly, interpersonal problems with peers, superiors, and subordinates can extend from the shop floor to the executive suite.

Exhibit 14-3 summarizes the sources of stress at various points in the organization.

REACTIONS TO ORGANIZATIONAL STRESS

In this section we shall examine the reactions that individuals who experience organizational stress might exhibit. These reactions can be divided into behavioral, psychological, and physiological responses.

Behavioral Reactions to Stress

Behavioral reactions to stress involve overt activities that the stressed individual uses in an attempt to cope with the stress. They include problem solving, withdrawal, and the use of addictive substances.

EXHIBIT 14-3   **Sources of stress at various points in the organization.**

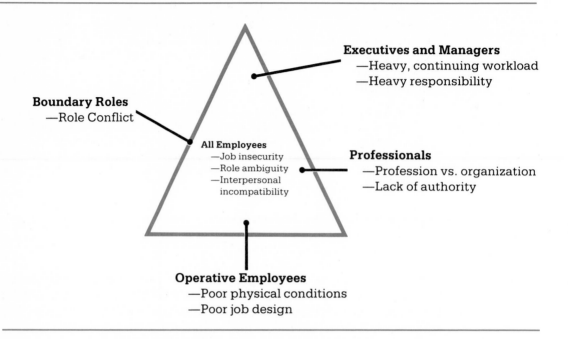

PROBLEM SOLVING.   We would hope that problem solving is the most typical response to organizational stress. In general, **problem solving** is directed toward terminating the stressor or reducing its potency, and not toward simply making the person feel better in the short run. Problem solving is reality oriented, and while it is not always effective in combatting the stressor, it reveals flexibility and realistic use of feedback. Thus, if an attempted solution to a stress problem is not effective, the person feels capable of trying another approach. Most examples of a problem-solving response to stress are undramatic, because problem solving is generally the routine, sensible, obvious approach that an objective observer might suggest. Some examples of problem-solving reactions to stress include the following:

- *Delegation.* A busy executive reduces her stress-provoking work load by delegating some of her many tasks to a capable subordinate.

- *Time management.* A manager who finds the day too short writes a daily schedule, forces his subordinates to make formal appointments to see him, and instructs his secretary to screen phone calls more selectively.

- *Talking it out.* A professional engineer who is experiencing stress because of poor communication with her nonengineer superior resolves to sit down with the boss and hammer out an agreement concerning the priorities on a project.

- *Asking for help.* A salesperson who is anxious about his company's ability to fill a difficult order asks the production manager to provide a realistic estimate of the probable delivery date.

- *Searching for alternatives.* A machine operator who finds his monotonous job stress-provoking applies for a transfer to a more interesting position, even though the pay is identical.

Whether or not these responses are effective in reducing stress depends on circumstances. However, it should be clear that problem solving is generally beneficial for both the individual and the organization.

WITHDRAWAL. Withdrawal from the stressor is one of the most basic reactions to stress. In organizations, this withdrawal takes the form of absence and turnover. Compared with problem-solving reactions to stress, absenteeism fails to attack the stressor directly. Rather, the absent individual is simply attempting some short-term reduction of the anxiety prompted by the stressor. When the person returns to the job, the stress is still there. From this point of view, absence is a dysfunctional reaction to stress for both the individual and the organization. The same can be said about turnover when a person resigns from a stressful job on the spur of the moment merely to escape stress. However, a good case can be made for a well-planned resignation where the intent is to assume another job that should be less stressful. This is actually a problem-solving reaction which should benefit both the individual and the organization in the long run. We are as yet unsure just how much absence and turnover represents specific withdrawal from stress. However, there is some evidence that stress-prone operative jobs are likely to prompt absence.[28] In addition, several potential stressors discussed earlier (role ambiguity and underutilization of potential) are associated with absence.[29] Turnover and turnover intentions have often been linked with stress and its causes.[30]

USE OF ADDICTIVE SUBSTANCES. Smoking, drinking, and drug use represent the least satisfactory behavioral responses to stress for both the individual and the organization. These activities fail to terminate stress episodes, and they leave employees less physically and mentally prepared to perform their jobs. We have all heard of hard-drinking newspaper reporters and advertising executives, and it is tempting to infer that the stress of their boundary role positions is responsible for their drinking. Unfortunately, like these, most reports of the relationship between stress and the use of addictive substances are anecdotal. However, there are some tentative indications that cigarette use and alcohol abuse are associated with the presence of work-related stress.[31]

Psychological Reactions to Stress

Psychological reactions to stress primarily involve emotions and thought processes, rather than overt behavior, although these reactions are frequently revealed in the individual's speech and actions. The most common psychological reaction to stress is the use of defense mechanisms. **Defense mechanisms** are psychological attempts to reduce the anxiety associated with stress. Notice that, by definition, defense mechanisms concentrate on *anxiety reduction,* rather than actually confronting or dealing with the stressor. The use of defense mechanisms is usually automatic and unconscious; the individual is unaware of his or her defensiveness. However, in some cases the person may be aware of such defensiveness or intentionally implement a defense. Some common defense mechanisms include the following:

- **Rationalization** involves attributing socially acceptable reasons or motives to one's actions so that they will appear reasonable and sensible, at least to oneself. For example, a male nurse who becomes very angry and abusive when learning that he will not be promoted to supervisor may justify his anger by claiming that the head nurse discriminates against men.

- **Projection** involves attributing one's own undesirable ideas and motives to others so that they seem less negative. For example, a sales executive undergoing conflict about offering a bribe to an official of a foreign government may reason that the *official* is corrupt.

- **Displacement** involves directing feelings of anger at a "safe" target rather than expressing them where they may be punished. For example, a construction worker who is severely criticized by the boss for sloppy workmanship may go home and kick the family dog.

- **Reaction formation** involves expressing oneself in a manner that is directly opposite to the way one truly feels, rather than risking negative reactions to one's true position. For example, a low-status member of a committee may vote with the majority on a crucial issue rather than stating his true position and opening himself to attack.

- **Compensation** involves applying one's skills in a particular area to make up for failure in another area. For example, a professor who is unable to get her research published may resolve to become a superb teacher.

- **Repression** involves preventing threatening ideas from becoming conscious, so that the stressor need not be confronted. For example, the assembly line worker who finds his routine but demanding job stressful may honestly forget to set his alarm clock and wake up too late to go to work.

You will recall that Alan Windsor responded defensively to the stress generated by his failure as an account executive when he blamed his support staff for his problems. This involved a combination of rationalization and projection. By projecting his own inadequacies onto them, he was trying to rationalize his inability to land accounts.

Is the use of defense mechanisms a good or bad reaction to stress? Used occasionally to temporarily reduce anxiety, they appear to be a useful reaction. For example, the construction worker who displaces aggression onto the family dog rather than attacking the frustrating boss may calm down, return to work the next day, and "talk it out" with the boss. (Note that this is a problem-solving reaction. We hope he would also make up with the dog!) Thus, the occasional use of defense mechanisms as short-term anxiety reducers probably benefits both the individual and the organization. In fact, those with "weak defenses" may be incapacitated by anxiety and resort to dysfunctional withdrawal or addiction.

When the use of defense mechanisms becomes a chronic reaction to stress, however, the picture changes radically. The problem stems from the very character of defense mechanisms—they simply don't change the objective character of the stressor, and the basic conflict or frustration remains in operation. After some short-term relief from anxiety, the basic problem remains unresolved. In fact, the stress may *increase* with the knowledge that the defense has been essentially ineffective. In addition, as the above examples illustrate, all defense mechanisms involve a certain degree of detachment from the *reality* of the stress episode. As defense is piled upon defense, it may be more and more difficult for individuals to accurately assess the true reason for their anxiety. In this case, they become less and less likely to engage in sensible problem-solving responses to the stressor.

Physiological Reactions to Stress

Can work-related stress kill you? This is clearly an important question for organizations, and it is even more important for individuals who experience excessive stress at work. Most studies of physiological reactions to stress have concentrated on the cardiovascular system, and specifically on the various risk factors that might prompt heart attacks. For example, there is evidence that work stress is associated with electrocardiogram irregularities and elevated levels of blood pressure, cholesterol, and pulse.[32] However, most of the studies have been correlational in nature, comparing the incidence of these risk factors across occupations that were *assumed* to differ in the presence of stressors. In Chapter 2 you learned that correlation does not imply causation, and it is possible that individuals who are already high coronary risks *choose* to go into certain occupations. In this case, certain occupations would indeed appear to promote adverse physiological reactions, but mainly because they attracted high-risk candidates.

One study of physiological reactions to stress is interesting because it confirms the intuitive notion that air traffic controllers are exposed to elevated levels of job stress. Compared with a group of second-class airmen, air traffic controllers had higher blood pressure and more diabetes and stomach ulcers. As for air traffic control attracting risk-prone individuals—among the controllers, high blood pressure and ulcer development were more common at airports with more traffic. This suggests that stress-provoking job demands were indeed responsible for adverse physiological reactions.[33]

Although you probably accept the fact that air traffic control is a stress-prone occupation, you may be surprised to learn that *dentists* also suffer from a fairly high rate of physiological problems that may be associated with stress. One study found that the difficulties of building a dental practice, the image of the dentist as an inflictor of pain, and a lack of appreciation from patients were related to various cardiovascular risks among dentists.[34]

ORGANIZATIONAL STRATEGIES TO REDUCE STRESS

This chapter would be incomplete without some discussion of the strategies that organizations might implement to try to reduce employee stress. However, this section has been written with a certain degree of caution. Earlier, we stated that scientific interest in organizational stress is relatively recent. More research activity is clearly needed, and one subject that has received little attention as yet is the interventions that organizations might implement to decrease the presence of stressors or reduce their impact. Below is an intuitive list of approaches that might be used, some of which correspond to the stressors discussed earlier. You should be aware, however, that their effectiveness in reducing stress is generally untested.

Prepare Employees for Stress

One approach to preparing employees for anticipated stress might be to institute *realistic job previews,* which attempt to clearly specify the nature of the work to be encountered before the person is hired (Chapter 9). In their zeal to hire people, many recruiters tend to gloss over negative aspects of a job, including its potential to induce stress. A realistic preview should permit those who feel incapable of coping with stress to decline a job offer or to go into a job adequately forewarned. Although such previews have been shown to facilitate job satisfaction and reduce turnover, their effects on stress have not been examined. Realistic job previews could also be used to inform candidates for promotion or internal transfer about possible stressors in the new job.

In a similar vein, many multinational firms have instituted seminars to help employees and their families prepare for the stress that might be encountered in moving to another country and experiencing culture shock. Such programs warn transferees about the difficulties that might be confronted and provide them with an arsenal of stress-preventing suggestions. Similar plans have also been implemented by the armed forces. For example, the U.S. Air Force introduces military families who are about to be transferred to a foreign base to a local "sponsor family" that is currently stationed at that base. This enables the departing family to obtain first-hand information about the kinds of problems that might be encountered in the foreign environment and provides an established connection for them once they arrive there.

Job Redesign

As indicated earlier, many jobs seem to have the potential for stress designed into them. For this reason, organizations might implement plans to redesign jobs so as to reduce their stressful characteristics. In theory, jobs anywhere in the organization could be redesigned to this end. Thus, an overloaded executive might be given an assistant to reduce the number of tasks he or she must perform. In practice, most formal job redesign efforts have involved enriching operative level jobs to make them more stimulating and challenging. As noted in Chapter 7, this is usually accomplished by giving employees more control over the pace of their work and permitting them to use more of their skills and abilities. Although enrichment often increases job satisfaction and reduces withdrawal, there have been almost no studies of the impact of enrichment on stress reduction or physiological indicators of stress. One exception is a study in the production and packing department of a candy producer that showed distinct improvements in employee mental health after job enrichment.[35] Such tests are important because it is conceivable that job enrichment could provoke stress rather than reduce it. In general, job redesign is an important method of dealing with stress, because it attempts to *remove* stressors rather than simply helping employees to *cope with* stressors.

Job Posting and Promotion from Within

Job posting refers to publicizing job openings within the organization and encouraging current employees to apply for the openings. A **promotion-from-within** policy refers to the notion that all jobs except those at the entry level will be staffed (if possible) by promoting those who are already employed by the organization. Effectively managed, these schemes may serve as stress reducers by allowing employees to gravitate to jobs that are compatible with their personalities and stress-tolerance characteristics. For example, job posting may allow a worker to request a lateral transfer (to a job at the same level) that is perceived as less stressful. Similarly, a promotion-from-within policy may permit an employee to escape the stress experienced in a routine, monotonous job. However, the promotion-from-within policy must be administered carefully to ensure that individuals do not feel *forced* to accept higher level jobs which may involve more responsibility and thus prove more stressful.

Sabbaticals

In a sense, *sabbaticals* represent ''time off for good behavior'' in the organizational environment. They have been popularized by colleges and universities, in which professors are relieved of their usual duties for several months in order to engage in research, writing, or travel. Presumably, sabbaticals permit self-development and rejuvenation by removing the individual from the stresses of the regular job. Sabbaticals have occasionally been used by business firms, usually at the executive level. For example, Xerox and IBM have permitted paid sabbaticals for community service projects. Other firms occasionally implement exchange programs with governments or universities to permit their executives to utilize their talents in different, less stressful settings. Sabbaticals would seem especially useful for combatting stress in burnout-prone jobs.

Stress Management Programs

In recent years, some organizations have begun to experiment with programs designed to help employees "manage" work-related stress. Some of these programs are designed to help physically and mentally healthy workers prevent problems due to stress. Others are therapeutic in nature, aimed at individuals who are already experiencing stress problems. Although the exact content of the programs varies, most involve one or more of the following techniques: meditation; training in muscle-relaxation exercises; biofeedback training to control physiological processes; skills training in areas such as time management; training to think more positively and realistically about sources of job stress.[36] Although each of these techniques has been shown to be useful in reducing anxiety and tension in other contexts, they have only recently been applied in the work setting. Tentative evidence suggests that these applications are useful in reducing physiological arousal, sleep disturbances, and self-reported tension and anxiety.[37]

Some authors, including some who have designed successful stress management programs, have raised questions about their ethical implications.[38] Many of these programs take job or role requirements as given and then train workers to cope with the resulting stress. This approach does not try to permanently remove sources of stress, as job redesign might do. Is this strategy ethical? To some degree the answer to this question depends on the situation. If one is dealing with a large number of Type A individuals, who are evidently especially sensitive to stressors, a stress management program seems sensible and ethical because the source of much stress is within the employee. On the other hand, if clear and obvious stressors to which almost anyone would object are present (such as extreme overload or horrible working conditions) stress management programs look a lot less ethical.

Exercise Programs

It is often argued that physical exercise can reduce stress and counteract some of the adverse physiological effects of stress. To this end, some organizations have established fitness programs for their members. These range from simple arrangements with local health clubs or YMCAs to complete in-house facilities with resident trainers.

> Companies like Xerox, Rockwell International, Weyerhaeuser, and Pepsi-Cola are spending tens of thousands of dollars for gyms equipped with treadmills, exercycles, and jogging tracks—and full-time staff. One of the more impressive operations is Kimberly-Clark, where $2.5 million have been invested in a 7,000 square foot health testing facility and a 32,000 square foot physical fitness facility staffed by fifteen full-time health care personnel.[39]

Physical fitness training is a strategy that has received some research attention. Studies have shown that fitness training is associated with improved mood, a better self-concept, reduced absenteeism, and reports of better performance.[40] Some of these improvements probably involve stress reduction.

SUMMARY

- Stressors are environmental conditions that have the potential to induce stress. Stress is a psychological reaction that can prompt threat or anxiety because an individual feels incapable of coping with the demands made by a stressor. Two basic forms of stress include frustration (blocked goals due to delays, lacks, losses, and failures) and conflict (competing goals or goals with both positive and negative features).

- Personality characteristics can cause some individuals to perceive more stressors than others, experience more stress, and react more negatively to this stress. In particular, persons with the Type A behavior pattern are prone to such reactions. Type A persons are aggressive, ambitious, and often hostile. They are preoccupied with their work and feel a great sense of time urgency.

- At the managerial or executive level, common stressors include role overload and high responsibility. Among professionals, conflict between professional demands and organizational demands, as well as lack of authority, may provoke stress. At the operative level, poor physical working conditions and underutilization of potential due to poor job design are common stressors. Boundary role occupants often experience stress in the form of conflict between demands from inside the employing organization and demands from outside. Burnout may occur when interaction with clients produces extreme physical, emotional, and mental exhaustion. Job insecurity, role ambiguity, and interpersonal incompatibility have the potential to induce stress in all organizational members.

- Behavioral reactions to stress include problem solving, withdrawal, and the use of addictive substances. Problem solving is most effective because it confronts the stressor directly and thus has the potential to terminate the stress episode. The most common psychological reaction to stress is the use of defense mechanisms to temporarily reduce anxiety. The most studied physiological reactions to stress are cardiovascular risk factors.

- Strategies that might be used to reduce organizational stress include preparation for anticipated stress, job redesign, job posting, promotion from within, sabbaticals, stress management programs, and exercise programs.

KEY CONCEPTS

Stressors
Stress
Stress reactions

Type A behavior pattern
Frustration
Intrapersonal conflict

Approach-avoidance conflict
Multiple approach-avoidance conflict
Avoidance-avoidance conflict
Role overload
Boundary roles
Burnout
Problem solving
Defense mechanisms
Rationalization

Projection
Displacement
Reaction formation
Compensation
Repression
Job posting
Promotion from within
Sabbaticals

DISCUSSION QUESTIONS

1. Two social workers just out of college join the same county welfare agency. Both find their case loads very heavy and their roles very ambiguous. One exhibits negative stress reactions, including absence and elevated alcohol use. The other seems to cope very well. Use the stress episode model to explain why this might occur.

2. Imagine that a person who greatly dislikes bureaucracy assumes her first job as an investigator in a very bureaucratic government tax office. Describe the stressors that may be encountered in this situation. Give an example of a problem-solving reaction to this stress. Give an example of a defensive reaction to it.

3. The jobs in the previous two questions are boundary role jobs. Explain this, and describe why boundary roles often prove stressful.

4. Give an example of a multiple approach-avoidance conflict that might provoke anxiety. Describe a problem-solving reaction to this anxiety.

5. Compare and contrast the stressors that might be experienced by an assembly line worker and the president of a company.

6. Discuss the advantages and disadvantages of hiring employees with Type A personality characteristics.

7. Discuss the following three propositions: a) Organizations have a moral obligation to their employees to make the organizational environment as stress-free as possible; b) Stress reduction in organizations makes good business sense; c) A stress-free organization would not only be impossible to achieve, but such an environment would not be entirely desirable for either the individual or the organization.

FOR FURTHER READING

Beehr, T. A., & Bhagat, R. S. (1985). *Human stress and cognition in organizations.* New York: Wiley.

> Uses a single cohesive framework to examine the causes, effects, and treatment of worker stress. Covers traditional concerns as well as stress encountered by working women, dual-career couples, retirees, and those facing budget cuts.

Neilsen, J. (1985, October 28). Management layoffs won't quit. *Fortune,* 46–49; Kessler, F. (1985, October 28) Managers without a company. *Fortune,* 51–56.

> The first article details how competitive pressures have led top corporations to thin their executive ranks as a cost cutting measure. The second relates the stress that managers experience when they find that their services are no longer wanted.

Oates, W. (1971). *Confessions of a workaholic.* New York: World Publishing.

> A personal account of one man's attempt to deal with stress and heart disease presumably provoked by his "addiction to work." Discusses meditation, reducing busywork, relying on others, and various strategies to confront stress head on.

Case Study

The Price of Success

"Kevin, what has happened to that unswerving drive of yours toward working your way to the top of our company?" asked his boss. "You are almost there. We have offered you a division presidency. Three years of success in that job and we might be able to bring you back to the corporate office as a Senior Vice President of Marketing. You are big league timber, Kevin. You are destined for greatness in our company.

"Ten years ago you came to us as an eager young business administration major just out of college. What an impression you created! Eager, intelligent, and, even at age 21, with an executive aplomb about you. We grabbed you right away for our executive training program. After two years in the field as a territory salesman, you moved effortlessly into a marketing research assignment. Within one year you became a Senior Market Analyst. After two years of brilliance in that position, we made you a Branch Manager. Again, after several years of sterling performance you then became the youngest Regional Manager in the history of our company. We figure you are now ready for the big jump—a general management assignment where you will be operating a profit center of your own. What more can a young executive want?

"We are sticking our necks out for you. Should you fail as a 31-year-old division president, the company could look foolish. Our offer is real. You can become President of the Cosmetics Division if you will just accept the position. I hear the excuses you are making about not being experienced enough for

Source: Reprinted with permission from Dubrin, A. J. (1977). *Casebook of organizational behavior.* New York: Pergamon Books Ltd.

the job, and that other people in the company are more deserving of the position, but I don't buy them. Something else is holding you back, Kevin. What is it?"

"Fred, you're pushing for a rapid answer to a major life decision. Becoming a company president isn't like buying a cabin cruiser or going on a two-week vacation to Bermuda. It's more like getting married or having triplets. It's one helluva change in your life style. An impulsive person shouldn't even be in such an assignment."

"Am I really talking to ambitious Kevin Brady, that hard charging, good-looking Irishman who hates to lose at anything? Two years ago, if I asked you to tackle a special assignment in Venezuela, you would have been on your way to the airport before we went over all the details of the job. I always had the impression that if you weren't in business you would be an automobile racing driver.

"Could it be that you are acting coy because you want us to up the ante a little? As I said, the job should pay about $42,000 a year in salary plus a healthy executive bonus, depending upon the profitability of your division. In a boom year you could increase your salary by one third with your bonus. Besides that, being a division president would give you a fast track to perhaps a bigger division presidency or the Senior Vice President of Marketing slot. It is conceivable that you could be set for life financially if you accept this assignment now."

"Fred, believe me. I'm not being an ingrate. I haven't turned down this magnificent offer. Yes, the challenge of a division presidency excites me. I believe in the product line of that division. For instance, my 14-year-old niece used that facial blemish cream and it really works. The improvement in her appearance actually raised her level of self-confidence. We are marketing something solid. Our cosmetic line does contribute something esthetic to society in its own way. I think our company performs a lot of social good, considering its record on environmental safety and equal employment opportunity.

"Yet a man contemplating becoming a president has to carefully evaluate what becoming a president will do to his life style. In other words, what am I really letting myself in for?"

"Kevin, you're speaking in generalities. Let's get down to the specifics of what's really holding you back from jumping at this once-in-a-lifetime opportunity. Be candid with me. I'm both your boss and your friend."

"A good way to begin, Fred, is to tell you about a recent experience my wife and I had at the Sales Executive Club. An industrial psychologist was giving a talk about the problems created by successful husbands. He wasn't putting down success, and he wasn't really putting down husbands. What he seemed to be saying was that being a successful career person can create a lot of problems in your personal life, particularly with your wife and children. When he finished his talk there was tension in the air. Husbands were grinning sheepishly at their wives. Most of the wives had a surprised expression as if this man was revealing their personal case history. One skeptic said this psychologist was way off base, that he was dramatizing a few isolated case histories of obsessed executives and their neurotic wives. That was hardly the reaction my wife or I had to the theme of the talk.

"As an aftermath to the talk, my wife and I began some serious dialogue about our relationship. She has some real concerns that if I become any more successful as an executive I might become a flop as a husband. A woman quoted at the talk said something that really hit home with my wife. Something to the effect, 'I think the husbands with the least success in their careers make the best husbands, because their wives and families are all they have.'

"Noreen thinks that I have paid progressively less attention to her as I have advanced in my career. She told me that I'm so preoccupied with business problems that I only pay surface attention to her problems. One night she told me that her gynecologist said she would need a hysterectomy. I expressed my sympathy. She retorted that this was the second time she told me about the pending hysterectomy.

"That conversation served as a springboard for an examination of many other things about our family life. Out of nowhere, she asked me to name the teachers of our three children. I struck a blank on all three. She then asked me what grade our daughter Tricia was enrolled in. I told her I thought the third grade. I was off by one grade, which she used as evidence that I'm not really participating in our children's worlds.

"Worse than that, Noreen then pointed out that I have been out of town on her last three birthdays. I feebly pointed out to her that her birthday just happens to take place during the time of our annual sales convention. My opinion is that a good many husbands who are going nowhere in their careers— even a few unemployed husbands—forget their wives' birthdays. We can't attribute all my shortcomings to my business success. But it did make me wonder if a company president can ever remember his wife's birthday, or maybe even his own."

"Okay, Kevin, you have the standard problems at home that an executive can anticipate. Just pay a little more attention to your wife and things will straighten out on that front."

"Fred, the problem of success interfering with my personal life goes beyond my relationship with my wife. I'm also worried about my physical health. I'm not a candidate for an ulcer or a heart attack, but the attention I have been paying to my career lately has taken its toll on my physical condition. I notice that I've gained a lot of weight owing to the amount of time I spend in bars and restaurants with customers and colleagues. Those hefty business lunches add more calories than most people realize. Not only am I gaining weight, but I don't look as sharp as I did when I devoted less time to the job.

"Part of the problem, of course, is that you have less time to exercise when you're immersing yourself in your job. When I am home on weekends, I have so much catching up to do on household tasks that I get less physical exercise. I wouldn't worry so much about having gained a few pounds and looking a little pale, if I didn't see a steady deterioration of my golf game. A few years ago, I heard a statement about golf and business that passed by me at the time, but now it makes a good deal of sense. According to the fellow making this statement, if your golf score gets over 85 you have no business playing golf. But if your golf score gets under 75, you have no business.

"Now I know what that character was talking about. As my income and level of responsibility has increased, so has my golf score. When I do play, I'm more erratic. My putting is ragged, I slice more than ever, and I've added about 10 points to my average score. I used to pride myself on my golf. Now I'm just a duffer who plays recreational golf. To get my game back in shape, I'll either have to sacrifice my job or my family. I know that the stereotype of a golfer is an affluent executive. More accurately, the affluent executive fits the stereotype of a duffer. My career is very important to me, but so is my golf game. It would seem unfeeling on my part to chip away at my time with the family in order to bring my game back to snuff."

"Of course, Kevin, if you don't keep raising your income you soon will not be able to afford golf. A person needs a lot of money to keep a golf game going, perhaps a few thousand a year, depending upon the particular club. If we give you a job as a clerk your game might return to its former level, but you would have to play in public parks. You'd spend so much time waiting to tee off, golf would then interfere with your personal life."

"Fred, I'm glad you brought up the topic of money. So far, the ever increasing amount of money I've earned hasn't had an overwhelming impact on my standard of living. In the 10 years I've been working for the company my income has more than tripled, but my standard of living has hardly tripled. My cost of living creeps up every year, and I need that big 10 to 15 percent salary increase just to stay even. Taxes go up at a much steeper rate than does your income.

"At times I find it both disturbing and embarrassing when I realize how little real financial security my ever increasing income has brought me. People think that as a Regional Manager for a large corporation, I have no financial worries. My in-laws think I'm stashing away about $1000 per month for the kids' college and our retirement. The truth is that except for programmed savings like the company retirement system and a mutual fund plan I'm enrolled in, many months go by without my saving any cash.

"What eats away at my insides the most is that some people grossing half as much money as I do seem to live about the same. Maybe they drive a Plymouth Duster instead of a Chrysler Cordova, but their car still performs the same function. Noreen, the children and I took a week's vacation to the Poconos last fall. We met loads of people there, such as foremen and school teachers, who make less than half my income and they had more dough to spend at the nightclub than I do. I'm beginning to wonder if the financial rewards associated with moving up in the executive ranks are real or illusory. Most of the bankruptcies I read about involve executives. Maybe there is something wrong with our system that subtly pushes up your expenses to meet your income."

"Kevin, maybe you're just having a bad day. Most of the problems you allude to are not as serious as you make them out to be. Perhaps you're overreacting."

"I don't entirely discount that possibility, Fred, but before I take the big plunge to a presidency there are certain things that would have to be ironed out in advance. Most important of all, what would be expected of a division president in this company? How many hours per week do I devote to the company? Who takes priority in my life, my company or my family? Do I get paid the same if I work 70 or 40 hours per week? What certainty do I have of that executive bonus? And how much of it will you guarantee?"

"Kevin, get hold of yourself. To succeed at the top you have to love every minute of the job. Digging in to the corporate problems should be your biggest source of kicks in life. All the concerns about the job and the little inconveniences at home are not the central issue. They are simply part of the price of success."

■ ■ ■

1. Is Kevin showing signs of work-related stress, or is he just having a bad day? First, answer the question intuitively and give your reasoning. Then, apply the stress model shown in Exhibit 14-1 to Kevin's situation, noting signs of stressors, stress, and stress reactions.
2. Does Kevin exhibit a Type A behavior pattern? Is he suffering from burnout?
3. Evaluate Fred's performance as a boss in the episode recounted in the case.
4. Under ideal conditions, what should Kevin and Fred do now?

REFERENCES

1. McGrath, J. E. (1970). A conceptual formulation for research on stress. In J. E. McGrath (Ed.), *Social and psychological factors in stress.* New York: Holt, Rinehart, Winston.

2. Roth, S., & Cohen, L. J. (1986). Approach, avoidance, and coping with stress. *American Psychologist, 41,* 813–819.

3. Anderson, C. R. (1977). Locus of control, coping behaviors and performance in a stress setting: A longitudinal study. *Journal of Applied Psychology, 62,* 446–451.

4. Friedman, M., & Rosenman, R. (1974). *Type A Behavior and your heart.* New York: Knopf.

5. Chesney, M. A., & Rosenman, R. (1980). Type A behavior in the work setting. In C. L. Cooper and R. Payne (Eds.), *Current concerns in occupational stress.* Chichester, England: Wiley.

6. Steinberg, L. (1985). Early temperamental antecedents of adult Type-A behaviors. *Developmental Psychology, 21,* 1171–1180.

7. Chesney & Rosenman, 1980.

8. Matthews, K. A. (1982). Psychological perspectives on the Type A behavior pattern. *Psychological Bulletin, 91,* 293–323. For a representative study see Ivancevich, J. M., Matteson, M. T., & Preston, C. (1982). Occupational stress, Type A behavior, and physical well-being. *Academy of Management Journal, 25,* 373–391.

9. Chesney & Rosenman, 1980.

10. Coleman, J. C. (1979). *Contemporary psychology and effective behavior* (4th ed.). Glenview, IL: Scott, Foresman.

11. See Parasuraman, S., & Alutto, J. A. (1981). An examination of the organizational antecedents of stressors at work. *Academy of Management Journal, 24,* 48–67.

12. Parasuraman & Alutto, 1981.

13. Mintzberg, H. (1973). *The nature of managerial work.* New York: Harper & Row, p. 30.

14. Rogers, E. M., & Larsen, J. K. (1984). *Silicon valley fever: Growth of a high-technology culture.* New York: Basic Books, p. 138.

15. An excellent review of managerial stressors can be found in Marshall, J., & Cooper, C. L. (1979). *Executives under pressure.* New York: Praeger.

16. La Porte, T. R. (1965). Conditions of strain and accommodation in industrial research organizations. *Administrative Science Quarterly, 10,* 21–38.

17. La Porte, 1965, p. 24.

18. Terkel, S. (1972). *Working,* New York: Avon, pp. 227–228.

19. Terkel, 1972, pp. 50–51.

20. Lawler, E. E., III. (1985). Education, managerial style, and organizational effectiveness. *Personnel Psychology, 38,* 1–26.

21. For a more optimistic view see Kirkland, R. I., Jr., (1985, June 10). Are service jobs good jobs? *Fortune,* 38–43.

22. Karasek, R. A., Jr. (1979). Job demands, job decision latitude, and mental strain: Implications for job redesign. *Administrative Science Quarterly, 24,* 285–308. Also see Kauppinen-Toropainen, K., Kandolin, I., & Mutanen, P. (1983). Job dissatisfaction and work-related exhaustion in male and female work. *Journal of Occupational Behaviour, 4,* 193–207.

23. Miles, R. H. Organizational boundary roles. In Cooper & Payne, 1980.

24. Much of this discussion of burnout relies on Pines, A. M., & Aronson, E. (with D. Kafry) (1981). *Burnout: From tedium to personal growth.* New York: The Free Press.

Also see Maslach, C., & Jackson, S. E. (1981). The measurement of experienced burnout. *Journal of Occupational Behaviour, 2,* 99–113.

25.   For a study of burnout among police personnel see Gaines, J., & Jermier, J. M. (1983). Emotional exhaustion in a high stress organization. *Academy of Management Journal, 26,* 567–586.

26.   Jackson, S. E., & Schuler, R. S. (1985). Meta-analysis and conceptual critique of research on role ambiguity and conflict in work settings. *Organizational Behavior and Human Decision Processes, 36,* 16–78. For a critique of some of this research see Fineman, S., & Payne, R. (1981). Role stress—a methodological trap? *Journal of Occupational Behaviour, 2,* 51–64.

27.   Terkel, 1972, pp. 115–116.

28.   Katz, D., & Kahn, R. L. (1978). *The social psychology of organizations* (2nd ed.). New York: Wiley.

29.   Gupta, N., & Beehr, T. A. (1979). Job stress and employee behavior. *Organizational Behavior and Human Performance, 23,* 373–387.

30.   See Kemery, E. R., Bedian, A. G., Mossholder, K. W., & Touliatos, J. (1985). Outcomes of role stress: A multisample constructive replication. *Academy of Management Journal, 28,* 363–375; Parasuraman, S., & Alutto, J. A. (1984). Sources and outcomes of stress in organizational settings: Toward the development of a structural model. *Academy of Management Journal, 27,* 330–350.

31.   Beehr, T. A., & Newman, J. E. (1978). Job stress, employee health, and organizational effectiveness: A facet analysis, model, and literature review. *Personnel Psychology, 32,* 665–699.

32.   Beehr & Newman, 1978. For a later review and a strong critique of this work see Fried, Y., Rowland, K. M., & Ferris, G. R. (1984). The physiological measurement of work stress: A critique. *Personnel Psychology, 37,* 583–615.

33.   Katz & Kahn, 1978.

34.   Cooper, C. L., Mallinger, M., & Kahn, R. (1978). Identifying sources of occupational stress among dentists. *Journal of Occupational Psychology, 51,* 227–234.

35.   Wall, T.D., & Clegg, C. W. (1981). A longitudinal field study of group work redesign. *Journal of Occupational Behaviour, 2,* 31–49.

36.   Murphy, L. R. (1984). Occupational stress management: A review and appraisal. *Journal of Occupational Psychology, 57,* 1–15.

37.   Murphy, 1984.

38.   Johnston, D. C., Mayes, B. T., Sime, W. E., & Tharp, G. D. (1982). Managing occupational stress: A field experiment. *Journal of Applied Psychology, 67,* 533–542.

39.   Ivancevich, J. M., & Matteson, M. T. (1980). *Stress at work: A managerial perspective.* Glenview, IL: Scott, Foresman, p. 215.

40.   Folkins, C. H., & Sime, W. E. (1981). Physical fitness training and mental health. *American Psychologist, 36,* 373–389; Falkenberg, L. E. (1987). Employee fitness programs: Their impact on the employee and the organization. *Academy of Management Review, 12,* 511–522.

Part Four

The Total Organization

Chapter 15

Organizational Structure

STEEL VERSUS SOLAR

Bill Donovan reflected on his first eight months at Solar Components Corporation with a sense of satisfaction. "Now I understand this company," he thought. "Now I understand my role here." As Donovan's thoughts imply, things had not always been this way. In fact, his first four months as sales manager at Solar had been the most perplexing and challenging in his business career.

After graduating from high school Donovan had obtained an engineering degree. However, he found the profession boring, and while working for one firm he began to pursue an M.B.A. degree part-time, hoping to move into management. He had especially enjoyed his marketing courses, and this led to a fairly radical career change. Upon graduating, Donovan quit the engineering firm and took a job as a sales representative for Ohio Valley Steel. Starting in the field had been a wise move. In two years, Donovan was promoted to sales manager for finished steel products. Two years after this, he became general sales manager, with the managers for finished products and bulk steel reporting to him. Donovan occupied this position until he quit to become sales manager at Solar Components. Solar developed, designed, and constructed custom solar heating and cooling devices for residential and commercial buildings.

Bill Donovan's recent experience at Solar had led him to think a lot about his five years at Ohio Valley. In retrospect, selling steel had been a pretty routine business. Ohio Valley's product line had remained the same for years, and selling consisted mainly of detailing existing customers and keeping one's eyes open for new prospects who could use what Ohio produced. Sales contracts were standard and routine, and Donovan had only encountered a couple of unusual cases in his whole career there. "After all," Donovan thought, "steel is steel. The winner in that business delivers on time and keeps quality high."

Ohio Valley Steel had been a formal, tightly controlled organization. Each position Donovan held had a detailed job description and a carefully written procedures manual. In addition, it had a long chain of command. Sales representatives reported to sales managers who reported to the general sales manager. In turn, he reported to the marketing director who then reported to the vice-president of marketing. Employees were encouraged to stick to the chain. This could be both comforting and frustrating. On one hand, there was always someone up the line to answer a question or deal with a problem. On the other, decisions could take *forever* to be made. In general, all important decisions were made at the top of the company. Donovan gradually came to understand the reason for this: Long production runs were most economical and easy to control in terms of quality. Only at the senior management level could sales orders be integrated into efficient production runs.

Even during his job interview, he was aware that things would be different at Solar Components. Asking to see written job descriptions for the sales manager and sales reps, he was told that there were none. Verbally, however, he learned that the jobs involved considerable latitude. He also realized that the chain of command at Solar was shorter than that at Ohio—just sales rep to sales manager to vice-president of marketing.

When he assumed his new job, it didn't take Donovan long to see the consequences of these differences. Unlike Ohio Valley's reps, the Solar sales reps had a high degree of technical training. Most were science graduates, and they worked closely with potential customers to develop custom solar systems suited to their individual needs. The solar technology was changing rapidly, and most salespersons consulted directly with the design department once a contact had been made. This procedure made Donovan nervous, so he asked to review all contacts before the reps went to design. Quickly, however, he realized that this didn't make any sense. Despite his engineering background, he simply didn't understand enough about solar systems to be helpful at this stage. Thus, he reinstituted the looser system of communication between sales and design.

Donovan also found out that the short chain of command discouraged pushing decisions "upstairs." When a sales rep came to him complaining about surface cracks in some solar panels that had just been delivered, he contacted his vice-president for advice. "I don't understand that stuff," he was told. "You and the rep get together with Michaels in production and Robbins in design and work it out. Whatever you decide is okay by me." Gradually, Donovan learned that such informal teamwork was common at Solar. Slowly, he settled into the job and learned to enjoy the system. Still, he wondered how two successful companies could be organized so differently.

This story reflects the common observation that different organizations are organized or structured differently. But why is this so? And how do these differences affect organizational members and the overall effectiveness of the organization? These are the kinds of questions we shall attempt to answer in this chapter and the next.

First, organizational structure will be defined, and the methods by which labor is divided and departments are formed will be discussed. Then we will consider some methods by which labor is coordinated. Traditional structural characteristics and the relationship between size and structure will be considered. Finally, we will review some early prescriptions concerning structure and some signals of structural problems.

A PROLOGUE: THE ROLE OF ORGANIZATIONAL STRUCTURE

In previous chapters we have been concerned primarily with the bits and pieces that make up organizations. First, we analyzed organizational behavior from the standpoint of the individual member—how his or her learning, perception, attitudes, and motivation affect behavior. Then we shifted our analysis to groups and to some of the processes that occur in organizations, including communication, leadership, and decision making. In this chapter we adopt yet another level of analysis by looking at the organization as a whole. Our primary interest is the causes and consequences of organizational structure.

Shortly we will discuss organizational structure in detail. For now, it is enough to know that it broadly refers to how the organization's individuals and groups are *put together* or *organized* to accomplish work. This is an important issue. It is entirely possible to conceive of a firm or institution that has well-motivated individual members and properly led groups and still fails to fulfill its potential because of the way their efforts are divided and coordinated.

We are not used to thinking about the structure of organizations and how it affects us. Frequently, we confuse the effects of structure with motivation, leadership, or communication. For example, consider the Master's level engineering student who must withdraw from a course that is cancelled because its enrollment is too small. She is able to withdraw from the course at the graduate office, but she is told that she must go to the accounts office to obtain a tuition refund. At the accounts office, she learns that she must have a note from the department that cancelled the course. Returning with a note from the electrical engineering department, she finds that she must also obtain a copy of her registration from the registrar's office before a refund can be granted. Ready to scream, she proceeds to give the poor accounts clerk a lecture on leadership, motivation, and communication. In fact, each of the subunits described in this example may be doing its own job perfectly well. It is the way the university is *structured* that is causing the student problems.

In Chapter 1 we defined organizations as social inventions for accomplishing goals through group effort. We also separated organizational goals into official goals (such as making a profit or curing the sick) and operative goals (such as keeping workers satisfied) that can assist in the achievement of official goals. In this chapter and the next we shall see that organizational structure intervenes between goals and organizational accomplishments, and thus influences organizational effectiveness.

WHAT IS ORGANIZATIONAL STRUCTURE?

Organizational structure is not the easiest concept to define precisely, because the concept covers so much territory. However, we can get a little more precise than our previous allusion to structure as being how an organization is ''put together'' or ''organized.''

Let's begin this way: In order to achieve its goals, an organization has to do two very basic things—divide labor among its members and then coordinate what has been divided. The university mentioned above divided its labor—some members taught electrical engineering, some ran the graduate program, some took care of accounts, and some handled registration. It is simply unlikely that anyone could do *all* of these things well. Furthermore, within each of these subunits labor would be further divided. For example, the registrar's office would include a director, secretaries, clerks, and so on. With all this division, some coordination is obviously necessary. Although the student didn't feel the coordination was adequate, a good organizational detective would spot evidence of its existence—everyone knew who she should see to solve her refund problem.

We can conclude that **organizational structure** is the manner in which an organization divides its labor into specific tasks and achieves coordination among these tasks.[1]

THE DIVISION AND COORDINATION OF LABOR

Labor must be divided because individuals have physical and intellectual limitations. *Everyone* can't do *everything,* and even if this were possible, tremendous confusion and inefficiency would result. There are two basic dimensions to the division of labor, a vertical dimension and a horizontal dimension. Once labor is divided, it must be coordinated to achieve organizational effectiveness.

Vertical Division of Labor

The **vertical division of labor** is concerned primarily with apportioning authority for planning and decision making—who gets to tell whom what to do? As shown in Exhibit 15-1, in a manufacturing firm the vertical division of labor is usually signified by titles such as president, manager, and supervisor. In a university it might be denoted by titles such as president, dean, and chairperson. Organizations

EXHIBIT 15-1   **The dimensions of division of labor in a manufacturing firm.**

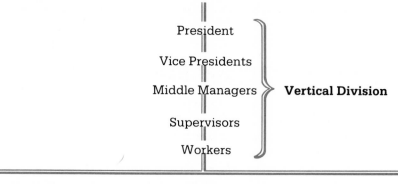

President

Vice Presidents

Middle Managers   **Vertical Division**

Supervisors

Workers

Making Goods Selling Goods Handling Finances Dealing with Personnel

Horizontal Division

differ greatly in the extent to which labor is divided vertically. For example, the U.S. Army has nine levels of command ranging from four-star generals to sergeants. Similarly, Bell Canada has seven levels ranging from president to first-level supervisors. On the other hand, an automobile dealership might have only three levels, and a university would usually fall between these extremes. Separate departments, units, or functions *within* an organization will also often vary in the extent to which they vertically divide labor. A production unit might have several levels of management ranging from supervisor to general manager. A research unit in the same company might have only two levels of management. A couple of key themes or issues underlie the vertical division of labor.

AUTONOMY AND CONTROL. Holding other factors constant, the domain of decision making and authority is reduced as the number of levels in the hierarchy increases. Put another way, managers have less authority over fewer matters. This was illustrated in the story that began the chapter. Ohio Valley Steel had quite a few levels in its marketing hierarchy, and Bill Donovan found his authority to make decisions restricted. Solar Components, with fewer levels, pushed such authority lower and even involved the sales representatives in decisions.

COMMUNICATION. A second theme underlying the vertical division of labor is communication or coordination between levels. As labor is progressively divided vertically, timely communication and coordination may become harder to achieve. Recall that decisions took "forever" at Ohio Valley Steel. Also recall our discussion of information filtering as a barrier to communication in Chapter 11. As the number of levels in the hierarchy increases, filtering is more likely to occur.

These two themes illustrate that labor must be divided vertically enough to ensure proper control but not so much as to make vertical communication and coordination impossible. The proper degree of such division will vary across organizations and across their functional units.

Horizontal Division of Labor

The **horizontal division of labor** involves grouping the basic tasks that must be performed into jobs and then into departments so that the organization can achieve its goals. The firm schematized in Exhibit 15-1 must produce and sell goods, keep its finances straight, and keep its employees happy. A hospital must admit patients, subject them to lab tests, fix what ails them, and keep them comfortable, all the while staying within its budget. Just as organizations differ in the extent to which they divide labor vertically, they also differ in the extent of horizontal division of labor. In a small business, the owner may be a "jack of all trades," making estimates, delivering the product or service, and keeping the books. As the organization grows, horizontal division of labor is likely, with different groups of employees assigned to perform each of these tasks. Thus, the horizontal division of labor suggests some specialization on the part of the work force. Up to a point, this increased specialization may promote efficiency. A couple of key themes or issues underlie the horizontal division of labor.

JOB DESIGN. The horizontal division of labor is closely tied to our earlier consideration of job design (Chapter 7). An example will clarify this. Suppose that an organization offers a product or service that consists of A work, B work, and C work (e.g., fabrication, inspection, and packaging). There are at least three basic ways it might structure these tasks:

- Form an ABC Department in which all workers do ABC work
- Form an ABC Department in which workers specialize in A work, B work, or C work
- Form a separate A Department, B Department, and C Department

There is nothing inherently superior about any of these three designs. Notice, however, that each has implications for the jobs involved and how these jobs are coordinated. The first design provides for enriched jobs in which each worker can coordinate his or her own A work, B work, and C work. However, this design may require highly trained workers, and it may be impossible if A work, B work, and C work are complex specialties that require (for example) engineering, accounting, and legal skills. The second design involves increased horizontal division of labor in which employees specialize in tasks and in which the coordination of A work, B work, and C work becomes more critical. However, much of this coordination could be handled by properly designing the job of the head of the department.

Finally, the third design offers the greatest horizontal division of labor in that A work, B work, and C work are actually performed in separate departments. This design provides for great control and accountability for the separate tasks, but it also suggests that someone above the department heads will have to get involved in coordination. There are several lessons here. First, the horizontal division of labor strongly affects job design. Second, it has profound implications for the degree of coordination necessary. Finally, it also has implications for the vertical division of labor and where control over work processes should logically reside.

DIFFERENTIATION.   A second theme occasioned by the horizontal division of labor is related to the first. As organizations engage in increased horizontal division of labor they usually become more and more differentiated. **Differentiation** is the tendency for managers in separate functions or departments to differ in terms of goals, time spans, and interpersonal styles.[2] In tending to their own domains and problems, these managers may develop distinctly different psychological orientations toward the organization and its products or services. A classic case of differentiation is that which often occurs between marketing managers and those in research and development. The goals of the marketing managers may be external to the organization and oriented toward servicing the marketplace. Those of R&D managers may be oriented more toward excellence in design and state-of-the-art use of materials. While marketing managers want products to sell *now,* R&D managers may feel that "good designs take time." Finally, marketing managers may believe that dispute resolution with R&D is best accomplished by interpersonal tactics learned when they were on the sales force ("Let's discuss this over lunch"). R&D managers may feel that "the design data speaks for itself" when a conflict occurs. The essential problem here is that the marketing department and the R&D department *need* each other to do their jobs properly![3]

Differentiation is a natural and necessary consequence of the horizontal division of labor, but it again points to the need for coordination, a topic which we will consider in more detail below. For now, let's examine more closely how organizations can allocate work to departments.

Departmentation

As suggested above, once basic tasks have been combined into jobs, a question still remains as to how to group these jobs so that they can be managed effectively. The assignment of jobs to departments is called departmentation, and it represents one of the core aspects of the horizontal division of labor. It should be recognized that "department" is a generic term that some organizations may also call unit, group, or division. There are several methods of departmentation, each of which has its strengths and weaknesses.

FUNCTIONAL DEPARTMENTATION.   This form of organization is basic and familiar. Under **functional departmentation,** workers with closely related skills and responsibilities (functions) are located in the same department (see Exhibit 15-2). Thus, those with skills in sales and advertising are assigned to the marketing department, those with skills in accounting and credit are assigned to the finance department, and so on. Under this kind of design, employees are grouped according to the kind of resources they provide to achieving the overall goals of the organization.[4]

What are the advantages of functional departmentation? The most-cited advantage is that of efficiency. When all of our engineers are located in an engineering department, rather than scattered throughout the organization, it is easier to be sure that they are neither overloaded nor underloaded with work. Also, support factors such as reference books, computer terminals, and laboratory space can be allocated more efficiently with less duplication. Some other advantages of functional departmentation include the following:

- Communication within departments may be enhanced, since everyone "speaks the same language."
- Career ladders and training opportunities within the function are enhanced.
- It may be easier to measure and evaluate the performance of functional specialists when they are all located in the same department.

What are the disadvantages of functional departmentation? Most of them stem from the specialization within departments that occurs in the functional arrangement. As a result, a high degree of differentiation can occur between functional departments. At best, this may lead to poor coordination and slow response to organizational problems. At worst, it may lead to open conflict between departments in which the needs of clients and customers are ignored. Departmental empires may be built at the expense of pursuing organizational goals.

EXHIBIT 15-2   Functional departmentation.

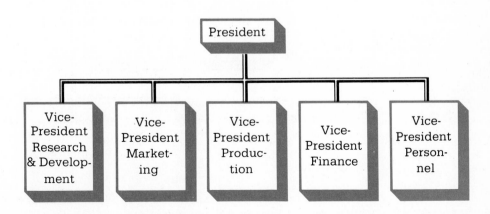

There is consensus that functional departmentation works best in small to medium-size firms that offer relatively few product lines or services. It can also be an effective means of organizing the smaller divisions of large corporations. When scale gets bigger and the output of the organization gets more complex, most firms gravitate toward product departmentation or its variations.

PRODUCT DEPARTMENTATION. Under **product departmentation,** departments are formed on the basis of a particular product, product line, or service. Each of these departments can operate fairly autonomously because it has its own set of functional specialists dedicated to the output of that department. For example, a computer firm might have a hardware division and a software division, each with its own staff of production people, marketers, and research and development personnel (see Exhibit 15-3).

EXHIBIT 15-3   Product departmentation.

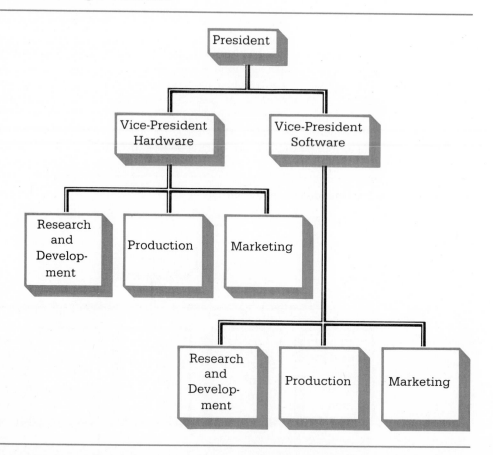

What are the advantages of product departmentation? One key advantage is better coordination among the functional specialists who work on a particular product line. Since their attentions are focused on one product and they have fewer functional peers, fewer barriers to communication should develop. Other advantages include flexibility, since product lines can be added or deleted without great implications for the rest of the organization. Also, product-focused departments can be evaluated as profit centers, since they have independent control over costs and revenues. This is not feasible for most functional departments (e.g., the research and development department doesn't have revenues). Finally, product departmentation often serves the customer or client better, since the client can see more easily who produced the product (the software group, not Ajax Computers).

Are there any disadvantages to product departmentation? Professional development may suffer without a critical mass of professionals working in the same place at the same time. Also, economies of scale may be threatened and inefficiency may occur if relatively autonomous product-oriented departments are not coordinated. R&D personnel in an industrial products division and a consumer products division might work on a similar problem for months without being aware of each other's efforts. Worse, product-oriented departments might actually work at cross-purposes to each other. At Hewlett-Packard, for instance, extensive product departmentation led to a proliferation of products that couldn't communicate with each other (In–Focus 15-1). This has led the company to back away from pure product departmentation.

OTHER FORMS OF DEPARTMENTATION. Several other forms of departmentation can be observed.[5] Two of these are simply variations on product departmentation. One is called geographic departmentation. Under **geographic departmentation,** relatively self-contained units deliver the organization's products or services in specific geographic territories (Exhibit 15-4). This form of departmentation shortens communication channels, allows the organization to cater to regional tastes, and gives some appearance of local control to clients and customers. National retailers, insurance companies, and oil companies generally exhibit geographic departmentation.

Another form of departmentation that is closely related to product departmentation is called customer departmentation. Under **customer departmentation,** relatively self-contained units deliver the organization's products or services to specific customer groups (Exhibit 15-5). The obvious goal is to provide better service to each customer group by specialization. For example, many banks have commercial lending divisions that are separate from the consumer loan operations. Universities may have separate graduate and undergraduate divisions. An engineering firm may have separate divisions to cater to civilian and military customers. In general, the advantages and disadvantages of geographic and customer departmentation parallel those for product departmentation.

IN–FOCUS 15-1　HEWLETT-PACKARD RETREATS FROM STRONG PRODUCT DEPARTMENTATION

After hinting for months that it was poised to fire its first salvos into the small but fast-growing computer-aided-engineering industry, Hewlett-Packard has spiked its cannon. The company's line of CAE hardware and software designed to speed the development of electronic systems won't start coming out as planned in November. In fact, H-P won't announce any CAE products this year and, according to William Parzybok, general manager of the design systems group, "prefers not to talk about introduction dates."

An upheaval in Hewlett-Packard's CAE ranks began last July, when the company undertook a tumultuous reorganization. This led to the dissolution of the division responsible for the new CAE product line late in September. Under the old organization, Hewlett-Packard operated as a loose agglomeration of small, autonomous businesses, each focused tightly on its own product line. The structure worked wonderfully as long as H-P pursued hundreds of niche markets. But as customers began demanding systems of H-P products that could work together, the structure turned into a liability. The CAE division, set up in early 1983, was given a special franchise to build systems out of hardware drawn from at least six other divisions, but people who left say they had trouble getting rival fiefdoms to cooperate.

With the reorganization, President John Young merged the product divisions into three large sectors aimed at different markets. Most of the CAE division was recently assigned to two design systems groups in Colorado, far from the division's old home in Cupertino, California. Embittered about the reorganization and reluctant to transfer, CAE engineers and managers began to leave for other jobs at H-P or to move to other companies. Résumés from disgruntled H-P employees, normally scarce, have been pouring into Silicon Valley CAE companies. Richard Moore, 50, a 23-year veteran of H-P and the head of the CAE division, went to Valid as president. By the time H-P closed the division, many top managers and engineers were gone.

But H-P hasn't abandoned its plan to be No. 1 in the CAE business, which Young considers strategically necessary.

Source: Edited from Uttal, B. (1984, October 29). Delays and defections at Hewlett-Packard. *Fortune*, p. 62. © 1984, Time Inc. All rights reserved.

Finally, it should be recognized that few organizations represent "pure" examples of functional, product, geographic, or customer departmentation. It is not unusual to see **hybrid departmentation** which involves some combination of these structures. For example, a manufacturing firm might retain personnel, finance, and legal services in a functional form at headquarters but use product departmentation to organize separate production and sales staffs for each product. Similarly, a large retail firm might departmentize buying functionally (all buyers working out of the same headquarters department) even though it otherwise relies on geographic departmentation. The hybrids attempt to capitalize on the strengths of various structures while avoiding the weaknesses of others.

EXHIBIT 15-4   Geographic departmentation.

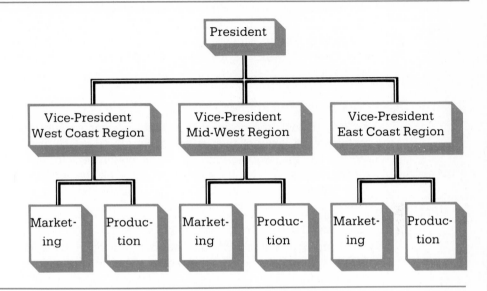

EXHIBIT 15-5   Customer departmentation.

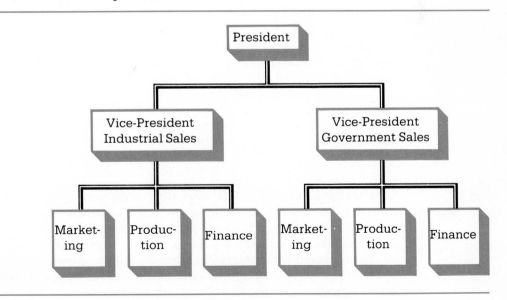

Basic Methods of Coordinating Divided Labor

When the tasks that will help the organization achieve its goals have been divided among individuals and departments, they must be coordinated so that goal accomplishment is actually realized. We can identify five basic methods of **coordination,** which is a process of facilitating timing, communication, and feedback.[6]

DIRECT SUPERVISION.   This is a very traditional form of coordination. Working through the chain of command, designated supervisors or managers coordinate the work of their subordinates. For instance, a production foreman coordinates the work of his or her subordinates. In turn, the production superintendent coordinates the activities of all the foremen. This method of coordination is closely associated with our discussion of leadership in Chapter 10.

STANDARDIZATION OF WORK PROCESSES.   Some jobs are so routine that the technology itself provides a means of coordination. Little direct supervision is necessary for these jobs to be coordinated. The automobile assembly line provides a good example. When a car comes by, worker X bolts on the left A-frame assembly and worker Y bolts on the right assembly. These workers do not have to interact with each other, and they require minimal supervision. Work processes can also be standardized by rules and regulations. The procedures manuals Bill Donovan found at Ohio Valley Steel are an example.

STANDARDIZATION OF OUTPUTS.   Even when direct supervision is minimal and work processes are not standardized, coordination can be achieved through the standardization of work outputs. Concern shifts from how the work is done to ensuring that the work meets certain physical or economic standards. For instance, workers in a machine shop may be required to construct complex valves that require a mixture of drilling, lathe work, and finishing. The physical specifications of the valves will dictate how this work is to be coordinated. Standardization of outputs is often used to coordinate the work of separate product or geographic divisions. Frequently, top management assigns each division a profit target. These standards ensure that each division "pulls its weight" in contributing to overall profit goals. Thus, budgets are a form of standardizing outputs.

STANDARDIZATION OF SKILLS.   Even when work processes and output cannot be standardized, and direct supervision is unfeasible, coordination can be achieved through standardization of skills. This is seen very commonly in the case of technicians and professionals. For example, a large surgery team can often coordinate its work with minimal verbal communication because of its high degree of interlocked training—surgeons, anesthesiologists, and nurses all know what to expect from each other because of their standard training.

MUTUAL ADJUSTMENT. Mutual adjustment relies upon informal communication to coordinate tasks. Paradoxically, it is useful for coordinating the most simple and the most complicated divisions of labor. For example, imagine a small florist shop that consists of the owner-operator, a shop assistant, and a delivery person. It is very likely that these individuals will coordinate their work through informal processes, mutually adjusting to each other's needs. At the other extreme, consider the team that was responsible for designing the heat-shield tiles for the U.S. space shuttle craft. This complicated task reached to the very edge of current technology, requiring the collaboration of physicists, chemists, computer specialists, and aeronautical engineers. Here we see a unique task and a radical mix of specialists with different backgrounds and training. Again, mutual adjustment would be necessary to coordinate their efforts, because standardization would be impossible (also, the more complex coordination mechanisms discussed below would be used). At Solar Components, Bill Donovan found that mutual adjustment was necessary to coordinate the efforts of sales, production, and design. The customized nature of the product dictated that this approach be used.

Now that we have reviewed the five methods of coordinating divided labor, a few comments are in order. First, as shown in Exhibit 15-6, the methods can be crudely ordered in terms of the degree of *discretion* they permit individual workers in terms of task performance; applied strictly, direct supervision permits little discretion. Standardization of processes and outputs permits successively more discretion. (However, these forms of standardization can be "beaten" by clever workers.) Finally, standardization of skills and mutual adjustment put even more control into the hands of those who are actually doing the work.

Notice that just as division of labor affects the design of jobs, so does the method of coordination employed. As we move from the left side to the right side of the continuum of coordination, there is greater potential for jobs to be designed in an enriched manner. By the same token, an improper coordination strategy can destroy the intrinsic motivation of a job. Traditionally, much work performed by

---

EXHIBIT 15-6 **Methods of coordination as a continuum of worker discretion.**

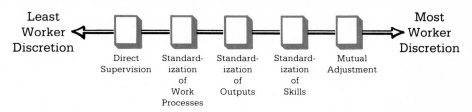

Source: From Mintzberg, H. (1979). *The structuring of organizations: A synthesis of the research.* Englewood Cliffs, NJ: Prentice-Hall, p. 198. © 1979. Reprinted by permission of Prentice-Hall, Inc., Englewood Cliffs, NJ.

professionals (e.g., scientists and engineers) is coordinated by their own skill standardization. If the manager of a research lab decides to coordinate work with a high degree of direct supervision, the motivating potential of the scientists' jobs may be damaged. *She* is doing work that *they* should be doing.

It can also be observed that the use of the various methods of coordination tends to vary across different parts of the organization. These differences in coordination stem from the way labor has been divided. For example, upper management relies heavily upon mutual adjustment for coordination. Where tasks are more routine, such as in the lower part of the production subunit, we tend to see coordination via direct supervision or standardization of work processes or outputs.[7] Advisory subunits staffed by professionals, such as the legal department or the marketing research group, often rely upon a combination of skill standardization and mutual adjustment.

Finally, methods of coordination may change as task demands change. Under peacetime conditions or routine wartime conditions, the army relies heavily on direct supervision through a strict chain of command. However, this method of coordination may prove ineffective for fighting units under heavy fire. Here, we might see a sergeant with a radio instructing a captain where to direct artillery fire. This reversal of the chain of command is indicative of mutual adjustment.

Other Methods of Coordination

The forms of coordination discussed above are very basic in that almost every organization uses them. After all, when do we see an organization that *doesn't* exhibit some supervision, some standardization, and some talking things out? Sometimes, however, coordination problems are such that more customized, elaborate mechanisms are necessary to achieve coordination. This is especially true when we are speaking of lateral coordination across highly differentiated departments. Recall that the managers of such departments may vary greatly in goals, time spans, and interpersonal orientation. Figuratively, at least, they often "speak different languages"! The process of obtaining coordination across differentiated departments usually goes by the special name of **integration.**[8] Good integration achieves coordination without reducing the differences that enable each department to do its own job well.[9] For example, in a high technology firm, we don't *want* production and engineering to be so cozy that innovative tension is lost.[10]

In ascending order of elaboration, three methods of achieving integration include the use of liaison roles, task forces, and full-time integrators.[11]

LIAISON ROLES.   A **liaison role** is occupied by a person in one department who is assigned as part of his or her job to achieve coordination with another department. In other words, one person serves as a part-time link between two departments. Sometimes the second department might reciprocate by nominating its own liaison person. For example, in a university library, reference librarians might be required to serve as liaison persons for certain academic departments or schools. In turn, an academic department might assign a faculty member to "touch base" with its liaison in the library. Sometimes liaison persons may actually be located physically in the corresponding department. For instance, a member of the engineering department may be assigned to an office in the plant to assist with production matters.

TASK FORCES. When coordination problems arise that involve several departments simultaneously, liaison roles are not very effective. **Task forces** are temporary groups set up to solve coordination problems across several departments. Representatives from each department are included on a full-time or part-time basis, but when adequate integration is achieved, the task force is disbanded. The introduction of a new product or service may stimulate the establishment of a task force because of the degree of confusion and uncertainty. It may enable design, engineering, production, and sales to get their respective roles and time frames hammered out without referring the problem up into the hierarchy where detailed knowledge may be lacking.

INTEGRATORS. **Integrators** are organizational members who are permanently installed between two departments that are in clear need of coordination. In a sense, they are full-time problem solvers. Integrators are especially useful for dealing with conflict between (1) highly interdependent departments (2) which have very diverse goals and orientations (3) in a very ambiguous environment. Such a situation occurs in many high technology companies.[12] For example, a solid-state electronics firm may introduce new products almost every month. This is a real strain on the production department, who may need the assistance of the design scientists to implement a production run. The scientists, on the other hand, rely on production to implement last-minute changes due to the rapidly changing technology. This situation badly requires coordination.

Integrators usually report directly to the executive to whom the heads of the two departments report. Ideally, they are rewarded according to the success of both units. A special kind of person is required for this job, since he or she has great responsibility but no direct authority in either department. The integrator must be unbiased, "speak the language" of both departments, and rely heavily on expert power.[13] An engineer with excellent interpersonal skills might be an effective integrator for the electronics firm.

TRADITIONAL STRUCTURAL CHARACTERISTICS

Every organization is unique in the exact way in which its labor is divided and coordinated. Few business firms, hospitals, or schools have perfectly identical structures. What is needed, then, is some efficient way to summarize the effects of the vertical and horizontal division of labor and its coordination on the structure of the organization. Over the years, management scholars and practicing managers have agreed upon a number of characteristics that summarize the structure of organizations.[14]

Span of Control

The **span of control** is the number of subordinates supervised by a superior. There is one essential fact about span of control: The larger the span, the less *potential* there is for coordination by direct supervision. As the span increases, the attention that can be devoted to each subordinate decreases. When work tasks are routine, coordination of labor through standardization of work processes or output often substitutes for direct supervision. Thus, at lower levels in production units it is not unusual to see spans of control ranging to over twenty. In the managerial ranks tasks are less routine, and adequate time may be necessary for informal mutual adjustment. As a result, spans at the upper levels tend to be smaller. Another factor may also be at work here. At lower organizational levels, workers with only one or a few specialties report to a supervisor. For instance, an office supervisor may only supervise clerks. As we climb the hierarchy, workers with radically different specialties may report to the boss. For example, the president may have to deal with vice-presidents of personnel, finance, production, and marketing. Again, the complexity of this task may dictate smaller spans.[15]

Flat Versus Tall

Holding size constant, a **flat organization** has relatively few levels in its hierarchy of authority, while a **tall organization** has relatively many levels. Thus, flatness versus tallness is an index of the vertical division of labor. Again, holding size constant, it should be obvious that flatness and tallness are associated with the average span of control. This is shown in Exhibit 15-7. Both schematized organizations have thirty-one members. However, the taller one has five hierarchical levels and an average span of two, while the flatter one has three levels and an average span of five. It is usually thought that flatter structures tend to push decision-making powers downward in the organization, because a given number of decisions are apportioned among fewer levels. We saw this earlier in the comparison of Ohio Valley Steel and Solar Components. Also, flatter structures generally enhance vertical communication and coordination (In–Focus 15-2).

Formalization

Formalization refers to the extent to which work roles are highly defined by the organization. A more formalized organization tolerates little variability in the way members perform their tasks. Some formalization stems from the nature of the job itself—the work requirements of the assembly line provide a good example of this. More interesting, however, is formalization that stems from rules, regulations, and

EXHIBIT 15-7 **The relationship between span of control and organizational flatness and tallness.**

Tall Organization: 31 Members; 5 Levels; Average Span of Control is 2

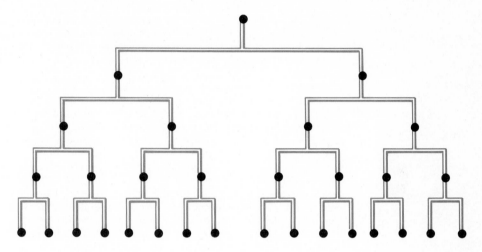

Flat Organization: 31 Members; 3 Levels; Average Span of Control is 5

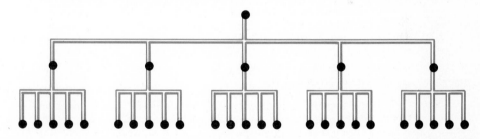

procedures that the firm or institution chooses to implement. Detailed written job descriptions, thick procedures manuals, and the requirement to "put everything in writing" are evidence of such formalization. Many government organizations use this method of formalization. So does the fast-food chain McDonald's:

> Rules and regulations are the gospel at McDonald's. The company's operating bible has 385 pages describing the most minute activities in each outlet. The manual prescribes that certain equipment—cigarette, candy, and pinball machines—is not permitted in the stores. It also prescribes strict standards for personal grooming. Men must keep their hair short and their shoes black and highly polished. Women are

IN–FOCUS 15-2   EATON COMPANY FLATTENS STRUCTURE

The T. Eaton Company is a large Canadian retail chain. President and Chief Executive Officer F. S. Eaton explains why Eaton flattened its structure.

At Eaton's we spent considerable time and effort last year designing exactly what kind of a company we wanted to both survive bad times and prosper. We then set about implementing an immediate reorganization.

In our first step, we began to simplify the management structure to remove layers or flatten it. This move lowered costs mainly through wage and benefit savings. It also improved communication by shortening the chain of command.

The organization flattening was achieved by removing one level of management from the store and functional organizations. Before we had four regional staffs. Now we have eliminated three of them and have one head office level. Within the stores themselves, we have eliminated one level of management. The improvement in job satisfaction and the increase in speed of decision making have been most dramatic. While this is the real benefit of the changes, our company has also achieved dramatic savings in annual management costs.

These steps were taken largely as a result of our personnel group interviewing our senior staff and middle and junior management on job satisfaction, a practice adopted in 1981, when sales were still buoyant. To our surprise, we found that one of the biggest dissatisfactions encountered by these levels of management and staff was the sense of having to wait for the boss to make a decision. The junior levels, while certain they knew what to do and were competent to do it, believed that if they took independent action the boss might feel threatened or be unhappy with the decision.

The removal of layers of management shortens the chain or command, thus reducing message loss down the chain. Many management experts have argued for years that there is a significant loss in the content of management directives as they pass through each level of management. Practical experience and interviewing by our personnel staff with all our management levels indicated that this is indeed the case at Eaton's. We wished to try to ensure that the corporation's objectives were getting to every level of management with maximum clarity, and the fewer levels they had to pass through the better.

An organization with fewer levels of management also gets better feedback from the lower, even lowest, levels. This is important, because the methods of achieving the corporation's objectives are often best understood by those people who have to achieve them. Thus, the objective is set by the corporation, but it should listen to the line manager who says, "Okay, that's what you want. Well, this is the best way I can achieve it."

Source: Edited from Eaton, F. S. (1983, Spring). Managing in tough times: How to survive and prosper. *The Canadian Business Review,* 17–19, p. 17. Reprinted by permission.

expected to wear hair nets and to use only very light makeup. The store manager is even provided with a maintenance reminder for each day of the year, such as "Lubricate and adjust potato-peeler belt."[16]

Centralization

Centralization refers to the extent that decision-making power is localized in a particular part of the organization. In the most centralized organization, the power for all key decisions would rest in a single individual, such as the president. In a more decentralized organization, decision-making power would be dispersed down through the hierarchy and across departments. One observer suggests that limitations to individual brainpower often prompt decentralization:

> How can the Baghdad salesperson explain the nature of his clients to the Birmingham manager? Sometimes the information can be transmitted to one center, but a lack of cognitive capacity (brainpower) precludes it from being comprehended there. How can the president of the conglomerate corporation possibly learn about, say, 100 different product lines? Even if a report could be written on each, he would lack the time to study them all.[17]

Of course, the information-processing capacity of executives is not the only factor that dictates degree of centralization. Some organizations may consciously pursue a more participative climate that can be achieved through decentralization. In others, top management may wish to maintain greater control and opt for stronger centralization.

Recalling the story that began the chapter, it should be obvious that Ohio Valley Steel was fairly tall, formalized, and centralized. Solar Components was flatter, less formal, and decentralized.

Complexity

Complexity refers to the extent to which organizations divide labor vertically, horizontally, and geographically.[18] A fairly simple organization will have few management levels (vertical division) and not many separate job titles (horizontal division). In addition, jobs will be grouped into a small number of departments, and work will be performed in only one physical location (geographic division). At the other extreme, a very complex organization will be tall, have a large number of job titles and departments, and may be spread around the world. The essential characteristic of complexity is *variety*—as the organization becomes more complex it has more kinds of people performing more kinds of tasks in more places, whether these places are departments or geographic territories.

ORGANIZATIONAL SIZE AND STRUCTURAL CHARACTERISTICS

It is perhaps trivial to note that the giant General Motors Corporation is structured differently from your small corner grocery store. But exactly how does organizational size (measured by number of employees) affect the structure of organizations?

In general, there is much evidence that large organizations are more complex than small organizations.[19] For example, a small organization is unlikely to have its own legal department or market research group, and these tasks will probably be contracted out. Economies of scale enable large organizations to perform these functions themselves, but with a consequent increase in the number of departments and job titles. In turn, this horizontal specialization often stimulates the need for additional complexity in the form of appointing integrators, creating planning departments, and so on. As horizontal specialization increases, management levels must be added (making the organization taller) so that spans of control do not get out of hand.[20] To repeat, size is associated with increased complexity.

Complexity means coordination problems in spite of integrators, planning departments, and the like. This is where other structural characteristics come into play. In general, bigger organizations are less centralized than smaller organizations.[21] In a small company, the president might be involved in all but the least critical decisions to be made. In a large company, the president would be overloaded with such decisions, and they could not be made in a timely manner. In addition, since the large organization will also be taller, top management is often too far removed from the action to make many operating decisions. How is control retained with decentralization? The answer is formalization—large organizations tend to be more formal than small organizations. Rules, regulations, and standard procedures help ensure that decentralized decisions fall within accepted bounds. This comparison of a small independent bank with a larger more complex bank with several branches illustrates the point nicely:

> Interestingly, the larger bank may be much more decentralized than the small bank. In the small bank, the president may give final approval on all loans simply because time is available to do so. In large banks with many branches no one person can examine all the loan applications, so the decisions are decentralized to officers within the branches. However, this delegation of responsibility is accompanied by *standard procedures* for evaluating loan applications. Decision rules are carefully worked out in advance and communicated downward through policy updates, newsletters, and other formal documents. In this way the large organization can control its lower levels.[22]

Two further points about the relationship between size and structure should be emphasized. First, you will recall that product departmentation is often preferable to functional departmentation as the organization increases in size. Logically then, organizations with product departmentation should exhibit more complexity and more decentralization than those with functional departmentation. A careful comparison of Exhibits 15-2 and 15-3 will confirm this logic. In the firm with the product structure, research, production, and marketing are duplicated, increasing complexity. In addition, since each product line is essentially self-contained, decisions can be made at a lower organizational level.

Finally, it should be recognized that size is only one determinant of organizational structure. Even at a given size, organizations may require different structures to be maximally effective. In the next chapter we will examine other determinants of structure.

Exhibit 15-8 summarizes the relationship between size and structural variables.

EMPLOYEE REACTIONS TO STRUCTURAL CHARACTERISTICS

What are the implications of structural characteristics for the job satisfaction of employees? The research literature provides us with some clues.[23]

There is no simple association between tallness or flatness and job satisfaction. Managers in organizations with less than 5000 employees seem to exhibit more job satisfaction when they operate under flatter structures. Those in organi-

---

EXHIBIT 15-8   **The relationship between size and structure.**

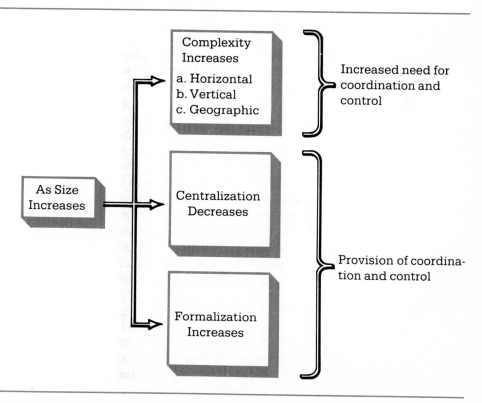

zations with over 5000 employees seem happier with taller structures.[24] We have noted that larger organizations tend to be taller. This suggests that exceptions to the general rule (i.e., small, tall organizations and large, flat organizations) prompt dissatisfaction. In the former, managers may have few opportunities for decision making. In the latter, coordination may be so poor that role ambiguity results.

Formalization often prompts job dissatisfaction, except for those individuals who have very strong needs for the security that rules provide.[25] Formalization is a particular problem for boundary role occupants who must deal directly with outsiders.[26] Salespeople, welfare officers, and courthouse desk clerks often find themselves held to rules and red tape that damage their relationships with clients and customers and thus provoke considerable disillusionment.

There is no simple, straightforward relationship between job satisfaction and degree of organizational centralization. This may be because different degrees of centralization are appropriate for different subunits and across various kinds of organizations.

There has been very little study of individual reactions to varying spans of control. However, one study of sales representatives found that role ambiguity increased as more reps reported to the same manager.[27] This suggests that spans that are too large may contribute to communication and coordination problems. On the other hand, very small spans may reduce employee autonomy and provoke dissatisfaction, especially among well-trained and experienced personnel.

One important mechanism by which structural characteristics influence job satisfaction is job design.[28] We saw earlier that job design is affected by the way in which labor is divided and coordinated. For example, extreme division of labor may reduce the task variety of individual jobs and prompt dissatisfaction. Similarly, coordination of this divided labor by high formalization may reduce autonomy, again stimulating dissatisfaction.

EARLY PRESCRIPTIONS CONCERNING STRUCTURE

For many years, those who were interested in organizational effectiveness concerned themselves with prescribing the "correct" way to structure an organization to achieve its goals. There were two basic phases to this prescription which might be called the classical view and the human relations view. The following sketch of these viewpoints is necessarily brief and thus does some injustice to the subtle thinking underlying them. Nevertheless, the basic caricatures are accurate.

The Classical View and Bureaucracy

Most of the major advocates of the classical viewpoint were experienced managers or consultants who took the time to set down their thoughts on organizing in writing. For the most part, this activity occurred in the early 1900s. Frederick Taylor, the father of Scientific Management (Chapter 7), can be considered a contributor to the classical school, although he was mainly concerned with job design and the structure of work on the shop floor.[29] You will recall that Taylor advocated extreme division of labor and specialization, even extending to the specialization of supervisors in roles such as trainer, disciplinarian, and so on. Also, he advocated careful standardization and regulation of work activities, rest pauses, and so on.

Other classical writers acquired their experience in military settings, mining operations, and factories that produced everything from cars to candy. Prominent names include Henri Fayol, James D. Mooney, and Lyndall Urwick.[30] Although exceptions existed, they tended to advocate a very high degree of specialization of labor and a very high degree of coordination. For example, they favored functional division of labor because this led to a high degree of specialization within departments. To coordinate these specialists, high formalization, a fairly tall structure, and an adequate degree of centralization were advocated. For the same reason, fairly small spans of control were suggested, except for lower-level jobs, where machine pacing might substitute for close supervision.

The practicing managers had an academic ally in Max Weber, the distinguished German social theorist. Weber made the term *bureaucracy* famous by advocating it as a means of rationally managing complex organizations. During Weber's lifetime (1864–1920) managers were certainly in need of advice. In this time of industrial growth and development, most management was by intuition, and nepotism and favoritism were rampant. According to Weber, a **bureaucracy** has the following qualities:

- A strict chain of command in which each member reports to only a single superior

- Selection and promotion on the basis of impersonal technical skills rather than nepotism or favoritism

- Detailed rules, regulations, and procedures ensuring that the job gets done regardless of who the specific worker is

- Strict specialization to match duties with technical competence

- The centralization of power at the top of the organization[31]

It is important to understand that Weber saw bureaucracy as an "ideal type" or theoretical model that would standardize behavior in organizations and provide workers with security and a sense of purpose. Jobs would be performed *as intended* rather than according to the whims of the specific role occupant, and in exchange for this conformity, workers would have a fair chance of being promoted and rising in the power structure. This sense of security was backed up by rules, regulations, and a clearcut chain of command that further clarified required behavior.

We can summarize the prescriptions of the classical theorists by saying that they advocated mechanistic structures.[32] As summarized in Exhibit 15-9, **mechanistic structures** tend toward tallness, narrow spans, specialization, high centralization, and high formalization. Other structural and personnel aspects are designed to complement these basic structural prescriptions. By analogy, the organization is to be structured as a mechanical device, each part serving its separate function, each part closely coordinated with the others.

The Human Relations View and a Critique of Bureaucracy

The human relations movement is generally conceded to have begun with the famous Hawthorne studies of the 1920s and 1930s.[33] These studies, conducted at the Hawthorne plant of Western Electric near Chicago, began in the strict tradition of industrial engineering. They were concerned with the impact of fatigue, rest pauses, and lighting on productivity. However, during the course of the studies,

EXHIBIT 15-9   Mechanistic and organic structures.

Organizational Characteristics	Types of Organization Structure	
Index	Organic	Mechanistic
Span of control	Wide	Narrow
Number of levels of authority	Few	Many
Ratio of administrative to production personnel	High	Low
Range of time span over which an employee can commit resources	Long	Short
Degree of centralization in decision making	Low	High
Proportion of persons in one unit having opportunity to interact with persons in other units	High	Low
Quantity of formal rules	Low	High
Specificity of job goals	Low	High
Specificity of required activities	Low	High
Content of communications	Advice and information	Instructions and decisions
Range of compensation	Narrow	Wide
Range of skill levels	Narrow	Wide
Knowledge-based authority	High	Low
Position-based authority	Low	High

SOURCE: From Seiler, J. A. (1967). *Systems analysis in organizational behavior.* Homewood, IL: Irwin, p. 168. © Richard D. Irwin, Inc. 1967. This exhibit is an adaptation of one prepared by Paul R. Lawrence and Jay W. Lorsch in an unpublished ''Working Paper on Scientific Transfer and Organizational Structure,'' 1963. The latter, in turn, draws heavily on criteria suggested by W. Evans. ''Indices of the Hierarchical Structure of Industrial Organizations,'' *Management Science,* Vol. IX (1963), pp. 468–77. Burns and Stalker, *op. cit.,* and Woodward, *op. cit.,* as well as those suggested by R. H. Hall, ''Intraorganizational Structure Variables,'' *Administrative Science Quarterly,* Vol. IX (1962), pp. 295–308. Reprinted by permission.

the researchers began to notice the impact that psychological and social processes had on productivity and work adjustment. This impact suggested that there were dysfunctional aspects to the mechanistic organization of work. One obvious sign was resistance to management through strong informal group mechanisms such as norms that limited productivity. Gradually, this cause was taken up by a number of other theorists and researchers (mostly academics) who proceeded to take a hard look at the potential problems of mechanistic organizations. Their views are usually described as a critique of bureaucracy, and some specific criticisms include the following:

- Strict specialization and strong formalization are incompatible with human needs for growth and achievement.[34] This can lead to employee alienation from the organization and its clients or customers.

- Strong centralization and reliance upon formal authority often fail to take advantage of the creative ideas and knowledge possessed by lower-level members.[35] As a result, the organization will fail to learn from its mistakes, and innovation and adaptation will be threatened. Resistance to change will occur as a matter of course.

- Formalization through strict, impersonal rules leads members to adopt the *minimum* acceptable level of performance that the rules specify.[36] If a rule states that at least eight claims a day must be processed, eight claims will become the norm, even though higher performance levels are possible.

■ Strong specialization combined with formalization causes employees to lose sight of the overall goals of the organization.[37] Forms, procedures, and required signatures become ends in themselves, divorced from the true needs of customers, clients, and other departments in the organization. This is the "red-tape mentality" that is sometimes observed in bureaucracies. The cost of such red tape is illustrated in In–Focus 15-3.

Obviously, not all mechanistic organizations exhibit these dysfunctions. However, they were observed commonly enough that human relations advocates and others began to call for the adoption of more organic organizational structures. As noted in Exhibit 15-9, **organic structures** rely upon less formalization, centralization, and specialization. Flexibility and informal communication are emphasized over rigidity and the strict chain of command.

The labels *mechanistic* and *organic* simply represent theoretical extremes, and organizational structures can obviously fall between these two extremes. Still, the question remains, is one structure superior to the other? A clue to the answer to this question can be found in the case that began the chapter. Ohio Valley Steel exhibited a more mechanistic structure, while Solar Components exhibited a more organic structure. However, both organizations were successful. In general, (as long as the problems noted above are avoided), mechanistic structures are called for when the organizational environment is fairly stable and the technology is fairly routine (as at Ohio Valley Steel). Organic structures tend to work better when the environment is less stable and the technology is less routine (as at Solar Components). In the next chapter we will examine in detail the impact of environment and technology on organizational structure. For now, it is enough to recognize that there is no "one best way" to organize.

A FOOTNOTE: SYMPTOMS OF STRUCTURAL PROBLEMS

At the beginning of the chapter, I observed that it is sometimes difficult to appreciate the impact of organizational structure on the behavior that occurs in organizations. Now that you have been through the basics of structure, your appreciation of this impact should be much improved. Let's conclude the chapter by considering some symptoms of structural problems in organizations.

■ *Bad job design.* As was noted at several points, there is a reciprocal relationship between job design and organizational structure. Frequently, improper structural arrangements turn good jobs on paper into poor jobs in practice. A tall structure and narrow span of control in a research and development unit may reduce autonomy and turn exciting jobs into drudgery. An extremely large span of control may overload the most dedicated supervisor.

■ *The right hand doesn't know what the left is doing.* If repeated examples of duplication of effort occur, or if parts of the organization work at cross-purposes, structure is suspect. One author gives the example of one division of a large organization laying off workers while another division was busy recruiting from the same labor pool![38] The general problem here is one of coordination and integration.

■ *Persistent conflict between departments.* Managers are often inclined to attribute such conflicts to personality clashes between key personnel in the warring departments. Just as often, a failure of integration is the problem. One clue here is if the conflict persists even when personnel changes occur.

■ *Slow response times.* Ideally, labor is divided and coordinated to do business quickly. Delayed responses may be due to improper structure. Centralization may speed responses when a few decisions about a few products are required (dictating functional departmentation). Decentralization may speed responses when many decisions about many products are required (dictating product departmentation).

■ *Decisions made with incomplete information.* In Chapter 12 we noted that managers generally acquire more than enough information to make decisions. After the fact, if we find that decisions have been made with incomplete information, and the information existed somewhere in the organization, structure may be at fault. It is clear that structural deficiencies were in part responsible for keeping top NASA administrators unaware of the mechanical problems that contributed to the 1986 explosion of the space shuttle *Challenger*.[39] This information was known to NASA personnel, but it did not move up the hierarchy properly.

■ *A proliferation of committees.* Committees exist in all organizations, and they often serve as one of the more routine kinds of integrating mechanisms. However, when committee is piled upon committee, or when task forces are being formed with great regularity, it is often a sign that the basic structure of the organization is being "patched up" because it doesn't work well.[40] A structural review may be in order if too many people are spending too much time in committee meetings.

SUMMARY

■ Organizational structure is the manner in which an organization divides its labor into specific tasks and achieves coordination among these tasks. Labor is divided vertically and horizontally. Vertical division of labor concerns the apportioning of authority. Horizontal division of labor involves designing jobs and grouping them into departments. While functional departmentation involves locating employees with similar skills in the same department, other forms of departmentation locate employees in accordance with product, geography, or customer requirements.

■ Basic methods of coordinating divided labor include direct supervision, standardization of work processes, standardization of outputs, standardization of skills, and mutual adjustment. Workers are permitted more discretion as coordination moves from direct supervision through mutual adjustment. More elaborate methods of coordination are aimed specifically at achieving integration across departments. These include liaison roles, task forces, and integrators.

■ Traditional structural characteristics include span of control, flatness versus tallness, formalization, centralization, and complexity. Larger organizations tend to be more complex, more formal, and less centralized than smaller organizations. Various structural characteristics influence the job satisfaction of the work force.

■ The classical organizational theorists tended to favor mechanistic organizational structures (small spans, tall, formalized, and fairly centralized). The human relations theorists, having noted the flaws of bureaucracy, tended to favor organic structures (larger spans, flat, less formalized, and less centralized). However, there is no one best way to organize, and both mechanistic and organic structures have their places.

■ Symptoms of structural problems include poor job design, extreme duplication of effort, conflict between departments, slow responses, too many committees, and decisions made with incomplete information.

KEY CONCEPTS

Organizational structure
Vertical division of labor
Horizontal division of labor
Differentiation
Functional departmentation
Product departmentation
Geographic departmentation
Customer departmentation
Hybrid departmentation
Coordination
Integration
Liaison role

Task force
Integrators
Span of control
Flat organization
Tall organization
Formalization
Centralization
Complexity
Bureaucracy
Mechanistic structures
Organic structures

DISCUSSION QUESTIONS

1. Discuss the division of labor in a college classroom. What methods are used to coordinate this divided labor? Do differences exist between very small and very large classes?

2. Is the departmentation in a small college essentially functional or product-oriented? Defend your answer. (Hint: In what department will the historians find themselves? In what department will the groundskeepers find themselves?)

3. Which basic method(s) of coordination is (are) most likely to be found in a pure research laboratory? On a football team? In a supermarket?

4. Most of the advocates of the classical approach to organizational structure were practicing managers or management consultants working in the early part of this century. Most of the advocates of the human relations approach were academics. How might these different backgrounds have affected their views about organizational structure?

5. Discuss the logic behind the following statement: "We don't want to remove the differentiation that exists between sales and production. What we want to do is achieve integration."

6. As Spinelli Construction Company grew in size, its founder and president Joe Spinelli found that he was overloaded with decisions. What two basic structural changes should Spinelli make to rectify this situation without losing control of the company?

7. Describe a situation where a narrow span of control might be appropriate and contrast it with a situation where a broad span might be appropriate.

8. Review some of the problems that bureaucratic or mechanistic structures may promote.

FOR FURTHER READING

Flax, S. (1985, January 7). Can Chrysler keep rolling along? *Fortune,* 34–39.
> An interesting account of how Chrysler Corporation trimmed its bureaucracy and provided complementary management support systems to speed the introduction of new car models to the market.

Miner, J. B. (1982). *Theories of organizational structure and process.* Chicago: Dryden.
> Provides a detailed but very readable account of a number of theories of organizational structure and the research evidence bearing on these theories.

Perrow, C. (1979). *Complex organizations: A critical essay* (2nd ed.). Glenview, IL: Scott, Foresman.
> Takes a pithy, critical look at the foundations of thinking on organizational structure, with particular emphasis on the interplay between classical theory, bureaucracy in particular, and the human relations model.

Van Fleet, D. D., & Bedian, A. G. (1977). A history of the span of management. *Academy of Management Review, 2,* 356–372.
> Discusses and evaluates prescriptions concerning the optimal size of the span of control as it has been debated over the years. Also covers textbook treatments and contemporary views.

Case Study

Trouble in the TV Division

You have recently taken over as Division Manager of the portable TV Division of the X Electronics Company. Several years earlier this Division was a leading contributor to company profits; now it is losing money and can't compete with other domestic companies or imports.

A simplified version of the organization chart of your Division is shown in Exhibit 1.

Your predecessor seemed to have good accounting records which enabled him to know on a bi-weekly basis when any group exceeded its budgeted expenses. You also have available daily production figures which enable you to spot problems in any area.

The work in your division encompasses the following activities: Sales deals with customers (wholesale appliance dealers) and provides inputs to Engineering on what features (and what prices) are desirable from a marketing point of view; and Production, of course, manufactures the sets.

New models are introduced annually. This means that the Systems group develops the circuitry (the underlying electrical engineering of the new set). The Components group converts these specifications and design features into actual component and subsystem specifications (e.g., transistors, tubes, capacitors, et cetera). The Chassis group designs the cabinetry and frame. Industrial Engineering determines the specific production techniques and

procedures that will be used. Automation designs and produces the equipment which makes the printed circuits and assembles components (with the goal of limited human intervention).

In reviewing past history, you note that the greatest problems seem to occur (and it is not surprising) during the introduction of the new models. This past year was the worst. Sales noted a new trend toward bright, pastel-colored cabinetry. When the Chassis group was consulted on changing its design for the cabinet, it reported that the type of plastics that could be obtained in the desired intense colors could not be molded with the appropriate tolerances into the size and shape cabinet that had been agreed to. More rounding would be required, which would require the Components people to relocate one of their subsystems. They, in turn, said that this would have other impacts and they wanted additional time to calculate these and assess their costs.

At the same time Production was pushing for final plans, saying that every day's delay meant that their final tooling and training would be off by an extra two weeks. You found a memo from Engineering saying that over the years Production had stepped up their requirements for lead time (final plans to first models off the line) from two months to four months. Production's response had been that the promised simplifications had not materialized, and that budget cutting in various efficiency programs had reduced the number of production specialists they had to guide the work force in making a smooth transition from last year's to this year's model. At the end a number of fruitless meetings were held in which Sales, Production, and Engineering endeavored to resolve their differences.

Source: Originally published as "Introducing a New Appliance Model" in Wegner, R. E. C., & Sayles, L. (1972). *Cases in organizational and administrative behavior.* Englewood Cliffs, NJ: Prentice-Hall.

EXHIBIT 1   **Organization chart of the portable TV division.**

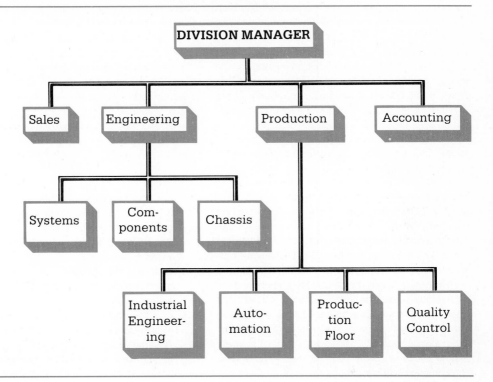

You found several other memos which indicated that the Systems group believed that the company's product was declining in quality; its reputation as the best in the industry was in jeopardy; and that good systems design was being sacrificed for what could be easily manufactured. They noted that the Automation group was harassing their design engineers, seeking to get a look at the early plans to see what they were like and to persuade the engineers to make modifications that would allow for greater use of automation, simpler printed circuitry, and more machine-controlled operations. This interfered with the design work and complicated it needlessly, noted the Systems manager.

Industrial Engineering said that there were a number of improved manufacturing techniques the company could employ if the Systems and Components people would call on them before introducing major new design features. Often minor changes in the design features would allow for very major man-

ufacturing improvements. The Systems and Components group argued that Industrial Engineering sought to dominate these discussions, and that if they employed reasonable effort and ingenuity they could find ways of converting reasonable plans into manufacturing procedures.

It is obvious that as Division Manager, your predecessor had spent a great deal of time on the production floor during the early part of any new model year, and during the preceding weeks, trying to resolve bottlenecks and speed decisions. During this time there were apparently a number of problems like these:

Inspection shows a badly crimped wire likely to break during shipping and production. The Supervisor asks his boss to get the wire shifted, reinforced, or changed in some other way. Production head calls Engineering office to see if design can be changed. After locating the man who originally specified that subsystem in Components, answer goes back to Production that a change can't be made. By the time the answer gets back, a large number of sets are backed up waiting for change or release. Production head then requests that either quality standard (for breakage) be lowered, or that Division manager require Components to change their specs. Also he requests that Accounting modify its costing to take into account that Components' delay in responding slows Production. (It should be noted that one of the reasons for an almost automatic rejection of Production's requests for Component changes is that engineers have already been reassigned to new projects, and that redesign would hurt the Components' expense budget.)

Another observation you make is that the head of Automation is a very forceful personality who managed to influence the work of Systems by getting your predecessor to agree that certain aspects of the circuitry would be checked out with Automation before being finalized as part of the Divisions's efforts to reduce manufacturing costs. Whenever a problem arose the Automation group spoke with a clear, single voice. The head of Systems, on the other hand, was a rather mild-mannered, theoretically oriented engineer. He rarely spoke in the name of his group but answered each charge or request in a very logical, systematic way. Over the past several years the company had lost a good many of its more ambitious circuit designers, and you wondered what was cause and what was effect.

Another problem revolved around the production methods and standards set by Industrial Engineering. When these seemed too tight to the production workers, the foremen often agreed with their men. Industrial Engineering would endeavor to get them accepted, noting that there was a learning curve and what seemed impossible at first, during the new model run, would seem easy after a few weeks. At times the workers would introduce "simplifications" in the job to meet the standard, and when these caused Quality problems at inspection time, it was not clear where the problem originated—from incorrect or ambiguous specifications by the Industrial Engineers, or the changes introduced by the workers or their foremen.

When Quality Control sought to have the problem investigated and the line stopped, the Sales group put pressure on Production to ignore this if dealer stocks had not yet been filled. At such times Production would argue that the company was dominated by a "sell now and don't worry about the product later" point of view, even though the company's market position had been attained through a combination of quality and technical pioneering. Sales reported that competition became keener each year, and that the end goal of the company was sales and not production.

■ ■ ■

1. Noting that the case involves only the TV Division of X Electronics, speculate about the structure of X Electronics as a whole. Use the concepts of complexity, centralization, and formalization. What form of departmentation does the firm as a whole rely upon?
2. Describe the horizontal division of labor and method of departmentation in the TV Division of X Electronics.
3. Use the concepts of differentation and integration to analyze the events in the TV Division.
4. Assume that you call in some outside consultants to help your analyze and solve the problems in the TV Division. Here are key sentences from the reports they provide:
   a. "The main problem is poor job descriptions. If every person knew his or her job, there would be few problems."
   b. "Several personality conflicts are the cause of the coordination problem in the division."
   c. "The situation here is natural and common, and it is unlikely to be improved."
   Critique each of these reports, speculating on its validity.
5. Outline the things that you, as the new manager, would do to make the operations of the TV Division more effective. Explain the reasons for your decisions.

REFERENCES

1. Mintzberg, H. (1979). *The structuring of organizations.* Englewood Cliffs, NJ: Prentice-Hall.

2. Lawrence, P. R., & Lorsch, J. W. (1969). *Organization and environment: Managing differentiation and integration.* Homewood, IL: Irwin.

3. For an extended treatment of the role of interdependence between departments see McCann, J., & Galbraith, J. R. (1981). Interdepartmental relations. In P. C. Nystrom & W. H. Starbuck (Eds.), *Handbook of organizational design* (Vol. 2). Oxford: Oxford University Press.

4. For a comparison of functional and product departmentation see McCann & Galbraith, 1981, and Walker, A. H., & Lorsch, J. W. (1968, November-December). Organizational choice: Product vs. function. *Harvard Business Review,* 129–138.

5. Contemporary treatment of these forms of departmentation can be found in Daft, R. L. (1986). *Organization theory and design* (2nd ed.). St. Paul, MN: West, and Robey, D. (1986). *Designing organizations* (2nd ed.). Homewood, IL: Irwin.

6. Mintzberg, 1979.

7. See Hall, R. H. (1962). Intraorganizational structural variation: Application of the bureaucratic model. *Administrative Science Quarterly, 7,* 295–308.

8. Lawrence & Lorsch, 1969.

9. Galbraith, J. R. (1977) *Organization design.* Reading, MA: Addison-Wesley.

10. See Birnbaum, P. H. (1981). Integration and specialization in academic research. *Academy of Management Journal, 24,* 487–503.

11. This discussion relies on Galbraith, 1977.

12. Lawrence & Lorsch, 1969.

13. Galbraith, 1977.

14. These definitions of structural variables are common. However, there is considerable disagreement about how some variables should be measured. See Walton, E. J. (1981). The comparison of measures of organizational structure. *Academy of Management Review, 6,* 155–160.

15. Research on these hypotheses is sparse and not always in agreement. See Dewar, R. D., & Simet, D. P. (1981). A level specific prediction of spans of control examining effects of size, technology, and specialization. *Academy of Management Journal, 24,* 5–24; Van Fleet, D. D. (1983). Span of management research and issues. *Academy of Management Journal, 26,* 546–552.

16. Daft, 1986, p. 178. Derived from Lucas, A. (1971, July 4). As American as McDonald's hamburger on the fourth of July. *New York Times Magazine,* and Culver, M., Mewis, L., & Vaughn, J. (1981). *McDonald's case study.* Unpublished manuscript, Texas A&M University.

17. Mintzberg, 1979, p. 182.

18. Daft, 1986.

19. Much of this research was stimulated by Blau, P. M. (1970). A theory of differentiation in organizations. *American Sociological Review, 35,* 201–218. For a review and recent test see Cullen, J. B., Anderson, K. S., & Baker, D. D. (1986). Blau's theory of structural differentiation revisited: A theory of structural change or scale? *Academy of Management Journal, 29,* 203–229.

20. Dewar, R., & Hage, J. (1978). Size, technology, complexity, and structural differentiation: Toward a theoretical synthesis. *Administrative Science Quarterly, 23,* 111–136; Marsh, R. M., & Mannari, H. (1981). Technology and size as determinants of the

organizational structure of Japanese factories. *Administrative Science Quarterly, 26,* 33–57.

21.   Mansfield, R. (1973). Bureaucracy and centralization: An examination of organizational structure. *Administrative Science Quarterly, 18,* 77–88; Hage, J., & Aiken, M. (1967). Relationship of centralization to other structural properties. *Administrative Science Quarterly, 12,* 72–91.

22.   Robey, 1986, p. 119.

23.   For comprehensive reviews see Berger, C. J., & Cummings, L. L. (1979). Organizational structure, attitudes, and behavior. *Research in Organizational Behavior, 1,* 169–208; Porter, L. W., & Lawler, E. E., III. (1965). Properties of organizational structure in relation to job attitudes and job behavior. *Psychological Bulletin, 81,* 23–51.

24.   Porter & Lawler, 1965.

25.   Crozier, M. (1964). *The bureaucratic phenomenon.* Chicago: University of Chicago Press.

26.   Merton, R. K. (1957). *Social theory and social structure* (rev. ed.). New York: Free Press.

27.   Chonko, L.B. (1982). The relationship of span of control to sales representatives' experienced role conflict and role ambiguity. *Academy of Management Journal, 25,* 452–456.

28.   Oldham, G. R., & Hackman, J. R. (1981). Relationships between organizational structure and employee reactions: Comparing alternative frameworks. *Administrative Science Quarterly, 26,* 66–83.

29.   Taylor, F. W. (1967). *The principles of scientific management.* New York: Norton.

30.   For a summary of their work and relevant references see Wren, D. A. (1979). *The evolution of management thought* (2nd ed.). New York: Wiley.

31.   Weber, M. (1947). *The theory of social and economic organization* (A. M. Henderson & T. Parsons, Trans.). New York: Free Press.

32.   The terms *mechanistic* and *organic* (to follow) were first used by Burns, T., & Stalker, G. M. (1961). *The management of innovation.* London: Tavistock Publications.

33.   Roethlisberger, F. J., & Dickson, W. J. (1939). *Management and the worker.* Cambridge, MA: Harvard University Press.

34.   Argyris, C. (1957). *Personality and organization.* New York: Harper.

35.   Likert, R. (1961). *New patterns of management.* New York: McGraw-Hill.

36.   Gouldner, A. W. (1954). *Patterns of industrial bureaucracy.* New York: Free Press.

37.   Selznick, P. (1949). *TVA and the grass roots: A study in the sociology of formal organizations.* Berkeley: University of California Press.

38.   Child, J. (1984). *Organization: A guide to problems and practice.* London: Harper & Row.

39.   Presidential Commission. (1986). *The report on the space shuttle Challenger accident.* Washington, DC: U.S. Government Printing Office.

40.   Pugh, D. (1979, Winter). Effective coordination in organizations. *Advanced Management Journal,* 28–35.

Chapter 16

Environment, Strategy, and Technology

GENERAL MOTORS' SATURN VENTURE

It was an amazing sight. Several prominent state governors appeared on the Phil Donahue show to argue publicly the case for their states' obtaining the new General Motors Saturn plant. Shortly thereafter, the suspense ended when GM announced that Spring Hill, Tennessee, would be the beneficiary of its projected $5 billion investment. The governors were obviously interested in the job opportunities (projected at 6000) and other economic spin-offs that would accrue if their states were chosen as the location for the Saturn plant. But what prompted GM to invest a projected $5 billion in a completely new car line, its first since the 1927 La Salle?

Saturn is a totally new corporation, a wholly owned GM subsidiary due to come on line in 1989. It is an autonomous division with its own sales and service operations, and it will not necessarily be tied to current GM dealerships. Why did GM decide to separate Saturn so decisively from the existing corporate structure, rather than just add yet another product line to its Chevrolet, Oldsmobile, Pontiac, Buick, and Cadillac lines? General Motors insiders and auto industry analysts cite two primary reasons. First, GM badly needs to find ways to cut costs to compete in the small car market, where current estimates suggest that Japanese manufacturers enjoy a $2000 advantage per car. Secondly, top GM executives hope to use the Saturn venture as a testing ground for innovations that can be applied throughout the rest of the organization, especially those that can get new models to the market more quickly. To accomplish both of these goals, the freedom of a completely "fresh start" and the protection offered by autonomy seemed to be essential.

Saturn observers have noted that the prototype cars themselves do not represent a radical departure for GM, although the final configuration of the 1989 models is far from clear. Rather, it is the process by which the cars are designed, built, and marketed that will be innovative. Even at the early design stages, representatives from engineering, manufacturing, and marketing are working together to ensure early coordination of efforts. This stands in sharp contrast to usual industry practice. In manufacturing, extensive use will be made of robotics and computers. Rather than moving on assembly lines, chassis will move along the floor on guided tracks that permit them to be stopped. Assembly will be done by self-managed work teams who will maintain their own equipment, order supplies, set work schedules, and even select new members. To control quality and reduce transport costs, much subassembly will be done by suppliers who will be located close to the plant or even within the plant. In the marketing domain, potential customers will be able to tailor their cars to their wishes via a computer terminal that will be linked directly to the Spring Hill factory. This will speed delivery and enable customers to obtain just the features they want. At the same time, dealers will be freed from carrying expensive inventories of new cars.

These changes in design procedure, manufacturing, and marketing will be supported by a number of departures from conventional structure, management style, and labor relations practices. The Saturn corporation will have a flatter management structure than the traditional GM divisions. A "paperless" operation of electronic mail and computerized storage of information should speed decisions and counter bureaucracy. Finally, GM has agreed to a truly ground-breaking labor contract with the United Auto Workers. Workers will be on salaries, although these salaries will average only 80 percent of industry hourly wages. In addition, restrictive work rules will be eliminated to support the team assembly concept. In exchange for these concessions, GM will devote 20 percent of the industry hourly wage to performance incentives and a profit-sharing plan for Saturn workers. In addition, 80 percent of the workforce will be granted lifetime employment security. Union representatives will sit on all planning and organizing committees.

Time will tell if GM's gamble on Saturn proves to be a pacesetter for the North American auto industry. The gamble is certainly sizable. The $5 billion investment represents about one half the assets of the entire Chrysler Corporation.[1]

The Saturn story illustrates the major themes of this chapter—how the external environment influences organizations, how a strategy must be developed to cope with this environment, and how technology and other factors can be used to implement strategy. In the previous chapter we concluded that there is no one best way to design an organization. In this chapter we will see that the proper organizational structure is contingent on environmental, strategic, and technological factors.

THE EXTERNAL ENVIRONMENT OF ORGANIZATIONS

In previous chapters we have been concerned primarily with the internal environments of organizations—those events and conditions inside the organization—that affect the attitudes and behaviors of members. In this section we turn our interest to the impact of the **external environment**—those events and conditions *surrounding* the organization that influence its activities.

There is ample evidence in everyday life that the external environment has tremendous influence on organizations. The OPEC oil embargo of 1973 and subsequent oil price increases shook Detroit automobile manufacturers to their foundations. Faced with gasoline shortages, increasing gasoline prices, and rising interest rates, consumers postponed automobile purchases or shifted to more economical foreign vehicles. As a consequence, American workers were laid off, plants were closed, and dealerships failed while the manufacturers scrambled to develop their fuel-efficient X-cars, J-cars, and K-cars. Advertising strategies changed from an emphasis on styling and comfort to economy and value. Significant portions of the manufacturers' environment (Middle East oil suppliers, American consumers, and Japanese competitors) prompted this radical regrouping.

Environmental conditions change, and by the mid-1980s an international oil surplus pushed gasoline prices down. Consumers responded with increased interest in size, styling, and performance. Auto industry analysts have noted that some manufacturers responded to this shift faster than others. Chrysler, trimmed of bureaucracy by its near demise several years earlier, responded quickly and scored a number of marketing coups. General Motors responded less quickly. Along with a massive reorganization of its traditional divisions, the Saturn project is an attempt to enable the company to respond more quickly to environmental trends.

Organizations as Open Systems

Organizations can be described as open systems. **Open systems** are systems that take inputs from the external environment, transform some of these inputs, and send them back into the external environment as outputs (Exhibit 16-1).[2] Inputs include capital, energy, materials, information, technology, and people, while outputs include various products and services. Some inputs are transformed (e.g., raw materials) while other inputs (e.g., skilled craftspersons) assist in the transformation process. Transformation processes may be physical (e.g., manufacturing

EXHIBIT 16-1   **The organization as an open system.**

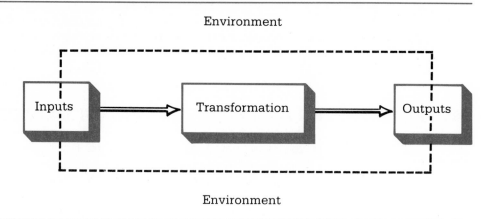

or surgery), intellectual (e.g., teaching or programming), or even emotional (e.g., psychotherapy). For example, an insurance company imports actuarial experts, information about accidents and mortality, and capital in the form of insurance premiums. Through the application of financial knowledge, it transforms the capital into insurance coverage and investments in areas such as real estate. Universities import seasoned scholars and aspiring students from the environment. Through the teaching process, educated individuals are returned to the community as outputs.

The value of the open systems concept is that it sensitizes us to the need for organizations to cope with the demands of the environment on both the input side and the output side. As we will see, some of this coping involves adaptation to environmental demands. On the other hand, some coping may be oriented toward changing the environment.

First, let's examine the external environment in greater detail.

Components of the External Environment

The external environment of any given organization is obviously a "big" concept. Technically, it involves any person, group, event, or condition outside the direct domain of the organization. For this reason it is useful to divide the environment into a manageable number of components.[3]

THE GENERAL ECONOMY.   Organizations that survive by selling products or services will often suffer from an economic downturn and profit by an upturn. When a downturn occurs, competition for remaining customers increases and needed capital improvements may have to be postponed. Of course, some organizations may thrive under a poor economy, including welfare offices and law firms that deal heavily in bankruptcies. In addition, if a poor economy is accompanied by high unemployment, some organizations may find it opportune to upgrade the quality of their staffs since they will have an ample selection of candidates.

A clear example of the impact of the general economy can be seen in what happened to many savings and loan companies during the last U.S. recession. Faced with double-digit inflation, they were forced to pay double-digit interest rates for capital while receiving only single-digit interest from the mature mortgages they held. Many companies failed due to this critical inability to manage inputs.

CUSTOMERS.   All organizations have potential customers for their products and services. Piano makers have musicians and consumer activist associations have disgruntled consumers. The customers of universities include not only students but the firms that employ their graduates and seek their research assistance. Organizations must be sensitive to changes in customer demands. For example, the small liberal arts college that resists developing a business school may be faced with declining enrollment.

Coca-Cola's past decision to introduce a ''new,'' sweeter Coke in place of the traditional soft drink encountered tremendous customer resistance and forced the company finally to market two products in place of one—the new product and the relabeled Coke Classic. Most industry observers were not impressed with this disregard of potential customer dissatisfaction. Successful firms are generally highly sensitive to customer reactions. Proctor & Gamble deleted the 103-year-old man-in-the-moon logo from its packaging after it was unable to squelch rumors that it had satanic connotations (In–Focus 16-1).

SUPPLIERS.   Organizations are dependent on the environment for supplies that include labor, raw materials, equipment, and component parts. Shortages can cause severe difficulties. For instance, the lack of a local technical school may prove troublesome for an electronics firm that requires skilled labor. Similarly, a strike by a company that supplies component parts may cause the purchaser to shut down its assembly line.

Jaguar, the British luxury car manufacturer, was almost forced out of the North American market because of its reputation for poor quality. Finally, Jaguar engineers traced many of the car's reliability problems to electrical accessories supplied by the Joseph Lucas company (Lucas, a prominent supplier of lighting equipment, has often been dubbed by unfriendly observers as the Prince of Darkness!). Jaguar threatened and worked with Lucas to improve reliability, and the firm now does extremely well in North America.[4]

COMPETITORS.   Environmental competitors vie for resources that include both customers and suppliers.[5] Thus, hospitals compete for patients and consulting firms compete for clients. Similarly, utility companies compete for coal and professional baseball teams compete for free agent ballplayers. Successful organizations devote considerable energy to monitoring the activities of competitors.

The economics of the U.S. soft drink industry provide an example of the

IN–FOCUS 16-1 PROCTOR & GAMBLE DELETES TRADITIONAL LOGO AND SUES RUMOR-MONGERS

CINCINNATI—Procter & Gamble Co. said it sued a minister, a school teacher and two others whom it charged with spreading "false and malicious" rumors that the company worships Satan.

The suits, filed in federal courts in Virginia, Pennsylvania and Kansas, are P&G's latest effort to squash seemingly irrepressible rumors that have haunted the consumer products company since the late 1970s.

The company alleged that James H. Johnson, a Baptist minister in Madison Heights, Va., George Embers, a school teacher in Wichita, Kan., and Mary and Clem Folejewski of Dunmore, Pa., libeled P&G's character and distributed literature claiming that P&G supports the church of Satan. The literature also maintains that the company's man-in-the-moon logo is a symbol of the devil, the suit said.

"We are determined to bring an end to these lies," said a P&G senior vice president, W. Wallace Abbott, in explaining the decision to sue. "Our investigations are continuing and additional suits will be filed if necessary." In the suits, P&G asked for unspecified damages and for the courts to keep the individuals from circulating the stories and literature.

Thousands of such leaflets advocating boycotts of P&G products, which include Ivory soap, Crisco oil and Mr. Clean, have been distributed throughout the U.S. in recent years. The stories sent consumers to their shelves to study the familiar P&G packages, only to discover the logo imprinted on every label. The 103-year-old trademark features a man-in-the-moon and 13 stars that are meant to represent the original 13 American colonies.

Calls to the company inquiring about the logo peaked at 15,000 a month in 1982, gradually fell off, and then rose again this year to 9,000 in April. P&G has conducted media campaigns, hired private detectives, collected testimonials from religious leaders and, in 1982, filed six other suits.

But last month P&G finally took the step it long had vowed it wouldn't: It began to remove the logo from the thousands of package labels on which it appears.

Source: P & G sues, alleges four libeled firm with devil rumors. (1985, May 17). *Wall Street Journal*, p. 8. © Dow Jones & Company, Inc. Reprinted by permission.

importance of the competitor component. One percent market share in this industry translates into $300 million in retail sales. Thus, it is no wonder that Coca-Cola recently spent $70 million in one year to promote the new Coke and PepsiCo spent $50 million to advertise Pepsi.[6] The majority of this expenditure goes toward countering the competition rather than expanding the overall market for soft drinks.

SOCIAL/POLITICAL FACTORS. Organizations cannot ignore the social and political events that occur around them. Changes in public attitudes toward racial integration, the proper age for retirement, or the proper role of big business will soon affect them. Frequently, these attitudes find expression in law through the political process. Thus, organizations must cope with a series of legal regulations that prescribe fair employment practices, proper competitive activities, product safety, and clients' rights.

One example of the impact of social trends on organizations involves the abuse of cocaine and other drugs. Many firms have found that drug abuse is responsible for low productivity, absenteeism, accidents, and security problems. In response, firms such as IBM instituted routine drug tests for new job applicants at all levels.[7]

An example of the conversion of a social trend into political and governmental action is seen in the 1978 deregulation of the U.S. airline industry. Part of a general trend that has reduced federal regulation of business, this action spurred a long series of market entries, fare wars, route wars, mergers, acquisitions, and bankruptcies. Many a harried airline executive felt the target of the ancient Chinese curse, "May you live in interesting times"!

TECHNOLOGY.   The environment contains a variety of technologies that are useful for achieving organizational goals. As we shall see, technology refers to ways of doing things, not simply to some form of machinery. The ability to adopt the proper technology should enhance the organization's effectiveness. For a business firm this may involve the choice of a proper computer system or production technique. For a mental health clinic it may involve implementing a particular form of psychotherapy that is effective for the kinds of clients serviced.

An example of the impact of technology on organizational life can be seen in the advent of computer-aided design (CAD). With CAD, designers, engineers, and draftspersons can produce quick, accurate drawings via computer. Data bases can be stored, and simulations can be run that produce visual records of the reaction of objects to stress, vibration, and design changes. Some firms have found that CAD reduces design lead times and increases productivity. Others have found that CAD systems have led to labor relations problems. Some traditional draftspersons have felt that their job security is threatened by CAD. Also, pay and status differences between those who learn CAD and those who do not may be difficult to resolve. In general, CAD seems destined to break down the traditional role differences between designers, engineers, and drawing technicians.

Now that we have outlined the basic components of organizational environments, a few more detailed comments are in order. First, this brief list does not provide a perfect picture of the large number of actual interest groups that can exist in an organization's environment. **Interest groups** are parties or organizations other than direct competitors who have some vested interest in how an organization is managed. For example, Exhibit 16-2 shows the interest groups that surround a small private college. As you can see, our list of six environmental components actually involves quite an array of individuals and agencies with which the college must contend. To complicate matters, some of these individuals and agencies may make competing or conflicting demands on the college. For instance, booster clubs may press the college to allocate more funds to field a winning football team, while scholarship sponsors may insist that the college match their donations for academic purposes. In–Focus 16-2 shows how interests groups in the political domain have exerted influence on universities.

Such competition for attention from different segments of the environment is not unusual. Iron City beer was boycotted by Pittsburgh area blacks who wanted

EXHIBIT 16-2   **Interest groups in the external environment of a small private college.**

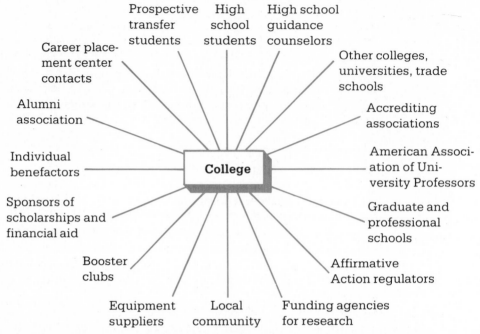

Source: From Brown, W. B., & Moberg, D. J. (1980). *Organization theory and management.*
New York: Wiley, p. 45. Copyright © 1980, by John Wiley and Sons, Inc. Reprinted by
permission.

the Pittsburgh Brewing Company to hire more blacks. When an agreement was
reached and the black boycott ended, a counter-boycott was begun by some
disgruntled whites![8] Similarly, while anti-drug organizations have sometimes supported the screening of employees for drug use, the American Civil Liberties Union
has taken a keen interest in the violation of privacy that such tests may involve.
Obviously, different interest groups evaluate organizational effectiveness according
to different criteria.[9]

A second point to consider about the basic components of an organization's
environment is that different parts of the organization will often be concerned with
different components. For instance, we can expect a marketing department to be
tuned in to customer demands and a legal department to be interested in regulations stemming from the social/political component. As indicated in the previous
chapter, coordination of this natural division of interests is a crucial concern for all
organizations. Also, as environmental demands change, it is important that power
shifts occur to allow the appropriate functional units to cope with these demands.

Finally, events in various components of the environment provide both constraints and opportunities for organizations. Although environments with many

IN–FOCUS 16-2 UNIVERSITIES FACE ENVIRONMENTAL PRESSURES

Great universities are not run by governors, budget analysts or legislators.

Yet increasingly, America's leading public institutions have fallen prey to legislative meddling and, in some cases, what can only be called genteel extortion.

A new study by Frank Newman—former President of the University of Rhode Island, now head of the Denver-based Education Commission of the States—finds that while there is a tendency for states to intrude in the affairs of the universities and a need for greater university autonomy, there is also a tendency for universities "to cause or invite intrusion."

Last year, the governors of 38 states cited economic development a top priority in their annual state-of-the-state address, and in every case a dependence on the quality of higher education was made clear. This year, at least 10 states are engaged in statewide studies related directly to how they can improve the governance of their higher education system, and in some cases the committees—appointed by governors and legislators—are viewed as yet another medium for intrusion.

At the outset, Newman confessed to hold "a simpler view of the issue" but has come to realize that state-university relations are of a highly complex nature. He found that evidence of intrusion generally fell into one of three categories:

☐ Bureaucratic—the accumulated weight of unnecessary or counterproductive regulations, which is the most common form of inappropriate intrusion.

☐ Political—the exercise of raw political power for self-interest rather than public interest, which is an important deterrent to quality in a minority of states.

☐ Ideological—the attempt to impede university activity on ideological grounds, which now seldom occurs as a result of state actions.

Newman shared a number of horror stories with reporters, citing cases in which key personnel appointments at some major state universities fell prey to political patronage.

"In the states that are expert at this, they don't even leave a mark on the body," said Newman.

Universities often cause unnecessary intrusion, Newman contends, warning institutions to avoid:

☐ End runs of the governance process to achieve campus goals.

☐ Institutional ambitions that run counter to the agreed institutional mission.

☐ Self-intrusion or limitation, as has occurred most notably in ideological intrusion, where it is the university itself rather than the state that tends to limit the freedom of discussion on campus.

"What is the right relationship?" asks Newman. "It has to be a function of trust. You can't get first class colleges if every move has to be checked with the state."

Using the case of affirmative action in collegiate women's athletics as a typical scenario, Newman outlined the process of intrusion.

"Society asks and the university does not respond," he said. "Like all social organizations, the university is made up of people with vested interests. Eventually, though, the university grudgingly gives in and accepts. But sometime later the university takes all the credit for implementing reform."

Source: Edited from McQuaid, E. P. (1986, June). South of the border. *CAUT Bulletin,* p. 9. Reprinted by permission.

constraints (e.g., high interest rates, strong competition, and so on) appear pretty hostile, an opportunity in one environmental sector may offset a constraint in another. For example, the firm faced with a dwindling customer base may find its salvation by exploiting new technologies that give it an edge in costs or new product development.

The Environment of Saturn

Let's return to the story that began the chapter and analyze some of the environmental components that shaped General Motors' plans regarding the Saturn project. A strong impetus for the Saturn venture was the $2000 cost advantage per small car that Japanese competitors held. However, cost reductions will mean little unless the quality of the Saturn automobile is comparable to that of Japanese makes. To enhance quality, GM has exercised particular control over parts suppliers, inducing them to locate within or near the plant to facilitate communication with Saturn engineering and manufacturing personnel. How work will actually be performed at the Saturn plant is strongly influenced by technological advances in robotics and computers.

During the recessionary early 1980s, the general economy faltered and unions lost considerable bargaining power. Union membership fell, and GM capitalized upon changing social attitudes toward unions to forge an innovative contract with the United Auto Workers. However, the legality of the contract was challenged by an interest group, the National Right to Work Legal Defense Foundation. This group, which provides legal aid to those who do not wish to join unions, argued that it was improper for GM to specify the United Auto Workers as a bargaining agent in advance of any workers having been hired.[10]

Finally, GM is gambling that its customer component is ready to order cars via computer assistance rather than choosing already-built models from a large inventory stocked at a dealership.

Clearly, Saturn is a product of environmental constraints and opportunities. But exactly how do such constraints and opportunities impinge on the organization? To answer this question, we turn to the concepts of environmental uncertainty and resource dependence.

Environmental Uncertainty

One of the themes implied in our earlier discussion of environmental components is the fact that environments have considerable potential for causing confusion among managers. Customers may come and go, suppliers may turn from good to bad, and competitors may make surprising decisions. The resulting uncertainty may be both challenging and frustrating. **Environmental uncertainty** exists when an environment is vague, difficult to diagnose, and unpredictable. We all know that some environments are less certain than others. Your hometown provides you with a fairly certain environment. There, you are familiar with the transportation system, the language, and necessary social conventions. Thrust into the midst of a foreign culture, such as that found in India, you encounter a much less certain environment. How to greet a stranger, order a meal, or get around town become significant issues. There is nothing intrinsically bad about this uncertainty. It simply requires you to marshal a particular set of skills in order to be an effective visitor.

Like individuals, organizations may find themselves in more or less certain environments. But just exactly what makes an organizational environment uncertain? Put simply, uncertainty depends upon the environment's *complexity* (simple versus complex) and its *rate of change* (static versus dynamic).[11]

- ■ *Simple environment.* A simple environment involves relatively few factors, and these factors are fairly similar to each other. For example, consider the pottery manufacturer that obtains its raw materials from two small firms and sells its entire output to three small pottery outlets.

- ■ *Complex environment.* A complex environment contains a large number of dissimilar factors that affect the organization. For example, the college shown in Exhibit 16-2 has a more complex environment than the pottery manufacturer. In turn, the Saturn organization has a more complex environment than the college.

- ■ *Static environment.* The components of this environment remain fairly stable over time. The small-town radio station that plays the same music format, relies on the same advertisers, and works under the same FCC regulations year after year has a stable environment. (Of course, no environment is *completely* static, and we are speaking in relative terms here.)

- ■ *Dynamic environment.* The components of a highly dynamic environment are in a constant state of change. This change is unpredictable and irregular, not cyclical. For example, consider the firm that designs and manufactures microchips for electronics applications. New scientific and technological advances occur rapidly and unpredictably in this field. In addition, customer demands are highly dynamic as firms devise new uses for microchips. A similar dynamic environment faces Saturn, in part due to the vagaries of the energy situation and in part due to the fact that marketing automobiles has become an international business rather than a national business. For example, fluctuations in the relative value of international currencies may radically alter the cost of competing imported cars quite independently of anything Saturn management does.

As shown in Exhibit 16-3, rate of change and complexity can be arranged in a matrix. A simple/static environment (cell 1) should provoke the least uncertainty, while a dynamic/complex environment (cell 4) should provoke the most. Some research suggests that change has more influence than complexity on uncertainty.[12] Thus, we might expect a static/complex environment (cell 2) to be somewhat more certain than a dynamic/simple environment (cell 3).

EXHIBIT 16-3   **Environmental uncertainty as a function of complexity and rate of change.**

		Complexity	
		Simple	**Complex**
Rate of Change	**Static**	CELL 1: *Low Perceived* *Uncertainty* 1. Small number of factors and components in the environment 2. Factors and components are somewhat similar to one another 3. Factors and components remain basically the same and are not changing	CELL 2: *Moderately Low* *Perceived Uncertainty* 1. Large number of factors and components in the environment 2. Factors and components are not similar to one another 3. Factors and components remain basically the same
	Dynamic	CELL 3: *Moderately High* *Perceived Uncertainty* 1. Small number of factors and components in the environment 2. Factors and components are somewhat similar to one another 3. Factors and components of the environment are in continual process of change	CELL 4: *High Perceived* *Uncertainty* 1. Large number of factors and components in the environment 2. Factors and components are not similar to one another 3. Factors and components of environment are in a continual process of change

Source: Duncan, R. B. (1972). Characteristics of organizational environments and perceived environmental uncertainty. *Administrative Science Quarterly, 17*, 313–327, p. 320.

Earlier it was stated that different portions of the organization are often interested in different components of the environment. To go a step further, it stands to reason that some aspects of the environment may be less certain than others. Thus, some subunits may be faced with more uncertainty than others. For example, the research and development department of a microchip company would seem to face a more uncertain environment than the personnel department.

Increasing uncertainty has several predictable effects on organizations and their decision makers.[13] For one thing, as uncertainty increases, cause and effect relationships become less clear. If we are certain that a key competitor will not match our increased advertising budget, we may be confident that our escalated ad campaign will increase our market share. Uncertainty about the competitor's response reduces confidence in this causal inference. Second, environmental uncertainty tends to make priorities harder to agree upon, and it often stimulates a fair degree of political jockeying within the organization. To continue the example, if the consequences of increased advertising are unclear, other functional units may see the increased budget allocation as "up for grabs." Finally, as environmental uncertainty increases, more information must be processed by the organization to make adequate decisions. Environmental scanning, planning, and formal management information systems will become more prominent. This illustrates that organizations will act to cope with or reduce uncertainty because uncertainty increases the difficulty of decision making and thus threatens organizational effectiveness. Shortly, we will examine in greater detail means of managing uncertainty. First we explore another aspect of the impact of the environment on organizations.

Resource Dependence

Earlier it was noted that organizations are open systems that receive inputs from the external environment and transfer outputs into this environment. Many inputs from various components of the environment are valuable resources that are necessary for organizational survival. These include things such as capital, raw materials, and human resources. By the same token, other components of the environment (such as customers) represent valuable resources on the output end of the equation. All of this suggests that organizations are in a state of **resource dependence** with regard to their environments.[14] Carefully managing and coping with this resource dependence is a key to survival and success.

Several points about resource dependence deserve our attention. First, although all organizations are dependent upon their environments for resources, some organizations are more dependent than others. This is because some environments are more *munificent* than others (that is, they have a larger amount of readily accessible resources). Speaking very generally, the computer industry is currently located in a munificent environment. Capital is readily available, human resources are being trained in relevant fields, and new uses for computers are continually being developed. On the other hand, many organizations in traditional "smokestack" industries encounter a much less munificent environment. Investors are wary, customers are disappearing, and skilled human resources are attracted to situations with better career prospects. A classic case of a highly resource-dependent organization is a newly formed small business. Cautious bank managers, credit-wary suppliers, and a dearth of customers all teach the aspiring owner the meaning of dependence.

Secondly, it should be noted that a given organization may encounter ready resources in one sector of its environment and limited resources in another. For example, the U.S. military has generally had free and easy access to the latest in technological advances. On the other hand, the advent of the all-volunteer service has presented the military with constant problems in attracting and retaining highly qualified human resources.

Third, resource dependence can be fairly independent of environmental uncertainty, and dealing with one issue will not necessarily have an effect on the other.[15] For example, although the computer industry generally faces a munificent environment, this environment is uncertain, especially with regard to rate of change. On the other hand, many mature small businesses exist in a fairly certain environment but remain highly resource-dependent.

Finally, competitors, regulatory agencies, and various interest groups may have a considerable stake in how an organization obtains and transforms its resources.[16] In effect, the organization may be indirectly resource-dependent upon these bodies and thus susceptible to a fair degree of social control. For example, since Saturn is an independent corporation, it could begin operations without unionization (the Nissan plant located in Tennessee is not unionized). However, other GM plants are organized by the United Auto Workers. In order to preclude labor difficulties and ensure the presence of committed human resources, GM agreed to United Auto Workers representation from the outset of the project.

The resource dependence concept does not mean that organizations are totally at the mercy of their environments. Rather, it means that they must develop strategies for managing both resource dependence and environmental uncertainty.

STRATEGIC RESPONSES TO UNCERTAINTY AND RESOURCE DEPENDENCE

Organizations devote considerable effort to developing and implementing strategies to cope with environmental uncertainty and resource dependence. **Strategy** can be defined as the process by which top executives seek to cope with the constraints and opportunities posed by the organization's environment. Some views of the strategic process portray it as very conscious, planned, and rational. Other views portray the process as more intuitive, emerging from a stream of decisions made over time. The actual process of strategy formulation usually incorporates both approaches.

Exhibit 16-4 outlines the nature of the relationship between environment and strategy. At the top, the objective organizational environment is portrayed in terms of uncertainty and available resources, as discussed above. However, much of the impact that the environment has on organizations is indirect rather than direct, filtered through the perceptual system of managers and other organizational members.[17] By means of the perceptual process discussed in Chapter 4, personality characteristics and experience may color managers' perceptions of the environment. For example, the environment may seem much more complex and unstable for a manager who is new to his job than one who has years of experience. Similarly, the optimistic manager may perceive more resources than the pessimistic manager.[18] It is the perceived environment that comprises the basis for strategy formulation.

Strategy formulation itself involves determining the mission, goals, and objectives of the organization. At the most basic level, for a business firm, this would even involve consideration of just what business the organization should pursue.

EXHIBIT 16-4   Environment and strategy.

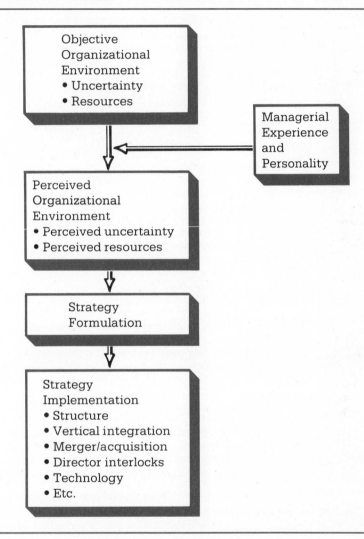

Then, the organization's orientation toward the perceived environment must be determined. This might range from being defensive and protective of current interests (such as holding market share) to prospecting vigorously for new interests to exploit (such as developing totally new products).[19] There is no single correct strategy along this continuum. Rather, the chosen strategy must correspond to the constraints and opportunities of the environment. Finally, the strategy must be implemented by selecting appropriate managers for the task and employing appropriate techniques as shown in Exhibit 16-4.

IN–FOCUS 16-3 PEOPLE EXPRESS CHANGES STRATEGY

NEW YORK—Founded just five years ago, People Express became one of the America's biggest airlines by aggressively courting passengers willing to give up free in-flight meals and other amenities for discount fares. Its announcement this week that it would change course and go after first-class customers as well, marked a realization by People that, having achieved its goal, it has outgrown that strategy.

Now the fifth-largest carrier in the United States—People has to attract more than its original market of students, retirees and other discount-minded passengers. Catering to that market, which is largely seasonal in nature, has meant that People's burgeoning fleet is overbooked during holiday periods and in the summer but flies with many empty seats at other times of the year.

Moreover, most older carriers are responding to the challenge from People and other cut-rate lines by paring their own costs and matching the lower fares, although with many restrictions.

Caught between a maturing market and a strong counterattack from the older lines, People has decided to join what could be the new mainstay of the airline industry, hybrid carriers, like Continental Airlines, that offer both unrestricted low fares and traditional services.

People was spawned by the 1978 deregulation of the American airline industry. The strategy of its founder and chairman, Donald Burr, called for quick and continued expansion of the non-union carrier.

The goal was to become large enough to control its hubs such as Newark and defend its niche in Denver against such large carriers as United and Continental.

That goal has been reached, but the strategy has also led to large losses recently. People reported a record loss of $32.2 million in the fourth quarter of 1985 and expects an even larger loss in the first quarter this year.

Many business travellers, most of whom travel at company expense, want to fly with all the trimmings, including first-class seats and frequent-flier programs that offer rewards to repeat customers.

While People came to symbolize what a new carrier under deregulation should look like, Dan Kasper, who was the director of international aviation for the Civil Aeronautics Board and is now an aviation consultant for Harbridge House, a management consultant firm, said that "the world has not stood still."

At the time of its founding in 1981, People's strategy was right, he said, and Burr was looked on as a "messiah."

Now, Kasper added, "the marketplace has clearly changed."

One organization that pursued an interesting strategy in response to environmental constraints and opportunities and then modified that strategy was People Express airlines (In–Focus 16-3). Born in the heady days of airline deregulation, People began by offering "no frills" service at discount prices rather than competing directly with established carriers for business customers. This strategy was successful for awhile, but as the established carriers responded with their own cut-rate fares, and the no-frills market became saturated, People changed its strategy also to cater to business travelers.[20] This change in strategy may have come too late, as People was shortly thereafter taken over by Texas Air. In its early days, People was small and had to pursue a strong cost-management strategy to reap profits from its low fares. To accomplish this, People had a remarkably organic structure, and it was not unusual to find pilots or flight attendants filling in as aircraft schedulers. As the airline got bigger, the structure became more formalized and mechanistic.[21] This is an example of using structure to implement strategy, a topic to which we now turn.

Organizational Structure as a Strategic Response

How should organizations be structured to cope with environmental uncertainty? Paul Lawrence and Jay Lorsch of Harvard University have studied this problem.[22]

Lawrence and Lorsch chose for their research more and less successful organizations in three industries—plastics, packaged food products, and paper containers. These industries were chosen intentionally because it was assumed that they faced environments that differed in perceived uncertainty. This was subsequently confirmed by questionnaires and interviews. The environment of the plastics firms was perceived as very uncertain because of rapidly changing scientific knowledge, technology, and customer demands. Decisions had to be made even though feedback about their accuracy often involved considerable delay. At the opposite extreme, the container firms faced an environment that was perceived as much more certain. No major changes in technology had occurred in twenty years, and the name of the game was simply to produce high-quality standardized containers and get them to the customer quickly. The consequences of decisions could be learned in a short period of time. The perceived uncertainty faced by the producers of packaged foods fell between that experienced by the plastics and container firms.

Going a step further, Lawrence and Lorsch also examined the sectors of the environment faced by three departments in each company: Sales (market environment); production (technical environment); and research (scientific environment). Their findings are shown in Exhibit 16-5. The crucial factor here is the *range* of uncertainty across the subenvironments faced by the various departments. In the container companies, producing, selling, and research (mostly quality control) were all fairly certain activities. In contrast, the range of uncertainty encountered by the plastics firms was quite broad. Research worked in a scientific environment that was extremely uncertain. On the other hand, production faced a technical environment that was a good bit more routine.

When Lawrence and Lorsch examined the attitudes of organizational managers, the impact of perceived environmental uncertainty became apparent. First of all, because the departments of the plastics firms had to cope with sectors of the environment that differed in certainty, the plastics firms tended to be highly differentiated (Chapter 15). Thus, their managers tended to differ rather greatly in

EXHIBIT 16-5 **Relative perceived uncertainty of environmental sectors in the Lawrence and Lorsch study.**

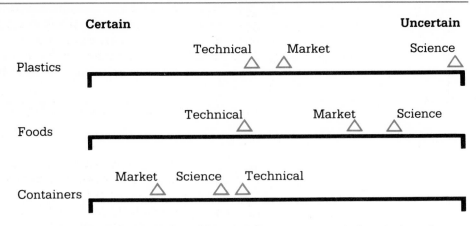

Source: Modified with permission from Paul R. Lawrence and Jay W. Lorsch, *Organization and Environment: Managing Differentiation and Integration.* Boston: Division of Research, Harvard University Graduate School of Business Administration, 1967, p. 91. (Republished as a Harvard Business School Classic: Boston: Harvard Business School Press, 1986)

terms of goals, interpersonal relationships, and time spans. For example, production managers were interested in immediate, short-term problems, while those in the research department were concerned with longer-range scientific development. Conversely, the container firms were not highly differentiated because the environmental sectors they dealt with were more similar in perceived certainty. The food-packaging firms were more differentiated than the container firms but less differentiated than the plastic companies.

Because they faced a fairly certain environment and because they were fairly undifferentiated, the container firms had adopted mechanistic structures. The most successful was organized along strict functional lines and was highly centralized. Coordination was achieved through direct supervision and formalized written schedules. All in all, this container firm conformed closely to the classical prescriptions for structure. At the other extreme, the most successful plastics companies had adopted organic structures. This was the most sensible way to deal with an uncertain environment and high differentiation. Decision-making power was decentralized to locate it where the appropriate knowledge existed. Coordination was achieved through informal mutual adjustment, ad hoc teams that cut across departments, and special integrators who coordinated between departments (Chapter 15). In addition, the departments themselves were structured somewhat differently, with research being the most organic and production the least organic.

The Lawrence and Lorsch study is important because it demonstrates a close connection between environment, structure, and effectiveness. However, follow-up research has not been entirely supportive of their findings, and several contradictory studies exist.[23] Part of the problem may rest in the difficulty of measuring uncertainty and in reconciling perceptions of the environment with objective environmental characteristics. How the "real" environment interacts with perceptions of the environment to affect strategy and structure remains to be determined.

Despite these spotty research findings, organizations very commonly tailor structure to strategy in coping with the environment. You may recall our discussion in Chapter 9 of the change in strategy and culture that was necessitated at AT&T as a result of its divestiture of local telephone companies. Forced to be more sales and marketing oriented, AT&T changed from a functional structure to a product structure to get close to its customers. The new structure is decentralized and more organic:

> To back up the new emphasis on sales, AT&T is changing its structure to point the corporation toward the market. Historically AT&T has been organized along functional lines—Bell Labs researched, Western Electric manufactured, and so forth. Insulated from the market, these units responded largely to their own inner needs. To banish this kind of thinking, AT&T is splitting up functional units to conform to the company's lines of business, and allowing product managers to stretch their authority across various functions to pull together the effort needed to get a product to market. . . . Robert J. Casale, a McGill recruit who is executive vice-president of Information Systems, says each line of business will have its own product-development, product-management, marketing, and distribution teams, and its own sales force.[24]

It is interesting to note that part of the GM Saturn organization's strategy involves reducing the development time for new models. This strategy helps to counteract the uncertainty of the marketplace. To implement it, GM is also opting for a flatter, more organic, less bureaucratic structure for Saturn.

The argument presented so far suggests that strategy always determines structure, rather than the other way around. This is a reasonable conclusion when considering an organization undergoing radical change (such as AT&T) or the formation of a new organization (such as Saturn). However, for ongoing organizations, structure may sometimes dictate strategy formulation. For instance, highly complex decentralized structures may dictate strategies that are the product of political bargaining between functional units. More centralized simple structures may produce strategies that appear more rational and less political (although not necessarily superior in effectiveness).[25]

Other Forms of Strategic Response

Variations on organizational structure are not the only strategic response that organizations can make. Structural variations are often accompanied by other responses that are oriented toward coping with environmental uncertainty or resource dependence. Some forms of strategy implementation appear extremely routine, yet they may have a strong effect on the performance of the organization. For example, economic forecasting may be used to predict the demand for goods and services. In turn, formal planning may be employed to synchronize the organization's actions to the forecasts. All of this is done to reduce uncertainty and to predict trends in resource availability. Simple negotiating and contracting are also forms of implementing strategy. The innovative agreement between GM and the United Auto Workers regarding Saturn is one such example. General Motors' strategy here involved guaranteeing itself a ready supply of flexible labor at somewhat less than the going wage rate at its other plants. Some more elaborate forms of strategic response are worth a more detailed look.

VERTICAL INTEGRATION.   Many managers live in fear of disruption on the input or output end of their organizations. A lack of raw materials to process or a snag in marketing products or services may threaten the very existence of the organization. One basic way to buffer the organization against such uncertainty over resource control is to use an inventory policy of stockpiling both inputs and outputs. For example, an automaker might stockpile chromium in anticipation of shortages due to political disruption in South Africa. At the same time, it might have thirty days' supply of new cars in its distribution system at all times. Both inventories serve as environmental "shock absorbers." A natural extension of this logic is **vertical integration,** the strategy of formally taking control of sources of supply and distribution. Major oil companies, for instance, are highly vertically integrated, handling their own exploration, drilling, transport, refining, retail sales, and credit.[26] Again, environmental shock absorption is the goal, and it is no mystery that the activities of OPEC bolstered vertical integration on the supply end of this chain! Vertical integration can reduce flexibility and attract antitrust legislation. Thus, some organizations are employing innovations to improve supply-side relations without actually producing supplies themselves. Recently, most auto manufacturers have developed much more cooperative relationships with their parts suppliers, offering elaborate technical assistance to improve product quality.

MERGERS AND ACQUISITIONS.   In recent years, we've seen the headlines again and again: General Electric acquires RCA; Nabisco is taken over by R. J. Reynolds; Philip Morris and General Foods merge. Such mergers of two firms or the acquisition of one firm by another are increasingly-common strategic responses. Some mergers and acquisitions may be stimulated by simple economies of scale. For example, a motel chain with one hundred motels may have the same advertising costs as one with fifty motels. Other mergers and acquisitions may be pursued for purposes of vertical integration. For instance, a paper manufacturer may purchase a timber company. When mergers and acquisitions occur within the *same* industry there is evidence that they are being effected partly to reduce the uncertainty prompted by competition. When they occur across *different* industries (a diversification strategy) the goal is often to reduce resource dependence on a particular segment of the environment. A portfolio is created so that if resources become threatened in one part of the environment the organization can still prosper.[27]

This discussion of mergers and acquisitions underlines the point that growth itself can be a strategic response. For example, large multinational corporations have a fair degree of control over the environment by virtue of their size and geographic dispersion. Because they interact with a wide variety of customers and suppliers, they are less susceptible to being damaged by any one group or firm. And because they employ large numbers of people they should have considerable influence in the social/political sphere. Conversely, the small business may find itself at the mercy of an inefficient supplier or a shift in customer demand. Furthermore, it should not be able to command much political clout.

INTERLOCKING DIRECTORATES.   If we added up all the positions on boards of directors in the country and then added up all the people who serve as directors, the second number would be considerably smaller than the first. This is because of **interlocking directorates,** the condition said to exist when one person serves as a director on two or more boards. Such interlocking is prohibited by law when the firms are direct competitors, but as you can imagine, a fine line may exist as to the definition of a direct competitor. It has long been recognized that interlocking directorates provide a subtle but effective means of coping with environmental uncertainty and resource dependence. The director's expertise and experience with one organization may provide valuable information for another. Sometimes the value of the interlock is more direct. This is especially true when it is a ''vertical interlock'' in which one firm provides inputs to or receives outputs from the other (for instance, a director might serve on the board of a steel company and an auto producer):

> In addition to reducing uncertainty concerning inputs or outputs, a vertical interlock may also create a more efficient method of dealing with the environment. The outside director might be able not only to obtain the critical input, but also to procure favorable treatment such as a better price, better payment terms, or better delivery schedules. In addition, the search costs or the complexity involved in dealing with the environment may be reduced.[28]

Interlocks can also serve as a means of influencing public opinion about the wealth, status, or social conscience of a particular organization. Highly placed university officials, clergy, or union leaders are effectively board members in their own organizations, and they may be sought as board members by business firms to convey an impression of social responsibility to the wider public.[29] Resources are easier to obtain from a friendly environment than from a hostile environment!

The preceding are just a few examples of the kinds of strategic responses that organizations can implement to cope with the environment. Now, let's examine in greater detail another such response—technological choice.

THE TECHNOLOGIES OF ORGANIZATIONS

The term *technology* brings to mind physical devices such as turret lathes, handsaws, computers, and electron microscopes. However, as pointed out earlier, this is an overly narrow view of the concept. To broaden this view, we might define **technology** as the activities, equipment, and knowledge necessary to turn organizational inputs into desired outputs. In a hospital, relevant inputs might include sick patients and naive interns, while desired outputs include well people and experienced doctors. In a steel mill, crucial inputs include scrap metal and energy while desired outputs consist of finished steel. What technologies should the hospital and the steel mill use to facilitate this transformation? And more important for our purposes, do different technologies require different organizational structures to be effective?

You will observe that the concepts of technology and environment are closely related.[30] The inputs transformed by the technology come from various segments of the organization's environment. In turn, the outputs that the technology creates are returned to the environment. In addition, the activities, equipment, and knowledge that constitute the technology itself seldom spring to life within the organization. Rather, they are imported from the technological segment of the environment to meet the organization's needs.

It should be emphasized that organizations choose their technologies.[31] In general, this choice will be predicated on a desired strategy. For example, the directors of a university mental health center may decide that they wish to deal only with students suffering from transitory anxiety or mild neuroses. Given these inputs, certain short-term psychotherapies would constitute a sensible technology. More disturbed students would be referred to clinics with different strategies and different technologies.

Finally, it should be noted that different parts of the organization rely on different technologies, just as they respond to different aspects of the environment as a whole. For example, the personnel department uses a different technology than the finance department. However, research has often skirted this problem by concentrating on the "core" technology used by the key operating function (e.g., the production department in manufacturing firms).

Basic Dimensions of Technology

Organizational technology has been defined, conceptualized, and measured in literally dozens of different ways.[32] Some analysts have concentrated on degree of automation while others have focused on the degree of discretion granted to workers. Here we will consider other classifications of technologies developed by Charles Perrow and James D. Thompson. These classification schemes are advantageous because they can be applied to both manufacturing firms and to service organizations such as banks and schools.

PERROW'S ROUTINENESS. According to Perrow, the key factor that differentiates various technologies is the routineness of the transformation task that confronts the department or organization.[33] **Technological routineness** is a function of two factors:

■ *Exceptions*. Is the organization taking in standardized inputs and turning out standardized outputs (few exceptions)? Or is the organization encountering varied inputs or turning out varied outputs (many exceptions)? The technology becomes less routine as exceptions increase.

■ *Problems.* When exceptions occur, are the problems easy to analyze or difficult to analyze? That is, can programmed decision making occur, or must workers resort to nonprogrammed decision making? The technology becomes less routine as problems become more difficult to analyze.

As shown in Exhibit 16-6, the exceptions and problems dimensions can be arranged to produce a matrix of technologies:

■ *Craft technologies* typically deal with fairly standard inputs and outputs. Cabinetmakers use wood to make cabinets, and public schools attempt to educate "typical" students. However, when exceptions are encountered (a special order or a slow learner) analysis of the correct action may be difficult.

■ *Routine technologies* such as assembly line operations and technical schools also deal with standardized inputs and outputs. However, when exceptions do occur (a new product line or a new subject to be taught) the correct response is fairly obvious.

■ *Nonroutine technologies* must deal frequently with exceptional inputs or outputs, and the analysis of these exceptions is often difficult. By definition, research units are set up to deal with difficult, exceptional problems. Similarly, psychiatric hospitals encounter patients with a wide variety of disturbances. Deciding on a proper course of therapy may be problematic.

EXHIBIT 16-6   **Perrow's matrix of technologies.**

		Exceptions	
		Few	Many
Problems	Difficult Analysis	**Craft Technology** Cabinet making Public School	**Nonroutine Technology** Research Unit Psychiatric Hospital
	Easy Analysis	**Routine Technology** Assembly Line Vocational Training	**Engineering Technology** Heavy machinery Construction Health Spa

Source: From Perrow, C. (1967, April). A framework for the comparative analysis of organizations, *ASR*, Vol. 32, No. 2, Figures 1 and 2, pp. 196, 198. Copyright © 1967 American Sociological Association. Reprinted by permission.

■   *Engineering technologies* encounter many exceptions of input or required output, but these exceptions can be dealt with using standardized responses. For example, individuals with a wide variety of physical conditions visit health spas, and each has a particular goal (e.g., weight loss, muscle development). Despite this variety, the recommendation of a training regimen for each individual is a fairly easy decision.

From most routine to least routine, Perrow's four technological classifications can be ordered in the following manner: Routine, engineering, craft, nonroutine. Shortly we will consider which structures are appropriate for these technologies. First, let's examine Thompson's technological classification.

THOMPSON'S INTERDEPENDENCE.   In contrast to Perrow, James D. Thompson was interested in the way in which work activities are sequenced or "put together" during the transformation process.[34] A key factor here is **technological interdependence,** the extent to which organizational subunits depend on each other for resources, raw materials, or information. In order of increasing interdependence, Thompson proposed three classifications of technology (Exhibit 16-7):

■   *Mediating technologies* operate under **pooled interdependence.** This means that each unit is to some extent dependent upon the pooled resources generated by the other units, but is otherwise fairly independent of those units. Thompson gives rather abstract examples, such as banks which mediate between depositors and borrowers and post offices which mediate between the senders and receivers of letters. However, the same argument can be applied more clearly to the branches of banks or post offices. The health of a bank as a whole may depend on the existence of several branches, but these branches operate almost independently of each other. Each has its own borrowers and depositors. Similarly, post office branches are dependent upon other branches to forward and receive mail, but this is the limit of their required interaction.

■   *Long-linked technologies* operate under **sequential interdependence.** This means that each unit in the technology is dependent on the activity of the unit that preceded it in a sequence. The transformed product of each unit becomes a resource or raw material for the next unit. Mass production assembly lines are the classic example of long-linked technology. However, many "paper processing" technologies, such as the claims department of an insurance company, are also sequentially interdependent (claims must be verified before they are adjusted, and adjusted before they are settled).

■   *Intensive technologies* operate under **reciprocal interdependence.** This means that considerable interplay and feedback must occur between the units performing the task in order to accomplish it properly. This is necessary because each task is unique, and the intensive technology is thus a customized technology. One example might be the technology employed by a multidisciplinary research team. Thompson cites a general hospital as a prime example of intensive technology:

At any moment an emergency admission may require some combination of dietary, x-ray, laboratory, and housekeeping or hotel services, together with the various medical specialties, pharmaceutical services, occupational therapies, social work services, and spiritual or religious services. Which of these is needed, and when, can be determined only from evidence about the state of the patient.[35]

As technologies become increasingly interdependent, problems of coordination, communication, and decision making increase. To perform effectively, each technology requires a structure tailored to facilitate these tasks.

EXHIBIT 16-7   Thompson's technology classification.

Mediating Technology (Pooled Interdependence):

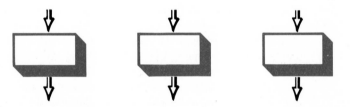

Long-Linked Technology (Sequential Interdependence):

Intensive Technology (Reciprocal Interdependence):

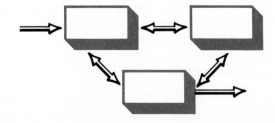

Structuring to Cope with Technology

How does technology affect organizational structure? According to Perrow, routine technologies should function best under more mechanistic structures, while non-routine technologies call for more organic structures. In the former case, few exceptions to the normal course of events and easily analyzable problems suggest high formalization and centralization. In the latter case, many exceptions and difficult problems suggest that decision-making power should be located "where the action is." The craft and engineering technologies fall between these prescriptions. Perrow encountered difficulties in actually measuring routineness according to the dimensions of exceptions and ease of analysis.[36] However, simplified measures have generally supported his notion that more routine technologies adopt more mechanistic structures.[37]

According to Thompson, increasing technological interdependence must be accompanied by increased coordination or integration mechanisms. There is research evidence to support this proposition.[38] Furthermore, the *methods* used to achieve coordination should be reflected in structural differences across the technologies. Mediating technologies, operating only under pooled interdependence, should be able to achieve coordination via standardization of rules, regulations, and procedures. This formalization is indicative of a mechanistic structure (consider banks and the post office). Long-linked technologies must also be structured mechanistically, but the increased demands for coordination prompted by sequential interdependence must be met by planning, scheduling, and meetings. Finally, intensive technologies require intensive coordination, and this is best achieved by mutual adjustment and an organic structure that permits the free and ready flow of information among units.[39]

Without a doubt, the most famous study of the relationship between technology and structure was performed by Joan Woodward. Woodward examined the technology, structure, and organizational effectiveness of one hundred firms in South Essex, England.[40] This study is especially interesting because it began as an attempt to test the classical argument that mechanistic structures will prove most effective in all cases. In brief, this test failed—there was no simple, consistent relationship between organizational structure and effectiveness, and many of the successful firms exhibited organic structures. Woodward then analyzed and classified the technologies of the eighty firms in her sample that had clear-cut, stable production processes. She used these classifications:

■ *Unit* (production of single units or small batches)
   - Custom-tailored units
   - Prototype production
   - Fabrication of large equipment in stages (e.g., locomotives)
   - Small batches to order

■ *Mass* (production of large batches or mass production)
   - Large batches on assembly lines
   - Mass production (e.g., bakeries)

■ *Process* (input transformed as an ongoing process)
 - Chemicals processed in batches
 - Continuous-flow production (e.g., gasoline, propane)

From top to bottom, this scale of technology seems to reflect both increasing smoothness of production and increasing impersonalization of task requirements.[41] Less and less personal intervention is necessary as machines control more and more of the work. Woodward's mass technology incorporates aspects of Perrow's routine technology and Thompson's long-linked technology. Her unit technology seems to cover Perrow's craft and engineering technologies and some aspects of Thompson's intensive technology. It is difficult to isolate Woodward's process technology in the Perrow or Thompson classifications.

Now for the key questions. Did organizational structures tend to vary with technology? If so, was this variance related to organizational effectiveness? The answer in both cases is yes. Each of the three technologies tended to have distinctive structures, and the most successful firms had structures that closely approximated the average of their technological groups. For instance, Woodward found that as the production process became smoother, more continuous, and more impersonal, the management of the system took on increasing importance. That is, moving from unit to mass to process, there were more managers relative to workers, more hierarchical levels, and lower labor costs. (See the top two diagrams in Exhibit 16-8). This is not difficult to understand. Unit production involves custom-tailored craftsmanship in which the workers can essentially manage their own work activity. However, it is very labor intensive. On the other hand, sophisticated continuous-process systems (such as those used to refine gasoline) take a great amount of management skill and technical attention to start up. Once rolling, a handful of workers can monitor and maintain the system.

Successful firms with unit and process technologies relied upon organic structures, while successful firms engaged in mass production relied upon mechanistic structures. For example, as shown in the bottom two diagrams of Exhibit 16-8, the latter firms had more specialization of labor, more controls, and greater formalization (a reliance on written rather than verbal communication). At first glance, it may strike you as unusual that the firms at the extremes of the technology scale (unit and process) both tended to rely on organic structures. However, close consideration of the actual tasks performed under each technology resolves this apparent contradiction. Unit production generally involves custom-building complete units to customer specifications. As such, it relies upon skilled labor, teamwork, and coordination by mutual adjustment and standardized skills. The work itself is not machine-paced, and far from mechanistic. At the other extreme, process production is almost totally automated. The workers are essentially skilled technicians who monitor and maintain the system, and they again tend to work in teams. While the machinery itself operates according to a rigid schedule, workers can monitor and maintain it at their own pace. Informal relationships with supervisors replace close control.

Woodward's research is a landmark in demonstrating the general proposition that structure must be tailored to the technology the organization adopts to achieve

---

EXHIBIT 16-8   **Woodward's study: Relationships between technology and structure for effective firms.**

Structural Characteristics	Technology-Structure Relationship
Number of levels of management Span of control of chief executive Ratio of managers to total personnel	*(graph: increasing line from U to P)* OC; axis U M P (T)
Ratio of direct to indirect labor Ratio of manual workers to clerical and administrative staff Ratio of wages and salaries to total costs Labor costs	*(graph: decreasing line from U to P)* OC; axis U M P (T)
Span of control of first-level production supervisor Separation of production administration from actual supervision of production operations Amount of written communications Use of control and sanction procedures Specializations between line and staff functions	*(graph: inverted-V peaking at M)* OC; axis U M P (T)
Amount of verbal communications Role ambiguity concerning duties and responsibilities (an index of organizational flexibility) Number of skilled workers	*(graph: V-shape low at M)* OC; axis U M P (T)

Note: OC = organizational structure characteristic; *T* = technology; *U* = unit-production system; *M* = mass-production system; *P* = process-production system.

Source: Adapted from Miles, R. H. (1980). *Macro organizational behavior.* Glenview, IL: Scott, Foresman, p. 58.

---

its strategic goals. Her findings have been replicated and extended by others.[42] However, there have been disconfirming studies, and a constant debate has gone on about the relative importance of organizational size versus technology in determining structure.[43]

The design of the Saturn organization shows evidence of an attempt to match structure to technology. In Woodward's terms, the core technology at Saturn is obviously mass production. However, the floor track system and the opportunity to stop car chassis mean that the technology is somewhat less routine (in Perrow's terms) than the conventional monolithic assembly line. To take advantage of this, the shop floor organization, with its work teams and reduced supervision, is more organic than is typical for the North American auto industry. This, then, is also reflected in the managerial and professional ranks, where the technology for designing cars will be modified. Instead of passing designs from department to department (Thompson's sequential interdependence), early involvement of all crit-

ical departments will be required (Thompson's reciprocal interdependence). Again,
this points to a more organic structure backed up by sophisticated electronic aids
to facilitate coordination and communication. In–Focus 16-4 shows that General
Motors is not the only company to change the technology of car design.

Some Implications of Advanced Technology

In concluding the chapter, it is important to consider some of the implications that
ongoing advances in technology may have for organizational behavior. Such advances include computerized work station networks, the deployment of robots,

computer-numerically-controlled machine tools, computer-aided design systems, computerized warehousing, and so on. Three major trends underlie such **advanced technology.**[44] The first is an obvious capitalization on computer intelligence and memory. The second is flexibility, in that these technologies are designed to accomplish a changing variety of tasks. This is often the product of an organizational strategy that involves finding and exploiting short-term "niches" in the marketplace rather than hoping to produce large volumes of the same product (or service) year after year. Finally, advanced technologies are increasingly being designed to be integrated with *other* advanced technologies used by the organization. For example, the computer-aided design system that is used to design and modify a product can also be used to design, operate, and modify its production process via computer-aided manufacturing programs (the result being a so-called CAD/CAM system). Ultimately, using most of the technologies mentioned here, flexible manufacturing systems that integrate and automate all aspects of design, manufacturing, assembly, and inspection can be put in place. In turn, computerized information systems can link these tasks to supply and sales networks.

What are the implications of such advanced technology for organizational behavior? First, let's ignore the exotic labels and examine the advanced technologies in terms of the basic dimensions discussed earlier. Advanced technologies tend to automate the more routine information-processing and decision-making tasks. What remains for operators are the more complex tasks of a nonroutine nature, those dealing with system problems and exceptions. In addition, task interdependence tends to increase under advanced technologies. For example, design, manufacturing, and marketing may become more reciprocally than sequentially interdependent in a flexible manufacturing system. Finally, let's remember that such advanced technologies are adopted in part to cope with a less certain environment. Thus, many advanced technological systems result in nonroutine, highly interdependent tasks that are embedded in an uncertain environment.[45]

ORGANIZATIONAL STRUCTURE.   What are the implications of this shift in technology? One is a movement toward flatter, more organic structures.[46] This corresponds to Woodward's finding that unit technologies require more organic designs than mass technologies, and the adoption of more flexible, short-term production batches is an example of unit technology. The expectation for flatter structures stems from the fact that more highly automated systems will handle information processing and diagnoses that were formerly performed by middle managers. Implications of advanced technology for centralization are interesting. On the one hand, matters such as ordering raw materials and scheduling production should become more highly centralized. This is both required by the flexibility of the system and permitted by the enhanced information-processing capability of the system. On the other hand, when problems or exceptions occur, or when new designs are conceived, decentralization may be called for to locate decision making in the hands of lower-level specialists. However, the whole thrust of advanced technology dictates greater integration among specialties such as design, engineering, production, and marketing. This may require a retreat from the rigid functional structures (Chapter 15) that are common in manufacturing firms. Minimally, it suggests the increased use of integrators, task forces, planning committees, and other mechanisms that stimulate coordination.

JOB DESIGN. In addition to its impact on organizational structure, advanced technology can be expected to affect the design of jobs, especially at lower organization levels. Early discussions of the possible impact of advanced technology frequently warned about the "deskilling" of jobs that could occur as computers took over skilled tasks formerly performed by workers. It is now clear that such deskilling can occur, but its occurrence is a signal of bad job design rather than bad hardware. For example, the firm that installs an expensive computer-aided design system only to have it used as a fancy drafting device by conventional draftspersons may be attacking their traditional skills and not fully exploiting the design capabilities of the hardware. Job design must be matched to the demands of advanced technology.

Since advanced technology tends to automate routine tasks, it is usually the case that operative workers must acquire advanced skills (e.g., computer skills). Also, since advanced technology tends to be flexible as well as expensive to operate, workers themselves must be flexible and fast to respond to problems. Extreme division of labor may be counterproductive in advanced technology. For example, operators simply may not be able to wait for someone else to perform routine maintenance, and may thus have to have the flexibility to do this themselves. Similarly, traditional distinctions between roles (electrical maintenance versus mechanical maintenance, or drafting versus design) begin to blur when the needs for coordination imposed by advanced technology are recognized.

All of this points to the design of jobs for advanced technology according to the principles of job enrichment discussed in Chapter 7. In turn, this suggests that proper training is critical and that pay levels be revised to fit the additional skills and responsibilities prompted by the technology. In production operations, many observers have recommended that self-managed teams be made responsible for setting up, running, and maintaining the system.[47] In fact, GM has adopted this scheme for the Saturn plant. Such teams permit cross-transfer of skills and provide the cross-task integration necessary to keep things working smoothly. The team concept also seems applicable to other aspects of advanced technology. For example, one company organized its CAD/CAM users into teams composed of two designers, a draftsperson, and a toolmaker.[48]

Most of the foregoing is admittedly speculative, since research has really just begun on the organizational behavior implications of advanced technology. However, there are many examples emerging of organizations that have had poor success in introducing advanced technology because they ignored the human dimension. This raises the issue of implementing change in organizations, the topic of the next chapter.

SUMMARY

- Organizations are open systems that take inputs from the external environment, transform some of these inputs, and send them back into the environment as outputs. The external environment includes all of the events and conditions surrounding the organization that influence this process. Major components of the environment include the economy, customers, suppliers, competitors, social/political factors, and existing technologies.

- One key aspect of the external environment is its uncertainty. More uncertain environments are vague, difficult to diagnose, and unpredictable. Uncertainty is a function of complexity and rate of change. The most uncertain environments are complex and dynamic—they involve a large number of dissimilar components which are changing unpredictably. More certain environments are simple and stable—they involve a few similar components that exhibit little change. As environmental uncertainty increases, cause-effect relationships get harder to diagnose and agreeing on priorities becomes more difficult because more information must be processed.

- Another key aspect of the external environment is the amount of resources it contains. Some environments are richer or more munificent than others, and all organizations are dependent upon their environments for resources.

- Strategy is the process by which executives seek to cope with the constraints and opportunities posed by the organization's environment, including uncertainty and scarce resources. One critical strategic response involves tailoring the organization's structure to suit the environment. In general, as demonstrated by the Lawrence and Lorsch study, mechanistic structures are most suitable for more certain environments, and organic structures are better suited to uncertain environments. Other strategic responses include vertical integration, mergers and acquisitions, interlocking directorates, and technological choice.

- Technology includes the activities, equipment, and knowledge necessary to turn organizational inputs into desired outputs. One key aspect of technology is the extent of its routineness. A routine technology involves few exceptions to usual inputs or outputs and readily analyzable problems. A nonroutine technology involves many exceptions that are difficult to analyze. Another key aspect of technology is the degree of interdependence that exists between organizational units. This may range from simple pooling of resources to sequential activities to complex reciprocal interdependence.

- The most famous study of the relationship between technology and structure was performed by Joan Woodward. She determined that unit and process technologies performed best under organic structures while mass production functioned best under a mechanistic structure. In general, less routine technologies and more interdependent technologies seem to call for more organic structures.

■   Advanced technology uses extensive computerization to create flexible, interrelated systems to accomplish work. Current thinking suggests that advanced technologies may be most effective when coupled with essentially organic structures, enriched, skill-enhanced jobs, and self-managed work teams.

KEY CONCEPTS

External environment
Open system
Interest groups
Environmental uncertainty
Resource dependence
Strategy
Vertical integration
Interlocking directorates

Technology
Technological routineness
Technological interdependence
Pooled interdependence
Sequential interdependence
Reciprocal interdependence
Advanced technology

DISCUSSION QUESTIONS

1. Construct a diagram of the various interest groups in the external environment of CBS Television. Discuss how some of these interest groups may make competing or contradictory demands on CBS.

2. Describe a real or a hypothetical organization with a very uncertain environment. Do the same for an organization with a fairly certain environment. Be sure to cover both the complexity and rate of change dimensions.

3. Give an example of vertical integration. Use the concept of resource dependence to explain why an organization might choose a strategic response of vertical integration.

4. Discuss how interlocking directorates might reduce environmental uncertainty and help manage resource dependence.

5. Explain why organizations operating in more uncertain environments require more organic structures.

6. Locate the technology of a branch bank situated in a shopping center in Perrow's technology matrix (Exhibit 16-6). Defend your answer.

7. Distinguish among pooled interdependence, sequential interdependence, and reciprocal interdependence in terms of the key problem each poses for organizational effectiveness.

8. Give an example of unit technology, mass technology, and process technology. For which type of technology are the prescriptions of the classical organizational theorists best suited?

9. Imagine that a company is converting from conventional mass technology to a highly flexible, computerized, integrated production system. List structural and behavioral problems that may have to be anticipated in making this conversion.

10. Summarize the environmental and technological conditions that favor mechanistic structures. Do the same for organic structures.

FOR FURTHER READING

Galbraith, J. R. (1982, Winter). Designing the innovating organization. *Organizational Dynamics,* 4–25.

> Discusses the proper design for organizations that wish to pursue strategies that involve innovation. Covers structural arrangements, reward systems, and personnel requirements. Includes an illustrative case study.

Hulin, C. L., & Roznowski, M. (1985). Organizational technologies: Effects on organizations' characteristics and individuals' responses. *Research in Organizational Behavior, 7,* 39–85.

> Reviews the relationship between technology and structure and then looks at the impact of subsystem technology on leadership, communications, and organizational climate. Discusses the relationship among technology, job characteristics, and employee responses.

Kanter, R. M., & Buck, J. D. (1985, Winter). Reorganizing part of Honeywell: From strategy to structure. *Organizational Dynamics,* 4–25.

> Describes how the Employee Relations department of Honeywell's largest division initiated a self-study to refine its strategy and choose a revised structure to match this strategy. Interesting because it concerns the strategy and structure of one department rather than a whole organization.

Marks, M. L., & Mirvis, P. H. (1986, October). The merger syndrome. *Psychology Today,* 36–42.

> Although mergers represent a popular corporate strategy, they can lead to problems when the organizational cultures of the merged firms clash. Presents examples of such clashes and provides a checklist of twelve signs of merger trouble.

Case Study

Letters of Credit

In 1970 New York's Citibank faced a problem common to many of North America's largest banks, a problem created in part by its own success. The economic upsurge of the 1950s and 1960s, coupled with the advent of high-capacity centralized computers, had resulted in a radical increase in banking volume. This increase in volume was accompanied by a corresponding increase in banking transactions, each of which generated considerable paperwork. To cope with this avalanche of paperwork, more and more clerks were hired. Generally inexperienced and less than extensively trained because of time constraints, these clerks were assigned to routine, repetitive paperhandling jobs. Single tasks with little apparent relationship to an entire banking transaction were performed over and over again. As a result of monotony, processing errors, discrepancies, and confusion became all too common, and on one occasion a backlog of 36,000 customer inquiries existed.

Not surprisingly, a 1970 Opinion Research Corporation survey ranked Citibank very low on customer service. Thus, despite its increased staffing and improved computer capacity, the bank was falling behind in the very area it had sought to maintain or improve—accurate, timely service. To add insult to injury, internal operating costs had been increasing at a rate of 15 percent a year.

The initial response of top management to Citibank's problems was a program that lasted from 1970 to 1975. The program involved recruiting a new

Source: This case is based on Matteis, R. J. (1979, March-April). The new back office focuses on customer service, *Harvard Business Review*.

management team from organizations not traditionally associated with banking—especially from manufacturing industries. The new managers, educated in quantitative methods and production management, examined Citibank from a fresh perspective. In this analysis, they tended to view Citibank as a factory—albeit a paper and data processing factory—and they concluded that major changes in organizational structure were necessary to improve the bank's position. These changes were implemented to increase management control over a situation that had gotten out of hand.

Prior to the new program, transactions were processed using what might be called a "centralized assembly line." That is, whether a transaction was initiated from a branch bank, a correspondent bank, or the Federal Reserve, it went into a first-come, first-served queue where it was sorted and processed in an assembly-line manner. The same applied whether the transaction involved a stock, bond, loan, or deposit. This meant that if a bottleneck in the processing occurred, the bank's entire operations would be affected. Furthermore, a functional manager (such as one responsible for dealing with loans issued by branch banks) would have a difficult time resolving processing errors, since they occurred outside of his or her line of authority.

In response to these problems, the new management program divided transactions into source (i.e., branch bank, correspondent bank, Federal Reserve) and type (e.g., loan, deposit, stock, bond) and then set up a separate processing unit under each division. Now, managers had control over the processing of transactions relevant to their own function from the time the transaction entered the bank until the customer was advised of its disposition. Quality control systems similar to those used in manufacturing were devised, and increased automation occurred, although the processing jobs remained essentially the same as they had before the transition—work was still fragmented. The centralized assembly line had been replaced by many parallel assembly lines.

By many standards, the program developed between 1970 and 1975 was successful. Despite inflation, the costs of processing transactions had stabilized. In addition, another customer survey in 1975 indicated improvements in accuracy and speed. However, management was still unhappy about the bank's current position, even though it had moved to the middle of the pack of surveyed banks. Also, this survey pointed out a particularly disturbing problem. Evidently, in improving the *efficiency* of its interaction with customers, the bank had acquired the image of being *less personal*. Especially when compared with smaller institutions, Citibank was seen as offering less personalized service in a business that is founded on such service. The factory metaphor was not the perfect one for the banking business, and even parallel assembly lines had their limitations.

To cope with the need to provide unique, personalized service to its customers, Citibank embarked on a second program—services management—in 1975. Services management consisted of three interrelated components. First, the market was segmented more carefully than it had been with the previous management program. A real attempt was made to tie customers who had particular needs (e.g., a British correspondent bank seeking credit for a chemical producer) to an appropriately specialized Citibank unit. This effectively moved expertise and decision-making power closer to the customer. Secondly, minicomputers were adopted to tailor the processing of transactions to this particular customer segment. Even the parallel assembly lines had relied upon standardized, centralized computing. Finally, and very importantly, processing jobs were redesigned to correspond to the new market segmentation and technology. When possible, the assembly lines were abolished.

The nature of the new services management program is well illustrated by the revision of the bank's letter of credit operation. A letter of credit is a complex financial instrument by which a bank in effect serves as an intermediary between one of its customers and a third party. The letter guarantees that the bank will pay the third party on behalf of its customer when certain conditions of a business transaction have been met. Letters of credit are commonly used in international trade. For example, a customer in Saudi Arabia may request a letter of credit to finance the shipment of oil drilling equipment from a Texas manufacturer. When the bank determines that delivery has been made according to agreed-upon conditions, it makes payment to the Texas firm's bank. The basic process of issuance of the letter and payment to the beneficiary is often complicated by intermediate amendments to the letter as the deal progresses and by inquiries from the customer concerning the status of the letter.

In 1975, a typical letter of credit required the sequential attention of at least fourteen clerks, managers, and officers. This preparation, checking, verifying, and approving involved over thirty separate processing steps and took several days to accomplish. If the customer then requested an amendment to the letter, the process was repeated by a revised cast of characters. A similar unwieldy, lengthy system was followed when it was time to make the payment guaranteed by the letter. This complex, specialized assembly line was simply too slow and fragmented. Employees who could process an issuance knew nothing about amendment, and customer service was handled separately from issuance, amendment, and payment. It was no wonder that customers questioned the personalization of Citibank's service.

In order to improve the letter of credit operation, a services management team began by taking a long, hard look at the actual work that went into processing a letter of credit. Beginning with the simplest, most straightforward examples, they had an experienced veteran process the letters before their eyes, questioning the need for every step, form, file, and rubber stamp. In addition, comprehensive interviews were conducted with other employees. Gradually, the management team was able to develop a streamlined basic letter of credit process which involved half the steps of its predecessor. This new process then became the foundation for simplifying yet more complex letters. It was concluded that a letter of credit could be processed by a single employee using a specially programmed minicomputer.

Careful planning was necessary to move the letter of credit operation from a fourteen-person assembly line to a one-person process. Clerks who were formerly familiar with only one or two steps in the process were to become full-fledged letter of credit professionals. First, minicomputer work stations were designed. Each included a telephone to answer customer inquiries. In addition, the computers themselves were programmed to provide the operator with complete data about his or her customers, so that the customers would no longer be an anonymous cipher on a form. After-hours training in computer operation was provided, and employees began to cross-train each other in the various aspects of letters of credit. Those who knew issuance trained those who knew amendment and vice versa. At all stages, pains were taken to communicate to employees what was happening, and their participation in decision making was sought. For example, workers were consulted extensively about the design of the new work stations. Employees who did not desire the revised jobs were permitted to transfer to other functions. Those who remained were given pay raises to correspond to their increased responsibility.

Now individual employees who were formerly clerks are responsible for all aspects of "their" letters of credit for "their" personal customers. If the customer has a problem to be solved or an amendment to be processed, it is done by the same person who issued the letter. Employees feel possessive about their work stations and often decorate them with souvenirs of the nations they serve. Less direct supervision is necessary since employees now have the knowledge and perspective to solve many problems on their own. In turn, managers in the letter of credit operation can devote their time to customer development rather than to coordinating a fragmented series of processing steps. Since the workers who process letters of credit now understand an important bank process in full, career paths into other aspects of the organization have opened up.

By almost all standards, Citibank considers its services management program a great success. Although the letter of credit processors enjoy their new jobs, some report feeling a certain sense of isolation from co-workers in doing the jobs individually. Gradually, this problem should be resolved as the bank moves toward a series of working units that will deal with *all* the financial needs of particular customers. These multiproduct work centers should provide employees with a sense of teamwork while furthering Citibank's goal of personalizing its services.

■ ■ ■

1. Discuss the environmental components of Citibank that are exerting influence at the time of the case.
2. Apply the concepts of environmental uncertainty, resource dependence, and strategy to the Citibank case.
3. Discuss Citibank's first program (1970–75) to improve its services, considering the interplay among strategy, structure, and technology. Why was this program partially successful? Why was it not more successful?
4. Discuss Citibank's second program (services management, begun in 1975) to improve its services, again considering the interplay among strategy, structure, and technology.
5. Discuss how advanced technology shaped the design of the letters of credit jobs. Were the jobs enriched? Support your answer.
6. Not all efforts at organizational change turn out successfully. What factors contributed to the success of the redesign of the letters of credit job at Citibank?

REFERENCES

1. This case is based on several sources: Fisher, A. B. (1985, November 11). Behind the hype at GM's Saturn. *Fortune,* 34–49; Lienert, P. (1985, April). The Saturn project. *Car and Driver,* 32; Saturn: GM's bold new plan. (1985, January 28). *Autoweek,* 4; Edid, M. (1985, August 5). How power will be balanced on Saturn's shop floor. *Business Week,* 48–49.

2. Katz, D., & Kahn, R. L. (1978). *The social psychology of organizations* (2nd ed.). New York: Wiley.

3. This list relies upon Duncan, R. (1972). Characteristics of organization environments and perceived environmental uncertainty. *Administrative Science Quarterly, 17,* 313–327.

4. Coates, L. (1986, July 5). High-flying Jags no longer such a pain to take care of. *The Gazette* (Montreal), F 1.

5. See Khandwalla, P. (1981). Properties of competing organizations. In P. C. Nystrom & W. H. Starbuck (Eds.), *Handbook of organization design* (Vol. 1). Oxford: Oxford University Press.

6. Williams, M. J. (1985, June 24). Soft drink wars: The next battle. *Fortune,* 70–72.

7. O'Connell, J. M. (with B. Arnold). (1985, February 18). Computers are starting to sniff out cocaine users. *Business Week,* 37.

8. Pfeffer, J., & Salancik, G. R. (1978). *The external control of organizations: A resource dependence perspective.* New York: Harper & Row.

9. Connolly, T., Conlon, E. J., & Deutsch, S. J. (1980). Organizational effectiveness: A multiple-constituency approach. *Academy of Management Review, 5,* 211–217.

10. Fisher, 1985.

11. Duncan, 1972; Just how to measure uncertainty has provoked controversy. See Downey, H. K., & Ireland, R. D. (1979). Quantitative versus qualitative: Environmental assessment in organizational studies. *Administrative Science Quarterly, 24,* 630–637. For advances in quantitative measurement see Snyder, N. H., & Glueck, W. F. (1982). Can environmental volatility be measured objectively? *Academy of Management Journal, 25,* 185–192, and Dess, G. G., & Beard, D. W. (1984). Dimensions of organizational task environments. *Administrative Science Quarterly, 29,* 52–73.

12. Duncan, 1972; Tung, R. L. (1979). Dimensions of organizational environments: An exploratory study of their impact on organization structure. *Academy of Management Journal, 22,* 672–693. For contrary evidence see Downey, H., Hellriegel, D., & Slocum, J. (1975). Environmental uncertainty: The construct and its application. *Administrative Science Quarterly, 20,* 613–629.

13. See also Leblebici, H., & Salancik, G. R. (1981). Effects of environmental uncertainty on information and decision processes in banks. *Administrative Science Quarterly, 26,* 578–596.

14. Pfeffer & Salancik, 1978.

15. Dess & Beard, 1984.

16. Pfeffer & Salancik, 1978.

17. See Yasai-Ardekani, M. (1986). Structural adaptations to environments. *Academy of Management Review, 11,* 9–21.

18. For an analog see Miller, D., Kets de Vries, M. F. R., & Toulouse, J. M. (1982). Top executive locus of control and its relationship to strategy-making, structure, and environment. *Academy of Management Journal, 25,* 237–253.

19. Miles, R. C., & Snow, C. C. (1978). *Organizational strategy, structure, and process.* New York: McGraw-Hill.

20. Salpukas, A. (1986, May 3). People Express goes for first class. *The Gazette* (Montreal). I-14.

21. Labich, K. (1985, November 25). How long can quilting-bee management work? *Fortune, 132.*

22. Lawrence, P. R., & Lorsch, J. W. (1967). *Organization and environment: Managing differentiation and integration.* Homewood, IL: Irwin. For a follow-up study see Lorsch, J. W., & Morse, J. J. (1974). *Organizations and their members: A contingency approach.* New York: Harper & Row.

23. For a review see Miner, J. B. (1982). *Theories of organizational structure and process.* Chicago: Dryden.

24. Main, J. (1984, December 24). Waking up AT&T: There's life after culture shock. *Fortune,* 66–74, p. 70.

25. Frederickson, J. W. (1986). The strategic decision process and organizational structure. *Academy of Management Review, 11,* 280–297.

26. Robey, D. (1986). *Designing organizations* (2nd ed.). Homewood, IL: Irwin.

27. Pfeffer & Salancik, 1978.

28. Schoorman, F. D., Bazerman, M. H., & Atkin, R. S. (1981). Interlocking directorates: A strategy for reducing environmental uncertainty. *Academy of Management Review, 6,* 243–251, p. 244.

29. Schoorman et al., 1981.

30. Rousseau, D. M. (1979). Assessment of technology in organizations: Closed versus open systems approaches. *Academy of Management Review, 4,* 531–542.

31. Child, J. (1972). Organizational structure, environment and performance: The role of strategic choice. *Sociology, 6,* 2–22.

32. Rousseau, 1979; Gillespie, D. F., & Mileti, D. S. (1977). Technology and the study of organizations: An overview and appraisal. *Academy of Management Review, 2,* 7–16.

33. Perrow, C. A. (1967). A framework for the comparative analysis of organizations. *American Sociological Review, 32,* 194–208.

34. Thompson, J. D. (1967). *Organizations in action.* New York: McGraw-Hill.

35. Thompson, 1967, p. 17.

36. Perrow, C. A. (1970). *Organizational analysis: A sociological view.* Belmont, CA: Wadsworth. For an update on measurement see Withey, M., Daft, R. L., & Cooper, W. H. (1983). Measures of Perrow's work unit technology: An empirical assessment and a new scale. *Academy of Management Journal, 26,* 45–63.

37. Gerwin, D. (1981). Relationships between structure and technology. In P. C. Nystrom & W. H. Starbuck (Eds.), *Handbook of organization design* (Vol. 2). Oxford: Oxford University Press.

38. Cheng, J. L. C. (1983). Interdependence and coordination in organizations: A role-system analysis. *Academy of Management Journal, 26,* 156–162.

39. Van de Ven, A. H., Delbecq, A. L., & Koenig, R., Jr. (1976). Determinants of coordination modes within organizations. *American Sociological Review, 41,* 322–338.

40. Woodward, J. (1965). *Industrial organization: Theory and practice.* London: Oxford University Press.

41. Mintzberg, H. (1979). *The structuring of organizations.* Englewood Cliffs, NJ: Prentice-Hall.

42. Marsh, R. M., & Mannari, H. (1981). Technology and size as determinants of the organizational structure of Japanese factories. *Administrative Science Quarterly, 26,* 33–57; Keller, R. T., Slocum, J. W., Jr., & Susman, G. J. (1974). Uncertainty and type of management in continuous process organizations. *Academy of Management Journal, 17,* 56–68; Zwerman, W. L. (1970). *New perspectives on organizational theory.* Westport, CT: Greenwood.

43. Gerwin, 1981.

44. Child, J. (1987). Organizational design for advanced manufacturing technology. In Wall, T. D., Clegg, C. W., & Kemp, N. J. (Eds.), *The human side of advanced manufacturing technology.* Sussex, England: Wiley.

45. Cummings, T. G., & Blumberg, M. Advanced manufacturing technology and work design. In Wall et al., 1987.

46. The following draws upon Child, 1987.

47. Cummings & Blumberg, 1987; Blumberg, M., & Gerwin, D. (1984). Coping with advanced manufacturing technology. *Journal of Occupational Behaviour, 5,* 113–130.

48. From an unpublished paper by C. A. Voss, cited in Child, 1987.

Chapter 17

Organizational Change and Development

FABER COLLEGE

Faber College was in trouble. Like many small, private colleges in the late 1980s, it was going broke. Located in the idyllic countryside of New Hampshire, Faber had been founded in 1912 by the wealthy philanthropist G. Roberts Faber. Its primary mission had always been to provide a high-quality undergraduate education in the liberal arts. However, in 1958 Faber had developed a Department of Economics and Business with funding from a local industrialist. With five faculty members, this department was the smallest in the college, and it had traditionally been regarded as the least prestigious and least powerful. However, this didn't inhibit its newfound popularity with students—the department's classes had been overflowing for the last three years. "Which is more than I can say for the other departments," thought Jean Marlow.

Dr. Jean Marlow had been president of Faber College for eighteen years. When she had been a professor of philosophy, and early in her reign as president, Faber had been fairly prosperous. Students had been eager to obtain the personalized education offered by Faber at a cost not much greater than that of large, anonymous state universities. However, with few economies of scale and an expansive, old-fashioned campus to maintain, Faber's tuition and room and board expenses had climbed radically in recent years, outstripping those of the state schools. In addition, in the 1980s students began to shift their interests to more practical, career-oriented courses, and Faber offered few of these. The net result was a sharp decline in enrollments and their accompanying fees. In fact, outside of the Department of Economics and Business, class enrollments had fallen to seminar-like levels. According to the Director of Finance, the writing was on the wall: Faber would be unable to meet its operating expenses within the next two years.

After long consultation with the board of regents, Jean Marlow called a general meeting of all Faber academic and support staff. She outlined Faber's dire economic situation, then made these points:

- Radical cuts would be made in support staff, strictly on a seniority basis.
- All academic departments except Economics and Business would have to reduce staff, beginning with untenured professors. Economics and Business would be expanded and marketed more aggressively to potential students.

- In some departments, tenured professors would be dismissed. She said that the guidelines set down by the American Association of University Professors would be followed, and she invited input from the Faber Faculty Association.
- All salaries would be frozen indefinitely.

The following weeks at Faber were filled with confusion, uncertainty, and conflict. Several excellent faculty members missed classes due to "personal business" which actually consisted of job hunting trips out of town. Three tenured faculty members who were threatened with dismissal filed lawsuits against Faber. A meeting of the Faculty Association broke up in hostility because opinions were so highly polarized. Learning that several popular untenured professors were to be dismissed, Faber students held a protest march on Jean Marlow's office. Members of the Department of Economics and Business avoided walks across campus, having become the target of open hostility from other faculty members. The chairperson of Economics and Business wondered how he could recruit new faculty members with indefinitely frozen salaries and an atmosphere of tension surrounding the college.

In her office, Jean Marlow began to wonder if some kind of a consultant could be hired to help Faber get through its identity crisis.

As this story illustrates, organizations must often come to grips with the need for change. It also shows that the prospect of change may be an unpleasant experience. Why did the Faber administration ignore the trends that led to its present problem? Why did various parties react so negatively to Jean Marlow's plans? Could she have proceeded in a more satisfactory manner? Could a consultant help Faber cope with change? These are the kinds of questions we will address in this chapter.

First, the concept of organizational change will be discussed, including the *whys* and *whats* of change. Then, the process by which change occurs will be considered and a number of problems involved in managing change will be examined. Following this, organizational development will be defined, and several development strategies will be explored. Finally, the success of organizational development will be evaluated.

THE CONCEPT OF ORGANIZATIONAL CHANGE

Common experience indicates that organizations are far from static. Our favorite small restaurant experiences success and expands. We return for a visit to our alma mater and observe a variety of new programs and new buildings. The local Oldsmobile dealer also begins to sell Toyotas. As consumers, we are aware that such changes may have a profound impact on our satisfaction with the product or service offered. By extension, we can also imagine that these changes have a strong impact on those who work at the restaurant, university, or car dealership. In and of themselves, such changes are neither good nor bad. Rather, it is the way the changes are *implemented* and *managed* that is crucial to both customers and members. This is the focus of the present chapter.

In previous chapters we have explored a number of specific techniques to improve organizational effectiveness, including job redesign, goal setting, and participative leadership. When such programs are introduced they surely represent a change from the status quo. But what prompts such changes? And what ensures that they will be effective?

Why Organizations Must Change

All organizations face two basic sources of pressure to change—external sources and internal sources. Although this distinction is somewhat arbitrary, it provides a convenient basis for discussing forces for change.

In Chapter 16 it was pointed out that organizations are open systems that take inputs from the environment, transform some of these inputs, and send them back into the environment as outputs.[1] Most organizations work hard to stabilize their inputs and outputs. For example, a manufacturing firm might use a variety of suppliers to avoid a shortage of raw materials and attempt to turn out quality products to ensure demand. However, there are limits on the extent to which such control over the environment can occur. In this case, environmental changes must be matched by organizational changes if the organization is to remain effective. For example, consider the successful producer of slide rules in 1960. In less than a decade, the slide rule market virtually disappeared with the advent of reasonably priced electronic calculators. If the firm was unable to anticipate this by developing a new product and a market, it would surely cease to exist.

Federal legislation often spurs organizational change. For instance, the abolition of the United States military draft required the "New Volunteer Army" to radically rethink its recruiting and selection procedures. How could an adequate number of recruits be attracted? Some selection standards were lowered, and this in turn required revisions in training and job design. Similarly, strict enforcement of Equal Employment Opportunity Commission regulations caused many firms to look carefully at hiring, promotion, and pay policies for women and minorities. How could inequalities be redressed without charges of reverse discrimination? A variety of changes in personnel policies were implemented.

The story that began the chapter also illustrates the impact of the external environment on organizational change. Faber College was forced to change because its outputs (liberal arts graduates) were in less demand. Therefore, it attracted fewer crucial inputs (students and their fees).

Change can also be provoked by forces in the *internal* environment of the organization. Low productivity, conflict, strikes, sabotage, and high absenteeism and turnover are some of the factors that may signal to management that change is necessary. For instance, a firm that has experienced dramatic growth may have promoted many persons to supervisory positions without adequate training. Production problems and labor strife may signal the need to develop a formal training program. Very often, internal forces for change occur in response to organizational changes that are designed to deal with the external environment. At Faber College, severe internal disruptions occurred when Jean Marlow announced her solution to the enrollment problem. These internal forces suggest that additional changes might be necessary at Faber.

Two final points about the forces for change should be emphasized. First, the internal and external environments of various organizations will be more or less dynamic (a point made in Chapter 16 with regard to the external environment). In responding to this, organizations will therefore differ in the amount of change they should exhibit (Exhibit 17-1). As shown, organizations in a dynamic environment must generally exhibit more change to be effective than those operating in a more stable environment. Secondly, change in and of itself is not a good thing, and organizations can exhibit too much change as well as too little (Exhibit 17-1). The company that is in constant flux fails to establish the regular patterns of behavior necessary for effectiveness.

What Organizations Can Change

In theory, organizations can change just about any aspect of their operations they wish. Since change is a broad concept, it is useful to identify several specific domains where modifications can occur. Of course, the choice of *what* to change

EXHIBIT 17-1   **Relationships among environmental change, organizational change, and organizational effectiveness.**

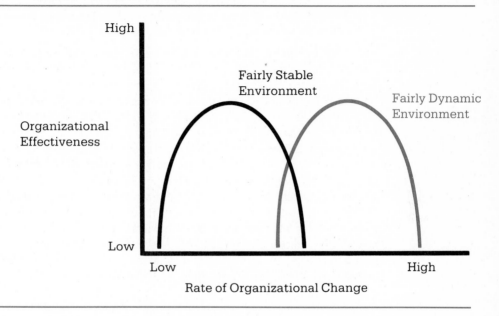

depends upon a correct analysis of the internal and external forces that signal that change is necessary:

- *Goals and strategies.* Organizations frequently change their goals and the strategies used to reach these goals. Expansion, the introduction of new products, and the pursuit of new markets represent such changes. At Faber College, the administration decided to expand the Economics and Business department to better tap the student market.

- *Technology.* Technological changes can vary from minor to major. The introduction of on-line computer access for bank tellers is a fairly minor change. The steel mill that switches from traditional large-batch technology (make steel, pour ingots, roll ingots into slabs) to continuous casting technology is undergoing a major technological change.

- *Job design.* Individual groups of jobs can be redesigned to offer more or less variety, autonomy, identity, significance, and feedback, as discussed in Chapter 7.

- *Structure.* Organizations can be modified from a functional to a product form or vice versa. Formalization and centralization can be manipulated, as can tallness and spans of control. Structural changes also include modifications in rules, policies, and procedures.

■ *People.* The membership of an organization can be changed in two senses. First, the actual *content* of the membership can be changed through a process of hiring and firing. This is often done to introduce "new blood." Secondly, the existing membership can be changed in terms of skills and attitudes by various training and development methods.[2]

Two important points should be made about the various areas in which change can be introduced. First, a change in one area very often calls for changes in others. Failure to recognize this systemic nature of change can lead to severe problems. For example, consider the functionally organized east coast chemical firm that decides to expand its operations to the west coast. To be effective, this goal and strategy change may require some major structural changes, including a more geographic form and decentralization of decision-making power.

Secondly, changes in goals, strategies, technology, structure, and job design almost always require that serious attention be given to people changes. As much as possible, necessary skills and favorable attitudes should be fostered *before* these changes are introduced. For example, although providing bank tellers with computer access is a fairly minor technological change, it may provoke anxiety on the part of those whose jobs are affected. Adequate technical training and clear, open communication about the change may do much to alleviate this anxiety. At Faber College, the administration decided on a change in goals and strategies without giving enough attention to people changes. This aroused anxiety, anger, and conflict. Preparing members for especially extensive change efforts may require detailed groundwork. Major work restructuring at Shell in Great Britain began this way:

> Work redesign was undertaken only after large amounts of organizational time had been spent in sessions developing and affirming a supportive managerial philosophy. Attitudes, in short, were changed before structure. . . . The second phase was intended to ensure that the operating philosophy was freely accepted by all 6000 members of the organization from senior managers to hourly workers. To accomplish this dissemination—involving active testing and consensus building—required 18 months, from fall 1965 to spring 1967—and a cascade of conferences.[3]

The Change Process

By definition, change involves a sequence of organizational events or a psychological process that occurs over time. The distinguished psychologist Kurt Lewin has suggested that this sequence or process involves three basic stages—unfreezing, changing, and refreezing.[4]

UNFREEZING. **Unfreezing** occurs when recognition exists that some current state of affairs is inadequate. This might involve the realization that the present structure, task design, or technology is ineffective or that member skills or attitudes are inappropriate. *Crises* are especially likely to stimulate unfreezing. A dramatic drop in sales, a big lawsuit, or an unexpected strike are examples of such crises.

At Faber College, the enrollment crisis unfroze the administration. In 1982, the Ford Motor Company's financial crisis unfroze the United Auto Workers' traditional attitudes toward union-company relations, and wage cutbacks were accepted to keep plants open. Of course, unfreezing may also occur without crisis. Regular attitude surveys and accounting data are often used to anticipate problems and initiate change before crises are reached.

CHANGE.   Change occurs when some program or plan is implemented to move the organization and/or its members to a more adequate state. The terms *program* and *plan* are used rather loosely here, since some change efforts reveal inadequate planning. Change efforts can range from minor to major. A simple skills training program or a revised hiring procedure constitute fairly minor changes in which few organizational members are involved. Conversely, major changes that involve many members might include extensive job enrichment, radical restructuring, or serious attempts at extending participation in decision making.

REFREEZING.   When changes occur, the newly developed behaviors, attitudes, or structures must be subjected to **refreezing** to become an enduring part of the organizational system. At this point, the effectiveness of the change can be examined and the desirability of extending the change further can be considered.

ISSUES IN THE CHANGE PROCESS

The simple sketch of the change process presented in the preceding section ignores several important issues that must be confronted during the process. These issues represent problems that must be overcome if the process is to be effective. Exhibit 17-2 illustrates the relationship between the stages of change and these problems.

Diagnosis

Accurate organizational diagnosis serves two important functions. First, **diagnosis** can provide information that contributes to unfreezing by showing that a problem exists. Secondly, once unfreezing occurs, further diagnosis can clarify the problem and suggest just what changes should be implemented. It is one thing to feel that "hospital morale has fallen drastically" but quite another to be sure that this is true and to decide what to do about it. These are critical decision points in the change process, and our discussion of decision making in Chapter 12 suggests the potential for many errors. This is especially true if unfreezing has been stimulated by a crisis. For instance, at Faber College the diagnosis of economic problems was correct, but the strategy to correct them was hotly disputed.

Diagnosis can take a variety of forms and be performed by a variety of individuals. Relatively routine problems might be handled through existing chan-

---

EXHIBIT 17-2   **The change process and change problems.**

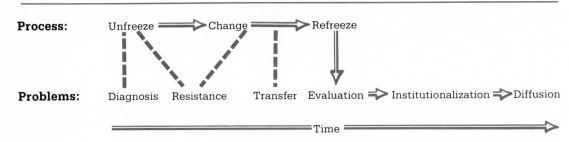

---

nels. For example, suppose the director of a hospital laboratory has reason to believe that many of his lab technicians do not possess adequate technical skills. In conjunction with the hospital personnel manager, the director might arrange for a formal test of these skills. A training program could be devised to correct inadequacies, and a more stringent selection program could be established to hire better personnel. At Faber College, a routine mechanism (the Board of Regents) was used to diagnose a very nonroutine problem.

For more complex, nonroutine problems, there is considerable merit in seeking out the diagnostic skills of a change agent. **Change agents** are experts in the application of behavioral science knowledge to organizational diagnosis and change. Some large firms have in-house change agents who are available for consultation. In other cases, outside consultants might be brought in. In any event, the change agent brings an independent, objective perspective to the diagnosis while working with those who are about to undergo change. For a relatively complete diagnosis of an organization anticipating major change, one experienced change agent recommends the following coverage:

- Genetic data
  - Identifying information (size, type, location of organization)
  - Historical data (developmental phases, past crises)
- Description of current organization
  - Structure
  - Processes (communication, decision making)
- Interpretation of current organization
  - Current functioning (perceptions and knowledge use)
  - Attitudes and relationships
- Analyses and conclusions[5]

Such information can be obtained through a combination of observations, interviews, questionnaires, and the scrutiny of records. As the next section will show, there is usually considerable merit in using questionnaires and interviews to involve the intended targets of change in the diagnostic process. The next section will also show why the change agent must be perceived as *trustworthy* by his or her clients.

The importance of careful diagnosis cannot be overemphasized. Properly done, diagnosis clarifies the problem, suggests *what* should be changed, and suggests the proper *strategy* for implementing change without resistance.

Resistance

As the saying goes, people are creatures of habit, and change is frequently resisted by those for whom it is targeted. More precisely, both unfreezing and change may be resisted. At the unfreezing stage, defense mechanisms (Chapter 14) may be activated to deny or rationalize the signals that change is needed. And even if there is agreement that change is necessary, any specific plan for change may be resisted. This occurred early in the Reagan administration. Even though there was considerable agreement in Congress that national economic strategies needed revision, specific programs such as a three-year tax cut encountered strong resistance. The faculty, staff, and students were doubtless aware of Faber College's financial troubles. Despite this, specific plans for change were opposed.

Resistance occurs because organizational members fear that the costs of change will outweigh its benefits. Such costs may be economic or social. For example, workers may resist conversion to a piecerate payment plan because they fear it will lead to reduced wages. Similarly, a change in organizational structure may be resisted because it revises reporting relationships and disrupts informal social contacts developed under the existing structure (see the cartoon).

Although the evidence is not in perfect agreement, it seems that resistance to change can be reduced by involving those who are the targets of the change in the change process (a point essentially ignored by the Faber College administration).[6] This strategy should increase commitment to change by giving the involved individuals "ownership" of the change process. Some of the most striking examples of using participation to overcome potential resistance have involved changes in pay systems. This is ironic because the design of pay systems has traditionally been considered by management as inappropriate for participation. In one study, part-time janitorial staff members who exhibited high absenteeism helped design a cash bonus plan to reward good attendance. When implemented, the plan led to significant reductions in absence, a goal that would traditionally provoke resistance.[7]

It is unrealistic to assume that active participation can be sought for every change that management wishes to introduce. This may be especially true of structure and technology changes. In these cases, some resistance may be countered by clear, ongoing communication about intended changes.

I'm not opposed to change, but I have an image to maintain.

Source: *Psychology Today,* August 1985, p. 14.

Transfer of Change to the Work Environment

Certain programs to induce change are conducted outside of the context of the job to which the "changed" individuals must return. This occurs for several reasons. First, it may be impossible to modify certain technical skills on the job without severe work disruption or safety problems. Secondly, in the case of interpersonal or human relations skills, it may be valuable to isolate trainees from their normal work environment to stimulate the unfreezing process. Finally, certain sources of change may only be available outside of the organization. The following examples illustrate change programs based outside of the regular work context:

- A company about to adopt a new continuous-process technology in its Houston plant sends key workers to its Atlanta plant to learn to run the new system.

- In order to increase the social skills of certain executives, an airline company sends them to a five-day sensitivity training session at an Aspen resort.

■ To broaden its administrative staff, a local government agrees to reimburse them for courses taken at a local university.

Transfer (from "transfer-of-training") refers to the extent to which changes which occur through methods such as these are actually translated to the job. This is an important issue—does valuable change survive (refreeze) in the home environment? Evidence suggests that effective transfer is most likely when:

■ The elements of the change process correspond to particular elements of the work environment.[8]

■ The change is immediately *useful* in the work environment.[9]

■ The changed attitudes or behaviors are *supported* by others in the work environment.[10]

To illustrate the meaning of these three points, consider the firm that feels absenteeism could be reduced and labor relations improved by training supervisors in human relations skills. The "corresponding elements" proposition simply means that the training program must concentrate on those human relations problems encountered on the job. If the supervisors have trouble giving compliments or administering discipline, the program must address these specific issues. However, corresponding elements do not guarantee transfer unless what is learned is perceived as useful on the job. In this case, practice in imitating skilled models giving compliments and administering discipline would probably build confidence (see Chapter 3). Finally, transfer may be inhibited if newly acquired skills are unrewarded (or even punished) by managers in the home environment. Even if the changes provided by human relations training prove useful for supervisors, they may refrain from using them if their bosses see such behavior as a waste of time. Again, this illustrates the need to consider the *systemic* nature of change and the value of careful diagnosis.

Evaluation

From the detached observer's point of view, evaluation stands out as the "bad boy" of most change efforts. This seems especially true of programs designed to change interpersonal skills or attitudes, such as human relations training programs. Organizations are quick to adopt faddish change programs and then reluctant to evaluate them critically:

> The fads center around the introduction of new techniques and follow a characteristic pattern. A new technique appears on the horizon and develops a large stable of advocates who first describe its "successful" use in a number of situations. A second wave of advocates busy themselves trying out numerous modifications of the basic technique. A few empirical studies may be carried out to demonstrate that the method "works." Then the inevitable backlash sets in and a few vocal opponents begin to criticize the usefulness of the technique, most often in the absence of data. Such criticism typically has very little effect. What does have an effect is the appearance of another new technique and a repetition of the same cycle.[11]

Ideally, plans for **evaluation** of change efforts would begin during the diagnostic stage, with some of the diagnostic data providing a baseline for measuring change. For programs concerned with changing skills or attitudes, we might be concerned with four principal variables:

- Reactions—Did participants like the change program?
- Learning—What was acquired in the program?
- Behavior—What changes in job behavior occurred?
- Outcomes—What changes in productivity, absence, etc., occurred?[12]

To some extent, reactions measure resistance, learning reflects change, and behavior reflects transfer and successful refreezing. Outcomes indicate whether refreezing is useful for the organization. Unfortunately, many evaluations of change efforts never go beyond the measurement of reactions. Part of the reason for this may be political. Those who propose the change effort fear reprisal if failure occurs. This is ironic, because, as we shall see, "soft" evaluations may actually threaten the continuity of a successful change effort.

Later in the chapter we shall consider the evaluation of select change efforts in more detail.

Institutionalization

If the outcome of change is evaluated favorably, the organization will wish to institutionalize that change. This means that the change becomes a permanent part of the organizational system, a social fact that persists over time despite possible turnover by the members who originally experienced the change.[13] In a sense, **institutionalization** represents the organization's seal of approval for refreezing.

Logic suggests that it should be fairly easy to institutionalize a change that has been deemed successful. Reality, though, indicates otherwise. In the previous section we noted that many change efforts go unevaluated or are only weakly evaluated. This means that without hard proof of success, it is very easy for institutionalization to be rejected by disaffected parties. This is a special problem for extensive, broad-based change programs that call for a large amount of commitment from a variety of parties (e.g., extensive participation, job enrichment, or work restructuring). It is one thing to institutionalize a simple training program, but quite another to do the same for these complex interventions that can be judged from a variety of perspectives.

Studies of more complex change efforts indicate that a number of factors may inhibit institutionalization. For example, promised extrinsic rewards (such as pay bonuses) may not be developed to accompany changes. Similarly, initial changes may provide intrinsic rewards that create higher expectations which cannot be fulfilled. Institutionalization may also be damaged if new hires are not carefully socialized to understand the unique environment of the changed organization. As turnover occurs naturally, the change effort may backslide. In a similar vein, key management supporters of the change effort may resign or be transferred. Finally, environmental pressures such as decreased sales or profits can cause management to regress to more familiar behaviors and abandon change efforts.[14]

It stands to reason that some of these threats to institutionalization can be anticipated during the diagnostic process. As we shall see shortly, some comprehensive organizational development efforts are designed to cope with such problems in an ongoing manner.

Diffusion

Many change efforts begin as limited experiments in one section or division of an organization. This is a cautious and reasonable approach. For example, an insurance company might begin a limited exploration of job enrichment by concentrating only on clerical jobs in the head office. Similarly, a manufacturing firm might introduce a nontraditional work structure and reduced supervision in a new plant. If such efforts are judged successful it seems logical to diffuse them to other parts of the organization. While institutionalization refers to permanently establishing a change where it was introduced, **diffusion** means institutionalizing the change in other portions of the organization as well. As you might guess from the previous section, this can be difficult.

Richard Walton of Harvard University has carefully studied the diffusion process of eight major change efforts in firms such as Volvo, Alcan, General Foods, Corning Glass, and Shell U.K. Each effort was fairly rigorous and broad-based, generally having the following characteristics:

> The work restructuring approach pursued in the eight cases studied embraces many aspects of work, including the content of the job, compensation schemes, scope of worker responsibility for supervision and decision making, social structure, status hierarchy, and so on. The design of each element is intended to contribute to an internally consistent work culture—one that *appropriately* enlarges workers' scope for self-management, enhances their opportunity for learning new abilities, strengthens their sense of connectedness with co-workers, increases their identification with the product and manufacturing process, and promotes their sense of dignity and self-worth.[15]

All of the pilot projects Walton studied were initially judged successful, and each received substantial publicity, a factor which often contributes to increased commitment to further change. Despite this, substantial diffusion occurred in only one of the observed firms—Volvo (see Chapter 7). What accounts for this poor record of diffusion? Walton identified these factors:

- Lack of support and commitment by top management.

- The technology or setting of the pilot project differs significantly from other units in the organization, raising arguments that "it won't work here."

- Attempts to diffuse particular *techniques* rather than *goals* that could be tailored to other situations.

- Management reward systems that concentrate on traditional performance measures while ignoring success at implementing change.

- Union resistance to extending the negotiated "exceptions" in the pilot project.

- Fears that pilot projects begun in nonunionized locations could not be implemented in unionized portions of the firm.

- Conflict between the pilot project and the bureaucratic structures in the rest of the firm (e.g., pay policies and staffing requirements).

Because of these problems, Walton raises the depressing spectre of a "diffuse or die" principle. That is, if diffusion does not occur, the pilot project and its leaders become more and more isolated from the mainstream of the organization and less and less able to proceed alone.

WHEN WILL CHANGE OCCUR? AND WHEN WILL IT BE SUCCESSFUL?

Can we draw any conclusions about when organizational change is likely to occur? One expert in changing organizations puts the odds this way:

$$Change = (D \times M \times P) > C$$

Where D = Dissatisfaction with the status quo
      M = A new model of managing and organization
      P = A planned process for managing change
      C = Cost of change to individuals and groups[16]

In other words, the forces for change include dissatisfaction (D), a clear alternative (M), and a plan to achieve that alternative (P). If the product of these forces outweighs the resistance associated with perceived social and economic costs (C), change should occur. But will such change be successful? Here are some conditions that are frequently associated with successful change efforts in improving the quality of work life:

- People in the organization must feel *pressure* in order to be ready to change.

- Participation and involvement of people in reexamining problems and practices are needed to build commitment to change, and to assure that behaviors and attitudes once changed remain changed without surveillance and control.

- Some new ideas, models, or concepts must be brought in from the outside to help people in the organization find new approaches to management and to work that will improve the quality of work life.

- To ensure early success and prevent massive failures that can slow the momentum of change, early innovations leading to improvements should be *limited* in scope.

- A skilled leader or consultant is often needed to bring in new ideas, catalyze the process of reexamination, and support individuals in the process of improving the quality of work life.[17]

Running through these stimuli for change and conditions for success is a key issue—*planning.* Let's now examine organizational development, a general label for techniques to effect planned change.

ORGANIZATIONAL DEVELOPMENT: PLANNED CHANGE, ETC., ETC.

The heading of this section is meant to convey some of the difficulty one encounters in trying to precisely define organizational development (OD). There is a message to be gained from this difficulty. OD is a continuously changing art and science which uses a wide variety of specific techniques and strategies to change organizations. As such, its character is difficult to summarize in a sentence. While all OD seeks to change organizations, not all change efforts can be classed as OD. With this preamble, I present a working definition which seems to synthesize current thinking:[18]

> **Organizational development (OD)** is a planned, ongoing effort to change organizations to be more effective and more human. It uses the knowledge of behavioral science to foster a climate of organizational self-examination and readiness for change. A strong emphasis is placed on interpersonal and group processes.

The fact that OD is *planned* distinguishes it from the haphazard, accidental, or routine changes that occur in all organizations. OD efforts tend to be *ongoing* in at least two senses. First, many OD programs extend over a long period of time, involving several distinct phases of activities. Secondly, if OD becomes institutionalized, continual reexamination and readiness for further change become permanent organizational properties. In trying to make organizations more *effective* and more *human,* OD gives recognition to the critical link between personal processes such as leadership, decision making, and communication, and organizational outcomes such as productivity and efficiency. The fact that OD uses *behavioral science knowledge* distinguishes it from other change strategies which rely solely upon principles of accounting, finance, or engineering. However, an OD intervention may also incorporate these principles. The *climate* of an organization refers to its prevailing norms, role relationships, and patterns of interaction. OD seeks to modify these so that the organization remains self-conscious and prepared for adaptation. Finally, a focus on *interpersonal* and *group* processes recognizes that all organizational change affects members and is implemented with their cooperation.

To summarize the above, we can say that OD recognizes that systematic attitude change must accompany changes in behavior, whether these behavior changes are required by revisions in tasks, work procedures, organizational structure, or business strategies.

A few words should be said about the values and assumptions espoused by change agents who practice OD. While generalizations are always suspect, it is fair to say that change agents have traditionally operated under the following set of values and assumptions:

- Most organizational members desire self-actualization.

- Most people desire to increase their contribution to the achievement of organizational goals.

- The open expression of feelings in organizations is desirable.

- The level of trust and cooperation in most organizations should be increased.[19]

Are these values and assumptions realistic? Do they mean that OD can only be implemented in certain organizations? Do they suggest one best way to manage and organize, which goes against the contingency notions we have discussed throughout the book?[20] In response to these questions, one OD expert proposes an alternative set of propositions which should enable change agents to help organizations clarify their *own* needs for development. Specifically, OD must:

- Help organizations generate valid data about the state of the organization in relation to its environment

- Help organizational stakeholders clarify desired outcomes

- Help organizations make strategic choices based on a diagnosis of the current state and desired outcomes.[21]

SOME SPECIFIC ORGANIZATIONAL DEVELOPMENT STRATEGIES

The organization seeking to "develop itself" has recourse to a wide variety of specific techniques, and many have been used in combination. Some of these techniques have been discussed earlier in the book. For example, work restructuring through systematic job enrichment and Management by Objectives (Chapter 7) are usually classed as OD efforts. In this section we will discuss five additional OD methods that illustrate the diversity of the practice. *Laboratory training* provides the clearest example of traditional OD values and illustrates the historical roots of OD. *Team building* illustrates the extension of the laboratory approach to solving specific organizational problems. *Quality circles* reveal how small groups can be used to improve organizational effectiveness. *Survey feedback* shows how OD can be conceived of as an ongoing applied research effort. Finally, *Grid OD* illustrates a structured, long-range approach to system-wide change and development.

Laboratory Training

Laboratory training, also called sensitivity training, is an OD method based upon the interaction that occurs in small face-to-face groups.[22] These groups are sometimes called encounter groups or T-groups. It was developed and refined by the National Training Laboratories in the late 1940s. Union Carbide and Esso Standard Oil were among the first industrial users. Along with survey feedback, the advent of laboratory training signaled the beginning of OD.[23] Although it is an OD method in its own right, laboratory training is also used to "loosen up" organizational members for other OD efforts.

A T-group usually consists of eight to twelve participants and the change agent. The initial experience may range from a weekend to two or three weeks, and the group often meets outside of organizational premises. Some T-groups are "stranger" groups in which participants are from different organizations. Others are "cousin" groups (members from the same organization who don't work with each other) or "family" groups (intact work groups).

What happens in a T-group? Aside from separate lecture and theory sessions, most groups begin interaction in an intentionally unstructured manner. The change agent might start with a brief speech that the goal of the group is to learn more about itself and then adopt a fairly inactive role. What happens subsequently varies from group to group, but a frequent pattern is the following: Casual small talk is begun but ceases fairly quickly because it seems to get nowhere. Signs of frustration appear. A leader emerges and proposes an agenda, note-taking, and other task-oriented responses. Unfortunately, the task isn't very clear, and this effort soon fizzles. More frustration occurs, and hostility is often directed at the change agent, who doesn't seem to be doing his or her "job." This gives the agent a chance to focus on an event (the hostility) that has occurred in the here and now. This pattern continues, and participants are encouraged to give feedback to each other about their interpersonal styles and functioning in the group. This can prove quite stressful, and the change agent tries to protect vulnerable members. However, some degree of anxiety seems necessary to unfreeze members and to get them "to learn to learn" about social processes.

Most versions of laboratory training are structured to achieve one or more of the following goals:

- Increased sensitivity to the behavior and feelings of others—How do I interpret others' actions? Am I accurate in my perceptions?

- Increased understanding of group processes—What causes groups to succeed or fail at their tasks? How do individuals influence group action?

- Increased social diagnostic skills—Ability to *use* the two previous abilities in social situations.

- Increased skill in *acting to influence* interpersonal and social situations in order to increase effectiveness and/or satisfaction.

- Increased skill in learning to continually analyze one's own and others' behavior in ongoing interpersonal situations.[24]

As we shall see shortly, there is evidence that laboratory training has the capacity to induce changes such as these. However, two problems associated with T-grouping deserve attention. First, there is some evidence that the high anxiety and realistic feedback experienced in the T-group can cause psychological problems for a certain proportion of trainees. These problems may be due to a combination of unskilled, overaggressive trainers and a history of psychological distress on the part of the affected trainees.[25] Secondly, traditional T-grouping seems especially likely to suffer from the transfer problem discussed earlier in the chapter. That is, interpersonal skills acquired in the off-the-job context of the group may be difficult to translate to a home environment that does not support the open expression of feelings and honest feedback. For this reason, T-group training has tended to become somewhat more structured and job-oriented (the "corresponding elements" principle). Methods to increase transfer include having participants apply what is learned in the group to cases and simulated organizational exercises or having them bring real organizational problems to work on in the group.

A major electronics and communications firm exposed managers to laboratory training to improve work coordination and communications. To enhance transfer-of-training, company trainer-consultants (TCs) collected data about how the managers were perceived by their peers and subordinates and brought it to the training session. This data, along with questionnaires completed by others undergoing training, provided managers with information about how they were perceived by others. The TCs observed the managers during group sessions and helped them integrate the knowledge they were acquiring. Then, the TCs helped each manager develop a program of changes in work procedures and communications to implement in the "back home" environment. During this implementation, the TCs acted as continuing consultants and sources of support for their managers.[26]

Even with such modifications, it is fair to say that laboratory training is best conceived as an unfreezing device. Thus, team building and Grid OD use laboratory methods as part of more complex change efforts.

Team Building

The team building approach to OD developed gradually in response to the transfer problems associated with orthodox laboratory training. The term *team* can refer to intact work groups, special task forces, new work units, or people from various parts of an organization who must work together to achieve a common goal. Although **team building** often involves aspects of traditional laboratory training with cousin or family groups, it is decidedly more *task-oriented*. In addition to modifying interpersonal processes, it focuses on clarifying goals and role relationships.[27] (What is our team trying to accomplish, and who is responsible for what?) As such, it should facilitate communication and coordination.

Team building usually begins with a diagnostic session, often held away from the work place, in which the team explores its current level of functioning. The team may use several sources of data to accomplish its diagnosis. Some data may be generated through sensitivity training and open-ended discussion sessions. In addition, "hard" data such as attitude survey results and production figures may be used. The goal at this stage is to paint a picture of the current strengths and weaknesses of the team. The ideal outcome of the diagnostic session is a list of needed changes to improve team functioning. Subsequent team building sessions usually have a decidedly task-oriented slant—How can we actually implement the changes indicated by the diagnosis? Problem solving by subgroups may be used at this stage. Between the diagnostic and followup sessions, the change agent may hold confidential interviews with team members to anticipate implementation problems. Throughout, the change agent acts as a catalyst and resource person.

The city government of Tacoma, Washington, assisted by external consultants, has made extensive use of team building to improve communications within and between existing departments.[28] Because the work of the personnel department affected that of all other departments, any errors made by personnel had a high degree of impact and visibility. As a result, personnel had become the scapegoat of the system. Initial team-building sessions concentrated on having department members identify and work out internal communication problems. In addition, clients of the personnel department from other city departments were invited to day-long sessions in which they aired their complaints to personnel and worked out solutions. One result of this was a system by which each client department was assigned to a particular member of the personnel department. This member then served as an ongoing "contact person" to expedite requests from clients.

Tacoma also used team building to improve communication among the top management of its fire department. This was a particular problem because the battalion chiefs were geographically decentralized in various fire stations and because they worked shifts. As a result of team building, it was decided to hold bimonthly meetings of all management staff to facilitate ongoing communication. Those who were off duty when meetings were held were paid overtime to attend.

When team building is used to develop *new* work teams, the preliminary diagnostic session may involve attempts to clarify expected role relationships and laboratory training to build trust among team members. In subsequent sessions the expected task environment may be simulated with role-playing exercises. One company used this integrated approach to develop the management team of a new plant.[29] In the simulation portion of the development, typical problems encountered in opening a new plant were presented to team members via hypothetical in-basket memos and telephone calls. In role playing the solutions to these problems, they reached agreement about how they would have to work together on the job and gained a clear understanding of each other's competencies. Plant startups were always problem-laden, but this was the smoothest in the history of the company.

Ideally, team building is a continuing process that involves regular diagnostic sessions and further development exercises as needed. This permits the team to anticipate new problems and to avoid the tendency to regress to less effective pre-development habits.

Quality Circles

Of all the techniques discussed in this chapter, quality circles represent the most recent addition to the North American OD scene. Also, they are the most common example of the importation of "Japanese management" techniques to our shores. Quality circles began in Japan as part of an effort to rebuild the country's industrial base following World War II. At this time, Japan was known widely as a producer of shoddy, slipshod merchandise, and Japanese managers were eager to change this reputation. American-developed statistical quality control techniques were embraced with great enthusiasm, and gradually a philosophy developed that all workers were responsible for quality control. Small groups of workers were formed into quality circles (or ''quality control circles'') throughout an organization and taught the statistical principles of quality control. They were then encouraged to detect and suggest solutions to quality problems in their own domains. This unusual mixture of participative management and industrial engineering has become something of a national movement in Japan.[30]

Faced with the reality of superbly constructed Hondas, Sonys, and Nikons, and with the phenomenal productivity growth of Japan, North American firms have shown great interest in the quality circle concept. The North American version of **quality circles** might be described as follows:

> *Small groups of people who perform similar work meet voluntarily on a regular basis, usually once a week, to analyze work-related problems and propose solutions to them. QC's are usually led by the supervisor or manager of the work unit in which they are located. Members receive training in problem solving, quality control and group dynamics to help them function well.*[31]

As you can see, there are elements of both participative management and team building in the quality circle concept. Circles are encouraged to find problems, devise solutions, and submit solutions for management approval. Despite their name, quality circles have gone well beyond quality problems and also focussed on safety, working conditions, productivity, and cost-cutting. For example, quality circles have often proposed how to reduce scrap costs and raw materials waste in manufacturing. In order to build commitment to the quality circle concept and avoid overt resistance, most programs are voluntary, but the circles typically meet on company time. Despite voluntary membership, quality circles are permanent and ongoing. Usually, a steering committee made up of managers, workers, union representatives, and supervisors who lead circles oversees the program. Individuals are appointed to act as facilitators between the steering committee and the quality circles.[32]

Training and management support are critical to the success of quality circles. Leaders of circles require thorough training in leading group discussions. Leaders and members need a thorough grasp of quality-control concepts, problem-analysis techniques, and team-building principles. Managers need a firm grounding in the philosophy of quality circles and need to be committed to seriously considering the suggestions that emanate from quality circles. Establishing quality circles requires substantial effort, and they actually represent something of a structural modification to the organization. Thus, there is much pressure for them to be successful, and nothing can dampen enthusiasm more than the rejection of good ideas.

One organization that reports considerable success with quality circles is Wedgwood, the esteemed English producer of fine china. Their experience shows that even traditional craftsmanship can be improved with new ideas. Circles have developed good ideas to avoid waste and spoilage. For example, one circle designed a new cart that reduced the risk of unfired pottery knocking together and breaking. Another designed a new brush for painting plates and worked with a brush supplier to have it produced. Yet another circle worked with the local bus company to improve service to the Wedgwood factory, effectively reducing commuting problems for employees.[33]

In–Focus 17-1 illustrates the successful application of quality circles in a service organization and shows how one company developed some different ideas about how to organize a quality circle program.

Later in the chapter we will review the evidence on the effectiveness of quality circles. For now, it is worth noting that some observers have questioned the general application of quality circles in Western cultures. Some have argued that the Japanese traditions of lifetime employment, company unions, paternalism, and concern with social harmony provide a special environment for the use of quality circles. Western cultures, with their emphasis on individualism and a more adversarial relationship between management and labor, may not provide such a conducive background for quality circles[34] (see the cartoon).

Survey Feedback

In bare-bones form, **survey feedback** involves collecting data from organizational members and feeding this data back to them in a series of meetings in which the data is explored and discussed.[35] The purpose of the meetings is to suggest or formulate changes that are suggested by the data. In some respects, survey feedback is similar to team building. However, survey feedback places more emphasis

"Something must have been lost in the translation."

Source: *TIP (The Industrial/Organizational Psychologist)* February 1983, p. 43.

IN–FOCUS 17-1 QUALITY CIRCLES AT THE PAUL REVERE INSURANCE GROUP

The Paul Revere Insurance Group uses a new type of Quality Circle (QC) that its managers believe overcomes many objections to traditional QC's. For one, participation on Revere's quality teams isn't voluntary, as it is with most QC's. Everyone, from the president to the newest hire, belongs to at least one team.

A second difference is that quality teams not only develop better ways of doing a job, but can implement them before notifying higher management. The Revere teams also receive greater recognition and rewards than are typical with QC's.

The 100 percent participation and ability to implement recommendations eliminate two problems that lessen the productivity of many QC's: resistance from managers who have no involvement with an idea until they are called on to approve it and resistance from workers who are often told to change the way they do things without having had a part in the decision or understanding the reasons for it.

When a suggestion seems promising, the leader logs it into the Quality Team Tracking Program (QTTP), using the nearest computer terminal. This makes the suggestion available to any other team leader, and "stealing" ideas is encouraged. An idea is first logged in with a status of "1," meaning that it is untested. As the team works on the idea, the status is changed to "2," meaning pending; to "3," meaning it has been rejected by the team; or to "4," meaning it has been accepted and implemented.

At this stage, one of the analysts at Quality Team Central (QTC) calls the team leader and schedules a meeting to review the idea and see whether it has actually improved things as well as saved time or money. If it has, the idea is certified and upgraded to "5" status on the QTTP. It then counts toward earning prizes for the team members.

Patrick Townsend, director of QTC, says that ideas have come from all areas of the company. One of the earliest successful ones was developed by a team in financial services. A new clerk there saw that the company was keeping as little money as possible in the checking accounts it maintained throughout the country to pay claims and other expenses. The procedure was apparently left over from the days before interest-bearing checking accounts, high charges for overdrafts and free services for maintaining a designated balance. The clerk estimated that the practice was costing the company $3,000 a year (later analysis upped this to $5,000) in lost interest and other expenses.

A suggestion to ship material to the company's Canadian offices by truck rather than air saved $27,000 annually. Another, to use reusable nylon mail bags rather than manila envelopes to send material to field claim representatives, saved $9,200 a year in postage and envelopes.

Townsend sums up Revere's experience with quality teams since 1984 as "a corporate revolution . . . vastly successful from a business viewpoint. In 1985 alone, the 1,220 employees of the Paul Revere home office implemented 5,703 ideas with an annual value of $7,500,000. . . . These are ideas that were already implemented before the company took note of them."

Source: Horn, J. C. (1986, August). Making quality circles work better. *Psychology Today,* p. 10.

on the collection of valid data and less emphasis on the interpersonal processes of specific work teams. Rather, it tends to focus on the relationship between organizational members and the larger organization.

As its name implies, survey feedback's basic data generally consists of either interviews or questionnaires completed by organizational members. Before collecting this data a number of critical decisions must be made by the change agent and organizational management. First, who should participate in the survey? Sometimes, especially in large organizations, the survey could be restricted to particular departments, jobs, or organizational levels where problems exist. However, most survey feedback efforts attempt to cover the entire organization. This approach recognizes the systemic nature of organizations and permits a comparison of survey results across various subunits.

Secondly, should questionnaires or interviews be used to gather data? The key issues here are coverage and cost. It is generally conceded that *all* members of a target group should be surveyed. This procedure builds trust and confidence in survey results. If the number of members is small, the change agent could conduct structured interviews with each person. Otherwise, cost considerations dictate the use of a questionnaire. In practice, this is the most typical data-gathering approach.

Finally, what questions should the survey ask? Two approaches are available. Some change agents use prepackaged, standardized surveys such as the University of Michigan Survey of Organizations.[36] This questionnaire covers areas such as communication and decision-making practices and employee satisfaction. Such questionnaires are usually carefully constructed and permit comparisons with other organizations in which the survey has been conducted. However, there is a real danger that prepackaged surveys may neglect critical areas for specific consideration. In and of itself, this is bad enough, but the apparent lack of relevance of a packaged survey may reduce the care members take in completing it or reduce trust in the final results. For these reasons, many change agents choose to devise their own custom-tailored surveys. They might begin with a series of interviews to determine potential problem areas. In some cases a task force of organizational members might also be enlisted to help develop the final version of the survey. Again, the goal is to build relevance, trust, and involvement in those who will be surveyed. This should guarantee valid data. To increase the involvement of managerial personnel, they might be asked to predict the results of the survey.

Feedback seems to be most effective when it is presented to natural working units in face-to-face meetings. This method rules out presenting only written feedback or feedback that only covers the organization as a whole. In a manufacturing firm, a natural working unit might consist of a department such as production or marketing. In a school district, such units might consist of individual schools. Many change agents prefer that the manager of the working unit conduct the feedback meeting. This demonstrates management commitment and acceptance of the data. The change agent attends such meetings and helps facilitate discussion of the data and plans for change.

An example of survey feedback occurred in a school district. The purpose of the exercise was to stimulate changes that would promote more effective problem solving by the faculty members of individual schools. Teachers completed questionnaires concerning their attitudes toward factors such as administrative practices, work load, students, facilities, and relationships with colleagues. In feedback sessions, teachers in individual schools were able to compare their average responses on individual survey questions with those of teachers in the district as a whole. In addition, the responses were grouped into categories and presented as shown in Exhibit 17-3, which compares the responses of "School Z" with those of the district overall. It was hoped that observed discrepancies would reveal strengths and weaknesses and stimulate the desire for appropriate changes. Although this occurred in certain schools, others were unable or unwilling to institutionalize mechanisms for improved problem solving.[37]

Grid® Organization Development

Grid Organization Development is a comprehensive, long-term effort directed toward changing the total organization. It was developed by Robert Blake and Jane Mouton of Scientific Methods, Incorporated.[38] The basic premise of **Grid OD** is that organizational excellence can be achieved through a *joint* concern with high performance and the maintenance of a psychologically healthy working climate. Ignoring either of these factors at the expense of the other will not promote true excellence.

Grid OD uses a building-block approach which consists of six phases. A large organization might take several years to pass through these phases. Blake and Mouton feel that poor communication and inadequate planning are responsible for most failures to achieve excellence. Thus, the first three Grid phases are oriented toward improving communication while the latter three are designed to foster careful planning and goal setting:

1. *Grid seminar.* This is a very structured laboratory training session designed to encourage individual organizational members to analyze their own management styles. The behavioral theory underlying Grid OD (discussed below) is taught. Top management usually attend the Grid seminar first.

2. *Teamwork development.* Natural work teams attend seminars designed to extend Grid concepts to improve team functioning. Again, this effort begins at the top and is highly structured.

3. *Intergroup development.* Work teams that must interface with each other attend seminars stressing conflict reduction and improved coordination.

4. *Development of an ideal strategic model.* Top management meets to evaluate the current state of the organization and develop a model for improvement. Key issues include policy, structure, and financial objectives.

5. *Planning and implementation of the ideal model.* Task forces of organizational members with relevant skills are formed to plan and implement the model developed by top executives. Management science techniques are used and outside experts are brought in if necessary.

EXHIBIT 17-3   Survey feedback to one school in a school district.

Group Profiled: School Z
No. in Group: 23

Legend: ● School
         △ District Overall

Percent favorable response

Category	0	10	20	30	40	50	60	70	80	90	100
1. Administrative Practices				△	●						
2. Professional Work Load					△		●				
3. Nonprofessional Work Load					●	△					
4. Materials and Equipment				△		●					
5. Buildings and Facilities			●		△						
6. Educational Effectiveness						△●					
7. Evaluation of Students				△		●					
8. Special Services				△●							
9. School—Community Relations			●		△						
10. Supervisory Relations					●	△					
11. Colleague Relations						●	△				
12. Voice in Educational Program			●△								
13. Performance and Development					△	●					
14. Students			●	△							
15. Reactions to Survey						△●					

Source: Mirvis, P. H., & Berg, D. N. (1977). *Failures in organization development and change.*
New York: Wiley, p. 152. Copyright © 1977, by John Wiley and Sons, Inc. Reprinted by
permission.

6. *Systematic critique.* The results of previous changes are evaluated using quantitative data, internal evaluation teams, and external independent evaluators. Plans for further OD efforts are based on this critique.

Since the initial Grid Seminar provides the conceptual basis for the whole of Grid OD, it is worth a closer look. These five-day seminars are conducted by line managers in the organization who have received previous training in Grid theory. Blake and Mouton feel that line managers are best at this job because their understanding of day-to-day organizational problems provides them with a high degree of credibility as trainers. In fact, the entire Grid program is conducted with in-house personnel, and the role of external change agents is downplayed. A major purpose of the Grid Seminar is to teach trainees the principles of the **Managerial Grid**® shown in Exhibit 17-4. According to the Grid, leadership is composed of two basic dimensions—concern for production and concern for people. Observe the extreme styles portrayed on the Grid: The 1,1 leader is a "do nothing" person who should exert little influence on subordinates. The 1,9 leader might be portrayed as a "country club" leader who is concerned primarily with easy interpersonal relations. The 9,1 leader is something of a "taskmaster." Finally, the 9,9 leader exhibits high concern for *both* interpersonal relations and the demands of the task. He or she is interested in maintaining high productivity while fostering an open, candid, trusting relationship with subordinates. Grid OD seeks to diffuse a 9,9 philosophy throughout the organization.

Several potential problems of Grid OD are worth noting. First, its prepackaged nature may not suit the development needs of every organization. Secondly, "concern for production" is very similar to initiating structure, while "concern for people" is very similar to consideration. From Chapter 10, you will recall that being high on both of these dimensions may not always be the optimal leadership strategy. Finally, a large number of changes obviously occur when the full Grid program is implemented. In evaluating the success of Grid OD, it is often very difficult to determine just which elements of the Grid program were responsible for any favorable outcomes.

DOES ORGANIZATIONAL DEVELOPMENT WORK?

For the final time in the book we again ask the critical question: Does it work? That is, do the benefits of OD outweigh the heavy investment of time, effort, and money? The answer to this question is important. In recent years OD has been extended from business and industry into more diverse settings, including international relations, domestic politics, health care delivery, schools, universities, and the military[39] (In–Focus 17-2). Is such extension justified, or is it an example of the faddishness in training and development discussed earlier?

At the outset, it should be reemphasized that most OD efforts are *not* carefully evaluated. Political factors and budget limitations may be prime culprits, but the

EXHIBIT 17-4   The Managerial Grid.®

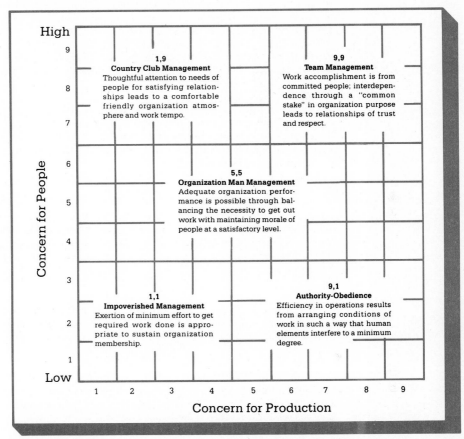

Source: Blake, Robert R., and Mouton, Jane Srygley. *The Managerial Grid III: The Key to Leadership Excellence*. Houston: Gulf Publishing Company, Copyright © 1985, page 12. Reproduced by permission.

situation is not helped by some OD practitioners who argue that certain OD goals (e.g., making the organization more human) are incompatible with impersonal, scientifically rigorous evaluation.

Laboratory training is the OD method that has received the most evaluation attention. An earlier review of such studies concluded the following:

■ Co-workers report that 30 to 40 percent of trained individuals exhibit changes in job behavior after training. Such changes include increased sensitivity, more flexibility, and more open communication.

IN–FOCUS 17-2 ORGANIZATIONAL DEVELOPMENT IN THE MILITARY?!

At first glance, the idea of OD in the military must seem pretty exotic and unlikely. After all, the traditional values associated with OD seem somewhat out of sync with the bureaucratic structure of the military. However, faced with the need to compete with private industry and other service branches to attract and retain quality personnel, each branch has experimented with its own version of OD. Denis Umstot has reviewed OD in the military.

Army

In the Army, OD is called OE (Organizational Effectiveness). Internal change agents are trained and dispersed to various installations to "sell" their services to local commanders. Techniques include team building and survey feedback, but avoid sensitivity training. OE seems to have the backing of the top Army command.

Navy

In the Navy, OD is called HRM (Human Resource Management). After poor results with outside change agents, the Navy began to train experienced line officers and senior noncommissioned officers as change agents. They work out of five established centers. Survey feedback is the major HRM technique, with an emphasis on increasing reenlistments and reducing disciplinary rates.

Air Force

OD in the Air Force is less formalized and centralized than in the other services. Although laboratory training, team building, and survey feedback have been used, job enrichment has received the most attention.

■ ■ ■

John Turney and Stanley Cohen have reviewed some of the problems involved in implementing OD in the military based on their experiences with Army OD efforts. They point out that the long chain of command in the military makes it difficult to decide just how far up one should go to get "top" management support for change efforts. They also point out that the total immersion twenty-four-hour environment of the military may include sources of dissatisfaction much more complex than those found in civilian life. Can OD efforts cope with a total military lifestyle? Many military units include both civilian and military personnel. The resulting "we-they" attitude of both groups may undermine some OD efforts. Finally, frequent personnel rotation and turnover may threaten the establishment and continuity of OD.

Sources: Umstot, D. D. (1980). Organization development technology and the military: A surprising merger? *Academy of Management Review, 5,* 189–201; Turney, J. R., & Cohen, S. L. (1978). Organizational implications for practicing OD in the army. *Personnel Psychology, 31,* 731–738.

- Laboratory training *may* lead to improved self-perception and increased sensitivity to others.
- Laboratory training does not lead to deep-rooted personality changes.[40]

Evidence for the effectiveness of quality circles can properly be described as *mixed*.[41] While some studies report clear-cut improvements in factors such as cost reduction or improved employee attitudes, other studies reveal no improvements. Given this result, it is not surprising that many firms have instituted and then abandoned quality circles. However, given the newness of the techniques and the faddishness noted earlier, failures are to be expected, and firms that are truly committed to quality circle programs will probably learn from those who have failed.

One review has contrasted the results of four OD techniques discussed in this chapter (laboratory training, team building, survey feedback, and Grid OD) as well as eclectic approaches that use a combination of several specific OD techniques.[42] The reviewers recognized the fact that various techniques might be targeted at changing various aspects of the organization or might work better in affecting certain aspects. Thus they looked for changes at four levels of analysis—those seen in individual organizational members, in leaders, in groups, and in the organization as a whole. In addition, changes in process variables and outcome variables were examined. Process variables include changes in trust, self-awareness, leadership, and decision making. They essentially affect *how* work is accomplished. Outcome variables refer to the assumed consequences of process variables, such as performance, job satisfaction, profits, and efficiency. Ignoring the exact type of OD intervention, Exhibit 17-5 shows the impact of OD on outcome and process variables at various levels of analysis. As you can see, positive changes are reported in many cases. Also, since most OD efforts tend to be group-focused, it is not surprising that the most substantial changes tend to occur at the group level.

Exhibit 17-6 contrasts changes in processes and outcomes for the various OD strategies. While each technique often induces change, simple laboratory training seems less likely than the others to do so. This may be due in part to the transfer problem.

Another review has examined the impact of laboratory training, team building, survey feedback, and combinations of these techniques on outcome variables such as work force behavior, monetary criteria, and productivity.[43] As shown in Exhibit 17-7, improvement was noted in many cases, although it was by no means universal. The author also reports that these interventions were more effective for blue-collar rather than white-collar workers.

Despite these generally encouraging results, research evaluations of the success of OD interventions continue to be plagued by weak methodologies, which leaves the exact impact of the interventions open to question.[44] In fact, some have argued that weaker evaluations are more likely to result in finding positive outcomes, although the actual evidence for this idea is negligible.[45] Still, several problems persist in OD evaluations:

EXHIBIT 17-5 **Effects of organizational development on outcome and process variables.**

Level of Analysis	Typical Outcome Variables	Number of Studies	Average Positive Change
Group	Performance; length and number of meetings	8	63%
Organization	Profit; return-on-investment; production efficiency	12	47%
Individual	Performance; satisfaction	14	42%
Leader	Performance	3	—
TOTAL		22	51%

Level of Analysis	Typical Process Variables	Number of Studies	Average Positive Change
Group	Trust; involvement	10	62%
Organization	Leadership; decision making	11	49%
Individual	Self-awareness; self-actualization	20	45%
Leader	Openness to influence; interaction facilitation	27	36%
TOTAL		35	46%

Source: From Porras, J. I., & Berg, P. O. (1978, April). The impact of organization development, *The Academy of Management Review*, Vol. 3, No. 2, pp. 254, 256. © 1978 by the Academy of Management.

EXHIBIT 17-6 **Positive changes in outcome and process variables for various organizational development interventions.**

Dominant Intervention	Percent Change	
	Process Variables	Outcome Variables
Eclectic approach	52% (5)	52% (5)
Team building	45% (14)	53% (3)
Managerial Grid	43% (4)	68% (3)
Survey feedback	48% (4)	53% (3)
Laboratory training	44% (8)	44% (8)

Note: Numbers of studies are in parentheses.

Source: From Porras, J. I., & Berg, P. O. (1978, April). The impact of organization development, *The Academy of Management Review*, Vol. 3, No. 2, p. 259. © 1978 by the Academy of Management.

EXHIBIT 17-7   **The impact of laboratory training, team building, and survey feedback on outcome variables.**

Variable	Number of Studies	Percent[a] Change
Work-force		
Turnover	7	71
Absenteeism	7	57
Grievances	1	0
Total	11	60[b]
Monetary		
Costs	2	0
Profits	2	100
Sales	1	100
Total	4	60
Productivity		
Efficiency	6	50
Effectiveness	3	33
Quantity	2	50
Total	10	45
Quality	4	50
Overall	15	54

[a]Percentage of variables measured in a category showing significant positive change.

[b]Of 15 variables measured in 11 studies, 60 percent (9) showed significant positive change.

Source: From Nicholas, J. M. (1982, October). The comparative impact of organization development interventions on hard criteria measures. *The Academy of Management Review*, Vol. 7, No. 4, p. 535. © 1982 by the Academy of Management. Reprinted by permission.

- OD efforts involve a complex series of changes. There is little evidence of exactly *which* of these changes produce changes in processes and outcomes.

- Novelty effects or the fact that participants receive special treatment may produce short-term gains which really don't persist over time.

- Self-reports of changes in processes after OD may involve unconscious attempts to please the change agent.[46]

For these reasons and others, OD continues to be characterized by both problems and promise. One hopes promise will overcome problems as organizations try to respond effectively to their increasingly complex and dynamic environments.

SUMMARY

- All organizations must change due to forces in the external and internal environment. Although more environmental change usually requires more organizational change, organizations can exhibit too much change as well as too little. Organizations can change goals and strategies, technology, job design, structure, and people. People changes are almost always required to accompany changes in other factors.

■ The general change process involves unfreezing current attitudes and behaviors, changing them, and then refreezing the newly acquired attitudes and behaviors. Several key issues or problems must be dealt with during the general change process. One is accurate diagnosis of the current situation. Another is the resistance that may be provoked by unfreezing and change. A third is the problem of ensuring that changes invoked outside of the job setting are transferred to the job. A fourth issue is performing an adequate evaluation of the success of the change effort. Many such evaluations are weak or nonexistent. If the change effort is considered favorable, it must be institutionalized, or made a permanent part of the organizational system. A final problem in inducing change involves diffusing the change to other parts of the organization. Change should occur when dissatisfaction, a new model for the organization, and a planned process for achieving the model exist, and their benefits outweigh the anticipated costs of the change.

■ Organizational development (OD) is a planned, ongoing effort to change organizations to be more effective and more human. It uses the knowledge of behavioral science to foster a climate of organizational self-examination and readiness for change. A strong emphasis is placed on interpersonal and group processes. The traditional values underlying OD are humanistic, but an alternative set of values argues that change agents must only help organizations clarify their own needs and alternatives for action.

■ Five popular OD techniques were discussed. Laboratory training involves the use of a fairly unstructured group experience to increase self-awareness and interpersonal sensitivity. Team building attempts to increase the effectiveness of work teams by concentrating on interpersonal processes, goal clarification, and role clarification. Quality circles involve small groups of workers in solving problems of quality, productivity, and costs. Survey feedback requires organizational members to generate data that is fed back to them as a basis for inducing change. Grid OD is a comprehensive long-term effort to change organizations which uses a systematic series of developmental phases to accomplish its goals. It is grounded in the Managerial Grid®, which emphasizes maximizing concern for productivity and concern for people.

■ In roughly half of all OD attempts that have been adequately evaluated, positive changes in processes and/or outcomes have been observed. Despite this, the careful evaluation of OD programs poses special challenges to researchers.

KEY CONCEPTS

Unfreezing	Diffusion
Refreezing	Organizational development (OD)
Diagnosis	Laboratory training
Change agent	Team building
Resistance	Quality circles
Transfer	Survey feedback
Evaluation	Grid OD
Institutionalization	Managerial Grid®

DISCUSSION QUESTIONS

1. Discuss how the introduction of computers has led to changes in organizations. Explain how this change in technology might require changes in job design and people.

2. Describe an example of resistance to change that you have observed. Why did it occur?

3. As pointed out in the chapter, many training and development programs are not carefully, objectively evaluated by organizations. Why do you think this is so? Discuss political, economic, and resource reasons.

4. Discuss why the sole use of participant reactions is a poor basis for evaluating change efforts (i.e., finding out whether participants liked the change program).

5. Suppose a job enrichment effort in one plant of a manufacturing firm is judged to be very successful. You are the corporate change agent responsible for the project, and you wish to diffuse it to other plants that have a similar technology. How would you sell the project to other plant managers? What kinds of resistance might you encounter?

6. What personal qualities and skills would be useful for an OD change agent to possess? Describe the relative merits of using an internal staff change agent versus an external consultant.

7. Explain why traditional laboratory training seems most susceptible to the transfer problem. Consider both the nature of the training and the organization's reaction to the trained individuals.

8. Imagine that the U.S. Marine Corps is forming a special hostage rescue unit to aid American hostages around the world. How could team-building principles be used to enhance the formation and functioning of this unit? What are some limitations to using this approach in the military?

9. Debate this statement: Survey feedback can be a problematic OD technique because it permits those who are affected by organizational policies to generate data that speaks against those policies.

10. Explain why top management commitment is necessary for an organization to proceed through all six phases of Grid OD. Discuss why Grid OD is divided into a number of distinct phases.

FOR FURTHER READING

Cobb, A. T., & Margulies, N. (1981). Organization development: A political perspective. *Academy of Management Review, 6,* 49–59.

> Argues that the practice of organizational development is inherently political, even though this is unrecognized by many OD practitioners. Discusses how an awareness of organizational politics can help OD efforts.

Dowling, W. F. (1975, Spring). To move an organization: The Corning approach to organization development. *Organizational Dynamics,* 16–34.

> A detailed discussion of the ambitious OD effort at Corning Glass. Describes the eclectic approach used and considers why a very successful effort in one plant did not diffuse to others.

Lawler, E. E., III. (1981). *Pay and organization development.* Reading, MA: Addison-Wesley.

> Argues that OD has traditionally ignored the role of pay in changing organizations. Contends that flexible benefit plans, gain sharing between management and labor, and plans that pay for acquired skills can enhance organizations. Discusses how changes in pay systems must often accompany other OD efforts.

Case Study

Talking in Circles!

As the only power company in a territory extending from Belleville, Ontario, in the west to the Quebec border in the east, and from the St. Lawrence River on the south along Highway 401, Southern Ontario Utility was firmly situated in the "golden corridor" which extends from Windsor, Ontario, to the Quebec-Ontario border. Although it held a monopolistic position, the Ontario provincial regulators kept user rates at a set level, and any attempts at the lucrative home-heating markets met with stiff competition from both the oil companies and the natural gas companies. The company also had little leeway with respect to labor costs. All of the nonmanagement employees belonged to a Canadian affiliate of the powerful International Union of Electrical Workers. Settlements with the unions were always based on parity across borders, and consequent high wage and benefit packages were the norm. Nor were suppliers noted for their charity, whether they were suppliers of machinery and materials or suppliers of capital. Suffice it to say, effective management of resources in the achievement of organizational goals was necessary, even in a monopoly.

To better serve its customers, Southern Ontario Utility divided its territory geographically into a number of districts. Each district contained all the line functions required to serve its customers (see Exhibit 1). The construction crews built new customer networks (e.g., placed poles, cables, and equipment) which were maintained subsequently by the repair crews. The testers located in the Brockville work center conducted network fault location in

support of the repair people. The clerks also worked in the center and dealt with customer service applications, bill payments, enquiries, and so on.

Results in key areas were published by the Corporate Accounting/M.I.S. group (Exhibit 1), and were a method of maintaining competition between district managers. Among the more progressive and innovative managers was Debbie Wilson, who was in charge of the Brockville, Ontario, district. She had risen quickly in the company and was known for getting results from her people. Although a review of her latest key indicators was positive, she felt more could be obtained from her staff and had decided to seek help from the Corporate Human Resources/Organizational Development group located in Kingston, Ontario (see Exhibit 1). Subsequently, organizational development consultants, along with Debbie and her four group managers, spent a whole day reviewing district operations. At the end of that meeting, a task force was established, composed of the two consultants and two of the group managers. Debbie's closing remarks to all participants were:

I'll tell you what I want. I'd like to see more smiling faces around here. And I don't just mean that human relations stuff. I believe people should enjoy their work and get a bang out of doing it. I believe that when people enjoy coming to work that there is a payoff to the company. So I'm not telling what to do. Just make sure that whatever you do, that our year-end results don't slip and that you stay within the budget. . . . you're the experts. . . . do something!

In the next four weeks, the task force moved quickly. A survey questionnaire was designed and administered to all managers and nonmanagement

---

Source: This case was prepared by Roland Leroux. Reprinted by permission.

EXHIBIT 1   Organization chart for Southern Ontario Utility.

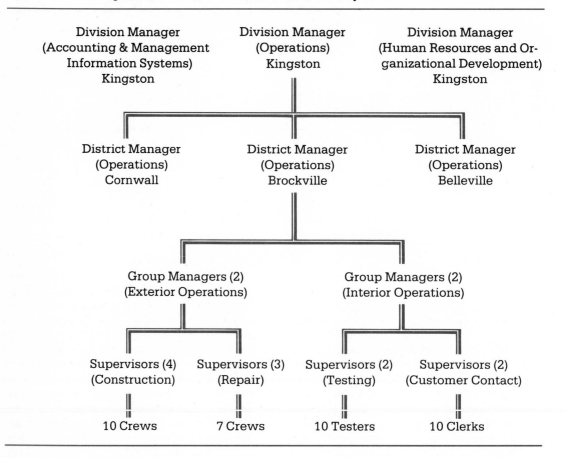

employees within the Brockville district. The responses were compiled and yielded the results shown to the right.

The task force analyzed the data and associated write-in comments, like:

. . . . you come in at 8:00, do your work, go home at 5:00. . . .

. . . . everyone just seems interested in their own turf. . . .

. . . . if it affects your results and you don't get credit for it, why help the other guy. . . . ?

They concluded that the chosen intervention should be one that allowed nonmanagement people to solve their own problems, brought diverse work groups together, and improved daily relationships between supervisors and subordinates.

Area Surveyed	Percent Negative Answers*
Interest in job	79%
Organizational structure	72%
Relations with supervisor	69%
Physical working conditions	43%
Stress/mental exertion	28%
Future/goal attainment	27%
Relations with associates	8%

*These percentages comprise answers to questions where the responses indicated "Most of the Time" and "Frequently". (See typical questions below.)

• How often do you feel your job is monotonous and routine?

• How often is it difficult to approach your supervisor for information you need to do your job?

• How often do you feel you have too little authority to carry out the responsibilities assigned to you?

A plan of action based on quality circles was agreed upon and included the following:

• Team building meetings for quality circle volunteers

• Brainstorming sessions to decide problem priorities

• Other skill-training sessions

• Presentation of recommendations to upper management

• Implementation (on approval) and monitoring of planned changes

This was approved by Debbie Wilson. A general meeting was held to which all employees in the district were invited. The entire program was outlined. Feedback of the survey and the explanation of the program were presented by one of the consultants. Enthusiasm was high, and enough volunteers came forward to start three quality circles of about ten employees each. The program was underway!

The decision to start with team building proved to be a wise one. The three quality circles were composed of persons who did not normally work together. Two were formed of men who worked outdoors and not necessarily from the same work crews. The other circle was a mixture of male testers and female clerks, all of whom worked within the work center. After two training sessions, the quality circles began to show signs of cohesiveness. Leaders were elected by the members, and basic work procedures for the groups had been agreed to. The consultants reported these successes to Debbie Wilson and anxiously moved forward to the next step of the program.

The brainstorming sessions were designed to help the quality circles decide on problem priorities. All three circles seemed to be having trouble dealing with the first three areas identified as problems (see Table above). The groups wanted to focus on the area of physical working conditions. The discussions rotated around items like parking spaces, work center temperature ("too hot in the summer, too cold in the winter"), lunchroom facilities, and so on. As one consultant said, "It is as if they just don't know how to handle issues like structure, authority, and interpersonal relationships with the boss." The task force decided to let the circles focus on the problems of basic working conditions, hoping then to move on to the "meatier" problem areas. Soon after, the quality circle members reported to the task force that their supervisors were questioning them about "what was going on" in the meetings and that they were acting to solve problems before the circles could make presentations of the problems and recommendations to higher management (e.g., one supervisor immediately placed fans in the work center when she heard of temperature problems). "They are acting awfully scared" was the remark of one circle leader.

No presentations had yet been made to higher management, but to the task force these seemed to be in the offing. The training portion of the circle meetings was becoming shorter and shorter. However, the time of the members was now spent attempting to really analyze problems that had provoked the most negative survey responses. They debated about and could not agree upon what to do. The discussion went around in circles ("No wonder they called them quality circles," one member remarked!) Their discussions carried beyond the circles to coffee breaks and lunch time and included anyone and everyone around. While membership in the circles had been open to all, the majority of employees had adopted a "wait and see" attitude. The quality circle volunteers represented about a third of the district forces. Now the other employees were not liking what they saw and heard. To them, they saw a group that was being given special treatment and extra training (even though much of it was on their own time), and who were becoming high-profile with management. Rumblings were being heard by the union stewards. The task force saw this as an understandable problem and said, "We'll issue a monthly newsletter, and that should clear it up."

Two weeks later the bomb dropped. The task force was summoned to Debbie Wilson's office. She announced, "Well, maybe the grand experiment is over. The president has just received a letter from the union protesting our unilateral implementation of a quality circle program. It is instructing any union stewards to avoid the program and, at the same time, advising all employees to do the same. Where do we go from here?".

■ ■ ■

1. What impact did the composition and the role of the task force have on the success of the change intervention?
2. What possible reasons could the union have had for its objection to the program?

3. What were some of the implementation errors made by the task force, and what would you have done differently?
4. If you were on the task force, what would you do now?

REFERENCES

1. Katz, D., & Kahn, R. L. (1978). *The social psychology of organizations* (2nd ed.). New York: Wiley.
2. This list relies mostly on Leavitt, H. (1965). Applied organizational changes in industry: Structural, technological, and humanistic approaches. In J. G. March (Ed.), *Handbook of organizations.* Chicago: Rand McNally.
3. Walton, R. E. (1975, Winter). The diffusion of new work structures: Explaining why success didn't take. *Organizational Dynamics,* 3–22, p. 5.
4. Lewin, K. (1951). *Field theory in social science.* New York: Harper & Row.
5. Levinson, H. (1972). *Organizational diagnosis.* Cambridge, MA: Harvard University Press.
6. For a review of evidence see Filley, A. C., House, R. J., & Kerr, S. (1976). *Managerial process and organizational behavior* (2nd ed.). Glenview, IL: Scott, Foresman. Also see Tichy, N. M., Hornstein, H., & Nisberg, J. N. (1976). Participative organization diagnosis and intervention strategies: Developing emergent pragmatic theories of change. *Academy of Management Review, 1,* 109–120.
7. Lawler, E. E., & Hackman, J. R. (1969). The impact of employee participation in the development of pay incentive plans: A field experiment. *Journal of Applied Psychology, 53,* 467–471.
8. Gagné, R. M. (1962). Military training and principles of learning. *American Psychologist, 18,* 83–91.
9. Goldstein, A. P., & Sorcher, M. (1974). *Changing supervisor behavior.* New York: Pergamon.
10. Fleishman, E. A., Harris, E. F., & Burtt, H. E. (1955). *Leadership and supervision in industry.* Columbus: Ohio State University Bureau of Educational Research.
11. Campbell, J. P. (1971). Personnel training and development. *Annual Review of Psychology, 22,* 565–602.
12. Catalanello, R. F., & Kirkpatrick, D. L. (1968). Evaluating training programs—the state of the art. *Training and Development Journal, 22,* 2–9.
13. Goodman, P. S., Bazerman, M., & Conlon, E. (1980). Institutionalization of planned organizational change. *Research in Organizational Behavior, 2,* 215–246.
14. Goodman et al., 1980.
15. Walton, 1975.
16. Beer, M. (1980). *Organization change and development: A systems view.* Glenview, IL: Scott, Foresman, p. 46.
17. Beer, M., & Driscoll, J. W. (1977). Strategies for change. In J. R. Hackman & L. L. Suttle (Eds.), *Improving life at work: Behavioral science approaches to organizational change.* Glenview, IL: Scott, Foresman.
18. For a review of various definitions see: Mapping the territory. In W. L. French, C. H. Bell, Jr., & R. A. Zawacki (Eds.) (1978), *Organization development: Theory, practice, and research.* Dallas: Business Publications.

19. French, W. L., & Bell, C. H., Jr. (1973). *Organization development.* Englewood Cliffs, NJ: Prentice-Hall.

20. See Connor, P. E. (1977). A critical inquiry into some assumptions and values characterizing OD. *Academy of Management Review, 2,* 635–644.

21. Beer, 1980, p. 43.

22. For a detailed discussion of laboratory training see Golembiewski, R. T. (1972). *Renewing organizations: A laboratory approach to planned change.* Itasca, IL: Peacock.

23. French & Bell, 1973.

24. Campbell, J. P., & Dunnette, M. D. (1968). Effectiveness of T-group experiences in managerial training and development. *Psychological Bulletin, 70,* 73–104.

25. Hartley, D., Roback, H. B., & Abramowitz, S. I. (1976). Deterioration effects in encounter groups. *American Psychologist, 31,* 247–255.

26. Dyer, W. G., Maddocks, R. F., Moffitt, J. W., & Underwood, W. J. (1970). A laboratory consultation model for organizational change. *Journal of Applied Behavioral Science, 6,* 211–227.

27. Beer, M. (1976). The technology of organizational development. In M. D. Dunnette (Ed.), *Handbook of industrial and organizational psychology.* Chicago: Rand McNally.

28. Bell, C. H., Jr., & Rosenzweig, J. (1978). Highlights of an organizational improvement program in a city government. In French et al.

29. Wakeley, J. H., & Shaw, M. E. (1965). Management training: An integrated approach. *Training Directors Journal, 19,* 2–13.

30. Munchus, G., III. (1983). Employer-employee based quality circles in Japan: Human resource policy implications for American firms. *Academy of Management Review, 8,* 255–261; Cole, R. E. (1980). *Work, mobility, and participation: A comparative study of American and Japanese industry.* Berkeley, CA: University of California Press.

31. Marks, M. L. (1986, March). The question of quality circles. *Psychology Today,* 36–46.

32. Crocker, O., Charney, C., & Chiu, S. L. (1984). *Quality circles: A guide to participation and productivity.* Toronto: Methuen; Robson, A. (1982). *Quality circles: A practical guide.* Aldershot, England: Gower.

33. Fletcher, D. (1984). Keeping going I: Wedgwood. In M. Robson (Ed.), *Quality circles in action.* Aldershot, England: Gower.

34. See Crocker et al., 1984.

35. This description relies upon Beer, 1980; Huse, E. F. (1980). *Organization development and change* (2nd ed.). St. Paul, MN: West; Nadler, D. A. (1977). *Feedback and organization development: Using data-based methods.* Reading, MA: Addison-Wesley.

36. Taylor, J., & Bowers, D. (1972). *Survey of organizations: A machine-scored standardized questionnaire instrument.* Ann Arbor, MI: Center for Research on Utilization of Scientific Knowledge, Institute for Social Research, University of Michigan.

37. Mohrman, S. A., Mohrman, A. M., Cooke, R. A., & Duncan, R. B. (1977). A survey feedback and problem-solving intervention in a school district: "We'll take the survey but you can keep the feedback." In P. H. Mirvis & D. N. Berg (Eds.), *Failures in organization development and change: Cases and essays for learning.* New York: Wiley.

38. The Managerial Grid figure from *The Managerial Grid III: The Key to Leadership Excellence,* by Robert R. Blake and Jane Srygley Mouton. Houston: Gulf Publishing Company, Copyright © 1985, page 12. Reproduced by permission.

39. Alderfer, C. P. (1977). Organization development. In M. R. Rosenzweig & L. W. Porter (Eds.), *Annual Review of Psychology, 28,* 197–223.

40. Campbell & Dunnette, 1968.

41. Steel, R. P., & Shane, G. S. (1986). Evaluation research on quality circles: Technical and analytical implications. *Human Relations, 39,* 449–468.

42. Poras, J. I., & Berg, P. O. (1978). The impact of organization development. *Academy of Management Review, 3,* 249–264.

43. Nicholas, J. M. (1982). The comparative impact of organization development interventions on hard criteria measures. *Academy of Management Review, 7,* 531–542.

44. Nicholas, J. M., & Katz, M. (1985). Research methods and reporting practices in organization development: A review and some guidelines. *Academy of Management Review, 10,* 737–749.

45. Woodman, R. W., & Wayne, S. J. (1985). An investigation of positive-findings bias in evaluation of organization development interventions. *Academy of Management Journal, 28,* 889–913.

46. White, S. E., & Mitchell, T. R. (1976). Organization development: A review of research content and research design. *Academy of Management Review, 1,* 57–73.

Chapter 18

Careers

JAN AND REGINALD

Jan Thompson and Reginald Wilson both graduated from university with bachelor's degrees in business. They wanted to get married and start careers together. Jan was viewed by her many friends as very sociable and "quite an actor," as well as someone who could "sell ice cubes to Eskimos." For her, a marketing major was a natural choice. Because of her good school record, achievements in extracurricular activities, and interpersonal skills, she had a number of job options upon graduation.

Reggie also established a good record while at university. He particularly excelled in accounting and finance because they allowed him to use his numerical abilities, and he thought those fields were "orderly and practical." When a guest speaker in one of his classes noted that people making it to high positions like chief executive officer increasingly had solid accounting backgrounds and a good eye for financial matters, he knew that his finance major and accounting minor were good choices. When he graduated he was happy to have almost as many job options as his socially hyperactive girlfriend.

Planning two careers simultaneously proved trying at times, but in the end Jan and Reggie were able to get good jobs in not only the same city but the same company. Reggie got a job in the finance department helping to manage the company's investment portfolio. While most of the work during the first year was fairly mundane, he was able to form a good relationship with his boss who eventually gave him more challenging assignments and even introduced him to the "movers and shakers" in the company. At the end of his third year, a position on the controller's staff in the accounting department opened up. His boss confided that even a junior position on the controller's staff is a "good place to get your ticket punched if you're serious about moving on to bigger and better things." Reggie decided to investigate further and to his surprise found that his boss had "greased the skids" well, and he got an acceptable offer in his first meeting with the area manager.

Jan's first job was in marketing. She called herself a rover because she was moved to different areas and projects wherever she was needed. After four years she got a chance to make a regional market test of a new line of hand soap. As product manager, she coordinated the whole show and made numerous price, promotion, and distribution decisions. She even had two subordinates to help with the various duties. After nine months of hard work, the hand soap was a clear success. Jan received plenty of credit and was the natural choice to manage the product line on a national level. This was a big step up the corporate ladder. To everyone's surprise Jan turned down the promotion. The need to move to the corporate headquarters in another city, with the complications that would cause in Reggie's career, was a factor, but the major reason she gave to the marketing vice-president was "I'm a marketer, not a manager. I get my kicks from figuring out people's preferences and selling them on the product. The job you're offering has some attractive qualities, but I know the required wrestling with the bureaucracy and digesting all the sales and cost data will do me in!"

Fifteen years later. . . . A number of challenges and changes have been confronted by both Reggie and Jan. Reggie has continued to climb the corporate hierarchy, but has moved to a new company. Lack of opportunity seemed to be his main reason for changing. "After ten years and four different positions, I knew that my chances for a high executive position were low. It seems everyone at the top has 'Made in Marketing' stamped on their personnel files. I had accepted a transfer to a marketing job just to pick up this experience, but it was clear that I needed more than a two-year hitch to get by. Even the M.B.A. I picked up in over five years of night classes couldn't compensate for my nonmarketing orientation. It wasn't a company in which I could really trade on my strengths." After this discovery, he looked around and found a general management position with a bank that liked his consumer industry experience and strong financial orientation.

Reggie's consistent and clear career focus is still a bit of a puzzle for Jan. After turning down the product manager's job she had taken on a number of interesting and challenging marketing assignments. However, at around age thirty she found herself very dissatisfied. She observed that "all of a sudden, the successes at work didn't mean as much as they did before. A big factor was that the company wanted all of me and just wasn't willing to take anything less. Reggie and I had always talked about having a couple of children when the time was right, but for the company there was never a 'right time.' The only option within the company was taking six weeks maternity leave and then jumping back into ten-hour work days with too many travel requirements. It just didn't fit the life I had envisioned for myself, so I quit." Leaving the work force was quite difficult for Jan. As Reggie put it, "when she became pregnant with our second child, it hit her like a ton of bricks. The previous two years as full-time mother and homemaker had been seen as a temporary thing, but with the second child on the way it started to feel like a permanent assignment."

Jan eventually looked around for another job and a company that would be flexible in terms of the level of time commitment required, yet provide interesting and challenging assignments. They just were not there! Finally, she discovered that large companies were not the only game in town and that small businesses needed occasional marketing expertise. She now works as a consultant out of her home. She confides, "It's not a perfect situation. The flexibility is great, and I enjoy promoting myself. Unfortunately, the consulting projects I've picked up aren't very challenging and the income is unpredictable, but hopefully this will change."

Organizations need people. Without people, organizations cannot achieve their goals and produce goods or services. In a similar way, people, like Jan and Reggie, need organizations. Without organizations, people would have few opportunities to satisfy their many needs, accomplish their varied goals, and engage in activities which enrich and add meaning to their lives. This mutual dependence on one another is the basis for the topic of this chapter. Careers provide organizations a way to channel people into needed areas and to develop their skills so they can continue to perform needed organizational functions. If this is done right, employees also gain. Careers can provide chances to have experiences and jobs which offer valued rewards and develop skills leading to other desirable opportunities and a brighter future. Consider your own case. Why are you in this class and reading this book? For many it is a chance to develop skills and gain knowledge which contribute to a successful and satisfying career. At a minimum, this course probably leads to a degree, which in turn will open a few doors. Organizations also have a stake in this process. The supply of graduates which schools produce allows organizations to acquire partially trained and socialized human resources (at what some students consider bargain basement prices!)

Schooling, however, is only the first step in many people's careers. Most of the interesting action that makes up career processes in people's lives starts after they check out of school and into their first career-oriented job. Accordingly, this chapter will focus on the patterns and consequences of careers in organizations. First, we will define the meaning of the term career, and discuss the major ways of conceiving individual career orientation. Then, career and adult life stages which depict changes people tend to go through will be presented. Following this, organizational practices and supervisory behavior associated with effective career management are discussed. The chapter concludes with an approach for students to plan and prepare for their own careers.

WHAT IS A CAREER?

A **career** is a sequence of work activities and positions, and associated attitudes and reactions, experienced over a person's life.[1] Thus, it involves a variety of objective events (e.g., promotions) and self-perceived reactions which occur throughout a lifetime. Three elements are important in fully understanding the meaning of a career. First, a career involves moving on a path over time. This path has two sides. One side is the more or less objective path which employees follow in an organization (sometimes called external careers because they can be seen by external observers).[2] The pattern of placing new graduates in a "contract administrator" position, promoting them into a "senior contract administrator" job and eventually into a "senior contract negotiator" position is an example of the prescribed **external career** in a contracts department in a West Coast aerospace firm. These paths may be orderly, like the three-position contracts sequence, or have major discontinuities of functional, as well as hierarchical level, position changes in which the duties in one position do not naturally build on the skills developed in the previous job. Frequently, these steps are not planned and seem to emerge over time. The other side of this path is the individual's subjective interpretation of the meaning of various work experiences, sometimes called the **internal career** because it can be known only from the point of view of the actor. Internal careers are the individual's reactions to the objective bench marks of the external career. The criteria people use to evaluate their progress changes over time. For example, being a contract administrator is likely to have a very different meaning to the new graduate at age twenty-two than it will at thirty-two after ten years of no movement. A position associated at one point in time with feelings of optimism and a brighter future can later be associated with feelings of being "stuck" or a failure.

The second key element of a career is that it is the interaction of individual and organizational factors. People's reaction to a given job is function of the fit between the individual's occupational self-concept (i.e., the pattern of needs, aptitudes, and preferences) and types of opportunities, constraints, and demands provided by that job. One person may find the contract administrator job interesting and challenging and a step to a brighter future. Another may find it stifling. Understanding these differences is critical to effectively managing one's own career, as well as helping others, such as subordinates, manage their careers.

The third important element of a career is that it is an occupational identity.[3] What people do in our society is very much a key element in who they are. When we are getting acquainted with someone new, "What do you do?" is often one of the first questions posed. People vary as to how important their occupational self-identity is to their overall identity, but for many it is the primary factor in how they define who they are.

INDIVIDUAL DIFFERENCES IN CAREER ORIENTATION

Fortunately for everyone concerned, people are not all the same. Each of us differs in terms of skills, values, goals, and preferred activities. However, as different as people are from one another, there are also a number of similarities between people. Consider the two people in the story at the beginning of this chapter. Although Jan and Reginald are markedly different in some respects, they are similar in a number of ways to a lot of other people. Useful information on these patterns of similarities and dissimilarities in career orientation would tell us:

■ What are the specific ways in which people are similar and/or different from one another?

■ How might knowledge of similarities and differences help us to understand how different types of people will react to certain work situations?

■ How can the answers to these two questions help individuals plan more satisfying careers and help organizations more effectively manage their human resources?

Scientists studying careers have developed a number of insights which help us answer these questions. Through a number of studies they have developed ways of categorizing people which capture major patterns of similarities and differences in people's career orientation. As depicted in Exhibit 18-1, **career orientation** is defined in terms of the preferred activities, talents, and attitudes which people have. Different career orientations are consistent with particular task demands and rewards presented in some work environments. The fit or consistency between one's career orientation and work environment has direct consequences in terms of people's job behavior and attitudes.

Holland's Theory of Career Types

Easily the most researched and best documented theory of career orientation is John Holland's **theory of career types.**[4] Years of studies have documented that

EXHIBIT 18-1   Career orientation and its consequences.

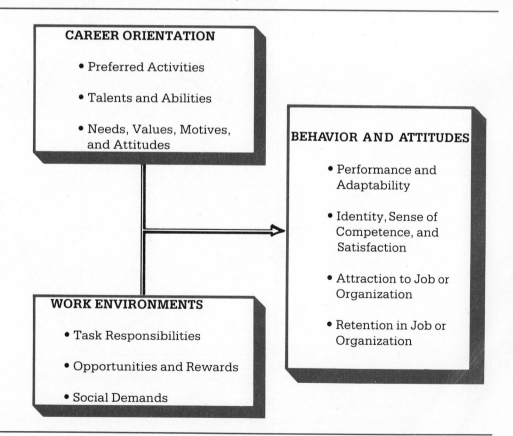

CAREER ORIENTATION

• Preferred Activities

• Talents and Abilities

• Needs, Values, Motives, and Attitudes

BEHAVIOR AND ATTITUDES

• Performance and Adaptability

• Identity, Sense of Competence, and Satisfaction

• Attraction to Job or Organization

• Retention in Job or Organization

WORK ENVIRONMENTS

• Task Responsibilities

• Opportunities and Rewards

• Social Demands

six distinct patterns explain many people's career orientation. These are presented in the hexagonal model in Exhibit 18-2. Some of these orientations or career types are almost the direct opposite of one another, while those adjacent to one another on the hexagonal model are more similar.

CONVENTIONAL.   The conventional orientation is probably the most dominant career type found in business occupations. This type of person prefers rule-regulated, orderly activities which generally include organizing written or numerical information or analyzing this information with an unambiguous set of procedures (e.g., computing financial ratios). These people are typically described as conforming, orderly, efficient, and practical. Less flattering descriptions include unimaginative, inhibited, and inflexible. Reggie, in the opening story, seemed to have a number of these qualities. Accounting and finance jobs, which require the precise

---

EXHIBIT 18-2   Holland's career types.

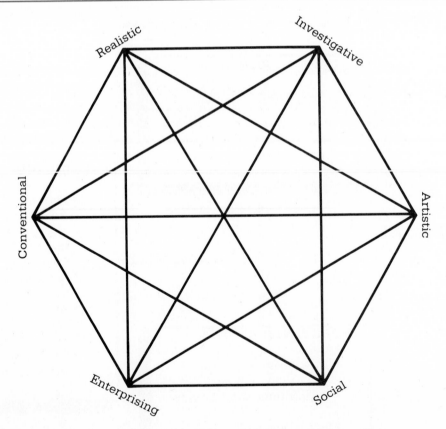

Source: Adapted from Holland, J. L. (1973). *Making vocational choices: A theory of careers.* Englewood Cliffs, NJ: Prentice-Hall, p. 23.

organization and evaluation of numerical information in a fairly stable work setting with clear operating procedures, typically fit people with a conventional orientation. The consequence is that they are attracted to, and perform well in, these work environments. Reggie's selection of a finance and accounting emphasis in school and finance and accounting jobs illustrates how career orientation and work environment fit can work.

ARTISTIC.   The artistic career orientation is the most dissimilar to the conventional type. These people prefer ambiguous and unsystematic activities which entail creating expressive written, spoken, or visual forms. These people are often described as imaginative, intuitive, and independent, as well as disorderly, emotional, and impractical. Painting, music, and drama are obvious artistic occupations. The most negative descriptions, like ''impractical,'' are characterizations which the opposite of an artistic type, a conventional career type, is more likely to make. Artistic types are, in turn, more likely than other types to return the favor by coming up with pejorative descriptions of conventional type people, like unimaginative and inflexible. While business organizations will have far fewer of these types, they could easily be exactly what graphics or advertising departments need.

REALISTIC.   The realistic career type prefers activities which require the physical manipulation of objects or tools in a well-ordered work environment with few social demands. These people usually have mechanical abilities and are most likely to be described as genuine, stable, and practical, as well as possibly shy, uninsightful, and conforming. This type of person is likely to be at home in semiskilled or crafts positions (e.g., carpenter, mechanic, assembly line worker, plumber) which present consistent task requirements and few social demands, such as negotiating and persuading.

SOCIAL.   The social type is the near opposite of the realistic career orientation. This type of person prefers activities which involve informing, helping, or developing others and has an aversion to well-ordered and systematic work environments. Besides being described as sociable, this person is typically characterized as tactful, friendly, understanding, and helpful. Less positive descriptions (which are most likely to be made by the opposite of this career type, the realistic type) include dominating and manipulative. Clearly Jan had a number of these qualities and, as a consequence, was attracted to a work situation in which she interacted with, and attempted to understand, other people in a fairly unstructured setting. Nursing and teaching are occupations in which jobs typically fit the social type. Within business firms, marketing, sales, and training and development are areas which often fit the unique needs of this career type.

ENTERPRISING.   The enterprising type is somewhat similar to the social career orientation in that they like to work with people. The main difference is that enterprising types prefer to focus their energies on leading and controlling others (versus helping or understanding) in order to reach specific organizational goals or obtain economic gains. Positive characterizations of these people include self-confident, ambitious, energetic, and talkative. Less flattering descriptions include domineering, power-hungry, and impulsive. Consider Jan, again. While she is primarily a social type, the "quite an actor" description and her efforts to successfully launch the new product line and starting a consulting practice fit the profile of the enterprising type. Perhaps, if the product line manager position she was offered had involved predominantly interpersonal influence requirements (which fit the enterprising type) and less "digesting" numerical data (which fits the conventional type), she would have found it harder to turn down.

INVESTIGATIVE.   The investigative is the near-opposite of the enterprising career orientation. People in this category prefer activities which involve observing and analyzing phenomena in order to develop knowledge and understanding. These people are seen as complicated, original, and independent as well as possibly disorderly, impractical, and impulsive, and have an aversion to repetitious activities and to selling. Science occupations, such as biologist, sociologist, and mathematician, are well suited to this career type. Within business organizations, these people are attracted to research and development positions and staff positions which require complex analyses with little need to persuade and convince others.

CAREER CHOICE.   Holland's theory is primarily concerned with career choice. It identifies specific types of people and particular types of work environments to which each type will be attracted. There is evidence that people who end up in work environments which are not consistent with their career orientation tend to be dissatisfied and either gradually shift their orientation (i.e., become more like the career type which is congruent with their work environment) or move to a new work situation. One can see an explicit attraction-selection process operating in Jan's and Reggie's early career choices. Each found positions which had work environments (e.g., task duties, rewards, and social demands) which fit each of their distinctly different orientations and choose those jobs over others they were considering. Being in a congruent work environment will also increase the likelihood that they will be satisfied, achieve a sense of competence, and stay with the organization.

At this point you may be wondering if all people neatly fit into one of the six career types. The real world is certainly more complicated than this. Many of these complexities are recognized in Holland's theory. He acknowledges that many people are like Jan and seem to be a combination of two, or perhaps three, career types. The combinations which most frequently develop are those which are adjacent to each other on the hexagonal model presented in Exhibit 18-2. Jan's social-enterprising combination is quite consistent with the theory. She was interested in both figuring out people and being involved with them (which is consistent with the social orientation), yet also enjoyed promoting the new product line and influencing people (which is characteristic of the enterprising type). Another consistent combination is the conventional-enterprising combination which fits many, but certainly not all, managerial positions. The most unlikely combinations are those involving types which are opposite to each other on the hexagonal model, such as conventional-artistic or investigative-enterprising.

Holland's theory even predicts which people are least likely to be attracted to, or more satisfied in, work environments which seemingly fit their career orientation. Research finds that people with an inconsistent combination of orientations (i.e., those which are opposite one another on the hexagonal model in Exhibit 18-2, such as the artistic-conventional combination) or those with an undifferentiated pattern (i.e., people who see themselves as a little bit like many types and not very dissimilar to any type) are the least likely to be strongly attracted to, or satisfied with, a particular work environment. They are also the ones who are most likely to stay and adjust their career orientation to an initially inconsistent work environment. Those with a less inconsistent or more differentiated combination of characteristics would have a stronger negative reaction to the specific work demands which are incongruent with their orientation and start searching for a better alternative.

Do people use Holland's theory? This theory is the basis for much vocational guidance counseling. Many students, in attempting to figure out what kinds of jobs they want (and what kind of college major they should choose), visit a guidance counselor and are given the Strong Vocational Interest Blank.[5] This instrument compares one's interests to those in a variety of occupations. These occupations are grouped into the six Holland career types. Thus, the test tells you if you have interests similar to those in occupations in each of the six career type categories. These results are used to guide students into majors and career paths that are consistent with their interests. In summary, the basic thrust of the counseling is to find out what career type you are, and then get yourself qualified for jobs which are congruent with that orientation. Doing this increases the chances of finding a career which requires you to use your strengths, fulfills your needs, and puts you into association with those with whom you are likely to have the most in common.

Schein's Theory of Career Anchors

A more recent development in the study of careers is Edgar Schein's **theory of career anchors.**[6] Unlike Holland's career types, anchors develop well after childhood and adolescence. Career anchors evolve and develop through the successive new trials and opportunities one faces in early work experiences. Gradually, as one gains more self-knowledge and a clearer occupational self-concept, a distinct pattern of self-perceived talents, motives, needs, and values emerges. These distinct patterns are called career anchors. The five patterns which have been documented by early research are: technical functional competence, managerial competence, security, autonomy, and creativity. Just as a boat's anchor keeps it from drifting, career anchors keep one centered around certain types of work activities. If people happen to take on inconsistent work assignments, their career anchor acts to pull them back to more consistent activities.

TECHNICAL/FUNCTIONAL COMPETENCE.   For people with this anchor the primary factor in their career choices and decisions is the actual content of work. A chance to move to a job which takes them away from their technical or functional area is unattractive. Consider Jan in the opening story. The so-called opportunity to move into general management and away from pure marketing activities was not an opportunity in her eyes. For her, the marketing area and the activities it required her to do were closely tied to her feelings of competence. Moving would have required her to engage in activities and develop skills which did not fit her basic occupational self-concept. As a result, she told her boss, "I'm a marketer, not a manager." Engaging in marketing activities is consistent with her values and motives and allowed her to use skills and talents in which she had grown confident.

MANAGERIAL COMPETENCE.   For people with this career anchor the ultimate goal is to rise to positions of managerial responsibility. Reggie developed a strong managerial competence anchor early in his career. The position on the controller's staff provided him an opportunity to develop analytical and interpersonal competencies and gain valued exposure while getting his "ticket punched" on the way to his real goal, general management. People with this anchor see their competence tied to three areas: 1) analytical competence with which they can identify and solve problems with incomplete and uncertain information, 2) interpersonal competence through which they can influence others toward the achievement of organizational goals, and 3) emotional competence in dealing with high levels of responsibility and the exercise of power (e.g., firing someone). There appears to be a connection between Holland's enterprising and conventional career types and this anchor. Interpersonal influence competence is consistent with the enterprising orientation, while analytical competence corresponds to some of the characteristics of the conventional type. One potential inconsistency is that the conventional person is attracted to an orderly and stable work environment. Schein often talks about the inherent uncertainty and disorderliness of many managerial work environments. This latter characteristic is most consistent with Holland's social career orientation. Early in Reggie's career it was unclear whether he would develop adequate interpersonal skills and tolerance for uncertainty and fully fit the characteristics of the managerial competence anchor. Perhaps he took some lessons from Jan along the way.

SECURITY.   For some people a key factor in career planning and decision making is the development of long-term work-life stability and security. A good benefits and retirement package, past employment stability (e.g., few cycles of mass layoffs and rehiring), and clear career paths such as explicit planned sequences of jobs for employees, are some organizational features which are particularly attractive to a person with this anchor. Opportunities to use certain technical skills or promotion prospects may be of some importance, if, and only if, they are seen as leading to long-term stability and security.

AUTONOMY.   For the autonomy-anchored person, the chance to stay in a technical area, steadily march up a corporate hierarchy, or gain guaranteed-for-life employment would not be a highly valued opportunity. For these people, movement up the organizational ladder could be a trade-off between freedom to pursue their own interests and life-style versus status, responsibility, and money. Managerial competence people will want more of the latter, even if it costs them some freedom and constrains their life-style. Autonomy-anchored people, however, are more likely to say no to advancement if it means giving up their independence and freedom. The people in this category in Schein's original study were very satisfied. Some found their freedom in consulting roles, while others pursued careers as a freelance writer, a small business proprietor, and a college professor. The size of the organizations they were attracted to was generally small.

CREATIVITY.   Creativity-anchored people differ from people in the other categories in a specific way. While many of them want some degree of autonomy or to exercise managerial or technical/functional competence, they are unique in their overarching desire to create something that is entirely of their own making. It may be a product or technical process or a company. The creative anchor can find expression in a number of ways. One is through entrepreneurship which could include starting a new business venture. The second is through "intrapreneurship" from within an established company (see the cartoon). As an intrapreneur, one might carve out a unique role which allows one to try out and develop new ideas. Edwin Land of Polaroid is a prototypic example of this. His role in the organization

Source: *Los Angeles Times*, August 21, 1985.

is to develop innovations. Another possible role is the manager who works on special projects which require such things as developing a new product idea or developing and implementing a new manufacturing process. For creativity-anchored people, inventing something new is a measure of worth and the key to their sense of competence.

Career anchors provide a way to understand and predict how a person (such as Jan or Reggie in the story at the beginning of this chapter) is going to react to a particular work situation. It is important to remember that in the short term, people with very different orientations can find fulfillment in the same job, perhaps working right next to each other. For example, Reggie could conceivably have opted for a marketing position instead of accounting. Thus, for awhile he could have comfortably worked in a position very similar to Jan's. However, over time the differences in the way they evaluate their self-perceived success will reveal very different reactions to similar jobs. Lack of movement or a transfer to another marketing position may be just what Jan wants but may suggest to Reggie that he has been sidetracked and is not succeeding.

Managerial Implications of Career Orientation

The explicit message of both Holland's and Schein's models of career orientation is that those who run organizations should take into account differences in orientation when managing their human resources. Managerial practices that treat all people the same, which on the surface may seem like the fair thing to do, inevitably treat some of those people in ways that are dissatisfying and detract from organizational effectiveness.

For example, high-level (managerial competence–anchored) managers who create human resource policies and practices sometimes make the mistake of assuming that all reasonable employees basically prefer the same things that they do. As a result, they create reward systems and promotion patterns which conflict with other people's career orientations. Technical/functional competence–anchored people may find that they must leave their technical positions and take on managerial roles in order to have higher levels of compensation, a company-provided car, status, and influence in the company. The lack of a nonmanagerial or technical route to greater prestige and rewards puts nonmanagerial-anchored people in a dilemma. If they choose to stay close to the technical work they love, they will feel a sense of inequity (see Chapters 5 and 6) and may lessen their effort (a key input in equity theory terms) or look for another employer who will treat them in what they consider a fair and just manner. The managerial competence–anchored manager may have a hard time appreciating how an employee who turns down a "good" promotion can feel mistreated! This stems from a lack of understanding of individual differences and the assumption that "people are either similar to me or weird." On the other hand, if the technical/functional competence–anchored person takes the temptation to move to a nontechnical job, the consequence may be some dissatisfaction in spite of the extra rewards and potential poor performance since the person's orientation does not match task demands. Presenting these types of dilemmas to employees results in not only human costs, but also in organizational costs associated with diminished motivation and a misallocation of human resources.

Treating different people differently can not only be satisfying to those involved, but can help the organization achieve its goals. Doing this requires managers to take some positive steps. These might include:

- Understand and identify key individual difference characteristics which will shape the way that employees will react to so-called opportunities
- Identify key job and situational factors which are congruent with each of these characteristics
- Develop ways of matching employees to congruent work environment factors

The first two steps have been the focus of the first part of this chapter, while approaches for matching individuals and work situations will be addressed below.

Before turning our attention to those issues, a bias present in both Schein's and Holland's theories must be corrected. Both suggest that people are rather static and once they develop their career orientations by their middle to late twenties, they stay the same for life. This is clearly not true. Careers, like lives, have a dynamic quality and evolve and change in some predictable ways across adulthood.

CAREER AND ADULT LIFE STAGES

Over the past few years, behavioral scientists have found evidence of specific patterns of change and development throughout the adult years. Theorizing and research have been directed to patterns of change in one's work role (career stages) and more broadly focused patterns of development which include nonwork issues. While no two people go through a career or life in exactly the same fashion, the patterns scientists have discovered are broadly descriptive of many people's careers and adult years. Awareness of these patterns provides a general "road map" of many issues and demands which a young adult will face over his or her adult years.

Adult Life Stages

Adult life stages have their basis in both biological factors associated with adult aging processes and patterns of social expectations which exist in society. Thus, these are referred to as **biosocial life stages** in that they are the product of both forces. For example, a decline in biological vitality and increased frequency of health problems confront the middle-aged adult with the realization that life is half over and that time, in a very real way, is limited. The sudden emotional realization of this fact of life can lead to a reassessment of prior life-style choices and result in rather major changes and reordering of personal priorities (sometimes this stage is called the mid-life crisis). A key social force that influences adult development is **age norms,** which are widely accepted expectations in society about what behavior is appropriate for a person at a given age.[7] People whose behavior does not fit existing age norms find that they are given cues (such as others asking questions like "How come you're not married?" or "Isn't it time to settle down and think about a career?") which put pressure on them to conform.

A number of life-stage theorists have developed theories which, in spite of some differences, are quite consistent with one another. They all generally present the notion that across the adult years there are fairly stable periods which are a time for playing out prior decisions and life-style commitments. These stable periods are followed by more dynamic transitional periods during which prior choices are reconsidered and adjustments to various aspects of one's general style of life are explored. Sometimes, but certainly not always, these transitions are fairly traumatic and constitute crises which prompt major changes in people's lives.

One popular view of adult life stages is summarized in Exhibit 18-3.[8] It starts with the "early adult transition" which involves moving from adolescence and the exploration of various work roles and life-style choices to settling into a relatively stable period, called "entering adulthood," in which these preliminary choices about one's life-style are more fully tested. Toward the end of the twenties comes a period when those earlier choices are reassessed. This "age 30 transition" can be a traumatic time of disillusionment and change (e.g., divorce, major occupational change), but for many people it is more a time of minor adjustments, not revolution. Jan, in the opening story, went through a definite age thirty transition. She found that events which were previously satisfying had less meaning. A combination of social forces, such as friends and family asking her if she is going to have children and awareness of biological realities which make childbearing more risky in the middle to late thirties, probably helped initiate this period of reassessment. She made rather dramatic changes in her life (i.e., quitting her job and becoming a full-time homemaker). It appears that Reggie's age thirty transition was very smooth and hardly noticeable.

After the age thirty transition, a more stable "settling down" period begins. A person in this stage often focuses on establishing a stable and secure niche in society, and planning and striving to achieve particular goals (such as owning a house in a particular area, having one's own business, making vice-president by a certain age, etc.). In Jan's case it was focusing on her goal of having a family, and then adding a limited outside work role. Her going back to paid work was not simply a return to the life-style and priorities she had in her twenties. Her work role in her thirties was important, but definitely a secondary element in her overall life. Much of the research on men's life stages paints a very different picture; "making it" on specific work role goals is a central focus in their lives.

Sometimes the relatively stable settling down stage comes to a rather dramatic conclusion with the onset of the "mid-life transition." In the study which established this theory of life stages, 20 percent of the participants went through a period of minor questioning and adjustments. However, for the remaining 80 percent this transitional period was a traumatic time in which forgotten values,

EXHIBIT 18-3   **Levinson's adult life stages.**

Approximate Age Range	Life Stage and Major Characteristics
17–22	*Early adult transition.* Leave adolescence, make a preliminary step into the adult world by exploring different life-style choices and lessen dependence on parents.
22–28	*Entering adulthood.* Select and test out a specific set of choices of life-styles and roles.
28–33	*Age 30 transition.* Reassess previous choices, often with a sense of urgency to sort out one's life and make important choices before it is too late; this may be a smooth transition or a painful crisis.
33–40	*Settling down.* Focus on a specific agenda for accomplishing goals and advance, in occupational or nonoccupational terms, to higher levels of status.
40–45	*Mid-life transition.* Reappraise past life-style choices and begin to eliminate negative elements and test new choices. Radical changes to major elements (e.g., marriage, occupation) can be the result of a major disillusionment with one's life called the "mid-life crisis."
45–60	*Middle adulthood era.* Carry out life-style changes resulting from the mid-life transition. Often people "shift gears" and direct more time into nonwork, leisure activities.
60+	*Late adult transition & late adult era.* Some evidence of a continued pattern of reassessing prior choices and incorporating new values, interests, and behaviors into an altered life-style. Little research has been conducted on the specific qualities of these changes.

Source: Adapted from Levinson, D. J., et al. (1978). *The seasons of a man's life.* New York: Alfred Knopf. These stages were identified through an intensive study of forty adult males in a number of occupations. Their relationship to women's adult life stages is not known.

identities, or fantasies were confronted. The realization of one's biological mortality and a sense of having a limited amount of time are key factors which can be triggered by such events as a death of a friend or parent or a major illness. After the crisis is resolved and ways of giving forgotten identities more expression are determined, the next stable period, "middle adulthood," begins. The research on life stages after this point is quite limited. No doubt that as people live longer and longer, more research on additional life stages will become available.

Career Stages

Careers are an important aspect of many people's lives. Thus, they are influenced by the evolving pattern of needs, interests, and concerns associated with adult life stages. There are, however, general patterns of developmental changes in work-role activities which are distinct from life stages. These are called **career stages.** While everyone's career contains unique demands which dictate highly specific steps to success, there are issues and key tasks which are of general importance to a wide range of people. Exhibit 18-4 summarizes four career stages: exploration, establishment, advancement and maintenance, and late career. Knowing about career stages, like knowing about life stages, provides a map of likely events and concerns which a young adult will face in the future. Having a map increases the likelihood that the journey will be successful.

EXPLORATION.   This stage is a time of discovery and choice. People often leave their adolescence with a wide range of ideas about what they want to do, and, generally, what is possible in the world of jobs and occupations. As they move into the adult world, they must leave behind unrealistic views and settle in on a configuration of roles (i.e., student, wife/husband, occupation) and develop a life-style which fits key elements of their identity. This involves leaving one's family of origin and developing a mix of talents, skills and complementary interests and

---

EXHIBIT 18-4   Career stages.

Approximate Age Ranges	Career Stage and Characteristics
16–28	*Exploration.* Explore various occupational roles and test out an initial occupational identity. Develop skills, establish a social network and mentor relationship, and cope with the emotional demands of early career.
22–42	*Establishment.* Become an individual contributor with a specific area of expertise. Work through work versus nonwork conflicts and develop a plan for achieving career goals.
32–55	*Advancement and maintenance.* Focus on achieving career goals and maintaining organizational progress. Revise career plan in light of progress. Re-determine the relative importance of work and nonwork roles. For many the top position in their career becomes evident, and few promotions are likely. Become a mentor.
55–retirement	*Late career.* Usually the highest position has been reached and people have started to shift more energy into nonwork pursuits. Their main source of contribution is breadth of knowledge and experience. Mentoring can continue throughout this stage.

Source: Adapted from Hall, D. T., (1976). *Careers in organizations.* Glenview, IL: Scott, Foresman, and Schein, E. (1977). *Career dynamics.* Reading, MA: Addison-Wesley. Note that the ranges identify the ages within which most people enter and complete each stage. The issues and concerns identified with each stage are based on research on technical, professional, and managerial careers and may have less relevance to craft and blue-collar careers.

values which are in demand by society. These choices are broader than establishing one's occupational identity, but often one's choice of work role is the major element.

During the early part of this stage, several trial runs (such as part-time work or summer jobs during college) in different work roles are explored. These set the stage for more focused exploration during one's first "real" job. For many, this is the first job after graduation from high school or college. This job often has an enduring influence on one's career. Successfully coping with three particular tasks seems to increase the likelihood that this influence will be positive. These are:

- Establishing a social network of relationships
- Getting a job which challenges one's skills and abilities
- Coping with the emotional side of work

A social network has two key elements, one's peers and a senior person who will be the person's mentor. Peers can provide information about ways to accomplish job assignments and give feedback about the consequences of different career strategies.[9] This can help make up for some of the limited experiences of a person in this career stage. Additionally, they can also be a source of friendship and emotional support during times of career or personal crisis. Substantial research has confirmed the importance of finding a mentor early in one's career. A **mentor** is a senior person in the organization who gives a junior person (called an **apprentice** or protégé) special attention. This can include giving advice and creating opportunities. An example of this is present in the opening story. Reggie might never have heard of the opportunity in the accounting department, let alone had someone to put in a good word for him, if he had not developed a special relationship with his supervisor. More on the topic of mentoring will be presented later in the chapter.

A challenging first job can have a lasting impact on people's careers.[10] In one study, a group of young managers was followed for a five- to seven-year period. Their performance at the end of the study, as measured by salary level and performance ratings, was directly tied to the level of challenge in the first job assignment. Those who had easy first assignments, even if more challenging assignments were later added, seemed to be at a distinct disadvantage. Unfortunately, providing an easy first job and then cautiously adding more stretching assignments seems to be the implicit policy of many companies.[11] Successfully completing the first job and getting an early first promotion also has a long-term impact on promotion opportunities ten years later.[12] Jan and Reggie, in the opening story, were both fortunate to land challenging first jobs. Reggie's steady career movement up the corporate hierarchy illustrates the positive consequence of having a challenging first assignment and also getting an early promotion before the others that joined the company at about the same time have been promoted and left him behind.

Dealing with the emotional side of work is also important. A common phenomenon faced by many young people entering the work force is **reality shock.** This is caused by the disparity between unrealistic expectations people often have and the reality they confront in their first job (see Chapter 9). The consequence can be strong dissatisfaction until new expectations are developed and more challenging elements are added to the new person's role in the organization. The inherent dependency position associated with being a subordinate can also evoke a negative emotional reaction. This occurs at a time when the person has often only recently left his or her family of origin. The dependencies one has on his or her bosses can often feel like a return to adolescence. Additionally, people just starting out their career normally feel a little insecure about their untried and untested skills and abilities. Testing those skills and developing more self-confidence requires people to cope with the emotional challenges of insecurity. Having a social network can go a long way in helping a person through these difficult times.

ESTABLISHMENT.   The second major career stage involves establishing oneself as an independent contributor in a fairly specific area of expertise. During the earlier period, people tend to try their hand at many tasks. Establishing a career identity involves setting priorities of skills and interests and focusing on key activities which are central to one's goals and plans. It is generally necessary to move away from a close relationship with a mentor at this time. Dealing with the independence of not having someone to closely check their work can provoke feelings of insecurity unless people have developed some sound skills during the earlier stage. Conflict between work and nonwork roles can also be a problem. For example, people with families may find growing adolescent children demanding much more of their time (school plays, recreation programs, etc.) at the very time at which their biological vitality has begun to decline. Role conflict (see Chapter 8) can result when meeting one's career goals also demands an extra investment of time and energy. See In–Focus 18-1 for a particular illustration of work and nonwork conflicts.

ADVANCEMENT AND MAINTENANCE.   After people establish themselves in a particular occupational role, they often enter a period in which they focus on advancing toward key career objectives such as making partner in an accounting firm or publishing a respected book. This is then followed by a period in which they are concerned with maintaining their status and position. In the early part of this stage, people often feel a sense of urgency to accomplish certain career goals. Final career strategy choices must be made, and unrealistic objectives must be recognized and eliminated. After this, people enter a phase in which they generally stay close to their proven skills and interests. People's main career assets are likely to be breadth of experience and a general knowledge of a variety of areas. Some people take on mentoring responsibilities and find satisfaction in training and developing the next generation. All must confront the fact that there is a younger generation of people who see them as old-timers.

LATE CAREER.   For a few, late career is a time for continued growth in status and influence within the organization, but for many it is a time when the highest level of responsibility and status has already been reached or is clearly in sight. Signs of aging are obvious in this stage and some people face serious health

IN–FOCUS 18-1 THE DARK SIDE OF CAREER SUCCESS

At 33, Bill O'Donnell Jr. had succeeded. He was vice-president of Bally Manufacturing, had an annual salary of $150,000, owned two Mercedes Benz automobiles and an expensive house in Winnetka, Ill.

He also cheated on his wife, missed meetings he had called and used four grams of cocaine a day.

"I was pursuing the American Dream, and I thought cocaine would get me there faster," he said. "I was running through life so fast I didn't see that my role as a husband and father to my three sons was disintegrating, that my business abilities were crumbling."

In the era of the 30-year-old multi-millionaire, when success and money are more fashionable and sought after than they have been since the 1950s, the fast track is luring more and more college graduates with promises of power, prestige and big payoffs. But in these high-pressure, high-reward jobs psychotherapists say that many executives soon lose all sense of balance between their work and the other aspects of their lives.

"More and more successful people are becoming troubled . . . or emotionally damaged by their work and career climb," said Douglas LaBier, a psychoanalyst in Washington who has studied the perils of success in several hundred men and women. Dr. LaBier contends that the corporation, rather than the individual, can be a large part of the problem. "What is needed, in many instances, is a change in the values of business leadership and decentralizing hierarchies," said Dr. LaBier. "If careerists feel trapped, they leave or withdraw their energies and hunker down for the money."

Psychotherapists say there are too many young people being coaxed into work habits that throw their lives badly out of balance. Worse, many find they are encouraged to betray their deepest values—a love of family life, perhaps, or simply their basic integrity—as they chase success and wealth.

The symptoms vary, but there is one common theme: work has become an obsession whose rewards overshadow those offered from other parts of life. It is usually a crisis, a divorce or a career in shambles, that catapults the person off the fast track long enough to look at the destruction elsewhere in his or her life.

The balance between a successful career and personal fulfillment is elusive for many. Some famous names in business have recognized the need for it, and have changed their worklife. James Wolfensohn, for example, who led Salomon Brothers of New York into the top ranks of corporate finance, left that company to found his own one-man investment firm. The reason he gave: "I wanted a more balanced life."

Despite its glamor and power, the grinding pressures of Mr. Wolfensohn's position—round-the-clock negotiations and endless crises—left him with little control over his personal time. He was chairman of Carnegie Hall and an accomplished cellist, and he longed for the freedom to pursue his private interests, particularly music. With his new business, Mr. Wolfensohn says, he is able to spend the time he wants on music and his other interests "and still make a comfortable living."

Source: Abridged from Goleman, D. (1986, September 2). Hitting bottom when you hit the top. *The Globe and Mail*. Originally from the *New York Times* Service. Copyrighted © 1986 by the New York Times Company. Reprinted with permission.

problems. Retirement plans and decisions on how to spend postretirement years are made at this point. As one faces pensions and loss of salary financial considerations can be a source of anxiety. People often withdraw energy and time from career pursuits in this stage and become more concerned with nonwork factors.

People in this stage can be a source of wisdom for the organization. At this point, most people move away from a detailed understanding of their technical area and, perhaps, branch into areas where their broad range of experience and general understanding of a variety of issues can be tapped. Mentoring, which may have begun in the previous stage, can continue throughout this final career stage.

CAREER PLANNING AND DEVELOPMENT: THE ORGANIZATION'S ROLE

Up to this point the focus of this chapter has been primarily on individuals. Specifically, career orientations, which describe how people differ in terms of motives and interests, and patterns of career change have been presented. Careers, however, involve more than people. Organizations have a large stake in the effective management of people's careers. Organizations can be managed in ways that help people more successfully meet their own career objectives, and, at the same time, contribute to organizational effectiveness.

Historically, most organizations have had an implicit "sink or swim" philosophy about managing human resources. This translates into a "the cream will naturally rise to the top" (or do nothing) approach toward facilitating the career development of employees. While this is still standard practice at a number of organizations, significant changes are taking place. Many are now deeply involved with a variety of career-related programs and actively encourage managers to take their employees' careers seriously. **Career management** activities are programs and systems which are designed to enhance individual **career development** (i.e., development of skills, identification of goals and strategies, and the realization of one's full potential).[13] The more widely used career management practices will be presented first, followed by a discussion of the manager's role in mentoring junior employees.

Career Management Programs

Every couple of months, personnel journals present new and different techniques related to career management. In general, these fit into several basic categories which have been around for some years. Large companies like Sears, IBM, and General Electric, may offer a number of such programs.

PERFORMANCE APPRAISAL/CAREER PLANNING PROGRAMS. One popular approach is to graft a career planning thrust onto an existing program. Performance evaluation systems which require a yearly appraisal meeting between supervisors and subordinates are a frequent target. For example, a number of business units in General Electric require managers to have their employees complete a self-evaluation which includes assessing career strengths and weaknesses as well as identifying career goals and objectives for the next three years. Managers are instructed to discuss the employee's input either during the regular appraisal session or during a separate meeting. A Management by Objectives (MBO) program (Chapter 7) is also a frequent target for adding on a career thrust. In one study, about 50 percent of the firms surveyed introduced career planning by grafting it on to existing human resource management programs.[14]

A number of supervisors probably handle the career-oriented appraisal or MBO meeting skillfully and conclude the session with some specific development suggestions. The basic problem with such programs is that they are solely dependent on the supervisor's skill and motivation. The fact that there is strong evidence that supervisors often do not carry out required yearly performance appraisal does not inspire confidence that merely linking career discussion to the performance appraisal or MBO discussion is the optimal approach to career development.

FORMAL CAREER PLANNING PROGRAMS.   In an effort to avoid such strong dependence upon supervisors, a number of organizations have developed formal programs in which experts give guidance and help employees through a structured sequence of planning steps. The following sequence is typical:

- *Individual identification of needs, goals, and abilities.* This helps the employees determine some of their key strengths and weaknesses as well as the general types of positions to which they aspire. Sometimes an educational component will be included, and theories on career orientation and stages will be presented.

- *Identification of alternative career options within the organization.* This can include identifying training opportunities (e.g., tuition reimbursement, management development seminars), education and skills required for various jobs, and lower-level jobs which are most likely to prepare a person for specific higher-level jobs (job paths).

- *Establishment of specific career goals.* This should involve both short-term and long-term objectives, and can include key future decision points between specific alternatives.

- *Determination of developmental activities needed to attain career goals.* These can include educational activities such as getting an M.B.A. degree or taking on new duties and responsibilities as part of one's current job.

Planning workshops which include, in varying degrees, each of the above steps have been conducted in many organizations. The extensiveness of the program is typically reflected in its length, which varies from a part of a day to one week. However, IBM has included many of these same steps in a computer-assisted program which can be done at the employee's convenience.[15] (See In–Focus 18-2 for other career planning programs.) Perhaps the greatest benefit of these programs is not the identification of specific goals, but rather a proactive, "make opportunities happen" orientation to managing one's career.

IN–FOCUS 18-2 VARIOUS CAREER MANAGEMENT PROGRAMS

• Recognizing that supervisors at NASA's Goddard Space Flight Center may need to acquire skills to carry out their career development responsibilities, a workshop series was designed. The objective of the workshop is to help utilize employees productively. The workshop is based on a collaborative career planning approach, emphasizing the critical link that line managers must play to insure the success of the organization career development program. Specific objectives include: (1) identifying work requirements and identifying employee skills, abilities and motivations; (2) matching employees to work; and (3) communicating with employees.

• The Career Development Series at Polaroid consists of a group orientation session and four formal career workshops. During the group orientation, employees share their expectations with the career staff and learn about what the Series can do for them. Interested employees can then enroll in the formal career workshops. The first of these is the Career Awareness Workshop, which involves participants in basic career and life planning exercises. This is followed by workshops in Resume Organization and Interview Skills, which give participants practice in organizing their skills and experience and presenting them to a hiring supervisor. The final Career Search Workshop then teaches employees how to gather information about Company job opportunities and how to best use the Job Posting System.

• Richway Department Stores in Atlanta, Georgia utilize a Career Development Workbook to help employees assess their skills in light of their work preferences and desired lifestyle. The career workbook lets employees see if their work preferences and desired lifestyle are congruent with the working world of retail. For example, if an employee prefers a 9:00 A.M. to 5:00 P.M. job, then that desire would not be congruent with the real world of work at Richway. The workbook is self-administered and therefore can be done at the employee's own pace. A career chart gives the employee a chance to outline two possible career paths which he/she may want to pursue at Richway. The employee then discusses the chart with his/her supervisor, who provides some reality counseling. If the employee feels uncomfortable discussing the career path with a supervisor, then he/she may talk with the Personnel Manager, their bosses' boss or the Store Manager. All are trained in career counseling.

• Individual counseling is available from specially trained managers at Lawrence Livermore Labs in California for any employee who requests this service. Employees seek counseling for a variety of reasons. These reasons range from request for simple factual information on available educational courses or for assistance in developing education and occupational goals, to request for feedback on the reality of career goals.

Source: From Kaye, B. (1982). *Up is not the only way.* Englewood Cliffs, NJ: Prentice-Hall, pp. 43, 45, 46, 61.

DEVELOPING HIGH-POTENTIAL EMPLOYEES. Some types of programs focus on selecting employees with high potential for key jobs (usually managerial positions), and then carefully managing their development. These programs are fairly exclusive and only a small percentage of employees are designated as high potential, or "high pots." Sometimes high pots are widely known. At the other extreme, this designation is a closely guarded secret and even those so designated may be unclear that they have this special status. Sometimes their selection is fairly informal, such as a supervisor's putting in good word for a subordinate with the personnel/human resources department. In a few cases, the selection is through a formal assessment center. In an assessment center, candidates demonstrate their skill levels in specially designed simulations of key job demands (e.g., group decision making, problem solving, counseling a poor performer) and are rated by multiple observers. Once selected, the development of high pots is usually taken very seriously. They are put into a position which develops key skills and then frequently moved to new positions in order to maintain optimal challenge and continuous learning. Supervisors frequently spend extra time with these people and give them special developmental assignments. Usually there is an emphasis on giving the high pot exposure to various parts of organization. One criticism of this fast-track approach to development is that people are moved too quickly and end up knowing a little bit about everything, but lack adequate depth of knowledge in any one area and never stay in one place long enough to really see the results of their efforts. As a consequence they might not develop the self-confidence necessary for high-level positions.[16] (See In–Focus 18-3 for fast-track organizations.)

CAREER COUNSELING.   Some organizations attempt to supplement informal career advisement by having career counselors, typically located in the personnel/ human resources department, available to answer employees' career-related questions. An advantage of this approach is that subordinates may not feel free to ask a supervisor about opportunities beyond the current job. Also, specially trained counselors may have more information about the range of career possibilities than the typical supervisor. Additionally, they may have better counseling skills and support material which will aid the employee in identifying career goals and needs. A disadvantage is that the career counselor is not likely to have as good an understanding of the subordinate's strengths and weaknesses as the employee's supervisor. To take better advantage of the supervisor's knowledge of the subordinate, some management development programs emphasize career counseling skills. Besides developing skills, they also provide general information on career alternatives within the company.

CAREER INFORMATION SYSTEMS.   These systems match information on people with information on positions to facilitate selection decisions. Information on people, sometimes referred to as skill inventories, identify job-related skills, abilities, and career goals. Information on positions should identify the skills, abilities, and educational level required to perform job duties. Developing these two types of information requires both a thorough analysis of job demands and sophisticated understanding of human skills and abilities. When a position becomes vacant, the information system generates a list of candidates whose personal characteristics match job requirements. This information is then used by the people making the selection decision in a way which strikes a balance between the twin objectives of selecting a qualified candidate who will perform well in the job and optimizing the employee's long-term development. Some candidates could comfortably carry out the job duties but may not develop in the new position. An ideal

IN–FOCUS 18-3   WHAT ARE THE TOP FAST-TRACK COMPANIES?

What are the top fast-track corporations in America? FORBES asked placement directors of America's top ten business schools. After some side-stepping and requests for anonymity, they named companies.

Some placement directors, such as the University of Chicago's John Adams, wondered whether any big corporation could still provide young people with rapid mobility. "If your primary concern is making it to the top in the shortest amount of time, I wouldn't be looking at corporate America," advises Adams. "The best bets are the fastest-growing companies, venture firms or starting your own company."

Nevertheless, some big companies were singled out as promising for new pathfinders. Mentioned most often: Proctor & Gamble, General Foods and General Mills, where it's "up or out" for young M.B.A.s. There were the high-tech favorites, IBM, Intel and Hewlett-Packard. Financial trendsetters Citicorp, American Express and Bankers Trust also placed high.

Harvard's Parker Llewellyn advised looking for companies with one or more of these characteristics:

• An increasing market share in a fast-growing industry. This means a need for sophisticated people. Analog Devices, an electronic components company leading its field, was singled out by Fred Way of Columbia, as was sleeper GTE, a favorite of UCLA Acting Director Becky Freeman: "Primarily because of the industry—telecommunications," she says. Ditto for many of the Bell operating companies.

• Turnarounds that have yet to bring back young management. "At this stage there are knotholes in the organization that create a vacuum just above where young people are entering. That vacuum sucks them right up," says Llewellyn. Example: J. P. Stevens, Burroughs, NCR, First Chicago and even Petro-Lewis Corp. in Denver. "I know Petro-Lewis sounds strange, but if they can ever get through their limited partnership hassles, and oil turns around again, they can provide great opportunities for young people," says Chicago's John Adams.

• Companies organized into many smaller divisions—divisions that tend to grow and split or clone themselves, so creating more top management positions. Try Rohm & Haas, for example, the diversified chemical and plastics producer, which is expanding through acquisition, and First Interstate Bancorp, a company heavily into franchising.

• Companies where M.B.A.s are still relatively scarce in management's ranks. Stanford's Ayse Manyas Kenmore picks Federated Department Stores, "a traditional retailer that is undermanaged." And advertising firm Young & Rubicam. "Advertising doesn't pay well in the beginning, but five to seven years down the line most of these M.B.A.s are doing better than the others," says one director.

Source: Abridged from Schifrin, A. (1984, September 10). Placement directors picks. *Forbes*, p. 180.

decision is one which meets both criteria. Some organizations use a committee to make this decision (sometimes called a selection board) and assign one person the role of emphasizing the employee development objective. This is intended to counterbalance others who may focus on selecting a high performer but ignore developmental issues. A key benefit of developing an information system is that employees who would otherwise be overlooked are, at least, considered in the earlier phases of the selection process. Without such systems, getting considered can be overly dependent upon employees hearing about a particular opening, or having a supervisor or friend nominate them. In other words, such systems take some of the randomness out of career development.

JOB PATHING.   This approach focuses on the types of skills required and developed in various jobs. Initially, an analysis is conducted to identify logical sequences of positions such that skills developed in an initial job provide the basis for further development and successful performance in the next job, and so on.[17] An ideal path is a sequence of positions which channel employees into new positions where they are qualified to perform, yet also challenged and developed by new job demands. These paths can link positions within a given functional area (e.g., marketing) or may cross functional boundaries. Additionally, there can be branches and interconnections in the paths which provide multiple routes to higher level positions. Sometimes the initial analysis can identify problems which can be eliminated only by redesigning jobs. An example is a sequence of jobs where a later position in a sequence does not adequately go beyond the task demands of earlier positions and adequately challenge employees. An opposite type of problem is a sequence where a later position requires such a dramatic change in skill requirements that employees moving through the sequence are likely to be overwhelmed. In either case, both current performance and long-term development are likely to be less than optimal. Sears and ARCO are examples of organizations that have used career pathing to further employee career development for a number of years.[18]

EFFECTIVE CAREER MANAGEMENT PROGRAMS.   Whatever the exact configuration of programs an organization selects, research suggests certain guidelines to increase the likelihood of success.[19] These include:

■ *Integrate the human resource management system.* Information generated and used for one human resource management activity should be available and, if applicable, utilized in other activities. Assessing people on their creative abilities during the selection process and then ignoring that quality and focusing on such things as consistency and punctuality during their performance evaluation gives people contradictory cues which will only hurt career development efforts.

■ *Balance long-term developmental needs and short-term productivity maximization.* Both of these objectives are important and will, at times, be in conflict with one another. If management always opts for short-term productivity when the two conflict, employees will quickly figure out what really counts. Doing this requires management to view human resource management expenditures as an investment in the organization's future.

■ *Link human resource activities to organizational strategic goals.* Organizational goals cannot be assumed to be constant. Ignoring possible strategic directions and related environmental changes in career development activities can produce a disaster equivalent to producing vacuum tube (1950s technology) specialists for a silicon chip world.

The Manager's Role in Mentoring Employees

The career success of individuals within an organization is obviously influenced by effective supervisor and subordinate relationships. One element of an effective relationship can be the development of an effective mentor-apprentice relationship. While someone other than the junior person's boss can serve as a mentor, often the supervisor is in a unique position to provide mentoring. A number of research efforts have documented the importance of having a mentor to people starting out their career.[20]

CAREER FUNCTIONS OF MENTORING. A mentor provides a number of career-enhancing benefits to the young apprentice.[21] These benefits are made possible by the senior person's experience, knowledge of how the organization works, and status and influence with powerful people in the organization. The career functions of mentoring include:

- *Sponsorship.* The mentor may nominate the apprentice for advantageous transfers and promotions.

- *Exposure and visibility.* The mentor may provide opportunities to work with key people and see other parts of the organization.

- *Coaching and feedback.* The mentor may suggest work strategies and identify strengths and weaknesses in the apprentice's performance.

- *Providing developmental assignments.* Challenging work assignments the mentor may provide can facilitate the development of key skills and knowledge crucial to further advancement.

These career functions are most likely to be provided by a mentor. Peers are infrequently in a position to be able to provide them.

PSYCHOSOCIAL FUNCTIONS OF MENTORING. In addition to helping directly with career progress, mentors can provide certain psychosocial functions which are helpful in developing the apprentice's self-confidence, sense of identity, and ability to cope with emotional traumas which can damage a person's effectiveness. These include:

- *Role modeling.* This provides a set of attitudes, values, and behaviors for the junior person to imitate.

- *Acceptance and confirmation.* The mentor may also provide encouragement and support which can help the apprentice gain confidence.

- *Counseling.* This provides an opportunity to discuss personal concerns and anxieties.

Providing these functions can turn an "all business" relationship, which may be suitable for accomplishing the various career functions, into one which provides for the emotional development of the apprentice.

While all mentors, by definition, provide some subset of the career functions, these psychosocial functions may not necessarily be provided by a mentor. A network of close peers can go a long way in providing functions which one's mentor is not providing. People starting out their careers in an organization should be aware of the importance of both of these career and psychosocial functions, and attempt to establish a set of relationships (referred to as a social network) which fulfills them. A mentor relationship is usually a key element in this broader set of relationships.

BENEFITS TO THE MENTOR.   An effective mentor-apprentice relationship also provides a number of benefits for the mentor. In fact, if these benefits are not forthcoming, the mentor is unlikely to be motivated to spend the time and take the risks which mentoring involves. The time requirements of coaching and counseling are fairly obvious. The risk to mentoring is that poor performance by the apprentice will suggest that the mentor has poor judgment or inadequate training and developmental skills. Some of the benefits are task oriented. A good apprentice will typically do a number of mundane tasks. These types of tasks (e.g., copying and collating) must be done accurately. Having a reliable apprentice who will handle these details frees the mentor for other concerns. Other benefits are related to the mentor's career and biosocial life stage. Often mentors are in the stage of their careers when promotions start slowing down. Developing an effective subordinate can contribute to his or her sense of competence and self-worth. Life-stage theorists have pointed out that at mid-life people often develop "generativity needs" which can only be satisfied by passing on one's wisdom and experience to the next generation. Effective mentoring will satisfy this need.

WOMEN AND MENTORS.   One factor which inhibits women's career development, relative to their male counterparts, is the difficulty they face in establishing an apprentice-mentor relationship with a senior person in the organization. The fact that Reggie (in the opening story) had a mentor and Jan apparently did not illustrates this unfortunate fact of organizational life. The problem goes well beyond the traditional sex-role stereotyping discussed in Chapter 4. It stems from the fact that senior people, in the best position to be a mentor, are frequently men. A young woman attempting to establish a productive relationship with senior male associate faces complexities which the male apprentice does not. Part of the problem is caused by the lack of experience many male mentor candidates have in dealing with a woman in some role other than daughter, wife, or lover. Often the concerns of a woman are going to be different than they were for her male mentor. As a result, the strategies that he models may have more limited relevance to the female apprentice. Perhaps the greatest complexity is associated with fears that their relationship will be perceived as involving sexual intimacy. Concerns about appearances and what others will say can make both uncomfortable and get in the way of a productive relationship. Preliminary research has shown that women who do make it to executive positions invariably have had a mentor along the way.[22] Thus, for women with these career aspirations, finding a mentor appears to be a difficult but critical task. (As discussed in In–Focus 18-4, finding a mentor is not the only career obstacle women face.)

FORMAL MENTORING PROGRAMS.   Many people have observed that mentors are often unavailable and have argued that organizational reward systems which focus on short-term outcomes tend to discourage mentoring. In an effort to counteract these forces and facilitate subordinate development, a few organizations have implemented formal mentoring programs. For example, the mentoring program at Merrill Lynch is part of their Management Readiness Program for new and prospective managers.[23] Young employees entering this program are assigned to a fairly high-level management volunteer who meets at least monthly with four such employees from different areas in the company. In preparation for this role, the mentors are given general directions and former mentors are invited in to discuss their experiences. Over the six-month period of the program the junior people and mentor meet individually and as a group. The most common activities to date

Source: Guisewite, C. (1986, September 19). Cathy. *Globe and Mail*.

IN–FOCUS 18-4 IS BUSINESS MISSING THE BOAT WITH WOMEN?

Fortune magazine signs on to the lament with a cover story about its survey of 1,039 women who received MBAs from 17 top U.S. schools in 1976. It found that 30 percent had jumped off their fast tracks and were either unemployed or self-employed. Similar findings are turning up in other surveys of women MBAs a decade or so beyond graduation.

Why have these highly talented, highly trained women opted out? *Fortune* and others offer several theories:

• *Women don't jump; they are pushed.* Hostility to women, open and covert, still exists in many corporate cultures and in the behavior of many male decision-makers. Even the most talented of woman executives can be shunted into support jobs, left out of information loops, expected to underperform males and made to feel uncomfortable in traditional male territory.

• *Women hit their heads on the ceiling.* Women executives still run into an invisible wall trying to move from middle to top management. Smart career women come to recognize this gentlemen's-agreement situation below the surface cordiality on the job and decide to bail out.

• *It really is a matter of biology, after all.* Women really don't have the genes for business. They can't bond like males, compete like males, think like males or talk sports like males. They are too soft, too shrill, too right-brained (or left-brained), too subjective, too out of place at golf outings, bars and board meetings.

But whatever the misconceptions and remnants of sexism, the most compelling reason why so many fast-track women drop out or slow down is that their priorities change.

They discover, usually to their surprise, that it's more satisfying and important to do a personal job of mothering a small child than to make a 2-percent gain in the year-over-year sales of the packaging division of Widget Inc. Small children love you back. Computer printouts don't. An executive is replaceable. A mother isn't.

The remedies *Fortune* ticks off are familiar. I have long pushed for changes in the workplace to fit the needs of the changing workforce: flexible hours; part-time work options, even at an executive level; four-day work weeks; stretched-out paths to partnerships; more use of telecommuting; flexible benefit systems that include help with child-care arrangements; more choices about unpaid leaves.

There is still another strategy to be put in place. Businesses that really want to benefit from the talents of top women should be thinking in much longer terms than 12-week maternity leaves.

Women's preoccupation with young children lasts only a small slice of an adult lifetime. Bright and talented women who jump off the fast-track at 28 or 30 may well want back on at 35 or 37. And business can profit by giving them a helping hand, especially as the baby-bust years cut into the supply of available working talent.

include advice about how to get ahead and alternative career paths; tours of key areas (e.g., New York Stock Exchange); and discussions about planning developmental activities, establishing networks, and the structure of the company.

Is a program like this likely to fulfill all of the career and psychosocial functions of mentoring? Definitely not! However, it might provide some of them and would certainly communicate that developmental relationships of this sort are important in the company. A nice side benefit may be that junior people will get to know peers in other areas. This is the start of a social network. Additionally, as a consequence of the program the formal mentor may be more likely to develop a true mentor relationship with people in his or her own area. Perhaps the program is more of a training ground for mentors than the actual accomplishment of mentoring.

A FOOTNOTE: PLANNING YOUR CAREER

Much of the information presented in this chapter is directly relevant to your own career. The sections on career orientation and career stages provide information useful in analyzing your own career needs and interests as well as how they may change in the future. The section on the organization's role provides information relevant to managing a career within an organization. Using this information will be greatly facilitated by cycling through the following steps to manage your career:

- *Know yourself.* The criterion for judging your career success is always a personal one. This first step involves determining what matters most to you. What activities do you like? Would you go crazy in a job where you often could not talk to other people? How about jobs where talking is all that you do? Figuring out your preferences, needs, values, strengths, and weaknesses is not an easy task. School counselors and self-help books can provide tests and exercises to help. This process requires plenty of time and introspection. Other people (family, friends, or teachers) can provide additional input. This is not something you do once, but something which will need frequent updating.

- *Know your career alternatives.* Successful careers involve achieving good fit between individuals and their work environments. To attain this, one must know about prospective work environments. One can find out plenty of information through reading about various careers. Once a general area is found, more focused reading is in order. Talking with people in particular jobs can provide insights about the social and emotional demands and skills required. People who know their own needs can ask focused questions. Finally, direct experience in related jobs can provide further detail.

- *Establish your career goals and attainment strategy.* Establishing specific long-term goals which take into account both your career orientation and knowledge of alternative work environments provides the target for an attainment strategy. Work and nonwork factors should be considered. This strategy should identify necessary educational activities, early jobs, establishment of social networks, and so on. The younger a person is, the wiser it is to try to build flexibility into the strategy. In other words, select preparatory activities which can serve a variety of goals.

■ *Enact your plan and constantly re-evaluate.* Nothing ever goes exactly according to plan. Unforeseen opportunities, needs, and constraints will appear. People and their work environments are dynamic. Companies go out of business, recessions happen, a divorce or death can occur, and forgotten interests emerge. A good plan is one that changes with new information. To get this information, one must frequently recycle through the above three steps.

SUMMARY

■ A career is a sequence of work activities, attitudes, and reactions experienced over a person's lifetime. It involves an objective sequence of positions as well as reactions, attitudes, and an occupational identity which emerge from the fit or interaction between people and their work environments.

■ Individual differences are a critical factor in determining the fit between people and their work environments. The two major perspectives on career orientation are Holland's theory of career types and Schein's theory of career anchors. These define the job and situational factors which fit each career orientation and increase the likelihood of an individual's attraction, retention, and sense of competence and satisfaction associated with a given work environment.

■ People and their careers are dynamic. As we age, we go through a sequence of biosocial life stages. Over the life course there appears to be a pattern of transitional periods, during which previous life-style choices are reconsidered, followed by stable periods during which previous choices are tested out. Careers also go through a sequence of stages: exploration, establishment, advancement and maintenance, and late career.

■ Organizations can facilitate the development of individual careers so that peoples' short-term productivity and long-term development are enhanced. Organizational practices can range from formalized individual planning workshops to identifying developmental sequences of positions. Effective career-oriented human resource efforts are integrated, balanced, and linked to organizational strategy.

■ An effective supervisor-subordinate relationship is crucial to an employee's career development. Research on mentoring identifies key career and psychosocial functions which supervisors and peers can provide. Women face unique problems in forming career-enhancing relationships with mentors.

■ Careers should not be left to luck but should be planned. This requires gaining knowledge of one's own needs and motives. Integrating self-understanding with knowledge of the work demands required by various career alternatives should result in identifying specific career goals and an attainment strategy.

KEY CONCEPTS

Career
External career
Internal career
Career orientation
Theory of career types (Holland)
Theory of career anchors (Schein)
Biosocial life stages
Age norms
Career stages
Mentor

Apprentice
Reality shock
Career management
Career development

DISCUSSION QUESTIONS

1. A career has a number of specific elements. What are these elements?

2. Compare and contrast Holland's career types and Schein's career anchors. Which are quite separate and distinct from one another? Which have some degree of overlap such that people who fit one category of Holland's might also have certain career anchors? What career types and anchors are likely to be negatively related?

3. The father of psychoanalysis, Sigmund Freud, is said to have observed that people are mostly fixed by age six and stay pretty much the same after their early formative years. Is this view consistent or inconsistent with various points presented in this chapter? Identify three different parts of the chapter which back up your answer.

4. Compare and contrast career stages and biosocial life stages. Which life stage is likely to be confronted in which particular career stage?

5. Review the final section on planning your career and discuss how the various career management programs (e.g., career counseling) are likely to either facilitate or ignore various steps in the planning process.

6. Review the formal mentoring program at Merrill Lynch presented in the mentoring section and discuss which specific mentoring functions are likely to be fulfilled by the program. What are some difficulties associated with formal mentoring programs?

7. What unique obstacles do women face in their career development? Why should organizations be concerned with these obstacles?

8. Career management effort by organizations requires that they know plenty about their employee's needs, goals, and even nonwork demands (e.g., the need to be home in the evening with children). Isn't this an invasion of privacy? Will employees truthfully provide this information or will they play a "tell management what they want to hear" game?

FOR FURTHER READING

Bolles, R. N. (1982). *What color is your parachute?* Berkeley, CA: Ten Speed Press.
   This career planning self-help book is packed with useful information. Numerous exercises which facilitate self-understanding and guidelines for evaluating occupations, organizations, and specific positions will help people intelligently plan careers and deploy their plans.

Derr, C. B. (1986). *Managing the new careerists*. San Francisco: Jossey-Bass.
   Discusses the diversity of careers today. Covers the politics of managing careers. Presents case studies of five career orientations and gives management strategies for dealing with them.

London, M., & Stumpf, S. A. (1982). *Managing careers*. Reading, MA: Addison-Wesley.
   This provides conceptual material, real cases, and examples of organizational practices which provide further information on career planning and guidelines for making human resources management practices more career-enhancing.

Terkel, S. (1972). *Working*. New York: Avon.
   This is a journalist's account of interviews with people from almost all types of jobs, from yacht broker to steelworker. They talk about their jobs and the satisfactions and frustrations they provide.

Exercise

Career Orientation

Below is an aerial view (from the floor above) of a room in which a party is taking place. At this party, people with the same or similar interests have (for some reason) all gathered in the same corner of the room—as described below.

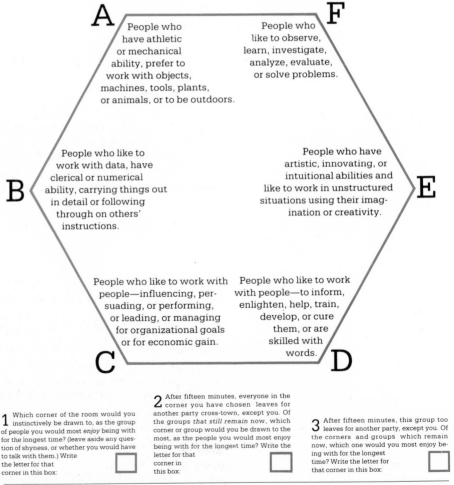

A People who have athletic or mechanical ability, prefer to work with objects, machines, tools, plants, or animals, or to be outdoors.

F People who like to observe, learn, investigate, analyze, evaluate, or solve problems.

B People who like to work with data, have clerical or numerical ability, carrying things out in detail or following through on others' instructions.

E People who have artistic, innovating, or intuitional abilities and like to work in unstructured situations using their imagination or creativity.

C People who like to work with people—influencing, persuading, or performing, or leading, or managing for organizational goals or for economic gain.

D People who like to work with people—to inform, enlighten, help, train, develop, or cure them, or are skilled with words.

1 Which corner of the room would you instinctively be drawn to, as the group of people you would most *enjoy* being with for the longest time? (leave aside any question of shyness, or whether you would have to talk with them.) Write the letter for that corner in this box:

2 After fifteen minutes, everyone in the corner you have chosen leaves for another party cross-town, except you. Of the groups *that still remain* now, which corner or group would you be drawn to the most, as the people you would most enjoy being with for the longest time? Write the letter for that corner in this box:

3 After fifteen minutes, this group too leaves for another party, except you. Of the corners and groups which remain now, which one would you most enjoy being with for the longest time? Write the letter for that corner in this box:

Source: Bolles, R. N., (1982). *What color is your parachute?* Berkeley, CA: Ten Speed Press. Reprinted by permission.

Exercise

Managing Careers— You're the Consultant

This exercise requires you to apply your understanding of career management and career development to some real situations. Read through each situation and take the role of a consultant who has been asked for help. For each situation (1) identify conceptual material which appears to be relevant and additional facts you would need to gather to do a thorough analysis, and (2) be ready to present your preliminary assessment and suggest some specific ways to meet the client's needs.

BAD TIMES AT MOBCORP

During your initial contact with Mobcorp the Human Resources Vice-President restated the facts which had emerged from last week's meeting of the top executive group. The basic concern of the executive group is that the turnover of technicians in various engineering categories has continued to grow. A similar labor category in a technically related area of manufacturing is evincing the same trend. Those leaving seem to be predominantly those who have spent several years in their positions and are in the thirty-five to forty-five age category. Management is concerned that younger employees are not ready to take over the duties of these senior technicians and that without experienced people to work with them, they may never be ready. A check of the salaries of the people leaving indicated that their wages were comparable to what other employers in the area were paying. Exit interviews have found that many simply wanted to try something new. One person put it this way: "Seven years ago when I started, my job was quite exciting. I faced a new challenge every week. I guess the problem is that I've changed and my job hasn't. Every problem I face, I've seen numerous times before. I hate it when people ask me what's new. I sometimes feel like saying that I'm getting older—that's all!"

CAREER PLANNING AT EDUCORP

Career planning programs certainly seem to be the thing to do these days. A few of your consulting clients have heard about other companies' efforts and have decided that it is time to test out a program. Your contacts say that the main pressure for this sort of program is from younger people who are not satisfied with letting their careers just happen and want the company to help them manage their own careers. One human resources executive came to the conclusion that "either we do it and give them more information on what the company has to offer, or the best ones will leave."

Source: Prepared by J. Bruce Prince. Used with permission.

You have come to the conclusion that, with so many clients wanting it, it is time you develop an approach to helping employees plan their careers. You have scheduled a lunch appointment with Fred Emery, Human Resource Vice-President at Educorp, for next week. It is now time to come up with a preliminary design of a career planning program to present to Fred. Also, you need to identify several specific areas in which you will need further information in order to complete the design of the program.

PROBLEMS AT STUKORP

John Davis, Manufacturing Vice-President at Stukorp, offered you a "free" lunch. You knew from past experience that these lunches are hardly ever free and that there is usually a pressing problem with which the person wants some help. Lunch with Davis was no exception. In between cocktails and coffee, he told you about Dan, the manager of the component reliability section who had spent over twenty-seven years with the company, serving in a number of capacities. Six years ago, he started his present position, and problems are now appearing. At the time of the transfer, the previous vice-president concluded that Dan's managerial competencies would be a real asset and would outweigh his lack of technical experience in the area. The component reliability section had always been staffed with junior people who were very technically qualified but had unknown managerial abilities and interests. Over the last couple of years, some top people had left the area with complaints that Dan did not give them adequate autonomy, tried to get too involved in the details of their work, and made some decisions which any good reliability engineer would know were wrong. Behind his back the employees referred to him as "Deadwood Dan" and considered him to be very defensive to the technically competent people in the department. Recently, Human Resources has had a hard time interesting people in transferring into the department. Morale and performance have been falling. Davis took a sip of coffee and said, "This whole problem is probably the company's fault, so I certainly can't fire him. Besides, he has given twenty-seven years of generally good service to the company. But I don't have any openings elsewhere for him." Davis paused for a few seconds, requested a second cup, and then asked, "Do you have any suggestions on how I should handle this?" He is now waiting for your reply.

Case Study

Weston Corporation: The Amherst Plant

Tom Newton stared at the three sobbing older women who sat before him and wondered what he could possibly do for them. The women, Joan, Alice,

9-482-043 Weston Corp.: The Amherst Plant
Copyright © 1981 by the President and Fellows of Harvard College. This case was prepared by Pam Posey under the direction of Jeffrey Sonnenfeld as a basis for class discussion rather than to illustrate either effective or ineffective handling of an administrative situation. Reprinted by permission of the Harvard Business School.

and Martha, were each in their early 60s and had been employed at Amherst for more than 30 years. They were close friends, having worked in the same operations area for 25 years. A few days before, they had been transferred to new departments separate from each other. Joan was put on the night shift for light maintenance work; Alice was put on a machine operating job, which had always frightened her; and Martha was put on a complex automated process which would require training to operate. All three were not only upset about the collapse of their department, but were dismayed in their assignments and separation. They felt that with so many years of dedicated service to the plant they deserved better consideration than this. Tom realized that their complaints might be symptomatic of the larger problems facing him at Amherst.

After the women left, Tom gazed out the office window toward the hazy skyline of Williston, and wondered about the future of the Amherst plant, Weston Corporation's oldest manufacturing facility. He had been the general manager at Amherst for three years, and had become increasingly aware of the special problems confronting a workforce employed in a plant which technological change was making obsolete. During his time as general manager, Tom had found himself caught in a bind between addressing the pressing operations problems created by new markets and technologies on one hand, and addressing the chronic personnel issues on the other.

THE AMHERST PLANT

The Weston Corporation, a producer of heavy industrial equipment, was founded in 1911. Its Amherst plant, the flagship of its three national manufacturing facilities, was the original company headquarters and occupied 150 acres of rolling meadows on the western border of the city of Williston. Amherst itself had been designed as a company town, with housing, stores, and recreational facilities located within the perimeter of company land. In the early 1900s, most employees had lived in the company-owned housing adjacent to the three manufacturing buildings. Amherst was a self-contained social and recreational center.

The environment generated a close-knit plant culture, which continued to grow and develop into the 1920s and 1930s. Amherst in the 1920s was so popular that, in spite of the general economic boom which the country enjoyed, special connections and family ties were often necessary to secure employment there. Employee relations were good, the plant was safe and efficient, and the market was healthy and growing. By 1935, the Amherst plant employed nearly 30,000 workers.

Following World War II, the situation began to change. The wide accessibility of transportation and increased mobility of the population created shifts in residential patterns. Employees began to move away from company housing and into more distant suburban areas. They were drawn away from the social amenities that had always been offered by Amherst. The plant became a job site rather than a family and social center. Technological advances had generated change in the manufacturing processes for the equipment produced at Amherst; and in 1965, the Weston Corporation decided that the new technologies demanded newer, more efficient production facilities. By 1970, new plants had been constructed near St. Louis and Houston, and many of Amherst's operations had been transferred to these sites. Many young workers, too, transferred to the new plants.

Amherst, in 1981, retained its core manufacturing processes. Operations had been consolidated into one building where newer technologically advanced production equipment had been installed. The other two buildings were shut down and boarded up: employees felt that these would be allowed to fall into the same state of dilapidation that the once-vital family housing units had suffered. The reduction of physical space needs was accompanied by large layoffs, and the current workforce was composed of fewer than 5,000 employees. The workers who remained after the layoffs were those with greatest seniority, and the average age of the Amherst work force was now over 50. Many workers were on the same jobs they had performed two or three decades ago, yet were using different technologies in a vastly different world. Fully one third were over age 55.

THE WORKFORCE

The older workers who once found Amherst to be the social center of their lives now spoke with anger about the lack of appreciation management had shown them by pulling them away from comfortable jobs they had mastered and placing them in new jobs with vastly different operation methods. Many of the older managers had been downgraded in rank so they could be retained through layoffs. They felt that their career opportunities, in spite of long service and good performance reviews, had eroded seriously. Although the Amherst plant remained profitable (sales had increased steadily by 10 percent per year since 1972), many workers were convinced that the plant would soon be closed completely.

Tom Newton had challenged these feelings, arguing that Amherst was still and would remain a significant operation for Weston Corporation. He did, however, state that new market pressures and continually developing technological changes were forcing the company to adopt different operating policies and procedures.

THE CURRENT SITUATION

The current plant problems were provoked by a changeover from an outdated technology to a more advanced and mechanized production process. More layoffs were imminent, retraining was a necessity, and some shifting of personnel to more complex and demanding tasks would have to occur.

Production operations previously performed by small work teams were now completed by new equipment requiring only a single operator. Development of new training programs designed to provide workers with skills needed to operate the new equipment met with resistance. Not only was the technology different, but old well-established social relationships were being broken up to better meet the demands of the new processes. Union-plant relationships were still positive, but union rules precluded replacing those employees having seniority with younger workers more accustomed to the newer production methods.

Tom knew he had to devise a plan to meet the needs of his plant and the Weston Corporation, but was worried about the apparently insurmountable obstacles facing him as plant manager. He had to devise a training program for workers to teach them the new production processes; yet the workers requiring training were resistant to the changes which had caused such upheaval in their lives. Employee morale was at an all-time low, further complicating the situation he faced.

Tom wondered if he should bring the union in, but was concerned about setting a precedent for future decisions. He wondered if part of the answer

lay in improved communications, yet knew that his management staff had already worked hard in this area.

Several days before, Tom had held a meeting with his employee development staff, and as he gazed out the window, he thought about the questions he had posed for them to consider.

How do we develop programs to retrain workers into new technologies when those workers resist the technological and work environment changes that necessarily result? Training programs are critical, but what types are most appropriate? We cannot replace the workers: they have seniority and most are not ready to retire even if we offered it early. The corporate culture supports a philosophy of lifetime employment, but I have a responsibility to keep this plant profitable as well as to the employees. How can we design and implement training programs capable of meeting both objectives now?

■ ■ ■

1. With the benefit of twenty-twenty hindsight, what are some career-related organizational practices that management could have begun ten to fifteen years ago to lessen some of the problems they now face?

2. Shifting personnel out of their present jobs seems to be inevitable. Present at least two organizational practices which will facilitate and improve the effectiveness of the transfer process.

3. How can concepts of career types and anchors and biosocial life and career stages be used to guide decisions which get made in the transfer process?

4. Management is currently focused on skill training. Does this approach reflect a full understanding of the meaning of a career? Remember that three key elements, discussed in the first part of the chapter, are important: External and internal careers, individual and organization interaction, and occupational identity.

REFERENCES

1.   Hall, D. T. (1976). *Careers in organizations.* Pacific Palisades, CA: Goodyear.
2.   Van Maanen, J., & Schein, E. J. (1977). Career development. In J. R. Hackman & J. L. Suttle (Eds.), *Improving life at work: Behavioral science approaches to organizational change.* Glenview, IL: Scott, Foresman.

3. Van Maanen, J., & Barley, S. R. (1984). Occupational communities: Culture and control in organizations. *Research in Organizational Behavior, 6,* 287–365.

4. Weinrach, S. G. (1984). Determinants of vocational choice: Holland's theory. In D. Brown & L. Brooks (Eds.), *Career choice and development.* San Francisco: Jossey-Bass; Holland, J. L. (1973). Making vocational choices: A theory of careers. Englewood Cliffs, NJ: Prentice-Hall.

5. Strong, E. K., Jr., & Campbell, D. P. (1981). *Strong-Campbell interest inventory.* Stanford, CA: Stanford University Press.

6. Schein, E. H. (1975). How "career anchors" hold executives to their career paths. *Personnel, 52,* 11–24; Schein, E. H. (1978). *Career dynamics.* Reading, MA: Addison-Wesley.

7. Neugarten, B. (1968). Adult personality: Toward a psychology of the life cycle. In B. Neugarten (Ed.), *Middle age and aging.* Chicago: University of Chicago Press.

8. Levinson, D. J., Darrow, C. N., Klein, E. B., Levinson, M. H., & McKee, B. (1978). *The seasons of a man's life.* New York: Alfred A. Knopf.

9. Kram, K., & Isabella, L. (1985). Mentoring alternatives: The role of peer relationships in career development. *Academy of Management Journal, 28,* 110–132.

10. Berlew, D. T., & Hall, D. T. (1966). The socialization of managers: Effects of expectations of performance. *Administrative Science Quarterly, 11,* 207–223.

11. Hall, D. T., & Lawler, E. E., III. (1969). Unused potential in research and development organizations. *Research Management, 12,* 339–354.

12. Rosenbaum, J. E. (1984). *Career mobility in a corporate hierarchy.* New York: Academic Press.

13. Gutteridge, T. G. (1986). Organizational career development systems: The state of the practice. In D. T. Hall (Ed.), *Career development in organizations.* San Francisco: Jossey-Bass.

14. Walker, J. W., & Gutteridge, T. G. (1979). *Career planning practices.* New York: American Management Association.

15. Minor, F. J. (1986). Computer applications in career development. In D. T. Hall (Ed.), *Career development in organizations.* San Francisco: Jossey-Bass.

16. Thompson, P. H., Baker, R. B., & Smallwood, N. (1986, Autumn). The derailment of fast-track managers. *Organizational Dynamics,* 41–48.

17. Morrison, R. F., & Hock, R. R. (1986). Career building: Learning from cumulative work experience. In D. T. Hall (Ed.), *Career development in organizations.* San Francisco: Jossey-Bass.

18. Wellbank, H. L., Hall, D. T., Morgan, M. A., & Hamner, W. C. (1978, March–April). Planning job progression for effective career development and human resources management. *Personnel,* 118–129.

19. Von Glinow, M. A., Driver, M. J., Brousseau, K., & Prince, J. B. (1983). The design of a career oriented human resource system. *Academy of Management Review, 8,* 23–32.

20. Dalton, G. W., Thompson, P. H., & Price, R. (1977, Summer). The four stages of professional careers—a new look at performance by professionals. *Organizational Dynamics,* 19–42.

21. Kram, K. (1985). *Mentoring at work.* Glenview, IL: Scott, Foresman.

22. Dennett, D. (1985, November). Risks, mentoring help women to top. *APA Monitor,* 26.

23. Farren, C., Gray, J. D., & Kaye, B. (1984, November–December). Mentoring: A boon to career development. *Personnel,* 20–24.

Name Index

Fichman, M., 422
Fiedler, F. E., 317, 321, 343, 344
Field, R. H. G., 345
Fierman, J., 390
Filley, A. C., 344, 345, 461, 612
Fineman, S., 496
Finger, J. R., Jr., 424
Fischhoff, B., 422, 423
Fisher, K., 479
Fiske, S. T., 112, 422
Fitch, H. G., 77
Fitzgerald, M. P., 224
Flax, S., 206, 338, 529
Fleishman, E. A., 612
Fleming, R. L., 65
Fletcher, D., 613
Folejewski, C., 540
Folejewski, M., 540
Folkins, C. H., 496
Foltz, R. G., 354, 381
Ford, H., 310
Ford, R. N., 225
Forsythe, S., 370, 382
Foushee, H. C., 244
Frantzich, S. E., 431
Fraser, S. C., 305
Frederickson, J. W., 573
Freedman, J. L., 305
Freeman, B., 638
Freeman, F. H., 23
French, J. R. P., Jr., 459
French, W. L., 612, 613
Freudenberger, H. J., 479
Fried, Y., 496
Friedman, M., 495
Futrell, C. M., 224

G

Gagné, R. M., 412
Gaines, J., 496
Galbraith, J. R., 533, 568
Gamboa, V. U., 77
Geis, R., 460
Gerard, H., 305
Gerard, H. B., 146, 266, 305
Gerver, I., 35, 42
Gerwin, D., 573, 574
Ghandi, 333
Ghiselli, E. E., 224
Gibson, J. L., 224
Gillen, B., 92
Gillespie, D. F., 573
Glueck, W. F., 348, 572
Golden, Larry, 110
Goldstein, A. P., 77, 78, 125, 146, 612
Golembiewski, R. T., 226, 613
Goodale, J. G., 226

Gooden, D., 65
Goodman, P. S., 147, 263, 612
Goodwin, J., 339
Gordon, M. E., 224
Gouldner, A. W., 534
Graen, G. B., 344
Grainger, Harvey, 110
Gray, J. D., 653
Gray, J. G., 43, 369
Grayson, Ollie, 41–43
Greed, J., 314
Greene, C. N., 345
Greenfield, Myra, 346–347, 353, 356, 357, 360
Greenhaus, J. H., 263, 267
Greenwald, A. G., 113, 423
Greenwood, R. J., 43
Gregory, K. L., 306
Greiner, J. M., 219
Griffin, R. W., 219, 271, 305, 345
Griffitt, W., 112
Griggs, Wayne, 230–232, 250
Grote, R. C., 67
Gruneberg, M. M., 77, 223
Guion, R. M., 147
Guisewite, C., 642
Gumpert, D. E., 306
Gupta, N., 496
Gustafson, D., 226, 413, 424
Gutteridge, T. G., 653
Guzzo, R. A., 183
Gyllenhammar, P. G., 202, 224

H

Hackett, Charles, 307–309, 310, 315, 316, 328
Hackett, R. D., 147
Hackman, J. R., 183, 196–197, 198, 199, 224, 305, 534, 612, 652
Hage, J., 533, 534
Haire, M., 112, 224
Hall, D. T., 630, 652, 653
Hall, R. H., 533
Hammond, K. R., 423
Hamner, W. C., 78, 653
Hampden-Turner, C., 179
Hampton, D. R., 417
Hanson, Rusty, 340–342
Hare, A. P., 266
Harris, E. F., 612
Hartley, D., 613
Hartley, E. L., 112
Hatch, M. J., 306
Hatry, H., 219
Hawkins, C., 267
Haynes, R. S., 77
Hedley, R. A., 182
Heider, F., 459

Heilman, M., 92
Hellriegel, D., 572
Hennessey, H. W., 460
Hermann, J. A., 77
Herzberg, F., 182
Heslin, R. 382
Hickson, D. J., 460
Hill, G. W., 266, 423
Hinings, C. R., 460
Hinrichs, J. R., 382
Hitler, A., 434
Hock, R. R., 653
Hoffman, E., 305
Holland, J. L., 383, 619, 620, 622, 623, 626, 627, 652, 653
Holland, W. E., 381
Hollander, E. P., 305
Hollman, T. D., 113
Hom, P. W., 224
Honig, W. K., 77
Hopkins, B. L., 77
Horn, J. C., 596
Hornstein, H., 612
House, J., 147
House, R. J., 224, 321, 322, 323, 333, 343, 344, 345, 612
Howe, Ann, 462–463
Howell, J. P., 345
Huber, G. P., 422
Hulin, C. L., 146, 224, 225, 568
Hunger, J. D., 461
Hunt, J. E., 333
Hunt, J. G., 344
Hunt, R. G., 143
Hunter, J. E., 182
Hurst, M. W., 147
Huse, E. F., 613
Huseman, R. C., 423

I

Iacocca, L., 62, 311, 333
Iaffaldano, M. T., 147
Ireland, R. D., 572
Isabella, L., 653
Isenberg, D. J., 415
Ivancevich, J. M., 34, 43, 78, 224, 226, 495, 496

J

Jablin, F. M., 381
Jackson, R. A. G., 474
Jackson, S. E., 266, 267, 496
Jago, A. G., 345, 381
Jamal, M., 147
James, R. M., 267
Janda, L. H., 92

Subject Index